Introduction to Public Librarianship

Introduction to Public Librarianship

THIRD EDITION

Kathleen de la Peña McCook
Jenny S. Bossaller

Foreword by Felton Thomas Jr.

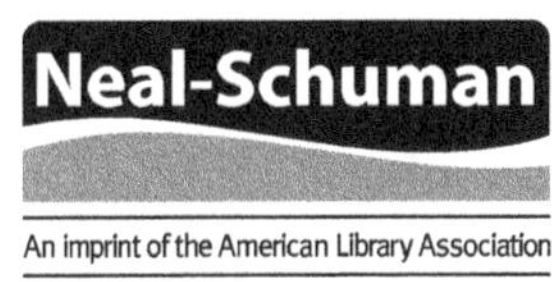

CHICAGO :: 2018

ISBNs
978-0-8389-1506-6 (paper)
978-0-8389-1665-0 (PDF)
978-0-8389-1664-3 (ePub)
978-0-8389-1666-7 (Kindle)

Library of Congress Cataloging-in-Publication Data
Names: McCook, Kathleen de la Peña, author. | Bossaller, Jenny S., 1972-, author.
Title: Introduction to public librarianship / Kathleen de la Peña McCook [and] Jenny S. Bossaller; with a foreword by Felton Thomas, Jr.
Description: Third edition. | Chicago: ALA Neal-Schuman, an imprint of the American Library Association, 2018. | Includes bibliographical references and index.
Identifiers: LCCN 2017041849 | ISBN 978-0-8389-1506-6 (print : alk. paper) | ISBN 978-0-8389-1665-0 (pdf) | ISBN 978-0-8389-1664-3 (epub) | ISBN 978-0-8389-1666-7 (kindle)
Subjects: LCSH: Public libraries—United States.
Classification: LCC Z731 .M355 2018 | DDC 027.473—dc23
LC record available at https://lccn.loc.gov/2017041849

Cover design by Kimberly Thornton; imagery © Adobe Stock. Text design and composition by Karen Sheets de Gracia in the Cardea and Acumin Pro typefaces.

♾ This paper meets the requirements of ANSI/NISO Z39.48-1992 (Permanence of Paper).

Printed in the United States of America
22 21 20 19 18   5 4 3 2 1

CONTENTS

List of Figures *xi*

Foreword, *by Felton Thomas Jr.* *xv*

Preface, *by Kathleen de la Peña McCook and Jenny S. Bossaller* *xvii*

Acknowledgments *xxi*

1 The American Public Library: Democracy's Hope and The Community's Commons *1*

by Kathleen de la Peña McCook

The Community's Commons: Heart, Anchor, Safe Haven *8*
Evolution *14*
Notes *17*
References *18*

2 Development of the Public Library in America: Colonial Times to the 1960s *23*

by Kathleen de la Peña McCook

Colonial Times to 1852 *23*
1852 to the Great War (World War I) *30*
State Library Commissions *35*
World War I (1918) to the Public Library Inquiry (1952) *37*
After World War II: The Public Library Inquiry *39*
From LSA to LSCA (1956 to 1966) *40*
Notes *42*
References *46*

3 People, Not Institutions: Toward Equity of Access (1960 to the Present) *53*

by Kathleen de la Peña McCook

Civil Rights and the Role of Public Libraries *53*
People and Community Focused Librarianship: Equity of Access Becomes a Core Value for America's Public Libraries *54*

A Strategy for Public Library Change: A Major Transformation of the Philosophy of Public Librarianship *56*
Steps toward Transformation: Roles, Responses, and Outcomes *57*
Thirty Years of the Library Services and Construction Act: 1966 to 1996 *59*
Transformation and Strategic Planning: 1996 to 2015 *61*
The New Outcome Era: 2015 to the Present *61*
The Public Library in the Twenty-First Century: Core Values and Trends *66*
Conclusion *72*
Notes *72*
References *75*

4 **The Public Library Journey to Accountability: Metrics and Outcomes to Demonstrate Value** *81*

by Kathleen de la Peña McCook

Measuring the Outcomes of Library Programs *81*
How Do We Convey the Importance of Public Libraries? *83*
State Public Library Standards *91*
Ratings and Awards *93*
Quality of Life and Human Development *96*
Notes *97*
References *100*

5 **"More and Better Libraries": Political, Legal, and Financial Aspects of the Public Library** *105*

by Kathleen de la Peña McCook

The Library in the Government *106*
State Library Administrative Agencies and the Institute of Museum and Library Services *114*
The Library Services and Technology Act *115*
Evaluations *121*
Advocacy and Federal Legislation *122*
Funding the Public Library *123*
Transforming the Perception of Libraries *136*
Notes *137*
References *140*

6 **The Public Library's People: Work Life and Commitment** *143*

by Kathleen de la Peña McCook

How Libraries Are Organized *143*
The Library Board of Trustees *144*

Trustee Organizations *150*
The Library Director *152*
The Library Staff *158*
Union Impact on Salaries and Working Conditions *174*
Friends of Libraries *174*
Volunteers *175*
Overarching Issues Relating to Staffing *176*
Continuing Education and Staff Development *181*
Recognizing Excellence in Staff and Trustee Development *183*
Notes *184*
References *187*

7 The Public Library Building: Emblem of Community Heritage and Embodiment of Community Courage *193*

by Kathleen de la Peña McCook

Civic Memory and Identity *193*
The Beginning of the Public Library Building *195*
Funds for Public Library Construction: Priming the Pump with LSCA *197*
Building Showcases *202*
Branches *206*
Resources on Building Design *208*
Accessibility and Universal Design *212*
Green and Sustainable Building *214*
Bookmobiles *215*
Disasters and Public Libraries *216*
Conclusion *219*
Notes *220*
References *223*

8 Youth Services in Public Libraries: History, Core Services, Challenges, and Opportunities *229*

by Alicia K. Long

History *230*
From Core Services to Civic Engagement and Innovation *234*
Youth Media Book Awards *243*
Key Books and Media Awards for Children and Young Adults in the United States *244*
Programs and Initiatives *247*
The Future of Youth Services: Challenges and Opportunities *250*
Notes *252*
References *253*

9 Reader and Adult Services: To Survive, to Flourish, to Create *257*

by Kathleen de la Peña McCook and Katharine Phenix

Inclusion and Accessibility *258*

Reader Services *259*

Adult Services during the Planning Era (1966 to 2015): Public Library Roles to Services Responses *275*

The Public Library as the Help Desk and Facilitator of Community Engagement *276*

Conclusion *279*

Notes *281*

References *285*

10 Collaboration and Consortia *293*

by Jenny S. Bossaller

Cooperating with Each Other: Consortia, State Libraries, and Cooperatives *294*

Local History: Cooperating with the Community and with Other Libraries *302*

Community Outreach: Cooperating with Other Groups *309*

Public Library Leadership *316*

Conclusion *316*

References *316*

11 Technology in Public Libraries: An Overview of the Past, Present, and Future *321*

by Richard J. Austin and Diane Austin

Information Technology in Public Libraries: A Brief History *323*

Public Librarianship and Technology Skills *325*

Information Technology in Public Libraries Today *328*

Kinds of Technology *330*

Connections: Library 2.0 and 3.0 *335*

Electronic Resources and Digital Libraries *340*

Conclusion *342*

Notes *343*

References *344*

12 Global Perspectives on Public Libraries *347*

by Clara M. Chu and Barbara J. Ford

History and Purpose of Public Libraries: A World View *349*

Worldwide Snapshot *350*

IFLA: A Global Voice for Public Libraries *353*

Implementing the Manifesto *364*

Impact and Advocacy *364*
Community Outreach and Services *370*
The Road Ahead for Public Libraries Worldwide *373*
References *375*

AFTERWORD: WHAT WE DO, *by Katharine Phenix* *379*

ABOUT THE AUTHORS AND CONTRIBUTORS *389*

INDEX *393*

LIST OF FIGURES

FIGURE 1.1 Library Services for and with Indigenous Peoples of the Americas: Tribal Community Libraries *3*

FIGURE 1.2 The Public Library: Democracy's Resource—A Statement of Principles *6*

FIGURE 1.3 Public Libraries in Puerto Rico *9*

FIGURE 1.4 Libraries Change Lives: Declaration for the Right to Libraries *15*

FIGURE 5.1 Percentage Distribution of Public Libraries by Type of Legal Basis and State: Fiscal Year 2014 *108*

FIGURE 5.2 Commonwealth of Massachusetts, General Laws, Chapter 78: Libraries *112*

FIGURE 5.3 State Allotments: Fiscal Year 2012 to 2017 *117*

FIGURE 5.4 Total Per Capita Operating Revenue of Public Libraries by Source of Revenue and State: Fiscal Year 2014 *125*

FIGURE 5.5 Per Capita Library Support Compared to Median Household Income *128*

FIGURE 5.6 Michigan City, Village, and Township Libraries Act 164 of 1877 (Excerpt) *129*

FIGURE 5.7 Oak Park (IL) Public Library Board of Trustees Budget, 2016 *130*

FIGURE 5.8 Saint Paul (MN) Public Library Agency, 2016 Adopted Budget *131*

FIGURE 6.1 Town of Bedford (MA) Organizational Chart *145*

FIGURE 6.2 Aurora (IL) Public Library Organizational Chart *146*

FIGURE 6.3 Denver Public Library 2016 Organizational Chart *147*

FIGURE 6.4 Akron-Summit County (OH) Public Library 2016 Organizational Chart *148*

FIGURE 6.5 New Hampshire Statutes: Library Trustees *150*

FIGURE 6.6 Voter Fever ("Save Our Library Committee" Cartoon) *153*

FIGURE 6.7 Knowledge, Skills, and Abilities of the Director *154*

FIGURE 6.8 Job Announcement: CEO, Hartford (CT) Public Library *157*

FIGURE 6.9 Number of Paid Full-Time Equivalent Staff and Paid Full-Time Equivalent Librarians of Public Libraries per 25,000 Population, by State: Fiscal Year 2014 *160*

FIGURE 6.10 Number of Paid Full-Time Equivalent Librarians with an ALA-Accredited MLS and Other Paid Full-Time Equivalent Staff of Public Libraries per 25,000 Population, by State: Fiscal Year 2014 *162*

FIGURE 6.11 Library and Information Studies and Human Resource Utilization: A Statement of Policy *164*

FIGURE 6.12 Selection of Public Library Position Titles, 2016 *165*

FIGURE 6.13 Sampling of Library Position Announcements, 2016 *166*

FIGURE 6.14 Number of Paid Full-Time Equivalent Staff in Public Libraries, by Type of Position, Percentage of Total Librarians and Total Staff with ALA-MLS Degrees, and Number of Public Libraries with ALA-MLS Librarians in the 50 States and the District of Columbia by Population of Legal Service Area: Fiscal Year 2014 *170*

FIGURE 6.15 Sample "Get Involved" Volunteer Search, California State Library, Zip Code 92704, Orange County *177*

FIGURE 6.16 Laura Bush 21st Century Librarian Program *178*

FIGURE 7.1 Image of Alice Virginia and David W. Fletcher Branch, Washington County, MD *196*

FIGURE 7.2 2017 AIA Kentucky Honor Award, Paris-Bourbon County (KY) Public Library *198*

FIGURE 7.3 Public Library Construction and Technology Enhancement Grants to State Library Agencies (CFDA No. 84.154) Funding History *199*

FIGURE 7.4 Chicago Public Library—Harold Washington Library Center *200*

FIGURE 7.5 Public Libraries: Five-Year Cost Summary *201*

FIGURE 7.6 Cedar Rapids (IA) Public Library *202*

FIGURE 7.7 Main Library, East Baton Rouge (LA) Parish Library at Goodwood *204*

FIGURE 7.8 Northeast Dade-Aventura Branch, Miami-Dade (FL) Public Library *204*

FIGURE 7.9 Mitchell Park Library and Community Center, Palo Alto, CA *205*

FIGURE 7.10 Corvallis-Benton County (OR) Public Library, Monroe Community Library *206*

FIGURE 7.11 The Southeast Branch, Nashville Public Library, Antioch, TN *207*

FIGURE 7.12 Number of Public Libraries with Branches and Bookmobiles, and Number of Service Outlets, by Type of Outlet and State: Fiscal Year 2014 *209*

FIGURE 7.13 Library Services for People with Disabilities (Excerpt) *213*

FIGURE 7.14 National Bookmobile Day, 2017 *215*

FIGURE 7.15 "Libraries as Acts of Civil Renewal": Excerpts from a Speech by Carnegie Corporation President Vartan Gregorian to the Kansas City Club *219*

FIGURE 8.1 Key Figures in the History of Youth Services *231*

FIGURE 8.2 ALSC Competencies *235*

FIGURE 8.3 YALSA Competencies *236*

FIGURE 8.4 Selected Book Awards *245*

FIGURE 9.1 The Workforce Innovation and Opportunity Act: Summary of Library Provisions *271*

FIGURE 9.2 Resolution Reaffirming ALA's Commitment to Basic Literacy *273*

FIGURE 9.3 Public Library Service Roles in the 1980s *276*

FIGURE 9.4 Public Library Service Responses in the 1990s *277*

FIGURE 9.5 Public Library Service Responses in 2008 *277*

FIGURE 9.6 Adult Attendance at Public Library Programs by State: Fiscal Year 2014 *280*

FIGURE 10.1 Profile: AMIGOS *297*

FIGURE 10.2 Profile: The Digital Public Library of America *306*

FIGURE 10.3 Profile: The Public Library Association (PLA) *307*

FIGURE 10.4 Huber's Community Hierarchy of Needs *311*

FIGURE 10.5 Presidents of the Public Library Association from 1945 to 2012 *317*

FIGURE 11.1 Major Technological Developments since the Introduction of Commercial Computers *325*

FIGURE 11.2 Examples of Current Web 2.0 Technologies and Applications *337*

FIGURE 12.1 UNESCO Public Library Manifesto *362*

FOREWORD

Felton Thomas Jr.

A public library saved my life. The audience is usually startled when I share that statement at the beginning of a speaking engagement, but they soon understand how libraries have altered my life's trajectory. I reveal to them that as a young boy I grew up in one of the poorest and most dangerous neighborhoods in Las Vegas. Drugs and gangs were starting to infiltrate my neighborhood as I began my teenage years. When my two best friends decided to join gangs, I had to make a decision quickly. There weren't many options. Much of my neighborhood was either abandoned or burned down, and the only institutions left standing were the churches and the public library.

After school, I would slip away from my friends by telling them that I had homework to do and would go to the library. It was only about 8,000 square feet, and had previously served as a space for social workers to provide services. The Las Vegas-Clark County Library system took it over when the welfare office chose to leave for a bigger space. Although small, it opened the larger world to me. As a young African-American boy from a very poor family, the closest I was going to get to other parts of our country and the world was from the books in the library.

By the end of my eighth-grade year, my friends had stopped asking me to join them, having realized that I was now on a different path. I started going to the library every day after school. Soon the children's librarian noticed me. "You are here so much, you should work here," she quipped. One month later, I began my career in public libraries. I count my blessings every day that I did not go down the same road as my two best friends, both of whose lives have been tragically altered by their choices.

Even now, I can barely believe that the young boy who started working in public libraries at the age of 13 to escape neighborhood gangs would one day be elected president of the Public Library Association, an organization with a membership of 9,000 public library professionals that supports over 16,000 public libraries throughout the country.

The public library hasn't just been a career path for me, it has been my life. This is why the work that is being done to train the next generation of librarians is so important to me. For libraries to continue to alter the lives of the many young people who look to it for salvation, they must be staffed by librarians who are properly prepared. Especially now, as librarians are watching a professional revolution take place right before our eyes, we need library professionals who understand the context of our history and how it influences our possibilities for the future.

In the previous edition of *Introduction to Public Librarianship,* Dr. Kathleen de la Peña McCook masterfully provided a blueprint for training our new professionals. That book adorned my small shelf of most-consulted books 10 years ago, when I was a mid-level manager. Yellow highlights streaked the articles I used to introduce my colleagues to some of the most important writing on public librarianship. The book is a treasure trove of citations and references for anyone who wants to understand public librarianship.

When I read the second edition of *Introduction to Public Librarianship*, I realized that the book encompassed the three most important concepts for the next generation of librarians and library professionals. First, it documented how libraries and librarians have shaped the intellectual landscape. Its detailed examination of the history of public librarianship is one of the most thorough assessments I've encountered. Second, the book provided a remarkable exploration of our core values. Public libraries will begin to falter when we forget the principles upon which they were founded, especially at this time in history, as the foundations upon which democracy was built are being challenged. Finally, and most important to me, Dr. McCook dedicated many pages to the discussion of diversity in our profession. Today's libraries are much more complex and open than their nineteenth- and twentieth-century counterparts, and therefore we must understand our ever-changing communities.

This third edition of *Introduction to Public Librarianship* shouldn't be read only by those choosing to join our profession. It is also a must-read for the most experienced library professional. Dr. Jenny Bossaller, a professor at the University of Missouri, has collaborated with Dr. McCook on this edition. Dr. Bossaller's commitment to the scholarship of community engagement is demonstrated throughout the new edition. Readers will continually find themselves having "aha!" moments, because Dr. McCook and Dr. Bossaller have revised the previous work in the context of a public library world that has become more global. I have worked in libraries for over 35 years, and have been a librarian for 25 years, but may be more excited about this new revision than I've been about a library resource to date.

Dr. McCook and Dr. Bossaller identify the public library's core values as lifelong learning, support for democracy, intellectual freedom, and Internet access. As I meet librarians from across the United States and around the globe, I'm heartened by their commitment to these principles. These librarians tell me that our professional associations must do more to speak to these important issues, which are under attack in many communities. I agree with them, but counter that although our associations and institutions must indeed do more, so must all library professionals. This third edition provides the resources we need to make this happen.

I often quote the author William Gibson, who once stated, "The future is already here—it's just unevenly distributed." We currently live in a society in which the divide between the haves and the have-nots is growing wider. The public library can remain the "Great Equalizer" only if we educate ourselves about our great history, our core values, and how to provide these resources inclusively.

I wish to thank Dr. McCook and Dr. Bossaller for pouring their hearts and passion into this work. The library profession owes them a great deal of gratitude.

PREFACE

Kathleen de la Peña McCook and Jenny S. Bossaller

The public library is an institution founded in a belief in universal education and opportunity. In the United States, there is no other institution that is as open and welcoming to every person regardless of age, abilities, or legal status. Today, public libraries are symbols of equality, democracy, and the public good. Our future is as much about the people in our communities as it is about the library as place and platform.

Introduction to Public Librarianship, Third Edition, presents readers with both historic and current pictures of public librarianship, with a focus on the United States. There has been much written about the public library, its purposes, and its various services. This volume is a synthesis and overview of many years of public library development. It focuses on the work done by public librarians to establish and strengthen an institution that aims to be for the good of all who wish to use its services.

Public libraries in the United States of America are in their third century of service at the heart of communities throughout the nation. The physical and online services, collections, and spaces all serve to enhance the cultural life of their communities. They strive to increase public participation and foster the public sphere though conversations, listening, and learning.

The literature of public librarianship is extensive, but it is also dispersed among many specializations such as management, lifelong learning, information technology, youth services, and community planning. In truth, public librarianship incorporates all of these specializations, just as public librarians work to serve all people—all backgrounds, all ethnicities, all ages, all religions or no religion, all abilities, all economic means. The universality of mission and responsibilities presents a grand challenge for putting together an introduction.

The public library of the twenty-first century is more complex than its nineteenth- and twentieth-century predecessors, with multiple formats, virtual mobile access, and the mandate to provide equitable service to all people. The larger community is made stronger by a vibrant public library and the library remains a positive indicator of the quality of life.

PURPOSE

This book provides the historical, sociological, and cultural background of the public library in the United States. It is also a guide to the extensive literature of the field's various areas of specialization. This book was written for students, new librarians, library trustees and friends, and members of the general public who wish to understand the foundations of different aspects of public librarianship. Readers of *Introduction to Public Librarianship* will gain a greater understanding of the following key areas:

- The history of American public librarianship within the broader historical and cultural movements of the times

- The landmark literature of public librarianship's development
- The evolution of accountability, including standards, planning, and outcomes for public library service
- The role of the political process in the growth of libraries and library services
- The people who work to make the library function—the board, library workers, and volunteers who come together to shape the public sphere in twenty-first-century communities
- The public library building as a symbol of civic memory and identity
- Public libraries' youth and adult services as reflections of changing societal trends
- Human rights and human capabilities as guiding beacons for public library service in the twenty-first century
- Cooperative social and technological structures that involve public libraries
- A macro-level overview of the technological environment of librarianship
- Public libraries internationally, framed within the United Nations' Millennium Development Goals that aim to eradicate poverty, tackle inequality and injustice, and promote environmental sustainability

ORGANIZATION

Each chapter provides a holistic approach to its subject with a historical background, an organizational context, and discussion about the development of public libraries.

Chapters 1 through 7 were written by Kathleen de la Peña McCook.

Chapter 1 provides readers with a context for understanding where we are today, emphasizing the narrative of the public library's contribution to the democratic process. This chapter also includes background information about services to Native Americans, a population that is increasingly receiving new service and support from the Institute of Museum and Library Services. There is also a brief section on the status of public libraries in the Commonwealth of Puerto Rico.

Chapter 2 reviews the historical antecedents and the legal basis for establishing tax-supported public libraries. It discusses the fundamental *Report of the Trustees of the Public Library of the City of Boston, 1852*, one of the key documents of librarianship in the United States. This chapter pays special attention to the important role played by women in the establishment of public library service across the United States.

Chapter 3 covers the history of public libraries from the 1960s to the present. It focuses on efforts to equalize opportunity through the growing role assumed by the American Library Association, the enactment of federal legislation (LSA, LSCA, and LSTA), and an expanded scope of activity for the public library. It also discusses the work of national and state library associations and the role of state library agencies as the growing voice of advocacy for libraries that resulted from these actions.

Chapter 4 explores the historical progress of public library statistics and reviews the development of standards for public library service developed by the American Library Association. It analyzes the evolution of current planning processes that have replaced standards and measurable outcomes, focusing instead on quality-of-life indicators in local communities.

Chapter 5 reviews the political and economic context in which the public library functions. This chapter pays due attention to the organizational, legal, and funding basis of the public library, noting the parallels to municipal government structures and the move to larger units of service. The importance of advocacy at all levels is emphasized.

Chapter 6 surveys the structure of library governance and legislation. It presents the responsibilities of the library director and the board, and the need for board diversity. The chapter also presents job descriptions for librarians, model organizational charts, staff recruitment and development, and the role of unions.

Chapter 7 looks at the history and symbolism of public library buildings. It also explores how the Library Services and Construction Act (LSCA) and the Library Services and Technology Act (LSTA) shifted emphasis from buildings (structure) to technology (infrastructure). This chapter summarizes design standards, including accessibility, and addresses security and disaster planning.

Chapter 8, by Alicia K. Long, reviews the history and current practice of services to young people in public libraries. It looks at youth services staff competencies, collaboration among organizations, collections and book awards, and library spaces for children and teenagers.

Chapter 9, by Kathleen de la Peña McCook and Katharine Phenix, presents current guidelines and innovative programming for adults, with special focus on readers' services, the development of adult literacy services, and adult lifelong learning.

Chapter 10, by Jenny S. Bossaller, defines cooperation between libraries and outside groups. It focuses on networking in public librarianship, including the role of professional organizations, state library agencies, and library consortia.

Chapter 11, by Richard J. Austin and Diane Austin, provides public library students and new public librarians with a macro-level overview of the technological environment they will likely see as they move into positions in public library systems in the United States. It provides an overview of technology used in daily workflow of staff.

Chapter 12, by Clara M. Chu and Barbara J. Ford, discusses the new international agenda of public libraries, with goals to eradicate poverty, tackle inequality and injustice, and manage climate change globally by the year 2030. It provides an overview of public library development and cooperation worldwide.

Introduction to Public Librarianship, Third Edition, provides essential information for future library workers to inherit the future of public libraries as developed by their past and to continue to follow the ideas, principles, and goals that have shaped over 150 years of public librarianship in the United States.

The book includes special sections by practicing librarians. The foreword is written by Felton Thomas Jr., the Executive Director and CEO of the Cleveland Public Library and 2016–2017 president of the Public Library Association. The afterword is authored by Katharine Phenix, an Adult Services Librarian (also known as an Adult Guide) at Colorado's Anythink Libraries, who reflects on her 30 years as a public librarian and her ideas for the future of public libraries.

ACKNOWLEDGMENTS

Many people assisted in the development of *Introduction to Public Librarianship*, Third Edition. We worked to gain insight and advice from librarians and scholars from all over the United States whose backgrounds are varied and experiences diverse. Their interest and suggestions made our book more robust. We are deeply grateful to all of them.

Great appreciation is due to the Public Library Association (PLA) for commitment to a sustained vision of equality and transformation, especially to Barbara Macikas, PLA Executive Director, who steers a big ship and launches many patrols. We are grateful to strategic thinker Sandra Nelson, who built the planning frameworks, and to *Public Libraries* editor, Kathleen M. Hughes who is always on point for the new and creates opportunity to explore traditions.

Those who helped on bibliographic and technical preparation include Shawn Otani and James Scholz, research associates at the University of South Florida, School of Information. Library resource verification for this book's extensive bibliography was obtained by the Inter-library department at the University of South Florida, Tampa Campus Library staff: Sandra Law, Brenda Raiford, Cat Camp, Beverlyn Harris-Johnson, Catherine Negron, and LeEtta Schmidt.

Maria Almaguer Treadwell, assistant director for the East Coast Program, University of South Florida, School of Information, read early versions of the manuscript and made substantive comments. Kim Miller of the Institute of Museum and Library Services provided technical insight to the statistical data gathering process. Jorg Jemelka provided analysis and suggestions about quantitative data.

Margaret Heim Christ and John Walter Christ provided technical assistance in manuscript development. They were efficient, capable, and added clarity.

We would like to thank the ALA Editions staff, especially Rachel Chance, Acquisitions Editor, for her wise and patient counsel; Angela Gwizdala, Director of Editing, Design, and Production; Helayne Beavers, intrepid and gracious copy editor; and Laurie Graulich for her keen eye and meticulous index. We would also like to thank Charles Harmon, executive editor at Rowman and Littlefield, who initiated the first edition of this book in 2004 for Neal-Schuman and who has remained a constant supporter of public librarianship.

The careful review by Advisory Committee members provided the basis for revisions and a strong final book. We are most grateful to Dr. Ismail Abdullahi, North Carolina Central University; Dr. Anthony Bernier, San Jose State University; Ms. Nancy Fredericks, Libraries Administrator Pasco County Library Cooperative, Hudson, Florida; and Dr. Maurice B. Wheeler, University of North Texas.

We would also like to thank public librarians everywhere, whose practice inspired us to tell the story of their life work. We dedicate this book to the public librarians of the future.

Kathleen de la Peña McCook
Athens, Georgia and Ruskin, Florida

Jenny S. Bossaller
Columbia, Missouri

JUNE 2017

CHAPTER 1

The American Public Library

Democracy's Hope and the Community's Commons

> The public library is an excellent model of government at its best. A locally controlled public good, it serves every individual freely, in as much or as little depth as he or she wants.
>
> **—John N. Berry, "A Model for the Public Sector," 2001**

The people of the United States of America established the public library on democratic principles, developed support for the public library as a public good, and placed the public library at the community center as a commons. In 2017 America supports 8,895 public library administrative units (as well as 7,641 branches and bookmobiles).[1] (ALA, 2017)

We are now in the third century since the founding of the first public libraries in New England. Assessment of the institution's past and present is essential to its future. Some of the questions we will answer in this book include:

- What do we mean when we say that the public library is *democracy's hope?*
- How did the public library overcome the segregation of the Jim Crow era?
- How did the public library shift its attitude towards immigrants from assimilation to multicultural affirmation?
- What do we mean when we call the public library the *community commons?*
- How, and why, did public librarians resist the government's unchecked power to examine library records under the National Security Act?
- How is the public library evolving as a vital hub for digital inclusion? (Digital Inclusion Survey, 2016; Cowan, 2006; Knott, 2015; Kranich, 2001; Jones, 1999; Widdersheim, 2015).

These questions frame the complexities and the challenges of the public library as a public good supported by tax revenue, open to all, and committed to inclusion. In the twenty-first century, the public library occupies a central, physical space in communities across the United States, much as it has for centuries. However, librarians' understanding of the user is shifting, and the UX (user experience) is changing the face of many libraries' services (Stara, 2016). It is our intention to convey both the rich history and the current developments in the always exciting and evolving field of public librarianship. This chapter examines myriad statements about what democracy means, or what it looks like, in public libraries.

Democracy's Hope as the People's University

"There can be no doubt that such reading [for the diffusion of knowledge] ought to be furnished to all, as a matter of public policy and duty, on the same principle that we furnish free education . . . it is of paramount importance . . . that the largest possible number of persons should be induced to read and understand questions going down to the very foundation of social order."

—Report of the Trustees of the Boston Public Library, 1852

The decision to establish tax-supported public libraries as a natural and right extension of public schools in the 1850s tied public libraries to the ideal of a democratic society. The narrative linking democracy and public libraries has been a consistent theme (with many variations) that can be seen in professional statements, landmark decisions, and library literature. Just as the Trustees of the Boston Public Library made the connection between libraries and democracy in 1852, so did Koehler in 2015: "For a political system to function effectively it is assumed that the electorate, however established, must be sufficiently knowledgeable to make informed and intelligent decisions" (p. 137).

This was the rationale around which women's clubs organized for political advocacy, widely expanding public library services across America between 1870 and 1930. The concept of the library spread westward primarily through the efforts of determined and dedicated women, resulting ultimately in fairly large-scale female participation in appointed political offices on library boards and commissions (Watson, 1994, p. 265). Their goal was to improve civic life and quality of life, which was critical to the establishment of the majority of the public libraries that exist across America today. They were also instrumental in raising funds to bring Carnegie libraries to communities (Swetnam, 2012).

Writing of this period of library development in *Arsenals of a Democratic Culture,* Sydney Ditzion (1947) observed that "The major ideological currents . . . were directed toward producing a unified nation based on the free informed choice of individuals rather than on measures of indoctrination on behalf of any particular group . . . It was hoped that these could be eased, or perhaps erased, by establishing agencies of enlightenment for adult and youth alike" (pp. 75–76).

In the years following World War I, public libraries became a force for cultural assimilation through the efforts of ALA's Committee on Work with the Foreign Born (Jones, 1999). Americanization and a strong focus on adult education were factors contributing to the connection of libraries to civic life in the first part of the twentieth century. In *The Public Library—A People's University,* Johnson described the public library as "one of the outstanding American contributions to civilization . . . which will be the sound bulwark of a democratic state" (Johnson, 1938, p. 79).

Parallel to these general efforts to support education in service of democracy were the struggles of minority groups to gain access to library services. Knott's study of African-Americans and libraries during Jim Crow, *Not Free, Not for All* (2015) and Patterson's "History and Status of Native Americans in Librarianship" (2000) provide important factual analysis of the failure of American librarianship to include all people in the first phases of library growth (see figure 1.1). The democratic public library would not be mandated to serve all the people of America until the 1960s (*Brown v. Louisiana,* 1966).[2]

Library Services for and with Indigenous Peoples of the Americas: Tribal Community Libraries

This book does not address libraries for the more than 500 tribal nations residing within the geographical boundaries of the United States. There are about 500 recognized tribes and more than 10 unrecognized tribes. Not every tribe has a reservation. Indigenous peoples have a parallel history of knowledge and wisdom that must be considered in its own context. For a broader understanding of this alternative tradition, read *Tribal Libraries, Archives and Museums: Preserving Our Language, Memory and Lifeways* (Roy, Bhasin, & Arriaga, 2011).

The United States government has addressed the heritage of "knowledge seekers" and "wisdom keepers" who live within Native American tribes and maintain links with traditional tribal knowledge and history; see the official report *Pathways to Excellence* (U.S. National Commission on Libraries and Information Science, 1992).

Targeted federal funding is provided through the Native American Library Services Program. The Institute of Museum and Library Services (IMLS) provides basic funds, assistance grants, and enhancement grants to serve the range of needs of Indian tribes and Alaskan Native villages. Separate IMLS funding is also available for Native Hawaiian library development. In 2016 IMLS announced 243 grants totaling $4,055,022 through three library programs aimed at supporting and improving services among Native American and Native Hawaiian institutions.

Research and projects such as TRAILS and Four Directions, conducted by Native American library scholars Lotsee Patterson and Loriene Roy, have supported tribal community libraries serving indigenous people. To understand the holistic approach to service development, review the papers presented at the biennial International Indigenous Librarians' Forum (Roy and Smith, 2002); participate in meetings of the American Indian Library Association; follow the work of the ALA Committee on Rural, Native, and Tribal Libraries of All Kinds; and view work done at the National Museum of the American Indian.

Roy (2000) has made the following observations about libraries serving American Indians:

> Indians are rediscovering or retaining their culture by establishing genealogy, reading and inventing literature, reclaiming their Native languages, and becoming involved with political and social issues such as natural resource management, reclamation and reburial of human remains, and protection of treaty rights.
>
> This renaissance is built partially by the work of the American Indian library community, which has labored for many years to find support for Native American educational needs.

FIGURE 1.1 Library Services for and with Indigenous Peoples of the Americas: Tribal Community Libraries [CONTINUED ON FOLLOWING PAGE]

FIGURE 1.1 [CONTINUED]

SOURCES AND FURTHER READING

American Library Association. American Indian Library Association (AILA). http://www.ailanet.org/.

Association of Tribal Archives, Libraries, and Museums. http://www.atalm.org/.

Grounds, R. A., Tinker, G. E., and Wilkins, D. E. (2003). *Native voices: American Indian identity and resistance*. Lawrence, KS: University Press of Kansas.

Hills, G. H. (1997). *Native libraries: Cross-cultural conditions in the circumpolar countries.* Lanham, MD: Scarecrow Press.

Huhndorf, S. M. (2009). *Mapping the Americas: The Transnational politics of contemporary Native culture*. Ithaca, NY: Cornell University Press.

Institute of Museum and Library Services. Native American/Native Hawaiian museum services. https://www.imls.gov/grants/available/native-americannative-hawaiian-museum-services-program.

Jorgensen, M., Morris, T. L., Feller, S., Association of Tribal Archives, Libraries, and Museums, & Institute of Museum and Library Services. (2014). *Digital inclusion in Native communities: The role of tribal libraries*. Oklahoma City, OK: Association of Tribal Archives, Libraries, and Museums.

Patterson, L. (2000). History and status of Native Americans in librarianship. *Library Trends, 49*(1), 182–193.

Patterson, L. (2001). History and development of libraries on American Indian reservations. In Robert Sullivan (Ed.), *International Indigenous Librarians' Forum Proceedings* (38–44). Auckland, New Zealand: Te Ropu Whakahau.

Patterson, L. (2008). Exploring the world of American Indian libraries. *Rural Libraries, 28*, 7–12.

Roy, L. (2000, Spring). To support and model Native American library services. *Texas Library Journal, 76*, 32–35.

Roy, L. (2006, January/February). Honoring generations: Recruiting Native students into careers in librarianship. *Public Libraries, 45*, 48–52.

Roy, L., and Smith, A. A. (2002, Spring). Supporting, documenting and preserving tribal cultural lifeways: Library services for tribal communities in the United States. *World Libraries, 12*, 28–31.

Roy, L., Bhasin, A., & Arriaga, S. K. (2011). *Tribal libraries, archives, and museums: Preserving our language, memory, and lifeways.* Lanham, MD: Scarecrow Press.

Rural, Native, and Tribal Libraries of All Kinds Committee of ALA. http://www.ala.org/groups/committees/ala/ala-ruralcom.

Talbot, S. (2015). *Native nations of North America: An indigenous perspective*. Boston, MA: Pearson.

TRAILS toolkit. Tribal library procedures manual. This manual was revised through the American Library Association's Office for Literacy and Outreach Services and Committee on Rural, Native, and Tribal Libraries of All Kinds. It is made possible with ALA's 2010 funding. www.ala.org/offices/sites/ala.org.offices/files/content/olos/toolkits/TRAILS3.pdf.

U.S. National Commission on Libraries and Information Science. (1992). *Pathways to excellence: A report on improving library and information services for Native American peoples.* www.ncli.gov/libraries/nata.html.

After World War II the multi-volume Public Library Inquiry was commissioned by the American Library Association to establish the contribution of public libraries to society. In his examination of this landmark report series, Raber observed that commitment and promotion of the freedom of inquiry were necessary for

> the creation and maintenance of democratic society. There was a hope and a belief that this was the library's most fundamental source of legitimacy, that the library actually

> did this, and that American society was still a democratic one in which people's opinions were still relevant to the formation of public policy. In this view, the library's purpose was intimately connected to an informed citizenry that was the source of power, wisdom, and rightness of American culture and politics. (1994, p. 51)

Democratic ideals remained fundamental to public librarianship as the Public Library Association of ALA issued standards for public libraries in 1956 and 1966 that emphasized the educational function of the public library. Federal legislation provided funds to expand services through the Library Services Act (1956) and the Library Services and Construction Act (1966). To some degree the shift from national standards to a community planning model that took place in the 1970s and 1980s lessened the centrality of democracy in the national dialogue. Recognizing this, PLA appointed a Public Library Principles Task Force.

In 1982 the Task Force published "The Public Library: Democracy's Resource" a document that identified the public library as offering access freely to all members of the community without regard to race, citizenship, age, education level, economic status, or any other qualification or condition (see figure 1.2). These principles defined the public library as an institution of American life through which our highest aspirations are expressed.

In a 1987 essay, "Toward a Broader Definition of the Public Good," Boston Public Library director Arthur Curley called for librarians to assert the relationship of libraries to basic democratic freedoms and the fundamental humanistic principles central to our way of life was crucial to alliances for the public good. He advocated alliances with other public goods to preserve freedom.[3]

The close relationship of libraries and democracy was emphasized in 1995 when ALA's magazine, *American Libraries,* published "12 Ways Libraries Are Good for the Country," and opened with the following:

> Libraries safeguard our freedom and keep democracy healthy . . . Democracy and libraries have a symbiotic relationship. It would be impossible to have one without the other. Democracy vests supreme power in the people. Libraries make democracy work by providing access to information so that citizens can make the decisions necessary to govern themselves. Libraries make knowledge and ideas available to all, regardless of age, race, creed, gender, or wealth. Libraries provide the information that promotes civil debate and fosters good citizenship.
>
> The public library is the only institution in American society whose purpose is to guard against the tyrannies of ignorance and conformity, and its existence indicates the extent to which a democratic society values knowledge, truth, justice, books, and culture. . . . The public library is a measure of a democracy's belief that these things should be available to all individuals . . . Without democracy, libraries cannot be free to offer access to knowledge and ideas. Without libraries, true democracy cannot exist.

Similarly, Kevin Mattson characterized the public library as society's last defense against the possibility of oppression and the only agency guaranteeing wide accessibility to all kinds of ideas (1998). In 1999 the American Library Association Council adopted the statement "Libraries: An American Value," which declared: "Free access to the books, ideas, resources, and information in America's libraries is imperative for education, employment, enjoyment, and self-government" (ALA, 1999).

At the turn of the millennium, ALA president, Nancy Kranich edited the book *Libraries and Democracy: The Cornerstones of Liberty* (2001), which focused on the role libraries play

The Public Library: Democracy's Resource

A Statement of Principles

The public library is unique among our American institutions. Only the public library provides an open and nonjudgmental environment in which individuals and their interests are brought together with the universe of ideas and information. The ideas and information available through the public library span the entire spectrum of knowledge and opinions. The uses made of the ideas and information are as varied as the individuals who seek them. Public libraries freely offer access to their collections and services to all members of the community without regard to race, citizenship, age, education level, economic status, or any other qualification or condition.

Free access to ideas and information, a prerequisite to the existence of a responsible citizenship, is as fundamental to America as are the principles of freedom, equality and individual rights. This access is also fundamental to our social, political and cultural systems. Our founding documents eloquently express the concepts of an open society in which the hopes and aspirations of individuals are best realized in a political system which honors the consent of the governed, the greatest good for the greatest number, and tolerance and acceptance of the diversity of human thought and endeavor.

Access to information and the recorded wisdom and experience of others has long been held a requirement for achieving personal equality, and for improving the quality of life and thought in the daily activities and relationships of individuals. Along with the freedoms of speech, press, and religious expression, and publicly supported schools freely open to all, the public library emerged as one of those "institutions" of American life through which our highest aspirations are expressed. These "institutions" are the visible signs of the nation's abstract beliefs in the right to "life, liberty and the pursuit of happiness." Today, public libraries are integral parts of their communities in the fifty states and territories of the United States.

Public libraries were founded and supported by appropriations from tax revenues for very practical reasons: to provide and conserve books and journals economically for community use. Today, public libraries continue to provide free access to, and promote the communication of, ideas and information so that individuals on their own behalf, and groups, agencies, organizations and institutions can take active control of their lives and affairs. Public libraries have multiple roles: they serve the entire community as a center for reliable information; they provide opportunity and encouragement for children, young adults, and adults to educate themselves continuously; they create opportunities for recreation and personal enrichment; and they provide a place where inquiring minds may encounter the rich diversity of concepts so necessary for a democratic society whose daily survival depends on the free and competitive flow of ideas.

To perform these varied roles, public libraries assemble, make available, and preserve organized collections of books, related materials and systems in which ideas and informa-

FIGURE 1.2 The Public Library: Democracy's Resource—A Statement of Principles

[CONTINUED ON FOLLOWING PAGE]

SOURCE: Adopted by the Public Library Association Board of Directors in Philadelphia, July 13, 1982.

FIGURE 1.2 [CONTINUED]

tion are recorded. Public libraries employ staff with special skills, knowledge, and abilities to help library users find the ideas, information and materials to meet their diverse interests. The public library initiates and promotes information services, program events, exhibits, story hours, film showings, discussion groups and many other activities. Public libraries use assessment and planning processes to determine community needs and interests, often in cooperation with other community agencies and organizations. Libraries develop services to meet those needs and interests.

As the forms in which ideas and information are stored change, and will continue to change, the challenge of making the widest possible range of information accessible to all remains constant. The ideals which brought free public libraries into existence are as vital now as when they were formulated. Public libraries continue to be of enduring importance to the maintenance of our free democratic society. There is no comparable institution in American life.

Public Library Principles Task Force:
Kenneth F. Duchac, Samuel F. Morrison, Gail M. Sage, Jean Barry Molz,
Patrick M. O'Brien, Joseph F. Shubert, Margaret E. Monroe, W. Boyd Rayward,
Ronald A. Dubberly, Chair.

in advancing deliberative democracy. She lays down the marker for librarians to act decisively to affect policy issues that are changing the way information is produced and distributed, noting that libraries strengthen democracy by facilitating access to information in all its forms (Kranich, 2001, pp. 93–94).

Democracy was reaffirmed as a core value of librarianship by ALA in 2004:

> A democracy presupposes an informed citizenry. The First Amendment mandates the right of all persons to free expression, and the corollary right to receive the constitutionally protected expression of others. The publicly supported library provides free and equal access to information for all people of the community the library serves. (ALA, 2004)

In 2012 Carolyn Lukensmeyer, founder of America Speaks, declared the public library the institution that is most essential to democracy with talented committed staff interested in making a difference in the community.

Although some writers have been quizzical about the power of association between democracy and public libraries (Jaeger, Gorham, Bertolt, & Sarin, 2014, pp. 42–43; Oltmann, 2016), the fact remains that democracy and libraries have been connected by everyday people, scholars, advocates, and the political class for three centuries. In its *Creating a Nation of Learners: Strategic Plan, 2012–2016*, the Institute of Museum and Library Services states, "A democratic society in the knowledge age demands that its citizens learn continually, adapt to change readily, and evaluate information critically" (IMLS 2013).

The *National Policy Agenda for Libraries* (2015), led by the American Library Association Office for Information Technology Policy, underscores the connection:

> Libraries also promote intellectual freedom through inclusive and diverse collections, noncommercial public spaces that encourage open information exchange and debate, protection of privacy and confidentiality, and advocacy for government transparency, uncensored communications networks, and free expression. These values of equity, opportunity and openness are quintessentially democratic values, as well.

In 2017 ALA President Julie Todaro issued a statement reaffirming ALA's commitment to serve all community members: "Our core values include access to information; confidentiality/privacy; democracy; equity, diversity and inclusion; intellectual freedom; and social responsibility" (Todaro, 2017).

THE COMMUNITY'S COMMONS: HEART, ANCHOR, SAFE HAVEN

This book looks at aspects of the public library—its history, its services, its governance, and its multiple roles in the community for people of all ages. But we start with the assertion that communities in America support and love their public libraries. The study *How Americans Value Public Libraries in Their Communities* reports impressive results:

- 95% of Americans ages 16 and older agree that the materials and resources available at public libraries play an important role in giving everyone a chance to succeed.
- 95% say that public libraries are important because they promote literacy and a love of reading.
- 94% say that having a public library improves the quality of life in a community. (Pew, December 2013).

The Library Services and Technology Act (LSTA) provides federal funding through the Institute of Museum and Library Services (IMLS) to public libraries in every state. The IMLS statistics used in this book do not include the Commonwealth of Puerto Rico, although Puerto Rico's nearly 4 million people are U.S. citizens and the Commonwealth receives LSTA Funds. After a recent period of crisis when several public libraries in Puerto Rico had to close their doors, a campaign initiated in 2016 at the Graduate School of Library Science and Technology at the University of Puerto Rico that seeks to bring awareness of the roles of libraries in communities. We have asked Puerto Rican-born Loida Garcia-Febo, 2017-2018 ALA president, to characterize public libraries in Puerto-Rico and share her insights (figure 1.3).

Heart

Public libraries are often referred to as "the heart of the community." Try Googling "public library+heart." You will find testimonials from politicians, government officials, and library users writing in newspapers and stating before cameras their love and passion about the public library in their communities. On one day in 2015, the following articles came up:

- "The Library—Keeping the Heart of the City Alive," University of California Riverside *Highlander*. October 6, 2015.

- "Nashville Public Library Reopens in Bordeaux after Renovations," WKRN News. October 21, 2015. "'In many ways, our libraries are both the heart and mind of our community,' [Mayor] Barry said to the crowd. 'They are the intellectual home of our neighborhoods and our city.'"
- "People around Orangeburg County, SC, Depend on the Library to Offer Services They May Not Have at Home," WLTX News, October 2, 2015. "This library is really the heart of the community," says the director. "We want people to be able to come here and access the power, and access the internet."

For a truly magnificent paean to public libraries see *Heart of the Community: The Libraries We Love* which presents photographs and essays as testimony to the library faith (Christensen & Levinson, 2007).

Another way to think about the public library as the "heart of the community" is through the care that librarians offer to their patrons. From multilingual story times to programs for older adults, libraries offer learning and entertainment opportunities for all citizens, from cradle to grave. The "heart" aspect might even be quite literal. Many libraries today have emphasized healthy communities as a mission, serving as a point for information about consum-

Public Libraries in Puerto Rico

Puerto Rico's first public library, The Biblioteca Insular, was established in 1903 in Old San Juan. It included collections and manuscripts dating from the Spanish-era government. Years later when Andrew Carnegie provided funds for a larger building and the Biblioteca Carnegie was opened in 1916, the collection from the Biblioteca Insular was transferred to that library, which was opened until very recently.

Currently, there are many public, municipal and community libraries distributed across the island. In 2016 a research team from the University of Puerto Rico's Escuela Graduada de Ciencias y Technologías de la Información [Graduate School of Information Sciences and Technologies] carried out a study of public libraries in Puerto Rico entitled "Al rescate de las bibliotecas Públicas de Puerto Rico" [To the rescue of public libraries in Puerto Rico"]. As a result, the visibility of public libraries increased with findings from the project presented at library conferences, and updates shared on social media and library listservs within the country. An interactive map with the location of all the libraries was produced and it is available on the project's website, https://bibliotecaspublicasenpuertorico.wordpress.com/mapa-de-bibliotecas-publicas-municipales-y-de-comunidad/.

There are two bilingual English/Spanish libraries in Puerto Rico. The Jane Stern Dorado Community Library is located in the town of Dorado in the north of the island. Founded by community activist Jane Stern, it is a bilingual learning center that provides after-school programs. The San Juan Community Library is located in the town of San Juan and maintains a Virtual Branch where users can download ebooks and audiobooks.

A number of municipal libraries include their own electronic catalogs, computer labs, after-school programs, and cultural events. Some of these include the Biblioteca Municipal

FIGURE 1.3 Public Libraries in Puerto Rico [CONTINUED ON FOLLOWING PAGE]

FIGURE 1.3 [CONTINUED]

Dr. Carlos Hernández Rodríguez in the town of Carolina in the north of Puerto Rico, Biblioteca Municipal de Manati in the town of Manati, and Biblioteca Publica Dr. Pedro Albizu Campus in the town of Caguas.

The Library and Information Services Program of the United States Department of Education provides leadership and support to Puerto Rico's libraries to satisfy the information needs of its residents by offering programs and services and by promoting the love of reading and lifelong learning, regardless of age, location, social or physical condition.

The Puerto Rico Department of Education, as the assigned SLAA, provides and establishes guidelines for the best use of the Library Services and Technology Act funds. It also works towards the promotion of an island wide library development plan to fulfill the goals and objectives presented in its Five Year Plan.

—Loida Garcia-Febo

Postscript: In September 2017, Hurricane Maria made landfall in Puerto Rico, causing catastrophic damage to the island's infrastructure and communities. For a personal account of the aftermath, read University of Puerto Rico librarian Evelyn Milagros Rodriguez's account of the ongoing tragedy at http://theconversation.com/im-a-librarian-in-puerto-rico-and-this-is-my-hurricane-maria-survival-story-86426.

REFERENCES

About public libraries in Puerto Rico. www.puertadetierra.info/edificios/biblio/biblioteca.htm.
Al rescate de las bibliotecas Publicas de Puerto Rico [To the rescue of public libraries in Puerto Rico]. https://bibliotecaspublicasenpuertorico.wordpress.com/sobreelproyecto/.
Biblioteca Municipal Dr. Carlos Hernández Rodríguez. www.carolina.gobierno.pr/index.php/enlaces-de-interes/dept-de-educacion/136.html.
Biblioteca Publica Dr. Pedro Albizu Campus. www.actiweb.es/bibliotecadrpac/.
Puerto Rico Five Year LSTA Plan: 2013–2017. https://www.imls.gov/sites/default/files/state-profiles/plans/puertoric05yearplan.pdf.
Jane Stern Library. www.jsdcl.org/index.html.
San Juan Community Library. www.yourlibrarysanjuan.org/.
San Juan Community Library Virtual Bibrary. www.yourlibrarysanjuan.org/about-2/virtual-branch-open-247/.

er health and mental health for individuals and families in need. A recent study (Morgan et. al., 2016) of the 54 libraries of Philadelphia found that their broad social reach to vulnerable populations, including "homeless people, people with mental illness and substance use, recent immigrants, and children and families suffering trauma," offered the community support and "untapped potential to improve population health" (p. 2030). The researchers found that the libraries were frequently more welcoming than other community agencies. From the 84,701 attendees of early literacy programs to the 5,500 people who attended nutrition and healthy culinary classes, they have created programs that are interventions to health problems across the lifespan. Carolyn Connuscio, who was part of the research team, stated: "Our work shows very clearly that libraries are vital, dynamic organizations that know their patrons well and respond creatively to community needs" ("Libraries Can Be a Health Lifeline," 2016). Another member of the team, Ellen Rubenstein, said, "Libraries function as the heart of their communities . . . They serve as valuable community centers that bring together diverse groups of people and enrich lives every day" ("Libraries Can Be a Health Lifeline," 2016).

Anchor

Community anchors are organizations with firm roots—they keep the community from floating away. They might be economic assets like large employers, or community assets like the farmer's market. At the outset of the new millennium, the public library began to be characterized as a community anchor because public officials recognized libraries as equity investments that play a vital role in a community's social and fiscal well-being (St. Lifer, 2001). The concept of library as anchor institution was stated most clearly by Chicago Mayor Richard M. Daley in partnership with Chicago Public Library Commissioner Mary Dempsey.[4] Daley (2005) explained their collaboration to revitalize the public library system:

> *Libraries today are community anchors.* When we go out and dedicate a new library, it is amazing how many new volunteers we get from the community itself and how many people look at that amount of investment in a library and see what it means . . . that we're investing that much money in the community. They in turn say, "We're going to start *investing our own time and effort in our own community.*" (Daley in Holt & Holt, 2010, p. 22)

The Federal Communications Commission (FCC) has identified "such entities as schools, libraries, hospitals, and other medical providers, public safety entities, institutions of higher education, and community support organizations that facilitate greater use of broadband by vulnerable populations, including low-income, the unemployed, and the aged" ("WCB Workshop," 2012). Rural libraries are able to expand Internet access to people who otherwise might have low bandwidth or poor access. Alemanne, Mandel, & McClure (2011) suggest that public libraries "embrace a role that includes serving as an anchor among anchors, that is, serving as a central and critical agency that can coordinate and facilitate community-based broadband planning, deployment, training, and awareness-raising efforts."

In 2011 the Institute of Museum and Library Services defined the role of "community anchor" as a Strategic Goal: "IMLS promotes museums and libraries as strong community anchors that enhance civic engagement, cultural opportunities, and economic vitality" (IMLS, 2013). In the IMLS Strategic Plan for 2012–2016, these anchors are described as providing services that connect people to information and ideas as well as strengthening the link between individuals and their communities.

Alan Inouye, director of the ALA Office for Information Technology, challenged presidential candidates: "Look to community anchor institutions as the front-line responders. How can we best position these formidable assets (e.g., there are 120,000 libraries in the United States) to bear on the challenge of fundamental changes in the economy and society?" (Inouye, 2015).

Safe Haven

The public library as a safe haven has many dimensions. It is a refuge during times of civic disturbance, a sanctuary after natural disasters, a safe place for children, and a welcoming space for poor people and the homeless. The library is the community's center in times of stress and anxiety. After the November 2016 general election, Mark Smith, director of the Texas State Library and Archives Commission, wrote in the *Midland-Reporter Telegram*, "Libraries can save divided America."

> Where do Americans find the authoritative, trusted information and connections they need to live productive fulfilled lives? To what safe and neutral space do Americans turn to reconnect with their communities and each other? The answer is: the library. Libraries are in a unique position to participate—even lead—the healing process in our country. (Smith, 2016)

Civil Disturbances

In 2014 the Ferguson (MO) Municipal Public Library became a model for all libraries in the way it reacted to the crisis and the aftermath of riots brought on by the shooting of Michael Brown, a young African-American man, by local police (Berry, 2015). Schools in Ferguson were closed for a week, but the library remained open to serve 200 children and businesses seeking state aid. A different view is that of Seale (2016), who views post-political neoliberalism as the root cause of conflict and acceptance of a democratic model as missing the point.[5] Seale does not address the library as a venue for civil discourse, a long-standing model most recently addressed by Kranich (2010, 2013).

In April 2015 riots broke out in Baltimore following the funeral service for Freddie Gray, an African-American man who died in police custody. People clashed violently with Baltimore law enforcement, burned cars, and looted businesses, and more than 200 arrests were recorded. The Enoch Pratt Free Library stayed open.[6] With the schools closed, children needed a place to go (Peet, 2015). The decision to stay open despite the threat of continued violence attracted praise and support both nationally and internationally, but librarian Melanie Townsend Diggs insisted it wasn't an act of heroism. She told *American Libraries:*

> This is our life every day. We are public servants every day. At the end of the day, what happened on Monday [during the height of the unrest] was service oriented . . . We were giving the best service to our customers and our community that we can give. We do that every day. (Cottrell, 2015)

Natural Disasters

Hundreds of events have been declared disasters by FEMA in the twenty-first century. Based on a governor's request, the president may declare that a major disaster or emergency exists, activating an array of federal programs to assist in the response and recovery efforts ("FEMA Declaration Process," n.d.). Hurricanes Katrina and Rita (2005); the Cedar Rapids Flood (2008); Hurricanes Gustav and Ike (2008); Tsunami American Samoa (2009); the Joplin tornado (2011), Superstorm Sandy (2012); the Oklahoma and Colorado wildfires (2012); Colorado floods (2013); California earthquake (2014); South Carolina floods (2015); and the Oregon severe winter storms, straight-line winds, flooding, landslides, and mudslides (2016) are just a few natural disasters that have affected communities and libraries ("FEMA Disaster Declaration Annual List," n.d.).

Libraries have been designated an essential service to meet immediate threats to life and property resulting from major disasters such as floods, hurricanes, or tornados by the Stafford Act, which authorizes FEMA to provide Federal assistance.[7] Public libraries, characterized by Bishop & Veil (2013) as post-crisis information hubs, provide Internet access to request aid, help find missing family and friends, file FEMA and insurance claims, and help residents begin rebuilding their lives.

Florida's public libraries were assisted in preparations to reduce the state's disaster risk during weather-related catastrophes by the Hurricane Preparedness and Response project, located at the Information Institute at Florida State University. This initiative sought to clarify and raise awareness of the roles of public libraries in hurricane/disaster preparedness and response, situating public libraries as essential service points in times of crisis (Brobst, Mandel, & McClure, 2012).

A bibliography maintained by the Disaster Information Management Research Center of the National Library of Medicine, "Librarians and Libraries Respond to Disasters," chronicles library support of communities during times of crises. At this writing, up-to-date information on the Flint, Michigan, water crisis is disseminated by the Flint Public Library (Greenberg, 2016).

A Safe Place for Children

All 27 of Seattle's public libraries have been designated a Safe Place where youth ages 12 to 17 can ask for help when in crisis (Seattle Public Library, n.d). Public libraries throughout America display the "Safe Place" sign. The National Safe Place Program is a network of services to help youth with problems like running away, homelessness, and abuse. Safe Place is a national youth outreach and prevention program for young people in need of immediate help and safety. As a community-based program, Safe Place designates businesses and organizations as Safe Place locations, making help readily available to youth in communities across the country.[8]

The ALA Gay, Lesbian, Bisexual, and Transgender Round Table sponsored the program "Fabulous Havens: Libraries as Safe Spaces for the Needs of LGBTQ Youth." A speaker from the Gay, Lesbian, and Straight Education Network (GLSEN) shared ways in which libraries can effectively reach out to LGBTQ youth. The answer to the first question—how can we ensure that users feel comfortable the moment they walk in the door?—is by having friendly, welcoming staff members who are trained and ready for them inside (Vaillancourt, 2013).

Homeless and Poor People

The public library eliminates barriers to service to provide a welcoming space for people in poverty. ALA's "Library Services to the Poor" policy statement begins:

> The American Library Association promotes equal access to information for all persons, and recognizes the urgent need to respond to the increasing number of poor children, adults, and families in America. These people are affected by a combination of limitations, including illiteracy, illness, social isolation, homelessness, hunger, and discrimination, which hamper the effectiveness of traditional library services. Therefore it is crucial that libraries recognize their role in enabling poor people to participate fully in a democratic society, by utilizing a wide variety of available resources and strategies.[9]

An overview of public library services for the homeless in *American Libraries* highlighted programs in Chicago; Atlanta; San Francisco; Madison, Wisconsin; Lombard, Illinois; and San Jose, California. These programs entailed working with social-service agencies to create spaces where homeless patrons feel welcome, intellectually engaged, and connected with their communities (Ruhlmann, 2014).

In collaboration with USDA, public library summer meal programs help ensure children and teens in low-income communities are healthy and engaged during the summer. These programs bring underserved families to the library and create new partnerships (Cole & Chamberlain, 2015; Lapides, 2012). To help libraries establish themselves as successful summer meal program sites, the California Summer Meal Coalition and California Library Association developed the Lunch at the Library program to provide children and teens with nourishment, enrichment, and learning during the summer months. Texas and Ohio have also sponsored summer lunch programs.[10]

EVOLUTION

Are public libraries in need of transformation? In retrospect, we can see that the public library has been in a continuous state of evolution since its inception. It has been characterized as an altar to the god of learning, a workshop, a laboratory for the mind, a temple, even as the feedwire on a trolley representing intellectual energy (Nardini, 2001). And for all these reasons, people who support libraries care deeply about the institution. Wiegand asserts that there are three reasons people love their libraries:

> for the useful information they have made accessible; for the public spaces they provided; and for the power of reading stories they circulated that helped users make sense of phenomena in the world around them. (2015, p. 3)

Foundational library services, such as print-based circulation, continue to persist as an essential public library role. But throughout the twentieth century, collections expanded to add audio and visual materials in changing formats (e.g., vinyl, cassettes, CDs, videos, DVDs, e-books, and streaming video). Library services have evolved as well to include readers' advisory, makerspaces, youth services, career support, economic development, computer access, Wi-Fi, genealogy, local history, literacy services, ESL classes, book groups, and social services connections.

"The public library has been evolving for three centuries. It is a community commons, a place for lifelong learning, a place for early childhood, emergent literacy, a creator space, and perhaps most subtly, a statement of community value" (LaRue, 2014). Ta-Nehisi Coates passionately describes the public library as "open, unending and free" (Coates, 2015).

In 2015 the American Library Association launched the "Libraries Transform" campaign to reassert that libraries are not obsolete or simply nice amenities, and that they are more than quiet places to do research, find a book, and read. The campaign focuses on the idea that "libraries are essential" and the centers of their communities, places to learn, create and share.[11] This project was organized in collaboration with the ALA Center for the Future of Libraries (Figueroa, 2015) and the ALA Center for Civic Life: Libraries Transforming Communities initiative (Brewer, 2015). These are extraordinary projects that will keep public libraries connected to the community and funders. Telling the story of libraries in the political and policy context is emphasized by Jaeger et al. as critical to future support (2014, pp. 96–97).

These projects are variations on long-valued themes in the progress of the public library's purpose. Over the years many scholars and advocates have declared a transformation in public library services. In 1998 the Public Library Planning for Results initiative was greeted as a "transformation process" in the way libraries defined mission and goals (Himmel & Wilson, 1998). The IMLS report *A Catalyst for Change: The Transformation of Library Services to the Public* is an assessment of the impact of the LSTA and the post-Internet transformation of public libraries:

> **▶ TASK**
>
> Find the mission and vision statements of your local library. How does your library state its place in the community?

> Libraries expanded their traditional mission of collecting and circulating physical holdings to one that also provides access to computers, software, a host of new services, and an ever-increasing pool of digital information resources. This change demanded major investments in staff development, capital construction, IT hardware and software, and other digital resources to effectively meet public demand. . . . Apart from sheer volume, the information resources available in today's public libraries are also more varied and provide greater depth than was possible with the traditional (pre-Internet) library service model. (Manjarrez, Langa, & Miller, 2009)

The authors of *Transforming Libraries, Building Communities* remind us that even in the late 1800s, visionaries saw the public library as a "means to extend civic involvement" (Edwards, Robinson, & Unger, 2013, p. 6). Their book focuses on case studies of programs of deep, sustained community engagement that show what the community-centered library means in relation to transformative community building. Although their ideas about what the library should do for the community are not necessarily new, they show how to work through partnerships to maximize the capabilities of public libraries as centers of sustainability, creativity, and civic action.

The cornerstone document of the 2013–2014 ALA President Barbara Stripling's presidential initiative, "Libraries Change Lives" (figure 1.4) was designed to build the public will and sustain support for America's right to libraries. Signing ceremonies where community members visibly declared their right to have vibrant libraries in their community were held

Libraries Change Lives: Declaration for the Right to Libraries

In the spirit of the United States Declaration of Independence and the Universal Declaration of Human Rights, we believe that libraries are essential to a democratic society. Every day, in countless communities across our nation and the world, millions of children, students and adults use libraries to learn, grow and achieve their dreams. In addition to a vast array of books, computers and other resources, library users benefit from the expert teaching and guidance of librarians and library staff to help expand their minds and open new worlds. We declare and affirm our right to quality libraries—public, school, academic,

FIGURE 1.4 Libraries Change Lives: Declaration for the Right to Libraries

[CONTINUED ON FOLLOWING PAGE]

SOURCE: Declaration for the Right to Libraries, 2013–2014 (www.ala.org/advocacy/declaration-right-libraries).

FIGURE 1.4 [CONTINUED]

and special—and urge you to show your support by signing your name to this Declaration for the Right to Libraries.

LIBRARIES EMPOWER THE INDIVIDUAL. Whether developing skills to succeed in school, looking for a job, exploring possible careers, having a baby, or planning retirement, people of all ages turn to libraries for instruction, support, and access to computers and other resources to help them lead better lives.

LIBRARIES SUPPORT LITERACY AND LIFELONG LEARNING. Many children and adults learn to read at their school and public libraries via story times, research projects, summer reading, tutoring and other opportunities. Others come to the library to learn the technology and information skills that help them answer their questions, discover new interests, and share their ideas with others.

LIBRARIES STRENGTHEN FAMILIES. Families find a comfortable, welcoming space and a wealth of resources to help them learn, grow and play together.

LIBRARIES ARE THE GREAT EQUALIZER. Libraries serve people of every age, education level, income level, ethnicity and physical ability. For many people, libraries provide resources that they could not otherwise afford—resources they need to live, learn, work and govern.

LIBRARIES BUILD COMMUNITIES. Libraries bring people together, both in person and online, to have conversations and to learn from and help each other. Libraries provide support for seniors, immigrants and others with special needs.

LIBRARIES PROTECT OUR RIGHT TO KNOW. Our right to read, seek information, and speak freely must not be taken for granted. Libraries and librarians actively defend this most basic freedom as guaranteed by the First Amendment.

LIBRARIES STRENGTHEN OUR NATION. The economic health and successful governance of our nation depend on people who are literate and informed. School, public, academic, and special libraries support this basic right.

LIBRARIES ADVANCE RESEARCH AND SCHOLARSHIP. Knowledge grows from knowledge. Whether doing a school assignment, seeking a cure for cancer, pursuing an academic degree, or developing a more fuel efficient engine, scholars and researchers of all ages depend on the knowledge and expertise that libraries and librarians offer.

LIBRARIES HELP US TO BETTER UNDERSTAND EACH OTHER. People from all walks of life come together at libraries to discuss issues of common concern. Libraries provide programs, collections, and meeting spaces to help us share and learn from our differences.

LIBRARIES PRESERVE OUR NATION'S CULTURAL HERITAGE. The past is key to our future. Libraries collect, digitize, and preserve original and unique historical documents that help us to better understand our past, present and future.

all over the country. The Declaration (ALA, 2013) is the most recent national commitment to this essential institution.

In any community, the public library provides a sense of place, a refuge, and a still point; it is a commons, a vital part of the public sphere, and an incubator of ideas and creativity. The public library supports family literacy, fosters lifelong learning, helps immigrants find a place, and gives a place to those for whom there is no other place to be. The public library provides a wide-open door to knowledge and information to people of all ages, genders, abilities, ethnicities, and economic status. People who use the public library, and even those who do not, will fight to maintain it even in hard budget times. Individuals afraid of the influence of ideas may attack the public library, but philanthropists and everyday people donate money to support the public library and politicians make proclamations about the public library as the heart of the community. In the United States, the public library exists in cities, towns, and rural areas due to many advocates who support democracy and dreams.

NOTES

1. The Institute of Museum and Library Services carries out data collection and analysis to extend and improve library services. Data used in this book were reported in 2016 based on data collected in 2013. The number of libraries is reported in table 3 of the 2016 report, supplementary tables, and p. 10. https://www.imls.gov/sites/default/files/fy2013_pls_tables_1_thru_35_and_staterank.pdf.
2. In her history of public libraries in the age of Jim Crow, Cheryl Knott notes: 1) racially segregated public libraries were not aberrations; they were routine in the Jim Crow era; 2) middle-class white women ensured that the newly created public libraries were "white spaces"; 3) counter to their own preference, African Americans created separate libraries for themselves, and library desegregation proceeded unevenly (Knott, 2015, pp. viii–ix).
3. The American Library Association holds an annual lecture in commemoration of Arthur Curley. He was a champion of the arts and of the library's role as a center that can transform the community. The lecture series commemorates his lifelong dedication to the principles of intellectual freedom and free public access to information. www.ala.org/awardsgrants/arthur-curley-memorial-lecture.
4. The Chicago Public Library during the Dempsey years was the focus of study as an exemplary community-building organization. See Putnam & Feldstein (2003).
5. The Ferguson Municipal Public Library was honored as the 2015 Gale/LJ Library of the Year. Library director Scott Bonner was awarded the 2015 Lemony Snicket Prize for Noble Librarians Faced with Adversity.
6. Dr. Carla D. Hayden, CEO of the Enoch Pratt Free Library in Baltimore, was selected by the Advisory Committee of the ALA Office for Diversity, Literacy, and Outreach Services in recognition of her efforts to keep the Enoch Pratt Free Library and its branches open and continually engaged with the Baltimore community during the civil unrest in the wake of the death of Freddie Gray to deliver the 2015 Jean E. Coleman Library Outreach Lecture. In 2016 she was named Librarian of Congress and the press noted her example as a leader during the civil unrest in Baltimore (Landgraf, 2016).
7. Section 403 of the Stafford Act authorizes FEMA to provide federal assistance to meet immediate threats to life and property resulting from a major disaster. Specifically, Section 403(a)(3)(D) allows for the provision of temporary facilities for schools and other essential community services, when related to saving lives and protecting and preserving property or public health and safety. Libraries have been designated an essential service. This change took place in 2011; it had its roots in the exception that was made in 2009 to assist the flood-damaged Cedar Rapids Library in Iowa (Kelley, 2011).

8. National Safe Place ensures an effective system of response for youth in crisis through public and private partnerships at a local, state, and national level (http://nationalsafeplace.org/what-is-safe-place/).
9. The Hunger, Homelessness, and Poverty Task Force of the ALA Social Responsibilities Round Table was established to promote and implement Policy 61 and to raise awareness of poverty issues. See www.ala.org/srrt/hunger-homelessness-and-poverty-task-force-hhptf.
10. For details of these programs, see USDA Summer Meals Toolkit (www.fns.usda.gov/sfsp/summer-meals-toolkit); California Library Association (http://lunchatthelibrary.org/program-overview/); State Library of Ohio (https://library.ohio.gov/services-for-libraries/library-programs-development/youth-services/summer-food-service-program/); Texas State Library (https://www.tsl.texas.gov/summerreading/summerfood).
11. The 2015–2018 Libraries Transform project included an awareness campaign and work with the Center for the Future of Libraries to aggregate tools and resources to help library professionals deal with the cultural implications of this transformation (Feldman, 2015).

REFERENCES

12 ways libraries are good for the country. (1995, December). *American Libraries, 26*, 1113–1119. www.ala.org/ala/alonline/selectedarticles/12wayslibraries.htm.

Alemanne, N. D., Mandel, L. H., & McClure, C. R. (2011). Chapter 3: The rural public library as leader in community broadband services. *Library Technology Reports, 47*(6), 19–28.

American Library Association. (1999) Libraries: An American value. www.ala.org/advocacy/intfreedom/americanvalue.

American Library Association. (2004). Core values of librarianship. www.ala.org/advocacy/intfreedom/statementspols/corevalues.

American Library Association (2013). Declaration for the right to libraries. www.ala.org/advocacy/declaration-right-libraries.

American Library Association. (2017). *The state of America's libraries 2017: A report from the American Library Association.* Kathy S. Rosa, ed. 2016. www.ala.org/news/state-americas-libraries-report-2017.

American Library Association, Office for Information Technology Policy. (2015). *National policy agenda for libraries.* www.ala.org/advocacy/sites/ala.org.advocacy/files/content/pdfs/NPAforLibraries1.pdf.

American Library Association, Office for Literacy and Outreach Services. (2012). *Extending our reach: reducing homelessness through library engagement.* www.ala.org/offices/extending-our-reach-reducing-homelessness-through-library-engagement-7.

Arthur Curley Memorial Lecture. Awards and Grants. (n.d.). www.ala.org/awardsgrants/arthur-curley-memorial-lecture.

Berry, J. N. (2001). A model for the public sector. *Library Journal, 126*(4), 6–59.

Berry, J. N. (2015). 2015 Gale/LJ library of the year: Ferguson Municipal Public Library, MO, courage in crisis. *Library Journal, 140*(10), 28–32.

Bishop, B., & Veil, S. R. (2013). Public libraries as post-crisis information hubs. *Public Library Quarterly, 32*(1), 33–45.

Boston Public Library. (1852). *Report of the Trustees of the Public Library to the City of Boston.* https://babel.hathitrust.org/cgi/pt?id=umn.31951000831516z;view=1up;seq=7.

Brewer, B. (2015, January/February). Libraries transforming communities. *American Libraries, 46*, 50–53.

Brobst, J. L., Mandel, L. H., & McClure, C. R. (2012). Public libraries and crisis: Roles of public libraries in hurricane/disaster preparedness and response. In C. Hagar (Ed.), *Crisis information management: Communication and technologies* (pp. 155–173). Cambridge, United Kingdom: Woodhead.

Brown v. Louisiana. (1966). 383 U.S. 131.

Coates, T. N. (2015). *Between the world and me.* New York, NY: Spiegel & Grau.

Cole, N. & Chamberlain, P. (2015). Nourishing bodies and minds when school is out. *Public Libraries, 54*(2), 22–28.

Christensen, K., & Levinson, D. (Eds.). (2007). *Heart of the community: The libraries we love.* Great Barrington, MA: Berkshire.

Cottrell, M. (2015, May 15). Libraries respond to community needs in times of crisis: Baltimore, Ferguson just two recent examples of libraries offering refuge. *American Libraries.* https://americanlibraries magazine.org/2015/05/15/libraries-respond-to-community-needs-in-times-of-crisis/.

Cowan, A. L. (2006, May 31). Four librarians finally break silence in records case. *The New York Times.* www.nytimes.com/2006/05/31/nyregion/31library.html.

Curley, A. (1987). Toward a broader definition of the public good. In E. J. Josey (Ed.), *Libraries, coalitions and the public good* (p. 37). New York, NY: Neal-Schuman.

Dana, J. C. (1902, August). The meaning of the public library in a city's life: Address at dedication of the Trenton Public Library. *Library Journal, 27,* 755–757.

Digital inclusion survey. (2016). http://digitalinclusion.umd.edu/.

Ditzion, S. H. (1947). *Arsenals of a democratic culture: A social history of the American public library movement in New England and the Middle States from 1850–1900.* Chicago, IL: American Library Association.

Edwards, J. B., Robinson, M. S., & Unger, K. R. (2013). *Transforming libraries, building communities: The community-centered library.* Lanham, MD: Scarecrow Press, 2013.

Ethnic and Multicultural Information Exchange Round Table (EMIERT). The multicultural library. www.ala.org/emiert/usefullinks/links.

Federal Emergency Management Agency. (n.d.) Disaster declarations by year. https://www.fema.gov/disasters/grid/year.

Federal Emergency Management Agency. (n.d.) Disaster declaration process. https://www.fema.gov/disaster-declaration-process.

Feldman, S. (2015, July/August). President's message. Libraries transform. *American Libraries, 46,* 5.

Figueroa, M. (2015, March/April). Forecasting the future of libraries. *American Libraries, 46,* 28–29.

Greenberg, W. (2016, March 31). Flint Public Library to archive stories of residents living through the water crisis. Michigan Radio [Internet]. http://michiganradio.org/post/flint-public-library-archive-stories-residents-living-through-water-crisis#stream/0.

Himmel, E., Wilson, W. J., with the ReVision Committee of the Public Library Association. (1998). *Planning for results: A public library transformation process.* Chicago, IL: American Library Association.

Holt, L. E., & Holt, G. E. (2010). *Public library services for the poor: Doing all we can.* Chicago, IL: ALA Editions.

Hudson, M. (2016). Quoted in Putnam, L. How libraries are curating current events, becoming community debate hubs. http://mediashift.org/2016/05/how-libraries-are-curating-current-events-becoming-community-debate-hubs/.

Inouye, A. S. (2015). Presidential candidates: Local economies in the digital age deserve attention [Blog post]. https://www.benton.org/blog/presidential-candidates-local-economies-digital-age-deserve-attention.

Institute of Museum and Library Services. (2013, 2011). *Creating a nation of learners: Strategic plan, 2012–2016.* https://www.imls.gov/sites/default/files/legacy/assets/1/AssetManager/StrategicPlan2012-16.pdf.

Institute of Museum and Library Services. American Institutes for Research. (2016). PLS web portal user's guide. Version 1.4. *Guide for reporting data for the Public Libraries Survey, FY2015 using the Web Public Library Universe System Software.* https://www.imls.gov/sites/default/files/pls_users_guide_fy2015_508.pdf.

Jaeger, P. T., Gorham, U., Bertot, J. C., & Sarin, L. C. (2014). *Public libraries, public policies, and political processes: Serving and transforming communities in times of economic and political constraint.* Lanham, MD: Rowman & Littlefield.

Johnson, A. (1938). *The public library—A people's university.* Chicago, IL: American Library Association.

Jones, P. A., Jr. (1999). *Libraries, immigrants, and the American experience.* Westport, CT: Greenwood Press.

Kelley M. (2011, January 19). ALA Midwinter 2011: Cedar Rapids new public library helped spur FEMA change. *Library Journal.*

Knott, C. (2015). *Not free, not for all: Public libraries in the age of Jim Crow.* Amherst, MA: University of Massachusetts Press.

Koehler, W. C. (2015). *Ethics and values in librarianship: A history.* Lanham, MD: Rowman & Littlefield.

Kranich, N. (Ed.). (2001). *Libraries and democracy: The cornerstones of liberty.* Chicago, IL: American Library Association.

Kranich, N. (2010, Fall). Promoting adult learning through civil discourse in the public library. *New directions for adult and continuing education, 127*, 15–24.

Kranich, N. (2013). Libraries and strong democracy: Moving from an informed to a participatory 21st century citizenry. *Indiana Libraries, 32*(1), 13–20.

Landgraf, G. (2016, November/December) America's librarian. *American Libraries, 47,* 40–43.

Lapides, S. (2012, July/August). Summer lunches program takes off. *Public Libraries, 52*, 8–9.

LaRue, J. (2014). Why build libraries? *Public Libraries, 53*(4), 12–17.

Libraries and the USDA Summer Food Service Program: TSLAC. (n.d.). https://www.tsl.texas.gov/summerreading/summerfood.

Libraries can be a health lifeline for people most at risk. (2016, November 11). www.foxnews.com/health/2016/11/11/libraries-can-be-health-lifeline-for-people-most-at-risk.html.

Lukensmeyer, C. J. (2012). Public libraries and the future of democracy. *National Civic Review, 101,* 13–14.

Manjarrez, C., Langa, L., & Miller, K. (2009). *A catalyst for change: LSTA grants to states program activities and the transformation of library services to the public.* IMLS-2009-RES-01. Washington, DC: Institute of Museum and Library Services. www.imls.gov/pdf/CatalystForChange.pdf.

Mattson, K. (1998). *Creating a democratic public: The struggle for urban participatory democracy during the Progressive Era.* University Park, PA: Pennsylvania State University Press.

Morgan, A., et. al. (2016). Beyond books: Public libraries as partners for population health. *Health Affairs,* 2030–2036.

Nardini, R. F. (2001). A search for meaning: American library metaphors, 1876–1926. *Library Quarterly 71*(2), 111–140.

National Commission on Libraries and Information Science. (1992). *Pathways to excellence: A report on improving library and information services for Native American Peoples.* www.ncli.gov/libraries/nata.html.

Oltmann, S. (2016). "For all the people": Public library directors interpret intellectual freedom. *Library Quarterly, 86*(3), 290–312.

Overview:|Lunch at the library. (n.d.). http://lunchatthelibrary.org/program-overview/.

Patterson, L. (2000, Summer). History and status of Native Americans in librarianship. *Library Trends, 49,* 182–193.

Peet, L. (2015, May). Baltimore's Enoch Pratt Free Library provides haven in troubled times. *Library Journal, 140*(8).

Pew Internet and American Life Project. (2013). *How Americans value public libraries in their communities.* http://libraries.pewinternet.org/2013/12/11/libraries-in-communities/.

Public Library Association, Public Library Principles Task Force. (1982, Fall). The public library: Democracy's resource, a statement of principles. *Public Libraries, 21,* 92.

Putnam, L. (2016) How libraries are curating current events, becoming community debate hubs. http://mediashift.org/2016/05/how-libraries-are-curating-current-events-becoming-community-debate-hubs/.

Putnam, R. D., & Feldstein, L. M. (2003). Branch libraries: The heartbeat of the community. In *Better together: Restoring the American community* (pp. 34–54). New York, NY: Simon and Schuster.

Raber, D. (1994). Inquiry as ideology: The politics of the Public Library Inquiry. *Libraries and Culture 29*(1), 49–60.

Rainie, L. (2016). *Libraries and learning.* Pew Research Center. www.pewinternet.org/2016/04/07/libraries-and-learning/.

Roy, Loriene. (2000, Spring). To support and model Native American library services. *Texas Library Journal, 76,* 32–35.

Roy, L., Bhasin, A., & Arriaga, S. K. (2011). *Tribal libraries, archives, and museums: Preserving our language, memory, and lifeways.* Lanham, MD: Scarecrow Press.

Roy, Loriene, & A. Arro Smith. (2002, Spring). Supporting, documenting and preserving tribal cultural lifeways: Library services for tribal communities in the United States. *World Libraries 12,* 28.

Ruhlmann, E. (2014). A home to the homeless. *American Libraries, 45*(11/12), 40–44.

Seale, M. (2016). Compliant trust: The public good and democracy in the ALA's "Core Values of Librarianship." *Library Trends, 64*(3), 585–603.

Seattle Public Library. (n.d.). Safe Place. www.spl.org/audiences/teens/safe-place.

Smith, M. (2016). Libraries can save divided America. *Midland Reporter-Telegram.* www.mrt.com/news/education/article/Libraries-can-save-divided-America-10614025.php.

St. Lifer, E. (2001, January). The library as anchor. *Library Journal, 126,* 59–61.

Stara, L. (2016). Improving your library's UX. http://publiclibrariesonline.org/2016/08/improving-your-librarys-ux/.

Summer Food Service Program, State Library of Ohio. (n.d.) https://library.ohio.gov/services-for-libraries/library-programs-development/youth-services/summer-food-service-program/.

Summer Meals Toolkit. (n.d.). Food and nutrition service. www.fns.usda.gov/sfsp/summer-meals-toolkit.

Swetnam, S. H. (2012). *Books, bluster, and bounty: Local politics and Intermountain West Carnegie Library Building Grants, 1898–1920.* Logan, UT: Utah State University Press.

Todaro, J. (2017). ALA opposes new administration policies that contradict core values.

www.ala.org/news/press-releases/2017/01/ala-opposes-new-administration-policies-contradict-core-values.

Vaillancourt, S. (2013). On my mind. Libraries as safe spaces. *American Libraries, 44*(1/2), 30.

Watson, P. D. (1994, July). Founding mothers: The contribution of women's organizations to public library development in the United States. *Library Quarterly, 64,* 237.

WCB cost model virtual workshop 2012—Community anchor institutions. (2012, June 1). https://www.fcc.gov/news-events/blog/2012/06/01/wcb-cost-model-virtual-workshop-2012-community-anchor-institutions.

Widdersheim, M. M. (2015). Governance, legitimation, commons: A public sphere framework and research agenda for the public library sector. *Libri: International Journal of Libraries and Information Services, 65*(4), 237–245.

Wiegand, W. A. (2015). *Part of our lives: A people's history of the American public library.* New York, NY: Oxford University Press.

Youth Runaway Prevention. (n.d.). What is Safe Place? http://nationalsafeplace.org/what-is-safe-place/.

CHAPTER 2

Development of the Public Library in America

Colonial Times to the 1960s

> Why should not this prosperous and liberal city extend some reasonable amount of aid to the foundation and support of a noble public library, to which the young people of both sexes, when they leave the schools, can resort for those works which pertain to general culture, or which are needful for research into any branch of useful knowledge?
>
> —***Report of the Trustees of the Public Library to the City of Boston,*** **1852**

How did the public library grow from small shared book collections in the 1700s to become the essential part of the educational ecosystem and a resource for promoting digital and information literacy that it is today?[1] Who were the people responsible for the growth of public libraries in the United States? What were the roles of Jesse Torrey, Alexandre Vattemare, Josiah Quincy, Andrew Carnegie, Elizabeth Putnam Sohier, Julius Rosenwald, Carl Milam, Julia Wright Merrill, Carlton Joeckel or Edith Green—just a few of the individuals who laid the groundwork for today's public library?

COLONIAL TIMES TO 1852

The early settlers on the northeastern shores of the New World were readers. Books were important to the development and stability of the seventeenth-century colonies, particularly in what would one day be Massachusetts, and were viewed as a means to provide a continuity of values. Many of the New England colonists had private libraries. By understanding the extent of reading among colonists we begin to realize the importance attached to the "culture of the Word" as described in *The Colonial Book in the Atlantic World* (Amory and Hall, 2000). The early settlers read for religious and secular purposes; this "reading public" has been the subject of studies that help us understand how the reading and intellectual lives of our forebears shaped our culture today.[2]

The best-documented example of books brought to the New World as the "carrier of inspiration" is the effort of English Anglican clergyman Thomas Bray, whose Society for Promoting Christian Knowledge, and under the Crown and Anglican Church, the Society for the Propagation of the Gospel in Foreign Parts. This gave him the means to establish 39 parish libraries along the Eastern seaboard in Maryland, Virginia, and South Carolina between 1695 and 1704. Bray initiated three types of libraries: provincial, parochial, and layman's libraries. These also functioned as lending libraries for the public at large (Knight, 1922; Laugher, 1973).

Since 1754 the reading public of New York City has been analyzed in detail that provides evidence of the integration of reading into daily life (Glynn, 2015). An overview of the "new nation" and its reading and print culture is provided in *A History of the Book in America: An Extensive Republic: Print, Culture, and Society in the New Nation, 1790–1840* (Gross & Kelley, 2010). People in colonial days were readers, and they found ways to have access to more books than they could afford individually. These habits created a context for the development of common access to books and reading materials. Reading took place in diverse settings in the colonies before they declared independence as the United States of America from Great Britain in 1776.

The work of library historians reinforces the importance of New England in the development of tax-supported public libraries, because much of the synthetic literature about the founding of public libraries is based upon accounts written by New Englanders. Charles Coffin Jewett's report of 1851, *Notices of Public Libraries in the United States of America* provided the foundation for many later studies.

Until 1876 the term "public library" meant any library not privately owned, whereas the phrase "free public library" was used to indicate libraries that were similar to the tax-supported public library of today. Yet in the years prior to laws enabling tax-supported public libraries in the mid-1800s, tens of thousands of libraries open to various publics were established in the United States.

Three Forerunners of the Public Library: Social, Circulating, and School District Libraries

Social Libraries

Social libraries and circulating libraries existed in the colonies by the early 1700s. Social library collections emphasized literature, history, science, and theology, whereas circulating libraries were comprised mainly of popular reading. For a detailed analysis (descriptions, statistics, etc.) of libraries prior to 1876, three works by Haynes McMullen (1987, 1991, 2001) provide comprehensive information on the founding and growth of hundreds of libraries including the middle and far West.

Social libraries trace their origins to the gentlemen's libraries and book clubs of the early 1700s (Raven & Howsam, 2011). The Library Company of Philadelphia, established in 1731 by Benjamin Franklin and the Junto (whose motto was "Communiter Bona profundere Deum est": "To pour forth benefits for the common good is divine"[3]) as a joint-stock company or proprietary library, is the most well-known social library. The establishment of the Charleston Library Society in South Carolina in 1748 demonstrates that book culture also existed outside of the Northeast.

Social libraries involved the coming together of individuals to fund and develop collections based on their interests. Athenaeums emphasized more scholarly collections and cultural programs. Mechanics' libraries and mercantile libraries were established to provide educational opportunities for workers (Raven, 2007). African-American literary societies also existed in New York, Massachusetts, Ohio, and Michigan, which offered lectures and access to books as part of membership (Porter, 1936). Although historians recount the stories of some social libraries, enabling us to imagine the intellectual and pragmatic pursuits of members, we know of many others from the barest of records.[4]

Studies of individual libraries and societies outside of New England, such as the Virginia Historical Society (Todd, 2001), or the St. Augustine, Florida, Library Association, located in the oldest city in the United States (Blazek, 1979), provide a clearer picture of particular places. Broader studies, such as "Women and the Founding of Social Libraries in California, 1859-1910" (Musmann, 1982), or Hoyt's (1999) "A Strong Mind in a Strong Body: Libraries in the German-American Turner Movement," give us a more sweeping look at the growth of social libraries.

Circulating Libraries

Circulating libraries that rented popular books originated in Germany, France, and England in the mid-1700s. There were a number of small circulating libraries in New England in the late 1700s. The proprietor generally sold another type of product—such as tea or newspaper vendors, music shops, or fabric stores. The proprietor also might have been a publisher or owned a press. They often included fiction, and were run by men or women (Kaser, 1980; Croteau, 2006), and they closed after just a few years. Digitization projects, such as the Library of Congress's Chronicling America, have made it possible to locate many instances of circulating libraries from the country's formative years.

Circulating libraries of popular books for rent were business enterprises such as the Boston Circulating Library (Glasgow, 2002). Some circulating libraries were affiliated with bookstores; some with coffee shops and others, for women, with millinery shops; and still others were freestanding enterprises.[5]

The institution spread through Massachusetts with circulating libraries established in Salem (1789) and Newburyport (ca. 1794) and elsewhere in New England: New London, Connecticut (1793); Keene, New Hampshire (1805); Providence, Rhode Island (1820); and Woodstock, Vermont (1821).

Profits followed the fiction market and analyses of collections based on catalogs of the time show fiction dominating the holdings. Meanwhile, reading rooms were popular in places like Lexington, Kentucky, described by a visitor in 1807 as subscribing to 42 newspapers from all over the United States. Other locations were as different as rooms in manufacturing towns established for factory workers (1844) or New England mill girls (Kaser, 1978, 1980; McCauley, 1971).

School District Libraries

School district libraries also laid the groundwork for a culture of reading. In 1815 Jesse Torrey, founder of New York's Juvenile Society for the Acquisition of Knowledge, urged that governments establish free circulating libraries accessible to all classes and both sexes. He believed that all people should be educated, not just the privileged. Torrey's progressive ideas provided the rationale for the eventual movement towards public libraries (Ditzion, 1940).

The Common School movement of the 1830s, which ensured that every child would have a basic tax-supported education, has been described as the product of social reform in an age of perceived social decline. Conceived as a bulwark of traditional values against the tide of immigrants, public schools, with the addition of district libraries, were viewed as the means to forge a new moral order by educating children properly (Fain, 1978). "The bridge between free schools and free libraries was omnipresent in the early documents of the public library movement," states Ditzion (1947, p. 22) in his history of early American public libraries.

The advocacy of New York governor De Witt Clinton (1835) for collections attached to common schools to be the basis of a tax on each district for a school library marks the first state law for tax-supported (though school-based) free library service (Joeckel, 1935, p. 9). In 1835 New York State passed a law providing tax-supported school-based free library service. Support for school district libraries as part of the common school movement formed the basis for secular, universal education. Horace Mann's efforts to provide access to education included strong pronouncements about the importance of books and reading (McCook, 2011).

By 1847 there were 8,070 school district libraries. The school district system promoted values that formed a basis for the idea of public libraries, including taxation. Linking libraries to education was an essential connection for the establishment of the tax-supported public library. The U.S. Bureau of Education's *Special Report* (U.S. Department of the Interior, Bureau of Education, 1876, 38-69) provides a summary of how far school district libraries had spread across the United States. Following the first such law enacted in New York in 1835, Massachusetts passed legislation providing for school district libraries in 1837, in large part due to the eloquence and earnestness of Horace Mann. Eight other states enacted laws by 1848.

Before the first law for tax-supported public libraries, 10 states had already identified the importance of tax support for school district libraries. The school district as a unit of governance was too small, staffing and location were volatile, and book procurement was uneven. Thus, its influence on future public library development was significant.[6] The school district system did much to establish certain principles that formed the basis for public libraries, including taxation and state aid to libraries. Support for libraries affiliated with school districts was critical in recognizing the library as an educational agency and an extension of the system of public education beyond the formal instruction offered by schools (Joeckel, 1935, pp. 8-13).[7]

Public Libraries Paid for by the People

The Boston Public Library is considered the first municipal library authorized by state law in the United States of America (though this has been debated). This was achieved by an act of the Massachusetts General Court in 1848.[8] *Report of the Trustees of the Public Library to the City of Boston* (1852), the founding document of the Boston Public Library, states:

> There can be no doubt that such reading [for the diffusion of knowledge] ought to be furnished to all, as a matter of public policy and duty, on the same principle that we furnish free education, and in fact, as a part, and a most important part, of the education of all.[9]

How did a new institution—a public library—become embedded as a tax-supported public good? We see that the social and circulating libraries supported a reading culture in New England. We see that support for district school libraries set a precedent for taxation. What else contributed to its establishment?

A detailed social history essential to understanding the context of the establishment of the public library is *Foundations of the Public Library: The Origins of the Public Library*

Movement in New England, which covers the years 1629–1855 (Shera, 1949). Factors that laid the groundwork for the public library included:

1. Economic Resources. The philanthropy of wealthy individuals and the prosperity of New England provided the financial basis for library development.
2. Scholarship. The desire to preserve the documents of the nation motivated public funding of libraries. Historical societies focused attention on preserving and building scholarly collections.
3. Local Pride. John Jacob Astor bequeathed $400,000 to establish a public library in New York created competition. Bostonian George Ticknor used the competition between the two cities to argue for a public library.
4. Universal Education. The acceptance of universal education as a public responsibility added strength to the argument for a tax-supported public library. Bostonian Edward Everett, former governor and congressman of Massachusetts, appointed Horace Mann as secretary of the Massachusetts Board of Education and oversaw the improvement of common schools and the extension of education throughout the state.
5. Self-Education. Josiah Holbrook based a plan for adult self-education on the idea of the lyceum, a plan that expanded to over 3,000 lyceums by 1835. The National American Lyceum adopted as its purpose "the advancement of education, especially in the common schools, and the general diffusion of knowledge." The general popularity of self-improvement gave weight to the idea of a public library.
6. Vocational Influence. Institutes that supported the education of working men usually included libraries.
7. Religion and Morality. Reading and religion were mutually supportive endeavors in New England. One of the goals of the American Sunday School Union, founded in 1817, was to provide communities with libraries for religious instruction (McCook, 2011, pp. 17–20).

These factors combined to create public receptivity to the idea of a public library as a means to extend educational opportunity after formal schooling. Shera concludes:

> Complex social agencies do not arise in response to a single influence; the dogma of simple causation is an easy and ever threatening fallacy. It cannot be said that the public library began on a specific date, at a certain town, as the result of a particular cause. A multiplicity of forces, accumulating over a long period of time, converged to shape this new library form. (Shera, 1949, p. 200)

The First Laws Establishing Public Libraries

The phrase "free public library," as used by McMullen (2000) in his study of the library past of the United States, most reflects the public library of today. McMullen identified two types: 1) ordinary libraries established by local governments, and 2) township libraries established by state governments but intended to be at least partially supported and controlled by local officials. Ordinary libraries resembled social libraries (and in fact were often converted from social libraries) in that their support came from users in the form of taxes paid to the local government. Public libraries as tax-supported community agencies enabled by law have existed since the mid-nineteenth century. Although by consensus the establishment of the Boston Public Library (enacted in 1848 by state law and opened in 1854) marks the beginning of the public library movement, we can point to earlier examples of free public libraries, such as the Peterborough Town Library in New Hampshire, which was granted support in 1833 from a general state fund. Nevertheless, because of the well-documented discussions about its establishment, by and large most historians consider the Boston Public Library to be the wellspring from which the principles for tax-supported public libraries flowed.

What laws laid the foundation for legislation to support public libraries? New Hampshire has the honor of being the first state to enact a law to provide for public libraries, in 1849: "An Act Providing for the Establishment of Public Libraries." Whether this was due to the successful town library in Peterborough (1833), funded initially from a state fund but continued with local monies, or perhaps the persuasion of French ventriloquist M. Nicholas-Marie Alexandre Vattemare,[10] who had addressed the New Hampshire state legislature the day before on the importance of international exchanges of books, we cannot deduce the precise reasons for the introduction of the Act at this time. Nevertheless, this was the watershed event in U.S. public library history.

The New Hampshire Act provided 1) that towns might appropriate funds for the establishment, housing, and maintenance of libraries; 2) that such libraries would be free to all; 3) that the town might receive, hold, and dispose of gifts or behests made to the library; and 4) that libraries established under the law would annually receive works published by the state (Shera, 1949, pp. 186–189).

The Massachusetts law enacted in 1851 that opened the way for Boston to establish its library had a different history. In 1847 Francis Wayland, Brown University president, donated funds to the town of Wayland, Massachusetts, to establish a library but the town had no authority to contribute to the library's upkeep from municipal funds. Reverend John Burt Wight drafted a bill that authorized towns to establish libraries. He argued that such a law would inspire more libraries to be founded throughout Massachusetts. These libraries would supplement the public-school system, provide utilitarian information, support moral and intellectual advance, preserve public documents, encourage creative writing, and increase the effectiveness of public instruction.

After the Act passed, Wight sent a circular throughout Massachusetts to encourage the creation of town libraries. In the circular Wight declaimed, with great bravado: "The universal establishment of such libraries in this Commonwealth—and may I not say in the new England states, in the United States, and throughout the entire civilized world—is a question only of time" (Wight 1851).

> **▶ FACT**
>
> On July 7, 1849, the New Hampshire Legislature passed the Act Providing for the Establishment of Public Libraries, earning the distinction of being known as the first state in the United States of America to pass such a law.

Boston Public Library

In Boston, the concentration of circulating and social libraries laid the foundation for the population's desire for access to books. The Boston Mercantile Library hosted the French ventriloquist M. Nicholas-Marie Alexandre Vattemare in 1841, who proposed the unification of Boston's major social libraries. A committee to investigate this idea was appointed by the mayor, Josiah Quincy (Richards, 1940). A joint special committee of the City Council presented a proposal to the General Court of the state in 1848 that approved a special act permitting the city of Boston to establish a public library.

This Act is the first legal recognition by a state for tax-supported municipal library service:

> The City of Boston is hereby authorized to establish and maintain a public library, for the use of the inhabitants of the said city: and the city council of the said city may, from time to time, make such rules and regulations, for the care and maintenance thereof, as they may deem proper; provided, however, that no such appropriation for the said library shall exceed the sum of five thousand dollars in any one year. (General Court of Massachusetts, 1848)

The decision of a major city to support a public library by taxation was of tremendous importance. As the city established functions related to the community's well-being (fire protection, education, health), Boston considered it to be a proper function of city government to support a public library.[11] In 1851 an election to create a board of trustees for the library moved plans ahead. In 1852 the trustees submitted the most important foundational document in the history of public librarianship in the United States, the *Report of the Trustees of the Public Library to the City of Boston*.[12]

The report observed that there is no provision to put books within the reach of young men and women when public education ends. It asked:

> Why should not this prosperous and liberal city extend some reasonable amount of aid to the foundation and support of a noble public library, to which the young of both sexes, when they leave the schools, can resort for those works which pertain to general culture, or which are needed for research into any branch of useful knowledge? (Boston Public Library, 1852, p. 8)

The trustees summarized the status of libraries in Boston (athenaeums, mercantile libraries, mechanics' libraries, apprentices' libraries, social libraries, circulating libraries, and Sunday school libraries), which do not satisfy the demands for healthy, nourishing reading, for "the great masses of people, who cannot be expected to purchase such reading for themselves . . . The public library is conceived as the crowning glory of our system of City schools."

A Boston city ordinance was passed in October 1852 stating that the method of governance was to be a board of trustees, with the librarian to be appointed annually by the city council. This ordinance laid the foundation for libraries throughout the United States to adopt the board plan of administrative management (Joeckel, 1935, pp. 20–21). The Boston Public Library opened to readers on May 2, 1854.

Criticism of Public Library Development

We cannot overlook some of the critical literature related to public library development, which reveal that the public library was conceived as an instrument for social control. In a 1973 revisionist essay, Michael Harris looks at the events that led to the founding of the Boston Public Library from a different perspective. He describes additional discussions by the standing committee of the Boston Public Library that are not usually described in general histories, notably expressions of concern by committee members about the increase in foreign populations, who were generally viewed as unlettered and ignorant. Harris asserts that George Ticknor, the intellectual Boston Brahmin who was the main author of the *Re-*

port of the Trustees of the Public Library to the City of Boston, was motivated to a large degree by the idea that establishing a public library in Boston would uplift the masses so they would be sober, righteous, conservative, and devout.

The motivations of librarians and library supporters has also been discussed in Dee Garrison's *Apostles of Culture: The Public Librarian and American Society, 1876–1920* (1979). Extending the Harris thesis, Garrison describes the first leaders of the American Library Association (ALA)—Justin Winsor (Boston Public Library, Harvard), William Poole (Boston Athenaeum, Cincinnati Public Library, Chicago Public Library, Newberry Library), and Charles Ammi Cutter (Harvard, Boston Athenaeum)—as well as those others from the gentry who assumed positions of responsibility for libraries just after the initial enabling legislation. These individuals placed great emphasis on moral norms as a way of shaping the moral values of a society. Their response to political upheaval and labor unrest after the Civil War was to impose on others their middle-class values of "thrift, self-reliance, industriousness, and sensual control," seeing themselves as the saviors of society.

In 1982 Miksa compared the standard histories of the development of librarianship in the United States—Shera's (1949) *Foundations of the Public Library* and Ditzion's (1947) *Arsenals of a Democratic Culture*—applying Harris's (1973) and Garrison's (1979) revisionist theories. Miksa noted that Ditzion, Harris, and Garrison focused on the human element and that such efforts must be viewed as somewhat lacking in their extrapolation of the parts to the whole. Miksa suggested studies of individual librarians would do much to enhance our knowledge of public library history. Jaeger has synthesized the range of scholarship that examines the motivations instrumental in founding American public libraries; he noted that by 1900 many city libraries had established a range of cultural and educational activities (Jaeger, Gorham, Bertot, & Sarin, 2014, pp. 27–28).

1852 TO THE GREAT WAR (WORLD WAR I)

Public Libraries in the Nineteenth Century: Expanding Service, but Not for Everyone

The acceleration in the establishment of tax-supported public libraries after the founding of the Boston Public Library has been described in *The Government of the American Public Library* (Joeckel, 1935). Home rule, commissions, and council-manager forms of local government were essential to the evolution of the legal status of public libraries. The growing influence of librarians in the late nineteenth century has been described in *Part of Our Lives: A People's History of the American Public Library* (Wiegand, 2015), which presents struggles between patrons who wanted popular fiction and librarians lamenting that fact. The Groton (CT) Public Library refused to stock fiction in its library (founded in 1867), but readers circulated a petition to override the librarians' paternalism in regard to their reading preferences (Wiegand, 2015, p. 41).

A watershed year in public library development occurred in 1876. The report, *Public Libraries in the United States of America: Their History, Condition, and Management* included a "Table of Public Libraries Numbering 300 Volumes or Upwards," (U.S. Department of the Interior, Bureau of Education, 1876). Many of these grew from social libraries.[13] In this same year, the American Library Association (ALA) was founded and the periodical *Library Journal* was established. The new journal and the ALA annual conferences provided forums for a growing national movement to establish public libraries. An essay on state legislation presented the common preference of public library authorities in the matter of government (Poole, 1877).

Each region, state, city, or even neighborhood has its own library history. Titles of books and articles such as "Public Library History on the Lewis and Clark Trail" (Jordan, 2015)[14]; "Library Programs in Indiana in the 1850s" (Fitch & Hovde, 2015); or "The Public Library in an Immigrant Neighborhood: Italian Immigrants' Information Ecologies in Newark, New Jersey, 1889–1919" (Pozzi, 2013) illustrate some of these local histories. Putting these pieces together gives us a record of diverse and purposeful library development.

The Library History Round Table (LHRT) of ALA compiles a bibliography of papers about library history.[15]

We must remember that dominant groups have controlled the historical record. Because women and members of minority groups, notably Native Americans and African Americans, were not in positions of authority during the first century of American public library development they were barely mentioned in the classic public library histories such as those by Shera and Ditzion. More recent research, notably Hildenbrand's *Reclaiming the American Library Past: Writing the Women In* (1996); Patterson's "History and Status of Native Americans in Librarianship" (2000); and Battles' *The History of Public Library Access for African Americans in the South* (2008) have explored the history of public librarianship against the backdrop of race, gender, and class. Public librarians and students of the public library's history should supplement twentieth-century texts with studies such as Malone's "Toward a Multicultural American Public Library History" (2000), and Knott's *Not Free, Not for All: Public Libraries in the Age of Jim Crow* (Knott, 2015).[16]

> **▶ TASK**
>
> Visit the LHRT's bibliography. Can you find any readings about libraries or librarians in the area where you live?

Women Open New Possibilities

Although the standard histories of the development of public libraries mostly neglect the role of women, a fuller understanding is provided by works like Carmichael's study of early women directors in Atlanta, Georgia (1986); Lewis's study of Julia Brown Asplund and the New Mexico Library Service (1996); and Pawley's study of Lutie Stearns and the traveling libraries of the Wisconsin Free Library Commission (2000).[17] Each state has its own library founders and timeline. The story of Alice Tyler, who facilitated the use of Carnegie funds from 1900–1913 for the Iowa Library Commission, provides a nuanced assessment of the way one state facilitated, yet questioned, the use of Carnegie monies (Stuart, 2013).

And behind the scenes, women's clubs that formed after the Civil War were a major force in the spread of new libraries. The growth of women's clubs for self-education and community service is part of the sociological context in which public libraries developed. The General Federation of Women's Clubs helped to establish 474 free libraries and 4,655 traveling libraries by 1904.

Paula D. Watson has identified and summarized the cultural initiatives of the women who organized libraries throughout America. She observes, "the awakening of public sentiment in favor of libraries was the chosen work of state federations of women's clubs and individual clubs throughout the United States" (Watson, 1994, p. 262). Grassroots efforts made by women in Michigan are documented in *Historical Sketches of the Ladies' Libraries Associations of the State of Michigan* (Bixby & Howell, 1876).

There were many pioneering women in librarianship, but the road to equality has been uneven. By the early 1900s, the profession was dominated by women, but they lagged behind men in assuming directorships and other positions of power. Scholarship critical of

Dewey (e.g., Wiegand, 1996) has found that his recruitment of women was founded in a desire for economy—that is, women could be hired for lower salaries (Gordon, 2005, p. 236).

Philanthropy as Catalyst and Andrew Carnegie's Role

As we saw in Massachusetts, donations from individuals were often instrumental in the establishment of public libraries. Philanthropy was viewed as a righteous path for the stewardship of wealth as discussed in *Money and the Moral Order in Late Nineteenth and Early-Twentieth Century American Capitalism* (Hamer, 1998). Donations to libraries may have been born of a generous spirit or, more cynically, were a "shrewd policy on the part of millionaires to expend a trifle of the gains which they made off the people in giving them public libraries" (Ditzion, 1947, pp. 136-137).

After the Civil War, with no income tax or corporate tax, vast fortunes were accumulated by industrialists, merchants, and financiers. During the heyday of the Gilded Age $36,000,000 was donated to libraries (Twain & Warner, 1873). Although local library histories relate many donations to library founding across America, no single donor made more of an impact on the growth of public libraries than Andrew Carnegie.

Between 1898 and 1919 Carnegie donated over $41,000,000 to build 1,679 libraries in 1,412 communities across the United States. These comprise the largest single group of buildings nominated to the National Register of Historic Places. Many of them were built in the classical revival style and have become architectural landmarks (McCook, 2011, p. 36). Carnegie, an immigrant from Dunfermline, Scotland, became one of the wealthiest capitalists in the world. His decision to give away all the money he earned set him apart from other industrialists (Nasaw, 2007), but he has been characterized as avaricious and contradictory (Ernsberger, 2015). The hiring of hundreds of Pinkerton agents to confront the Amalgamated Association of Iron and Steel Workers at the Homestead Steel Workers resulted in death and destruction in 1892.[18] Yet even as workers were attacked and killed, Carnegie had already begun funding public libraries in 1886.

> ▶ **FACT**
>
> Andrew Carnegie donated over $41,000,000 for the erection of 1,679 libraries in 1,412 communities across the United States between 1898 and 1919.

What were Carnegie's reasons for choosing libraries as a focus of his philanthropy? As a young man in Pittsburgh he had been allowed to use the workingman's library, which helped convince him of the importance of access to books to educate and inspire workers.[19] Later in life, Carnegie wrote the "Gospel of Wealth," which presented his philosophy of stewardship and the belief that wealth should be used to help those who would help themselves (Carnegie, 1901). Carnegie's library philanthropy granted funds for library buildings but required that communities furnish a site and pledge ongoing support. Carnegie initially (from 1886 to 1896) gave buildings with endowments—the "retail period"—to communities in which his industries were located, but changed to a "wholesale" approach from 1896 through 1919, which required community support (Bobinski, 1969, pp. 13-23). In 1901 $5.2 million in U.S. Steel bonds were delivered from Carnegie to John Billings, director of the New York Public Library, to establish a branch library system for New York (Dierickx, 1996).

James Bertram was hired by Carnegie to oversee the library program. Communities requesting a library were sent a short questionnaire.[20] If their response was satisfactory they were asked to supply a letter describing the site and vouching that it was purchased and paid in full. Communities had to pledge at least 10% of the amount of the grant for annual maintenance. Forty-six states built libraries in 1,679 communities with Indiana building the most—164. A case study of the Carnegie library brought to Brazil, Indiana, illustrates the confluence of two factors: women's commitment and Carnegie's philanthropy.

The intersection of women and community leadership in securing Carnegie libraries in Idaho, Utah, Nevada, Arizona, Montana, Wyoming, Colorado, Washington, California, and New Mexico between 1898–1920 has been studied in *Books, Bluster, and Bounty: Local Politics in the Intermountain West and Carnegie Library Building Grants* (Swetnam, 2012). Increasingly we have come to understand that the development of the American public library owes a great deal to women working at the grass roots level. Individual library histories document this fact, although the major synthetic histories of American library history do not. The work of women in securing Carnegie libraries in western states has also been noted by Passet (1994) in *Cultural Crusaders: Women Librarians in the American West* and in Held's (1973) study of the rise of public libraries in California.

Brazil, Indiana: From the Coal Mines to a Carnegie Library, 1878–1904

by Lynn C. Westney

Between 1901 and 1918, 164 Carnegie public libraries were endowed in Indiana from grant proposals submitted to the Carnegie Foundation from 156 individual Indiana communities. Carnegie gave $2,508,664.38 to these 164 libraries. Other states received more money from the Carnegie Foundation, but no other state has as many libraries that received Carnegie gifts as did Indiana (Ksander, 2007).

Carnegie's philanthropy coincided with the rise of women's clubs in the post-Civil War period. Club women looked around their towns, saw what needed to be done, and helped to create libraries, health clinics, schools, sanitation systems, and decent roads. In doing so, they developed skills that made them the first generation of women to be elected and appointed in significant numbers to local and statewide offices. Women's organizations led the establishment of 75 to 80% of the libraries in communities across the United States (Scheer, 2002).

Brazil, Indiana, was one of Carnegie's fortunate recipients. The Village of Brazil was founded in 1866. It is located in the heart of the Midwest, today an hour's drive from Indianapolis. At one time, there were 13 coal mines and 11 clay factories operating in this small Indiana hamlet. A group of Brazil's women were inspired to start a public library, especially for the mostly uneducated mine workers. In 1878, Mary B. Schultz and Mary B. Richardson collected books to start a circulating library. Strawberry festivals and ice cream socials were held to raise money for the acquisition of additional books.

Brazil's first library board was established in 1879. In 1901, Mrs. Crawford, the wife of a library board member, traveled to New York City to request the gift of a library grant from Andrew Carnegie. In February 1902 Mrs. Crawford received a letter from Carnegie's

[CONTINUED ON FOLLOWING PAGE]

[CONTINUED FROM PREVIOUS PAGE]

secretary. The required information was forwarded to Carnegie and the $25,000 grant was promptly awarded to the community of Brazi1.

On April 14, 1902, a committee of six citizens was appointed to help the library board select a site for the new building. The present location was purchased from a Mrs. Carter for $2,400.00. On January 7, 1904, the board met in a special session and appointed Agnes McCrea as its first librarian. Built of Indiana limestone, the building was formally dedicated on October 18,1904, and stands today as a testament to the efforts of these tireless women.

Brazil, Indiana, is only one of the many examples of the success of these dedicated and determined women to the contribution of the history and development of Carnegie public libraries, not only in Indiana, but across the entire United States.

SOURCES

Blair, K. J. (1980). *The clubwoman as feminist: True womanhood redefined, 1868–1914.* New York and London: Holmes and Meier.

Ksander, Y. (2007). Indiana's Carnegie libraries. Moment of Indiana history. http://indianapublicmedia.org/momentofindianahistory/indianas-carnegie-libraries/.

Scheer, T. J. (2002). The "praxis" side of the equation: Club women and American public administration. *Administrative Theory and Praxis,* 24(3) 519–536.

Travis, W. (1909). History of Brazil, Clay County, Indiana. http://history.rays-place.com/in/clay-brazil-c1.htm.

Some communities refused the money, which they considered tainted by Carnegie's repressive labor policies, while others could not meet the financial obligation of the annual pledge. In *Carnegie Denied* (Martin, 1993), scholars have analyzed those communities that applied for building grants but did not complete projects. In their study of Carnegie libraries in New York, Stielow and Corsaro (1993) examined the work of the Progressives, including Melvil Dewey, to promote the library cause, thus melding the pseudo-aristocratic robber barons with the ideals of a new social awareness.

During the era of Jim Crow and racial segregation, African Americans were not permitted to use public libraries in many states. Carnegie funds supported the first library to serve African Americans in Louisville, Kentucky. The Western Branch Library opened in 1905 with Reverend Thomas Fountain Blue—the first African American to head a public library—serving as director (Thompson-Miller, Feagin, & Picco, 2015; McCook, 2011, p. 37). The history of the Colored Carnegie Library in Houston, which opened in 1907, demonstrates that the fund provided some relief from segregated facilities (Malone, 1999). The Library for the Colored Citizens of Savannah, built with Carnegie funds, was opened in 1913.[21]

Ditzion's assessment of Carnegie's contribution as a stimulus, not an initiator, is astute. Because the public library as an entity began on firm footing in New England, growth might have slowed as communities waited for big donors. Carnegie's great contribution to the idea of the public library was that it needed to be supported by the people of a community through taxation. "Popular initiative, participation and control were the desired aims" (Ditzion, 1947, p. 150). Philanthropy and the growing involvement of women in the political process were the fuel that moved the public library idea to catch fire.

The vast expansion of public libraries around the turn of the twentieth century was fueled by a progressive spirit and an influx of philanthropic donations. However, as Carnegie predicted, public libraries require regular funding to remain viable. He would not simply donate funds for a building; his donation required cities and towns to provide a plan for their own investment.

STATE LIBRARY COMMISSIONS

Another great impetus to the growth of public libraries occurred in 1890 with the passage of the Massachusetts law creating a state Board of Library Commissioners charged to help communities establish and improve public libraries. The law included a grant of $100 to begin collections in towns that did not have libraries. Elizabeth Putnam Sohier, a driving force in the legislative process, was appointed to the first Massachusetts Free Library commission and is representative of the importance of women in lobbying for the enactment of library legislation throughout America (Watson, 2003, p. 75). Similar laws were passed in New York in 1892 and in Maine, New Hampshire, and Connecticut in 1893.

In 1893 in New York, Melvil Dewey, then director of the state library, set up a system of traveling libraries to provide 100-volume collections for communities that had no libraries. Women's clubs in Delaware and Maryland set up similar programs likely paving the way for state library commissions. In her scholarly analysis of the role of women's clubs in establishing libraries, "Valleys without Sunsets: Women's Clubs and Traveling Libraries" Paula D. Watson provides comparative state-by-state data on the establishment of traveling libraries by state (2003).[22] A case study of the influence of women and their work in traveling libraries is Christine Pawley's 2000 article, "Advocate of Access: Lutie Stearns and the Traveling Libraries of the Wisconsin Free Library Commission: 1895–1914."

FACT

Elizabeth Putnam Sohier was the first woman appointed to a state library commission in Massachusetts in 1890.

The traveling library projects were closely tied to efforts across the country to establish state library commissions. Watson (1994) notes, "There is little doubt that the state federation of women's clubs can claim credit for the passage of legislation in many states to establish library commissions" (p. 244) and then details the efforts of women in Kentucky, Georgia, Illinois, Indiana, Maine, and Wisconsin. This inspired the appointment of women as commissioners or trustees to these commissions. In his assessment of library law and legislation, Alex Ladenson (1982, pp. 55–57) views the major expansion of public libraries after 1890 as attributable to the passage of legislation for the state library commissions.

As Martin and Lear (2013) point out in their volume on state libraries:

> the history of many state libraries is intertwined with the stories of state-level library associations and with county and public libraries. Historically, state governments, library associations, and county or public libraries all shared an interest in public library development, professional standards, interlibrary cooperation, and grant funding. (p. 4).[23]

Librarianship Gets Organized

During the period from 1876 through 1918, the founding and growth of the American Library Association, coupled with the entry of women into the profession, contributed to an increase in the number of public librarians, who in turn were active in helping to expand the number of public libraries. In his study of the development of librarianship in America, *The Politics of an Emerging Profession,* Wiegand (1986) tells the story of the founding of the American Library Association (established 1876), which formed the basis for the growth of the field and advocacy to support the establishment of new libraries throughout America. ALA members developed recommended reading lists and collection guides so that libraries might support best reading. These early librarians have been viewed as helping to lay the foundation for growth "as they spread the gospel of public culture to small towns across the United States, public libraries would acquire the status as a public good, worthy of tax support" (2001, p. 12).

The first formal education institute for librarians, the School of Library Economy, was opened by Melvil Dewey in 1886 at Columbia University, and admitted women students. However, Columbia administrators denied women access to education. Dewey moved to Albany when he became the secretary of the University of the State of New York and director of the state library in 1888. The School of Library Economy went with him (Vann, 1961). Librarian education programs proliferated (some affiliated with large libraries, some with higher education, and some as summer training programs), and the creation of these programs made the profession more accessible to women (Grotzinger, Carmichael, & Maack, 1994).[24] The employment of women is viewed as a factor in librarianship's shift to a community focus. This included opening shelves, youth services, and services to the foreign born (Mattson, 2000; Pawley, 2000).

ALA's practice of moving annual conferences throughout the nation stimulated interest in library matters. Certainly, discussions and programs held by the association made an impact on the way librarians thought about the services they were providing. By the early 1900s, progressive library leader John Cotton Dana observed that members of the public could forge their own use of the library in ways that they determined, an observation substantiated Lutie Stearns' work in Wisconsin to provide more democratic library services (Mattson, 2000; Pawley, 2000).

The ALA Committee on Work with the Foreign-Born, established in 1918, showed librarianship's increasing focus on working people and immigrants. Jones's 1999 study of libraries and the immigrant experience notes that in the first quarter of the twentieth century, the ALA Committee on Work with the Foreign-Born had an effect on library service: "Ironically, then, as immigrants were being transformed into Americans, librarians were also being transformed through their contacts with immigrants. . . . In the process they, too, were changed, metamorphosed into more tolerant Americanizers, more progressive citizens, and more responsive professionals" (p. 30). In the period between founding until World War I, the internal debates and personal beliefs of U.S. librarians within ALA demonstrated a slow but concerted evolution toward a greater commitment to access, as the needs of immigrants, working people, and children began to receive focus and attention.

World War I, also known as the Great War, gave librarians a new raison d'être with the establishment of the Library War Service. No longer were librarians criticized for supplying commonplace reading; they enlisted themselves to supply books to the armed forces. (Wiegand, 2015, p. 107; Young, 1981). The entry of the United States into the war gave librarians the opportunity to collaborate with other community agencies in the war effort. This period has been characterized by Wiegand as "an exhilarating experience that constituted a capstone to the public library movement in Progressive America." (1989, p. 133). During World War I ALA's Library War Service's work in training camps and in Europe, broadened the general public's appreciation for library service (Kelly, 2003). At the close of the war, the public library was broadly accepted as an essential municipal service.

The American Library Association, encouraged by the success of its Library War Service, planned for national fundraising and an Enlarged Program to "encourage and promote the development of library service for all Americans" (Thomison, 1978, pp. 70–71). Although the Enlarged Program did not come about, the philosophical and political ideas of growth and expansion for public library service continued to shape the profession's post-WWI future.

WORLD WAR I (1918) TO THE PUBLIC LIBRARY INQUIRY (1952)

The number of public libraries steadily grew during the first decades of twentieth century. By 1923 there were 4,046 public libraries with over 3000 volumes, and by 1929 this had increased to 6,031. Kevane and Sundstrom's (2014) quantitative assessment of library growth from 1887 through 1930 attributes growth to urbanization, immigration, and state library commissions.[25] U.S. public libraries expanded outlets, extended service areas, and defined broad goals as a vital and necessary community agency during the early twentieth century. After World War I the history of public libraries in the United States and ALA as a factor in the development of public libraries became intertwined with the actions of local and state governments.

The Public Library as the People's University: Extending Service to All

The Smith-Towner bill to mandate federal funds to extend public libraries for educational purposes and create a bureau of libraries at the federal level was proposed in 1919, but it was not enacted (Magill, 1920). This bill did create a context for future federal involvement in public library growth, however (Molz, 1984, p. 75). ALA's "Enlarged Program" concept, the experience of a national role for libraries during World War I, and the ALA Council's ongoing discussion of federal support for libraries expanded the scope of discussion about the role of public libraries. Two publications laid the groundwork tying public libraries to education:

- *The American Public Library and the Diffusion of Knowledge* noted that "the free public library is already an accepted and cherished figure in American intellectual life," and suggested ALA provide support for the growth and expansion of smaller libraries (Learned, 1924, pp. 75–80).
- *Libraries and Adult Education.* The principle that the public library was an agency of education for adults was affirmed, and ALA established the Board on Library and Adult Education (ALA, 1926).[26]

Inspired by these books and discussions at conferences, the ALA Committee on Library Extension (established in 1925) worked to extend library services to unserved areas in the United States. In 1936, the ALA Committee on Library Extension appointed Tommie Dora Barker as the regional field agent for the South, supported by funding from a Carnegie Corporation Grant. The League of Library Commissions (established in 1904 and affiliated with ALA, eventually becoming the State Library Agency of the Extension Division in 1942) worked on rural issues before and during the Depression-era New Deal. The citizens' library movement, especially in North Carolina, demonstrated a grassroots desire for library service ("Library Projects," 1933). During the 1920s and 1930s, ALA embraced the idea of libraries as a means to provide adult educational opportunities and combined this idea with many efforts to extend library service to unserved areas.[27]

The League of Library Commissions worked on rural issues before and during the New Deal. Studies that detail extension activities fostered by state libraries include California (Kunkle, 1969) and Illinois (Sorensen, 1999). In 1933 the first national standards for public libraries were issued—in a brief two-page statement in the *Bulletin of the American Library Association* (Martin, L.A., 1972)—that declared libraries should be available to all.

Julia Wright Merrill served over 20 years working to extend library services. She represented the American Library Association, traveling across the United States and Canada preaching a gospel of public library service for rural communities from 1925 to 1946 (Latham, in press; Sandoe, 1946). The backstory to the extension of library services to unserved areas has been explored by Latham (2010) who has analyzed the shift from local control to association control of the public library mission.

In 1934 John Chancellor was hired at ALA headquarters to foster adult education development in public libraries. A comparative study by Peich and Fletcher (2015) examines parallels between public libraries and cooperative extension in their connection to local communities.

During the Depression there were over 2,300 Works Progress Administration (WPA) library projects, which employed 14,500 people in 45 states. These were usually coordinated by state library commissions, which used the federal funds to extend library services to unserved areas. Traveling libraries were supported in rural areas. Packhorse libraries served 15 counties in rural Kentucky and employed 232 people. A houseboat on the Yazoo River in Mississippi stopped at riverbanks and distributed books.

> A WPA state-wide project in Ohio has made possible a circulation of some 70,000 books and magazines to approximately 300 back country centers in the State. A WPA carrier who operates out from West Union, the county seat of Adams County, follows a route where many of the roads are little more than wagon trails. During bad weather she is forced to change from her flivver, throw her books in a sack, and mount the saddle of her pony to ford the creeks and reach the one-room schoolhouses. (Woodward, 1938)

These WPA projects demonstrated the value of library services. Arkansas, which had only minimal service prior to the Depression, passed legislation to support public libraries after the WPA showed residents the value of local public libraries. As the WPA programs closed in the early 1940s, reports like "Platte votes for county library service following WPA demonstration" in Missouri presented tangible evidence that libraries, once experienced, became community priorities (Page, 1942). A complete analysis that demonstrates the influence of WPA support in extending the recognition of the value of public libraries is *Library Extension under the WPA: An Appraisal of an Experiment in Federal Aid* (Stanford, 1944). Swain (1995) has documented the expansion of readers' services during the New Deal, including supervised reading rooms, bookmobiles, and rural library services.

"What Should Be the Federal Government's Relation to Libraries?"

Here are the milestones in public library development that engaged the federal government after the Great War/World War I.

1929—Carl H. Milam, ALA executive secretary, sent a memorandum, "What Should Be the Federal Government's Relation to Libraries?" to the ALA Council.[28]

1934—The ALA executive board appointed a National Planning Committee in 1934, which developed the National Plan for Libraries.[29] Molz has observed, "The issuance of the National Plan was the first time that the Association itself entered the national political arena to state a plank as a public policy actor" (Molz, 1984, p. 37).

1936—An ALA statement, *The Equal Chance: Books Help to Make It,* compared per capita income to public library availability and urged people to get involved in state and national planning for library support to achieve the "equalizing of library opportunity." (ALA, 1936).[30]

1936-1941—The first federal monies to local libraries were granted through WPA projects (Kramp, 2010, p. 28).

1937—The U.S. Department of Education created the Library Services Division, which was responsible for leadership in nation-wide library development (Joeckel, 1938, quoted in Knight and Nourse, 1969, p. 468).

1943—*Post-War Standards for Public Libraries,* developed during World War II as part of the national initiative to plan for progress, asserted the importance of the public library and recommended that public library service should be universally available in the United States and its territories (Joeckel, 1943).[31]

1945—ALA established a Washington National Relations Office to strengthen influence with Congress and the U.S. Department of Education (Howard, 1945).

1948—The National Plan for Public Library Service, prepared for the Committee on Postwar Planning of the American Library Association, proposed nation-wide minimum standards including equalization of financial support. The state library agency was deemed central to achieving adequate, purposeful public library service. The National Plan proposed "a nation-wide minimum standard of service and support below which no library should fall" and called for equalization of financial support: "Very great inequalities among the states in per capita expenditures for public libraries are a dominant characteristic of American library development . . . Some degree of national equalization of these great differences between the states in library support must be a major concern in library planning" (Joeckel and Winslow, 1948, p. 30; p. 160).

AFTER WORLD WAR II: THE PUBLIC LIBRARY INQUIRY

"What should be the role of the public library after World War II?" was a question deliberated by library leaders, especially ALA executive secretary Carl Milam. ALA leadership developed plans for a study "to define legitimate library activity by adapting the traditional educational purposes of libraries to new social conditions and the public's willingness to pay for such services" (Raber, 1997, p. 43). A major research project, the Public Library Inquiry, was undertaken to find answers. Robert D. Leigh of the University of Chicago was selected to carry out the multipart project between 1947 and 1952. Douglas

Raber (1999), who has written extensively on the sociopolitical aspects of the Public Library Inquiry postulated:

> Postwar conditions offered both new promises and new threats. War-driven technological progress was combining with pervasive political and social change to create a volatile and uncertain world, not unlike our own, characterized by instability. Milam and others developed the idea of the Public Library Inquiry as a means to assess the condition of the public library in America, to determine if it had achieved its goals, and to chart a course for it in the postwar world.

The Public Library Inquiry consisted of seven volumes published by Columbia University Press between 1949 and 1952. The volumes included:

- Bernard Berelson, *The Library's Public* (1949)
- Alice I. Bryan, *The Public Librarian* (1952)
- Oliver Garceau, *The Public Library in the Political Process* (1949)
- Robert D. Leigh, *The Public Library in the United States* (1950)
- J. L. McCamy and J. T. McCamy, *Government Publications for the Citizen* (1949)
- William Miller, *The Book Industry* (1949)
- Gloria Waldron, *The Information Film* (1949)[32]

The Public Library Inquiry was a landmark in the history of the development of the philosophy of librarianship. It was undertaken a century after the establishment of the public library movement and signaled a shift in the way librarians thought about their mission.[33] In *Books and Libraries in American Society during World War II,* Becker (2005) assesses the shift from top-down assertion of library purpose to locally based needs as having paved the way for a more community focused institution (pp. 204-205).

At a forum on the inquiry held in 1949, Bernard Berelson, author of the inquiry volume *The Library's Public,* responded to concerns about his findings that the library reached only a minority of the population—the better educated (Asheim, 1970, p. 62). The inquiry contributed to the reformulation of the public library's service mission during the 1950s by acting as one of many catalysts that stimulated the innovative outreach efforts of the late 1960s and early 1970s (Maack, 1994).

It should be emphasized that much work to expand library service took place in every U.S. state during the 1950s. See, for example, the process by which California developed statewide cooperative systems led by the sweeping and dramatic work of state librarian Carma Zimmerman Leigh and University of California Berkeley School of Librarianship professor Edward A. Wight. The result was the Public Library Development Act of 1963, but the process also created a deeply committed culture of commitment to library access (Mediavilla, 2013).

FROM LSA TO LSCA (1956 TO 1966)

The Library Services Act (1956) and the Library Services and Construction Act (1966) were the central federal legislation that opened the way to equalize library access to all people in America.

How did this important legislation develop and what was the social context of the decades from 1956 to 1966?

> ▶ **FACT**
>
> In 1956, just prior to the passage of Library Services Act, 26 million people in rural areas were without public library service.*
>
> *A survey was undertaken by the U.S. Office of Education in 1956 just prior to the passage of the Library Services Act. In brief, 26 million people in rural areas were without any public library service, 50 million more had inadequate service as measured by State standards, and over 300 rural counties were without any public library within their borders. U.S. Office of Education (1958).

Civil Rights and Public Libraries

The classic public library histories (Ditzion, 1947; Shera, 1949) written prior to civil rights legislation in the 1960s barely mention the racial segregation that prevailed in libraries throughout much of the United States in the first 65 years of the twentieth century. When southern cities developed library systems, many excluded black patrons altogether, and others offered racially segregated service (Crestwell, 1996).[34]

For fuller understanding of this period of American library history, the following studies provide a wide range of views:

- E. Atkins Gleason. *The Southern Negro and the Public Library* (1941)
- E. J. Josey, *The Black Librarian in America* (1970)
- J. M. Tucker. *Untold Stories: Civil Rights, Libraries and Black Librarianship.* (1998)
- D. M. Battles. *The History of Public Library Access for African Americans in the South: Or, Leaving behind the Plow* (2008)
- C. Knott. *Not Free, Not for All: Public Libraries in the Age of Jim Crow.* (2015)

After Civil Rights legislation passed and became law in 1964, library historians began to explore the history of segregation and how Jim Crow laws impacted public libraries as public accommodations. P. T. Graham wrote of Alabama (2002); C. K. Malone of Houston (2007), and K. Cook of Mississippi (2013). Alma Dawson (2000) has written a celebratory study of African-American achievement, and P. Roughen (2014) has explored the influence of the Julius Rosenwald Library Service in the South.

Legislation for Libraries

> The Department of Defense is asking this year [1956] for over $1.4 billion to develop better weapons... What better weapon can we have in a struggle based on science, technology—and above all on ideas—than educated minds? Books for the education of young people are as much our strength in time of war as is armament for tanks and planes.
>
> **—Representative Edith Green (D.OR), May 8, 1956.[35]**

Elizabeth G. Meyer, state librarian of Rhode Island, took Congressman John F. Fogarty on a bookmobile ride. Fogarty, a former bricklayer, was so impressed with the library's role in people's lives that he went on to work with Senator Lister Hill to see through the passage of the Library Services Act (LSA) in 1956 (Healy, 1974, pp. 79–80). Representative Edith Green and Senator Lister Hill—with the bipartisan sponsorship of 27 representatives and 16 senators—introduced the legislation for the Library Services Act. On June 19, 1956, the bill was signed into law by President Dwight D. Eisenhower (Fry, 1975).

The LSA provided funds to support library services to people in rural and other unserved areas. The Federal Government paid part of the cost with a "Federal share"; and a state's matching percentage was based on the per capita income of the state as related to the national per capita income. This was intended to stimulate state and local governments to develop their own library programs (U.S. Office of Education, 1958). Each state was required to provide a plan for library development.[36] State library agencies and state library association chapters were key factors in implementing the LSA. Between 1956 and 1961, more than 5 million books were added to rural communities. Approximately 200 new bookmobiles extended library services to people in remote areas. Many county and regional library projects reported increased book circulation of 40% or more (Fry, 1975).

On January 29, 1963, President John F. Kennedy sent to Congress a special education message requesting enactment of legislation to amend the Library Services Act by authorizing a three-year grant program for the construction and operation of urban and rural libraries (*ALA Washington News Letter*, 1963, p. 6). Although President Kennedy did not live to see his dream realized (he was assassinated four days before the legislation was passed), his recommendation planted the idea of what was to become the most influential library legislation in the nation's history—the 1964 Library Services and Construction Act (LSCA) (Fry, 1975, p. 15).

On February 11, 1964, President Lyndon B. Johnson signed the Library Services and Construction Act (LSCA). It became P.L. 88-269,[37] which was amended and expanded in 1966 to include urban libraries and library cooperation, construction, services to the blind, physically handicapped, and institutionalized. The LSCA was the catalyst for a wide range of library development (Holley & Schremser, 1983). States were given flexibility to adapt to their own needs within federal priorities, which included adaptation of new technologies for library services and outreach to special segments of the population—such as the disadvantaged, those with disabilities, the elderly and homebound, those in institutions, those with limited English-speaking ability, those who needed literacy services, residents of Indian reservations, children in child care centers, and latchkey children (McCook, 2011, p. 54).[38] In 1970 the LSCA was extended to provide special library services for disadvantaged persons, to provide assistance to state library administrative agencies and to strengthen metropolitan libraries.

NOTES

1. *Libraries at the Crossroads,* a Pew report by J. Horrigan (2015), notes that large majorities of Americans see libraries as part of the educational ecosystem and as resources for promoting digital and information literacy.
2. For in-depth analysis of the reading world of the colonies see: Thompson (1952); Lehmann-Haupt, Wroth, and Silver (1952); Laugher (1973); Williams (1999); Lehuu (2000); and Brown, M. P. (2007). For background on reading in Spanish territories see Elliott (2006, pp. 205- 207).
3. The Junto was a discussion group of young men seeking social, economic, intellectual, and political advancement. *At the Instance of Benjamin Franklin: A Brief History of the Library Company of Philadelphia* (2015). www.librarycompany.org/about/Instance.pdf.
4. Founding dates and locations of a sample provide an indication of the scope of social libraries prior to the advent of tax-supported public libraries. Mechanics' and apprentices' libraries were

established in Newport, Rhode Island (1791); Detroit, Michigan, and Portland, Maine (1820); Lowell, Massachusetts (1825); and 30 years later in San Francisco, California (1855). Athenaeums were founded in Boston (1807); Philadelphia (1814); Providence, Rhode Island (1836); Zanesville, Ohio (1828), and Minneapolis (1859). Mercantile libraries included Boston and New York (1820); Philadelphia (1822); Albany, New York, and Detroit (1833); Cincinnati (1835); St. Louis (1846); Milwaukee (1847); San Francisco (1853); Peoria, Illinois (1855); and Dubuque, Iowa (1866). The single most enlightening document on a variety of social libraries is the U.S. Bureau of Education's *Public Libraries of Ten Principal Cities* (U.S. Department of the Interior, Bureau of Education, 1876: 837–1009). This article includes sketches on the founding and development of diverse social libraries such as the New York Historical Society Library (1804), Boston Athenaeum (1807), Cincinnati Circulating Library (1811), Apprentices' Library of Brooklyn (1823), Young Men's Association Library of Chicago (1841), Baltimore Mercantile Library Association (1842), Mercantile Library of San Francisco (1853), and Portland, Oregon Library Association (1864). Included for many of the libraries highlighted are membership rolls, budgets, and collection descriptions.

5. Circulating libraries spread through New England Salem (1789), Newburyport (ca. 1794) and New London, Connecticut (1793), Keene, New Hampshire (1805), Providence, Rhode Island (1820), and Woodstock, Vermont (1821) (McCook, 2011, p. 15).
6. Although most discussions of the history of public libraries address the school district library, many considerations of the development of libraries in the United States largely dismiss the school district library, because it was not particularly successful when actually delivered. However, the spread of this concept in connection with tax-supported schools across the nation certainly was a factor in creating a fertile opportunity for governments to establish public libraries in the following years. To understand the ongoing research in this area, see Wiegand (2007).
7. Freeman (2003) has written of the development of collections for these libraries and includes title lists that illustrate the scope of reading for common school students.
8. The Peterborough (NH) Town Library is accorded the distinction of being the first public library to be established from the start as a publicly supported institution in 1833. See Jewett (1851) and McMullen (2000).
9. See *Report of the Trustees of the Public Library to the City of Boston*, 1852.
10. French ventriloquist M. Nicholas-Marie Alexandre Vattemare is one of the most interesting personalities in U.S. library history. He was indefatigable in his efforts to establish an international system of exchanges of books and documents. From 1839 to 1849 he campaigned for this idea and was successful in creating an exchange system with the Library of Congress, as well as many states. We can only imagine, looking back, how much influence a persuasive idealist like Vattemare had on the public library idea. Sometimes a charismatic individual can successfully promote an ideal. For background on the connections of ventriloquism and the ideas of the enlightenment see Schmidt (1998). On the idea of Alexandre Vattemare and his system of international exchanges see Richards (1940).
11. "The Report of the Joint Special Committee to the Boston City Council of December 6, 1847" is reprinted in Wadlin (1911, 8–9).
12. *Report of the Trustees of the Public Library to the City of Boston, 1852*, is reproduced in Shera (1949/1965: 267–290). The Boston Public Library maintains a website of all historical documents relating to the library's founding: www.bpl.org/govinfo/online-collections/regional-boston-and-massachusetts/boston-public-library-documents-1852-1998/. Other essential writings include Ditzion (1947, pp. 5–7); Joeckel (1935, pp. 16–22); Ladenson (1982, pp. 7–9); Wadlin (1911); Whitehill (1956); F. R. Knight (2000); Davis (2002).
13. This report is available in digital form at the University of Wisconsin digital collection (http://digicoll.library.wisc.edu/cgi-bin/History/History-idx?type=header;pview=hide;id=History.PublicLibs).

14. Jordan looked at libraries in Missouri (8); Kansas (3); Nebraska (3); Iowa (3); South Dakota (3); North Dakota (4); Montana (14); Idaho (3); Oregon (6); and Washington (7).
15. Those interested may join the Library History Round Table of the American Library Association and keep current on new historical works through its *Bibliography of Library History* (www.ala.org/lhrt/popularresources/libhistorybib/libraryhistory).
16. Knott's *Not Free, Not for All: Public Libraries in the Age of Jim Crow* (2015) received the 2016 Eliza Atkins Gleason Book Award (www.ala.org/lhrt/awards/gleason-book-award). She previously wrote under the name Cheryl Knott Malone.
17. The contributions of women are largely ignored in Shera (1949), Ditzion (1947), and Harris (1995). Garrison's (1979) treatment of women was, as Francis Miksa (1982) demonstrates, somewhat speculative. For comprehensive bibliographic treatment see the bibliographic series issued by the ALA Feminist Task Force and the ALA Committee on the Status of Women in Librarianship; Weibel, Heim, and Ellsworth (1979); Heim and Phenix (1984); Phenix and Heim (1989); later years by Goetsch and Watstein (1993); Kruger and Larson (2000; 2006).
18. The Homestead Strike of June 1892 still stands as one of the bloodiest incidents in U.S. labor history, as Pinkerton guards sent to break the strike killed steel workers who worked at Carnegie's plants. See Nasaw (2007, pp. 405-427), "The Battle for Homestead."
19. A letter by the young Carnegie sent to the *Pittsburgh Dispatch* on May 9, 1853 provides insight to his passion for self-education (Nasaw, 2007, pp. 43–44).
20. Reproduced in Bobinski, 1969, pp. 203-206.
21. I was unable to find an article in the literature of librarianship to provide stable documentation but reproduce here the text of the historical marker dedicated in Savannah, Georgia., November 12, 2014. The marker reads: "Colored Library Association of Savannah." In 1906, 11 African-American men formed the Colored Library Association of Savannah and established the Library for Colored Citizens. They acquired the original collection from personal libraries and public donations of books and periodicals. In 1913, the Association successfully petitioned the Carnegie Corporation of New York for funds to build a permanent home for the collection. Dedicated in 1914 and completed in 1915, the library was designed by local architect Julian deBruyn Kops and is one of Savannah's few examples of Prairie School architecture. One of only two Carnegie library projects for African Americans in Georgia, this was the home library to James Alan McPherson, Pulitzer Prize-winning short story writer and essayist, and Clarence Thomas, Associate Justice of the Supreme Court of the United States. Erected by the Georgia Historical Society and Live Oak Public Libraries.
22. Between 1898 and 1905 300 traveling libraries were maintained in Illinois before state legislation passed. By 1904, 34 states with women's federations were overseeing over 300,000 volumes in 4,655 traveling collections.
23. In conjunction with the state library issue of *Information and Culture, 48*(1), Bernadette Lear (2013) compiled an extensive bibliography on the history of state libraries that is at the journal's website: www.infoculturejournal.org.
24. See also Rayward (1968); Churchwell (1975); and Davis and Dain (1986).
25. Kevane and Sundstrom (2014) assembled and coded data on individual libraries from special reports on libraries issued intermittently by the U.S. Bureau of Education. These reports included extensive tables of information on individual libraries gathered from surveys conducted by the bureau. The surveys covered were conducted in 1875, 1885, 1891, 1896, 1900, 1903, 1908, 1913, 1923, and 1929.
26. ALA, Commission on the Library and Adult Education (1926). For additional background on the Adult Education Board meetings and minutes through its history, see ALA archives under Reference and User Services Association. In 1926 ALA established the Board on Library and Adult Education (later the Adult Education Board) and published reports in the *ALA Bulletin*. The concept of the library as an agency of ongoing education for adults was firmly established.

27. National leaders, such as Louis R. Wilson of North Carolina, were able to speak out for citizen involvement. Connected to ALA's extension efforts, see Graham (1932). For an overview of this effort in North Carolina, South Carolina, Georgia, Kentucky, Mississippi, Tennessee, and Virginia, see Anders (1958). For an in-depth study of the North Carolina Citizens' Library Movement, see Eury (1951).
28. Milam was ALA executive secretary from 1920–1948. His service on the U.S. National Advisory Committee on Education gave him background on the possibility of federal aid to libraries (Sullivan, 1976, p. 165).
29. The National Plan examined the inequity of tax support for public libraries and sought provision of financial support so that library materials might be available throughout the nation (Sullivan 1976, p. 165; Milam, 1934). The National Plan was discussed at ALA Council during the 1934 annual conference, and though a sticking point was the locus of control (federal versus state and local), the committee made revisions affirming state and local responsibility and continuance and increase of local support. The National Plan was approved ("A National Plan for Libraries," 1935).
30. The work done by ALA's Library Extension Board laid much of the groundwork for a national vision of library service driven by a clearer idea of equity of financial support. Beginning in 1929, the Library Extension Board's occasional mimeographed newsletter, *Library Extension News*, was subtitled *Equalizing Library Opportunities*. The idea of equalization was clearly addressed in the 1936 publication issued jointly by ALA and the Library Extension Board and the Committee on Planning, *The Equal Chance: Books Help to Make It*. Using line drawings and charts, *The Equal Chance* compared per capita income to public library availability and declared, "It is increasingly true in our modern world that knowledge is power and that the uninformed man not only is handicapped in making a living, but is a liability as a citizen, for whose ignorance we all pay" (ALA, 1936, p. 15).
31. *Post-War Standards for Public Libraries* (Joeckel, 1943) were developed by ALA at the request of the National Resources Planning Board (NRPB). "Public Libraries Deserve Support That Will Enable Them Adequately to Fulfill Their Functions as Major Instruments of Adult Education" (U.S. NRPB, 1943: 70). The work of Joeckel (1935), the ALA Committee on Post-War Planning, and the New Deal National Resources Planning Board is viewed as laying the groundwork for federal legislation for library funding. Molz's (1984, pp. 95–96) characterization of Joeckel's rational planning approach and Milam's pragmatic incremental approach provide insight into the evolution of federal support. See also Sullivan (1976: 135–140); records in the ALA Archives: Post-War Planning Committee File, 1941–1948, including correspondence, reports, drafts, minutes, budgets, statistics, surveys, lists, proposals, and plans concerning a restatement of public library standards. *Post-War Standards for Public Libraries* (Joeckel, 1943), undertaken by ALA at the request of the National Resources Planning Board (NRPB). Adequate provision for library service had been recognized in the National Resources Development Report for 1943, issued by the NRPB in the section "Equal Access to Education," in which it was stated: "Public libraries deserve support that will enable them adequately to fulfill their functions as major instruments of adult education. Thirty-five million Americans, most of whom reside in rural areas, have no library service. Those to whom libraries are available receive service costing, on the average, little more than a third of the $1.50 per capita estimated to be required to maintain a reasonably good library." (U.S. NRPB, 1943, 70).
32. Raber (1997), "The Public Library and the Postwar World," pp. 23–36, and "The Beginnings of the Public Library Inquiry," pp. 37–49. The Public Library Inquiry consisted of seven volumes published by Columbia University Press: Bernard Berelson, *The Library's Public* (1949); Alice I. Bryan, *The Public Librarian* (1952); Oliver Garceau, *The Public Library in the Political Process* (1949); Robert D. Leigh, *The Public Library in the United States*, 1950; J. L McCamy and J. T McCamy, *Government Publications for the Citizen* (1949); William Miller & Social Science Research Council, *The Book Industry* (1949); and Gloria Waldron, *The Information Film* (1949). Supplementary reports

were issued on library finance, public use of the library, and effects of the mass media, music materials, and work measurement. For complete list, see Raber (1997, p. 82).

33. Bernard Berelson, author of *The Library's Public*, noted a split between the professed and practiced (Asheim, 1970, 62).
34. From *Plessy v. Ferguson* (1896) through *Brown v. Board of Education* (1954), many public libraries had separate and unequal facilities for African Americans—if they had any at all.
35. See *Congressional Record*, 84 Cong., 2 Sess. (1956), CII, Pt. 6, p. 7691.
36. *State Plans under the Library Services Act* (1960) is available as an ERIC document: http://files.eric.ed.gov/fulltext/ED543968.pdf.
37. See U.S. Senate. Committee on Labor and Public Welfare. Committee Print, The Library Services and Construction Act of 1964, 88 Cong., 2 Sess. (1964).
38. There were four titles added in 1966. Title I—Public Library Services: as in the 1964 act, matching-grant funds may be used for books and other library materials, library equipment, salaries, and other operating expenses. Title II—Public Library Construction: requested $40 million for fiscal year 1967, and for each of the next four fiscal years, such sums as Congress may determine. Title III—Interlibrary Cooperation: this section was a new title in the LSCA for establishment and maintenance of local, regional, state or interstate cooperative networks of libraries. Title IV—Specialized State Library Services: this new title was designed to assist states in providing greatly needed specialized state library services. It was to be divided in two parts: (1) state institutional library services, and (2) state plans for library services to the physically handicapped.

REFERENCES

A national plan for libraries. (1935, February). *ALA Bulletin, 29*, 91-98.

ALA Washington Newsletter. (1963, February 7).

American Library Association. (1936). *The equal chance: Books help to make it.* Chicago, IL: American Library Association.

American Library Association, Commission on the Library and Adult Education. (1926). *Libraries and Adult Education.* Chicago, IL: American Library Association.

Amory, H., & Hall, D. D. (Eds.). (2000). *A history of the book in America. Vol. 1 of The Colonial Book in the Atlantic World.* Cambridge, MA: Cambridge University Press.

Anders, M. A. (1958). *The development of public library service in the southeastern states, 1895-1950* (Doctoral dissertation). Columbia University, New York, NY.

Asheim, L. (1970). *A forum on the Public Library Inquiry.* Westport, CT: Greenwood Press. (Original work published 1950).

August, T. (2001, Fall). American libraries and agencies of culture. *American Studies, 42,* 12.

Battles, D. M. (2008). *The history of public library access for African Americans in the South: Or, leaving behind the plow.* Lanham, MD: Scarecrow Press.

Becker, P. C. (2005). *Books and libraries in American society during World War II: Weapons in the war of ideas.* New York, NY: Routledge.

Berelson, B. (1949). *The library's public.* New York, NY: Columbia University Press.

Bixby, A. F., & Howell, A. (1876). *Historical sketches of the ladies' library associations of the State of Michigan.* Adrian, MI: Times and Expositor Steam Print.

Blazek, R. (1979). The development of library service in the nation's oldest city: The St. Augustine Library Association, 1874-1880. *Journal of Library History, 14,* 160-182.

Bobinski, G. S. (1969). *Carnegie libraries: Their history and impact on American library development.* Chicago, IL: American Library Association.

Boston Public Library. (1852). *Report of the Trustees of the Public Library to the City of Boston.* https://babel.hathitrust.org/cgi/pt?id=umn.31951000831516z;view=1up;seq=7.

Brown, M. P. (2007). *The pilgrim and the bee: Reading rituals and book culture in early New England.* Philadelphia, PA: University of Pennsylvania Press.

Bryan, A. I. (1952). *The public librarian: A report of the Public Library Inquiry.* New York, NY: Columbia University Press.

Carmichael, J. (1986). Atlanta's female librarians, 1883-1915. *The Journal of Library History (1974-1987), 21*(2), 376-399.

Carnegie, A. (1901). *The gospel of wealth, and other timely essays* (New York, NY: Century).

Churchwell, C. D. (1975). *The shaping of American library education.* Chicago, IL: American Library Association.

Congressional Record, 84 Cong., 2 Sess. (1956), CII, Pt. 6, p. 7691.

Cook, K. (2013). Struggles within: Lura G. Currier, the Mississippi Library Commission, and library services to African Americans. *Information and Culture, 48*(1), 134-156.

Crestwell, S. (1996, Summer/Fall). The last days of Jim Crow in southern libraries. *Libraries and Culture, 31,* 557-573.

Croteau, J. (2006). Yet more American circulating libraries: A preliminary checklist of Brooklyn (New York) Circulating Libraries. *Library History, 22*(3), 171-180.

Davis, D. G., Jr. (2002). *Winsor, Dewey, and Putnam: The Boston experience.* Champaign, IL: Graduate School of Library and Information Science, University of Illinois at Urbana-Champaign.

Davis, D. G., Jr., & Dain, P. (1986). History of library and information science education. *Library Trends, 34*(3).

Dawson, A. (2000, Summer). Celebrating African-American librarians and librarianship. *Library Trends, 49,* 49-87.

Dierickx, M. B. (1996). *The architecture of literacy: The Carnegie libraries of New York City.* New York, NY: Cooper Union for the Advancement of Science and Art and the New York City Department of General Services.

Ditzion, S. H. (1940). The district school library, 1835-1855. *Library Quarterly, 10,* 545-547.

Ditzion, S. H. (1947). *Arsenals of a democratic culture: A social history of the American public library movement in New England and the Middle States from 1850-1900.* Chicago, IL: American Library Association.

Elliott, J. H. (2006). *Empires of the Atlantic world: Britain and Spain in America 1492-1830.* New Haven, CT: Yale University Press.

Ernsberger, R. (2015, February). Andrew Carnegie: Robber baron turned Robin Hood, *American History 49,* 33-41.

Eury, W. (1951). *The Citizens' Library Movement in North Carolina* (Unpublished master's thesis). George Peabody College for Teachers.

Fain, E. (1978, Winter). The library and American education: Education through secondary school. *Library Trends,* 327-352.

Fitch, John W., & Hovde, D. M. (2015, December). Library programs in Indiana in the 1850s. *Indiana Magazine of History* 111, 422-453.

Freeman, R. S. (2003). *Harper & Brothers' family and school district libraries, 1830-1846* (R. S. Freeman & D. M. Hovde, Eds.). Jefferson, NC: McFarland.

Fry, J. W. (1975). LSA and LSCA, 1956-1973: A legislative history. *Library Trends, 24*(1), 7-28.

Garceau, O. (1949). *The public library in the political process: A report of the Public Library Inquiry.* New York, NY: Columbia University Press.

Garrison, D. (1979). *Apostles of culture: The public librarian and American society, 1876-1920.* New York, NY: Free Press. Reprint, University of Wisconsin Press.

General Court of Massachusetts. (1848). Chapter 52. In *Massachusetts acts and resolves.* Boston, MA: State of Massachusetts.

Glasgow, E. (2002). Circulating libraries. *Library Review, 51*(8/9), 420-423.

Gleason, E. A. (1941). *The Southern Negro and the public library: A study of government and administration of public library service to Negroes in the South.* Chicago, IL: University of Chicago Press.

Glynn, T. (2015). *Reading publics: New York City's public libraries, 1754-1911.* New York, NY: Empire State Editions, an imprint of Fordham University Press.

Goetsch, L. A., & Watstein, S. B. (1993). *On account of sex: An annotated bibliography on the history of women in librarianship, 1987-1992.* Metuchen, NJ: Scarecrow Press.

Gordon, L. G. (2005). Education and the professions. In Nancy A. Hewitt (Ed.), *A companion to American women's history* (pp. 227-249). Malden, MA: Blackwell Publishing.

Graham, F. P. (1932, May). Citizen's library movements. *Library Extension News, 14,* 2.

Graham, P. T. (2002). *A right to read: Segregation and civil rights in Alabama's public libraries, 1900-1965.* Tuscaloosa, AL: University of Alabama Press.

Gross, R. A., & Kelley, M. (2010). *A history of the book in America: An extensive republic: print, culture, and society in the new nation, 1790-1840,* Volume 2. Chapel Hill: Published in Association with the American Antiquarian Society by the University of North Carolina Press.

Grotzinger, L. A., Carmichael, J. V., & Maack, M. M. (1994). *Women's work: Vision and change in librarianship.* Champaign, IL: University of Illinois.

Hamer, J. H. (1998, July). Money and the moral order in late nineteenth and early-twentieth century American capitalism. *Anthropological Quarterly, 71,* 138-149.

Harris, M. H. (1973, September 15). The purpose of the American public library: A revisionist interpretation of history. *Library Journal, 98,* 2509-2514.

Harris, M. H. (1995). *History of libraries in the Western world* (4th ed.). Lanham, MD: Scarecrow Press.

Healy, J. S. (1974). *John E. Fogarty: Political leadership for library development.* Metuchen, NJ: Scarecrow Press.

Heim, K. M., & Phenix, K. J. (1984). *On account of sex: An annotated bibliography on the history of women in librarianship, 1977-1981.* Chicago, IL: American Library Association.

Held, R. E. (1973). *The rise of the public library in California.* Chicago, IL: American Library Association.

Hildenbrand, S. (Ed.). (1996). *Reclaiming the American library past: Writing the women in.* Norwood, NJ: Ablex.

Holley, E. G., & Schremser, R. F. (1983). *The Library Services and Construction Act: An historical overview from the viewpoint of major participants.* Greenwich, CT: JAI Press.

Horrigan, J. (2015). *Libraries at the crossroads.* Pew Research Center. www.pewinternet.org/2015/09/15/Libraries-at-crossroads/.

Howard, P. (1945). There's work to be done in Washington. *Library Journal, 70,* 878-879.

Hoyt, D. J. (1999). *A strong mind in a strong body: Libraries in the German-American Turner movement.* New York, NY: Peter Land.

Jaeger, P. T., Taylor, N. G., Gorham, U., Kettnich, K., Sarin, L. C., & Peterson, K. (2014). Library research and what libraries actually do now: Education, inclusion, social services, public spaces, digital literacy, social justice, human rights, and other community needs. *Library Quarterly, 84*(4), 491-493.

Jaeger, P. T., Gorham, U., Bertot, J. C., & Sarin, L. C. (2014). *Public libraries, public policies, and political processes: Serving and transforming communities in times of economic and political constraint.* Lanham, MD: Rowman & Littlefield.

Jewett, C. C. (1851). Report on the public libraries of the United States of America, January 1, 1850. In *Report of the board of regents of the Smithsonian Institution.* Washington, DC: Smithsonian Institution.

Joeckel, C. B. (1935). *The government of the American public library.* Chicago, IL: University of Chicago Press.

Joeckel, C. B. (1943). *Post-war standards for public libraries.* Chicago, IL: American Library Association.

Joeckel, C. B., & Winslow, A. (1948). National plan for public library service. Chicago, IL: American Library Association.

Jones, P. A., Jr. (1999). *Libraries, immigrants, and the American experience.* Westport, CT: Greenwood Press.

Jordan, M. W. (2015). Public library history on the Lewis and Clark Trail. *Public Library Quarterly, 34*(2), 162-177.

Josey, E. J. (1970). *The Black librarian in America.* Metuchen, NJ: Scarecrow Press.

Kaser, D. (1978). Coffee house to stock exchange: A natural history of the reading room. In H. Goldstein (Ed.), *Milestones to the present: Papers from library history seminar V* (pp. 238-254). Syracuse, NY: Gaylord Professional Publications.

Kaser, D. (1980). *A book for a sixpence: The circulating library in America.* Pittsburg, PA: Beta Phi Mu.

Kelly, M. S. (2003, Fall). Revisiting C. H. Milam's "What libraries learned from the war and rediscovering the library faith." *Libraries and Culture, 38*, 378-388.

Kevane, M., & Sundstrom, W. A. (2014). The development of public libraries in the United States, 1870-1930: A quantitative assessment. *Information and Culture, 49*(2), 117-144.

Knight, D. M., & Nourse, E. S. (Eds.). (1969). *Libraries at large: Traditions, innovations and the national interest; the resource book based on the materials of the National Advisory Commission on Libraries.* New York, NY: R. R. Bowker.

Knight, E. W. (1922). *Public education in the South.* Boston, MA: Ginn and Company.

Knight, F. R. (2000). *A palace for the people: The relationships that built the Boston Public Library* (Doctoral dissertation). University of Oxford, Oxford, United Kingdom.

Knott, C. (2015). *Not free, not for all: Public libraries in the age of Jim Crow.* Amherst, MA: University of Massachusetts Press.

Kramp, R. S. (2010). *The Great Depression: Its impact on forty-six large American public libraries: An inquiry based on a content analysis of published writings of their directors.* Duluth, MN: Library Juice Press.

Kruger, B., & Larson, C. (Eds.). (2000). *On account of sex: An annotated bibliography on the status of women in librarianship, 1993-1997.* Lanham, MD: Scarecrow Press.

Kruger, B., & Larson, C. (Eds.). (2006). *On account of sex: An annotated bibliography on the status of women in librarianship, 1998-2002.* Lanham, MD: Scarecrow Press.

Kunkle, H. J. (1969). *A historical study of the extension activities of the California State Library with particular emphasis on its role in rural library development, 1850-1966.* (Doctoral dissertation). Florida State University, Tallahassee, FL.

Ladenson, A. (1982). *Library law and legislation in the United States.* Metuchen, NJ: Scarecrow Press.

Latham, J. M. (out for review). Creating a constituency: Julia Wright Merrill and Public Library Extension, 1925-1946.

Latham, J. M. (2010, July). Clergy of the mind: Alvin S. Johnson, William S. Learned, the Carnegie Corporations, and the American Library Association. *Library Quarterly, 80*, 249-265.

Laugher, C. T. (1973). *Thomas Bray's grand design.* Chicago, IL: American Library Association.

Learned, W. S. (1924). *The American public library and the diffusion of knowledge.* New York, NY: Harcourt.

Lehmann-Haupt, H., Wroth, L., & Silver, R. G. (1952). *The book in America: A history of the making and selling of books in the United States.* New York, NY: R. R. Bowker.

Lehuu, I. (2000). *Carnival on the page: Popular print media in Antebellum America.* Chapel Hill, NC: University of North Carolina Press.

Leigh, R. D. (1950). *The public library in the United States: The general report of the Public Library Inquiry.* New York, NY: Columbia University Press.

Lewis, Linda K. (1996). Julia Brown Asplund and New Mexico library service. In S. Hildenbrand, (Ed.). (1996). *Reclaiming the American library past: Writing the women in.* Norwood, NJ: Ablex.

Library projects under public works, civil works and relief administrations. (1933). *ALA Bulletin, 27*, 539-546.

Library Services Branch. (1960). *State plans under the library services act: A progress report, the first three years: Fiscal years 1957, 1958, 1959: Supplement 2.* Washington, DC: U.S. Department of Health, Education, and Welfare.

Maack, M. N. (1994, Winter). Public libraries in transition: Ideals, strategies and research. *Libraries and Culture, 29*, 79.

Magill, H. S. (1920). Smith-Towner Bill unlike other federal aid measures. *The Journal of Education, 91*(8 (2268)), 199-200. https://www.jstor.org/stable/i40106721.

Malone, C. K. (1999). Autonomy and accommodation: Houston's colored Carnegie Library, 1907-1922. *Libraries and Culture, 34*(2), 95-112.

Malone, C. K. (2000). Toward a multicultural American public library history. *Libraries & Culture, 35*(1), 77-87.

Malone, C. K. (2007). Unannounced and unexpected: The desegregation of Houston Public Library in the early 1950s. *Library Trends, 55*(3), 665-674.

Martin, L. A. (1972, October). Standards for public libraries. *Library Trends, 21*, 164-177.

Martin, R. S. (Ed.). (1993). *Carnegie denied: Communities rejecting Carnegie library construction grants, 1898-1925*. Westport, CT: Greenwood Press.

Martin, R. S., & Lear, B. A. (2013). Manley, L.1., & Holley, R. P. (2012). History of the Ebook: The changing face of books. *Technical Services Quarterly, 29*(4), 292-311. *Information and Culture, 48*(1), 1-7.

Mattson, K. (2000, Fall). The librarian as secular minister to democracy: The life and ideas of John Cotton Dana. *Libraries and Culture, 35*, 514-534.

McCamy, J. L., & McCamy, J. T. B. (1949). *Government publications for the citizen*. New York: Columbia University Press.

McCauley, E. B. (1971). *The New England mill girls: Feminine influence in the development of public libraries in New England, 1820-1860*. (Doctoral dissertation). Columbia University, New York, NY.

McCook, K. (2011). *Introduction to public librarianship* (2nd ed.). New York, NY: Neal-Schuman Publishers.

McMullen, H. (1987). Prevalence of libraries in the northeastern states before 1876. *Journal of Library History 22*, 312-337.

McMullen, H. (1991). The prevalence of libraries in the Middle West and Far West before 1876. *Libraries and Culture, 26*, 441-463.

McMullen, H. (2000). *American libraries before 1876*. Westport, CT: Greenwood Press.

Mediavilla, C. (2013). Carma Zimmerman Leigh and the diffusion of cooperation through California libraries, 1951-1972. *Information and Culture, 48*(1), 157-177.

Miksa, F. (1982). The interpretation of American public library history. In J. Robbins-Carter (Ed.), *Public librarianship: A reader* (pp. 73-90). Littleton, CO: Libraries Unlimited.

Milam, C. H. (1934, February). National planning for libraries. *ALA Bulletin, 28*, 60-62.

Miller, W., & Social Science Research Council. (1949). *The book industry; A report of the Public Library Inquiry*. New York, NY: Columbia University Press.

Molz, R. K. (1984). *National planning for library service, 1935-1975: From the national plan to the national program*. Chicago, IL: American Library Association.

Musmann, V. K. (1982). *Women and the founding of social libraries in California, 1859-1910* (Doctoral dissertation). University of Southern California, Los Angeles, CA.

Nasaw, D. (2007). *Andrew Carnegie*. New York, New York, NY: Penguin USA.

A national plan for libraries. (1935, February). *ALA Bulletin*, 29, 91-98.

Page, H. M. (1942). Platte votes for county library service following WPA demonstration. *Missouri Library Association Quarterly*, 339-340.

Passet, J. E. (1994). *Cultural crusaders: Women librarians in the American West, 1900-1917*. Albuquerque, NM: University of New Mexico Press.

Patterson, L. (2000, Summer). History and status of Native Americans in librarianship, *Library Trends, 49*, 182-193.

Pawley, C. (2000, Summer). Advocate of access: Lutie Stearns and the traveling libraries of the Wisconsin Free Library Commission: 1895-1914. *Libraries and Culture, 35*, 434-458.

Peich, A., & Fletcher, C. N. (2015), Public libraries and cooperative extension as community partners for lifelong learning and learning cities. *New Directions for Adult and Continuing Education, 2015* (145), 45-55.

Phenix, K., & Heim, K. M. (1989). *On account of sex: An annotated bibliography on the history of women in librarianship, 1982-1986*. Chicago, IL: American Library Association.

Poole, W. F. (1877). State legislation in the matter of libraries. *Library Journal, 2,* 7.

Porter, D. B. (1936, October). The organized educational activities of Negro literary societies, 1828-1846. *Journal of Negro Education 5,* 555-576.

Pozzi, E. M. (2013). *The public library in an immigrant neighborhood: Italian immigrants' information ecologies in Newark, New Jersey, 1889-1919* (Doctoral dissertation). Rutgers University Graduate School, New Brunswick, NJ.

Raber, D. (1997). *Librarianship and legitimacy: The ideology of the Public Library Inquiry*. Westport, CT: Greenwood Press.

Raber, D. (1999, August). Everything old is new again. *American Libraries 30,* 52-54.

Raven, J. (2007). Social libraries and library societies in eighteenth-century North America. In T. August & K. Carpenter (Eds.), *Institutions of reading: The social life of libraries in the United States* (pp. 24-52). Amherst, MA: University of Massachusetts Press.

Raven, J., & Howsam L., (Eds.) (2011). *Books between Europe and the Americas: Connections and communities, 1620-1860*. London, United Kingdom: Palgrave Macmillan.

Rayward, W. B. (1968). Melvil Dewey and education for librarianship. *Journal of Library History, 3,* 297-313.

Richards, E. M. (1940). Alexandre Vattemare and his system of international exchanges. *Bulletin of the Medical Library Association, 32,* 413-448.

Roughen, P. (2014). Julius Rosenwald: A review of the literature on his motivations and impact in redefining library service in the South. *Southeastern Librarian, 62*(2), 2-9.

Sandoe, M. W. (1946). Open letter to Julia Wright Merrill. *Library Journal,* p. 394.

Schmidt, L. E. (1998, June). From demon possession to magic show: Ventriloquism, religion, and the Enlightenment. *Church History, 67,* 274-304.

Shera, J. H. (1949). *Foundations of the public library: The origins of the public library movement in New England, 1629-1855*. Chicago, IL: University of Chicago Press.

Sorensen, M. W. (1999, Summer). The Illinois State Library: Extension, reorganization and experimentation, 1921-1955. *Illinois Libraries 81,* 131-138.

Stanford, E. B. (1944). *Library extension under the WPA: An appraisal of an experiment in federal aid.* Chicago, IL: University of Chicago Press.

Stielow, F. J., & Corsaro, J. (1993). The Carnegie question and the public library movement in Progressive Era New York. In R. S. Martin (Ed.), *Carnegie denied: Communities rejecting Carnegie library construction grants, 1898-1925* (pp. 35-51). Westport, CT: Greenwood Press.

Stuart, S. L. (2013). "My duty and my pleasure": Alice S. Tyler's reluctant oversight of Carnegie Library philanthropy in Iowa. *Information and Culture: A Journal of History,* (1), 91.

Sullivan, P. (1976). *Carl H. Milam and the American Library Association.* New York, NY: H. W. Wilson.

Swain, M. H. (1995). A new deal in libraries: Federal relief work and library service, 1933-1943. *American Libraries, 30,* 265-283.

Swetnam, S. H. (2012). *Books, bluster, and bounty: Local politics in the Intermountain West and Carnegie Library Building Grants, 1898-1920.* Logan, UT: Utah State University Press.

Thomison, D. (1978). *A history of the American Library Association, 1876-1972.* Chicago, IL: American Library Association.

Thompson, C. S. (1952). *Evolution of the American public library, 1653-1876.* Washington, DC: Scarecrow Press.

Thompson-Miller, R., Feagin, J. R., & Picco, L. H. (2015). *Jim Crow's legacy: The lasting impact of segregation.* Lanham, MD; Boulder; New York; London, United Kingdom: Rowman & Littlefield.

Todd, E. B. (2001, Fall). Antebellum libraries in Richmond and New Orleans and the search for the practices and preferences of real readers. *American Studies, 42,* 195-209.

Tucker, J. M. (1998). *Untold stories: Civil rights, libraries, and black librarianship.* Champaign, IL: Publications Office, University of Illinois Graduate School of Library and Information Science.

Twain, M., & Warner, C. D. (1873). *The gilded age.* Garden City, NY: Nelson Doubleday, Inc.

U.S. Department of the Interior, Bureau of Education. (1876). *Public libraries in the United States of America: Their history, condition, and management. Special report.* Champaign, IL: Government Printing Office. Reprint, as Monograph Series, no. 4.

U.S. National Resources Planning Board. (1943). *National resources development report for 1943.* Washington, DC: U.S. Government Printing Office.

U.S. Office of Education. (1958). *State plans under the Library Services Act.* U.S. Government Printing Office, Washington, DC.

U.S. Senate Committee on Labor and Public Welfare. Committee Print, The Library Services and Construction Act of 1964: 88 Cong., 2 Sess. (1964).

U.S. Senate Committee on Labor and Public Welfare (1964). *The Library Services and Construction Act of 1964: A Compilation of Materials Relevant to Public Law 88-269.* https://books.google.com/books?id=pNHAS275hicC.

Vann, S. K. (1961). *Training for librarianship before 1923: Education for librarianship prior to the publication of Williamson's report on training for library service.* Chicago, IL: American Library Association.

Wadlin, H. G. (1911). *The Public Library of the City of Boston: A history.* Boston, MA: The Trustees.

Waldron, G. (1949). *The information film: A report of the Public Library Inquiry [in co-operation with the Twentieth Century Fund].* New York, NY: Columbia University Press.

Watson, P. D. (1994, July). Founding mothers: The contribution of women's organizations to public library development in the United States. *Library Quarterly, 64,* 237.

Watson, P. D. (2003). Valleys without sunsets: Women's clubs and traveling libraries. In R. S. Freeman & D. M. Hovde (Eds.), *Libraries to the people: Histories of outreach* (pp. 73-95). Jefferson, NC: McFarland.

Weibel, K., Heim, K., & Ellsworth, D. J. (1979). *The status of women in librarianship, 1876-1976.* Phoenix, AZ: Oryx Press.

Whitehill, W. M. (1956). *Boston Public Library: A centennial history.* Cambridge, MA: Harvard University Press.

Wiegand, W. A. (1986). *The politics of an emerging profession: The American Library Association, 1876-1917.* New York, NY: Greenwood Press.

Wiegand, W. A. (1989). *An active instrument for propaganda: The American public library during World War I.* New York, NY: Greenwood Press.

Wiegand, W. A. (1996). *Irrepressible reformer: A biography of Melvil Dewey.* Chicago, IL: American Library Association.

Wiegand, W. A. (2007). The rich potential of American public school library history: Research needs and opportunities for historians of education and librarianship. *Libraries and the Cultural Record, 42*(1), 57-74.

Wiegand, W. A. (2015). *Part of our lives: A people's history of the American public library.* New York, NY: Oxford University Press.

Wight, J. B. (1851). Public libraries. *Common School Journal 13,* 257-264.

Williams, J. H. (1999). *The significance of the printed word in early America.* Westport, CT: Greenwood Press.

Wolf, E. (1976). *At the instance of Benjamin Franklin: A brief history of the Library Company of Philadelphia, 1731-1976.* The Library Company of Philadelphia. www.librarycompany.org/about/Instance.pdf.

Woodward, E. M. (1938). WPA library projects. *Wilson Bulletin for Librarians, 12,* 518-520.

Young, A. P. (1981). *Books for Sammies: The American Library Association and World War I* (No. 15). Beta Phi Mu Chapbooks.

CHAPTER 3

People, Not Institutions

Toward Equity of Access (1960 to the Present)

Equity of access as a central value of public library service emerged after 1960. This value was activated over the next decades by a series of government actions that carried significant funding. The Library Services and Construction Act (LSCA) replaced the Library Services Act in 1964. The LSCA was replaced by the Library Services and Technology Act (LSTA) in 1996, the same year the Institute of Museum and Library Services (IMLS) was established. These Acts demonstrate federal commitment to changing priorities in libraries.

ALA also expanded advocacy efforts during this time, shifting from national standards to community-based planning. Public librarians developed a number of self-study tools to measure the outputs and results of their efforts, such as the Planning for Results series of the 1990s. These tools were created to help librarians measure and demonstrate their value to their community as well as funding agencies. The focus of these tools and library services was on the individual using the library, rather than the library as an institution.

This chapter will look at the main forces outside and inside of the library profession that have shaped libraries over the past 50 years, a time of rapid technological advancement and social change.

CIVIL RIGHTS AND THE ROLE OF PUBLIC LIBRARIES

> At a time when our public is challenged on multiple fronts, we need to recommit ourselves to the ideal of providing equal access to everyone, anywhere, anytime, and in any format. . . . By finally embracing equity of access we will be affirming our core values, recognizing realities, and assuring our future.
>
> **—Carla D. Hayden, ALA President, 2003–2004**

The struggles of minority groups to gain access to library services continued until passage of the Civil Rights Act of 1964 (Risen, 2014). In *Not Free, Not for All: Public Libraries in the Age of Jim Crow* (2015), Cheryl Knott chronicles restriction of African Americans' access to public libraries. Lotsee Patterson's "History and Status of Native Americans in Librarianship" (2000) provides important factual analysis of the failure of American librarianship to include tribal people in the first century of library growth. It would not be until the 1960s that the democratic public library was mandated to serve all the people of America regardless of race (*Brown v. Louisiana,* 1966). It has been more than 50 years since the passage of legislation that ended discrimination based on race. How did American librarians work to end discrimination? How did they move to realize the oft-stated commitment to democratic values?

Today public libraries focus on people and communities, not institutions. The change began with the elimination of American Library Association national standards in 1966. The increased local flexibility of the Library Services and Construction Act (LSCA) gave individual libraries that received some funding through their state libraries the resources to encourage creativity and increase service to diverse populations. In the 1970s PLA initiated changes in how libraries planned services. The future was explored at the White House Conferences sponsored by the National Commission of Libraries and Information Science (NCLIS) in 1979 and 1991, which brought America to a new age in public library service at the turn of the millennium.

The work of state library agencies, usually in collaboration with state associations, has been central to overall national public library development. The 1966 report *The Library Functions of the States* (based on a 1960 survey) recognized the importance of state library agencies in their intermediary role between the federal government and local libraries, and recommended that state library agencies strengthen their positions (Monypenny, 1966).

These changes to the warp and woof of modern public librarianship can be found in state library association journals and conference programs. These provide important historical documentation of public library development. The flow of new ideas up from the grass-roots in the states is revisited and renewed by policy-makers.[1] PLA continued to be an important voice in library development after the 1960s, but was no longer the primary authority for the way things should be. How did public librarians who had been issuing national standards since the 1930s move to a national philosophy that was committed to equity of access?

PEOPLE AND COMMUNITY FOCUSED LIBRARIANSHIP: EQUITY OF ACCESS BECOMES A CORE VALUE FOR AMERICA'S PUBLIC LIBRARIES

The equity era of librarianship began in the 1960s with two major milestones, the 1963 *Access Study* and enactment of the Library Services and Construction Act (LSCA) in 1964. These two events gave voice to the changes in librarianship that were reflected in the larger society: equity of information for all people and the financial and ideological support to activate this ethos (McCook, 2002).

1963 Access Study

Desegregation of the Atlanta Public Library took place in 1959, led by Irene Dobbs Jackson.[2] There was little reporting of this in the library literature at the time (Lefever, 2005, pp. 10–12). However, the national library press faced the issue at long last in 1960, with *Library Journal* editor Eric Moon engaging Rice Estes, who characterized segregation as the most pressing problem facing the nation and criticized librarians for their failure to address the issue (Estes, 1960; Kister, 2002, pp. 152–164).

Moon's efforts were the catalyst for an ALA policy passed at the 1962 annual conference to "urge libraries which are institutional members not to discriminate among users on the basis of race, religion, or personal belief and if such discrimination now exists to bring it to an end as speedily as possible" (Highlights of the Detroit Conference, 1965). The policy also contained a provision to obtain accurate information about segregation that was the impetus behind the 1963 Access Study.

This study was the first national review of racial inequality in librarianship. The "Statement on Individual Members, Chapter Status and Institutional Membership" gave impetus to the 1963 Access Study, commissioned by the ALA Library Administration Division (LAD) to gather information on free access to library buildings, resources, and services. It was intended to provide an analysis of the extent of the problem and to give a valid basis for working toward improvement (Tucker, 1963; McCook, 2002). The study found direct discrimination (complete exclusion), and indirect discrimination practiced by branch libraries in northern cities that were so differentiated in terms of quantity and quality that one group was more limited in its access to the library resources of a community than another. Of these findings, Virginia Lacy Jones commented, "No one should have been surprised that branch libraries discriminate against Negroes, since all public institutions in the United States had discrimination against Negroes built into them. This fact is well known in the South; it is time the North woke up to it" (Jones, 1963, p. 744).

One of the last cases addressing segregation in libraries was *Brown v. Louisiana* (1966), a U.S. Supreme Court case based on the First Amendment to the U.S. Constitution. Four African-American men had requested a book from the Audubon Regional Library, sat down when told it was not available, and were arrested. The decision held that protesters have a First and Fourteenth Amendment right to engage in a peaceful sit-in at a public library.

There are many other important articles and books about the Civil Rights era in librarianship—both stories of heroism or resistance (e.g., Robbins, 2000; Graham, 2001) and stories of compliance (e.g., Harris, 2003).

1964 Library Services and Construction Act

On February 11, 1964, President Lyndon B. Johnson signed the Library Services and Construction Act (LSCA, successor to LSA), P.L. 88-269. The LSCA and its extensions included urban libraries and construction; library cooperation; services to the institutionalized, blind, and people with physical disabilities; special library services for disadvantaged persons; and assistance to state library administrative agencies (Fry, 1975).

The LSCA legislation provided some financial and philosophical support for public libraries to address consistent discrimination in library services that had been identified in the Access Study. The realization that public librarianship needed to be transformed became starkly clear when the *Minimum Standards for Public Library Systems* (PLA, 1967) were immediately found to fail to address the problems of inequality. Social historian Toni Samek has observed: "In the late 1960s, a number of American librarians argued that library collections lacked balance, that a purist moral stance on intellectual freedom was an example of hands-off liberalism, and that the library served mainstream social sectors, not the whole community" (Samek, 2001, p. 46).[3]

In 1966 library cooperation was added to the scope of the LSCA, as were services to the institutionalized, the blind, and people with physical disabilities. The LSCA stimulated a wide variety of innovative library development. States were given considerable flexibility to adapt to their own needs within federal priorities, which included public library construction and renovation; interlibrary cooperation and resource sharing; adaptation of new technologies for library services; and outreach to special segments of the population—including the disadvantaged, those with disabilities, the elderly and homebound, those in institutions, those with limited English-speaking ability, those who needed literacy services, residents of Indian reservations, children in child care centers, and latchkey children.

With LSCA providing some support to begin new programs, and an emphasis on the eradication of poverty, ALA members had the means and impetus to establish new round tables and organizations to address social needs. For instance, the Social Responsibilities Round Table was formed in 1968, and its members appointed a Coordinating Committee on Library Service to the Disadvantaged in 1970 (Lippincott & Taffae, 1996). Affiliate librarian organizations were established to address specific needs of ethnic minorities:

- American Indian Library Association (AILA), founded 1979
- Asian/Pacific American Librarians Association (APALA), founded 1980
- Black Caucus of the ALA (BCALA), founded 1970
- Chinese American Librarians Association (CALA), founded 1973, merged 1983
- REFORMA—National Association to Promote Library and Information Services to Latinos and the Spanish Speaking, founded 1971

Each of these affiliates provide support to develop services with a focus on the underserved.

Equality of service to people regardless of gender or sexual orientation also began to be addressed at this time by the creation of new groups within the American Library Association. The Feminist Task Force of the Social Responsibilities Round Table was established in 1970, the Task Force on Gay Liberation in 1970 (now the Gay, Lesbian, Bisexual, and Transgender Round Table), and the Committee on the Status of Women in Librarianship in 1976. Taken together, these determined, focused groups within ALA and its affiliates were influential forces that looked to the expansion of services by attending to the needs of groups of people who had been marginalized (Weibel, Heim, & Ellsworth, 1979; McCook. 2000; Carmichael, 1998). Their work to document discrimination and to advocate for positive actions changed the direction of the profession to a focus on all people rather than on institutions.

An important assessment of the role of the LSCA in the state of Illinois provides a substantive case study of the impact of this federal legislation. In her introduction to a special report on the history of the LSCA in Illinois, state librarian Bridget L. Lamont wrote, "During the LSCA years . . . countless LSCA projects of exceptional merit were undertaken, including expansion of public library services to underserved areas, special library services to nursing homes and other special populations, automation/technology initiatives and training grants" (1998, p. 93).

A STRATEGY FOR PUBLIC LIBRARY CHANGE: A MAJOR TRANSFORMATION OF THE PHILOSOPHY OF PUBLIC LIBRARIANSHIP

The atmosphere of social change in the 1960s affected the way public librarians thought about service. The *Minimum Standards for Public Library Systems, 1966* (PLA, 1967) did not provide the guidance needed in a changing world. PLA realized national standards no longer worked. After much internal deliberation and discussion, PLA published *A Strategy for Public Library Change* (A. B. Martin, 1972).[4] The focus on community-based planning moved public library discourse to acceptance of the innovation of local planning models that took place in the 1970s (Lynch, 1981). This was a major transformation of the philosophy of public librarianship.[5]

Background to the transformation of public library goals was provided by the work of the National Advisory Commission on Libraries (NACL), appointed in 1966 by President Lyndon B. Johnson. The NACL report was massive and comprehensive, entitled *Libraries At Large: Tradition, Innovation, and the National Interest.* The report recommended that the American people "should be provided with library and informational services adequate to their needs, and that the Federal Government, in collaboration with state and local governments and private agencies, should exercise leadership assuring the provision of such services." (Knight & Nourse, 1969).[6] To do this, the National Commission on Libraries and Information Science (NCLIS) was established to be a continuing Federal planning agency.

The effect of social change on libraries was addressed in a 1970 report, "Response to Change: American Libraries in the Seventies," by Mathews and Lacy. They identified two important ways in which libraries would be able to meet the challenges of the future: use of computers to automate the library's acquisitions, cataloging, circulation, inventory, and statistical work and by going out, both psychologically and physically into the community that is to be served and learning to operate in ways meaningful to those they are trying to reach. Especially engaging was their assertion that librarians should "serve as both the motivator and supplier of aspirations for the dispossessed and disorganized" (p. 42).

STEPS TOWARD TRANSFORMATION: ROLES, RESPONSES, AND OUTCOMES

How did public libraries transform their structural approach to planning and developing services after 1966? The answer is complex. The dynamic among library leaders in PLA, library science faculties, and the library press inspired an intensification of passion, commitment, and dedication to developing equitable library services for all. At the federal level, policy development and studies by the National Commission on Libraries and Information Science helped to create a vibrant, intellectual era of nationwide commitment to library services. From the first White House Conferences on Library and Information Science keynoted by President Jimmy Carter in 1979 to the second in 1991, libraries were important to the national conversation on lifelong learning.

The National Commission on Libraries and Information Science and the White House Conferences (1970–2008)

NCLIS began its work in 1970 with the goal:

> To eventually provide every individual in the United States with equal opportunity of access to that part of the total information resource which will satisfy the individual's educational, working, cultural and leisure-time needs and interests, regardless of the individual's location, social or physical condition or level of intellectual achievement. (National Commission on Libraries and Information Science, 1975)[7]

NCLIS issued a plan in 1975, *Toward a National Program for Library and Information Services: Goals for Action,* which declared a mandate to develop basic library services to meet the needs of all local communities. The *National Program* was widely distributed and formed a critical part of the policy framework for national public library planning for the last quarter of the twentieth century. NCLIS was responsible for organizing the first White House Conference on Library and Information Services (WHCLIS) in 1979.[8]

In that pre-Internet era, the level of face-to-face community and librarian engagement that took place all over America in nearly every state was nothing short of astounding. State conferences were held in 1977 and delegates included state and local officials, community and business leaders, educators, and library advocates. Each state conference developed its own resolutions and selected its own delegates to take those resolutions to Washington for the WHCLIS. It included a pre-conference on service to Native Americans.

> **▶ FACT**
>
> In preparation for the 1979 White House Conference on Libraries and Information Services, 3,000 resolutions were passed at 57 pre-conferences. Over 50 professional societies participated, as did community stakeholders (King Research, 1979).*
>
> *King Research (1979) includes a list of all the pre-conferences. Most lasted three days.

The resolutions that were passed at the WHCLIS called for change and a reshaping of library services to serve people usefully and conveniently. There was a call for more focus on literacy and serving ethnic groups. There was an emphasis on improving access to information for all, including blind persons, physically handicapped persons, and others not adequately served.[9] The WHCLIS helped bridge the gap between the interests of library professionals and those of grass-roots library users (Mathews, 2004).

NCLIS convened the second White House Conference on Library and Information Services in 1991, which had three themes: literacy, democracy, and productivity. The Executive Director of ALA's Washington Office, Carol C. Henderson, explained the importance of the 1991 Conference as a treasure lode:

> For the long term, the ALA Washington Office views the 95 recommendations from the 1991 White House Conference on Library and Information Services as a rich treasure lode to be mined throughout the 1990s. The recommendations are impressive citizen ammunition in support of policies, programs, and funding to foster improved library and information services. (Henderson, 1992)

The conference report *Information 2000* (NLCIS, 1991) laid the foundation for new library legislation introduced in 1996, the Library Services and Technology Act (LSTA). To some degree, NCLIS was a library think tank that provided opportunities for policy discussions, conferences, and programs on many aspects of librarianship. Before NCLIS was consolidated into the Institute of Museum and Library Services (IMLS) in 2008, John Berry wrote a cogent analysis in *Library Journal* noting the political component that pervaded the work that had been done (Berry, 2007).

The Public Library Mission Statement and its Imperatives for Service and the Public Library Development Program (PLDP)

Running parallel to federally supported discourse on the role of libraries in society fostered by NCLIS and the WHCLIS, the most powerful documentation of the ideas of change can be found in PLA's 1979 publication *The Public Library Mission Statement and Its Imperatives for Service.* In releasing the Mission Statement, PLA acknowledged that the future emphasis of public libraries would be on needs and services for people—not for institutions (Rohlf, p. 1982).

The *Public Library Mission Statement and Its Imperatives for Service* (PLA, 1979) listed these actions:

1. Provide access to the human record through collections and networking.
2. Organize the human record from a myriad of directions.
3. Collect, translate, and organize the human record on all intellectual levels in print and nonprint packages.
4. Dramatize the relevance of the human record with public information, guidance, and group activities.
5. Develop policies for preserving the record.
6. Take leadership in defining a new statement of ethics.
7. Coordinate acquisition policies.
8. Create a network for access to the record regardless of location.
9. Develop procedures for all to use the record.
10. Ensure that all will have access regardless of education, language, ethnic or cultural background, age, physical ability, or apathy.

The *Mission Statement* identified factors in U.S. society that called for a radical shift in the public library's emphasis: runaway social change, the exponential increase in the human record, total egalitarianism, and depletion of natural resources. It identified actions necessary for public libraries to be viable, seemingly anticipating the changes that the World Wide Web would bring to libraries.

After this major statement and much deliberation, PLA executive board decided to end the development of national standards to support local community-based planning in 1981. Manuals for local planning were published, which guided public libraries through the 1980s:

- *Planning Process for Public Libraries,* outlining methods for community analysis (Palmour, Bellassi, & DeWath, 1980)
- *Output Measures for Public Libraries,* describing data collection and the use of quantitative measures (Zweizig & Rodger, 1982)[10]

The next stage in the move toward adoption of the planning model was the introduction of the Public Library Development Program (PLDP) in 1986. The initial component was *Planning and Role Setting for Public Libraries: A Manual of Options and Procedures,* which identified eight potential roles for public libraries (McClure, 1987).[11] This phase lasted from the 1980s through 1996 and has been characterized as the Planning and Role Setting for Public Libraries Model (McCook, 2011, p. 87).

THIRTY YEARS OF THE LIBRARY SERVICES AND CONSTRUCTION ACT: 1966 TO 1996

At the time the NCLIS, PLA, and state library associations were planning for change, funding from the Library Services and Construction Act provided resources for local development under the aegis of each state's library agency. A 10-year evaluation of LSCA was funded by NCLIS in 1976. The effectiveness of the LSCA was measured by a state-by-state analysis of public library finance characteristics and an inventory of state public library aid programs. This included a review of the impact of revenue sharing on local and state public library support (Government Studies and Systems, 1976). The story of the impact of the LSCA over its 30 years must be pursued for each state because library development is responsive to state needs. This would require examination of state plans, reports, and state library journals. There was been little meta-analysis of the role of the states.[12]

Native Americans: Pathways to Excellence

In 1978 NCLIS sponsored the Indian White House Pre-Conference. A direct result was legislation—a rewritten Title IV of the Library Services and Construction Act (LSCA) targeted for tribal Indians (Patterson, 2000).[13] In 1992 *Pathways to Excellence: A Report on Improving Library and Information Services for Native American Peoples* was published by NCLIS. It provided a strategic long-range action plan developed to assist Native American leaders and tribal communities in the development and improvement of library and information services for all American Indians, Alaska Natives, and Native Hawaiians. The study found the full range of library and information needs of Native Americans were not being adequately met. They did not have effective access to specialized information resources that reflect the distinct cultural identities inherent in their heritage (*Pathways*, 1992).

> **▶ FACT**
>
> One-third of Americans, disproportionately low-income and members of minority groups, remain excluded and increasingly isolated from our digital society. "Public libraries are vital community technology hubs that millions of Americans rely on for their first and often only choice for internet access" (Shen, 2013).

Library Services for Poor People

The "Policy on Library Services to the Poor" was first passed by the ALA Social Responsibilities Round Table (SRRT) and then by ALA Council in 1990; it is in the ALA Policy Manual as B.8.10. The background to passage and difficulty in implementation has been summarized by Sanford Berman (1998). The Hunger, Homelessness, and Poverty Task Force of SRRT was formed in 1996.[14]

In 2000, *American Libraries* devoted a special issue to concerns about the "Policy on Library Services to the Poor." The Policy has kept inclusion and information equity high on the agenda of library policy makers, but these challenges require commitment and purposeful transformation (Holt & Holt, 2010; 2015).

> **▶ TASK**
>
> Go to the American FactFinder (census.gov). What are the demographics of your community? How many people are living in poverty?

TRANSFORMATION AND STRATEGIC PLANNING: 1996 TO 2015

In 1996 PLA appointed a ReVision Committee to update the PLDP process, which resulted in *Planning for Results: A Public Library Transformation Process* (Himmel & Wilson, 1998). The eight roles for public libraries that had been identified in 1986 were expanded to 13 "library service responses."[15] A streamlined approach to the planning process was published in 2001 as *The New Planning for Results* (Nelson) and a series of volumes, the Results series followed.[16]

In 2008 new planning guides with a more flexible strategic approach, *Strategic Planning for Results* and *Implementing for Results,* were published. They emphasized change and gave guidance for transforming strategic plans into reality. The service responses increased to 18 (Nelson, 2008, 2009).[17] This phase lasted from 1996 to 2015 and has been characterized as the New Planning for Results (NPFR) model.

THE NEW OUTCOME ERA: 2015 TO THE PRESENT

In 2015 the planning phase of PLA leadership concluded, and public libraries moved to an outcomes model. The Institute of Museums and Library Services requires Outcomes Based Evaluations (OBE) for grants.[18] Outcome Based Evaluation demonstrates good stewardship of IMLS resources. The process validates program expansion and support for new programs.

Project Outcome is a PLA initiative launched in 2015 to help public libraries understand and share the true impact of essential library services and programs. It will help librarians show the impact made by public libraries in their communities and to demonstrate the value of public librarians to residents and policy makers (Teasdale, 2015).

As public librarians developed various models to plan and position their agencies to enter the new millennium, the impact of digital technologies and networking changed the face of practice. In the next section of the history of public libraries, we review the milestones that moved libraries to the networked world.

Office for Information Technology Policy (OITP), Library Services and Technology Act (LSTA), E-Rate (Universal Service), the Gates Foundation, and Digital Inclusion

During the 1990s, as we have discussed above, public librarians created and implemented planning structures to accommodate local community needs just as world-changing technological disruptions emerged—namely, the Internet and the World-Wide Web. In 1991, about the same time that these new technologies exploded on the library scene, the second White House Conference on Library and Information Services convened. The conference had three themes: library and information services for literacy, democracy, and productivity. Task forces from ALA, the Urban Libraries Council, and Chief Officers of State Library Agencies identified two major goals: improvement of information access through technology and the educational empowerment of those who live outside the mainstream of quality library service (McCook, 1994).

Public librarians were digital risk takers and produced pilot programs such as free-nets, public information e-networks, and networked information resources with support from the National Telecommunications and Information Administration (McCook, 2004,

p. 179). These projects, as well as national discussions about the national information infrastructure, paved the way for broad understanding and acceptance of the shift from the brick-and-mortar age of the LSCA to the technological focus of the Library Services and Technology Act (LSTA). Milestones introduced since include establishment of the Office for Information Technology Policy of ALA, LSTA, Universal Service, and Bill and Melinda Gates Library funding.

Office for Information Technology Policy (OITP) of the American Library Association

The Office for Information Technology Policy (OITP) of ALA was founded in 1995. It has functioned as an advocacy organization working closely with librarians to implement legislation and support technological developments in concert with library programs. The mission of the office has had a profound effect on public library technology. Its mission is to:

> Advance ALA's public policy activities by helping secure information technology policies that support and encourage efforts of libraries to ensure access to electronic information resources as a means of upholding the public's right to a free and open information society. It works to ensure a library voice in information policy debates and to promote full and equitable intellectual participation by the public. (ALA, OITP)

A recent statement issued under the aegis of OITP, the *National Policy Agenda for Libraries* (2015) calls for strengthened national digital infrastructure sharing among libraries of all types, as well as other community and cultural institutions, to increases economic and operational efficiencies over stand-alone systems. It states that technological advances enable a broad range of data and information production and distribution opportunities (e.g., open access-based models) for libraries and their communities that extend beyond the confines of traditional models or silos.

Library Services and Technology Act (LSTA)

In 1996, the passage of the Library Services and Technology Act (LSTA) as Section B of the Museum and Library Services Act moved the administration of federal aid to public libraries from the Department of Education to a new agency, the Institute of Museum and Library Services (IMLS).[19] Congress's passage of H.R. 4278, an omnibus funding measure, mandated that the LSTA become the mechanism to provide federal funds to libraries. The American Library Association's (ALA) Washington Office played a leading role in the move from the Library Services and Construction Act (LSCA) to the Library Services and Technology Act. Besides the LSCA/LSTA transition, the new law called for an $8-million increase in federal library funding, from roughly $92 million in FY96 to more than $100 million in FY97. (Congress Passes Reconstituted Funding, 1996).

The LSTA built on the strengths of previous federal library programs, but sharpened the focus to two key priorities for libraries—information access through technology and information empowerment through special services. By locating federal support for libraries within the IMLS, since 1996 the government has emphasized the community-based role of libraries, and included lifelong learning as central to the mission of the public library

(Martin, 2001).[20] The shift from the Department of Education to IMLS has given libraries the opportunity to ally with museums and other cultural heritage organizations. The 2015 Every Students Succeeds Act (ESSA), successor to the Elementary and Secondary Education Act (ESEA), includes school libraries and literacy. As this funding becomes available, there will be more opportunity for creative public library school partnerships.[21]

The reauthorization of the Museum and Library Services Act in 2003, 2010, and 2015 updated the LSTA to promote improvements in all types of libraries; to facilitate access to, and sharing of, resources; and to achieve economical and efficient delivery of service for the purpose of cultivating an educated and informed citizenry. The LSTA links libraries electronically and helps provide users access to information through state, regional, national, and international networks (ALA, Office of Government Relations).

The major features of the LSTA are 1) to promote improvements in library services in all types of libraries in order to better serve the people of the United States; 2) to facilitate access to resources and in all types of libraries for the purpose of cultivating an educated and informed citizenry; and 3) to encourage resource sharing among all types of libraries for the purpose of achieving economical and efficient delivery of library services to the public (United States, Public Law 108-81, http://uscode.house.gov/statutes/pl/108/81.pdf).

Funding for LSTA was increased in FY17 to $183.6 million. Grants to states received an increase in FY17 to $156.1 million from $156 million in FY16. Native American grants ($4.1 million) and Laura Bush 21st Century Librarian ($10 million) received level funding. Overall funding for the Institute of Museum and Library Services was increased to $231 million ("LSTA Nets Small Increase," 2017).

E-Rate (Schools and Libraries Universal Support Mechanism)—1996

The Telecommunications Act of 1996 provided for discounted services to schools and libraries beginning in 1997. The E-Rate has played a pivotal role in helping libraries connect their users to the Internet. In 1996 only 28% of library systems offered public access to the Internet in at least one branch. Today, virtually all our nation's libraries offer Internet access, including Wi-Fi access, to the public. The E-Rate has helped change the public library's information technology landscape (ALA, E-Rate, n.d.).

However, this funding was linked to the Children's Internet Protection Act (CIPA) in 2000 (Menuey, 2009). Universal Service Fund recipients must block access to images that are harmful to minors with filtering software (Universal Service Administrative Company, 2016). For public libraries, this means filtering software must be installed if the library receives E-Rate discounts for Internet access costs, E-Rate discounts for internal connections costs, LSTA funding for direct Internet costs, or purchasing technology to access the Internet (Lawrence & Fry, 2016; Jaeger and McClure, 2004).

E-Rate modernization began in 2014 when the FCC adopted the Second E-Rate Modernization Order to maximize options for schools and libraries seeking to purchase high-speed broadband (Federal Communications Commission, 2016).

Bill and Melinda Gates Foundation

The Bill and Melinda Gates Foundation was the catalyst to wire the nation's communities through public libraries beginning in 1997.

The program focused on libraries that serve populations where 10% earn below the federal poverty line; it reached into nearly every low-income area and isolated public library in America. Louisiana was one of the first states to receive Gates funding. At least one workstation was placed in every public library in the state—over 1000 in all. Along with the computer hardware and software the Gates provided training for the librarians in one- or two-day sessions (Gillane, 1999). This provided the necessary infrastructure to public librarians in Louisiana that made possible the State Library's funding of broadband Internet access for every public library in the state.[22]

Writing of the Gates legacy, Miller (2014) observed:

> This initiative dovetailed with the intensification of the digital revolution, and it anticipated the potential for libraries to be in the forefront. It gave libraries momentum and capacity at a critical moment and worked to speed the identification of libraries as tech hubs—just as the digital divide began to yawn. In short, mission met mission. No doubt the Gates Library Foundation program was only one source of technology and training that got us to the next level, but libraries have not been the same since.

> ▶ **FACT**
>
> The Gates Program was the largest gift to U.S. public libraries since Carnegie. The program brought computers into the majority of public libraries in all 50 states—40,000 computers in about 10,000 eligible facilities plus funds for training. (Gordon, Gordon, Moore, & Heuertz, 2003).

Digital Literacy, Broadband Adoption, and Digital Inclusion

In 2014 the Chief Officers of State Libraries Agencies (COSLA) issued a guide to national projects associated with digital inclusion, digital literacy, and broadband adoption. This guide provides a broad overview of the concerns of public libraries in the new millennium. The brief summaries of key initiatives that follow lead to detailed reports and evaluations that describe digital initiatives in public libraries.

1. *DigitalLearn.org site.* This is PLA's online hub for digital literacy support and resources for libraries and other community organizations. The site includes self-directed tutorials for end-users as well as resources and a community of practice for digital literacy support providers and trainers.
2. *Digital Inclusion Survey.* Equitable access to and participation in the online environment are essential for success in education, employment, finance, health and wellness, civic engagement, and a democratic society. The Digital Inclusion Survey addresses the efforts of public libraries to address disparities and provide opportunity to individuals and communities by providing free access to broadband, public access technologies, digital content, digital literacy learning opportunities, and a range of programming that helps build digitally inclusive communities (http://digitalinclusion.umd.edu/).
3. *The Edge Initiative,* led by the Urban Libraries Council, is a nationally recognized leadership and management tool designed for public libraries.

It provides powerful new strategies and resources that help libraries strengthen their public access technology services and provide greater value to their communities (www.libraryedge.org/).

4. *The Impact Survey* is an online tool that makes the "Opportunity for All" survey instrument available to all public libraries to use for data collection with their online and public access technology users This service will fuel enhanced evaluation and advocacy efforts in public libraries by allowing them an easy to way to find out how their patrons are using library technology and the impact of that use on patrons and the community (https://impactsurvey.org/).
5. *Pew Research Center Internet Project.* The Pew Research Center conducted research to understand the role of libraries in the lives of the patrons and communities. This includes studies of Americans' technology use, reading, use of libraries and library websites and measures of public attitudes about libraries and library services (http://libraries.pewinternet.org/).
6. *U.S. Unified Community Anchor Network (U.S. UCAN*). The United States Unified Community Anchor Network (U.S. UCAN) is an Internet2 program working with regional research and education networks across the country to connect community anchor institutions, including schools, libraries, health care facilities and other public institutions, to advanced broadband capabilities (www.internet2.edu/vision-initiatives/initiatives/us-ucan/).
7. *Connected Learning (ConnectedLib).* An IMLS-funded professional development program to "help librarians incorporate digital media into their work with youth to promote connections across learning contexts" (http://connectedlib.ischool.uw.edu/connected-learning-in-libraries).

Five-Year Plans Submitted to IMLS by the States

The overarching vantage point from which to assess the current status of public libraries in America, is the five-year plans submitted to IMLS by individual states.[23] These provide powerful, clear statements of planning and projects. Some examples that stand out are:

- The Michigan Reads! Statewide early literacy program helps provide quality program kit to approximately 600,000 students and young children.
- South Dakota's citizens and libraries will be supported with appropriate online databases to meet educational and research needs as well as those that improve quality of life.
- Seamless, stable access to North Carolina's special and unique library collections will be available through the Digital North Carolina Digital Heritage Center.
- New Mexican print-disabled patrons will have access to reading for information, education, and recreation using digital technology.

Statistics show the status of American libraries today, but the planning documents are a testament to public librarians' commitment to people of all ages, background, and abilities.[24]

THE PUBLIC LIBRARY IN THE TWENTY-FIRST CENTURY: CORE VALUES AND TRENDS

Established in the mid-1850s, U.S. public libraries are now in the third century of service and can look back on a history based on commitment to democratic ideals, lifelong learning, and facilitation of access to the world's cultural heritage and knowledge.

The Core Values of Librarianship, as defined by ALA, are Access; Confidentiality/Privacy; Democracy; Diversity; Education and Lifelong Learning; Intellectual Freedom; Preservation; the Public Good; Professionalism; Service and Social Responsibility (ALA, Core Values). Each of these has an impact on the public library mission. These core values are central to the future of public libraries.

Access and Advocacy

Local, state, and federal funding have all contributed to the expansion of access to library services, but because libraries are ultimately funded locally, there are still gaps in service and equity. Library advocates identify gaps in services and methods for resolving those gaps. State-level legislative action committees and ALA's Office for Library Advocacy support resource development and peer-to-peer library advocacy at all levels. We saw how astute leaders connected library issues to federal programs during the New Deal to gain a place for libraries in postwar planning efforts. The library community has continued to hold this position at the federal level by communicating with legislators about the importance of funding, which led to a series of acts and legislation. Today's library leaders use a variety of methods, including social networking tools, to deliver their message about the importance of libraries.

Education and Lifelong Learning

Support for public libraries in the United States initially came from a desire to maintain social order and promote education for adults. But perhaps more importantly, lifelong learning and education was foundational to maintaining principles of a democratic government; an educated society is better able to make good decisions about its government.

The core values of Education and Lifelong Learning are supported through current IMLS funding:

> Through the collections, services, and spaces they provide, libraries offer us a lifelong opportunity to gain the knowledge, skills and experiences that will enrich our lives. With the increased availability of online resources, libraries are now positioned to re-imagine services and spaces, to increase their reach to and impact on the communities they serve. (IMLS Focus, 2015)

Public Librarians as Defenders of Intellectual Freedom

Intellectual freedom means freedom to read. The Office for Intellectual Freedom and the Freedom to Read Foundation emphasize libraries' role in promoting people's ability to "engage in free inquiry, to consider different ideas and perspectives, and to research more and better information" as prerequisites of a healthy democracy (Freedom to Read Foundation, 2016). Every year during Banned Books Week libraries celebrate freedom to read and provide education to the public by holding readouts of censored materials, such as *Bury My Heart at Wounded Knee* (Dee Brown) or *Their Eyes Were Watching God* (Zora Neale Hurston) (www.bannedbooksweek.org/). Librarians have not always celebrated freedom to read, though. Recall that, initially, the public library was seen as a tool for social stability. Many librarians interpreted this duty as being bound with censorship—they were to stock the shelves with books that were morally uplifting. Board oversight, too, encouraged "safety" in selection. Although we might be tempted to dismiss threats to intellectual freedom as coming from small-minded individuals in the community, in actuality threats come from within the profession, from boards of trustees, and even from the government.

Geller (1984), in *Forbidden Books in American Public Libraries, 1876 to 1939,* characterizes 1923 to 1930 as the period when a critical shift by public librarians moved toward a more expansive philosophy of collection development. In 1931 George F. Bowerman, director of the Washington, DC, Public Library, addressed the issue of censorship and reminded librarians that classics like Eliot's *Adam Bede,* Hardy's *Jude the Obscure,* and Whitman's *Leaves of Grass* were once deemed worthy of condemnation. He characterized censorship as repugnant to public librarians and noted that the public library is "not an institution for the inculcation of standardized ideas. . . . It stands for free opinion and to that end it supplies material on both or all sides of every controversial question of human interest" (pp. 5-6).

The man who would later be named poet laureate of the United States, Stanley J. Kunitz, also editor of the *Wilson Bulletin for Libraries* from 1928 to 1943, provided unyielding defense of the freedom to read. In his ongoing column, "The Roving Eye," Kunitz was critical of librarians who did nothing to oppose censorship. Although he cherished democracy, Kunitz (1939) opposed intolerance, intellectual provincialism, and protection of the status quo. His editorials are a legacy to the community of public librarians striving to define intellectual freedom as a professional ethic.

In 1936 the Chicago Public Library issued the first formal intellectual freedom policy to be published by a library in the United States in response to challenges from the local Polish and Russian communities that the collection include works by Marx and Lenin. Latham (2007) explained: "The Public Library asserts its right and duty to keep on its shelves a representative selection of books on all subjects of interest to its readers and not prohibited by law, including books on all sides of controversial questions" (p. 15). Forrest Spaulding, director of the Des Moines (IA) Public Library, developed the Library Bill of Rights in 1938. He was inspired by Bernard Berelson's 1938 essay "The Myth of Library Impartiality," which exposed the inadequacy of instructions to collect books "on both sides of the issue." Spaulding's Bill of Rights was adapted and was approved for the profession by ALA at the 1939 San Francisco conference. *The Grapes of Wrath,* by John Steinbeck, was published in March 1939 and immediately banned at some libraries because of its social criticism (Lingo, 2003). After passage of the Library Bill of Rights, the ALA Adult Education Board distributed copies to libraries to help fight against requests to censor. Because of the rash of book banning across the nation, ALA appointed a committee to study censorship and recommend policy. In 1940 that committee reported that intellectual freedom and professionalism were linked and recommended a permanent committee, which was established as the Committee on Intellectual Freedom to Safeguard the Right of Library Users to Freedom of Inquiry (changed in 1947 to the Committee on Intellectual Freedom).

Censorship of fiction generally focuses on propriety, whereas national interests during wartime present a different reason for censorship. As mentioned above, the Chicago Public

Library fought to include controversial political works in their collection. However, many librarians were actively involved in book banning at the end of World War I. Wayne Wiegand (1989) explained that "librarians willingly but quietly pulled from their shelves any title that might raise suspicions of disloyalty. Some librarians burned these titles, many of which were classic works of German philosophy, books advocating American pacifism, and simple German language texts" (p. 6). In his study of propaganda and the public library from the 1930s to World War II, Lincove (1994) describes discussions in the field that addressed fascist propaganda as a threat to democracy and capitalism. The core of debate was whether the library should censor based on moralism and control versus a philosophy that would provide access to mainstream and controversial ideas, especially foreign and domestic political propaganda.

Following World War II, the loyalty programs implemented by President Truman, the establishment of the House Un-American Activities Committee, and the general Cold War atmosphere presented new threats to intellectual freedom. Librarians responded with a renewed commitment to fight censorship. A revised Library Bill of Rights issued in 1948 included a far stronger statement of the librarian's responsibility to defend freedom of inquiry (Berninghausen, 1948). State intellectual freedom committees were formed, the "Statement on Labeling" was adopted (1951), and a national conference was held in 1952. Events that brought about the Freedom to Read Statement (1953) included the overseas library controversy (Robbins, 2001) and attacks on the International Information Administration's libraries, all of which were instrumental in the identification of librarians as defenders of intellectual freedom (Robbins, 2001).

The passage of the USA PATRIOT Act (an acronym for the Uniting and Strengthening America by Providing Appropriate Tools Required to Intercept and Obstruct Terrorism) after the 2001 terror attacks put librarians across the country on high alert. Four courageous librarians—the Connecticut Four—resisted censorship and privacy violations. In 2005, Library Connection, a nonprofit consortium of 27 libraries in Connecticut, received a National Security Letter (NSL) from the FBI that demanded library patrons' records accompanied by perpetual gag order. George Christian, executive director of Library Connection, and three members of the executive committee of the board engaged the American Civil Liberties Union (ACLU) to file suit to challenge the constitutional validity of the NSL. Because Section 505 of the USA PATRIOT Act, which authorizes the FBI to demand records without prior court approval, also forbids, or gags, anyone who receives an NSL from telling others about it, they also challenged the validity of the gag order.

For almost a year, the ACLU fought to lift the gag order, challenging the government's power under Section 505 to silence four citizens who wished to contribute to public debate on the PATRIOT Act. In May 2006, the government finally gave up its legal battle to maintain the gag order. On June 26, 2006, the ACLU announced that, after dropping its defense of the gag provision accompanying the NSL request, the FBI abandoned the lawsuit entirely. The Connecticut Four were honored by ALA with the 2007 Paul Howard Award for Courage for their challenge to the National Security Letter and gag order provision of the USA PATRIOT Act. The Connecticut Four are:

1. George Christian, executive director of Library Connection
2. Peter Chase, vice president of Library Connection, director of the Plainville (CT) Public Library, and chairman of the Connecticut Library Association's Intellectual Freedom Committee
3. Barbara Bailey, president of Library Connection and director of the Welles-Turner Memorial Library in Glastonbury, Connecticut

4. Jan Nocek, secretary of Library Connection and director of the Portland (CT) Library

In a summary of the actions of the Connecticut Four and their challenge to the USA PATRIOT Act, Barbara M. Jones (2009, p. 223) noted that "librarians need to understand their country's legal balance between the protection of freedom of expression and the protection of national security. Many librarians believe that the interests of national security, important as they are, have become an excuse for chilling the freedom to read." Recognizing that in less than a century librarians have progressed from participating in censorship to fighting it in the Supreme Court, we see that a change in philosophy regarding intellectual freedom between the end of World War I and the years following World War II marked the growth of U.S. public librarianship as a profession (Robbins, 1996).

In 2016 Steven Woolfolk, the director of public programming and marketing at the Kansas City Public Library, was arrested during a library event for defending a patron's First Amendment rights (Eberhart, 2016). Honored with the BORDC/DDF Patriot Award for his defense of free speech, Woolfolk observed, "We're going to be living in a different kind of country . . . if people can be arrested for asking questions at a library." This story emphasizes the current centrality of the Library Bill of Rights to librarians' daily practice (Oltmann, 2016). Woolfolk has also been honored with the 2017 Paul Howard Award for Courage and the 2017 Lemony Snicket Prize for Noble Librarians Faced with Adversity.

Since the adoption of the Freedom to Read statement in 1953, library workers have faced and coped with many challenges. New interpretations of the Library Bill of Rights have been issued, including "Access to Electronic Information Services and Networks" (1996), "Access to Library Resources and Services Regardless of Gender or Sexual Orientation" (2000), and "Importance of Education to Intellectual Freedom" (2009). The ninth edition of the *Intellectual Freedom Manual* includes expanded interpretations of the Library Bill of Rights, including 34 ALA policy statements and documents addressing patron behavior, Internet use, copyright, exhibits, use of meeting spaces, and other common concerns (Magi, Garnar, & ALA, 2015). These and other amplifications of the basic tenets of intellectual freedom define the "active advocacy" that librarians accept when they join the profession (Conable, 2002, p. 43).

Sense of Place and the Public Library as Public Sphere

A sense of place is the sum total of all perceptions—aesthetic, emotional, historical, supernal—that a physical location and its associated activities and the emotional responses it invokes in people. The public library provides a sense of place that transcends new development, big-box stores, and malls to help a community retain its distinct character. The growing emphasis on sustainable and livable communities encourages the creation of public spaces that are true community places. The editors of *The Library as Place: History, Community, and Culture* (Buschman & Leckie, 2007) explored this idea and extended the concept to address the impact of technology. The importance of the public library as a commons is part of the larger metaphor of the public sphere in democratic societies developed in the work of philosopher Jürgen Habermas, who has described the significance of people connecting ideas through broad discussion.

Public libraries that recognize the importance of sustaining the public sphere will respond to their community members' desire for a place to address critical issues in their lives. However, real threats to the availability of information for public discourse do exist. In *Dismantling the Public Sphere,* Buschman (2003) provides a critique of librarianship in light of increasing commercialization of information and the broad reach of authoritarian populism. Taken together, the provision of a commons, materials in all formats to support exploration of important issues, and opportunities for communities to come together are important public library contributions to a rich public sphere. If discourse becomes more democratic through consensus building, it is partly because authentic discourse enables people to move from personal opinions to informed ideas. The complexity of the public sphere and the public library's role as commons has recently been explored by Widdersheim & Koizumi (2016), who view the library as a public sphere institution acting as a platform to support discourse.

The Topeka and Shawnee County (KS) Public Library (TSCPL) was named the 2016 Gale/Library Journal Public Library of the Year, in part because of its engagement in every discussion in its community. For the area's Community Conversation on Poverty in 2014 and 2015, TSCPL provided facilitators to lead sessions and assess how the library could take a role in action to improve the situation. In 2016, the library was asked to provide facilitators for the conversations, which demonstrated the community's commitment to the library (Berry, 2016).

Bossaller commenting on public library facilitation of community engagement before the 2016 presidential election has noted, "Librarians can and should capitalize on the truth that can be fostered through dialogue, combating apathy and indifference and nourishing civic education" (2017, p.207).

Convergence of Cultural Heritage Institutions

Libraries are stewards of cultural heritage, information, and ideas, but so are archives, museums, and historical societies. The IMLS was created to bring these together under a single funding mechanism. Marcum (2014) noted, "However one reads the past, today's information technologies open opportunities never equaled before to make the world's cultural heritage accessible, usable, and valuable." This convergence of cultural heritage institutions is not only a manifestation of technological possibilities, but also the result of a new way of looking at learning and cultural participation across the lifespan. Within public libraries, we have seen projects such; participation in the network of hubs that make up the Digital Public Library of America (Cohen, 2016), and training and engagement with Wikipedia to reinforce the library's role "as stewards of quality information, standard bearers for information literacy and curators of authoritative collections" ("Wikipedia + Libraries: Better Together," 2016).

A recent example of public libraries preserving cultural heritage is Culture in Transit, a joint project of the Brooklyn Public Library, Queens Library, and the Metropolitan New York Library Council. It delivers digitization equipment and expertise to smaller libraries and community organizations throughout the city in an effort to help neighborhoods define and catalog their histories. In addition to digitizing institutional archives, Culture in Transit helps people in New York preserve their own historical memorabilia, which they may then share with local collections and submit to the Digital Public Library of America. The Knight News Challenge on Libraries funds library projects that preserve cultural heritage; build more knowledgeable communities; and encourage innovation, creativity, entrepreneurship, and education.

Commitment to Human Rights and Social Justice

Public libraries have sought to extend library services to all community residents for many years. Equity of access is a simple concept, but complex in implementation. There are over 39 million people (12.6% of the population) in the United States with some sort of disability; over 14 million (21.5% of the population) five years and older speak a language other than English in the home; and over 21 million (14.7% of the population) live below the poverty level (U.S. Census Bureau, 2015). Each of these groups presents a set of special service requirements if the public library is to provide equity of access. National policy statements such as "Library Services for People with Disabilities Policy" and "Library Services for the Poor" show the official view of librarians and ALA. Associations such as the National Association to Promote Library and Information Services to Latinos and the Spanish Speaking (REFORMA) focus on the special reading and information needs of people from diverse cultures. It becomes a task for librarians in different communities to identify the demographic composition of the population and develop responsive services.

Social justice is activated when librarians work to provide all community members with inclusive services regardless of age, ethnicity, language, physical or mental challenges, or economic class (Mathuews, 2016). Whether ensuring that there is online access in rural public libraries or bringing bookmobiles to urban centers, public librarians contribute to human development and enrichment. The respect that librarians give to all members of their communities is a rare yet precious mode of daily work. Commitment to human rights includes sensitivity to racial issues such as Libraries4BlackLives (Peet, 2016); homelessness (Bardoff, 2015); or immigration status (REFORMA, Toolkit). Access to information and library services has been posited as a human right by Mathiesen (2013). The "virtuous circle"—intersecting issues of diversity, inclusion, rights, justice, and equity—is viewed by Jaeger et al. (2015) as a complementary set of actions that will move the field toward a human rights commitment.

Two recent volumes are important to the ethical aspects of public library commitment to these principles. *Libraries, Human Rights, and Social Justice: Enabling Access and Promoting Inclusion* examines issue in terms of efforts to support equity in communities as a whole and efforts intended to promote equity in specific disadvantaged or marginalized populations, such as the homeless, immigrants, people with disabilities, and the socioeconomically disadvantaged (Jaeger, Taylor, & Gorham 2015). *Human Rights and Social Justice* outlines human rights and social justice issues as a powerful conceptual framework for policy and practice, urging the creation of a human rights culture as a "lived awareness" of human rights principles, including human dignity, nondiscrimination, civil and political rights, economic, social, and cultural rights, and solidarity rights (Wronka, 2017).

National groups such as the ALA Social Responsibilities Round Table, the Progressive Librarians Guild, and ethnic associations such as the American Indian Library Association, Asian Pacific Librarians Association, Black Caucus, Chinese American Library Association, and REFORMA have been organized to frame and address issues of human rights and social justice as a key factor in developing service models.

Public librarians committed to the continuation of this most democratic of all institutions face the future with the charge of maintaining a sense of place, sustaining an open and active public sphere, and working with other cultural institutions while promoting social justice and human rights. The public library is endowed with a history of grassroots support for its development, the ongoing commitment of friends and users, and staffs comprised of thoughtful and engaged individuals who tend to its future. Public librarians work passionately to establish the public library as an essential community agency and to defend the ideals of free inquiry.

CONCLUSION

As we have seen, it took over a century from the founding of tax-supported public libraries for the institution to become open to all people. In spite of the soaring rhetoric we saw in documents like the *Report of the Trustees of the Boston Public Library* (1852), the public library did not embrace its role as open to all until after passage of Civil Rights Legislation in 1964.

Technologies have been a major priority in funding for libraries. The LSCA recognized borrowing and lending between libraries facilitated by technologies. The LSTA enhanced technology infrastructure in libraries. The formation of the IMLS formalized the convergence of museums, libraries, and cultural heritage institutions that technologies have facilitated.

The IMLS and other funding agencies want proof that their investments are being spent well. Thus, the methods for determining the library's effectiveness have evolved. The PLA's former national standards for measuring library effectiveness evolved into the Planning for Results model, and to today's Project Outcome initiative. These strategies have encouraged local libraries to identify their own priorities based on the needs of their communities. This flexibility allows librarians to be responsive, which ensures that the library is an institution that remains the heart of the community, and is rooted firmly as a community anchor.

NOTES

1. Most states published a printed journal prior to the Internet. These were wonderful projects that involved and engaged librarians in each state where volunteer librarian editors and reporters would focus on issues large and small and strive to integrate policy and publishing and technological developments to reflect state goals and traditions. These included *Alabama Librarian, Bay State Librarian, California Librarian, Florida Libraries, Georgia Librarian, Idaho Librarian, Illinois Libraries, Kansas Library Bulletin, Kentucky Libraries, Louisiana Library Association Bulletin, Maine Library Bulletin, Maryland Libraries, Michigan Librarian, Nebraska Library Association Quarterly, New York Libraries, Oklahoma Libraries, North Carolina Libraries, Wisconsin Library Bulletin, Wyoming Library Roundup*. Reviewing the contents of these journals provides insight into public library development on the ground.
2. In "A Quiet Case of Social Change," Howard Zinn (1997), then teaching at Spelman College, summarized these events. See also Blackburn-Beamon (1982/83); Wiegand, (2017).
3. In *White Trash* (Isenberg, 2016) describes the persistent class structure in the United States. Reaching out to the rural and urban white working class is also a challenge. See McCook 2017.
4. This turbulent time is remembered through the annual award of PLA's Allie Beth Martin Award (www.ala.org/pla/awards/alliebethmartinaward).
5. The 1970s were a time of passionate discussion among members of PLA. The dialogue arose from the decision to discontinue standards in favor of community planning (PLA, Goals, Guidelines, and Standards Committee, 1973). The PLA Design for Diversity focused on planning for the future rather than reporting on the past, managing rather than comparing, and addressing a new concern for output (Blasingame and Lynch, 1974). For an analysis see Pungitore (1995).
6. This report has been compared to the 1876 U.S. Bureau of Education's Special Report on the conduct of the nation's libraries (interview with D. M. Knight, 1967).

7. Molz has characterized the NCLIS National Program as the lineal descendant of the National Plan of 1934 (1984, p. 120).
8. White House Conferences are a mechanism to bring together experts and advocates to develop policy recommendations on an important topic. White House Conferences have been held on topics as diverse as aging, productivity, and travel and tourism. The first proposal for a White House Conference on Library and Information Services (WHCLIS) was in 1957. It took more than 20 years of advocacy to obtain the authorization for the first White House Conference on Library and Information Services, which took place on November 15-19, 1979 (Davenport & Russell, 2008, p. 34).
9. Those interested in the intellectual and philosophical commitment of librarians at this time will find the complete list of resolutions of interest. See U.S. NCLIS. White House Conference on Library and Information Services (1980). Summary: The final report.
10. A series of programs and workshops sponsored by PLA took place in the early 1980s to disseminate the process. The change in the method of developing goals and plans for libraries had moved from national standards to local planning (PLA, Public Library Principles Task Force, 1982).
11. These are 1) community activities center; 2) community information center; 3) formal education support center; 4) independent learning center; 5) popular materials library; 6) preschoolers' door to learning; 7). reference library; 8) research center (McClure, 1987).
12. ERIC reports are the best public record of LSCA by state. See, for example, North Dakota State Library Commission, (1970); North Dakota State Plan for Library Programs under the Library Services and Construction Act; and Ohio State Library (1975); The Ohio Long Range Program for Improvement of Library Services as Assisted by the Federal Library Services and Construction Act; Oklahoma State Department of Libraries (1978); Oklahoma Long-Range Program for Library Development, 1979-1984; Michigan State Department of Education, L. S. (1982); Long-Range Program; The State Plan for Michigan State Library Services, 1982-1987; Michigan Library. (1997); Library Services & Construction Act. LSCA Report for 1996; Information Partners for the 21st Century; Jaques, T. F., & Louisiana State Library, B. R. (1998); and Improving Information Access through Technology: A Plan for Louisiana's Public Libraries. These are just a few examples of state reports available at ERIC. http://eric.ed.gov/.
13. National Commission on Libraries and Information Science (1981); Task Force on Library and Information Services to Cultural Minorities: Hearings. Washington, DC: USGPO. ERIC Document Reproduction Service No. ED 241 015. Lotsee Patterson's 2000 article, "History and Status of Native Americans in Librarianship," provides a chronology of the foundation of funding for tribal libraries including the role of NCLIS.
14. In 1996, members of the Social Responsibilities Round Table (SRRT) formed the Hunger, Homelessness and Poverty Task Force to Promote and Implement the Policy on Library Services to the Poor (www.hhptf.org/archive).
15. These are 1) basic literacy; 2) business and career information; 3) commons; 4) community referral; 5) consumer information; 6) cultural awareness; 7) current topics and titles; 8) formal learning support; 9) general information; 10) government information; 11) information literacy; 12) lifelong learning; 13) local history and genealogy (Himmel & Wilson, 1998). Training and workshops were held at state conferences and sponsored by state library agencies to assist in adoption of procedures. A companion volume, *Managing for Results,* was issued in 2000 to help turn plans into reality (Nelson, Altman, and Mayo, 2000).
16. The Public Library Association Results series (Chicago, IL, American Library Association) comprises:
    - E. Himmel & W. J. Wilson, *Planning for Results: A Public Library Transformation Process* (1998)

- D. Mayo & S. Nelson, *Wired for the Future: Developing Your Library Technology Plan* (1999)
- S. Nelson, E. Altman, & D. Mayo, *Managing for Results: Effective Resource Allocation for Public Libraries* (2000)
- S. Nelson, *The New Planning for Results: A Streamlined Approach* (2001)
- D. Mayo & J. Goodrich, *Staffing for Results: A Guide to Working Smarter* (2002)
- S. Nelson & J. Garcia, *Creating Policies for Results: From Chaos to Clarity* (2003)
- R. J. Rubin, *Demonstrating Results: Using Outcome Measurement in Your Library* (2005)
- D. Mayo, *Technology for Results: Developing Service-Based Plans* (2005)
- C. Bryan, *Managing Facilities for Results: Optimizing Space for Services* (2007)
- S. Nelson, *Strategic Planning for Results* (2008)
- S. Nelson, *Implementing for Results: Your Strategic Plan in Action* (2009)

17. These are:
    1. Be an informed citizen: local, national, and world affairs
    2. Build successful enterprises: business and nonprofit support
    3. Celebrate diversity: cultural awareness
    4. Connect to the online world: public Internet access
    5. Create young readers: early literacy
    6. Discover your roots: genealogy and local history
    7. Express creativity: create and share content
    8. Get facts fast: ready reference
    9. Know your community: community resources and services
    10. Learn to read and write: adults, teens, and family literature
    11. Make career choices: job and career development
    12. Make informed decisions: health, wealth, and other life choices
    13. Satisfy curiosity: lifelong learning
    14. Stimulate imagination: reading, viewing, and listening for pleasure
    15. Succeed in school: homework help
    16. Understand how to find, evaluate, and use information: information fluency
    17. Visit a comfortable place: physical and virtual spaces
    18. Welcome to the United States: services for new immigrants (Nelson, 2008)
18. See the IMLS website for the model of outcomes-based planning and evaluation (https://www.imls.gov/grants/outcome-based-evaluation/basics).
19. The Museum and Library Services Act of 1996 (https://www.imls.gov/sites/default/files/1996.pdf) established the Institute of Museum and Library Services. The new agency combined the Institute of Museum Services, which had been in existence since 1976, and the Library Programs Office, which had been part of the Department of Education since 1956. See the IMLS Timeline (https://www.imls.gov/about-us/legislation-budget/timeline).
20. In 2008 NCLIS was incorporated into the IMLS. Its final report, *Meeting the Information Needs of the American People: Past Actions and Future Initiatives,* provides a history of NCLIS since its establishment in 1970 (Davenport and Russell, 2008). John Berry (2007) has provided insight into the politics of NCLIS. Achievement of a national voice for public libraries resulted from ongoing collaboration among librarians organized in national and state library associations.
21. The Every Student Succeeds Act (ESSA) was signed by President Obama on December 10, 2015. It reauthorized the 50-year-old Elementary and Secondary Education Act (ESEA), the nation's national education law and longstanding commitment to equal opportunity for all students (www.ed.gov/essa). The impact on school libraries is discussed by Peet (2016).
22. Interview with Sara M. Taffae, retired computing consultant, State Library of Louisiana, 2016. Sara coordinated the team that implemented the Gates grants in Louisiana through the state library.

Her work throughout Louisiana to create the public library computing infrastructure from the 1980s through 2010 is emblematic of public librarians throughout America who quietly changed the field through their willingness to take risks and implement numerous changing technologies.

23. See IMLS "State Profiles" (https://www.imls.gov/grants/grants-state/state-profiles) and COSLA "Member Profiles" (www.cosla.org/profiles/).
24. The Grants to States program is the largest source of federal funding support for library services in the U.S. Using a population based formula, more than $150 million is distributed among the State Library Administrative Agencies (SLAAs) every year. The Library Services and Technology Act requires each SLAA to submit a plan that details library services goals for a five-year period. SLAAs must also conduct a five-year evaluation of library services based on that plan. These plans and evaluations are the foundation for improving practice and informing policy (https://www.imls.gov/grants/grants-states).

REFERENCES

American Library Association. (2004). Core values of librarianship. www.ala.org/advocacy/intfreedom/statementspols/corevalues.

American Library Association. (2016). E-Rate and Universal Service. www.ala.org/advocacy/telecom/erate.

American Library Association. (2017). Record-setting Senate support needed to save federal library funding! www.ala.org/advocacy/advleg/federallegislation/fight-for-libraries.

American Library Association, Office for Information Technology Policy. OITP General Information. www.ala.org/advocacy/pp/info.

American Library Association, Office for Information Technology Policy. (2015). *National policy agenda for libraries*. www.ala.org/advocacy/sites/ala.org.advocacy/files/content/pdfs/NPAforLibraries1.pdf.

American Library Association, Office of Governmental Relations. (n.d.). www.ala.org/offices/wo.

Banned Books Week (n.d.). www.bannedbooksweek.org.

Bardoff, C. (2015). Homelessness and the ethics of information access. *Serials Librarian 69*, 3-4, 2015.

Berelson, B. (1938). The myth of library impartiality. *Wilson Library Bulletin, 13,* 87-90.

Berman, S. (1998). "Foreword." In K. M. Venturella (Ed.), *Poor people and library services*. Jefferson, NC: McFarland.

Berninghausen, D. K. (1948, July/August). Library Bill of Rights. *ALA Bulletin, 42*, 285.

Berry, J. N. (2007, March). The politics of NCLIS. *Library Journal, 132,* 10.

Berry, J. N. (2016, June 7). 2016 Gale/LJ Library of the Year: Topeka & Shawnee County Public Library, KS, leveraging leadership. *Library Journal*. http://lj.libraryjournal.com/2016/06/awards/2016-galelj-library-of-the-year-topeka-shawnee-county-public-library-ks-leveraging-leadership/.

Blackburn-Beamon, J. (1982/83). The library card. *Spelman Messenger,* p. 41.

Blasingame, R., Jr., & Lynch, M. J. (1974). Design for diversity: Alternatives to standards for public libraries. *PLA Newsletter, 13,* 4-22.

Bossaller, J.A. (2017). Alternatives to apathy and indifference: Civic education in public libraries. *Library Quarterly, 87*(3), 195–210.

Boston Public Library. (1852). *Report of the Trustees of the Public Library to the City of Boston.*

Bowerman, G. F. (1931). *Censorship and the Public Library: With Other Papers*. Freeport, NY: Books for Libraries Press.

Brown v. Louisiana. 1966. 383 U.S. 131 (1966).

Bryan, C. (2007). *Managing facilities for results: Optimizing space for services*. Chicago, IL: ALA Editions.

Buschman, J. (2003). *Dismantling the public sphere: Situating and sustaining librarianship in the age of the new public philosophy*. Westport, CT: Libraries Unlimited.

Buschman, J., & Leckie, G. J. (Eds.). (2007). *The library as place: History, community, and culture.* Westport, CT: Libraries Unlimited.

Carmichael, J. V., Jr. (1998). *Daring to find our names: The search for lesbigay library history.* Westport, CT: Greenwood Press.

Carter, J. (1979). White House conference on libraries and information services remarks at a meeting of the Conference, November 16, 1979. *The American Presidency Project.* www.presidency.ucsb.edu/ws/?pid=31696.

Chief Officers of State Library Agencies. (2014). Reference guide to national projects: Digital literacy, broadband adoption, and digital inclusion. www.cosla.org/documents/NationalProjectGuide1.pdf.

Cohen, D. (2016). The Digital Public Library of America (DPLA), Part 2: A conversation with Dan Cohen. *Preservation, Digital Technology and Culture, 45*(3), 145–146.

Conable, G. (2002). Public libraries and intellectual freedom. In *Intellectual freedom manual* (6th ed.). Chicago, IL: American Library Association.

Congress passes reconstituted federal library funding bill. (1996). *Library Journal,* 12113–12114.

Davenport, N., & Russell, J. (2008). *Meeting the information needs of the American people: Past actions and future initiatives.* Washington, DC: National Commission on Libraries and Information Science. ERIC 500878.

Eberhart, G. (2016, October 3) Kansas City Public Library embroiled in free-speech case. *American Libraries.* https://americanlibrariesmagazine.org/blogs/the-scoop/kansas-city-public-library-embroiled-in-free-speech-case/.

Estes, R. (1960, December 15). Segregated libraries. *Library Journal,* 4418–4421.

Federal Communications Commission. (2016). Universal Service program for schools and libraries. https://www.fcc.gov/general/universal-service-program-schools-and-libraries-e-rate.

Freedom to Read Foundation (2016). Issues. www.ftrf.org/?page=Issues.

Fry, J. W. (1975). LSA and LSCA, 1956–1973: A legislative history. *Library Trends, 24*(1), 7–28.

Geller, E. (1984). *Forbidden books in American public libraries, 1876–1939: A study in cultural change.* Westport, CT: Greenwood Press.

Gillane, D. (1999). The Gates Library Foundation in Louisiana. *Louisiana Libraries, 62*(1), 11–12.

Gordon, A. C., Gordon, M. T., Moore, E., & Heuertz, L. (2003, March 1). The Gates legacy. *Library Journal,* 44–48.

Government Studies and Systems, Inc., & United States. (1976). *Evaluation of the effectiveness of federal funding of public libraries: A study.* Washington, DC: National Commission on Libraries and Information Science.

Graham, P. T. (2001). Public librarians and the civil rights movement: Alabama, 1955–1965. *Library Quarterly, 71*(1), 1–27.

Harris, S. R. (2003). Civil Rights and the Louisiana Library Association: Stumbling toward integration. *Libraries and Culture, 38*(4), 322–350.

Hayden, C. D. (2003) "Presidential Initiative: Equity of Access," as quoted in Osborne, R., (2004). *From outreach to equity: Innovative models of library policy and practice,* p. xi. Chicago, IL: American Library Association.

Henderson, C. C. (1992). ALA and the 1991 WHCLIS recommendations. *Government Information Quarterly, 9*(3), 333–335.

Highlights of the Detroit Conference. (1965). *ALA Bulletin 59*(7), 617-629; 632-642.

Himmel, E., Wilson, W. J., with the ReVision Committee of the Public Library Association. (1998). *Planning for results: A public library transformation process.* Chicago, IL: American Library Association.

Holt, G. E., & Holt, L. E. (2015). Library card campaigns and sustaining service: How do public libraries best serve poor children? *Public Library Quarterly, 34*(3), 270–278.

Holt, L. E., & Holt, G. E. (2010). *Public library services for the poor: Doing all we can.* Chicago, IL: ALA Editions.

IMLS Focus: Learning in Libraries (2015). ttps://www.imls.gov/sites/default/files/publications/documents/imlsfocuslearninginlibrariesfinalreport.pdf.

Isenberg, N. (2016). *White trash: The 400-year untold history of class in America.* New York, NY: Viking.

Jaeger, P. T., Cooke, N. A., Feltis, C., Hamiel, M., Jardine, F., & Shilton, K. (2015). The virtuous circle revisited: Injecting diversity, inclusion, rights, justice, and equity into LIS from education to advocacy. *Library Quarterly, 85*(2), 150-171.

Jaeger, P. T., Taylor, N. G., & Gorham, U. (2015) *Libraries, human rights, and social justice: Enabling access and promoting inclusion.* Lanham, MD: Rowman & Littlefield.

Jaeger, P. T., & McClure, C. (2004). Potential legal challenges to the application of the Children's Internet Protection Act (CIPA) in public libraries: Strategies and issues. *First Monday 9*(2). http://firstmonday.org/ojs/index.php/fm/article/view/1117/1037.

Jones, B. M. (2009). Librarians shushed no more: The USA PATRIOT Act, the "Connecticut Four," and professional ethics. *Newsletter on Intellectual Freedom, 58*(6), 221-223.

Jones, V. L. (1963, September). The access to public libraries study. *ALA Bulletin, 57,* 742-745.

King Research. (1979). Issues and resolutions: A summary of pre-conference activities: Graphic presentation. Washington: National Commission on Libraries and Information Science.

Kister, K. F. (2002). *Eric Moon: The life and library times.* Jefferson, NC: McFarland.

Knight, D. M. (1967). Interview, by K. Molz. *Wilson Library Bulletin, 42,* 56-64.

Knight, D. M., & Nourse, E. S. (Eds.). (1969). *Libraries at large: Traditions, innovations and the national interest; the resource book based on the materials of the National Advisory Commission on Libraries.* New York, NY: R. R. Bowker.

Knott, C. (2015). *Not free, not for all: Public libraries in the age of Jim Crow.* Amherst, MA: University of Massachusetts Press.

Kunitz, S. (1939, December). That library serves best. *Wilson Library Bulletin,* 314.

LSTA nets small increase in shutdown—Avoiding FY17 Omnibus Spending. (2017, May 5). www.districtdispatch.org/2017/05/lsta-nets-small-increase-in-shutdown/.

Lamont, B. L. (1998, Summer). The legacy of the Library Services and Construction Act in Illinois. *Illinois Libraries, 80,* 193-184.

Latham, J. M. (2007). *White collar read: The American public library and the Left-led CIO: A case study of the Chicago Public Library, 1929-1952* (Doctoral dissertation). University of Illinois at Urbana-Champaign.

Lawrence, E., & Fry, R., (2016). Content blocking and the patron as situated knower: What would it take for an Internet filter to work? *Library Quarterly, 86*(4), 403-418.

Lefever, H. G. (2005). *Undaunted by the fight: Spelman College and the civil rights movement*, 1957/1967. Macon, GA: Mercer University Press.

Lemony Snicket Prize for Noble Librarians Faced with Adversity. (n.d.) www.ala.org/awardsgrants/lemony-snicket.

Lincove, D. A. (1994, Summer). Propaganda and the American public library from the 1930s to the eve of World War II. *RQ, 33,* 510-523.

Lingo, M. (2003, Fall). Forbidden fruit: The banning of *The Grapes of Wrath* in the Kern County Free Library. *Libraries and Culture, 38,* 351-377.

Lippincott, K., & Taffae, S. M. (1996). *25 Years of outreach: A Bibliographic timeline of the American Library Association, Office for Literacy and Outreach Services.* ED 396 755 IR 055 926.

Lynch, M. J. (1981, Summer/Fall/Winter). The Public Library Association and public library planning. *Journal of Library Administration, 2,* 29-41.

Magi, T. J., Garnar, M., & American Library Association. (2015). *A History of ALA policy on intellectual freedom: A supplement to the Intellectual Freedom Manual,* 9th edition. Chicago, IL: ALA Editions.

Marcum, D. (2014). Archives, libraries, museums: Coming back together? *Information and Culture, 49*(1), 74-89.

Martin, A. B., Public Library Association, & American Library Association. (1972). *A strategy for public library change: Proposed public library goals—Feasibility study*. Chicago, IL: American Library Association.

Martin, R. S. (2001). 21st Century Learners Conference, Institute of Museum and Library Services, held November 7, 2001. Reprinted in K. McCook, *Introduction to public librarianship* (2nd ed.), pp. 469-473. New York, NY: Neal-Schuman.

Mathews, V. H. (2004). Libraries, citizens & advocacy: The lasting effects of two White House Conferences on Library and Information Services. Washington, DC: White House Conference on Libraries and Information Services Taskforce.

Mathews, V. H., and Lacy, D. (1970) Response to change: American libraries in the seventies. ERIC ED044131.

Mathiesen, K. (2013). The human right to a public library. *Journal of Information Ethics, 22*(1), 60-79.

Mathuews, K. (2016). Moving beyond diversity to social justice. *Progressive Librarian, 44,* 6-27.

Mayo, D. (2005). *Technology for results: Developing service-based plans*. Chicago, IL: American Library Association.

Mayo, D., & Goodrich, J. (2002). *Staffing for results*. Chicago, IL: American Library Association.

Mayo, D., Nelson, S. S., & Public Library Association. (1999). *Wired for the future: Developing your library technology plan*. Chicago, IL: American Library Association.

McClure, C. R. (1987). *Planning and role setting for public libraries: A manual of options and procedures*. Chicago, IL: American Library Association.

McCook, K. (1994). *Toward a just and productive society: An analysis of the recommendations of the White House Conference on Library and Information Services*. Washington, DC: National Commission on Libraries and Information Science.

McCook, K. (2000, Summer). Ethnic diversity in library and information science. *Library Trends, 49,* 1-214.

McCook, K. (2002). *Rocks in the whirlpool: Equity of access and the American Library Association*. ERIC database, ED462981.

McCook, K. (2004). *Introduction to public librarianship*. New York, NY: Neal-Schuman Publishers.

McCook, K. (2011). *Introduction to public librarianship* (2nd ed.). New York, NY: Neal-Schuman Publishers.

McCook, K. (2017, July) From the one mule tenant farmer to the hillbilly highway: How librarians can support the white working class. *Library Quarterly, 87*.

Menuey, Brendan P. (2009). CIPA: A brief history. *Computers in Schools: Interdisciplinary Journal of Practice, Theory, and Applied Research, 26*(1): 40-47.

Miller, R. (2014). The Gates impact. *Library Journal, 139*(10), 8.

Molz, R. K. (1984). *National planning for library service, 1935-1975: From the national plan to the national program*. Chicago, IL: American Library Association.

Monypenny, P. (1966). *The library functions of the states*. Chicago, IL: American Library Association.

National Commission on Libraries and Information Science. (1975). *Toward a national program for library and information services: Goals for action*. Washington, DC: U.S. Government Printing Office.

National Commission on Libraries and Information Science. (1981). Task force on library and information services to cultural minorities: Hearings. Washington, DC: USGPO. ERIC Document Reproduction Service No. ED 241.

National Commission on Libraries and Information Science. (2000). Information 2000: Library and information services for the 21st century. (Washington, DC: NCLIS, 1992).

National Commission on Libraries and Information Science, White House Conference on Library and Information Services. (1980). *Summary: The final report*. Washington: National Commission on Libraries and Information Science.

Nelson, S. (2001). *The new planning for results: A streamlined approach*. Chicago, IL: American Library Association.

Nelson, S. (2008). *Strategic planning for results*. Chicago, IL: American Library Association.

Nelson, S. (2009). *Implementing for results: Your strategic plan in action.* Chicago, IL: American Library Association.

Nelson, S., Altman, E., & Mayo, D. (2000). Managing your library's staff. In *Managing for results: Effective resource allocation for public libraries* (pp. 29–110). Chicago, IL: American Library Association.

Nelson, S., & Garcia, J. (2003). *Creating policies for results: From chaos to clarity.* Chicago, IL: American Library Association.

Oltmann, S. (2016). "For All the People": Public library directors interpret intellectual freedom. *Library Quarterly, 86*(3), 290–312.

Palmour, V. E., Bellassi, M. C., & DeWath, N. V. (1980). *A planning process for public libraries.* Chicago, IL: American Library Association.

Pathways to excellence: A report on improving library and information services for Native American peoples. (1992). Washington, DC: National Commission on Libraries and Information Science.

Patterson, L. (2000, Summer). History and status of Native Americans in librarianship. *Library Trends, 49,* 182–193.

Paul Howard Award for Courage. www.ala.org/awardsgrants/paul-howard-award-courage.

Peet, L. (2016). Libraries4BlackLives to support activism. *Library Journal, 141*(14), 14–15.

Public Library Association. (1967). *Minimum standards for public library systems, 1966.* Chicago, IL: American Library Association.

Public Library Association, Goals, Guidelines and Standards Committee. (1973). Community library services: Working papers on goals and guidelines. *Library Journal, 96,* 2603-2609.

Public Library Association, Goals, Guidelines and Standards Committee. (1979). *The public library mission statement and its imperatives for service.* Chicago, IL: American Library Association.

Public Library Principles Task Force. (1982, Fall). The public library: Democracy's resource, a statement of principles. *Public Libraries, 21,* 92.

Pungitore, V. L. (1995). *Innovation and the library: The adoption of new ideas in public libraries.* Westport, CT: Greenwood Press.

REFORMA. (2006). Librarian's toolkit for responding effectively to anti-immigrant sentiment. www.reforma.org/ToolkitPartI.pdf.

Risen, C. (2014). *The bill of the century: The epic battle for the Civil Rights Act.* New York, NY: Bloomsbury Press.

Robbins, L. S. (1996). *Censorship and the American library: The American Library Association's response to threats to intellectual freedom: 1939-1969.* Westport, CT: Greenwood Press.

Robbins, L. S. (2000). *The Dismissal of Miss Ruth Brown: Civil rights, censorship, and the American library.* Norman, OK: University of Oklahoma Press.

Robbins, L. S. (2001, Winter). The overseas library controversy and the freedom to read: U.S. librarians and publishers confront Joseph McCarthy. *Libraries and Culture, 36.* 27–39.

Rohlf, R. (1982, Summer). Standards for public libraries. *Library Trends*, pp. 65–76.

Rubin, R. J. (2005). *Demonstrating results: Using outcome measurement in your library.* Chicago, IL: ALA Editions.

Samek, T. (2001). *Intellectual freedom and social responsibility in American librarianship, 1967-1974.* Chicago, IL: American Library Association.

Shen, L. (2013). Out of information poverty: Library services for urban marginalized immigrants. *Urban Library Journal, 19*(1), 1–12.

Taffae, S.M. Interview with retired computing consultant who implemented Gates grant, State Library of Louisiana, October 2016, by Kathleen McCook.

Teasdale, R. (2015, May 28). Project Outcome launch: Seven surveys to measure impact. *Public Libraries Online.* http://publiclibrariesonline.org/2015/05/project-outcome-launch-seven-surveys-to-measure-impact/.

Tucker, H. W. (1963, September). The access to public libraries study. *ALA Bulletin, 57,* 742–745.

U.S., Public Law 108-81, Title II—Library Services and Technology, September 25, 2003.

U.S. Census Bureau (2015). Poverty. http://factfinder.census.gov/bkmk/table/1.0/en/ACS/15_1YR/S0201.

Universal Service Administration Company (2016). Applicant Process. Step 5 Starting Services. https://usac.org/sl/applicants/step05/cipa.aspx.

Warburton, B. (2015, February 10). All eyes on IMLS. *Library Journal.* http://lj.libraryjournal.com/2015/02/shows-events/ala/all-eyes-on-imls-priorities-for-2015-ala-midwinter-2015/#_.

Weibel, K, Heim, K., & Ellsworth, D. J. (1979). *The status of women in librarianship, 1876–1976.* Phoenix, AZ: Oryx Press.

Widdersheim, M. M., & Koizumi, M. (2016), Conceptual modelling of the public sphere in public libraries. *Journal of Documentation, 72*(3), 591–610.

Wiegand, W. A. (1989). *An active instrument for propaganda: The American public library during World War I.* New York, NY: Greenwood Press.

Wiegand, W.A. (2017, June 1). Desegregating libraries in the American South: Forgotten heroes in civil rights history. *American Libraries.* https://americanlibrariesmagazine.org/2017/06/01/desegregating-libraries-american-south/.

Wikipedia + Libraries: Better together: Connecting libraries and Wikipedia (2016). www.webjunction.org/explore-topics/wikipedia-libraries.html.

Wronka, J. (2017). *Human rights and social justice: Social action and service for the helping and health professions.* Los Angeles: Sage.

Zinn, H. (1997). A quiet case of social change. In *The Zinn reader: Readings on disobedience and democracy* (pp. 31–39). New York, NY: Seven Stories Press.

Zweizig, D. L., & Rodger, E. J. (1982). *Output measures for public libraries.* Chicago, IL: American Library Association.

The Public Library Journey to Accountability

Metrics and Outcomes to Demonstrate Value

Public libraries in the United States were established in the nineteenth century as components of the great democratizing of American life as an extension of public education. Initially funded by taxes to extend educational opportunity to entire communities, today public libraries must make their case in new ways to compete for scarce resources and demonstrate accountability to the taxpayers that provide money and support.

> **▶ FACT**
>
> E-circ is a newly established data element reported in the *Library Journal* series, America's Star Libraries. In 2017 the series will include Wi-Fi usage. Forty percent of the rating will be based on virtual use (Lyons & Lance, 2016).

This chapter highlights Project Outcome, the Public Library Association (PLA) initiative launched in 2015 to help public libraries understand and share the true impact of essential library services and programs. Public librarians have made sincere and sustained efforts to respond to the challenges of the larger world—wars, elections, depressions, and economic booms and busts. Therefore, the historical path to Project Outcome is reviewed to obtain perspective to identify the roles, service responses, and focuses that have been delineated by librarians over time to characterize the broad spectrum of public library daily actions.

To provide context, a summary is included of how public librarians moved from counting service, to measuring service, to assessing service impact through outcomes assessment. The committed and sustained effort of public librarians in communities, associations, and state agencies who have spent thousands of hours discussing, revising, and developing systematic techniques to define, evaluate, and make the case for public library services is reviewed.[1]

MEASURING THE OUTCOMES OF LIBRARY PROGRAMS

The Institute of Museum and Library Services (IMLS) provides funds to local public libraries through the conduit of state library administrative agencies. IMLS advocates an outcomes-based approach to evaluation to demonstrate in a compelling manner that strong public libraries enhance the lives of people and their communities (Shepherd, 2000). The landscape of outcomes assessment has been summarized by the authors of *Library Journal's* annual Index of Public Library Service (Lyons and Lance, 2014). Of outcomes assessments that have taken place in recent years the Public Library Association's Project Outcome has the most far-reaching implications for American public library accountability (Thomas, 2016).[2]

Project Outcome is an initiative of PLA. It grew from a 2013 Task Force charged to develop standardized measures of effectiveness for library services and to promote training and implementation tools for using the data collected (Anthony 2013, 2014). Project Outcome was launched at the American Library Association conference in 2015 to help librarians show the impact made by public libraries in their communities and to demonstrate the value of public librarians to residents and policy makers. Seven areas of focus to measure outcomes were selected:

- Civic/Community Engagement
- Digital Inclusion
- Early Childhood Literacy
- Economic Development
- Education/Lifelong Learning
- Job Skills
- Summer Reading (Teasdale, 2015)

The PLA Performance Measurement Task Force (PMTF), which developed Project Outcome, introduced a special section on performance measures in the 2014 Public Library Data Service survey, thus tying together two PLA projects. The survey was designed to determine the extent to which they understood the importance of measuring program outcomes and if they were able, or willing, to do so (Reid, 2015). Parker's thoughtful essay, written from the vantage point of a medium-sized public library director, presented additional perspective on the process as needing to differentiate for specific library environments (2014).

In 2015 PLA presented Project Outcome at six different conferences, while simultaneously presenting nine webinars to nearly 1,000 attendees on various outcome-measurement topics. Project Outcome has quickly met the public library demand and desire for standardized performance measures and continues to expand toward more advanced data collection.

The webinar, *Project Outcome: An Integral Part of the Planning Process,* guides participants through the four-step outcome measurement process: 1) set goals, 2) measure outcomes, 3) review results, and 4) take action. It is available on the PLA website as are additional resources (PLA, 2016). To better support a library's assessment needs, the Public Library Association's Project Outcome also partnered with the Urban Libraries Council's (ULC) Edge Initiative and the University of Washington's Impact Survey to host the webinar, *Measurement Matters: Using Edge, Project Outcome, and the Impact Survey to Assess and Improve Community Outcomes.*[3] These can be viewed On Demand at the PLA website.

Carolyn Anthony, writing on the first year of Project Outcome implantation noted that

> the real outcomes of the project will be realized as individual libraries are able to show local funding authorities the difference the public library is making in the lives of local residents and then, as data is aggregated, to reveal the true impact of the public library on people throughout states and regions. (Anthony, 2016)

Annual reports for Project Outcome are posted at the PLA website. The 2016 report describes how Project Outcome provided libraries with ready-to-use patron surveys for seven essential library service areas. Surveys measure immediate patron benefit following a library service or program, and longer-term behavior change. More than 225 library systems implemented Project Outcome surveys in their communities. Over 17,000 survey responses were collected within the first year across 774 programs and services—an average of 64 surveys every month. The most popular surveys were on Summer Reading, Education and Lifelong Learning, and Early Childhood Literacy (Examine PLA's First Project Outcome Annual Report, 2017; PLA Project Outcome Year in Review, 2016).

How did Project Outcome evolve from two centuries of public library measurement? This book is intended to put current initiatives in historical perspective and to provide documentation of public librarianship and its deeply thought-out path to the present forms of evaluation.

HOW DO WE CONVEY THE IMPORTANCE OF PUBLIC LIBRARIES?

In *The Public Library and the Political Process,* written as part of the mid-twentieth-century Public Library Inquiry, Oliver Garceau (1949) wrote about the "library faith"—the belief that libraries support reading and democracy—that grew and intensified as public libraries were founded throughout the United States (pp. 50-52). This faith inspired librarians and community members to raise funds to establish public libraries, but data and numbers were required to make the case for continuance.

Today data collection is a mandate under the Museum and Library Services Act, which states that "current, accurate and ongoing collection of library data is an essential foundation for quality library services in the United States."[4] How did the mandate for data collection evolve? The history of public library evaluation illuminates the public library story in America.

> **▶ FACT**
>
> The history of public library statistics development falls into five periods: exploratory (1870-1937); developmental (1938-1956); broadened responsibility (1956-1965); diversified responsibility (1965-1989); and the current era, which began in 1989 when the National Center for Education Statistics (NCES) initiated a formal library statistics program.*
>
> *See Schick, 1971; Chute, 2003; Library Research Service, 2009, McCook (2011). See Appendix D for a bibliography of national statistics gathered and reported for U.S. public libraries from 1853 to the present. See also the work of Herbert Goldhor (1983) and Robert V. Williams (1991). Williams and McLean (2008), who have identified, described, and provided bibliographic information on compilations of statistical information about libraries in the United States.

Counting and Comparing Public Libraries

1851 to 1988

As we have seen in the preceding chapters on the history of the public library, the establishment of the library as an essential tax-funded agency became widely accepted during the nineteenth and early-twentieth centuries. Wiegand's 2015 book, *Part of Our Lives: A People's*

History of the American Public Library, stated that Americans have valued libraries not only as civic institutions, but also as social spaces for promoting and maintaining community.

The first major effort to count the number of libraries open to the public was conducted for the Smithsonian Institution's *Report on the Public Libraries of the United States of America* (Jewett, 1851). The *Report* is the foundational document in American library enumeration. It included over 2 million volumes in state libraries, athenaeum libraries, academic libraries, church libraries, ladies' libraries, society libraries, literary societies, apprentices' libraries, and mechanics' libraries. This assessment coincided with the establishment of the first tax-supported public library in a major city—Boston. The Smithsonian *Report* reviewed the extent of libraries in the United States at the time when tax-supported municipal libraries began to be considered a community service.

In 1876 the massive report *Public Libraries in the United States of America: Their History, Condition, and Management* differentiated between general libraries and public libraries that were supported by communities through taxation and reported their findings in a combined table (U.S. Bureau of Education. 1876, p. 1010). From 1876 to 1989 the U.S. government and other entities issued over 250 statistical reports on public libraries in a variety of formats (McCook, 2011, pp. 483-492).

The passage of the Library Services Act in 1956 gave impetus to an ongoing statistical responsibility in the U.S. Office of Education that was eventually coordinated by the National Center for Education Statistics using the Library General Information System (LIBGIS) to collect data (Williams, R. V., 1991, pp. 468–470).

The "Public Libraries Survey" and the Z39.7 Standard

In 1988 the Public Libraries Survey was administered by the National Center for Education Statistics (NCES) using the Federal State Cooperative System FSCS.[5] The survey used the Z39.7 Standard, which identifies and defines the basic data collection categories used to collect library statistical data at the national level.[6] In 2007 the responsibility of administering the "Public Libraries Survey" moved from NCES to the Institute of Museum and Library Services (IMLS).[7] The process is advised by the Library Statistics Working Group, whose members are state librarians, state library data coordinators, and representatives of professional associations.[8]

The Z39.7 standard, *Information Services and Use: Metrics and Statistics for Libraries and Information Providers Data Dictionary,* was revised in 2013. It identifies categories for basic library statistical data reported at the national level, and provides associated definitions of terms. It deals with:

- reporting unit and target population
- human resources
- collection resources
- infrastructure
- finances
- services

In addition, the 2013 update of the Z39.7 standard identified new measures associated with networked services, databases, and performance (National Information Standards Organization. Approved: March 26, 2013).

State data coordinators from each state library agency submit data from each public library in their respective states—a universe of over 9,200 public libraries in 50 states, the District of Columbia, and the outlying areas—for the annual Public Libraries Survey[9] The IMLS releases the collected results in annual reports and data files. The data are used for planning, research, evaluation, and policymaking decisions by federal, state, and local officials, professional associations, researchers, educators, local practitioners, and other interested users. Data are submitted electronically using the PLS Web Portal at the American Institutes for Research (AIR).[10]

Public Libraries Surveys from 1988 to the present are available online at the IMLS website. *Public Libraries in the United States* is a national-level analysis that aggregates data from all 50 states and the District of Columbia to provide national estimates and trends. Each survey includes a section on public library indicators that provides an overall level of performance for key metrics and serves as a gauge to evaluate important changes in public library use, services, and resources.[11] These surveys provide sophisticated data analysis. The 2012 report used statistical modeling to examine the relationship between investment in and use of public libraries, which was found to be consistent for all libraries (IMLS, 2014, FY 2012, p. 13).

In October 2016 IMLS and the Chief Officers of State Library Agencies (COSLA) announced *Measures that Matter,* a project that will develop a Library Data and Outcomes Action Plan with key library stakeholder groups for a more coordinated approach to the collection of public library data nationally. The project's ultimate goal is to create a framework within which outcomes, outputs, and indicators can be drawn upon to consistently and effectively demonstrate the role, value, and impact of public libraries ("IMLS & COSLA Announce Project," 2016).

One additional initiative should be highlighted—The Research Institute for Public Libraries (RIPL).[12] The RIPL vision is to create a culture shift in public libraries, so that they are purposeful in gathering, analyzing, and using data for decision-making, strategic planning, and demonstrating impact. RIPL educates change agents who will go back to their libraries with the tools, competencies, and commitment to lead evidence-based practice by designing outcome-based evaluation of programs and services. The RIPL Institute coordinates with Project Outcome and other evaluation strategies.

The Public Library Data Service

The Public Library Data Service (PLDS) is a voluntary survey published annually by PLA (Reid, 2016). In 2015 over 1,800 libraries were included in the report. The PLDS identifies top-performing libraries, compares service levels and technology usage, and provides documentation for funding requests. Categories include financial information, library resources and per capita measures, annual use figures, and technology in public libraries. Special surveys are included in different years to address such topics as the use of outcome measures, library facilities, finance, young adult services, or strategic planning.

PLA*metrics* is the subscriber portal to the Public Library Data Service Statistical Report digital database, which provides access to all the yearly PLDS data currently available from FY2002 to the present and access to the IMLS data (FY2000 to the present). Additional support with using the PLA*metrics* is provided by *Managing with Data,* which demonstrates how to move towards outcomes assessments while simultaneously embracing values (Hernon, Dugan, & Matthews, 2015).[13]

National Standards for Public Library Service in the Twentieth Century: 1933, 1943, 1956, and 1966

From 1933 through 1966 U.S. public librarians developed standards to define the appropriate metrics for public libraries. In chapter 3 we addressed the meta-narrative that saw public libraries moving to a planning model, but for a deep understanding of the realities of library practice we now present a review of the standards as they developed in the twentieth century.

> ▶ **FACT**
>
> Carlton B. Joeckel summarized the various types of county library systems and developed the case for larger units of library service in his study *The Government of the American Public Library* (1935). His ideas influenced future planning for cooperative library projects.

1933 Standards

The 1933 "Standards for Public Libraries" defined the rationale for the public library: "in order that every man, woman and child may have the means of self-education and recreational reading" (American Library Association, 1933). The move to develop public library standards in the 1930s occurred at the same time that the library profession began efforts to develop a national plan for public library service.

Recommended numbers of books for each public library collection were:

- 3 per capita for cities with populations under 10,000
- 2 per capita for cities with populations of 10,000 to 200,000
- 1.5 per capita for cities with populations over 200,000

Recommended standards for lending and library registration were to be measured statistically:

- 50% registration and 10 books per capita for cities with populations under 10,000
- 40% registration and 9 books per capita for cities with populations of 10,000 to 100,000
- 35% registration and 8 books per capita for cities with populations of 100,000 to 200,000
- 30% registration and 7 books per capita for cities with populations of 200,000 to 1,000,000
- 25% registration and 5 books per capita for cities with populations over 1,000,000

Income was recommended at $1 per capita and at least $25,000 total, though it was recognized that smaller towns would usually need to spend more or enlarge the unit of service (ALA, 1933).

At this time there was much discussion of the size of local government required to support public libraries. Should public libraries be supported by towns, by counties, or by other entities? (Fair, 1934). Carlton B. Joeckel summarized the various types of county library systems and developed the case for larger units of library service in his study *The Government of the American Public Library* (1935). His ideas influenced future planning for cooperative library projects.

1943: Post-War Standards for Public Libraries and the 1948 National Plan for Public Library Service

In 1938 the U.S. government created the Library Services Division of the U.S. Office of Education, which provided a federal vantage point for national-level planning in collaboration with the National Resources Planning Board. ALA, anticipating the postwar period in which public library service would be seen as a responsibility of democratic government, appointed Joeckel chair of its Committee on Postwar Planning to 1) oversee the development of postwar standards, 2) coordinate data collection on the status of the U.S. public library, and 3) develop a national plan for public library service.

Post-War Standards for Public Libraries were based on the ideal that "public library service should be available without exception to all people and in all political jurisdictions throughout the nation" (Joeckel, 1943, p. 15). The Post-War Standards covered services, administration, size and area, finance, buildings, collection, personnel, and technical processes. They also included an inventory and evaluation of selected public libraries (McCook, 2011, p. 80).

Specificity included recommended percentages of registered borrowers, the number of books for children and adults that should circulate each year, hours of service, and collection size as a function of community served. Financial standards were addressed in terms of "limited," "reasonably good," and "superior" service with much attention to the necessity of a minimum of $25,000 to maintain basic service. The second phase of the Post-War Planning Committee's work was a report of the inventory and evaluation of selected public libraries in 1943, titled "Taking Stock of the American Public Library."

At the close of World War II, national per capita public library support was $0.72, and 35 million people were still unserved by any library. The National Plan for Public Library Service, which built on the Post-War Standards, changed the direction of the public library movement. The National Plan for Public Library Service is of particular importance to the discussion of standards because it used the standards in place at the time to characterize library service in general as mediocre, and also provided a platform from which to argue for the strengthening of library services throughout the United States in support of the goal "to bring into the life of every American an adequate, purposeful public library . . . to be achieved by the joint efforts of local, state and federal governments" (Joeckel & Winslow, 1948, p. 152). In the foreword to the National Plan, Carl H. Milam observed:

> This book can change the course of the Public Library Movement in North America. In particular, it can hasten the day when there will be no millions without good local public library service. But the book will not do it unaided. From here on the success of this planning effort will rest primarily with the state library organizations and library extension agencies.

In *The Public Library in the United States,* the report of the Public Library Inquiry, the idea of moving from municipalities to library systems was based philosophically on the 1948 National Plan (Leigh, 1950). It was the wellspring of the case for federal support for legislation through the Library Services Act (LSA) in 1956. It also set forth much of the rationale for developing standards in the context of systems.

1956: Public Library Service: A Guide to Evaluation with Minimum Standards

Early in the 1950s the Public Libraries Division of ALA was formed and immediately sought funding to revise and restate the 1943 standards. This movement also took place in the states. The California standards issued in 1953 were characterized by Shaughnessy (1975) as foreshadowing the next set of national standards, which emphasized a central library in addition to more access in rural areas. He also viewed emphasis on state planning as a precursor of wider commitment. This prediction came true at a national level in 1956.

A Coordinating Committee on Revision of Public Library Standards was convened in 1954 by the Public Libraries Division. By 1956, after several meetings and solicitation of profession-wide comment, the committee issued its recommendations, *Public Library Service: A Guide to Evaluation with Minimum Standards.* These standards incorporated ideals from the 1943 Post-War Standards and the National Plan, but went further to emphasize the educational function of the public library, the quality of service, and the organization of service. The concept of library systems was defined, and took note of the fact that while some large cities could provide excellent library services, smaller jurisdictions could not generate enough fiscal support to do so. Thus the 1956 standards advocated that "libraries working together, sharing their services and materials, can meet the full needs of their users and stated forcefully: This cooperative approach on the part of libraries is the most important single recommendation of this document" (ALA, PLD, Coordinating Committee, 1956, p. xv). Data on costs were issued as a supplement that was updated periodically.

Direct aid to public libraries in rural communities and small towns came with the passage of the Library Services Act in 1956 and extended to urban areas and construction in 1964 (the Library Services and Construction Act). Other federal legislation, such as Operation Headstart, a part of the Economic Opportunity Act, funded library projects in response to the 1960's War on Poverty. The federal aspect of funding for public libraries and the recognition of the changing context of service were very much on the minds of the Standards Committee of PLA at the time of the issuance of the *Minimum Standards for Public Library Systems,* 1966 (PLA, Standards Committee, 1967).

1966: Minimum Standards for Public Library Systems

Minimum Standards for Public Library Systems, 1966 were issued but were little changed from the 1956 standards (PLA, Standards Committee, 1967). The public library community recognized immediately that the 1966 Standards reflected the past and did not anticipate the future. Lowell Martin wrote of the 1966 standards:

> In the middle of the 1960s few people foresaw the threatened position in which the public library would find itself five years later. Those who did have forebodings had not conceived a fresh direction or role for the public library which could form the foundation of a genuinely new statement of standards. (L. A. Martin, 1972)

ALA had received the results of the report *Access to Public Libraries* in 1964 (ALA, 1963), the self-audit on the restriction of freedom of access to public libraries based on race, and was digesting this report's implications at the time the 1966 standards were released.

Planning for Library Service: 1966 to 2014

The 1966 standards were issued amid growing societal recognition that the United States was split into a nation of rich and poor, as clearly described in *The Other America: Poverty in the United States* (Harrington, 1962). The Civil Rights Act of 1964 had been signed into law. The spirit of the times galvanized ALA members to establish the Social Responsibilities Round Table and to appoint a Coordinating Committee on Library Service to the Disadvantaged.[14] The 1966 standards did not address the needs of all the people public libraries purported to serve, that is, *all* people. Change was needed.

The Public Library Association conducted a study that launched a transformation in how we think about public library service, *A Strategy for Public Library Change* (A. B. Martin, 1972). A new focus on community-based planning helped shift the profession's discourse to the idea of local models—a shift that began a nearly 50-year stage of public library development based on planning.

> **▶ FACT**
>
> To fill the gap between the 1966 standards to the 1975 "Goals and Guidelines for Community Library Service," a PLA committee issued *The Public Library Mission Statement and Its Imperatives for Service.*

The Standards Committee of PLA secured funding from the U.S. Office of Education for the study *Measurement of the Effectiveness of Public Libraries,* which was reported in the volume *Performance Measures for Public Libraries* (De Prospo et al., 1973). These studies changed the measurement focus of public librarians from input to output. In her analytic monograph *Innovation and the Library,* Verna L. Pungitore described the profession's response to this shift (1995).[15] The focus was to be planning for the future rather than reporting on the past, managing rather than comparing, and a new concern for output (Blasingame and Lynch, 1974).

The Public Library Mission Statement and Its Imperatives for Service, produced by a PLA Committee chaired by Peter Hiatt,[16] served as a bridge from the 1966 standards to the 1975 "Goals and Guidelines for Community Library Service" (PLA, GGSC, 1979). *The Public Library Mission Statement and Its Imperatives for Service* identified factors in U.S. society that called for a radical shift in emphasis of the public library: runaway social change, exponential increase in the human record, total egalitarianism, and depletion of natural resources. The move to a planning model and local definitions of service characterized public librarianship for the next 50 years.[17]

In 1980 PLA published *A Planning Process for Public Libraries,* a manual outlining methods for community analysis and planning for services (Palmour et al., 1980). Community-based planning was to be the new innovation that replaced national public library standards. A companion volume, *Output Measures for Public Libraries,* defining the use of quantitative measures, was released in 1982 (Zweizig and Rodger, 1982).[18]

The Public Library Association revised its Statement of Principles in 1982 with respect to planning (PLA, Public Library Principles Task Force, 1982). The next stage in the move toward adopting the planning model was the introduction of the Public Library Development Program (PLDP) in 1986 (Balcom). The initial component of PLDP was *Planning and Role Setting for Public Libraries: A Manual of Options and Procedures* (McClure, 1987), which identified eight potential roles for public libraries and a choice of levels of effort for the process, a revision of the output measures manual, and a data service (PLA, Public Library Data Service, 1992–present). The eight roles selected formed the basis for much library planning from 1987 to 1998.

1. Community activities center
2. Community information center
3. Formal education support center
4. Independent learning center
5. Popular materials library
6. Preschoolers' door to learning
7. Reference library
8. Research center

The broad acceptance of the PLDP among public librarians was reported in a 1993 survey of state agencies' use of the process (Smith, 1994). Douglas Raber (1995) characterized the process as a conflict of cultures moving from tradition to planning.[19]

The Public Library Association evaluated the effectiveness of the PLDP in 1995 with a national survey that concluded that the planning model was working and its use had done much to include the community and staff in the direction library services would evolve (Johnson, 1995). A "ReVision" Committee developed a new manual, *Planning for Results: A Public Library Transformation Process* (Himmel and Wilson, 1998). The eight roles for public libraries identified in 1986 were expanded to 13 "library service responses," defined as what a library does for, or offers to, the public to meet a set of well-defined community needs.

1. Basic literacy
2. Business and career information
3. Commons
4. Community referral
5. Consumer information
6. Cultural awareness
7. Current topics and titles
8. Formal learning
9. General information
10. Government information
11. Information literacy
12. Lifelong learning
13. Local history and genealogy

Planning for Results placed a greater focus on resource allocation. Training and workshops were held at state conferences and sponsored by state library agencies to assist in adopting procedures. A companion volume, *Managing for Results,* was issued in 2000 to help turn plans into reality (Nelson, Altman, and Mayo, 2000). A streamlined approach, *The New Planning for Results,* was issued in 2001 (Nelson, 2001). To support the implementation of the planning process, PLA launched a series of volumes, the Results series, offering a consistent set of themes.[20]

In 2006 PLA began a review of the 1998 service responses. In 2007 drafts of 18 proposed service responses were posted at the PLA blog for comment. The companion volumes, *Strategic Planning for Results* (2008) and *Implementing for Results* (2009) (Nelson, 2008, 2009) were published. Both emphasized change and gave guidance to transform strategic plans into reality. *Strategic Planning for Results* increased the number of service responses to 18 (Nelson, 2008, pp. 143-217):

1. Be an informed citizen: local, national, and world affairs
2. Build successful enterprises: business and nonprofit support
3. Celebrate diversity: cultural awareness
4. Connect to the online world: public Internet access
5. Create young readers: early literacy
6. Discover your roots: genealogy and local history
7. Express creativity: create and share content
8. Get facts fast: ready reference
9. Know your community: community resources and services
10. Learn to read and write: adults, teens, and family literature
11. Make career choices: job and career development
12. Make informed decisions: health, wealth, and other life choices
13. Satisfy curiosity: lifelong learning
14. Stimulate imagination: reading, viewing, and listening for pleasure
15. Succeed in school: homework help
16. Understand how to find, evaluate, and use information: information fluency
17. Visit a comfortable place: physical and virtual spaces
18. Welcome to the United States: services for new immigrants

These 18 service responses formed the national approach to public library services until 2015. The planning era from 1966 to 2015 changed the way librarians carried out their work. The public library became the public library in all ways.[21]

STATE PUBLIC LIBRARY STANDARDS

State level public library standards are an essential component of public library development. The national Public Library Association (PLA) decision to end standards development after 1966 did not mean rejection of standards in practice. At the state level, data and statistics have often been used to create standards to collaborate with the planning process and to establish the case for library support at the local level.

Public librarians recognize that it is compelling to make their case for funding to city councils, county commissions, and regional boards with clear standards. In fact, the enormous effort of librarians at the state level to craft standards has provided the field with a deeply understood philosophy of service that has been discussed at state conferences, in regional meetings, and in local communities.

Although the actions of the national Public Library Association have been central to what is discussed in this book, the PLA's work is by no means the entire story of the development of the public library's mission and direction in the United States. State library agencies are all participants in the constant process of deliberating on the goals and standards of public libraries through their own long-range planning in collaboration with the Institute of Museum and Library Services, state library associations, multitype library consortia, library systems, and local libraries and their boards ("IMLS & COSLA Announce Project," 2016).

In a 2011 paper, Houghtaling reported that at least half of the states in the U.S. tie state funding to standards. A complete set of standards is posted at the Public Library Standards committee site.[22] The COSLA (Chiefs of State Library Agencies) site also provides links to state standards as well as to individual states' long-range plans.[23]

The process by which each state compiles standards in itself contributes to the professionalism and knowledge base of the librarians in each state. For instance, the Indiana State Library (n.d.) has a comprehensive set of resources on its website that provides a systemic review of the standards process and also names participants, which indicates a cross-section of active engaged librarians from libraries of all sizes.

Similarly, the State Library of North Carolina posts standards that are benchmarks of conditions necessary for effective library service in North Carolina. These benchmarks are organized into five sections: Administration, Facilities, Human Resources, Resources, and Services; within each section, the benchmarks are organized by three categories:

- Public Value—practices that demonstrate effective stewardship of public funds and establish the Library's relevance and impact in the community
- Management—practices that result in effective and sustainable library operations
- Community Engagement—practices that build collaborative relationships and involve community members in planning, developing, using and evaluating library services (NC State Library, 2012)

A study posted at the COSLA website by Hamilton-Pennell (2010) reviewed the standards of all 50 states and identified the key reasons that state-level standards continue to be developed:

1. Assist in planning efforts
2. Provide an evaluation and mechanism tool for public accountability
3. Provide a philosophical context for quality public library service
4. Serve as a library development tool by stimulating growth and development
5. Serve as a tool to identify strengths and select areas for improvement
6. Provide a shared vision for library service
7. Assist in determining whether resources are sufficient
8. Set minimum guidelines for receipt of state aid

There are not many overviews or academic studies about state public library standard development. But I can add a personal note. As a member of the Florida Library Association Standards committee in 1993 and again in 2003, I visited many libraries and I engaged with many librarians and library users. I know that for decades the commitment of librarians across all of the states in America has been essential to the level of understanding and intellectual involvement of library workers at the front desks, in the processing room, and when speaking to elected officials and the public. I watched with great interest as Florida's librarians worked to revise standards in 2015—a process that engaged librarians throughout the state. When adopted, the minutes of the Florida Library Association were approved and posted on Facebook. This official notice by the Florida Library Association Board of Directors should be an example of the intense work by librarians all over the United States to develop standards for excellent service:

> With great pride the board voted to approve the *Florida Public Library Outcomes and Standards 2015* created by the FLA Standards and Outcomes Committee. The document will be posted on the FLA website. Region 6 Director, and committee liaison Stephen Grubb acknowledged the hard work and dedication of the committee, and committee

chairs, Ruth O'Donnell and Susan Dillinger. The board also expressed its gratitude to long time FLA partner, Harvard Jolly Architecture for proofreading and formatting the document. (from the Facebook page of the Florida Library Association.)

RATINGS AND AWARDS

Public library performance has also been highlighted over time by ratings and awards. Although these may vary in methodology, they draw attention to excellence that is variously defined.[24]

"America's Star Libraries," the annual *Library Journal* (LJ) Index of Public Library Service. was launched in 2009. This measurement tool for public libraries assesses library service output statistics based on five types of per capita use: visits, circulation, public access computer use, program attendance, and electronic circulation. The LJ Index scores and star ratings are based on data reported annually by public libraries to their state library agencies and compiled nationally by the Institute of Museum and Library Services (IMLS). Star Library ratings of five, four, and three stars are awarded to libraries that generate the highest combined per capita outputs among their spending peers (Lyons & Lance, 2016).

In 2016 the top ranked "Star Libraries" libraries by spending category were:

- Cuyahoga (OH) County Public Library ($30,000,000+)
- Allen County (IN) Public Library ($10,000,000 to $29,999,999)
- Washington County Cooperative Library ($5,000,000 to $9,999,999)
- Avalon (NJ) Free Public Library ($1,000,000 to $4,999, 999)
- Foley (AL) Public Library ($400,000 to $999,999)
- Red Hook (NY) Public Library ($200,000 to $399,999)
- Flomaton (AL) Public Library ($100,000 to $199,999)
- Real County (TX) Public Library ($50,000 to $99,999)
- Vincent (AL) Lalouise F. McGraw Library ($10,000 to $49,999)

For the scores for all libraries included in the LJ Index, links are provided to download a spreadsheet with the libraries rated, their ratings, and the data from which the ratings were derived (Lyons & Lance, 2016).[25]

An interview with Donna Dziedzic, director of the consistently award-winning Naperville (IL) Public Library. inquired how the library had gained the community's understanding and support. Dziedzic responded:

> Being a valuable service that's also a great value for the tax dollar was part of nearly every community presentation given by key staff for close to fifteen years. The NPL board

> and staff are committed to being good stewards of the taxpayers' dollars. The library has also been able to buttress that concept with hard numbers that demonstrate clearly its dedication to a positive cost to service/operation ratio. (Sloan, 2012)

We can learn from the wisdom of library directors whose libraries are recognized for excellence. Naperville Public Library has combined the various evaluation mechanisms to gain and keep public support.

The National Medal for Museum and Library Service

> Day after day, year after year, our nation's libraries and museums are here for our communities. And at the end of the day, you all don't measure your impact by the number of books on your shelves or pieces in your exhibits, but by the young people you inspire, the lives you transform, and the impact you have every single day on your communities.[26]
>
> **—First Lady Michelle Obama at the 2016 National Medal for Museum and Library Service Ceremony**

Former first lady Michelle Obama delivers remarks during the 2016 National Medal for Museum and Library Service award ceremony in the East Room of the White House, June 1, 2016.
Photo by Earl Zubkoff for IMLS.

The National Medal is the nation's highest honor. It is awarded to libraries for service to the community. The award celebrates institutions that present extraordinary and innovative approaches to public service that make a difference for individuals, families, and communities. The honorees in 2016 exemplify the nation's great libraries and demonstrate outstanding impact and quality of programs, services, and partnerships, exceeding the expected levels of community outreach. Comments made by honorees are inspiring and encouraging.

Brooklyn (NY) Public Library

> If you have the inclination and curiosity to open our doors, the world's knowledge is at your fingertips. It doesn't matter where you start. At Brooklyn Public Library our motto is "Start Here," and the fact is you can just walk in, and wherever you are comfortable, we will begin with you . . . we will find something to improve your life.
>
> **—Linda E. Johnson, President & CEO**

Madison (WI) Public Library

> Our community engagement approach enables us to stand out among our colleagues. We have partnered with an enormous variety of organizations that reach out to the library after hearing about the amazing things we've done, and our flexibility allows us to work with just about any organization that wants to work with us.
>
> **—Gregory Mickells, Library Director**

Otis Library (Norwich, CT)

> We always want to be pursuing community needs and making sure we are engaging the community on a regular basis to address what they want from a library. That summarizes why Otis is successful. We are not a passive organization, but an extremely proactive, dynamic one. That is what we pride ourselves on the most.
>
> **—Bob Farwell, Executive Director**

Santa Ana (CA) Public Library

> When people ask what I call this library, I say, la biblioteca milagrosa, which means the miracle making library. We customize the little resources we do have to fit our needs, and, more importantly, the needs of the community where we are ingrained.
>
> **—Gerardo Mouet, Executive Director, Santa Ana Department of Parks, Recreation and Community Services**

These exemplary libraries, which were honored with the 2016 National Medal, represent the scope and range of public library service that all public libraries make their goal and inspiration.

LJ Library/ Gale Cengage Learning Library of the Year

Library Journal gives annual competitive awards that provide another example of national excellence. Their nomination form states: All libraries are good, some are great. *LJ* is looking for role-model libraries to vie for the honor of being the *Library Journal*/Gale Cengage Learning Library of the Year. The prize celebrates the library that most profoundly demonstrates: service to the community; creativity and innovation in developing specific community programs or a dramatic increase in library usage; and leadership in creating programs that can be emulated by other libraries.[27]

Recent Library of the Year Winners

2016 Topeka & Shawnee County (KS) Public Library
2015 Ferguson (MO) Municipal Public Library
2014 Edmonton (Alberta, Canada) Public Library
2013 Howard County (MD) Library System
2012 San Diego (CA) County Library
2011 King County (WA) Library System
2010 Columbus (OH) Metropolitan Library

Association Awards

PLA also recognizes outstanding public libraries with the EBSCO Excellence in Small and/ or Rural Public Library Service Award, and many state association bestow honors, such as the Connecticut Library Association Excellence in Public Library Service Award, Florida Library of the Year Award, and Missouri Library of the Year Award.[28]

Innovation awards given annually by the Urban Libraries Council (ULC) showcase a wide range of services and programs that ULC members have developed to connect people to technology, address key community issues, and support participatory learning experiences across a lifetime. In 2016 honorees included the St. Paul (MN) Public Library's Saint Paul Public Library Racial Equity Initiative; King County Library System's Older Adults: Inspire, Engage, Connect; Queens Library's Helping Adults Finally Achieve that High School Diploma; and Sno-Isle Libraries' TEDxSnoIsle Libraries 2015.[29]

QUALITY OF LIFE AND HUMAN DEVELOPMENT

It is now time to step back and look at the bigger questions we are trying to address with these various efforts at analysis—how do public libraries contribute to a better quality of life for all the people they serve? What is it that the library does to help each person be able to do and to be? In her study *Creating Capabilities,* Nussbaum (2011) defines the capabilities-approach to quality of life assessment as taking each person as an end (p. 18).[30]

What we are really trying to figure out is how to demonstrate to our communities that libraries have the capacity to enhance human capabilities through human development. This is a global concern. It places human capabilities above economic indicators. The mission of the UN Human Development Report Office (HDRO) is to contribute to the expansion of opportunities, choice, and freedom. This reflects the same goals as public libraries. The UN Human Development Report process introduced a new approach for advancing human well-being. It is about expanding the richness of human life, rather than simply the richness of the economy in which human beings live. It is an approach that is focused on people and their opportunities and choices (UN Human Development, n.d.).

So, when all is said and done, we have reviewed over 150 years of library accountability. We are working to be able to demonstrate the value of the public library.

In an essay in *Library Journal,* "Outcomes, Impacts, and Indicators," Becker (2015a) notes,

> While deeply held values of our profession [democracy, intellectual freedom, love of reading] should guide our ethics and decision-making, we still have a need and an obligation to measure what outcomes we can and demonstrate our impact on the multitudes who benefit from public libraries in real and significant ways.

What Becker is suggesting is a manifestation of the capabilities approach. This may be realized through a number of current initiatives that will help us to make a case to our user communities to sustain and increase funding. They are more pragmatic than the human capabilities approach, but they have similar goals.[31]

After reviewing the history and recent means by which librarians tell the stories about the value of public libraries to their communities, we are able to identify the methods most helpful to us. We can also select from a variety of projects that will enable us to make the best case for the future of public libraries and the people they serve. How we frame what the library does matters. It shapes the public perception of the library and its services (Why Outcomes Matter, 2017).

Finally, the observation of Frances Stewart, Emeritus Professor of Development Economics at the University of Oxford, leave us with a larger consideration:

We all live embedded in social institutions—in the family, the neighbourhood, the nation. These and the social norms we face deeply affect the nature and quality of our daily life. In other words, we can't get away from society and retreat into a monadic existence of autonomous individuals. And if we did, we would be immeasurably impoverished. That being so, the study of and policy towards social institutions must form an essential component of our approach to human development.[32]

NOTES

1. At the 2016 Annual American Library Association conference, thousands of librarians met to discuss current issues and challenges including outcomes. If any one factor accounts for the success of the American public library, it may well be the dedication of librarians who take the time to participate in state and national meetings to analyze and refine library services, as they have done for nearly 200 years. We cannot thank these librarians enough for their dedicated commitment to meet and analyze strategies to improve library service.
2. Three major initiatives have taken place in recent years: The IMPACT Survey based at the University of Washington (Becker, 2015b); the Urban Libraries Council Edge Project (2015); and PLA's Project Outcome (2015).
3. PLA's Project Outcome creates webinars in partnership with the Edge and Impact Survey to support library assessment needs. These three field-driven tools help support libraries' various assessment needs: Edge, an online assessment that helps library leaders align library technology services to the needs of the community and communicate the library's value to community leaders; Project Outcome, a series of outcome-focused surveys about library programs, along with training, a portal for administering surveys, and an online data dashboard; and the Impact Survey, an online tool to help libraries better understand their communities and how people use their public technology resources and services. These are available on demand at the PLA website (www.ala.org/pla/onlinelearning/webinars/ondemand/assessment-evaluation).
4. See the Museum and Library Services Act of 2010, 20 U.S.C sec. 9108 (analysis of impact of museum and library services, policy research, analysis, data collection and dissemination) in SEC 210.
5. It was not until 1968 that the gathering of public library statistics was codified. Standardization in the United States is coordinated by the American National Standards Institute (ANSI; www.ansi.org). Over 175 entities are accredited by ANSI, each issuing American National Standards (ANSs). The entity most closely allied with libraries is the National Information Standards Organization (NISO; www.niso.org/home/),which was founded in 1939 and accredited by ANSI to identify, develop, maintain, and publish technical standards that manage information in the changing and ever more digital environment. NISO has issued many ANSs; those most notable for this discussion are Information Services and Use: Metrics and Statistics for Libraries and Information Providers—Data Dictionary (Z39.7), which was formerly called "Library Statistic." (National Information Standards Organization, 2013; Davis, D. M. 2004).
6. For a comprehensive summary see "The Federal-State Cooperative System for Public Library Data Chronology 1980-Current" (http://plsc.pbworks.com/f/LSCP1988-present.pdf).
7. In 1985 the NCES and the ALA conducted a pilot project in 15 states to assess the feasibility of a federal-state cooperative program for collecting public library data. The project was jointly funded by NCES and the U.S. Department of Education's former Library Programs (LP) office. In 1987, the project's final report recommended the development of a nationwide data collection system. The Hawkins-Stafford Elementary and Secondary School Improvement Amendments of

1988 (P.L. 100-297) charged NCES with developing a voluntary Federal-State Cooperative System (FSCS) for the annual collection of public library data. The NCES and the National Commission on Libraries and Information Science (NCLIS) formed a task force to carry out this mandate, and the FSCS was established in 1988. The 1988 NCES–NCLIS task force evolved into the FSCS Steering Committee. This committee has been integral to the design and administration of the survey. Its membership has included State Data Coordinators (SDCs), representatives of the Chief Officers of State Library Agencies (COSLA), the NCLIS, ALA, IMLS, the U.S. Census Bureau (the data collection agent), and NCES. With the transition of the collection from NCES to IMLS the steering committee was renamed the "Public Library Statistics Cooperative (PLSC)" (IMLS, 2014, p. 1). Mary Jo Lynch, director of ALA's Office for Research and Statistics from 1978 to 2003, was central to the establishment of the federal-state cooperative system for public library data and served on its steering committee for 20 years ("LPN Talks," 2004).

8. In 2015 the Library Statistics Working Group members included COSLA representatives from the Arkansas State Library, Oregon State Library, Minnesota State Library, Delaware Division of Libraries, and Kentucky Department for Libraries and Archives. State Data coordinators include representatives from the State Library of Louisiana, Wisconsin Department of Public Instruction, State Library and Archives of Florida, Carolina State Library, and the Arizona State Library, Archives and Public Records. Representatives also included members from the American Library Association's Office for Research and Statistics and from the Association of Research Libraries (Library Statistics Working Group Wikispace. 2014; http://lswg.wikispaces.com/Members).
9. Each state library collects data from every public library in its state, then reports to IMLS through a web portal. For example, the Library Research Service has posted the instructions for each public library in Colorado (*Colorado State Library: Public Library Annual Report Information and Help;* https://www.lrs.org/data-tools/public-libraries/public-library-annual-report-information-and-help/). The form the Colorado State Library used to gather are posted at https://www.lrs.org/wp-content/uploads/2013/01/PLAR_2015_Survey.pdf.
10. Until 2014 data were entered using WebPLUS into a database stored on a server at the Census Bureau for the IMLS (IMLS, 2016, pp. 22–25). For the FY2015 data collection, IMLS selected the American Institutes for Research (AIR) to collect the data for the PLS. This transition from the U.S. Census Bureau resulted in minimal changes in the PLS Web Portal2 interface and functionality. Changes that did occur between the FY2014 and FY2015 administrations are summarized in section 1.3 PLS, Web Portal Revisions. (Institute of Museum and Library Services. American Institutes for Research, 2016).
11. The Public Libraries in the United States Survey examines when, where, and how library services are changing to meet the needs of the public. These data, supplied annually by more than 97% of public libraries across the country, provide information that policymakers and practitioners can use to make informed decisions about the support and strategic management of libraries (www.imls.gov/research/pls_publications.aspx).
12. The Research Institute for Public Libraries (https://ripl.lrs.org/2016/) was launched in 2015 by the Colorado State Library and the Colorado Library Consortium. The Research Institute for Public Libraries is a singular event for public library leaders and others interested in public library data and evaluation. In this immersive, boot-camp-style event, participants learn practical, strategic methods of gathering, analyzing, and using data for planning, management, and communicating impact. Participants in the Institute will assess the needs of the local community; learn techniques for tracking public library data and using these data for planning, management, and demonstrating the library's worth; use data and stories to document the impact of the library; and align evaluation reports with existing initiatives such as Edge Benchmarks, Impact Survey, and Project Outcome.

13. The Public Library Data Service (PLDS) annual survey is conducted by Counting Opinions (SQUIRE) Ltd. on behalf of PLA. This survey of public libraries from the United States and Canada was collected in 2015 for the fiscal year 2014 (FY2014). (Reid, 2016).
14. For additional background see Harrington (1962); American Library Association, Committee on Economic Opportunity Programs (1969); Samek (2001); and McCook (2002).
15. Combined with working papers of the PLA's Goals, Guidelines, and Standards Committee (GGSC—previously called the Standards Committee), the goals feasibility and performance measures studies were key arguments in favor of community planning (PLA, Goals, Guidelines, and Standards Committee, 1973).
16. In 1975 the GGSC consolidated its working papers into "Goals and Guidelines for Community Library Service," for use while the PLA developed new tools to enable librarians to analyze, set objectives, make decisions, and evaluate achievements.
17. Pungitore's analysis of innovation is essential reading to understand the shift from standards to the planning model (1995: 92–94).
18. The Public Library Association revised its Statement of Principles in 1982, with reference to planning (PLA, Public Library Principles Task Force, 1982).
19. In her study of the profession's move from standards to the adoption of the PLDP, Pungitore (1995, p. 180) concluded that innovation can be facilitated and that public libraries can be "revitalized and reinvigorated" to assume a significant role.
20. The Public Library Association Results series is listed in chapter 3, note 16.
21. PLA made a clear distinction between the Planning and Role Setting for Public Libraries (PRSPL) model (which was introduced in 1980 and continued until 1995) and the New Planning for Results (NPFR) model, which began in 1996 and continued until 2015. The PRSPL model separated planning goals and service goals and indicated they could be developed separately. The NPFR approach was based on the premise that resource allocation decisions must be driven by the library's service priorities (McCook, 2011, pp. 86–88).
22. The Public Library Statistics Cooperative website provides links to each set of state standards. See http://plsc.pbworks.com/w/page/7422647/Public%20library%20standards%20by%20state.
23. In addition to state standards, the COSLA website links to long-range plans and state statistical data. See www.cosla.org/profiles/.
24. Hennen's American Public Library Ratings (HALPR) Index appeared in *American Libraries* from 1999 through 2010. When *Library Journal's* America's Star Libraries series began in 2009, there was much discussion about the two initiatives. The backstory on the development of these two comparative ratings methods provides insight into issues of statistical validity, robust data, and interpretation. The HALPR index was developed by Thomas J. Hennen Jr. In his assessment of the tenth anniversary edition, Hennen (2009) summarized the impact of the index and identified those libraries that had scored highly in all 10 years. Hennen's methodology has been questioned by Lance and Cox (2000), who use a bivariate correlation to demonstrate the lack of validity of the HAPLR. The Hennen ratings had broad visibility from 1999 to 2010.
25. See America's Star Libraries (2016) in the *Library Journal.* The series is based on data gathered and evaluated by Ray Lyons, an independent consultant and statistical programmer whose articles on library statistics and assessment have appeared in *Public Library Quarterly, Public Libraries,* and *Evidence Based Library and Information Practice.* He blogs on library statistics and assessment at libperformance.com. Keith Curry Lance is an independent consultant. He also consults with the Colorado-based RSL Research Group. In both capacities, he conducts research on libraries of all types for state library agencies, state library associations, and other library-related organizations (http://lj.libraryjournal.com/2016/11/managing-libraries/lj-index/class-of-2016/americas-star-libraries-2016-top-rated-libraries/).

26. See the IMLS website at https://www.imls.gov/issues/national-initiatives/national-medal-museum-and-library-service. The press release on the 2016 ceremony is posted at https://www.imls.gov/news-events/news-releases/first-lady-michelle-obama-honors-extraordinary-museums-libraries.
27. *Library Journal* features libraries and librarians among its honorees. http://lj.libraryjournal.com/awards/.
28. See PLA Awards (www.ala.org/pla/awards). For details on these state awards, see Connecticut Library Association, Excellence in Public Library Service Award (http://ctlibraryassociation.org/content.php?page=Awards__Scholarships___Grants); the Florida Library Association's Florida Library of the Year (www.flalib.org/awards.php#anchor3); and the Missouri Library Association, Missouri Library of the Year (http://molib.org/awards/missouri-library-of-the-year-award/).
29. The 2016 award is described at Urban Libraries Council. Innovations Initiative (www.urbanlibraries.org/2016-innovations-pages-522.php).
30. *The Journal of Human Development and Capabilities* is a resource that aims to stimulate innovative development thinking that is based on the premise that development is fundamentally about improving the well-being and agency of people by expanding the choices and opportunities they have.
31. The initiatives taking place today among public librarians that have a human capabilities orientation. For example, see the Aspen Institute's Dialogue on Public Libraries (www.aspeninstitute.org/policy-work/communications-society/our-work/dialogue-public-libraries); the Edge Initiative (www.libraryedge.org); Project Outcome (https://www.projectoutcome.org); the Research Institute for Public Libraries (https://ripl.lrs.org/wp-content/uploads/2015/10/ripl_flyer_2016.pdf); and the U.S. Impact Study (http://impact.ischool.uw.edu/us-public-library-study.html).
32. United Nations Development Programme. Human Development Report Office. Frances Stewart is Emeritus Professor of Development Economics at the University of Oxford. Her books include *Technology and Underdevelopment* (Macmillan, 1976) and *Planning to Meet Basic Needs* (Macmillan, 1985). She was a co-author of UNICEF's influential study Adjustment with a Human Face (OUP, 1987) and War and Underdevelopment (OUP, 2000). See Stewart (2013).

REFERENCES

American Library Association. (1933, November). Standards for public libraries. *ALA Bulletin, 27*, 513–514.

American Library Association. (1963). *Access to public libraries study.* Chicago, IL: American Library Association.

American Library Association, Committee on Economic Opportunity Programs. (1969). Library service to the disadvantaged: A study based on responses to questionnaires from public libraries serving populations over 15,000. Chicago, IL: American Library Association.

American Library Association, Public Libraries Division, Coordinating Committee on Revision of Public Library Standards. (1956). *Public library service: A guide to evaluation with minimum standards.* Chicago, IL: American Library Association.

Anthony, C. (2013). New measures for a new era. *Public Libraries, 52*(4), 5–6.

Anthony, C. (2014, May/June). Moving toward outcomes. *Public Libraries, 53,* 5–7.

Anthony, C. (2016). Project Outcome—Looking back, looking forward. *Public Libraries Online.* http://publiclibrariesonline.org/2016/01/project-outcome-looking-back-looking-forward/.

Balcom, K. M. (1986, June 15). To concentrate and strengthen: The promise of the public library development program. *Library Journal, 111,* 36–40. http://nces.ed.gov/pubs98/98310.pdf.

Becker, S. (2015a). Outcomes, impacts, and indicators. *Library Journal, 140*(15), 26–30.

Becker, S. (2015b). Impact survey. *Public Libraries, 54*(3), 35-37.

Blasingame, R., Jr., & Lynch, M. J. (1974). Design for diversity: Alternatives to standards for public libraries. *PLA Newsletter, 13,* 4-22.

Bryan, C. (2007). *Managing facilities for results: Optimizing space for services.* Chicago, IL: American Library Association.

Civic Impulse. (2016). H.R. 5—100th Congress: Augustus F. Hawkins-Robert T. Stafford Elementary and Secondary School Improvement Amendments of 1988. https://www.govtrack.us/congress/bills/100/hr5.

Chute, A. (2003). National center for education statistics library statistics program. In *The Bowker annual library and book trade almanac* (pp. 95-102). New York, NY: R. R. Bowker.

Davis, D. M. (2004). NISO standard Z39.7—The evolution to a data dictionary for library metrics and assessment methods. *Serials Review, 30*(1), 15-24.

De Prospo, E. R., Altman, E., & Beasley, K. (1973). *Performance measures for public libraries.* Chicago, IL: American Library Association.

Examine PLA's first project outcome annual report. (2017). *American Libraries, 48*(1/2), 17.

Fair, E. M. (1934). *Countywide library service.* Chicago, IL: American Library Association.

Garceau, O. (1949). *The public library in the political process: A report of the Public Library Inquiry.* New York, NY: Columbia University Press.

Goals and guidelines for community library service. (1975). *PLA Newsletter, 14,* 9-13.

Goldhor, H. (1983). U.S. public library statistics in series: A bibliography and subject index. In *Bowker Annual of Library and Book Trade Information* (28th ed.), pp. 327-335. New York, NY: R. R. Bowker.

Hamilton-Pennell, C. (2007, 2010). Public library standards: A review of standards and guidelines from the fifty states of the U.S. for the Colorado, Mississippi, and Hawaii state libraries. In *Mosaic Knowledge Works.* Chief Officers of State Library Agencies.

Harrington, M. (1962). *The other America: Poverty in the United States.* New York, NY: Macmillan.

Hennen, T. J., Jr. (2009). *HALPR 2009: 10th anniversary edition.* www.haplr-index.com/haplr_2009_10thAnniv_AmerLibrArticle.htm.

Hernon, P., Dugan, R. E., & Matthews, J. R. (2015). *Managing with data: Using ACRLMetrics and PLAmetrics.* Chicago, IL: ALA Editions.

Himmel, E., & Wilson, W. J., with the ReVision Committee of the Public Library Association. (1998). *Planning for results: A public library transformation process.* Chicago, IL: American Library Association.

Houghtaling, J. (2011). State standards and public libraries: An overview. *Current Studies in Librarianship, 31*(1), 37-53.

"IMLS and COSLA Announce Project to Develop Public Library Data and Outcomes Plan." (2017). *Library Administrator's Digest, 52,* 5-6.

Institute of Museum and Library Services. (2014). *Public libraries survey: Fiscal Year 2012.* www.imls.gov/research/public_libraries_in_the_us_fy_2012_report.aspx.

Institute of Museum and Library Services, American Institutes for Research. (2016). PLS Web Portal User's Guide. Version 1.4. Guide for Reporting Data for the Public Libraries Survey, FY2015 Using the Web Public Library Universe System Software. https://www.imls.gov/sites/default/files/pls_users_guide_fy2015_508.pdf.

Jewett, C. C. (1851). Report on the public libraries of the United States of America, January 1, 1850. In *Report of the Board of Regents of the Smithsonian Institution.* Washington, DC: Smithsonian Institution.

Joeckel, C. B. (1935). *The government of the American public library.* Chicago, IL: University of Chicago Press.

Joeckel, C. B. (1943). *Post-war standards for public libraries.* Chicago, IL: American Library Association.

Joeckel, C. B., & Winslow, A. (1948). A national plan for public library service. Chicago, IL: American Library Association.

Johnson, D. W. (1995). An evaluation of the public library development program. (Unpublished report) Public Library Association.

Leigh, R. D. (1950). *The public library in the United States: The general report of the Public Library Inquiry*. New York, NY: Columbia University Press.

Library Research Service. (2009). *National public library statistics*. www.lrs.org/public/national.php.

Library Services and Construction Act of 1964, PL 88-269, 20 USC §§ 351 et seq.

LPN talks with retiring ORS director Mary Jo Lynch. (2004, Winter). *Library Personnel News, 16*, 2–3.

Lyons, R., & Lance, K. (2014). America's libraries: The LJ index of public library service 2014. *Library Journal, 139*(18), 22–28.

Lyons, R., & Lance, K. C. (2016, November 1). America's Star Libraries, 2016: Top-Rated Library Journal. http://lj.libraryjournal.com/2016/11/managing-libraries/lj-index/class-of-2016/americas-star-libraries-2016-top-rated-libraries/.

Martin, A. B. (1972). *A strategy for public library change: Proposed public library goals—feasibility study*. Chicago, IL: American Library Association.

Martin, L. A. (1972, October). Standards for public libraries. *Library Trends, 21*, 164–177.

Mayo, D. (2005). *Technology for results: Developing service-based plans*. Chicago, IL: American Library Association.

Mayo, D., & Goodrich, J. (2002). *Staffing for results*. Chicago, IL: American Library Association.

Mayo, D., Nelson, S. S., & Public Library Association. (1999). *Wired for the future: Developing your library technology plan*. Chicago, IL: American Library Association.

McClure, C. R. (1987). *Planning and role setting for public libraries: A manual of options and procedures*. Chicago, IL: American Library Association.

McCook, K. (2002). Rocks in the whirlpool: Equity of access and the American Library Association. ERIC database, ED462981.

McCook, K. (2011). *Introduction to public librarianship* (2nd ed.). New York, NY: Neal-Schuman Publishers.

McCook, K. & Jones, M. A. (2002, Summer). Cultural heritage institutions and community building. *Reference and User Services Quarterly, 41*, 326–329.

Museum and Library Services Act of 2010 as stated in 20 U.S.C sec. 9108.

National Information Standards Organization (2013, March 26). Information services and use: Metrics and statistics for libraries and information providers—Data dictionary. www.niso.org/apps/group_public/download.php/11282/Z39-7-2013_metrics.pdf.

National Information Standards Organization. Information services and use: Metrics and statistics for libraries and information providers—Data dictionary. (2013). NISO Z39.7. http://z39-7.niso.org.

Nelson, S. (2001). *The new planning for results: A streamlined approach*. Chicago, IL: American Library Association.

Nelson, S. (2008). *Strategic planning for results*. Chicago, IL: American Library Association.

Nelson, S. (2009). *Implementing for results: Your strategic plan in action*. Chicago, IL: American Library Association.

Nelson, S., Altman, E., & Mayo, D. (2000). Managing your library's staff. In *Managing for results: Effective resource allocation for public libraries* (pp. 29–110). Chicago, IL: American Library Association.

Nelson, S. S., & Garcia, J. (2003). *Creating policies for results: From chaos to clarity*. Chicago, IL: American Library Association.

Nussbaum, M. C. (2011). *Creating capabilities: The human development approach*. Cambridge, MA: Belknap Press of Harvard University Press.

Palmour, V. E., Bellassi, M. C., & DeWath, N. V. (1980). *A planning process for public libraries*. Chicago, IL: American Library Association.

Parker, J. B. (2014). Measuring good. *Journal of Library Administration, 54*(8), 700–708.

Project Outcome: Year in review. (2016). https://www.projectoutcome.org/annual-report.

Public Library Association. (1967). *Minimum standards for public library systems, 1966*. Chicago, IL: American Library Association.

Public Library Association. (2015). *Project Outcome: Measuring the true impact of public libraries.* https://www.projectoutcome.org.

Public Library Association. (2016) *Project Outcome: An integral part of the planning process.* (Webinar.) www.ala.org/pla/onlinelearning/webinars/archive/projectoutcomeplanning.

Public Library Association, Goals, Guidelines and Standards Committee. (1973). Community library services: Working papers on goals and guidelines. *Library Journal, 96,* 2603-2609.

Public Library Association, Goals, Guidelines and Standards Committee. (1979). *The public library mission statement and its imperatives for service.* Chicago, IL: American Library Association.

Public Library Association, Public Library Data Service. (1992-present). *Statistical Report.* Chicago, IL: Public Library Association. http://cirss.lis.illinois.edu/Surveys/plds.html (Continues *Public library data service statistical report.* Chicago, IL: Public Library Association, 1988-1991).

Public Library Association, Public Library Principles Task Force. (1982, Fall). The public library: Democracy's resource, a statement of principles. *Public Libraries, 21,* 92.

Pungitore, V. L. (1995). *Innovation and the library: The adoption of new ideas in public libraries.* Westport, CT: Greenwood Press.

Raber, D. (1995, Fall). A conflict of cultures: Planning vs. tradition in public libraries. *RQ, 35,* 50-63.

Reid, I. (2015, March/April). The 2014 Public Library Data Service Statistical Report. *Public Libraries, 54,* 30-41.

Reid, I. (2016, May/June). The 2015 Public Library Data Service Statistical Report. *Public Libraries, 55,* 24-33.

Research Institute for Public Libraries. https://ripl.lrs.org/wp-content/uploads/2015/10/ripl_flyer_2016.pdf.

Rubin, R. J. (2005). *Demonstrating results: Using outcome measurement in your library.* Chicago, IL: ALA Editions.

Samek, T. (2001). *Intellectual freedom and social responsibility in American librarianship, 1967-1974.* Chicago, IL: American Library Association.

Schick, F. L. (1971). Library statistics: A century plus. *American Libraries, 2,* 727-741.

Shaughnessy, T. W. (1975). *An overview of the development of larger units of service and the central library concept.* Arlington, VA: ERIC Document Reproduction Service. ED 102 997.

Shepherd, B. (2000). Perspectives on outcome-based evaluation for libraries and museums. Washington, DC: Institute of Museum and Library Services. www.imls.gov/assets/1/AssetManager/PerspectivesOBE.pdf.

Sloan, T. (2012). What makes an award-winning public library successful? *Public Libraries, 51*(3), 30-47.

Smith, N. M. (1994, July/August). State library agency use of planning and role setting for public libraries and output measures for public libraries. *Public Libraries, 33,* 211-212.

Stewart, F. (1976). *Technology and underdevelopment.* London, United Kingdom: Macmillan.

Stewart, F. (1985). *Planning to meet basic needs.* London, United Kingdom: Macmillan.

Stewart, F. (2013) *Capabilities and human development: Beyond the individual—the critical role of social institutions and social competencies.* United Nations Development Programme. Human Development Report Office. Occasional Paper 2013/03. http://hdr.undp.org/sites/default/files/hdro_1303_stewart.pdf.

Stewart, F., Cornia, G. A., Jolly, R., & Stewart, F. (1987). *Adjustment with a human face: protecting the vulnerable and promoting growth.* Oxford, United Kingdom: Clarendon Press, 1987-1988.

Stewart, F., & Fitzgerald, V. (2000). *War and Underdevelopment: Country Experiences* (Vol. 2). Oxford University Press, USA.

Teasdale, R. (2015, May 28). Project Outcome launch: Seven surveys to measure impact. *Public Libraries Online.* http://publiclibrariesonline.org/2015/05/project-outcome-launch-seven-surveys-to-measure-impact/.

Thomas, F. (2016). Measuring the impact of public libraries. *Public Libraries, 55*(4), 5-6.

U. N. Human Development Programme. Human Development Report Office. Annual Reports. http://hdr.undp.org/en.

U.S. Department of the Interior, Bureau of Education. (1876). *Public libraries in the United States of America: Their history, condition, and management. Special report.* Champaign, IL: Government Printing Office. Reprint, as Monograph Series, no. 4.

Urban Libraries Council. (2015). Edge. www.urbanlibraries.org/edge-toolkit-pages-200.php; see also Edge Benchmarks 1.0. www.libraryedge.org/sites/default/files/Edge%20Benchmarks%20V1.pdf.

Why outcomes matter: An update on PLA's "Project Outcome." (2017, January). *Library Administrator's Digest,* 1.

Wiegand, W. A. (2015). *Part of our lives: A people's history of the American public library.* New York, NY: Oxford University Press.

Williams, R. V. (1991, Spring). The making of statistics of national scope on American libraries, 1836-1986: Purposes, problems, and issues. *Libraries and Culture, 26,* 464-485.

Williams, R. V., & McLean, M. K. (2008). *A bibliographical guide to a chronological record of statistics of national scope on libraries in the United States.* Columbia, SC: University of South Carolina, School of Library and Information Science.

Zweizig, D. L., & Rodger, E. J. (1982). *Output measures for public libraries.* Chicago, IL: American Library Association.

CHAPTER 5

"More and Better Libraries"*

Political, Legal, and Financial Aspects of the Public Library

> When library service is at last available at every crossroads throughout the land yours will be much of the glory.
>
> **—On the retirement of Julia Wright Merrill, ALA, Library Extension Division, February 4, 1946****

A successful public library requires a staff that can work effectively with all levels of government—local, state, and federal. The public library staff needs a clear understanding of the structure of political, economic, and social components in which the library operates and should engage with ideas that concern municipal policy makers. 2015's theme for the National League of Cities was the "Year of Connecting." The National Association of Counties' priorities were building healthy, vibrant, safe, and fiscally resilient counties. These are all ideas that resonate strongly in library practice and are often reflected in mission statements and planning documents (National League of Cities, 2015; National Association of Counties, 2015).

The necessity of political acumen is not new. In 1949, Oliver Garceau wrote in *The Public Library in the Political Process,* a volume of the mid-twentieth-century assessment, the Public Library Inquiry, that "Public librarians are inescapably a part of government and involved in 'politics'" (p. 239). This book remains a foundational assessment of how the public librarian must operate in a political environment.

How is the public library legally located in its community and how did the public library become a tax-supported essential service? We have seen the philosophical and historical reasons that libraries were established, but what of the process of creating a tax base and ensuring ongoing funding? Funding and political survival are essential to sustainabil-

* "More and Better Libraries" was the slogan of the Citizen's Library Movement of Louisiana, which was formed April 24, 1937, in Shreveport. The objectives were "the creation of interest throughout the state in libraries; state aid for existing libraries; and the promotion of the general welfare of all Louisiana libraries" (Culver & Gittinger, 1954, p. 20).

** See "An Open Letter to Julia Wright Merrill" in the March 1946 *Library Journal.* Merrill was a national leader in the extension of public library service. The Wisconsin Library Hall of Fame provides more information (http://heritage.wisconsinlibraries.org/entry/julia_wright_merrill_18811961).

ity. If we believe in the mission of the public library, we must learn how the political, legal, and financial aspects fit together to provide an effective basis for operation.

> ▶ **FACT**
>
> President Jimmy Carter's first public position was as the trustee of the Sumter County Library in Georgia.*
>
> ---
>
> *Jimmy Carter. White House Conference on Libraries and Information Services. Remarks at a Meeting of the Conference. November 16, 1979. www.presidency.ucsb.edu/ws/?pid=31696.

THE LIBRARY IN THE GOVERNMENT

A logical governing structure and a secure funding base are essential components for the library's survival within its larger governing legal entity—town, city, county, district, or multijurisdictional. Public libraries are a component of local governments in various configurations. In the United States, there are 9,091 public library administrative units with 16,545 stationary service outlets and 669 bookmobiles (IMLS, 2016, table 3). The legal basis of each library refers to the type of local government structure within which the library functions.

Additionally, the public library may be part of a multitype cooperative or regional entity for sharing resources. The local library has fiscal and legal connection to the state library agency of its state. And finally, the federal government plays a role by channeling funds through state library agencies to local libraries as well as implementing laws that affect public libraries, such as Universal Service and the E-Rate program.[1] Then there are opportunities for libraries to work on programs that can include them such as the Workforce Innovation and Opportunity Act.[2]

Legal Basis of Libraries Today

In the United States today, the majority of public libraries (as administrative units) are part of municipalities by legal basis. But it is often the case that the majority of people are served by the county or other larger units of service such as multicounty districts. In Florida, for example, county libraries serve over 15,000,000 people, municipal libraries 2,388,000, and others are served by multicounty or cooperative agreements.[3] So, even though municipal libraries may outnumber libraries under other legal bases, the number of people served in county or cooperative structures is larger.

According to IMLS (2016) here is the current distribution of libraries by legal basis:[4]

Municipal government. An organized local government authorized in a state's constitution and statutes and established to provide general government for a specific concentration of population in a defined area (53.1%).

County/Parish. An organized local government authorized in a state's constitution and statutes and established to provide general government (10.1%).

City/County. A multi-jurisdictional entity that is operated jointly by a county and a city (1%).

Multi-jurisdictional. A public library that is operated jointly by two or more units of local government under an intergovernmental agreement (3.3%).

Nonprofit association or agency libraries. A public library that is privately controlled but meets the statutory definition of a public library in a given state (13.8%).

School district. A public library that is under the legal basis of a school district (1.9%).
Library district. A local entity other than a county, municipality, township, or school district that is authorized by state law to establish and operate a public library (15.3%).
Other. Includes libraries under the legal basis of Native American Tribal Government and combined public/school libraries (1.5%).

As we see from figure 5.1, the type of legal basis varies by state. Indiana is 100% based on library districts; Maryland mostly county-based (95.8%); Georgia majority multi-jurisdictional (55.6%); and Iowa nearly completely municipal (99.1%). Each of these different legal bases presents a different set of challenges to the community to gain and maintain support. A county-wide or district basis requires representation from a broader geographic area than a defined municipality. In many cases, each branch library will have its own Friends group of supporters.

Historical Development of the Legal Basis of the Public Library

There were no models of governance when the first public libraries were established in the 1850s (Hall, 1992). The Board of Trustee structure of oversight used by the Boston Public Library, which prevails today, was developed in a piecemeal fashion with the municipality or even a school district as basis of organization.

In his 1935 treatise *Government of the American Public Library*, Joeckel described how the library movement in America paralleled the development of municipal government. From 1850 to 1890 boards (of trustees, of directors, of education) were the primary citizen mechanism that exercised stewardship over functions, services, and finances. Communities often chose this structure for public library oversight.

State library laws that enabled taxation and delineated responsibilities of trustees began to be passed in the second half of the nineteenth century. These took the form of short laws giving cities and towns great latitude, as well as long laws, like those enacted in Illinois in 1871 that detailed specific mill taxes for library purposes.[5]

When state library administrative agencies were established, "home rule" municipalities and commission government were encouraged by state library agencies to extend development of new libraries to unserved areas.[6] The Library Extension Board of ALA, established in 1925 by the ALA council, was created because ALA believed that providing adequate library service to the general public was an indispensable part of a national program of education. It was the Library Extension Board's responsibility to work for complete coverage of the United States with public library service by:

- developing a statewide systems of public libraries organized in large units with resources adequate for service throughout their areas
- strengthening responsibility and leadership through state library agencies, grants, and legislation for library development
- cooperating with the many national, regional, and state educational and social agencies, whose programs include, or might well include, library service, and with library trustee organizations and citizens' library committees
- promoting coordination, on national and state levels, purposes, and activities of other library agencies and groups with similar objectives

		Type of legal basis[1]								
State	Number of Public Libraries	Municipal government[2]	County/ parish[3]	City/ county[4]	Multi-jurisdictional[5]	Nonprofiy association or agency libraries[6]	School district[7]	Library district[8]	Other[9]	Response rate[10]
Alabama	218	76.1	7.8	0.5	15.6	0	0	0	0	100.0
Alaska	79	41.8	19.0	0	8.9	21.5	0	0	8.9	100.0
Arizona	90	51.1	7.8	10.0	1.1	6.7	0	3.3	20.0	100.0
Arkansas	58	25.9	41.4	1.7	27.6	0	0	0	3.4	100.0
California	184	64.7	23.9	2.2	2.7	0	1.6	4.9	0	100.0
Colorado	113	33.6	10.6	0	6.2	0	0.9	48.7	0	100.0
Connecticut	182	56.0	0	0	0	44.0	0	0	0	100.0
Delaware	21	14.3	28.6	4.8	0	0	0	52.4	0	100.0
District of Columbia	1	100.0	0	0	0	0	0	0	0	100.0
Florida	82	42.7	39.0	1.2	14.6	0	0	2.4	0	100.0
Georgia	63	0	44.4	0	55.6	0	0	0	0	100.0
Hawaii	1	0	0	0	0	0	0	0	100.0	100.0
Idaho	102	48.0	0	0	0	0	0	52.0	0	100.0
Illinois	623	48.0	0	0	0	0	0	52.0	0	100.0
Indiana	237	0	0	0	0	0	0	100.0	0	100.0
Iowa	534	99.1	0.6	0	0	0	0	0	0.4	100.0
Kansas	318	91.2	4.4	0	0.9	0	0	2.8	0.6	100.0
Kentucky	119	0	10.9	0	0.8	0	0	88.2	0	100.0
Louisiana	68	5.9	88.2	1.5	2.9	0	1.5	0	0	100.0
Maine	228	39.9	0	0	0	60.1	0	0	0	100.0
Maryland	24	4.2	95.8	0	0	0	0	0	0	100.0
Massachusetts	368	93.2	0	0	0.3	6.5	0	0	0	100.0

FIGURE 5.1 Percentage Distribution of Public Libraries by Type of Legal Basis and State: Fiscal Year 2014 [CONTINUED ON FOLLOWING PAGE]

		Type of legal basis[1]								
State	Number of Public Libraries	Municipal government[2]	County/ parish[3]	City/ county[4]	Multi-jurisdictional[5]	Nonprofiy association or agency libraries[6]	School district[7]	Library district[8]	Other[9]	Response rate[10]
Michigan	388	50.5	4.4	0	0	0	4.1	41.0	0	100.0
Minnesota	137	79.6	10.2	2.9	7.3	0	0	0	0	100.0
Mississippi	52	3.8	38.5	23.1	32.7	1.9	0	0	0	100.0
Missouri	149	9.4	0	0	0	0	0	90.6	0	100.0
Montana	82	34.1	32.9	15.9	13.4	0	0	3.7	0	100.0
Nebraska	263	95.8	3.8	0	0.4	0	0	0	0	100.0
Nevada	21	0	52.4	0	0	0	0	42.9	4.8	100.0
New Hamp-shire	219	95.9	0	0	0	3.2	0.9	0	0	100.0
New Jersey	281	80.4	5.0	0	2.1	12.5	0	0	0	100.0
New Mexico	87	65.5	1.1	2.3	0	9.2	0	0	21.8	100.0
New York	756	26.1	0.8	0	0	47.0	0.1	25.5	0.5	100.0
North Carolina	80	13.8	60.0	3.8	17.5	2.5	0	0	2.5	100.0
North Dakota	73	61.6	11.0	11.0	16.4	0	0	0	0	100.0
Ohio	251	8.8	23.5	0	0	7.6	59.0	0.4	0.8	100.0
Oklahoma	117	88.0	5.1	0.9	6.0	0	0	0	0	100.0
Oregon	129	58.1	10.1	0	0	2.3	2.3	27.1	0	100.0
Pennsylvania	455	0	0.2	0	0	85.5	0	0	14.3	100.0
Rhode Island	48	50.0	0	0	0	50.0	0	0	0	100.0
South Carolina	42	2.4	92.9	0	4.8	0	0	0	0	100.0
South Dakota	112	69.6	10.7	0.9	14.3	0.9	0	0	3.6	100.0
Tennessee	186	56.5	40.3	3.2	0	0	0	0	0	100.0
Texas	548	58.2	19.7	2.0	2.2	15.1	0	2.6	0.2	100.0

FIGURE 5.1 [CONTINUED ON FOLLOWING PAGE]

SOURCE: Institute of Museum and Library Services, Public Libraries Survey, Fiscal Year 2014. https://www.imls.gov/sites/default/files/fy2014_pls_tables.pdf.

FIGURE 5.1 [CONTINUED]

		Type of legal basis[1]								
State	Number of Public Libraries	Municipal government[2]	County/ parish[3]	City/ county[4]	Multi-jurisdictional[5]	Nonprofiy association or agency libraries[6]	School district[7]	Library district[8]	Other[9]	Response rate[10]
Utah	72	62.5	34.7	2.8	0	0	0	0	0	100.0
Vermont	155	58.1	0	0	5.8	35.5	0	0.6	0	100.0
Virginia	91	25.3	40.7	0	24.2	9.9	0	0	0	100.0
Washington	62	56.5	1.6	0	0	0	0	41.9	0	100.0
West Virginia	97	47.4	34.0	3.1	15.5	0	0	0	0	100.0
Wisconsin	381	89.2	2.1	0.8	6.6	0	0.3	0	1.0	100.0
Wyoming	23	0	100.0	0	0	0	0	0	0	100.0
Outlying areas										
American Samoa	1	0	0	0	0	0	0	100.0	0	100.0
Guam	1	100.0	0	0	0	0	0	0	0	100.0
Total[11]	9,070	53.1	10.1	1.0	3.3	13.8	1.9	15.3	1.5	100.0

1. Type of legal basis refers to the type of local government structure within which the library functions.
2. An organized local government authorized in a state's constitution and statutes and established to provide general government for a specific concentration of population in a defined area.
3. An organized local government authorized in a state's constitution and statutes and established to provide general government.
4. A multi-jurisdictional entity that is operated jointly by a county and a city.
5. A public library that is operated jointly by two or more units of local government under an intergovernmental agreement.
6. A public library that is privately controlled but meets the statutory definition of a public library in a given state.
7. A public library that is under the legal basis of a school district.
8. A local entity other than a county, municipality, township, or school district that is authorized by state law to establish and operate a public library.
9. This includes libraries under the legal basis of Native American Tribal Government and combined public/school libraries.
10. Response rate is calculated as the number of libraries that reported type of legal basis, divided by the total number of libraries in the survey frame. For item(s) with response rates below 100 percent, data for nonrespondents were imputed. Data were not imputed for the outlying areas.
11. Total includes the 50 states and the District of Columbia but excludes outlying areas and libraries that do not meet the FSCS Public Library Definition.

NOTE: Detail may not sum to totals because of rounding. Data were not reported by the following outlying areas (Northern Marianas and Virgin Islands). Missing data were not imputed for nonresponding outlying areas.

- encouraging experimentation with various types of organization and service in different sections of the country.[7]

The story of library development in each state has a cast of hundreds of civilians working in their own communities to forge library services. For instance, Jumonville's (2013) detailed and scholarly narrative described the quiet epic unfolding, through floods and depressions and unpaved roads, the creation and success of the Louisiana Library Commission through the efforts of small-town attorney J. O. Modisette, who chaired the Commission and advocated for library development through the Citizens Library Movement (Culver and. Gittinger, 1954).

> ▶ **TASK**
>
> Find out how your public library is funded. Is it municipal? Multi-jurisdictional? Is your public library part of a regional consortium?

By 1934 most states had taken responsibility for extending public library services (Wachtel, 1933).

It is noteworthy that although municipal libraries account for the majority of legal entities, county services serve far more people. Ohio, Maryland, Wisconsin, and California were among the first states to provide legal means for a tax base set by a larger unit than a city or town.

County library service in California demonstrates the historical progress to a county rather than municipal basis for public library service to the majority of people. Ray Held's *The Rise of the Public Library in California* (1973) provides a thorough analysis of the county as a legal basis for service in a state that has been an example of innovative library service.

Economies of scale based on larger units of service addressed the needs of regions where municipal or even county organization did not offer sufficient funding. These include library districts authorized by state law to provide library service and multi-jurisdictional libraries.[8]

Library Laws and Legislation

The American Library Association published *Library Law and Legislation in the United States* focusing on the three basic areas of law that relate to libraries—constitutional, statutory, and administrative (Ladenson, 1970, 1982). Today the library legislation for each state is available online at the COSLA (Chief Officers of State Library Agencies) website (COSLA Member Profiles, n.d.). This site provides a profile of each state library agency including the current website and links to the legislation for libraries currently in force for the state.[9]

For instance, the Code of Virginia states:

> **§ 42.1-33. Power of local governments to establish and support libraries.**
> The governing body of any city, county or town shall have the power to establish a free public library for the use and benefit of its residents. The governing body shall provide sufficient support for the operation of the library by levying a tax therefor, either by special levy or as a fund of the general levy of the city, county or town. The word "support" as used in this chapter shall include but is not limited to, purchase of land for library buildings, purchase or erection of buildings for library purposes, purchase of library books, materials and equipment, compensation of library personnel, and all maintenance expenses for library property and equipment. Funds appropriated or contributed for public library purposes shall constitute a separate fund and shall not be used for any but public library purposes. (Code of VA, chapter 2)

The legislation passed in each state relating to libraries varies, but a topical list of the sections of the laws of Massachusetts—one of the oldest state library administrative agencies—gives us an idea of the scope of legislation (see figure 5.2).

Commonwealth of Massachusetts, General Laws, Chapter 78: Libraries

- Section 1 Existing corporations
- Section 2 Organization of county law libraries
- Section 3 Use by residents of county
- Section 4 Source of funds
- Section 5 Right to receive legislative documents
- Section 6 Right to receive other books and documents
- Section 7 Establishment by cities and towns; records
- Section 8 Use of facilities by non-residents
- Section 9 Return of unwanted state publications
- Section 10 Town libraries; selection of trustees and officers
- Section 11 Board of trustees; powers and duties
- Section 12 Annual report of trustees
- Section 13 Applicability of sections relating to trustees
- Section 14 Board of library commissioners; members; appointment; term; by-laws; reimbursement; officers; staff
- Section 15 Duties relating to management and maintenance of libraries
- Section 16 to 18 Repealed, 1960, 429, Sec. 5
- Section 19P Powers, duties and status of board
- Section 19A State aid; determination
- Section 19B State aid; annual reports by libraries; requisites for aid
- Section 19C Regional public library service; annual appropriation
- Section 19D Regional public library service; council of members
- Section 19E Library media services; comprehensive statewide program; funds; standards
- Section 19F Regional public library service; arrangement for delivery and retrieval of materials or services
- Section 19G State assistance for public library projects
- Section 19H Definitions
- Section 19I Application for and distribution of funds
- Section 19J Allocation of funds; priorities
- Section 19K Gifts and grants
- Section 19L Massachusetts library and information network

FIGURE 5.2 Commonwealth of Massachusetts, General Laws, Chapter 78: Libraries

[CONTINUED ON FOLLOWING PAGE]

SOURCE: Commonwealth of Massachusetts. Title XII. Education, Chapter 78. Libraries. https://malegislature.gov/Laws/GeneralLaws/PartI/TitleXII/Chapter78.

FIGURE 5.2 [CONTINUED]

- Section 19M Statewide advisory council on cooperative library programs
- Section 19N Rules and regulations
- Section 20 Librarians; appointment; examination; registration
- Section 21 Inapplicability of certain sections to cities
- Section 22 Certification of librarians
- Section 23 Board meetings; quorum
- Section 24 Definitions applicable to Secs. 22 to 31
- Section 25 Rules and regulations
- Section 26 Repealed, 1977, 565, Sec. 6
- Section 27 Clerical assistance, etc.; expenditures
- Section 28 Duties of board
- Section 29 Librarians; qualifications
- Section 30 Fees
- Section 31 Status of existing librarians; certificates
- Section 32 Library staff members; leaves of absence for study or research
- Section 33 Policy for selection and use of library materials and facilities
- Section 34 Employment contracts for library employees

A student of public library law can have an enjoyable time reading and reviewing the statutes of each state.[10] These statutes reflect each state's particular philosophy and embed library values in the legislation that oversees the life of the public library in the state. Collaboration among local governments also takes place with state regulation. For instance, Wisconsin has a particularly interesting set of standards relating to organization of library systems that provides for regulations regarding single-county federated public library system, a multicounty federated public library system, or a single-county consolidated public library system.[11]

Local Ordinances and Cooperatives

Home rule is the right to local self-government, including powers to regulate for protection of public health, safety, morals, and welfare; to license; to tax; and to incur debt.[12] Powers granted under home rule vary in each state by government functions and the ability of local governments to raise taxes or impose regulations.[13] Some municipalities and counties have passed local ordinances relating to library governance.

A few examples of public library regulations give an idea of specific instances of local ordinances:[14]

- Keokuk, Iowa. Keokuk Municipal Code. Chapter 2.85: Board of Library Trustees.2.85.010. The purpose of this chapter is to provide for the creation and appointment of a city library board of trustees, and to specify that board's powers and duties (Ord. 1177 § 1, 1975).
- Boise, Idaho. The Boise City Code, Chapter 2, Section 4, specifically outlines the ordinances governing the Boise Public Library. All members of the

board are appointed by the Mayor and approved by the Council. Ordinance number 5942, passed by Boise City Council on September 28, 1999, empowers the Mayor to appoint a youth member to Boise City Department Boards as a nonvoting member.

- Oxnard, California. This ordinance protects the rights of library customers, staff and volunteers. They have at least the following rights: (A) To use library buildings, materials and services without being unreasonably disturbed or impeded by others; (B) To use and work in library buildings that are safe, secure, sanitary, and attractive; and (C) To use and work with library materials and equipment, which are accessible and in good condition in a quiet and orderly atmosphere conducive to every customer's exercise of his or her right to receive and read recorded communication.

Laws and legislation that support multitype library cooperation enable collaborative work between local governments with state regulation. See, for example, the Massachusetts Regulations for Regional Library Systems, which establishes minimum eligibility standards for regional reference and research centers relating to strength, accessibility, and use of resources, along with level of performance.[15] Another example is Nebraska, which organizes multitype regional library systems as nonprofit corporations to foster and conduct regional cooperative library programs and services (Nebraska Library Commission, 2011). One of the best-documented case studies of multitype collaboration is that of the regional library systems of Illinois, which are well-known for advocacy and cooperation (Byrnes, 2005).

New collaborations, such as the Bridges Library System of Wisconsin, which is composed of the Waukesha County Federated Library System and the Jefferson County Libraries, set a precedent for future library system reinvention across the state. The system was awarded a 2016 achievement award by the National Association of Counties (Building Bridges: The Creation of a New Library System, 2016).

STATE LIBRARY ADMINISTRATIVE AGENCIES AND THE INSTITUTE OF MUSEUM AND LIBRARY SERVICES

State library administrative agencies (SLAA), under various names and in various departments of state governments, are the connection between federal agencies and local public libraries.[16] SLAAs are official agencies charged by law with the extension and development of library services. A directory of state library agencies is at the website of the Chief Officers of State Library Agencies (www.COSLA.com). The sample list below demonstrates the variety of names as well as the different organizational location in the government of different states.[17]

- Georgia Public Library Service—Unit of the Board of Regents, University System of Georgia
- Kentucky Department for Libraries and Archives—Agency of the Education and Workforce Development Cabinet
- Washington State Library—Secretary of State
- Wisconsin Division for Libraries and Technology—Department of Public Instruction
- Wyoming State Library—Department of Administration and Information

State library agencies provide leadership, continuing education, and support in library development. In a 2013 special issue of the journal *Information and Culture,* Martin and Lear note:

> Every state in this country has a state library agency, and yet these institutions are among the least studied and least understood agencies in the library constellation. While library education programs offer multiple courses on school, public, academic, and special libraries, not one offers a course on state libraries. Most practicing librarians are only vaguely aware of their state library, and the historical literature on state libraries is scant. Yet state libraries are extremely important, if for no other reason than that they administer the federal funds directed to each state under the Library Services and Technology Act (LSTA, n.d.).

As we have seen, state library administrative agencies were instrumental in extending library services throughout America. The most recent survey on the status of state library administrative agencies by IMLS notes that "an SLAA is the official agency of a state that is charged by state law with the extension and the development of public library services throughout the state and has adequate authority under state law to administer state plans in accordance with the provisions of LSTA" (Swan et al., 2014). Once national federal legislation was passed in 1956, each state was required to submit a state plan. Federal funds have been tied to this requirement since 1956 as part of the Library Services Act and the subsequent legislation, the Library Services and Construction Act. This continues today as a requirement of the Library Services and Technology Act.

The Museum and Library Services Act (MLSA) of 1996 established the Institute of Museum and Library Services by combining the Institute of Museum Services and the Library Programs Office, which had been part of the Department of Education since 1956. Today the federal legislation that provides funding to libraries is the Museum and Library Services Act of 2010. The Library Services and Technology Act (LSTA), Chapter 72 of Title 20 of the U.S. Code, is specific to libraries. The purposes of the Act are essential for today's public librarians to recognize the potential and challenges posed by collaboration.

So much of the context of American public libraries is shaped by the LSTA. Its purposes overarch state long-range plans and drive federal funding, which in turn affects state aid in each state. A review of LSTA purposes puts current library priorities in perspective.

THE LIBRARY SERVICES AND TECHNOLOGY ACT[18]

The Fiscal Year 2017 Appropriations Request to the United States Congress from IMLS provides an overview of the work that the LSTA will accomplish in years to come.

> **§9121. Purpose**
>
> It is the purpose of this subchapter—
>
> (1) to enhance coordination among Federal programs that relate to library and information services;
>
> (2) to promote continuous improvement in library services in all types of libraries in order to better serve the people of the United States;
>
> (3) to facilitate access to resources in all types of libraries for the purpose of cultivating an educated and informed citizenry;

(4) to encourage resource sharing among all types of libraries for the purpose of achieving economical and efficient delivery of library services to the public;

(5) to promote literacy, education, and lifelong learning and to enhance and expand the services and resources provided by libraries, including those services and resources relating to workforce development, 21st century skills, and digital literacy skills;

(6) to enhance the skills of the current library workforce and to recruit future professionals to the field of library and information services;

(7) to ensure the preservation of knowledge and library collections in all formats and to enable libraries to serve their communities during disasters;

(8) to enhance the role of libraries within the information infrastructure of the United States in order to support research, education, and innovation; and

(9) to promote library services that provide users with access to information through national, State, local, regional, and international collaborations and networks.[19]

▶ FACT

In 2016 the total distribution of federal monies to the states as part of the LSTA was over $150,000,000.*

*IMLS, https://www.imls.gov/grants/grants-states.

Grants to States Programs

The LSTA authorizes the IMLS to administer several grant programs. The Grants to States Program is the largest source of federal funding support for library services in the United States. The program uses a population-based formula to distribute funds among the states through State Library Administrative Agencies. Each year, over 2,500 "Grants to States" projects support the purposes and priorities outlined in the LSTA. These include:

- expanding services for learning and access to information and educational resources in a variety of formats, in all types of libraries, and for individuals of all ages to support needs for education, lifelong learning, workforce development, and digital literacy skills
- establishing or enhancing electronic and other linkages to improve quality and access to library and information services
- developing public and private partnerships with other agencies and community-based organizations
- targeting library services to individuals of diverse geographic, cultural, and socioeconomic backgrounds, and to individuals with limited functional literacy or information skills
- targeting library and information services to persons having difficulty using a library and to underserved urban and rural communities
- developing library services that provide all users access to information through local, state, regional, national, and international collaborations and networks ("LSTA Grants," n.d.)

Funds may be used to support statewide initiatives and services. Partnerships with community organizations are encouraged, such as computer instruction, homework centers, summer reading programs, digitization of special collections, access to e-books and adaptive technology, bookmobile service, and development of outreach programs to the underserved.[20] Figure 5.3 details how the Grants to States program allocates a base amount to

State	FY 2012	FY 2013	FY 2014	FY 2015	FY 2016	FY 2017 Request
AL	$2,501,154	$2,416,705	$2,499,013	$2,476,238	$2,496,884	$2,457,603
AK	$952,947	$941,340	$955,925	$952,890	$956,117	$950,147
AZ	$3,250,835	$3,024,120	$3,152,086	$3,173,382	$3,233,171	$3,177,971
AR	$1,800,586	$1,742,394	$1,792,501	$1,778,761	$1,793,619	$1,769,542
CA	$15,029,503	$14,309,664	$15,030,377	$15,052,678	$15,317,151	$15,000,691
CO	$2,641,949	$2,530,270	$2,636,913	$2,663,845	$2,720,339	$2,676,226
CT	$2,038,047	$1,974,810	$2,034,387	$2,012,231	$2,022,715	$1,993,685
DE	$1,023,258	$1,008,026	$1,025,955	$1,026,557	$1,033,707	$1,026,059
FL	$7,871,982	$7,571,343	$7,967,170	$8,048,596	$8,259,897	$8,096,017
GA	$4,495,213	$4,229,250	$4,422,103	$4,420,116	$4,499,572	$4,416,992
HI	$1,159,084	$1,177,141	$1,205,222	$1,205,813	$1,215,308	$1,203,736
ID	$1,280,599	$1,253,142	$1,281,957	$1,285,415	$1,298,817	$1,285,438
IL	$5,664,245	$5,333,615	$5,536,935	$5,451,043	$5,488,648	$5,384,684
IN	$3,161,761	$3,036,565	$3,146,080	$3,123,514	$3,155,251	$3,101,735
IA	$1,844,037	$1,787,353	$1,839,676	$1,830,898	$1,848,098	$1,822,843
KS	$1,773,974	$1,718,260	$1,768,651	$1,755,667	$1,768,730	$1,745,191
KY	$2,350,899	$2,259,990	$2,332,425	$2,314,771	$2,334,644	$2,298,870
LA	$2,424,055	$2,334,293	$2,415,973	$2,117,896	$1,907,797	$2,388,732
ME	$1,185,547	$1,160,282	$1,181,411	$1,172,672	$1,177,066	$1,166,320
MD	$2,889,137	$2,787,551	$2,899,835	$2,893,697	$2,863,959	$2,877,374
MA	$3,233,374	$3,062,100	$3,114,756	$3,178,539	$3,220,591	$3,165,663
MI	$4,504,022	$4,251,300	$4,328,074	$4,350,678	$4,390,280	$4,310,063
MN	$2,717,086	$2,612,740	$2,709,174	$2,701,369	$2,732,686	$2,688,306
MS	$1,819,928	$1,757,051	$1,806,004	$1,789,025	$1,798,902	$1,774,711

FIGURE 5.3 State Allotments: Fiscal Year 2012 to 2017 [CONTINUED ON FOLLOWING PAGE]

SOURCE: IMLS, Fiscal Year 2017 Appropriations Request to the United States Congress. Grants to State Program, Table 2: State Allotments for FYs 2012–2017. https://www.imls.gov/sites/default/files/publications/documents/fy17cj_0.pdf.

State	FY 2012	FY 2013	FY 2014	FY 2015	FY 2016	FY 2017 Request
MO	$2,994,821	$2,853,508	$2,951,676	$2,925,990	$2,954,825	$2,905,643
MT	$1,057,408	$1,040,956	$1,059,170	$1,059,140	$1,066,243	$1,057,893
NE	$1,377,353	$1,346,312	$1,299,115	$1,376,920	$1,389,029	$1,373,700
NV	$1,702,212	$1,664,773	$1,720,752	$1,731,619	$1,760,954	$1,737,583
NH	$1,189,626	$1,156,668	$1,178,215	$1,171,459	$1,177,545	$1,166,788
NJ	$4,042,569	$3,869,793	$4,023,991	$3,990,753	$4,029,608	$3,957,188
NM	$1,463,144	$1,432,947	$1,466,728	$1,452,508	$1,459,670	$1,422,814
NY	$8,146,018	$7,718,754	$7,632,818	$7,929,546	$8,082,104	$7,922,067
NC	$4,322,143	$4,171,823	$4,173,865	$4,363,304	$4,229,540	$4,354,046
ND	$931,737	$927,315	$943,921	$953,909	$963,032	$956,914
OH	$5,120,439	$4,854,737	$5,034,831	$4,974,547	$5,022,527	$4,928,640
OK	$2,114,098	$2,051,036	$2,119,065	$2,116,453	$2,073,540	$2,110,919
OR	$2,164,574	$2,080,092	$2,150,954	$2,150,600	$2,186,528	$2,153,956
PA	$5,544,252	$5,287,918	$5,494,791	$5,416,459	$5,467,151	$5,363,652
RI	$1,086,948	$1,060,158	$1,076,202	$1,070,842	$1,074,974	$1,066,435
SC	$2,450,059	$2,372,043	$2,461,931	$2,469,980	$2,510,782	$2,471,200
SD	$995,771	$977,994	$994,366	$996,021	$1,001,001	$994,061
TN	$3,120,490	$2,995,498	$3,115,490	$3,105,919	$3,148,004	$3,094,645
TX	$10,388,436	$9,964,148	$10,510,319	$10,665,018	$10,951,336	$10,729,266
UT	$1,769,981	$1,698,728	$1,757,101	$1,770,068	$1,800,243	$1,776,023
VT	$919,668	$906,522	$916,150	$912,082	$914,092	$909,031
VA	$3,741,963	$3,607,790	$3,693,415	$3,764,107	$3,671,769	$3,746,824
WA	$3,277,624	$3,149,790	$3,281,761	$3,295,633	$3,262,304	$3,303,192
WV	$1,382,914	$1,350,913	$1,379,918	$1,365,372	$1,358,725	$1,354,653
WI	$2,862,663	$2,745,416	$2,840,170	$2,663,262	$2,670,703	$2,791,379

FIGURE 5.3 [CONTINUED ON FOLLOWING PAGE]

FIGURE 5.3 [CONTINUED]

State	FY 2012	FY 2013	FY 2014	FY 2015	FY 2016	FY 2017 Request
WY	$890,868	$885,450	$897,440	$896,374	$899,159	$894,422
DC	$915,107	$903,472	$918,531	$924,058	$931,362	$925,927
Puerto Rico	$2,140,076	$2,020,366	$2,038,457	$1,928,368	$1,564,119	$1,950,990
American Samoa	$81,378	$80,076	$80,642	$80,129	$80,264	$79,826
Northern Marianas	$80,748	$79,484	$79,303	$79,389	$79,993	$79,560
Guam	$121,361	$117,625	$120,499	$119,926	$120,853	$119,537
U.S. Virgin Islands	$100,971	$98,477	$99,510	$98,364	98,496	$97,663
9131(b) (3)(C) Poolz	$254,658	$250,113	$254,300	$253,590	$254,576	$252,964
TOTAL	$156,365,300	150,000,000	$154,848,000	$154,848,000	$155,789,000	$154,848,000

Section 9131(b)(3)(C) of the Museum and Library Services Act directs that funds allotted based on the populations of the Republic of the Marshall Islands, the Federated States of Micronesia, and the Republic of Palau be used to award grants on a competitive basis taking into consideration recommendations from the Pacific Region Educational Laboratory in Hawaii. These three freely-associated states, along with the U.S. Virgin Islands, Guam, American Samoa, and the Commonwealth of the Northern Marianas, are eligible to compete for the grants.

each of the SLAAs plus a supplemental amount based on population. For each of the 50 states, Puerto Rico, and the District of Columbia, the base amount is $680,000 each, and for the U.S. Territories the base amount is $60,000 each.[21]

Each state library agency is required by the Library Services and Technology Act to submit a plan that details library services goals for a five-year period. This continues the requirement of the LSA and LSTA. These plans are the foundation for improving practice and informing policy. All plans are posted at the IMLS website. Each plan includes a mission statement. Some examples are:[22]

Alabama. The mission of the Alabama Public Library Service (APLS) is to provide the services and leadership necessary to meet the educational, informational, cultural and economic needs of Alabama's citizens of all ages by providing "leadership, guidance and support for the development and maintenance of local public libraries in funding resources and programs; and through service as the information resource center for state government, including the Governor, the legislature, elected and appointed officials and state employees."

Nebraska. The mission of the Nebraska Library Commission is statewide promotion, development, and coordination of library and information services. As the state library agency, the Commission is an advocate for the library and information service needs of all Nebraskans.

Utah. The Utah State Library develops, leads, and delivers exceptional library services while optimizing Utah's investment in libraries.

Section 9131(b)(3)(C) of the Museum and Library Services Act directs that funds allotted based on the populations of the Republic of the Marshall Islands, the Federated States of Micronesia, and the Republic of Palau be used to award grants on a competitive basis taking into consideration recommendations from the Pacific Region Educational Laboratory in Hawaii. These three freely associated states, along with the U.S. Virgin Islands, Guam, American Samoa, and the Commonwealth of the Northern Marianas, are eligible to compete for the grants.

The following list contains a few highlights from state plans to demonstrate the targeted, innovative plans that SLAAs coordinate in order to make the best use of federal funds.[23]

$4,350,678.00—Michigan

> **▶ TASK**
>
> Find out how much money your state received through the Grants to States program.

Plan offered state residents a core set of information tools to use free of charge at their local libraries or via the Internet anywhere, anytime. With something for nearly every information need, this access meant opportunities for Michigan citizens to advance and enhance their lives as workers, students, citizens, family members, and lifelong learners. The databases include full-text articles, abstracts, electronic versions of reference books, and other formats that allow academic, school, and public libraries to offer consistent, high-quality materials to their patrons. Some of the databases offered geoauthentication by recognizing the physical location of the patron's IP address, thus allowing direct access to Michiganders who then did not need to use a login screen. Other databases authenticated via a local library card number or a state driver's license number.
IMLS Funds: $2,308,500.

$1,452,508.00—New Mexico

Rural Library Services. This statewide project provided library services to rural and remote populations with little or no other library service, including two counties with no public library. It carried out services using three regional bookmobiles and a books-by-mail program. During the project period, LSTA funds supported 12 full-time staff and covered the costs of collection development, cataloging, facilities, operations management, and outreach services. The New Mexico State Library maintains an automated library catalog for Rural Services using an open source integrated library system (ILS).

$8,513,873.00—New York

Brooklyn Public Library's Ready Set Kindergarten! Program was an extension of its popular Weekend Preschool Storytime project. Targeted to working parents, low-income families, and foreign-born families, the program sought to convey the importance of reading to children at an early age; offered ways to engage children in simple, developmentally appropriate math and science activities; and promoted the availability of early literacy services and local library resources. As part of the program, children engaged in fun, interactive storytimes to build skills for kindergarten readiness. Among parents of participating children, 83% reported that the activities, resources, and information had helped to improve their children's literacy, and 70% said they gained new ideas to use with their children. The project's focus on school readiness has also enabled Brooklyn Public Library to collaborate more with the New York City Department of Education's early childhood initiatives.

EVALUATIONS

State library administrative agencies are required to submit a five-year evaluation of library services based on the execution of their five-year plans. Measuring Success is a tool developed by IMLS in 2011 that provides IMLS and SLAAs a robust method for reviewing and analyzing grant-supported library activities (IMLS Measuring Success, n.d.). To date, Measuring Success has involved over 70 volunteers from 54 state library administrative agencies who collaborate to identify trends and share best practices in federally supported library activities. From these reports, strategies are developed to ensure that these activities deliver high-quality public service. These reports are not publicized and are discussed infrequently, but they provide an abundance of detailed analyses and narratives that provides a foundation of library services in each state. The evaluations also tie together the components of LSTA funding.

As an example, the most recent California evaluation includes an exhaustive review and analysis of the reports, data, and evaluative studies relating to the various grant projects in the state. Quantitative data were analyzed for both meaningful and statistically significant results. Qualitative and anecdotal data, including that gathered through stakeholder interviews, focus groups, and an online survey, were reviewed for common themes and causal relationships. The evaluative metrics were linked to the specific Outputs and Outcomes included in the CSL LSTA Five Year Plan by Goal and Program. The study is organized by IMLS Priority and then addresses each Priority using the applicable CSL LSTA Plan Goal, Program, and metric (CA State Library, 2012).

Each state five-year report is available at the IMLS website. These reports include original research, community-based evaluative information, and much statistical data. They convey a deep local understanding of the importance of libraries to people's lives, and include information on specialized services such as digitization projects, service to the blind and physically handicapped, bookmobiles, or services to refugees.[24]

ADVOCACY AND FEDERAL LEGISLATION

All federal legislation that impacts libraries is closely followed by the ALA Washington Office of Government Relations. The office works to ensure that libraries are consistently involved in the legislative and policy decision-making processes by

1. Informing government of the needs and concerns of the library community;
2. Providing library supporters with up-to-date information on government actions or proposals;
3. Building coalitions with Washington-based representatives of other groups with similar concerns; and
4. Developing grassroots networks to lobby legislators and further library interests (ALA Office for Govt. Relations, n.d.).

The formation of grassroots networks of librarians who can speak with lawmakers about library issues are supported by events such as National Library Legislative Day, held each May in Washington, DC., which brings together librarians, library board members, and library friends to advocate on behalf of libraries. A Virtual Library Legislative Day is held at the same time.[25]

This national event is the culmination of similar events at each state legislature. The ALA Office for Library Advocacy (OLA) supports the efforts of advocates who seek to improve libraries of all types by developing resources, a peer-to-peer advocacy network, and training for advocates at the local, state, and national level. In order to achieve this goal, OLA works closely with the Public Awareness Office, the Chapter Relations Office, the Office of Government Relations, and other ALA units involved in advocacy (ALA Office for Advocacy, n.d.).

A highly publicized involvement of libraries at the level of federal law was ALA's effort to prevent the linkage of universal service (e-rate) funding to Internet filtering. The Telecommunications Act of 1996 provided discounts of telecommunication costs to schools and libraries. However, passage of the Children's Internet Protection Act (CIPA, 47 U.S.C. 254) required libraries receiving federal funds to filter Internet access. ALA challenged CIPA in federal court as unconstitutional, but the decision was upheld by the Supreme Court. The study *Fencing out Knowledge: Impacts of the Children's Internet Protection Act 10 Years Later* (Batch, 2014) noted:

> Those who rely on public libraries for some or all of their internet access likewise are disproportionally affected by internet filtering policies. Libraries in low-income communities often serve as the primary means by which youth and adults can gain free access to digital tools and to training in using them effectively. Public libraries are recognized by other government agencies and programs as primary outlets for fulfilling a policy of "digital inclusion" that encompasses both digital access and digital literacy.

> Yet libraries that choose to preserve open and equal access to the internet must forego opportunities for federal funding.

Federal advocacy, including legal actions by ALA, and policy decisions in local libraries demonstrate the library profession's commitment to advocacy for all aspects of government policy that affect library service.

Articulation of Legal Considerations

Understanding the expansion of the legal basis of the U.S. public library over the past 160 years requires a knowledge of the continuum of government from the local to the federal levels. Librarians interact most closely with the government of the community served, and state library agencies act as the link between local activity and the federal government through the collaborative development of state library plans. Through state library associations, programs sponsored by state library agencies, and efforts by ALA, support for public libraries is integrated across all levels of government. The activation involves citizens, who oversee the policies and growth of the library, through their collaborative service on library boards (Minow & Lipinski, 2003; Miller & Fisher, 2007).

Librarian support of net neutrality (*United States Telecom Association, et al., v. Federal Communications Commission and United States of America*) is an example of a policy initiative that contributes to freedom of information ("Library Groups Fight for Net Neutrality," 2015). Similar support for the Freedom of Information Act (FOIA) Improvement Act to expand public access to government documents by codifying the "presumption of openness" will strengthen the U.S. Office of Government Information Services. ALA president Julie Todaro stated:

> The new law is a win-win for the public and the library community; it will improve government transparency by opening the window on the workings of our government wider, but the law also will advance librarians' efforts in making that vital information available to the public. Nationwide, libraries are often the first places that Americans visit to gain access to government information, records, and resources. We look forward to working collaboratively with all government agencies to make more of their records available in support of the public's fundamental right to know. (Todaro, 2016)

Advocacy for information policies extends the role of librarians in the public sphere and is an important aspect of the role librarians play as defenders of access to information and information equity.

FUNDING THE PUBLIC LIBRARY

The American public library is mainly funded by local taxes. This local support is a result of voter willingness to approve ongoing taxation. State support is a result of library advocates working with state legislators to provide state level funds. Private support is the result of Friends groups, foundations, and individual donors contributing to the library's resources. Federal support is the result of nearly a century of campaigns for America's libraries to serve the unserved (DeRosa, Johnson, & OCLC, 2008).

Overview of Public Library Funding

American public libraries operate with an average of $39.34 per person to provide library services. Public library revenue is generated from four sources: local government, state government, other sources (monetary gifts and donations), and federal government funding. Nationally, local governments provide $33.50; state governments $2.77; other sources $2.91, and the federal government, $0.15 (see figure 5.4).[26]

> ▶ **FACT**
>
> Texas public libraries collectively were found to provide $2.407 billion in benefits while costing less than $0.545 billion, a return on investment of $4.42 for each dollar invested.*
>
> *Texas Public Libraries: Economic benefits and return on investment. https://www.tsl.texas.gov/roi.

Comparing state profiles, we see that family median income and per capita library support are not comparable or correlational. New York, which provides the nation's greatest per capita support for libraries at $69.24, is eighteenth in state median household income. Maryland, with the highest median family income ($89,678), is thirteenth in per capita library support, at $52.41.[27] Mississippi ranks lowest in spending per capita ($17.35). Figure 5.5 provides comparative data for top and bottom ranked states in per capita support.

These disparate statistics are the result of historical support, efforts of state library associations, commitment of trustees and advocates, and political philosophy. Libraries have begun to assert their economic worth with valuation studies that demonstrate return on investment. The 2014 IMLS report on public libraries found a connection between investment in libraries and use as measured by visitation, circulation, computer use and program attendance (Swan et al., 2014, pp. 11-13). Wilson (2016) has explained the importance of the Return on Investment (ROI) model as presented in *Worth Their Weight: An Assessment of the Evolving Field of Library Valuation* (Imholz & Arns, 2007).

Local Funding

Public library funding most frequently comes from taxation or from a general fund. The assessment level a property tax generates is cited in state laws. The millage rate is the total number of mills (1 mill=1/1,000 of $1) that can be levied by each taxing authority. The primary support for public libraries is the property tax.

In Michigan the City, Village, and Township Libraries Act 164 of 1877 is one example of legislation that mandates taxation for public libraries (figure 5.6).

It is the responsibility of the library board and the library staff to ensure that the public is aware of the budgeting process and that it is open and transparent. The Oak Park (IL) Public Library shares its budget information online (figure 5.7).

Another outstanding example of budget transparency is the annual website report of the Saint Paul Public Library, which provides a clear step-by-step presentation to taxpayers. We include this process because it is one of the best publicly available examples we have been able to find that demonstrates how the budget process works at the local level (figure 5.8).

Referenda and Raising Funds

When libraries need to renew or expand financial support the referendum process is employed. State library associations and state library agencies provide support to local libraries on referenda. For examples, see California Library Association, "Why Support Your Pub-

		Total per capita operating revenue[1]									
		Total		Federal[2]		State		Local		Other[3]	
State	Number of public libraries	Total	Response Rate	Total	Response Rate	Total	Response Rate	Total	Response Rate	Total	Response Rate
Total[5]	9,070	39.34	98.2	$0.15	98.5	$2.77	98.4	$33.51	98.4	$2.91	98.3
Alabama	218	21.89	100.0	0.23	100.0	0.95	100.0	18.90	100.0	1.82	100.0
Alaska	79	57.89	100.0	1.78	100.0	1.68	100.0	49.93	100.0	4.51	100.0
Arizona	90	25.26	83.3	0.30	90.0	0.24	88.9	23.66	87.8	1.05	87.8
Arkansas	58	28.29	93.1	0	93.1	2.08	93.1	24.46	93.1	1.75	93.1
California	184	35.36	99.5	0.12	99.5	0.36	99.5	33.01	99.5	1.87	99.5
Colorado	113	54.85	99.1	0.15	100.0	0.24	100.0	51.30	99.1	3.16	100.0
Connecticut	182	55.07	97.8	0.10	97.8	0.42	97.8	47.44	97.8	7.12	97.8
Delaware	21	27.74	100.0	#	100.0	4.32	100.0	21.41	100.0	2.01	100.0
District of Co-lumbia	1	82.24	100.0	1.39	100.0	0	100.0	80.58	100.0	0.27	100.0
Florida	82	25.99	91.5	0.06	91.5	1.18	91.5	23.71	91.5	1.04	91.5
Georgia	63	19.46	100.0	0.05	100.0	2.62	100.0	15.43	100.0	1.36	100.0
Hawaii	1	24.19	100.0	1.18	100.0	21.29	100.0	0	100.0	1.72	100.0
Idaho	102	38.13	100.0	0.02	100.0	1.00	100.0	34.05	100.0	3.06	100.0
Illinois	623	68.70	99.5	0.29	99.5	3.83	99.7	61.20	99.5	3.38	99.5
Indiana	237	54.60	99.6	0.15	99.6	3.54	99.6	48.27	99.6	2.64	99.6
Iowa	534	39.93	96.8	0.28	96.8	0.84	96.8	35.36	96.8	3.44	96.8
Kansas	318	48.53	97.8	0.10	99.7	1.61	99.1	42.06	99.4	4.76	98.1
Kentucky	119	40.19	100.0	0.14	100.0	1.25	100.0	36.86	100.0	1.94	100.0
Louisiana	68	51.60	100.0	0.14	100.0	1.37	100.0	48.82	100.0	1.28	100.0
Maine	228	38.00	99.1	0.04	99.1	0.31	99.1	27.90	99.1	9.74	99.1
Maryland	24	52.41	100.0	0.17	100.0	8.81	100.0	38.40	100.0	5.04	100.0

FIGURE 5.4 Total per Capita Operating Revenue of Public Libraries by Source of Revenue and State: Fiscal Year 2014 [CONTINUED ON FOLLOWING PAGE]

SOURCE: Institute of Museum and Library Services. 2014. Public Libraries Survey. https://www.imls.gov/sites/default/files/fy2014_pls_tables.pdf.

		Total per capita operating revenue[1]									
		Total		Federal[2]		State		Local		Other[3]	
State	Number of public libraries	Total	Response Rate	Total	Response Rate	Total	Response Rate	Total	Response Rate	Total	Response Rate
Massachusetts	368	43.36	98.6	0.08	98.6	1.05	98.6	38.23	98.6	4.00	98.6
Michigan	388	40.35	97.7	0.05	99.0	1.13	99.0	36.58	99.0	2.59	97.7
Minnesota	137	38.98	98.5	0.02	99.3	1.65	99.3	33.64	99.3	3.68	98.5
Mississippi	52	17.35	100.0	0.50	100.0	2.71	100.0	12.02	100.0	2.12	100.0
Missouri	149	44.52	100.0	0.40	100.0	0.74	100.0	40.79	100.0	2.59	100.0
Montana	82	27.42	100.0	0.01	100.0	0.58	100.0	24.88	100.0	1.95	100.0
Nebraska	263	36.18	81.0	0.16	81.0	0.36	81.0	33.56	81.0	2.10	81.4
Nevada	21	32.17	100.0	0.38	100.0	7.75	100.0	22.76	100.0	1.28	100.0
New Hampshire	219	50.08	97.3	#	98.2	0.05	98.2	46.43	98.2	3.59	97.3
New Jersey	281	54.36	94.0	0.10	94.0	0.43	94.0	$51.70	94.0	$2.13	94.3
New Mexico	87	29.10	97.7	0.13	97.7	1.61	97.7	25.76	97.7	1.60	100.0
New York	756	69.24	100.0	0.30	100.0	3.26	100.0	55.78	100.0	9.89	100.0
North Carolina	80	21.56	100.0	0.16	100.0	1.40	100.0	18.57	100.0	1.42	100.0
North Dakota	73	28.17	100.0	0.02	100.0	2.38	100.0	23.88	100.0	1.90	100.0
Ohio	251	65.77	98.8	0.04	100.0	29.94	100.0	28.85	98.8	6.94	100.0
Oklahoma	117	35.99	100.0	0.19	100.0	0.71	100.0	33.28	100.0	1.80	100.0
Oregon	129	53.57	100.0	0.21	100.0	0.34	100.0	50.18	100.0	2.84	100.0
Pennsylvania	455	27.67	99.6	0.15	99.6	4.62	99.6	17.98	99.6	4.93	99.6
Rhode Island	48	44.63	100.0	0.40	100.0	7.63	100.0	30.51	100.0	6.09	100.0
South Carolina	42	28.06	100.0	0.07	100.0	1.44	100.0	25.48	100.0	1.08	100.0
South Dakota	112	33.20	99.1	0.51	100.0	0	100.0	31.49	99.1	1.20	100.0
Tennessee	186	17.70	100.0	0.03	100.0	0.06	100.0	16.57	100.0	1.03	100.0
Texas	548	20.00	100.0	0.02	100.0	#	100.0	19.19	100.0	0.79	100.0

FIGURE 5.4 [CONTINUED ON FOLLOWING PAGE]

FIGURE 5.4 [CONTINUED]

		Total per capita operating revenue[1]									
		Total		Federal[2]		State		Local		Other[3]	
State	Number of public libraries	Total	Response Rate	Total	Response Rate	Total	Response Rate	Total	Response Rate	Total	Response Rate
Utah	72	36.41	93.1	0.13	93.1	0.41	93.1	34.50	93.1	1.38	93.1
Vermont	155	37.25	99.4	0.06	99.4	0	99.4	30.33	99.4	6.86	99.4
Virginia	91	34.32	100.0	0.23	100.0	1.90	100.0	30.75	100.0	1.45	100.0
Washington	62	58.45	100.0	0.07	100.0	0.01	100.0	56.47	100.0	1.91	100.0
West Virginia	97	21.09	100.0	0.22	100.0	5.31	100.0	13.97	100.0	1.59	100.0
Wisconsin	381	39.89	100.0	0.11	100.0	0.75	100.0	36.69	100.0	2.34	100.0
Wyoming	23	55.10	100.0	0.01	100.0	#	100.0	51.83	100.0	3.26	100.0
Outlying areas											
American Samoa	1	7.91	100.0	1.40	100.0	6.29	100.0	0	100.0	0.23	100.0
Guam	1	7.39	100.0	0	100.0	0	100.0	6.95	100.0	0.44	100.0

Rounds to zero.

1. Per capita is based on the total unduplicated population of legal service areas.
2. This includes federal funds, such as Library Services and Technology Act (LSTA) funds, that are distributed to public libraries through state library agencies. Other federal funds that are used by state library agencies or library cooperatives to provide services that benefit local public libraries are not included in the table because they are not received as income by public libraries.
3. This includes monetary gifts and donations received in the current year, interest, library fines, fees for library services, or grants.
4. Response rate is calculated as the number of libraries that reported the item, divided by the total number of libraries in the survey frame. For item(s) with response rates below 100 percent, data for nonrespondents were imputed and are included in the table. Data were not imputed for the outlying areas.
5. Total includes the 50 states and the District of Columbia but excludes outlying areas and libraries that do not meet the FSCS Public Library Definition.

NOTE: Detail may not sum to totals because of rounding. Data were not reported by the following outlying areas (Northern Marianas and Virgin Islands). Missing data were not imputed for nonresponding outlying areas.

1	New York	$69.24	$71,115	(18)
2	Illinois	$68.70	$71, 796	(16)
3	Ohio	$65.77	$62,300	(30)
4	Washington	$58.45	$74,193	(13)
5	Alaska	$57.89	$71,583	(4)
47	West Virginia	$21.09	$52,413	(49)
48	Texas	$20.00	$62,830	(28)
49	Georgia	$19.46	$58,885	(41)
50	Tennessee	$17.70	$55,557	(45)
51	Mississippi	$17.35	$50,178	(51)

Figure 5.5 Per Capita Library Support Compared to Median Household Income

SOURCES: Institute of Museum and Library Services, Supplementary Tables: Public Libraries Survey Fiscal Year 2014, July 2016 (https://www.imls.gov/sites/default/files/fy2014_pls_tables.pdf and table 44, p. 119); American Community Survey, U.S. Census Bureau, 2014 (https://www.census.gov/acs/www/data/data-tables-and-tools/ranking-tables).

lic Library?" (2014); Maine State Library, "Advocacy and Community Relations" (n.d.); and Pennsylvania Library Association, "Learn to Be a Library Advocate" (n.d.).

United for Libraries, a division of the American Library Association, is the national network of library supporters that unites advocates as real force to be reckoned with at the local, state, and national levels.[28] The free webinar, Anatomy of a Successful Library Campaign: Real World Tips for Getting the Funding You Need, and other resources are available at the United for Libraries website (www.ala.org/united/). At the national level, PLA provides advocacy tools to help local libraries argue for library support (www.ala.org/pla/advocacy).

EveryLibrary is a nonprofit social welfare organization chartered to work on local library ballot initiatives. It works with the staff and the elected or appointed leadership of libraries on planning and executing effective campaigns. EveryLibrary advises and consults to Get Out the Vote and voter engagement for library measures.[29]

Successful strategies for tax campaigns for the support of public libraries have been outlined by Comito et al. (2012) and Turner (2000). A 14-point approach to engage political, policy-making, and fundraising processes on behalf of public libraries has been set forth by Jaeger, Gorham, Bertot, & Sarin (2014, pp. 120–123).

Initiatives to maintain and expand library funding are tracked by the American Library Association. Kathy Rosa, the director of ALA's Office for Research and Statistics, observed, "Referenda funds are used to build new libraries, renovate existing facilities, and maintain library operations. In addition, the funds can provide opportunities to update technologies and expand collections and services to meet the changing needs of library patrons" (Rosa, 2016). In 2016, 150 library referenda took place in 22 states, which resulted in 122 wins (Rosa & Henke, 2017). The annual *American Libraries* roundup provides state-by state results.

In addition to taxation, library board members and Friends of Libraries organizations enhance local budgets through a variety of initiatives. These include fundraising through library endowment development, book sales, and other philanthropic efforts.

Michigan City, Village, and Township Libraries Act 164 of 1877 (Excerpt)

397.210a Free public library in city; establishment; petition for tax; notice; library fund; preparing and reporting estimate of money necessary for support and maintenance; tax additional to tax limitation.

Sec. 10a.

(1) Fifty voters of a city may present to the clerk of the city a petition asking that a tax be levied for the establishment of a free public library in that city and specifying a rate of taxation not to exceed 2 mills on the dollar. The tax may be of unlimited duration or the petition may specify the number of years for which the tax shall be levied. The clerk, in the next legal notice of the regular election in that city, shall give notice that at the election every voter may vote upon the proposition. The notice shall specify the rate and any duration of taxation mentioned in the petition.

(2) If a majority of all the votes cast in the city upon the proposition is for the tax for a free public library, the tax specified in the notice shall be levied and collected in the same manner as other general taxes of that city for the period, if any, specified in the petition, and shall be placed in a fund to be known as the "library fund."

(3) If the free public library is established under this section, and a governing board is elected and qualified as provided in section 11, the board, on or before the first Monday in September in each year, shall prepare an estimate of the amount of money necessary for the support and maintenance of the free public library for the ensuing year, not to exceed 2 mills on the dollar of the taxable property of the city. Unless any period specified in the petition for the levy of the tax has expired, the governing board shall report the estimate to the legislative body of the city. The legislative body shall raise by tax upon the taxable property in the city the amount of the estimate in the same manner that other general taxes are raised in the city.

(4) A tax levied under this section shall be in addition to any tax limitation imposed by a city charter.

FIGURE 5.6 Michigan City, Village, and Township Libraries Act 164 of 1877 (Excerpt)

SOURCE: Michigan Legislature, City, Village, and Township Libraries (Excerpt) Act 164 of 1877, Section 397.210a. (http://legislature.mi.gov/doc.aspx?mcl-397-210a).

Community library foundations are a growing mechanism to enhance library support. The primary reason to form a foundation is to create a significant funding source that is separate and distinct from the regulations and restrictions that apply to any governmental institution. A foundation can establish its own rules, buy equipment, or provide services for the library without regard to competitive bidding, committee approvals, and so forth (UFL Fact Sheet, n.d.).

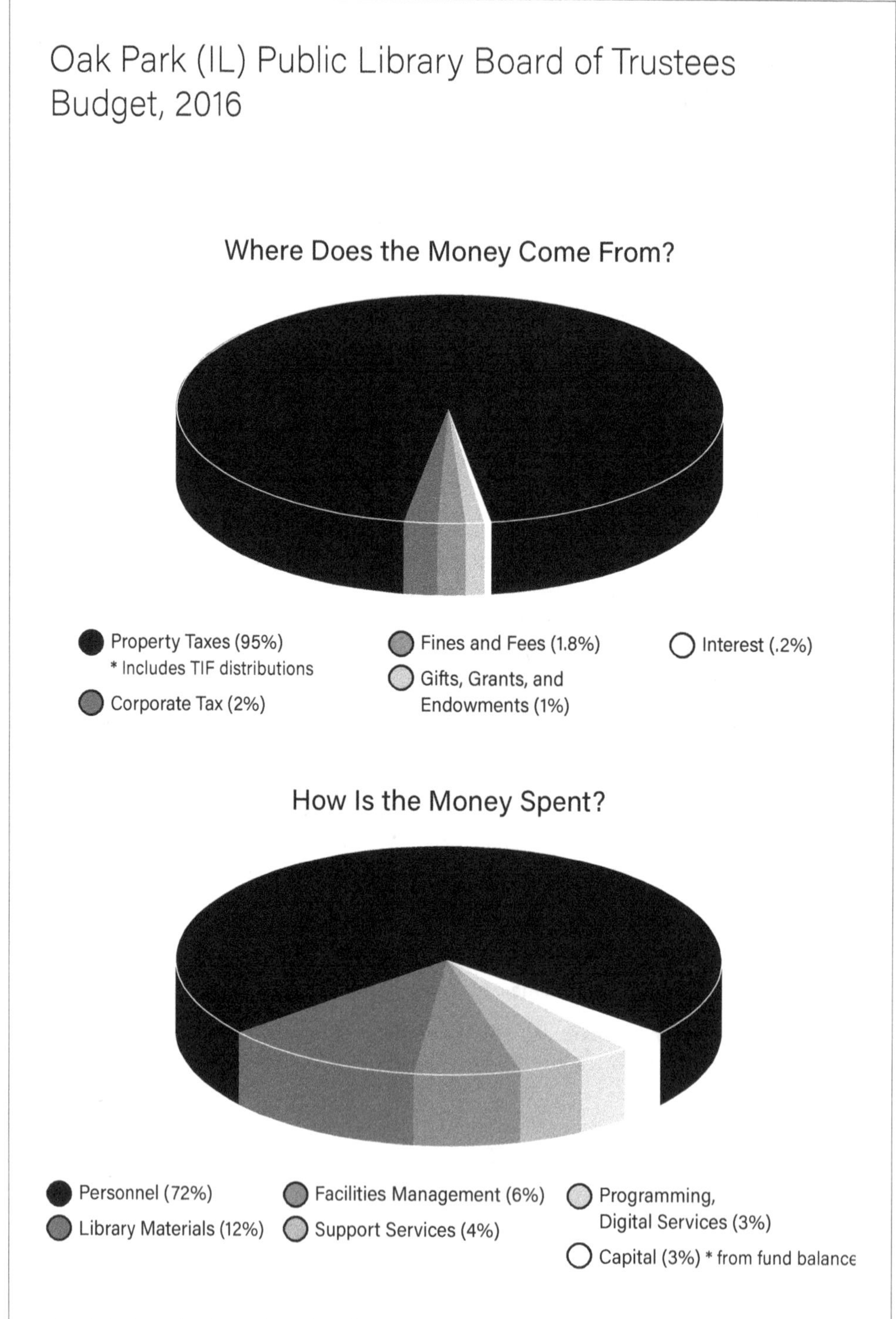

FIGURE 5.7 Oak Park (IL) Public Library Board of Trustees Budget, 2016

SOURCE: Board of Trustees Budget 2016 (http://oppl.org/about/budget). Courtesy of Oak Park Public Library.

Saint Paul (MN) Public Library Agency, 2016 Adopted Budget

The Budget Process is designed to conform with Minnesota law, the City charter, and the legislative code. The process to develop the budget commences in February.

January—March
The budget for following year is finalized during this time. This includes preparing, printing and distributing books reflecting the adopted budget. The accounting section of the Office of Financial Services prepares the annual financial report for the previous year. During this time, the "base budget" for the upcoming year is identified.

April—June
The Library Director presents a needs and resource assessment to the Library Board with priorities, no later than April 1st. Forms, instructions, printouts and the Mayor's guidelines are distributed. These tools are used to plan for and develop the operating budget. The department management and staff identify objectives, performance indicators and the resources needed to accomplish goals. Services are reviewed to determine purpose, need and cost-saving ideas. The department request for the following year's budget is submitted to the Office of Financial Services in June. After that, the department's budget is analyzed by the OFS budget staff. The Mayor meets with the Director to discuss needs, and to ensure the budget meets the service level and taxing objectives that have been established for the City.

July—September
The budget staff finalizes the Mayor's recommendation and the Mayor's proposed budget is produced. The Mayor then presents the recommended budget to the Library Board within one week of the deadline for the City budget presentation, as required by the city charter.

In August, the Library Board begins reviewing the Mayor's proposed budget. The Board will hold meetings with the Director, management and staff to obtain a clear understanding of the department's goals, service priorities and objectives that are represented in the proposed budget. As required by state law, the Library Board sets the maximum property tax levy in September. Governmental units can adjust budgets, resulting in property taxes that are less than, but not more than, the maximum levy.

October—December
The Library Board holds public hearings on the budget. Ramsey County [which includes St. Paul] mails property tax statements to property owners indicating the maximum

FIGURE 5.8 Saint Paul (MN) Public Library Agency, 2016 Adopted Budget

[CONTINUED ON FOLLOWING PAGE]

SOURCE: 2016 Adopted Budget (www.sppl.org/sites/default/files/rcl/pdf/budget/2016/2016_adopted.pdf). Courtesy of Saint Paul Public Library Agency,

FIGURE 5.8 [CONTINUED]

amount of property taxes that the owner will be required to pay. These statements also indicate when the budget and property tax public hearings will be held. State law requires a meeting be held to give residents the opportunity to comment on the information in their notices. This meeting is held in early December. The Library Board then adopts a recommended budget and tax levy for the Library Agency. The adopted budget represents changes made by the Library Board to the Mayor's proposed budget. The Mayor has veto authority over the Library Board-adopted budget.

State Funding

State funding for public libraries ranges from $0.00 to over $30.00 per capita (see, again, figure 5.3). State funding accounts nationally for 7% of library funding. The money each state provides to its public libraries is connected to federal funding.

There is no single source that summarizes yearly State Aid to Public Libraries, but the annual Pubic Library Survey Tables do give state by state amounts (IMLS, 2016). The purpose of State Aid is to supplement, not replace, local libraries' budgets. This requires a maintenance of effort to ensure that state funds are not replaced. State library agencies verify each individual public library's maintenance of effort. Annual reviews in *Library Journal* and *American Libraries* help us to see variation, but report only intermittently on specific states such as "Cut in Arkansas State Aid to Public Libraries" (Crow, 2015) or "Missouri Library Funds Restored" (Warburton, 2015).

Common characteristics of state library administrative agencies (SLAA) often called "state libraries" have been discussed by Wilkins (2011). Some SLAAs provide supplemental support for direct service, interlibrary loan, construction, or multitype library services. There is no overview of methods used by SLAAs to distribute state funds (Himmel, 2000). Most state library agencies require that public libraries meet compliance requirements (e.g., hours of service, paid employees, submission of annual reports and statistical data) and then generally distribute state aid funds based on level of compliance. This process establishes minimum levels of public library service within a state.

Because the state contribution to the funding of public libraries is so idiosyncratic, each state's documentation must be reviewed to gain an outline of the fiscal contribution. This includes the state library's website, reports to IMLS, state library association journals, and often fact sheets and information prepared for each state's legislative advocacy day.

Federal Funding

Federal funds for local public libraries are primarily administered through state library administrative agencies as LSTA funds. We have seen in the section on state funding (above) that federal funds are tied to public library maintenance of effort. In 2015, the total distribution of federal funds to states was $154,848,000—less than 1% of total budgets.

The State Library of North Carolina publishes "New Public Library Directors: State Aid Guide," which provides additional clarification:

> State Aid is intended to promote, aid, and equalize public library service in North Carolina.
>
> These grants are available to any public library, including municipal libraries, that establishes its eligibility according to the Rules and Regulations for the Allocation of State Aid to Public Libraries. The State Library's role in State Aid is to determine eligibility annually. It is also charged with receiving this funding from the legislature and allocating it to all eligible libraries based upon a formula approved by the North Carolina Library Commission. State Aid payments to eligible libraries are dispersed twice a year, in October and April.
>
> The North Carolina State Aid to Public Libraries is allocated among all eligible NC public libraries according to a formula:
>
> 50% of the total State Aid to Public Libraries appropriation is allocated in equal block grants to each eligible county, plus an additional block grant to each multi-county regional library. The remaining 50% of the State Aid fund is allocated as per capita income equalization grants.
>
> In other words, both the library's service area population and per capita income have an impact in determining the amount of State Aid allocated to your library. These factors recognize that if you have more people or poor people, then you need more money to provide library service. State Aid grant amounts are recalculated each year to take into consideration changes in population and per capita income.
>
> Another factor impacting the amount of State Aid the library may receive is Maintenance of Effort (MOE). . . . Maintenance of Effort (MOE) demonstrates that your local funders are maintaining or expanding their support of the cost of local library service. MOE is based on the average of the previous 3 year total local support. Each local funder must report the library's budgeted allocation on the Declaration of MOE form. If the budgeted MOE for the upcoming fiscal year is less than the average of the previous 3 years the library's allocation of state aid will be reduced according to the percentage loss. (State Library of NC, n.d.)

These funds are distributed by the SLAA to each state that coordinates and distributes federal funds from the Grants to States program. These federal funds, which are authorized by LSTA, are used directly by an SLAA or through sub-grants and cooperative agreements that operate at or below the state level. Details of each SLAA are reported in the *State Library Administrative Agencies Survey* (Swan et al., 2014).

The 2009 IMLS report, *A Catalyst for Change: LSTA Grants to States Program Activities and the Transformation of Library Services to the Public,* underscored the value of the LSTA grants to state programs to help libraries embrace technology, establish new service models, and engage the public (Manjarrez, Langa, & Miller, 2009).

Other federal agencies have played important roles in public library support. Outside of IMLS, the most notable may be the National Endowment for the Humanities (NEH). Funded projects have included collaborations with the Public Programing Office of ALA for national programs such as StoryLines: A Radio/Library Partnership Exploring Our Regional Literature (ALA Public Programs, n.d.) and "Let's Talk About It," which engages participants in discussion of a set of common texts selected by nationally known scholars for their relevance to larger, overarching themes.[30] *Bridging Cultures* is an NEH initiative that engages the power of the humanities to promote understanding and mutual respect for people with diverse histories, cultures, and perspectives within the United States and abroad. In 2013, 843 libraries and state humanities councils across the country received a complete set of materials in the Bookshelf collection.

Foundation Funding

Library foundations are nonprofit, 501(c)(3) organizations established to help secure the future of the public library through systematic and strategic fundraising. The money, opportunities, and visibility that a successful foundation brings to the library system are essential to long-term success. For some systems, foundations generate millions of dollars that help libraries achieve their visions. A successful library-foundation partnership will have a shared vision about the library's future (Urban Libraries Council, 2013).[31]

> **▶ FACT**
>
> The New York Public Library has assets of $1.1 billion but does not use a foundation structure. Seattle has the largest public library foundation with $53.4 million.*
>
> ———
>
> *Seattle has the largest public library foundation with $53.4 million, putting it seventh overall in terms of assets among all investment portfolios of libraries with and without foundations. It is followed by the San Diego Public Library Foundation at $40.7 million. (Burr, 2014)

Dillingham's 2013 study of library foundations observed: "Library fundraising foundations are an important tool for public libraries, and they should be focused on a diversified fundraising plan that also includes strategies around major gifts, planned giving, and legacy societies."

Examples of robust foundations can be large, like Ohio's Public Library of Cincinnati and Hamilton County Library Foundation, which is "dedicated to ensuring a great library system by raising, managing, and allocating funds to expand and enhance the programs and services of our library in the areas of Children's Literacy; Helping Teens Succeed; Family Outreach; Senior Services; and Collection Enrichment" (http://foundation.cincinnatilibrary.org). Or they may be modest, like Maine's Orono Pubic Library Foundation, which supports the Orono Public Library's mission "to serve as a community resource and to support the educational, cultural, and informational needs of the people of Orono. The Foundation is committed to strengthening the Orono community and enhancing the quality of life for all Orono citizens" (www.oronolibraryfoundation.org/about/).

Here is a selected short list of a diverse group of active, supportive foundations in urban and small communities:

- Public Library Foundation of Beaufort County (http://beaufortlibraryfoundation.org)

- Broward Public Library Foundation (www.bplfoundation.org)
- Chicago Public Library Foundation (www.cplfoundation.org)
- Cincinnati Library Foundation (http://foundation.cincinnatilibrary.org)
- Euclid Public Library Foundation (www.euclidlibrary.org/about-us/library-foundation)
- Houston Public Library Foundation (www.houstonlibraryfoundation.org)
- Indianapolis Public Library Foundation (https://www.indyplfoundation.org)
- Lexington Public Library (www.lexpublib.org/foundation)
- The Library Foundation of Los Angeles (http://lfla.org)
- Madison Public Library Foundation (https://mplfoundation.org)
- Nashville Public Library Foundation (http://nplf.org)
- Newport Beach Public Library Foundation (www.nbplfoundation.org)
- Omaha Public Library Foundation (www.omahalibraryfoundation.org)
- San Antonio Public Library Foundation (www.saplf.org)
- St. Louis Public Library Foundation (http://slplfoundation.org)
- Stayton Public Library (www.staytonlibraryfoundation.org)
- Wolfeboro Public Library Foundation (www.wolfeborolibraryfoundation.org)

The websites for these foundations are inspired examples of communities and libraries working together to develop programs and provide resources.

Also, many communities have multipurpose foundations that can provide additional funding for library projects. The report *Community Foundations and the Public Library,* published by Libraries for the Future, provides historical background (Schull and Zeisel, 2011).

For example, the Community Fund of Tomkins County, New York, made Community Foundation Library Grants of $138,394 to 21 of the 33 libraries in the Finger Lakes Library System in 2015. Pennsylvania's Erie Community Foundation includes several library endowments, and provides investment management, audit, and other related services for these funds. These foundations are sometimes fostered at the state level. "Fund Iowa" is a mechanism wherein the library doesn't have to go through the process and expense of establishing its own foundation and its own foundation board.

Public and private foundations also provide funding for public libraries. Private foundations generally award grants for special projects or demonstrations. The Bill and Melinda Gates Foundation brought 40,000 computers to libraries in all 50 states, increasing computer access for all U.S. residents, with a focus on the most impoverished, between 1997 and 2003.[32] The computer initiative anticipated the potential for libraries to be in the forefront giving them momentum and capacity to speed the identification of libraries as tech hubs—just as the digital divide began to yawn. The foundation pursued more intense efforts as it turned from direct technology support toward assisting with extending the capacity of libraries to foster greater sustainability. It also restored libraries destroyed by hurricanes Katrina and Rita (Miller, 2014).

In 2011 the Gates Foundation awarded over $12 million in grants to libraries in the United States, including funding efforts such as COSLA's development of its strategic plan, and providing nearly $1 million to the Digital Public Library of America to support librarian training programs and $1 million to the American Library Association for advocacy efforts. In 2014 it announced that it was concluding its support of libraries (Chant, 2014).

There are a number of sources of grant funding nationally and locally. The John S. and James L. Knight Foundation with projects such as the 2016 News Challenge awarded libraries $3 million to answer "How might we leverage libraries as a platform to build more knowledgeable communities?"[33] The Andrew Mellon Foundation has supported the Digital Public Library of America (DPLA) with multiple grants ("DPLA Announces Funding" 2014).

TRANSFORMING THE PERCEPTION OF LIBRARIES

Public libraries exist within a nested and overlapping structure of local, regional, state, and national political entities. At each level, librarians must work to inform policymakers about the fiscal and legal needs of libraries. From the enactment of the first laws for tax-supported libraries in the 1850s to the testimony for reauthorization of the LSTA in 2016, the political process has been central to the progress of public library development.[34]

ALA president E. J. Josey (1984–1985) edited a series of classic books on the library and the political process that laid out the intricate and interlocking effort that librarians must make to ensure that politicians understand the needs of libraries (Josey, 1980, 1987; Josey & Shearer, 1990). ALA presidents Patricia Schuman (1991–1992) and Carol Brey-Casiano (2004–2005) made advocacy the centerpiece of their presidential years and wrote compellingly about the librarian's role in the political process. ALA president Camila Alire (2009–2010) was elected after chairing ALA's Committee on Legislation. Her 2009–2010 presidential initiative was Front Line Advocacy—to educate and train librarians to seize opportunities at all levels and especially from the front lines to promote the value of libraries. The Office for Library Advocacy (www.ala.org/offices/ola) supports the efforts of advocates seeking to improve libraries of all types by developing resources, a peer-to-peer advocacy network, and training for advocates at the local, state, and national level. Advocacy University (www.ala.org/advocacy/advocacy-university) is a comprehensive clearinghouse of advocacy tools and resources for all types of libraries from the American Library Association.

> ▶ **FACT**
>
> *Turning the Page: Supporting Libraries, Strengthening Communities* is a free complete training package that includes an Advocacy Training Implementation Guide and an Advocacy Action Plan Workbook for Public Libraries.*
>
> *Public Library Resources. www.ala.org/advocacy/advocacy-university/public-library-resources

The Public Awareness Office of ALA promotes libraries and works effectively on advocacy. National Library Week celebrates libraries and publicizes the contributions of the nation's libraries and librarians to promote library use and support. In 2017 the National Library Week theme was "Libraries Transform."[35]

Public libraries have been effective in maintaining funding and support at the local, state, and federal levels. The Libraries Transform Campaign, an initiative of the American Library Association, was designed to increase public awareness of the value, impact, and services provided by libraries and library professionals. The campaign will ensure there is one clear, energetic voice for the profession, by showcasing the transformative nature of today's libraries and elevating the critical role libraries play in the digital age. The main idea is that libraries today are less about what they *have* for people and more about what they *do* for and with people (Feldman, 2015, 2016).[36]

NOTES

1. Universal service is the principle that all Americans should have access to communications services. Universal service is also the name of a fund and the category of FCC programs and policies to implement this principle. The Telecommunications Act of 1996 expanded the traditional goal of universal service to include increased access to both telecommunications and advanced services—such as high-speed Internet—for all consumers at just, reasonable, and affordable rates. The Act established principles for universal service that specifically focused on increasing access to evolving services for consumers living in rural and insular areas and for consumers with low incomes. Additional principles called for increased access to high-speed Internet in the nation's schools, libraries, and rural health care facilities. The schools and libraries universal service support program, commonly known as the E-Rate program, helps schools and libraries to obtain affordable broadband. See https://www.fcc.gov/general/universal-service-program-schools-and-libraries-e-rate.
2. The Workforce Innovation and Opportunity Act (PL 113-128) will help job seekers and workers access employment, education, training, and support services to succeed in the labor market. This legislation now recognizes the part libraries can play in assisting these job seekers and be integrated into the state and local plans to deliver these crucial services. See www.ala.org/advocacy/advleg/federallegislation/workforce.
3. See table 1 of the Florida Department of State Division of Library and Information Services, Library Data and Statistics. http://dos.myflorida.com/library-archives/services-for-libraries/more-programs/library-data-and-statistics/. Comparable data for each state's statistics agency show the distribution by legal basis and population.
4. IMLS issued its report based on 2013 data in April 2016. In August 2016, a new set of tools based on 2014 data was distributed. See https://www.imls.gov/research-evaluation/data-collection/public-libraries-survey/find-your-library.
5. Illinois, *Public Laws,* 1871-72, pp. 609-11. A mill is the amount of tax payable per dollar of the assessed value of a property. The mill rate is based on "mills." Because each mill is one-thousandth of a currency unit, one mill is equivalent to one-tenth of a cent, or $0.001.
6. For discussion of the concept of home rule, see Berman (2003).
7. See State Aid Publications in the ALA archive: 1935–1945(http://archives.library.illinois.edu/alaarchon/index.php?p=collections/controlcard&id=7037), including summaries of library extension legislation (1939-45); *Bulletin* reports on state aid (1936-42); printed & mimeographed material including State Grants to Libraries (1936-37, 1942); references on state aid for public libraries (1937-43); circular letters (1936-38); ALA resolutions (1935-36); lay agency issuances (1936-37); state aid bills (1941-42).
8. For example, the Alachua Library district in Florida is funded as an independent taxing district and is not a county agency (www.aclib.us/special-taxing-district).
9. For historical research, see *Library Law and Legislation in the United States*, a concise introduction to the three basic areas of law that relate to libraries—constitutional, statutory, and administrative (Ladenson, 1970, 1982).
10. This may sound "wonky," but it is very interesting to see how laws are set forth to support libraries in the various states.
11. Wisconsin. Updated 2013, 14 Wis. Stats. Published and certified under s. 35.18. November 6, 2015. Chapter 43. Libraries. Consolidated Public Library Systems.
    43.57. (4) METHOD OF ORGANIZATION.
    (a) A public library system may be organized as a single-county federated public library system, a multicounty federated public library system, or a single-county consolidated public library system.

Two public library systems may merge with the approval of each public library system board and the county boards of the participating counties. For the complete text see Wisconsin Statutes (http://docs.legis.wisconsin.gov/statutes/statutes/43.pdf).

12. See entry for "Home Rule" in *West's Encyclopedia of American Law,* 2nd edition (2008).
13. To put home rule in context for each state, review *Home Rule in America* (Krane, Rigos, & Hill, 2001).
14. For details, see the Keokuk, Iowa, Municipal Code. Chapter 2.85: Board of Library Trustees (www.keokuk.lib.ia.us/about/policies/admin-gov/ordinance); the Boise, Idaho, City Code, Chapter 2 Section 4 (www.boisepubliclibrary.org/info/board-of-trustees/); and Oxnard, California Ordinance 2888 (http://oxnard.granicus.com/MetaViewer.php?view_id=46&clip_id=2974&meta_id=146627).
15. Massachusetts Board of Library Commissioners. 605 CMR 7.00: Regional Library Systems (http://mblc.state.ma.us/mblc/laws/code/605cmr7.php).
16. They may provide important reference and information services to state governments, administer state libraries state archives, libraries for the blind and physically handicapped, and the State Center for the Book (Wilkins, 2011).
17. For details, see Georgia Public Library Service (www.cosla.org/stateinfo.cfm?StateIndex=GA; www.georgialibraries.org); Kentucky Department for Libraries and Archives (www.cosla.org/stateinfo.cfm?StateIndex=KY; http://kdla.ky.gov/Pages/default.aspx); Washington State Library (www.cosla.org/stateinfo.cfm?StateIndex=WA; www.sos.wa.gov/library/); Wisconsin Division for Libraries and Technology (www.cosla.org/stateinfo.cfm?StateIndex=WI; http://dpi.wi.gov/dlt); and Wyoming State Library (www.cosla.org/stateinfo.cfm?StateIndex=WY; http://ai.wyo.gov/state-library).
18. 20 U.S.C. United States Code, 2010 Edition. Title 20—EDUCATION. CHAPTER 72—MUSEUM AND LIBRARY SERVICES. SUBCHAPTER II—LIBRARY SERVICES AND TECHNOLOGY.
19. See the legislative timeline at the IMLS site (https://www.imls.gov/about-us/legislation-budget/timeline) as well as the 2010 Subchapter II- LSTA, 9121, and "Purpose" (https://www.imls.gov/sites/default/files/mlsa_2010_asamended.pdf).
20. See details on the IMLS website: https://www.imls.gov/grants/available/grants-state-library-administrative-agencies and https://www.imls.gov/grants/grants-states.
21. See the Institute for Museum and Library Services Appropriations Request to the United States Congress for fiscal year 2017 (https://www.imls.gov/sites/default/files/publications/documents/fy17cj_0.pdf).
22. Profiles, plans, and evaluations for all states are available at https://www.imls.gov/grants/grants-state/state-profiles. For more details on Alabama, see https://www.imls.gov/grants/grants-state/state-profiles/alabama-0; on Nebraska, https://www.imls.gov/grants/grants-state/state-profiles/nebraska; and on Utah, https://www.imls.gov/grants/grants-state/state-profiles/utah.
23. Profiles, plans, and evaluations for all states are available at https://www.imls.gov/grants/grants-state/state-profiles. For more details on Michigan, see https://www.imls.gov/grants/grants-state/state-profiles/michigan; on New Mexico, https://www.imls.gov/grants/grants-state/state-profiles/new-mexico; and on New York, https://www.imls.gov/grants/grants-state/state-profiles/new-york.
24. A helpful flowchart, Flow Chart of the Grants to States Program Administration, included in Manjarrez, C., Langa, L., & Miller, K. (2009) and is reprinted in McCook (2011, p. 117).
25. For information on these events, see National Library Legislation Day.www.ala.org/advocacy/advleg/nlld and Virtual Library Legislation Day. www.ala.org/united/advocacy/virtuallegday.
26. For more information from the FY 2014 Public Libraries Survey of over 9,000 public library systems and 17,000 public library outlets, see IMLS (2016), ***Supplementary Tables: Public Libraries Survey Fiscal Year 2014*** (https://data.imls.gov/view/ckgu-babp). https://www.imls.gov/sites/default/files/fy2014_pls_tables.pdf.

27. The sources of this information are IMLS's *Supplementary Tables: Public Libraries Survey Fiscal Year 2014,* July 2016 (https://www.imls.gov/sites/default/files/fy2014_pls_tables.pdf, table 22, p. 67), and the *American Community Survey,* U.S. Census Bureau, 2014 (https://www.census.gov/acs/www/data/data-tables-and-tools/ranking-tables/).
28. On February 1, 2009, Friends of Libraries U.S.A. (FOLUSA) and the Association for Library Trustees and Advocates (ALTA) joined forces to become an expanded division of ALA known as the Association of Library Trustees, Advocates, Friends and Foundations, now United for Libraries. Through this partnership, United for Libraries (www.ala.org/united/advocacy/altaffresources) brings together libraries' voices to speak out on behalf of library services and free public access to information. www.ala.org/united/about.
29. Since its founding in 2012, EveryLibrary has helped secure over $100 million in stable tax revenue with 27 wins (http://everylibrary.org/library-communities-everylibrary-history/).
30. The Bridging Cultures Bookshelf is a project of NEH conducted in cooperation with the ALA Public Programs Office with support from Carnegie Corporation of New York. Additional support was provided by the Doris Duke Foundation for Islamic Arts.
31. A foundation executive helps build and sustain a successful library-foundation partnership by shaping and implementing a fundraising strategy with input from the library director, staying well-informed about library priorities, working closely and regularly with the director, and running an effective organization that is respected by potential donors. As foundations become more and more essential to the financial strength of public libraries, these six leadership roles are particularly important for the foundation executive: 1) Partner to the library director; 2) Ambassador about the library's value and impact; 3) Matchmaker between the library's vision and donor interests; 4) Manager who runs an efficient, effective, and well-respected organization; 5) Educator about the value of philanthropy; and 6) Catalyst for fundraising action (Urban Libraries Council, 2013).
32. See also McCook, 2011, endnote 3.
33. 12th Knight News Challenge, on libraries, asked the question, "How might we leverage libraries as a platform to build more knowledgeable communities?" (www.knightfoundation.org/blogs/knightblog/2015/1/30/22-projects-win-knight-news-challenge-libraries/) p. 127.
34. For current examples, see documents at the website of the ALA Washington Office such as support for the appropriations bill of $186.6 million for the Library Services and Technology Act (LSTA) under the Institute of Museum and Library Services (IMLS), and $27 million for the Innovative Approaches to Literacy (IAL) program under the Department of Education (DOE). See also testimony submitted by Emily Sheketoff, Executive Director, ALA Washington Office, before the Senate Appropriations Subcommittee on Labor, Health and Human Services, Education, and Related Agencies (April 15, 2016). ALA Office of Government Relations. (www.ala.org/offices/ogr; www.ala.org/advocacy/advleg/federallegislation/libraryfunding).
35. The ALA Public Awareness Office (PAO) manages the public awareness efforts of the association through the Libraries Transform Campaign, which delivers key messages to external audiences about the value of libraries and library professionals. PAO also communicates ALA's key messages through media relations and crisis communications, and offers public relations counsel and editorial services. It develops and shares tools with librarians to help advance ALA's strategic directions and works with the ALA Public Awareness Committee (www.ala.org/offices/pao/).
36. Libraries Transform's broad objectives are:
    Awareness: Increase awareness of and support for the transforming library; *Perception:* Shift perception of library from "obsolete" or "nice to have" to essential; and *Engagement:* Energize library professionals and build external advocates to influence local, state and national decision makers (www.ilovelibraries.org/librariestransform/).

REFERENCES

20 U.S.C. United States Code, 2010 Edition. Title 20—Education. Chapter 72—Museum and Library Services. Subchapter II—library services and technology.

Advocacy University (n.d.). www.ala.org/advocacy/advocacy-university.

American Community Survey. U.S. Census Bureau. (2014). https://www.census.gov/acs/www/data/data-tables-and-tools/ranking-tables/.

American Library Association. Office for Advocacy (n.d.). www.ala.org/offices/ola/.

American Library Association, Public Programs Office. (n.d.). www.ala.org/programming/pastprograms/storylines/storylinesamerica.

American Library Association, Washington Office of Government Relations. (n.d.). www.ala.org/offices/org.

Andrew W. Mellon Foundation. (n.d.) https://mellon.org.

Batch, K. R., & American Library Association. (2014). *Fencing out knowledge: Impacts of the Children's Internet Protection Act 10 years later.* Washington, D.C: Office for Information Technology Policy, American Library Association.

Berman, D. R. (2003). *Local government and the states: Autonomy, politics and policy.* Armonk, NY: M. E. Sharpe.

Building bridges: The creation of a new library system (2016). National Association of Counties. www.uscounties.org/cffiles_web/awards/program.cfm?SEARCHID=2016libr49.

Burr, B. (2014, February 12). Library foundation assets of $2.5 billion tallied in Wilmington research. *Pensions and Investments.*

Byrnes, S. M. (2005, December). Advocacy and Illinois regional library systems. *Illinois Libraries, 86,* 80–81.

California Library Association. (2014). Why support your local library? www.cla-net.org/?page=457.

California State Library. (2012). *Evaluation of the Use of Library Services and Technology Act (Institute of Museum and Library Services) Funding in California FY 2006/2007–FY 2010/2011.* https://www.library.ca.gov/grants/lsta/docs/LSTAEvaluation2006-2011.pdf.

Chant, I. (2014, May 22). Gates Foundation prepares to exit library ecosystem. *Library Journal.*

Chief Officers of State Library Agencies. Member profiles (n.d.). www.cosla.org/profiles.

Civic Impulse. (2016). H.R. 803—113th Congress: Workforce Innovation and Opportunity Act. https://www.govtrack.us/congress/bills/113/hr803.

Code of Virginia. (2017). Title 42.1. Libraries. Chapter 2. Local and Regional Libraries. http://law.lis.virginia.gov/vacode/title42.1/chapter2/.

Comito, L., Geraci, A., & Zabriskie, C. (2012). *Grassroots library advocacy.* Chicago, IL: American Library Association.

Crow Sheaner, K. (2015). Cut in Arkansas state aid to public libraries. *Arkansas Libraries, 72*(2), 10–11.

Culver, E.M., & Gittinger, M. (1954, Winter). A history of the citizens' library movement. *Bulletin of the Louisiana Library Association, 17,* 18–20.

DeRosa, C., Johnson, J., & OCLC. (2008). *From awareness to funding: A study of library support in America: A report to the OCLC membership.* Dublin, OH: OCLC.

Dillingham, W. J. (2013). *Public libraries in the United States: Overview and insights on library foundations.* New York, NY: Wilmington Trust.

Directors: State Aid Guide (n.d.). http://statelibrary.ncdcr.libguides.com/c.php?g=217273&p=1435338.

DPLA announces $594,000 in new funding from the Andrew W. Mellon Foundation to research and pursue sustainability model. (2014). https://dp.la/info/2014/03/31/dpla-announces-new-funding-mellon-foundation/.

Feldman, S. (2015). Libraries transform: Making a difference for our profession. *American Libraries, 46*(7/8), 5.

Feldman, S. (2016). Libraries transform: Community disruption is leading to new roles for libraries. *American Libraries, 47*(1/2), 6.

Garceau, O. (1949). *The public library in the political process: A report of the Public Library Inquiry.* New York, NY: Columbia University Press.

Hall, P. D. (1992). *Inventing the nonprofit sector and other essays on philanthropy, voluntarism, and nonprofit organizations.* Baltimore, MD: Johns Hopkins University Press.

Held, R. E. (1973). *The rise of the public library in California.* Chicago, IL: American Library Association.

Himmel, E. E., Wilson, W. J., & DeCandido, G. (2000). *The functions and roles of state library agencies.* Chicago, IL: American Library Association.

Home rule. *West's Encyclopedia of American Law* (2nd ed.). Thomson-Gale.

Illinois, *Public Laws,* 1871–72.

Imholz, S., & Arns, J. W. (2007). *Worth their weight: An assessment of the evolving field of library valuation.* New York, NY: Americans for Libraries Council.

Institute of Museum and Library Services. (n.d.) Grants. https://www.imls.gov/grants/.

Institute of Museum and Library Services. Measuring Success Initiative in the Grants to States Program. (n.d.). https://www.imls.gov/research-evaluation/program-evaluation/grants-state-library-agency/measuring-success-initiative.

Institute of Museum and Library Services. (1996). *Museum and Library Services Act of 1996.* www.imls.gov/about/abt_ 1996.htm.

Institute of Museum and Library Services. (2014). Public Libraries Survey. Washington, DC: Institute of Museum and Library Services. https://www.imls.gov/sites/default/files/fy2014_pls_tables.pdf.

Institute of Museum and Library Services. (2016, July). *Supplementary Tables: Public Libraries Survey Fiscal Year 2014.* https://www.imls.gov/sites/default/files/fy2014_pls_tables.pdf.

Jaeger, P. T., Gorham, U., Bertot, J. C., & Sarin, L. C. (2014). *Public libraries, public policies, and political processes: Serving and transforming communities in times of economic and political constraint.* Lanham, MD: Rowman & Littlefield.

Joeckel, C. B. (1935). *The government of the American public library.* Chicago, IL: University of Chicago Press.

Josey, E. J. (1980). *Libraries in the political process.* Westport, CT: Oryx Press.

Josey, E. J. (1987). *Libraries, coalitions, and the public good.* New York, NY: Neal-Schuman.

Josey, E. J., & Shearer, K. D. (1990). *Politics and the support of libraries.* New York, NY: Neal-Schuman.

Jumonville, F. (2013). "Interested in public libraries": J. O. Modisette and the contributions of a Louisiana Library Commissioner. *Information and Culture, 48*(1), 112–133.

Keokuk, Iowa. Municipal Code. Chapter 2.85: Board of Library Trustees. www.keokuk.lib.ia.us/about/policies/admin-gov/ordinance.

Krane, D., Rigos, P. N., & Hill, M., Jr. (2001). *Home rule in America: A fifty state handbook.* Washington, DC: CQ Press.

Ladenson, A. (1970). Library legislation: Some general considerations. *Library Trends, 19*(2), 175–181.

Ladenson, A. (1982). *Library law and legislation in the United States.* Metuchen, NJ: Scarecrow Press.

The Library Foundation of Cincinnati and Hamilton County. (n.d.). http://foundation.cincinnatilibrary.org.

Library groups continue fight for net neutrality. (2015). *Newsletter on Intellectual Freedom, 64*(6), 139.

Library Services and Technology Act. LSTA-Grants to States Priorities (20 U.S.C. § 9141).

Maine State Library. (n.d.). Advocacy and community relations. www.maine.gov/msl/libs/advocacy/index.shtml.

Manjarrez, C., Langa, L., & Miller, K. (2009). *A catalyst for change: LSTA grants to states program activities and the transformation of library services to the public.* IMLS-2009-RES-01. Washington, DC: Institute of Museum and Library Services. www.imls.gov/pdf/CatalystForChange.pdf.

Manley, L.1., & Holley, R. P. (2012). History of the ebook: The changing face of books. *Technical Services Quarterly, 29*(4), 292–311.

Martin, R. S., & Lear, B. A. (2013). The origins of a state library. *Information and Culture, 48*(1), 1–7.

Massachusetts Board of Library Commissioners. 605 CMR 7.00: Regional Library Systems. http://mblc.state.ma.us/mblc/laws/code/605cmr7.php.

McCook, K. (2000). *A place at the table: Participating in community building.* Chicago, IL: American Library Association.

McCook, K. (2011). *Introduction to public librarianship* (2nd ed.). New York, NY: Neal-Schuman Publishers.

Michigan Legislature. Section 397.210a. City, Village, and Township Libraries (Excerpt) Act 164 of 1877. http://legislature.mi.gov/doc.aspx?mcl-397-210a.

Miller, E. G., & Fisher, P. H. (2007). *Library board strategic guide.* Lanham, MD: Scarecrow Press.

Miller, R. (2014). The Gates impact. *Library Journal, 139*(10), 8.

Minow, M., & Lipinski, T. A. (2003). *The library's legal answer book.* Chicago, IL: American Library Association.

National Association of Counties. (2015). Legislative priorities. www.naco.org.

National League of Cities. (2015). *2015 Annual Report.* www.nlc.org.

Nebraska Library Commission. (2011). *Rules and regulations of the Nebraska Library Commission: Title 236.* Chapter 2.002.07. www.nlc.state.ne.us/mission/rules.html#General%20Information.

Orono Public Library. (n.d.). About. www.oronolibraryfoundation.org/about/.

Oxnard, California. (2015, January 27). Ordinance 2888.

Pennsylvania Library Association. Learn to be a library advocate. (n.d.). https://www.palibraries.org/?page=Advocacy1.

Public Library Association. Advocacy. (n.d.). www.ala.org/pla/advocacy.

Rosa, K. (2016). Referenda roundup. *American Libraries, 47*(1/2), 54-59.

Rosa, K. & Henke, K. (2017). Referenda roundup 2017. *American Libraries, 48*(1/2), 36-41.

Schull, D.S., & Zeisel, W. (2011). Community foundations and the public library. Libraries for the Future, 1990–1991. In McCook, *Introduction to public librarianship.* (pp. 475–482). New York, NY: Neal-Schuman Publishers.

State Library of North Carolina. (n.d.) New public library directors: State aid guide. http://statelibrary.ncdcr.libguides.com/c.php?g=217273&p=1435338.

Swan, D. W., Grimes, J., Owens, T., Miller, K., & Bauer, L. (2014). *State Library Administrative Agencies Survey: Fiscal Year 2012* (IMLS-2014-SLAA-01). Washington, DC: Institute of Museum and Library Services. https://www.imls.gov/assets/1/AssetManager/2012%20SLAA%20Report.pdf.

Todaro, J. B. (2016). ALA lauds FOIA law signing. *American Libraries, 47*(7/8), 9.

Turner, A. M. (2000). *Vote yes for libraries: A guide to winning ballot measure campaigns for library funding.* Jefferson, NC: McFarland.

United for Libraries Advocacy. (n.d.). www.ala.org/united/advocacy/altaffresources.

United for Libraries. Friends & foundations fact sheets. (n.d.). www.ala.org/united/foundations/factsheets.

United States. (2003). Children's Internet Protection Act, Pub. L. 106-554: Study of technology protection measures in section 1703: Report to Congress. Washington, DC: Department of Commerce, National Telecommunications and Information Administration.

Urban Libraries Council. (2013). *Leadership brief: Maximizing the library-foundation partnership.* www.urbanlibraries.org/filebin/pdfs/Library_Foundation_Part_Nov13.pdf.

Wachtel, L. (1933). State provisions for the support of municipal public libraries. *Library Quarterly 3.*

Warburton, B. (2015). MO library funds restored; FY16 in flux. *Library Journal, 140*(8), 12.

Wilkins, B. (2011) State libraries and state library agencies. In *Encyclopedia of library and information sciences* (3rd ed.). Boca Raton, FL: CRC Press.

Wilson, P. (2016). Demonstrating the library's ROI. *Public Libraries Online.* http://publiclibrariesonline.org/2016/07/demonstrating-the-librarys-roi/#.V47JU9ryu4Q.

The Public Library's People

Work Life and Commitment

Library workers activate the mission of the public library through the library's collections, community partnerships, and one-on-one services. The library is able to support lifelong learning to people of all ages through hiring, training, and cultivating a qualified and committed staff. Many people—members of the library board, library workers, and volunteers—come together to shape a library that functions as the heart of the twenty-first-century community.

This chapter is about library personnel. It presents model organizational charts to illustrate the relationships between the library board, municipality, and staff. It describes the roles and responsibilities of the library board, giving special consideration to citizen representation and diversity among board members. It also provides details about the characteristics of the library director. The chapter addresses the organization of the library staff based on aggregated national data. It addresses the role of unions. Finally, it describes recruitment and staff development.

HOW LIBRARIES ARE ORGANIZED

Public librarians must conceive of the administration and staffing of public libraries in the context of the overall organizational structure, which exists as a function of municipal, county, or district governance. Due to their local nature, these differ from community to community; therefore, there is no single preferred way to organize a library's staff and chain of command (which is sometimes dictated by state statutes). However, we can begin by stating that, generally, the public library director reports to an elected or appointed Board of Trustees or Board Directors, or a Commission. For example, the director of the Denver (CO) Public Library reports to an eight-member Commission appointed by the mayor. The Charlotte Mecklenburg (NC) Library (North Carolina) operates under an 11-member board of trustees, 10 of whom are appointed by the Board of County Commissioners and one of whom is appointed by the Board of Education. The residents of Idaho's Madison Public Library District vote trustees to six-year terms.[1] Trustees are, therefore, near the top of the hierarchy: they hire, evaluate, and fire the director.

> **▶ TASK**
>
> There are multiple ways in which public library trustees are selected. Find out the method used by your local library.

In most states, public libraries operate as departments or units of municipal, county, or district governance. Figure 6.1, the organization chart of the Town of Bedford, Massachusetts, serving about 14,000 people, shows the board system at work via the Board of Assessors, the Board of Health, the Planning Board, and the Library Board all reporting to the voters and overseeing their respective areas of service.

> ▶ **TASK**
>
> There are many variations on the organizational structure of public libraries. What is the organization structure of your local public library?

The organization chart of the Aurora Public Library (figure 6.2) shows the structure of a municipal library serving about 200,000, which includes branch management and functional supervisors.

The consolidated city-county organizational chart of Denver, Colorado, serves approximately 680,000. Figure 6.3 shows a structure that includes community engagement, immigrant services, a community technology center, and western history. Figure 6.4 shows the organizational chart of the Akron-Summit County, Ohio, system, which serves 540,000 people.

THE LIBRARY BOARD OF TRUSTEES

The library board of trustees (or library board) is the citizen body prevalent in the oversight of American public libraries. It has its roots in the structure of the Boston Public Library. The enabling legislation for public libraries in each state generally specifies the composition and method used to appoint the library board. Commonly appointed by a governing body, but sometimes elected, the library board has responsibility for a range of functions:

- analysis of community needs
- hiring, recommending, and evaluating the public library director
- acting in an advocacy role to develop community support for bond issues and taxation
- budget review and approval
- policy review and approval
- commitment to freedom of inquiry and expression
- formulation of long-range planning

In her handbook for successful trustees, Moore (2010) outlined what it means to be a trustee, focusing on advocacy, policy development, director hiring and evaluation, strategic planning, budgeting, and fundraising. Miller & Fisher (2007) have developed a strategic guide that demonstrates how the director-board relationship fulfills a social contract with the community. In what is perhaps the most insightful of all writing on trustees Holt and Holt (2014) describe board members as the most important library volunteers, on whom institutional success depends (pp. 11–12). The board must first understand the complex political environment in order to forge policy and support for service (Henricks & Henricks-Lepp, 2014).

The Board of Trustee governance of public libraries—citizen oversight of budget and policies—has been in place since the first tax-supported libraries were established in the 1850s. The Board represents the people of the library's community. State library laws in-

Town of Bedford (MA) Organizational Chart

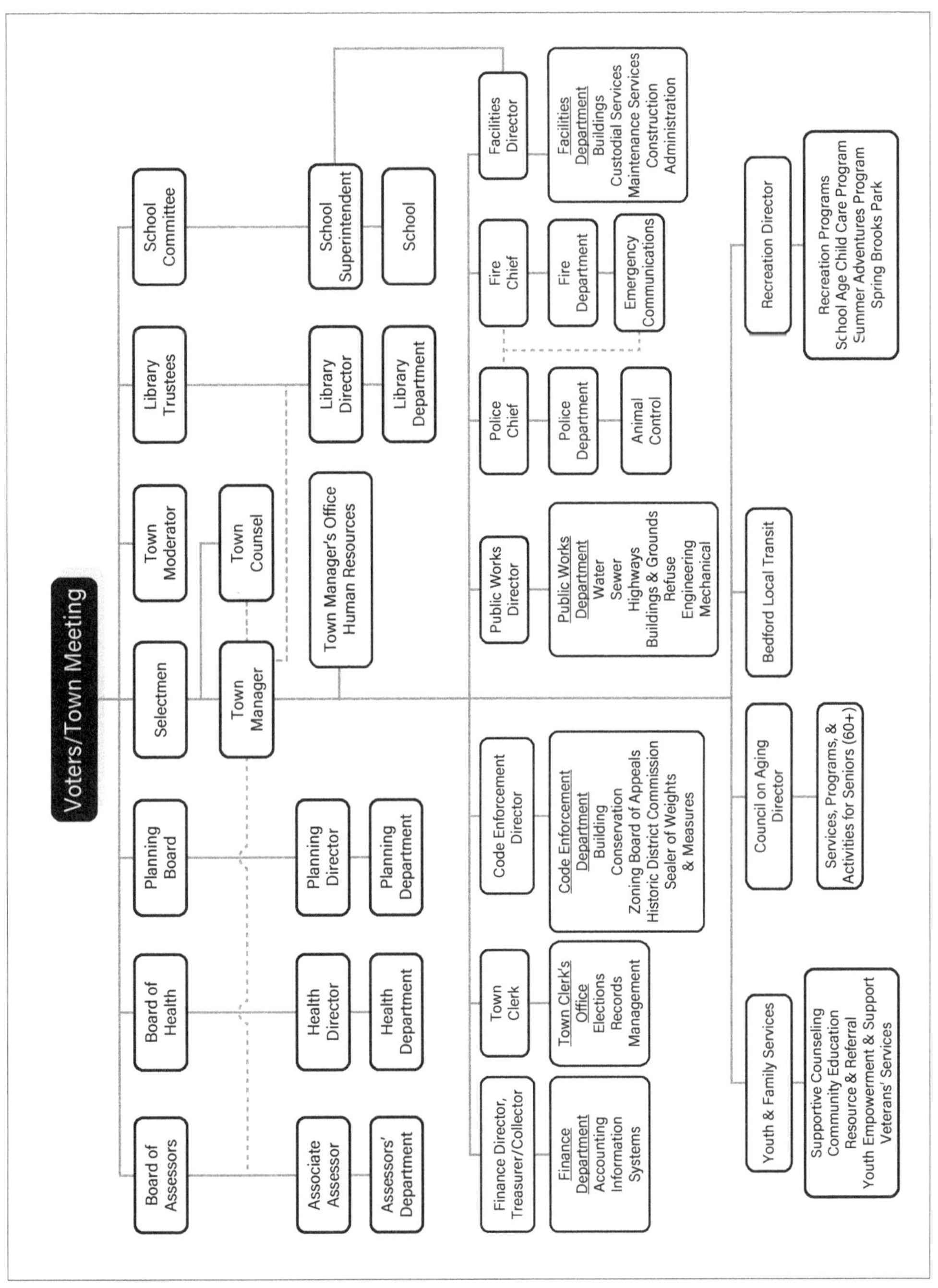

FIGURE 6.1 Town of Bedford (MA) Organizational Chart

SOURCE: Reprinted with the permission of the Town of Bedford, Massachusetts (www.bedfordma.gov/sites/bedfordma/files/file/file/townof2.pdf).

Aurora (IL) Public Library Organizational Chart

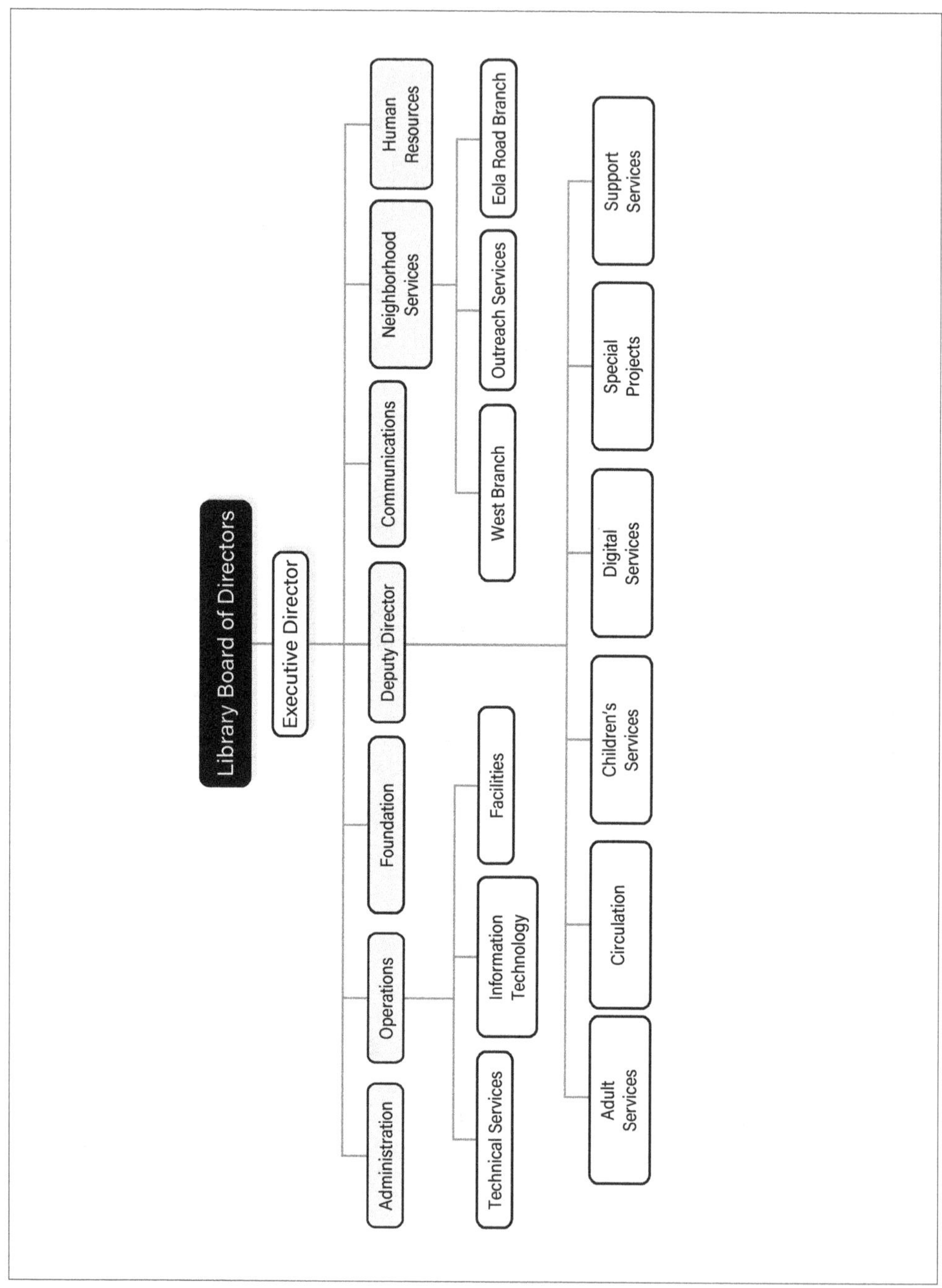

FIGURE 6.2 Aurora (IL) Public Library Organizational Chart

SOURCE: Courtesy of Aurora (IL) Public Library (www.aurorapubliclibrary.org).

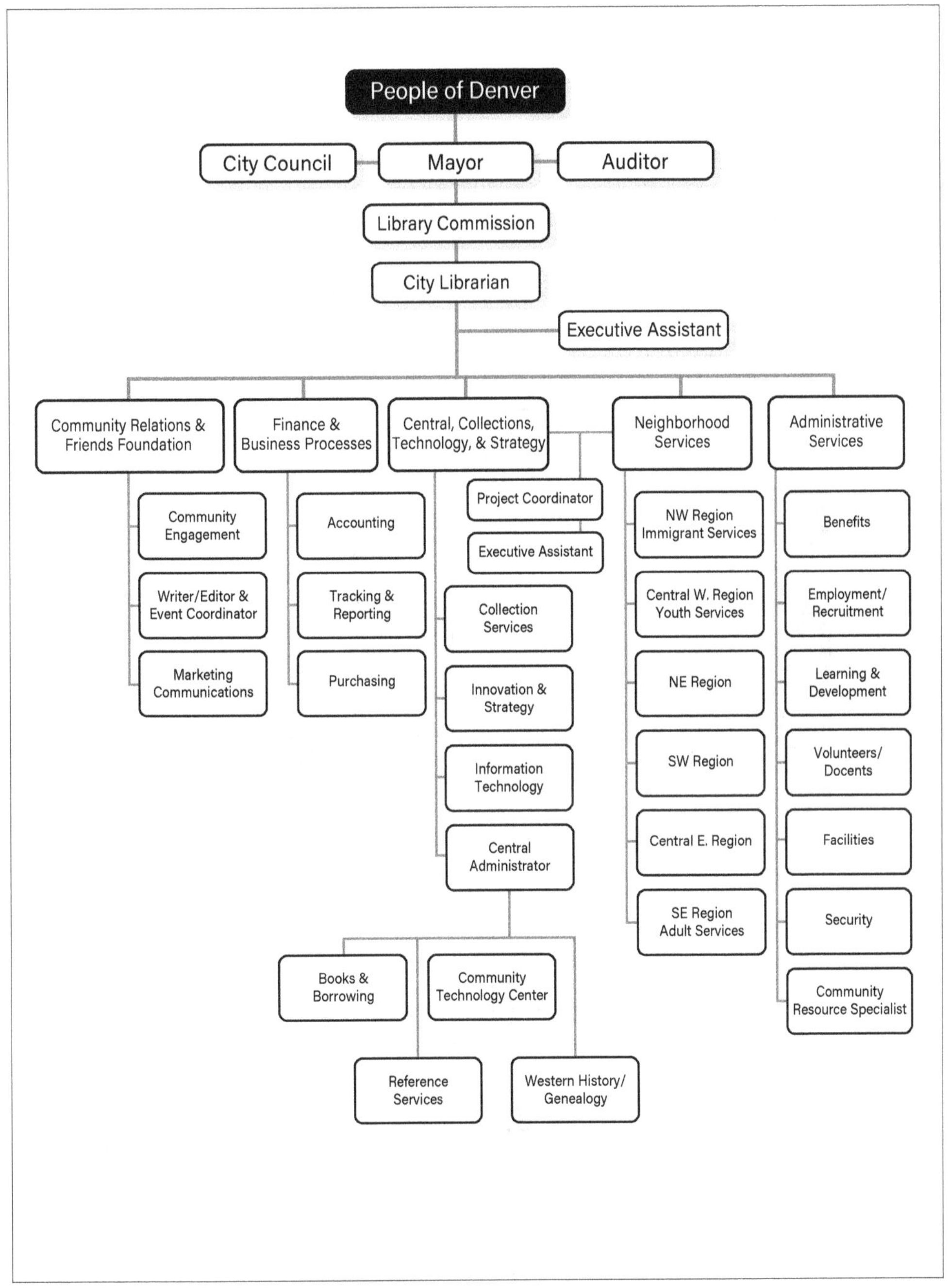

FIGURE 6.3 Denver Public Library 2016 Organizational Chart

SOURCE: Courtesy of Denver Public Library (https://www.denverlibrary.org/sites/dplorg/files/2016-05/org_chart_0516.pdf).

Akron-Summit County (OH) Public Library 2016 Organizational Chart

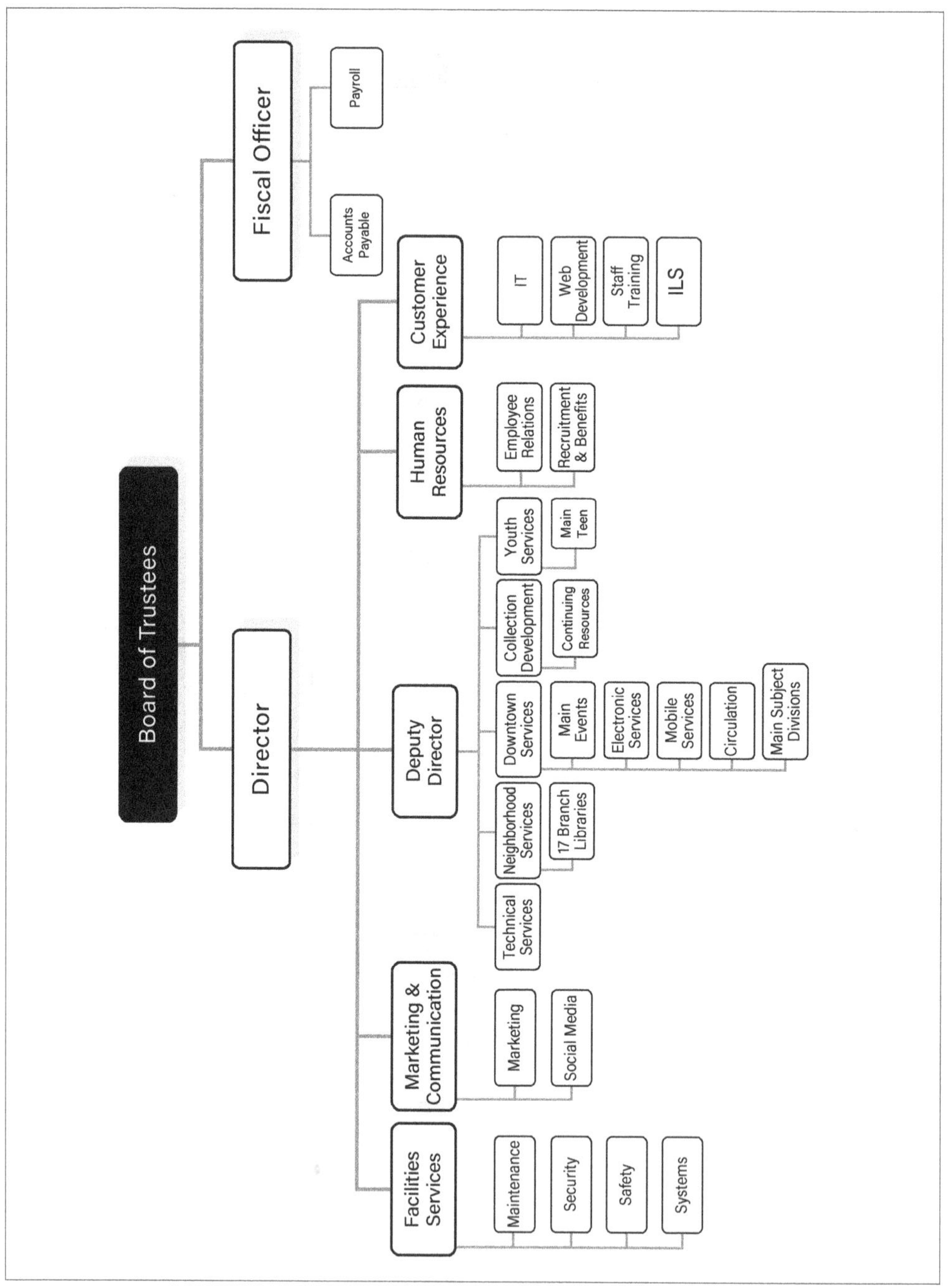

FIGURE 6.4 Akron-Summit County (OH) Public Library 2016 Organizational Chart

SOURCE: Courtesy of the Akron-Summit County (OH) Public Library (www.akronlibrary.org/images/pdfs/OrgChartRevised_8_18_16.pdf).

clude regulations about Board responsibilities. The New Hampshire Statute on Library Trustees identifies typical duties (figure 6.5).

The New Hampshire statute is similar to the statutes of other states throughout America, where the scope of trustee responsibilities includes budget, hiring the director, policy review, advocating for library support, and planning.

Who are trustees? There is not a great deal of historical or sociological information about trustee demographics. Eighty years ago, Joeckel's study of the governance of the American public library provided baseline information in his "Personnel of Library Boards." He reported 78% were men and the median age was 56, with more than 10% older than 70. Board members were long-serving, with 40% having served more than 10 years. The majority (70%) had college, graduate, or professional degrees. Members' occupational groups included lawyers, doctors, clergy, professors, engineers, bankers, and government service. Interestingly, one large group were simply listed as "married women" (Joeckel, 1935, pp. 236–247).

> **▶ FACT**
>
> Caucasians comprised 84% of nonprofit governance boards in 2010. African-Americans made up 8%; Latinos 4%; Asian-Americans 3%; American Indians 1%; two or more ethnicities-0.7%; and Native Hawaiian or Pacific Islanders 0.2%.*
>
> *Walker, V. L., & Davidson, D. J. *Vital Voices: Lessons Learned from Board Members of Color* (2010), https://www.boardsource.org/ewe. This publication provides survey and focus group results of 550 people of color serving on library boards. It did not provide data about library trustees. Searches conducted by the authors of this book yielded no data on the ethnicity of library trustees, but anecdotal observations suggested that boards are majority Caucasian.

Little detailed information of board composition has been compiled since. We know that boards of trustees still tend to be homogeneous and that the few studies done have shown they are comprised of older, well-educated, community minded individuals.[2] Most literature about Boards describes the kind of people needed. A 2013 survey of 777 subscribers to the United for Libraries trustee discussion list inquired why they decided to serve; what they consider to be the most important qualities and responsibilities of a trustee; and which trends and challenges are faced by today's libraries. No demographics were included, but desirable qualities were reported: integrity; willingness to listen and learn; understanding the library's mission and needs; and being knowledgeable about finances, legislative issues, legal matters, and board meeting etiquette (Rzepczynski, 2013).

> **▶ TASK**
>
> Find out about your local library's board of directors. How are they selected? What are their professions and backgrounds? Can you learn anything about how they are trained to perform their duties?

Why should we be concerned with diversity in relation to library boards? Amy Garmer, director of the Aspen Institute's Dialogue on Public Libraries, observed that libraries are "critical connectors for communities and connectors to others" that can help introduce different organizations or ethnic groups to one another in towns with changing demographics, or which can pull in marginalized members of the community who may be disconnected from the library. Trustees are the people entrusted to network on the library's behalf (Traska, 2015). Rutledge has examined strategies for library boards to become more inclusive (2013), which is important because they represent the community.[3]

TRUSTEE ORGANIZATIONS

The national organization for library trustees, United for Libraries, is a division of the American Library Association. (Note also that there are sections for trustees in every state library association.) It supports citizens who govern, promote, advocate, and fundraise for all types of libraries.[4] The specific responsibilities of United for Libraries are:

- educating through a continuing and comprehensive program for library Trustees to enable them to discharge their responsibilities in a manner best fitted to benefit the public and the libraries they represent

New Hampshire Statutes: Library Trustees

202-A: 11 Powers and Duties.—Except in those cities where other provision has been made by general or special act of the legislature, the library trustees of every public library in the state shall:

I. Adopt bylaws, rules and regulations for its own transaction of business and for the government of the library;

II. Prepare an annual budget indicating what support and maintenance of the free public library will be required out of public funds for submission to the appropriate agency of the municipality. A separate budget request shall be submitted for new construction, capital improvements of existing library property;

III. Expend all moneys raised and appropriated by the town or city for library purposes and shall direct that such moneys be paid over by the town or city treasurer pursuant to a payment schedule as agreed to by the library trustees and the selectmen or city council. All money received from fines and payments for lost or damaged books or for the support of a library in another city or town under contract to furnish library service to such town or city, shall be used for general repairs and upgrading, and for the purchase of books, supplies and income-generating equipment, shall be held in a nonlapsing separate fund and shall be in addition to the appropriation;

IV. Expend income from all trust funds for library purposes for the support and maintenance of the public library in said town or city in accordance with the conditions of each donation or bequest accepted by the town or city;

V. Appoint a librarian who shall not be a trustee and, in consultation with the librarian, all other employees of the library and determine their compensation and other terms of employment unless, in the cities, other provision is made in the city charter or ordinances.

FIGURE 6.5 New Hampshire Statutes: Library Trustees

SOURCE: New Hampshire Statutes (www.gencourt.state.nh.us/rsa/).

- encouraging and assisting the formation of and development of Friends of Library groups and Library Foundations
- providing a means for trustees to have access to information and ideas that will prove useful to them in the governance of their libraries
- providing Friends of Library groups and library foundations access to information and ideas that will prove useful to them in fundraising, library promotion and the operation of their organizations
- promoting strong state and regional trustee and Friends of Library organizations
- providing to all who value libraries the materials and support they need to be effective advocates for their libraries on the local, state, and national levels
- making the public aware of the existence of formalized citizen groups such as trustees, Friends of Library groups, and library foundations and the services they perform to encourage and develop expanded citizen participation in the support of libraries across the country

The "Public Library Trustee Ethics Statement: Official Statement from United for Libraries" states:

> Public library Trustees are accountable for the resources of the library as well as to see that the library provides the best possible service to its community. Every Trustee makes a personal commitment to contribute the time and energy to faithfully carry out his/her duties and responsibilities effectively and with absolute truth, honor and integrity.[5]

Library advocacy is a central activity of trustees. Trustees advocate for libraries at the local and state levels, and join with United for Libraries to participate in national legislative initiatives. State library associations and state library agencies also provide programs for library board members, which focus on state issues and organize programs, produce handbooks, and provide other means of support for the work of shared governance. The members of the library board articulate the importance of the library to the general public; therefore, board members' recognition of local and state issues is essential. Each state develops support that reflects its context. A few samples of state trustee handbooks provide the essence of state level trustee expectations.

Maine Library Trustee Handbook (2015)

> This handbook consists of basic information needed by you, the trustee, to be an effective board member and library advocate. . . . It is the responsibility of each Maine library to understand its legal status based on its establishment documents.

Handbook for Library Trustees of New York State (2015)

> Forward-looking, informed trustees are needed to guide their libraries. Reinforcing the traditional services of libraries and welcoming the new, expanded opportunities of broadband Internet access, makerspaces and other technologies, trustees must position their libraries as essential and vital resources for individual and community success.

Trustee Essentials: A Handbook for Wisconsin Public Library Trustees (2016)

> It has been written that the core of effective politics is the building of rapport. Since local politics are personal, your contacts on behalf of the library with public officials from the municipality, the county, and the state will advance the cause of your institution.

It is the persistence and advocacy of library boards that create the community support for building programs, increased taxes, or even new operational structures. An Illinois survey found that the state's trustees contributed over 250,000 hours of time in a single year. They are instrumental in making the case for funding (Kohn, 2016). When a municipality needs new or increased library space, the trustees play an important role. As Ames and Heid (2009) note, the library board of trustees is the owner of the construction program and represent the community; they are as necessary to the design and construction as the library director, staff, architect, and contractor.

We can identify various examples of the dynamic nature of trustee efforts, often through their firsthand accounts. Shirley Lang (2008), of the Syosset, New York, board of trustees and a longtime member of ALTA, has written insightfully on the relationship between directors and trustees.[6] Library board members' contagious enthusiasm and hope are emblematic of the committed, dedicated citizen, who has worked side by side with librarians to establish, develop, and strengthen library services. Looking at the role of trustees, we remember that libraries are not mandated by law; they are enabled and voluntary—the roots are nurtured and rise from the people.

The "Save Our Library Committee" cartoon (figure 6.6) in the June 2016 *ILA Reporter* demonstrates how a simple message in Alpha Park, Illinois, area newspapers helped to win 63% of the referendum vote in favor of capital repair and improvement projects (Kohn, 2016).

THE LIBRARY DIRECTOR

> A top skill for tomorrow's librarians—"to articulate our value in communities and the ability to speak about all of our offerings and how those offerings can practically impact people's lives."
>
> **—Nicolle Ingui Davies, executive director of the Arapahoe Library District, Centennial, CO, and the 2016 *LJ* Librarian of the Year, quoted in Schwartz (2016)**

Library directors have complicated jobs. They are leaders, managers, and visionaries. Library directors (in consultation with the board and staff) are responsible for setting priorities and maintaining relationships with community leaders. Marcum (2016) predicts that digital leadership, fostering user engagement, communication, and attention to the cultural fit of the library in the community will be the central skills of library directors in future years. Directors of very small public libraries might also be responsible for everything from collection development to website management and building maintenance.

Brian Kenney (2015) offers some useful tips to librarians who want to make the transition to library director:

CSI the library—"pull every document you can find about the library—annual report, state report, board audits, newsletters" (para. 6); look for a stable board that is capable of making decisions (read their minutes to find out). Examine the organizational chart to gain a sense of the infrastructure. Look at the numbers (budget, input, an output). Learn as much as you can about the library's culture to see what you might be walking into. Finally, look at the "Love Factor": does the city love the library? Have you fallen in love with the job? If so, you might be ready to apply. Two recent doctoral dissertations—Michele Leininger's "From Librarian to Proficient Manager: The Journey of Public Library Front-Line Managers" and Sharon P. Morris's "Reflecting on the Core Values and Defining Moments of Public Library Directors" provide scholarly insight as to qualities and affective characteristics of the director (Rosa, 2016).

The library director is most often selected by the board of trustees. A resource produced by COSLA, *Hiring a New Library Director: The Trustee Toolkit* (2015), is intended for use by trustees when selecting a new leader to run their library. Hiring a director is one of the primary responsibilities of many boards—a process important for success, which sets a trajectory for the future course of the library and the community it serves. Sample tools and templates included in the *Trustee Toolkit* are only a starting point that is intended to be modified for local use. The knowledge, skills, and abilities of a new director as characterized by the COSLA Toolkit are reprinted in figure 6.7.

FIGURE 6.6 Voter Fever ("Save Our Library Committee" Cartoon)

SOURCE: *ILA Reporter*, June 2016, p. 5. Design by Dean Patton and Jennifer Hattermann. Courtesy of Alpha Park Public Library District.

Knowledge, Skills, and Abilities of the Director

Responsibilities and Duties

A. Provides friendly, courteous and accurate service to all users
B. Provides a leadership role in the library
C. Responds to patron requests, suggestions and complaints
D. Evaluates operations and activities of the library, plans for future needs, develops library collections and services and adopts and implements new services
E. Advocates for the library by serving as the official representative of the library in the community and throughout the library field and by speaking before community, civic and other groups about the library's services
F. Establishes and maintains effective working relationships with library patrons, other governmental agencies, civic and community groups and the general public
G. Develops staff job descriptions, recommends and administers personnel policies involving hiring, evaluating, promoting and terminating staff
H. Directly supervises the Management Team; indirectly supervises all library employees
I. Defines expectations for staff performances, oversees and implements the staff evaluation process
J. Promotes staff morale through communication, staff meetings, in-service programs and staff trainings
K. Supervises and encourages staff members' continuing education
L. Maintains neatness of public areas including desks, counters, shelves, tables and personal space visible to public
M. Attends library board meetings and committee meetings and serves as a resource for the library board
N. Develops and submits an annual budget and monthly financial reports to the library board
O. Formulates and recommends policies to the library board and implements board adopted policies and library procedures
P. Monitors and approves appropriations and expenditures
Q. Prepares legal documents, files required documents, publishes required notices
R. Oversees grant proposals and submissions
S. Creates, organizes and implements solicitation of donations and/or gifts to the library, reviews and acknowledges receipt of donations and/or gifts
T. Monitors, oversees and evaluates the cost and adequacy of insurance coverage, services provided by insurance companies and insurance proposals and provide recommendations for the library board

FIGURE 6.7 Knowledge, Skills, and Abilities of the Director [CONTINUED ON FOLLOWING PAGE]

SOURCE: © 2015 Chief Officers of State Library Agencies. Hiring a New Library Director: Resource Packet for Public Library Board of Trustees. http://www.cosla.org/documents/HiringDirectorResourcePacket1.pdf.

FIGURE 6.7 [CONTINUED]

U. Oversees the automation and technology needs and maintenance of the library, implements new technology as appropriate

V. Attends library and professional meetings and participates in regional and statewide professional activities

Knowledge, Skills and Abilities

A. Knowledge of library philosophies, practices, procedures and technologies
B. Ability to set priorities, make decisions, and exercise discretion with patrons and staff
C. Ability to think analytically and to exercise initiative
D. Ability to prioritize work, meet established deadlines, delegate duties and attend to detail as appropriate
E. Ability to handle multiple and simultaneous tasks
F. Ability to develop and implement policies and procedures
G. Ability to establish and maintain effective relationships with staff and with local and regional media
H. Ability to hire, train, supervise, discipline and evaluate staff at all levels of experience
I. Ability to work effectively as a team
J. Knowledge of library budgetary and fiscal practices and library law
K. Knowledge of computers and the Internet, especially integrated library systems software, Microsoft Office, and similar software programs
L. Ability to communicate effectively, both in writing and orally and to prepare and present reports and other information in the appropriate format
M. Ability to work the hours needed to complete responsibilities of Library Director

Additionally, ALA's Library Career website identifies library director requirements, including

- the desire to meet and serve the library's user community
- the ability to think analytically and to develop new or revised systems, procedures, and work flow
- the ability to exercise initiative and independent judgment
- a knowledge of computers, the Internet, and commercially available library software
- the ability to prepare comprehensive reports and present ideas clearly and concisely in written and oral form
- the ability to make administrative decisions, interpret policies, and supervise staff

- the ability to motivate, establish, and maintain effective working relationships with associates, supervisors, volunteers, other community agencies and the public
- a knowledge of the philosophy and techniques of library service
- the ability to organize job duties and work independently
- a demonstrated knowledge of library materials and resources
- the creativity to develop and implement library programs and services
- the ability to communicate both orally and in writing
- the skill to employ management techniques effectively in directing, planning, organizing, staffing, coordinating, budgeting, and evaluating the library's operation*

One formal educational option for librarians who want to become administrators is the Certified Public Library Administrator certification. This program was authorized by the American Library Association-Allied Professional Association (ALA-APA), and is a post-MLS certification program for public librarians with three years or more of supervisory experience. CPLA certification is not measured in PLS statistics. The ALA-APA provides the certification that enables public librarians to:

- further their professional education and development
- move to a higher level of practical professional experience
- improve career opportunities through professional expertise
- demonstrate to colleagues, trustees and boards of directors, patrons, and the wider information community that the certified person has acquired a nationally and professionally recognized body of knowledge and expertise in public library administration
- improve the quality of library service through the provision of practical knowledge and skills essential to successful library management.[7]

> **▸ FACT**
>
> Salaries for public library directors ranged from $20,000 to $310,000, with the median registering at $59,000 in a 2014 report.*
>
> *Girmscheid, L., & Schwartz, M. (2014). Pay day. *Library Journal, 139*(12), p. 22.

Analysis of announcements for library director positions demonstrates that library boards value experience with multicultural communities, knowledge of digital technologies, and understanding the importance of community involvement, as well as experience working with an advisory board and community groups and elected officials. Figure 6.8 is a 2015 announcement from the Hartford (CT) Public Library. Directors are expected to be leaders with strong interpersonal, communication, staff development, and collaborative skills.

---

* American Library Association. www.ala.org/educationcareers/careers/librarycareerssite/whatyouneeddirector www.ala.org/educationcareers/careers/librarycareerssite/whatyouneeddirector.

Job Announcement:
CEO, Hartford (CT) Public Library

Chief Executive Officer (CEO), Hartford Public Library
Hartford, Connecticut
Salary: $140,000 to $160,000
Status: Full-time
Posted: 11/20/15
Deadline: 01/17/16

Chief Executive Officer (CEO)

Find Your Place at a Place Like No Other—The award-winning Hartford Public Library seeks a charismatic and experienced leader to provide vision and continued collaboration within the City of Hartford as the Library's next Chief Executive Officer (CEO).

The successful candidate will have an entrepreneurial focus and a strong background in fundraising and developing beneficial partnerships. In addition to external engagement, the new CEO will work with a committed, talented staff providing leadership and direction for the Library's continued success as a vital civic institution.

Current programs at the Library include YOUmedia Hartford—a digital learning place for teens; The American Place—designed to welcome immigrants and ease their transition to their new home city; CTWorks@HPL—a collaborative one-stop career center; The Kitchen at Hartford Public Library—a non-profit partnership pairing farm-to-table job training and permanent job placement; the Hartford History Center; Baby-Grand Jazz Series—a series of 16 free jazz concerts now in its 12th year; and ArtWalk—one of the largest and most stunning exhibition spaces in greater Hartford, featuring up to four exhibitions per year.

New projects and collaborations include two major branch construction projects and creation of the UCONN Hartford campus within the Downtown library, Itty Bitty Hartford—a childhood education play-and-learn destination inside the Downtown library, and an expanded partnership with the Hartford Public Schools.

A 2002 IMLS National Service Medal winner, the Library was also a finalist for the medal in both 2013 and 2014. Hartford Public Library, a 501c3 nonprofit, serves 124,775 residents with ten branches and a $9.6 million annual budget. In FY14, the library staff (104FTE) hosted 833,000 visits and circulated nearly 500,000 items. The Hartford Public Library is nationally recognized as one of the top libraries in the United States.

Compensation. The hiring salary range for the position is $140,000–$160,000 annually (with placement dependent upon qualifications) and includes a competitive employee benefits package.

FIGURE 6.8 Job Announcement: CEO, Hartford (CT) Public Library

SOURCE: Courtesy of Hartford Public Library.

THE LIBRARY STAFF

> In the midst of this painful time (Baltimore Civil Unrest in spring 2015) and in the epicenter of it all, Carla and her staff showed the world that libraries are safe havens and community anchors.
>
> **—Amundsen (2015)**[8]

Library staff are honored on the Tuesday of National Library Week to recognize the hard work, dedication, and expertise of library support staff and librarians. The contributions of library staff in times such as the Baltimore Civil unrest or during disaster response may receive national recognition, but day after day, in ways large and small, the people who work in our public libraries keep the enterprise at the heart of our communities (Disaster Information Model, n.d.).

Library staff are generally part the civil service systems of the government to which they report (e.g., city or county). Position requirements are usually created in collaboration with a larger government unit. These differ from community to community. There are no nationally or even state uniform position titles or job descriptions for librarians. The most common requirement for librarians is a degree from a graduate program accredited by the American Library Association.[9] The number of ALA-accredited degree holders at each public library is a data element collected by the Institute of Museums and Library services in its annual survey (Swan et al., 2015).

Who Are Public Library Workers?

Public library workers are at the frontlines of their communities' education, economic well-being, and safety. Librarians provide daily support for many aspects of community service, including collection development, basic literacy, lifelong learning, educational support, adult job seekers, digital access, cultural heritage, early learning, and local history. At times of community crisis—civil unrest, floods, fires, hurricanes, technology disruption—public librarians provide a sanctuary and safe haven. To fulfill individuals' needs—for books, vocational materials, music, health insurance information, or simply shelter from the heat or cold—public librarians provide guidance in intellectual development or sources for survival assistance.

> **▶ FACT**
>
> The median pay of a public librarian is $52,000.*
>
> *U.S. Bureau of Labor Statistics. Occupational Outlook Handbook, Librarians. www.bls.gov/ooh/education-training-and-library/librarians.htm#tab-5. See also ALA-APA Salary Survey Database at www.ala.org/cfapps/salarysurvey/login/login.cfm.

For public library workers, the mission of the public library is a daily reality. According to the Bureau of Labor Statistics (2016), a public librarian should have the following abilities:

- reading skills
- communication skills
- computer skills to help patrons research topics, to classify resources, create databases, and perform administrative duties

- initiative
- interpersonal skills
- problem-solving skills

The *Public Libraries in the United States Survey* (PLS), the IMLS annual report, publishes data about the public library workforce. The PLS states:

> Staff at public libraries ensure that resources, services, and facilities are accessible, available, and well managed. Moreover, beyond collection development and resource management, library staff address information needs by providing programming, answering reference questions, and supporting research. (IMLS, 2016, p. 14)

▶ FACT

Total public library staff per 25,000 people served vary across states as high as Wyoming (20.6) to as low as Nevada (6.1).*

*Public library staff consists of librarians (both those librarians with an ALA-accredited degree and those librarians that do not have an ALA-accredited degree) and other paid support staff (including paraprofessionals, IT, operations, and maintenance staff). In the Public Library Survey staffing is reported as paid full-time employment (FTE) positions. The total staff per capita indicator is defined as the total number of all paid staff divided by the people in the legal service area. For this, it is divided by each 25,000 people in the legal service area. (IMLS, 2014, pp. 53–54).

There are no national standards that govern staffing patterns for public libraries.[10] State-level standards often include guidelines about staffing. The Wisconsin Public Library Standards suggest:

> The public library staff should project an image of competence and friendliness to all members of the public. Public library staff members should understand the service goals of the library, should be aware of all library policies, and should be well trained in the practices and procedures required by their individual positions. (2010, p. 23)

In the national Public Library Survey report, public library staff are reported in three categories: librarians, ALA-MLS librarians,[11] and other paid staff. Indicators associated with public library staffing find nationwide that per 25,000 people served there are a total of 11.3 staffers, of which 3.9 were librarians. We can compare library patterns using the PLS data shown in figure 6.9.

▶ TASK

See how your state compares to the national average. Are there any requirements or recommendations for training or education for librarians in your state?

The distribution and ratio of public librarians with ALA-accredited Masters of Library and Information Studies (MLS) degrees varies across America. Public libraries in densely populated and urbanized areas are more likely to employ a librarian with an ALA-MLS accredited degree. Over two-thirds of all public libraries have a librarian with an accredited degree on staff. These metrics help to indicate whether there is enough staffing to address the needs of the population and measure professionalism in librarianship (IMLS, 2014, p. 54). Figure 6.10 provides ranking by state.

The American Library Association key document "Library and Information Studies and Human Resource Utilization: A Statement of Policy" is the most overarching statement on human resources for librarianship. It is presented in figure 6.11.

State	Ranking	Total Paid FTE Staff Per 25,000 Population[1]
TOTAL[2]	**†**	**11.29**
District of Columbia[3]	1	21.63
Wyoming	2	19.86
Ohio	3	19.38
Illinois	4	18.45
Indiana	5	17.94
New Hampshire	6	17.45
Kansas	7	17.27
New York	8	16.08
Connecticut	9	16.06
Colorado	10	15.70
Vermont	11	14.73
Maine	12	14.70
Iowa	13	14.39
Missouri	14	14.34
Maryland	15	14.29
Louisiana	16	14.23
Idaho	17	14.10
Massachusetts	18	14.08
Rhode Island	19	13.91
Washington	20	13.56
New Jersey	21	13.55
Wisconsin	22	13.32
Nebraska	23	12.87
Kentucky	24	12.39
Michigan	25	12.20
Oregon	26	12.00
Virginia	27	11.80
South Dakota	28	11.70
Alaska	29	11.65
Oklahoma	30	11.64
Utah	31	10.79
South Carolina	32	10.26
New Mexico	33	10.04
Arkansas	34	9.96
Minnesota	35	9.86
Alabama	36	9.83
Hawaii4	37	9.75
Montana	38	9.69
North Dakota	39	9.47
Pennsylvania	40	8.94
Delaware	41	8.92
West Virginia	42	8.72
Mississippi	43	7.88
Florida	44	7.70
Arizona	45	7.62
California	46	7.57
Nevada	47	7.48
North Carolina	48	7.37
Tennessee	49	7.17
Texas	50	6.97
Georgia	51	6.61

FIGURE 6.9 Number of Paid Full-Time Equivalent Staff and Paid Full-Time Equivalent Librarians of Public Libraries per 25,000 Population, by State: Fiscal Year 2014

[CONTINUED ON FOLLOWING PAGE]

SOURCE: Institute of Museum and Library Services (U.S.), (2016). *Supplementary Tables: Public Libraries Survey Fiscal Year 2014*. July 2016. https://www.imls.gov/sites/default/files/fy2014_pls_tables.pdf.

FIGURE 6.9 [CONTINUED]

State	Ranking	Paid FTE librarians per 25,000 population[1]
TOTAL[2]	†	**3.85**
New Hampshire	1	10.23
Vermont	2	8.89
Iowa	3	8.07
Wyoming	4	7.74
Connecticut	5	7.56
Maine	6	7.31
Kansas	7	7.02
Massachusetts	8	6.83
Kentucky	9	6.82
Illinois	10	6.75
South Dakota	11	5.96
Rhode Island	12	5.91
Indiana	13	5.88
Nebraska	14	5.80
Maryland	15	5.79
Louisiana	16	5.66
Ohio	17	5.64
District of Columbia[3]	18	5.58
Oklahoma	19	5.39
Mississippi	20	5.28
New York	21	5.26
North Dakota	22	5.18
Wisconsin	23	4.98
West Virginia	24	4.88
Montana	25	4.81

State	Ranking	Paid FTE librarians per 25,000 population[1]
Michigan	26	4.53
Colorado	27	4.40
Alaska	28	4.33
New Mexico	29	4.29
New Jersey	30	4.02
Alabama	31	3.96
Idaho	32	3.84
Missouri	33	3.64
Minnesota	34	3.58
Oregon	35	3.32
Delaware	36	3.29
South Carolina	37	3.24
Utah	38	3.14
Hawaii4	39	3.06
Washington	40	3.01
Virginia	41	3.01
Pennsylvania	42	2.98
Arkansas	43	2.71
Texas	44	2.51
Florida	45	2.46
Tennessee	46	2.21
California	47	2.09
Arizona	48	2.05
North Carolina	49	1.96
Nevada	50	1.82
Georgia	51	1.45

† Not applicable.

1. Per 25,000 population is based on the total unduplicated population of legal service areas.
2. Total includes the 50 states and the District of Columbia but excludes outlying areas and libraries that do not meet the FSCS Public Library Definition.
3. The District of Columbia, although not a state, is included in the state rankings. Special care should be used in comparing its data to state data.
4. Caution should be used in making comparisons with the state of Hawaii, as Hawaii reports only one public library for the entire state.

State	Ranking	Paid FTE librarians with ALA-MLS per 25,000 population[1]
TOTAL[2]	†	11.29
District of Columbia[3]	1	5.58
Connecticut	2	5.29
Rhode Island	3	4.92
Massachusetts	4	4.79
New Hampshire	5	4.78
Illinois	6	4.60
New York	7	4.43
Ohio	8	4.12
Indiana	9	3.85
Maine	10	3.38
New Jersey	11	3.37
Colorado	12	3.20
Michigan	13	3.15
Hawaii[4]	14	3.04
Wisconsin	15	2.99
Washington	16	2.85
Kansas	17	2.80
Maryland	18	2.79
Vermont	19	2.79
Oregon	20	2.74
Virginia	21	2.72
South Carolina	22	2.55
Wyoming	23	2.50
Louisiana	24	2.47
Iowa	25	2.44

State	Ranking	Paid FTE librarians with ALA-MLS per 25,000 population
Minnesota	26	2.40
Pennsylvania	27	2.34
Oklahoma	28	2.32
Alaska	29	2.26
Florida	30	2.14
Kentucky	31	1.99
California	32	1.94
New Mexico	33	1.91
Utah	34	1.88
Nebraska	35	1.87
Montana	36	1.82
North Carolina	37	1.82
Alabama	38	1.78
Idaho	39	1.77
Arizona	40	1.73
Texas	41	1.72
Delaware	42	1.72
North Dakota	43	1.54
Nevada	44	1.49
South Dakota	45	1.49
Georgia	46	1.45
Arkansas	47	1.34
West Virginia	48	1.28
Missouri	49	1.23
Mississippi	50	1.10
Tennessee	51	1.03

FIGURE 6.10 Number of Paid Full-Time Equivalent Librarians with an ALA-Accredited MLS and Other Paid Full-Time Equivalent Staff of Public Libraries per 25,000 Population, by State: Fiscal Year 2014 [CONTINUED ON FOLLOWING PAGE]

SOURCE: IMLS, 2016a.: *Public Libraries Survey Fiscal Year 2014,* July 2016 (https://www.imls.gov/sites/default/files/fy2014_pls_tables.pdf).

FIGURE 6.10 [CONTINUED]

State	Ranking	Other paid FTE staff per 25,000[1] population[1]
TOTAL[2]	†	**7.44**
District of Columbia[3]	1	16.05
Ohio	2	13.74
Wyoming	3	12.12
Indiana	4	12.06
Illinois	5	11.70
Colorado	6	11.30
New York	7	10.83
Missouri	8	10.69
Washington	9	10.55
Idaho	10	10.26
Kansas	11	10.25
New Jersey	12	9.52
Virginia	13	8.78
Oregon	14	8.67
Louisiana	15	8.57
Maryland	16	8.50
Connecticut	17	8.50
Wisconsin	18	8.34
Rhode Island	19	8.00
Michigan	20	7.67
Utah	21	7.65
Maine	22	7.39
Alaska	23	7.32
Arkansas	24	7.25
Massachusetts	25	7.25
New Hampshire	26	7.22
Nebraska	27	7.07
South Carolina	28	7.02
Hawaii[4]	29	6.69
Iowa	30	6.33
Minnesota	31	6.28
Oklahoma	32	6.25
Pennsylvania	33	5.96
Alabama	34	5.87
Vermont	35	5.84
New Mexico	36	5.74
South Dakota	37	5.74
Nevada	38	5.67
Delaware	39	5.63
Arizona	40	5.57
Kentucky	41	5.57
California	42	5.47
North Carolina	43	5.41
Florida	44	5.23
Georgia	45	5.16
Tennessee	46	4.96
Montana	47	4.88
Texas	48	4.46
North Dakota	49	4.29
West Virginia	50	3.84
Mississippi	51	2.60

† Not applicable.

1. An ALA-MLS is a master's degree from a program of library and information studies accredited by the American Library Association. Per 25,000 population is based on the total unduplicated population of legal service areas.
2. Total includes the 50 states and the District of Columbia but excludes outlying areas and libraries that do not meet the FSCS Public Library Definition.
3. The District of Columbia, although not a state, is included in the state rankings. Special care should be used in comparing its data to state data.
4. Caution should be used in making comparisons with the state of Hawaii, as Hawaii reports only one public library for the entire state.

The Library and Information Studies and Human Resource Utilization statement asserts that the ALA-accredited MLIS is the appropriate professional degree for librarians. The *2015 Standards for Accreditation* "protect the public interest and provide guidance for educators. Prospective students, employers recruiting professional staff, and the general public concerned about the quality of library and information services have the right to know whether a given program of education is of good standing. By identifying those programs meeting recognized standards, the Committee offers a means of quality control in the professional staffing of library and information services."[12]

Many libraries reserve certain duties for librarians who hold the MLS or similar degree, but they rely on both full-time and part-time support staff for many positions that do not require the MLS. ALA's list of support staff positions includes positions that would be held in public libraries, such as "Assistant Circulation Manager, Catalog Maintenance Supervisor, Computer Specialist, Inter-Library Loan Specialist, Information Assistant, Library Aides, Assistants, Clerks, Information specialists, Technicians, Small branch managers, Programmer analysts, Personnel administrators, Secretaries, Technical services assistants, and Volunteer coordinators (see figure 6.12)."

Some state libraries offer training for support staff, and many libraries involve all staff in professional development activities. There is also national certification for support staff: the Library Support Staff Certification (LSSC) Program is provided nationally by the ALA

Library and Information Studies and Human Resource Utilization: A Statement of Policy

To meet the goals of library service, both professional and supportive staff are needed in libraries. Thus, the library occupation is much broader than that segment of it which is the library profession, but the library profession has responsibility for defining the training and education required for the preparation of personnel who work in libraries at any level, supportive or professional.

Skills other than those of library and information studies also have an important contribution to make to the achievement of superior library service. There should be equal recognition in both the professional and supportive ranks for those individuals whose expertise contributes to the effective performance of the library.

The title "Librarian" carries with it the connotation of "professional" in the sense that professional tasks are those which require a special background and education. (American Library Association. Policy Manual, B.9.1).

Additionally:

The master's degree from a program accredited by the American Library Association (or from a master's level program in library and information studies accredited or recognized by the appropriate national body of another country) is the appropriate professional degree for librarians. (American Library Association. Policy Manual, B.9.2).

FIGURE 6.11 Library and Information Studies and Human Resource Utilization: A Statement of Policy

SOURCE: American Library Association Policy Manual. B.9 Library Personnel Practices.

Selection of Public Library Position Titles, 2016

- Adult Programs and Services Librarian
- Automated Network Services
- Branch Volunteer Coordinator
- Business Librarian
- Cataloger
- Children's Librarian
- Children's Services Manager
- Communication and Marketing Specialist
- Community Librarian
- Cultural and Community Affairs
- Customer Experience Librarian
- Digital Learning Coordinator
- Early Literacy Librarian
- Genealogy Librarian
- Head of Information and Digital Services
- Information Technology Director
- Online Experience Coordinator
- Operations Manager
- Outreach and Youth Services Manager
- Patron Services Technician
- Public Services Librarian
- Reference and Public Services Librarian
- Technology and Media Supervisor
- Teen Librarian
- Web Developer
- Youth Services Librarian

FIGURE 6.12 Selection of Public Library Position Titles, 2016

Allied Professional Association (ALA-APA), a nonprofit organization that promotes "the mutual professional interests of librarians and other library workers."[13] Establishment of the ALA-APA was authorized by the ALA Council in 2001 to enable the certification of individuals in specializations beyond the initial professional degree. In 2002, with the approval of preliminary bylaws, the scope of the organization was broadened to include advocacy for the "mutual professional interests of librarians and other library workers."[14]

Many states require certificates or certification for public library workers. These standards and requirements vary from state to state. Because these change, it is best to review each state. For example, there is a Kentucky State Board for the Certification of Librarians whose purpose is to upgrade the library profession, enrich the individual librarian, and promote quality library service. The certification board was established by the Kentucky General Assembly in 1938. Pennsylvania also requires certification of public library directors depending on population size as defined by the state's Public Library code. (See www.ala.org/offices/library-support-staff-certification-information-state.)

The best way to see the variety of public library positions and current salary ranges is to examine online job listings. A scan of several major services such as the ALA Job List, California Library Association, Florida Library Jobs, Jobzone (*Library Journal*) Library Jobline (Colorado), New York Job Openings, and RAILS (Illinois) during September 2016 netted a variety of position titles that demonstrate the evolving nature of public librarian worklife (figure 6.12).[15]

Three library position announcements are presented in figure 6.13: Adult Learning and Literacy at the Sacramento (CA) Public Library, Programming Manager at the Cedar Rapids (IA) Public Library, and Head of Youth Services at the Greene County (OH) Public Library. The Adult Learning and Literacy position does not require an accredited master's degree, but requires relevant adult education experience. Note that each position description includes a characterization of the local community.

Sampling of Library Position Announcements, 2016

Sacramento Public Library Adult Learning and Literacy Supervisor
Apply By: Thursday, September 22, 2016, on www.calopps.org
Pay: $26.59–$35.63 DOQ

The Sacramento Public Library is building a new future, transforming the library into our community's most valued resource and building the best staff there is. We are recruiting for an Adult Learning and Literacy Supervisor to oversee the Adult Literacy efforts for Sacramento Public Library, including Adult Basic Literacy, English as a Second Language (ESL), General Education Development (GED) tutoring, and the Career Online High School program.

The ideal candidate will have an understanding of the needs and challenges of adult learners, and will be an effective recruiter, trainer, and mentor for volunteer tutors. This candidate must have exceptional interpersonal skills, be unafraid to speak the truth, and understand that creative and constructive conflict is necessary to achieve success. A strong sense of humor is essential. Sacramento Public Library's organizational values of innovation, respect, excellence, accountability, and diversity should resonate with the successful candidate's personal values. The ideal candidate should have a strong desire to be part of a culture committed to customer service for those inside and outside of the organization.

The successful Adult Learning and Literacy Supervisor will enjoy building supportive and positive relationships with library staff, volunteer tutors, potential learners, and partner organizations. The Adult Learning and Literacy Supervisor will oversee a staff of two Literacy Associates to provide training and support to volunteer tutors for Adult Basic Literacy, ESL, and GED programs, including matching tutors and learners, tracking learner progress, and meeting all reporting requirements of the California State Library Literacy Services program (CLLS).

Requirements: Bachelor of Arts (BA)/Bachelor of Science (BS) degree in education, adult education, reading, literacy, social services, or a closely related field is required from an accredited college or university. Three (3) years' experience in adult literacy or basic adult education is required. Supervisory experience and grant-writing experience preferred. The salary is competitive, the benefits are excellent, and the staff is terrific. Sacramento, located in the heart of Northern California within easy driving distance of Lake Tahoe and San Francisco, is an incredible place to work and live, offering a variety of outdoor recreational activities along with a vibrant cultural core that showcases the best in music, art, and theater.

Licenses, Certifications, Bonding, and/or Testing Required: Possession of a valid Class C California Driver License and proof of satisfactory Department of Motor Vehicle (DMV) clearance is required.

FIGURE 6.13 Sampling of Library Position Announcements, 2016
[CONTINUED ON FOLLOWING PAGE]

SOURCE: Courtesy of Sacramento Public Library Authority; Cedar Rapids Public Library; and Greene County Public Library.

FIGURE 6.13 [CONTINUED]

Cedar Rapids Public Library Programming Manager

Job Description: You are the champion of lifelong learning. From story time to STEAM program, adult coloring night to cooking club, you have a passion for the participatory library and can lead a team of professionals who create and deliver innovative experiences.

Who You Are:

- You have a passion for youth services, but understand that adults need some fun, too.
- You are a positive motivator.
- You love to play, learn, and explore.
- You inspire fun in the people around you.
- You get programming and have experience in designing, preparing, promoting, implementing, delivering, and evaluating programs.
- You make friends and find opportunities to create partnerships.
- You love how the right details make the big picture come together.
- You're a natural communicator, whether in a small group or in front of a crowd.
- You are a creative problem solver.
- You are a lot of things to a lot of people—coach, leader, mentor, and entertainer.
- You know that playing is learning and the experiences patrons have in our libraries make lifelong learners.
- You engage well with others and are passionate about providing an exemplary customer experience.
- You are a team player who thinks quickly on your feet and can lead from within a team.
- You are a connector, working with stakeholders to enhance library programs and services.
- You are fearless, always willing to tackle challenges and handle surprises with grace.
- You are excited about leading others in a changing environment.

Your Work:

- You embrace the library's mission, vision, and values, and can apply them to your daily operations and team.
- You develop goals, plans, programs, services, and procedures for lifelong learning at the library.
- You are a strong manager, able to coach and lead a superb team.
- You take charge with grace and confidence.
- You understand how to budget for your department and advocate for resources.
- You strategize and develop the best staffing plan to best serve our customers' needs.

FIGURE 6.13 [CONTINUED]

- You take the initiative, working together with your team to find solutions.
- You embrace innovations, including tools and practices to produce an effective and efficient operation.
- You understand the strength of collaboration and support your team in bringing great ideas to life.
- You understand our community's needs and how the library's services can meet those needs.
- You have the energy to juggle many tasks with a smile; you are out on the floor, giving a tour, scheduling programs, coordinating with staff, or planning outreach.
- You build your team with job recruiting, hiring, and retaining a diverse and brilliant group of library employees and volunteers.
- You are brilliant at coaching your super-talented library team honestly, directly, and consistently to achieve new levels of success.
- You demonstrate excellent communication skills with staff, customers, community partners, and library leadership.
- You do the right thing. Every decision you make and action you take is an opportunity to demonstrate our collective integrity.

Do You Have What It Takes?

- Master's Degree in Library Science from an ALA accredited or approved equivalent graduate school.
- Considerable supervisory experience in a medium or large library environment.
- Experience organizing all aspects of a program and delivering programs, events, or outreach services in a library, educational institution, community non-profit or adult learning organization.

We are guided by our mission to be passionate advocates of literacy and lifelong learning.

About Our Community: Cedar Rapids, Iowa, is a vibrant urban hometown in the heart of east central Iowa. With a population of 128,000, we are the second largest city in Iowa, and home to some of the busiest libraries. Cedar Rapids is an award-winning city with opportunities for arts, culture, recreation, and community engagement.

Head of Youth Services, Greene County Public Library, Fairborn, OH
$23.70 an hour
Job Title: Head of Youth Services
Starting Rate: $23.70 per hour. Pay Grade: 24
Location / Department: Fairborn Community Library/Youth Services
Reports to: Fairborn Head Librarian
Employment Status: Full Time
FLSA Status: Exempt
Hours: Full time, 80 hours per pay period (schedule includes daytime, evening, and weekend hours)

FIGURE 6.13 [CONTINUED]

Job Objective: To promote the mission and values of the Greene County Public Library. To carry out objectives and goals of the strategic plan to better serve the community. To serve as the Head of Youth Services of a large-sized library in the system. To evaluate materials collection, plans, and provide services and activities for youth and those who serve youth. To supervise and participate in all operations of the Youth Services Department's tasks, programs, and services.

Requirements—Essential Job Functions:

- Plans, designs, promotes, presents, and evaluates library activities for children, young adults, parents, and adults who work with children.
- Interviews, selects, and trains new employees. Supervises and evaluates subordinates' performance and counsels them on the solution of new or difficult problems. Conducts staff meetings to transmit information about policies and procedures; solves departmental problems and solicits staff input.
- Assists in developing the community's library collection through: (1) analyzing and evaluating the collection's strengths and weaknesses, (2) selecting materials for removal from the collection, (3) identifying community information needs and selects materials to meet them.
- Gathers statistics, prepares reports, and completes other projects as assigned.
- The supervisor may require other related duties. These duties are nonessential functions of this position.
- Represents the Library and serves as an advocate for youth to community agencies and organizations. Acts as a liaison with schools and educators.
- Provides reference services and reader's advisory service to the public and conducts necessary research in print and electronic sources.
- Instructs and aids adults, young adults, children, and community groups in the use of the library and of reference tools; provides both one-to-one assistance and group presentations.
- Develops program and budget plan for community library or department for Director's consideration; is responsible for facilitating the approved plan.
- Plans and/or prepares displays, bibliographies, pathfinders, and other informational materials.
- Attends meetings of Children's Council and/or Young Adult Council and participates in system-wide children's services.
- In the absence of the head librarian, may perform supervisory tasks, and/or act as person in charge as needed.
- Keeps abreast of current developments in the field through attendance and participation in conferences and workshops and through programs of continuing education, professional reading, and participation in professional groups.
- Attend conferences, workshops, seminars, and training to maintain knowledge as reflected in training curriculum.
- Keeps abreast of information by regularly reading email, minutes, and staff website as well as attending staff meetings.

FIGURE 6.13 [CONTINUED]

Skills, Knowledge and Abilities:

- Ability to maintain good relations with the public and other staff, individually and in general, shows tact and courtesy.
- Ability to multitask, work in a fast-paced environment, and handle difficult situations.
- Ability to handle routine problems under guidance of supervisor and keep supervisor informed of departmental needs and concerns.
- Ability to utilize developmentally appropriate practices in services and programs for youth ages 0–17 and adults who work with youth. This includes early literacy programs and services.
- Proven knowledge of computers and ability to operate and troubleshoot AV, computer, and other equipment.
- Ability to communicate clearly; listen, understand, speak, and write effectively.

Qualifications:

- Master of Library Science degree from an ALA accredited school required. Experience demonstrating success with groups of youth, teens, and strong knowledge of children's and YA literature preferred.
- Two years supervisory experience strongly preferred.

Environmental Conditions:

- Work is performed in an office-like setting, but with need for considerable mobility: light lifting, bending, stooping, stretching, and sitting at a variety of desks and service points.
- Employee may be scheduled to work evening and weekend hours, including Sundays; schedules may be altered depending on the needs of the library.

Note: These announcements were provided on employer websites and submitted to job lines in 2016. The examples here are intended to demonstrate the variety of positions available.

There is a wide variation of staffing patterns throughout the United States. Figure 6.14 shows that the states with the highest percentage of staff with ALA-accredited degrees are Rhode Island (35.4%), Massachusetts (34%), and Connecticut (32.9%). States below 15% include South Dakota, Idaho, Wyoming, and Missouri.

Differences in staffing levels are due to different states' long-term approaches to lifelong learning and education. The "Advocating for Better Salaries Toolkit"[16] updated and

FIGURE 6.14 (OPPOSITE PAGE) Number of Paid Full-Time Equivalent Staff in Public Libraries, by Type of Position, Percentage of Total Librarians and Total Staff with ALA-MLS Degrees, and Number of Public Libraries with ALA-MLS Librarians in the 50 States and the District of Columbia by Population of Legal Service Area: Fiscal Year 2014

State	Number of public libraries	Paid FTE staff[1]									Percentage of total FTE librarians with ALA-MLS	Percentage of total FTE librarians with ALA-MLS	Number of public libraries with ALA-MLS librarians
		Total		Librarians				Other				
						Librarians with ALA-MLS[2]		Percentage of total	Percentage of total			
		Total	Response rate[3]	Total	Response rate[3]	Total	Response rate[3]	Total	Response rate[3]			
Total[4]	9,070	138,332.2	98.0	47,194.9	98.2	32,064.2	97.2	91,137.3	98.4	67.9	23.2	4,769
Alabama	218	1,802.8	100.0	725.7	100.0	325.6	100.0	1,077.0	100.0	44.9	18.1	85
Alaska	79	303.0	100.0	112.5	100.0	58.8	100.0	190.5	100.0	52.3	19.4	18
Arizona	90	2,031.5	93.3	546.2	93.3	461.3	93.3	1,485.3	93.3	84.5	22.7	46
Arkansas	58	1,053.5	96.6	286.4	96.6	142.0	96.6	767.1	96.6	49.6	13.5	45
California	184	11,598.1	99.5	3,209.7	99.5	2,976.5	99.5	8,388.3	99.5	92.7	25.7	175
Colorado	113	3,250.7	100.0	910.6	100.0	663.2	100.0	2,340.1	100.0	72.8	20.4	63
Connecticut	182	2,192.7	97.8	1,032.6	97.8	721.8	97.8	1,160.1	97.8	69.9	32.9	151
Delaware	21	330.0	100.0	121.7	100.0	63.6	100.0	208.3	100.0	52.2	19.3	15
District of Columbia	1	570.0	100.0	147.0	100.0	147.0	100.0	423.0	100.0	100.0	25.8	1
Florida	82	5,992.3	91.5	1,917.9	91.5	1,669.7	91.5	4,074.4	91.5	87.1	27.9	80
Georgia	63	2,734.3	100.0	598.1	100.0	598.1	100.0	2,136.2	100.0	100.0	21.9	63
Hawaii	1	547.5	100.0	172.0	100.0	171.0	100.0	375.5	100.0	99.4	31.2	1
Idaho	102	764.5	100.0	208.5	100.0	96.2	100.0	556.0	100.0	46.1	12.6	28
Illinois	623	8,617.7	95.0	3,153.5	95.0	2,146.2	80.4	5,464.2	99.4	68.1	24.9	332
Indiana	237	4,377.8	99.6	1,435.3	99.6	940.6	99.6	2,942.4	99.6	65.5	21.5	158
Iowa	534	1,754.5	96.8	983.2	96.8	296.9	96.8	771.3	96.8	30.2	16.9	104
Kansas	318	1,722.7	99.7	700.3	99.7	279.2	99.7	1,022.5	99.7	39.9	16.2	74
Kentucky	119	2,178.4	100.0	1,199.8	100.0	349.4	100.0	978.6	100.0	29.1	16.0	63
Louisiana	68	2,634.6	98.5	1,048.2	100.0	457.5	100.0	1,586.4	98.5	43.6	17.4	52
Maine	228	677.7	99.1	337.2	99.1	155.8	99.1	340.5	99.1	46.2	23.0	79
Maryland	24	3,331.2	100.0	1,348.9	100.0	651.1	100.0	1,982.3	100.0	48.3	19.5	24
Massachusetts	368	3,708.4	98.6	1,798.6	98.6	1,260.7	98.6	1,909.9	98.6	70.1	34.0	294
Michigan	388	4,790.7	99.0	1,777.9	99.0	1,238.1	99.0	3,012.8	99.0	69.6	25.8	232
Minnesota	137	2,137.0	100.0	775.2	100.0	519.2	100.0	1,361.8	100.0	67.0	24.3	68

FIGURE 6.14 [CONTINUED ON FOLLOWING PAGE]

State	Number of public libraries	Paid FTE staff[1]								Percentage of total FTE librarians with ALA-MLS	Percentage of total FTE librarians with ALA-MLS	Number of public libraries with ALA-MLS librarians
		Total		Librarians				Other				
						Librarians with ALA-MLS[2]		Percentage of total	Percentage of total			
		Total	Response rate[3]	Total	Response rate[3]	Total	Response rate[3]	Total	Response rate[3]			
Mississippi	52	940.6	100.0	630.3	100.0	130.8	100.0	310.3	100.0	20.7	13.9	46
Missouri	149	3,138.4	100.0	797.5	100.0	270.3	100.0	2,340.9	100.0	33.9	8.6	51
Montana	82	383.1	100.0	190.3	100.0	72.1	100.0	192.9	100.0	37.9	18.8	22
Nebraska	263	793.3	81.7	357.5	81.7	115.4	81.7	435.8	81.7	32.3	14.6	52
Nevada	21	836.9	100.0	203.1	100.0	166.5	100.0	633.9	100.0	82.0	19.9	13
New Hampshire	219	808.0	99.1	473.6	99.1	221.3	98.6	334.4	99.1	46.7	27.4	95
New Jersey[5]	281	4,672.5	94.0	1,387.7	94.0	1,161.5	94.0	3,284.8	94.0	83.7	24.9	237
New Mexico	87	659.3	97.7	282.0	97.7	125.6	97.7	377.2	97.7	44.5	19.1	27
New York	756	12,464.9	100.0	4,073.9	100.0	3,437.2	100.0	8,391.0	100.0	84.4	27.6	434
North Carolina	80	2,906.8	100.0	771.6	100.0	718.9	100.0	2,135.2	100.0	93.2	24.7	79
North Dakota	73	245.3	100.0	134.3	100.0	39.9	100.0	111.0	100.0	29.7	16.3	12
Ohio	251	8,934.8	100.0	2,598.9	100.0	1,901.0	99.2	6,335.9	100.0	73.1	21.3	190
Oklahoma	117	1,469.1	100.0	679.9	100.0	293.5	100.0	789.2	100.0	43.2	20.0	39
Oregon	129	1,801.2	100.0	499.0	100.0	411.1	99.2	1,302.2	100.0	82.4	22.8	80
Pennsylvania	455	4,443.5	95.8	1,481.5	99.6	1,164.3	99.3	2,962.0	95.8	78.6	26.2	295
Rhode Island	48	585.1	100.0	248.5	100.0	207.0	100.0	336.6	100.0	83.3	35.4	48
South Carolina	42	1,909.1	100.0	602.4	100.0	475.2	100.0	1,306.7	100.0	78.9	24.9	41
South Dakota	112	356.1	100.0	181.5	100.0	45.2	100.0	174.7	100.0	24.9	12.7	19
Tennessee	186	1,817.3	98.4	560.5	98.4	261.6	100.0	1,256.8	100.0	46.7	14.4	46
Texas	548	6,787.8	100.0	2,443.3	100.0	1,676.8	100.0	4,344.5	100.0	68.6	24.7	243
Utah	72	1,238.8	95.8	360.4	95.8	215.5	97.2	878.3	95.8	59.8	17.4	28
Vermont	155	339.2	99.4	204.7	99.4	64.2	98.1	134.5	99.4	31.4	18.9	50
Virginia	91	3,816.0	100.0	974.4	100.0	878.7	100.0	2,841.6	100.0	90.2	23.0	85
Washington	62	3,721.9	100.0	826.9	100.0	783.0	100.0	2,895.0	100.0	94.7	21.0	48
West Virginia	97	646.1	100.0	361.6	100.0	95.1	100.0	284.6	100.0	26.3	14.7	40

FIGURE 6.14 [CONTINUED ON FOLLOWING PAGE]

FIGURE 6.14 [CONTINUED]

State	Number of public libraries	Paid FTE staff[1]								Percentage of total FTE librarians with ALA-MLS	Percentage of total FTE librarians with ALA-MLS	Number of public libraries with ALA-MLS librarians
		Total		Librarians				Other				
						Librarians with ALA-MLS[2]		Percentage of total	Percentage of total			
		Total	Response rate[3]	Total	Response rate[3]	Total	Response rate[3]	Total	Response rate[3]			
Wisconsin	381	3,052.7	100.0	1,142.2	100.0	684.7	100.0	1,910.5	100.0	59.9	22.4	183
Wyoming	23	462.9	100.0	180.5	100.0	58.3	100.0	282.4	100.0	32.3	12.6	15
Outlying areas												
American Samoa	1	12.0	100.0	7.0	100.0	2.0	100.0	5.0	100.0	28.6	16.7	1
Guam	1	21.0	100.0	0	100.0	0	100.0	21.0	100.0	0	0	0

SOURCE: Institute of Museum and Library Services July 2016, Supplementary Tables: Public Libraries Survey Fiscal Year 2014. Number of Paid Full-Time-Equivalent (FTE) Staff in Public Libraries, by Type of Position, 2014. IMLS (2014a, table 19). https://www.imls.gov/sites/default/files/fy2014_pls_tables.pdf.

1. The Institute of Museum and Library Services is the source of the original data only. Although the data in this table come from a census of all public libraries and are not subject to sampling error, the census results may contain nonsampling error. Additional information on nonsampling error, response rates, and definitions may be found in Appendix B of the report for the Public Libraries Survey. Paid staff were reported in FTEs. To ensure comparable data, 40 hours was set as the measure of full-time employment (for example, 60 hours per week of part-time work by employees in a staff category divided by the 40-hour measure equals 1.50 FTEs). FTE data were reported to two decimal places but rounded to one decimal place in the table. Paid staff is one of four criteria used in the Public Libraries Survey to define a public library. Some states report public libraries that do not have paid staff but meet the definition of a public library under state law.
2. ALA-MLS: A Master's degree from a graduate library education program accredited by the American Library Association (ALA). Librarians with an ALA-MLS are also included in total librarians.
3. Response rate is calculated as the number of libraries that reported the item, divided by the total number of libraries in the survey frame. For item(s) with response rates below 100 percent, data for nonrespondents were imputed and are included in the table. Data were not imputed for the outlying areas.
4. Total includes the 50 states and the District of Columbia but excludes outlying areas and libraries that do not meet the FSCS Public Library Definition.
5. The number of "certified" librarians was reported in the Librarians with ALA-MLS column, as the state does not distinguish between Master's degrees from programs of library and information studies accredited by the American Library Association (ALA) and all other Master's degrees in library science awarded by institutions of higher education. Nationally, 7441 Master's degrees in library science were awarded by institutions of higher education in 2011–12. (Digest of Education Statistics, 2013, [NCES 2015011], Table 323.10. U.S. Department of Education, National Center for Education Statistics. Washington, DC: Government Printing Office).

NOTE: Detail may not sum to totals because of rounding. Data were not reported by the following outlying areas (Northern Marianas and Virgin Islands). Missing data were not imputed for nonresponding outlying areas.

revised by the members of the ALA-APA Standing Committee on the Salaries and Status of Library Workers assists libraries in demonstrating the value of library staff to the community (ALA-APA, 2014).

UNION IMPACT ON SALARIES AND WORKING CONDITIONS

Unions contribute to a stable, productive workforce. They give workers a voice and the means to improve their jobs. Library workers have unionized for better wages, working conditions, and benefits (McCook, 2010). Union members earn more money, have more benefits, and have more input about the best ways to get work done. The historical paternalism of the library workplace has sometimes allowed libraries to keep salaries below market value and sustained a hierarchical workplace. Unions clarify work rules, working conditions, and salaries.[17]

In 2015 11.3% of all workers in the United States belonged to unions but a far greater percentage of library and education workers did so—35.9% were represented by a union (U.S.B.L.S., 2016, Table 3).

ALA has taken action to advocate for librarians' working conditions and pay within the ALA-APA, which provides direct support of comparable worth and pay equity initiatives as well as other activities designed to improve the salaries and status of librarians and other library workers. ALA-APA also provides information about starting a union.

Some unions that represent public librarians include:

- American Federation of Government Employees (AFGE) afge.org
- American Federation of State, County and Municipal Employees (AFSCME) afscme.org
- Communications Workers of America (CWA) cwa-union.org
- International Brotherhood of Electrical Workers (IBEW) ibew.org
- International Federation of Professional and Technical Engineers (IFPTE) ifpte.org
- Office and Professional Employees Union (OPEIU) opeiu.org
- Retail, Wholesale and Department Store Union (RWDSU) rwdsu.org
- Service Employees International Union (SEIU) seiu.org[18]

"The Role of the Union in Promoting Social Justice" has been characterized as an aspect of the public library commitment to the promotion of human rights (Barriage, 2016).

FRIENDS OF LIBRARIES

Friends of Libraries groups fill many roles in public libraries. They raise money for buildings, renovations, and resources. Their members are advocates, fundraisers, and volunteers. Public libraries benefit from Friends groups, which increase available resources to serve the public. Friends extend a library's capacity through dollar gifts, book sales program support, and political advocacy.

According to United for Libraries, Friends groups work to achieve the following objectives:

- Direct additional financial assistance for needs not normally covered in the library's operating budget.
- Advocate for the library at the local level for increased financial support by the community.
- Encourage gifts.
- Raise money or pass bond issues for building and other capital projects.
- Provide volunteer services to the library.
- Increase community awareness about the library (Reed, 2012).

One way that Friends groups have traditionally raised money is through used book sales. Many people donate books to the public library, and they cannot all find a place on the bookshelves. They do get a second life, though, in the sales. Auctions, courses, sales of baked goods at coffee shops, and gift shops are alternative ways of generating income for the library (Neale, 2013).

The people in the Friends groups work in collaboration with trustees and library staff to provide library services to the community. Often members of Friends groups also act as volunteers or as volunteer coordinators such as the San Luis Obispo Friends group. which has a creative and informative website at www.slofol.org.

VOLUNTEERS

The United States has long fostered a culture of engagement and volunteerism. The Corporation for National and Community Service was established in 1993. Its goals are to improve lives, strengthen communities, and foster civic engagement through service and volunteering.[19] In *The Politics and Civics of National Service: Lessons from the Civilian Conservation Corps, Vista, and AmeriCorps,* Bass (2013) presents a panoramic view of volunteering. Public libraries have long been a popular organization for people to choose as a volunteer opportunity.

Library volunteers contribute hundreds of thousands of hours in time each year. The Charlotte-Mecklenberg Library (North Carolina) estimated 1,600 volunteers donated 62,000 hours of their time, valued at more than $1.4 million in donated services during 2015.[20] Many libraries have websites that recruit volunteers and provide an accessible application process. See, for instance, the Fargo (ND) Public Library website, which hosts a short video, "Gather Books and Be a Hero!"; the Provo City (UT) Library website, which includes extensive descriptions of opportunities such as Spanish Story Time volunteer or Teen Code Club volunteer; and the Ridgefield (CT) Library whose opportunities to volunteer include Talking Book Sound Editors and Homebound Delivery Service.[21]

Volunteerism by young adults in public libraries has been assessed by Bernier (2009), who observed that the degree of public value may frequently be underappreciated by libraries, supervisors, and administrators. He suggests that library staff may benefit from better volunteer administration skills and planning, and points out that volunteering is a mechanism that will more powerfully connect young people with their libraries and communities.

In many libraries, coordinators are assigned to organize and make the best use of these community-minded volunteers. "Recruitment, Retention and Recognition" is discussed in *Success with Library Volunteers* (Holt & Holt, chapter 5, 2014). At the Waukegan Public Library, one of the library's primary recruitment goals is to "make it easier for prospective volunteers to understand the numerous opportunities within the library" (Throgmorton, 2016).

One example of a matching service for volunteers and opportunities is the California State Library's "Get Involved." This is a statewide initiative in collaboration with Volunteer Match, the web-based volunteer engagement network that supports five million volunteers and more than 110,000 nonprofits designed to expand the visibility and contributions of skilled volunteers through public libraries. Potential volunteers input their zip code and receive a list of opportunities. A search for "Santa Ana, CA 92704" retrieved opportunities in four categories, as shown in figure 6.15.

King County Library System (Washington) has received national recognition for the breadth and quality of its volunteer program and has created documents and policies that are models for development of programs including administrative capacity for coordinating services.

Volunteers can be essential in times of crisis. For instance, in 2015, volunteers helped keep the library open in Ferguson, Missouri, after the shooting of an unarmed teenager by a police officer set off a string of protests and civil unrest. With the help of volunteers, Teach for America, church groups, and local educators, the library offered educational programming and served up to 200 children per day (Carlton, 2015).

OVERARCHING ISSUES RELATING TO STAFFING

Recruitment

Careers in public librarianship are publicized on PLA's website, "Careers in Public Librarianship," and by ALA's LibraryCareers.org. The need for funds to educate new librarians resulted in more than over $100 million dollars in grants through the Laura Bush 21st Century Librarian (LB21) program, funded by the Institute of Museum and Library Services (IMLS) beginning in 2003 and continuing through today (figure 6.16). The program recognizes the key role of libraries and librarians in maintaining the flow of information critical to support formal education and to create a climate for democratic discourse. Support to educate the next generation of librarians has focused on public librarians, certification of rural librarians, recruitment of people of color, and youth services librarians. Diversity and innovation were central drivers.

For example, the first 15 "Librarians Build Communities" (LBC) scholars began classes in August 2008 at Georgia's Valdosta State University's Master of Library and Information Science program. The program provided scholarships to prepare 45 students to be public librarians who would develop expertise in community building. It was funded for three cohorts (Most, 2011).

A 2013 evaluation of the LB21 program included assessment of the Public Urban Library Service Education Project (PULSE)—a collaboration between the Brooklyn Public Library and Pratt Institute's School of Information and Library Science (ICF, p. 42). A diverse library workforce is one of the most important discussions related to the effect of the LB21 grants on recruitment (LB21 Grant Evaluation, 2003-2009). Some examples of diversity-related LB 21 grants include "Preparing Librarians to Serve Diverse Communities Along Our Nation's Borders" (San Jose State University); "Librarians Build Communities," which provided expertise in community- building (Valdosta State University and Georgia Public Library Service) and "Project Recovery," a program for libraries in southern Louisiana that incurred staffing shortages as a result of the damage Hurricane Katrina (Louisiana State University, Dawson & McCook, 2006).[22]

State library associations and LIS programs also recruit and fund new librarians. For example, the Alabama School of Library and Information Studies has a public library scholarship; the Idaho Commission for Libraries has a public library grant; and the Louisiana State University School of Library and Information Science and Friends of the Lafayette Parish Public Library sponsor a Fellowship (ALA, COE, 2016).

Diversity

The responsibility of the library to help reduce inequities in the community suggests that library staff should represent the diversity of the communities they serve as well as take

Sample "Get Involved" Volunteer Search

California State Library, Zip Code 92704, Orange County

Welcome to the Library VolunteerMatch website!

Explore the many volunteer possibilities available in your community by **scrolling through the highlighted opportunities below.** They are divided into four categories:

Strengthen libraries: Libraries serve the entire community with diverse programs, services, & volunteer opportunities & need help in all areas.

- This fall help another OC adult "get back to learning" at the OC Public Libraries—Fountain Valley Branch Library.

Impact adult and family literacy: Help new readers of all ages discover the joys & benefits of reading.

- Book Organizer with Huntington Beach Public Library

Engage in other community opportunities: Discover how you can help support the causes & community organizations you care about.

- Personal Shop for Homeless Families and Individuals with Illumination Foundation.
- Volunteer as a personal shopper in our newly designed Illumination Foundation Donation Room for families and individuals who are homeless.

Opportunities for teens: Teens should be community minded & are often required to complete community service as part of their academic programs.

- Elders Need Helpers in the Santa Ana Community: Volunteer to Help Seniors Today!

FIGURE 6.15 Sample "Get Involved" Volunteer Search, California State Library, Zip Code 92704, Orange County

SOURCE: https://libraries.volunteermatch.org.

Laura Bush 21st Century Librarian Program

§9165. Laura Bush 21st Century Librarian Program

(a) Purpose

It is the purpose of this part to develop a diverse workforce of librarians by

1. recruiting and educating the next generation of librarians, including by encouraging middle or high school students and postsecondary students to pursue careers in library and information science;
2. developing faculty and library leaders, including by increasing the institutional capacity of graduate schools of library and information science; and
3. enhancing the training and professional development of librarians and the library workforce to meet the needs of their communities, including those needs relating to literacy and education, workforce development, lifelong learning, and digital literacy.

(b) Activities

From the amounts provided under section 9123(a)(2) of this title, the Director may enter into arrangements, including grants, contracts, cooperative agreements, and other forms of assistance, with libraries, library consortia and associations, institutions of higher education (as defined in section 1001 of this title), and other entities that the Director determines appropriate, for projects that further the purpose of this part, such as projects that

1. increase the number of students enrolled in nationally accredited graduate library and information science programs and preparing for careers of service in libraries;
2. recruit future professionals, including efforts to attract promising middle school, high school, or postsecondary students to consider careers in library and information science;
3. develop or enhance professional development programs for librarians and the library workforce;
4. enhance curricula within nationally accredited graduate library and information science programs;
5. enhance doctoral education in order to develop faculty to educate the future generation of library professionals and develop the future generation of library leaders; and
6. conduct research, including research to support the successful recruitment and education of the next generation of librarians.

FIGURE 6.16 Laura Bush 21st Century Librarian Program

SOURCE: 20 USC 9165: Laura Bush 21st Century Librarian Program. Text contains those laws in effect on September 1, 2016. From Title 20-EDUCATION.CHAPTER 72-MUSEUM AND LIBRARY SERVICES SUBCHAPTER II-LIBRARY SERVICES AND TECHNOLOGY. Part 4-Laura Bush 21st Century Librarians. http://uscode.house.gov/browse/prelim@title20/chapter72/subchapter2&edition=prelim.

steps to reflect this diversity (Brown, 2015). "Diversity" is a broad term that covers, according to the ALA Manual, "race, age, sex, sexual orientation, gender identity, gender expression, creed, color, religious background, national origin, language of origin or disability." Vinopal (2016) reports that the demographics of professional librarians "have barely shifted in decades" (para. 3); clearly, we still have work to do as a profession. Some methods for enhancing diversity are attracting a diverse workforce, and then retaining diversity through policies that maintain a space that is inclusive for both patrons and staff.

Racial/Ethnic Diversity

The most recent ALA diversity report lists a total of 118,666 credentialed librarians, of whom 6,160 are African-American and 3,661 are Latino. That means about 8% of working librarians represent more than 40% of our population (Hastings, 2015). Public librarians and their associations continue to work to broaden the diversity of staff at all levels to reflect the diversity of the U.S. population. One initiative designed to attract people of color to librarianship is the SPECTRUM scholarship program, which was established by ALA's Office for Diversity, Literacy and Outreach Services in 1997 to address this critical need. The scholarship, as of 2016, offers $5,000 to students enrolled in an ALA-accredited program. Its aim is to increase the number of racially and ethnically diverse professionals working as leaders in the field of library and information science to best position libraries and institutions at the core of today's culturally diverse communities.[23] PLA Executive Director Barbara Macikas explained the PLA commitment and historical support of the SPECTRUM Scholarship program in anticipation of the 2016 PLA conference.

Scholarships and mentoring for people of color are provided by the ethnic affiliate organizations of ALA: American Indian Library Association (AILA); Asian/Pacific American Librarians Association (APALA); Black Caucus of the ALA (BCALA); Chinese American Librarians Association (CALA); and REFORMA—National Association to Promote Library and Information Services to Latinos and the Spanish-Speaking.[24] Each affiliate holds conferences, recognizes excellence, and provides a venue for focus on cultural competence.

These efforts have yet to provide a profession-wide profile that reflects the changing U.S. population at large, but have reversed the sentiment that diversity issues have been deferred (Roy, 2006). The people who work in our public libraries are committed to outreach to all people of their communities. The "Diversity Counts" project results are posted at the website of the Office for Diversity, Literacy, and Outreach Services of the American Library Association (ALA-ODLOS, 2012). These results show that the library workforce does not reflect demographics of many communities at large.

In a provocative essay at the blog *In the Library with the Lead Pipe,* Jennifer Vinopal makes a bold suggestion:

> Make diversity and social justice a genuine and regular part of the organization's work. Rather than just paying lip service to the concept of diversity, include diversity initiatives in the library's strategic plan and then make time and provide support for staff to accomplish them. (2016)

PLA's strategic goal of inclusivity has been framed by Mehra and Davis in their study "Strategic Diversity Manifesto for Public Libraries in the 21st Century," in which they emphasize the need for public library to be culturally competent.

Disability

Libraries can be excellent places for people with a wide range of physical disabilities to work. There are many model policies and ideas at the website of the Office of Disability Employment Policy of the U.S. Department of Labor, which has the vision of "a world in which people with disabilities have unlimited employment opportunities" (Disability Employment Resources, n.d.).

Human resources departments should be familiar with associated statutes and codes of ethics regarding the employment and career counseling of people with disabilities (Mainzer & Dipeolu, 2015). After the long wars in the Middle East there are many veterans with disabilities; libraries could utilize the many talents and skills that veterans bring to the workforce and enable veterans to enjoy a more fulfilling work life and career (Stone & Stone, 2015).

Hiring library workers with disabilities has not been a major focus of librarianship, but the Association of Specialized and Cooperative Library Agencies does offer the ASCLA Century Scholarship that funds services or accommodation for library school students with disabilities admitted to an ALA-accredited library school. Chrystna Hunter (2016), reporting on a survey of 10 state library associations, found mixed response about hiring librarians with disabilities. She noted:

> In our profession, we work hard to include everyone who walks through the front door of the public library. But what about the back door? There have been a number of efforts via research, webinars, and conferences to evaluate and create programs for patrons with varying disabilities. Why can't the same be done for professionals in the same field? Until we highlight that there are indeed librarians with disabilities in the profession and make note of how to welcome more of them into the vocation, we could lose potentially valuable future members.

Sexual/Gender Orientation/Expression

The Bathroom Wars of 2016 brought sexual expression to the forefront of the American consciousness. Neil J. Young (2016) said that "in 2016, at least 15 states have considered 'bathroom bills' similar to the legislation recently enacted in North Carolina, which blocks transgender people from using bathrooms that don't correspond to the sex listed on their birth certificates." Legislators on both sides of the political aisle spoke in favor of or against the laws; people caught in the crossfire saw the law not as a law against bathroom use, but rather a law against their right to live a safe life as a transgender person. Such laws impact both library workers and patrons. ALA, as a national body, and groups within the organization, have spoken out against laws that discriminate or intimidate.

The Gay, Lesbian, Bisexual, and Transgender Round Table (GLBTRT) of the American Library Association is committed to serving the information needs of the GLBT professional library community. The group serves as an advocate for gender expression for library staff and patrons, as well as the right to find information and reading related to the needs and entertainment of people of all sexual orientations and gender identities. Just as American law is based on interpretation, GLBTRT has interpreted the Library Bill of Rights in relation to services, materials, and programs.

The GLBTRT hosts events and programs for librarians at conferences and also sponsors forums for GLBT librarians to connect, such as social networking and the GLBTRT

Buddy Program at ALA's Midwinter and Annual conferences. Grassroots opportunities like these are invaluable opportunities for a new librarian to feel a sense of community and brainstorm about ways to make the workplace friendlier for everyone.

CONTINUING EDUCATION AND STAFF DEVELOPMENT

Continuing education for public librarians may be reframed in light of the newly released *National Agenda for Continuing Education and Professional Development across Libraries, Archives, and Museums* (Drummond, 2016). The *National Agenda* provides a broad planning and evaluation framework for the systemic strengthening of continuing education and professional development (CE/PD) across the landscape of funders, professional associations, program administrators, and trainers. The project was supported by IMLS, the Bill and Melinda Gates Foundation, and OCLC.

Library staff may have mandated continuing education. In New York individuals certified as public librarians must be able to demonstrate completion of continuing education and training equal to or greater than 60 hours within each five-year period to maintain their certification as specified in the New York State Board of Regents Commissioner's Regulation §90.7.[25] Other states, such as New Mexico and Montana, encourage but do not mandate continuing education by law.[26] Stewart et al. (2013) present an overview of the importance of staff development from various vantage points in librarianship and discuss strategies for building and implementing a staff development program.

American Library Association

Continuing education is critical to the development of excellent library service. There are multiple options to fulfill the need for staff to develop their knowledge, skills, and abilities throughout their careers. The American Library Association evaluates programs according to the continuing education unit (CEU) standards set forth by the International Association for Continuing Education and Training (IACET). The IACET maintains a searchable online database of the colleges, universities, and other organizations that have continuing education courses that meet its criteria. ALA is an authorized provider of IACET-compliant CEUs. The Mission of the ALA Learning Round Table is to promote quality continuing education and staff development for all library personnel.

Within ALA, the Office of Human Resources Development and Recruitment sponsors programs such as Emerging Leaders, which enables newer library workers from across the country to participate in problem-solving work groups and network with peers to serve the profession in a leadership capacity (ALA Continuing Education, 2013a).[27]

Public Library Association

PLA also provides ongoing staff development and continuing education for public librarians via national conferences, meetings, and publications. In 2016, for example, the national PLA conference included programs on "Practical Community Engagement," "Project Outcome Enrollment Workshop: Simple Tools to Measure Our True Impact on the People We Serve," and "AnyAbility: Taking Ordinary Service for Adults with Disabilities to an Extraordinary

Level." In fact, a historical review of PLA programs at ALA conferences as well as at national PLA conferences illustrates an ongoing panorama of staff development topics (PLA 2016).

In collaboration with the International City/County Managers Association (ICMA), the PLA Leadership Academy emphasizes the broader community perspective. It teaches library leaders how to work in partnership with other community leaders to achieve community goals (Anthony, 2013). In 2017, the topic of the PLA Academy was "Navigating Change, Building Community." The academy empowers participants with the skills and information to be innovative and successful change leaders. It focuses on developing skills to work with municipal officials to enhance the position of the library within the community.

PLA Online learning provides webinars based on conference programs such as "Beyond Bilingual Storytime and ESL: Digging Deeper into Your Spanish Speaking Community" or "Developing Truly Effective Performance Evaluations."

Note that some programs are free to the public, others are free for members, and some are for-fee with varying rates for individuals or groups.

WebJunction

WebJunction, a project of OCLC, is the online destination for public library staff to gather to build the knowledge, skills, and support to power relevant, vibrant libraries. Since its launch in 2003, WebJunction has enrolled more than 80,000 library staff to build the knowledge and skills required to deliver transformational services to their communities. Support for WebJunction comes from IMLS, the Bill and Melinda Gates Foundation, and the Paul G. Allen family foundation.

State and Regional Library Associations

Every U.S. state and certain regions hold annual library conferences that provide geographically convenient opportunities for continuing education and staff development. A complete list appears at the ALA chapter site and each state's chapter website.

Librarians toured the Arizona Historical Society in Tucson; heard a program by Miguel Figueroa, head of the Center for the Future of Libraries in Sacramento, California; learned about marketing to the elusive teen in Indianapolis; and discussed the "accidental cataloger" at the joint meeting of the Wyoming Library Association and the Mountain Plains Library Association in Cheyenne. Most conferences have author keynotes, fundraisers for scholarships, and provide opportunities to learn about new technologies and service options.

The Texas Library Association conference is one of the major state conferences; see its website for information on:

- goals for conference goals;
- program planning do's and don'ts;
- the Program Committee's role, rubric, and process;
- timelines for conference planning;
- tips for contacting publishers; and
- instructions for creating and completing your program proposals in the online database.[28]

Some conferences offer CEUs and provide information on applications and process. Surfing state and regional conference websites highlights the hours of planning and development carried out by so many, year after year, to help keep practitioners up-to-date and ready to provide patrons with current services.

Affiliates and Ethnic Library Associations

Affiliate organizations of the American Library Association hold conferences and provide continuing education opportunities. Those of special interest to public librarians include the

- American Indian Library Association
- Asian/Pacific American Librarians Association
- Association for Rural and Small Libraries
- Association of Bookmobile and Outreach Services
- Black Caucus of ALA
- Chinese American Librarians Association
- Joint Conference of Librarians of Color
- National Storytelling Network
- ProLiteracy Worldwide
- REFORMA

Each of these affiliate organizations can provide resources and support for different service missions and targeted continuing education and staff development opportunities for different communities within the public library field.

For example, REFORMA–The National Association to Promote Library and Information Services to Latinos and the Spanish-Speaking, sixth national conference in 2017's theme is "Building Communities: Saving Lives." (www.rnc6.com/).

RECOGNIZING EXCELLENCE IN STAFF AND TRUSTEE DEVELOPMENT

Awards given to librarians, support staff, and trustees are based on excellent service to the field. They may be given at the national, state, or local level. They are meant to honor the recipient and inspire others in the field. The process of nominating, reviewing, and selecting individuals is itself a source of continuing education for the juries. At the time the award is given the awarding organization acknowledges its criteria for excellence.

A sample of recent public library award winners includes:

Barbara A.B. Gubbin, director of the Jacksonville (FL) Public Library, won the 2017 ALA Ernest A. Dimattia Jr. Award for innovation and service to community and profession, which is awarded to a public librarian who demonstrates leadership in anticipating emerging trends in services, products, and technologies that will enhance the library's position in its community.

Maureen Millea Smith, librarian at the Hennepin County (MN) Public Library -PLA's 2017 Allie Beth Martin Award for public librarians who demonstrate extraordinary range and depth of knowledge about books or other library materials and have a distinguished ability to share that knowledge.

Jill Bourne, Director of the San Jose Public Library, was honored with the *Library Journal* 2017 Librarian of the Year Award. San Jose Mayor Liccardo noted, "Jill has served as a tireless community advocate, a responsible steward of our treasured library system, and a strong voice for innovation." (Berry, 2017.)

Linda Crowe, co-founder of Califa Group and CEO of the Pacific Library Partnership, was inducted into the California Library Association Hall of Fame in 2016 for leading the merger of the four cooperative library systems (BALIS, PLS, MOBAC, and SVLS) in the San Francisco Bay Area and for her tireless advocacy of robust broadband connectivity at the state and national levels.

Isabel Huerta of the Addison Public Library was the recipient of the Illinois Library Association's Robert P. Doyle Award for Support Staff for her advocacy for education for the library's Latino community and building strong rapport with families.

Tonya Garcia of the Long Branch Free Public Library was named the New Jersey Library Association Librarian of the Year for serving as a role model, enhancing the image of librarianship, and advancing the positive visibility of libraries to the community.

Victoria Gerstenfeld of the Marple Public Library won the Pennsylvania Library Association's Trustee of the Year Award, which is presented to a public library trustee in recognition of outstanding leadership and service to library development at the local, system, district, and/or state level.[29]

The websites of all state chapter library associations offer readers the humbling opportunity to review the tremendous amount of work done by librarians in communities large and small, rural and urban. As individuals are awarded for extraordinary effort, all library workers are elevated by coming together to recognize excellence and gain inspiration from our common goals.

NOTES

1. For details see Denver Public Library, Organizational Structure (https://www.denverlibrary.org/content/organizational-structure); Charlotte Mecklenburg Library (https://www.cmlibrary.org/about/board-trustees?utm_source=footer&utm_medium=link&utm_campaign=board-trustees); and Madison Public Library District, Library Board of Trustees (http://madisonlib.org/board-of-trustees/).
2. These include Garceau (1949), Kelley (1999), and Applegate et al. (2007).
3. The lack of diversity in public library boards is similar to other cultural organizations. Aldo Guerrero's 2015 study of the Boards of National Public Radio, "National Plutocrat Radio: Corporate One-Percenters Dominate NPR Affiliates' Boards," reported that "two out of three board members are male, and nearly three out of four are non-Latino whites. Fully three out of every four trustees of the top NPR affiliates belong to the corporate elite" (http://fair.org/home/national-plutocrat-radio/).
4. The first trustee-focused division of the American Library Association was the American Library Trustees Association, which was founded in 1890. The name changed in 1999 to the Association for

Library Trustees and Advocates (ALTA). In 1975 a separate organization, Friends of Libraries USA (FOLUSA) was formed. In 2007 a meeting was held with the Executive Director of ALA and ALTA leadership to discuss a proposal to bring FOLUSA back to ALA and to combine these two advocacy groups under one Division. In 2009 ALTA and Friends of Libraries U.S.A. became the Association of Library Trustees, Advocates, Friends and Foundations. Today, this division is named "United for Libraries." See "New Voice for America's Libraries/A Rich History—United for Libraries," by Peggy Danhof, ALTA President 2008–2009; ALTAFF Co-President 2009 (www.ala.org/united/sites/ala .org.united/files/content/about/history.pdf).

5. Approved by the United for Libraries Board in January 2012. See www.ala.org/united/sites/ala.org .united/files/content/trustees/orgtools/Ethics%20Statement.pdf.
6. Examples include the story of a county rural district formed in Stevens County, Washington (Hague, 1999); a trustee's views of a campaign to pass a library bond issue (Glennon, 1997), and Louisiana trustee Jeanne T. Kreamer's (1990) credo on trustee activism. The literature needs more of these testimonies.
7. Descriptions of the two programs are available at http://ala-apa.org/certification-news/.
8. Dr. Carla D. Hayden, CEO of the Enoch Pratt Free Library in Baltimore, was named the 2015 "Jean E. Coleman Library Outreach Lecturer" by the ALA Office for Diversity, Literacy, and Outreach Services in recognition of her efforts to keep the library and its branches open and continually engaged with the Baltimore community during the civil unrest in the wake of the death of Freddie Gray in April: "In the midst of this painful time and in the epicenter of it all, Carla and her staff showed the world that libraries are safe havens and community anchors" (Amundsen, 2015). Dr. Hayden was appointed Librarian of Congress in 2016. Engagement and community concern were a hallmark of her time as leader of staff at a large urban library.
9. See *Standards for Accreditation of Master's Programs in Library and Information Studies,* adopted by approval of the Council of the American Library Association, February 2, 2015 (www.ala.org/ accreditedprograms/standards).
10. The Workload Measures and Staffing Patterns Committee of PLA conducted a survey in 2003 and determined that "if excellence is defined by meeting locally identified and defined needs, then there can be no 'one size fits all' answers or externally defined standards" (Goodrich, 2005, p. 280).
11. ALA-accredited master's programs can be found at colleges and universities in the United States, Canada, and Puerto Rico. These programs offer degrees with names such as Master of Library Science (MLS), Master of Arts (MA), Master of Librarianship, Master of Library and Information Studies (MLIS), and Master of Science (MS). ALA accreditation indicates that the program has undergone an external review and meets the ALA Committee on Accreditation's Standards for Accreditation of Master's Programs in Library and Information Studies (www.ala.org/ accreditedprograms/directory).
12. The *Accreditation Process, Policies and Procedures,* 4th edition, is used in conjunction with the *Standards for Accreditation of Master's Programs in Library and Information Studies* to guide the ALA's accreditation process. It is provided for use and reference by program and institutional representatives, members of the ALA Committee on Accreditation, and External Review Panelists. See www.ala.org/accreditedprograms/standards/AP3.
13. See the Library Support Staff Certification (LSSC) FAQ:

    8. What do I have to do to be certified? Successfully complete six of the ten competency sets established by LSSC, three required and three electives. 9. What are the competency sets? Required: Foundations of Library Services, Communication and Teamwork, Technology. Electives (choose any three): Access Services, Adult Readers' Advisory Services, Cataloging and Classification, Collection Management, Reference and Information Services, Supervision and Management, Youth Services. (http://ala-apa.org/lssc/about-lssc/faq/#1).

14. ALA and ALA-APA are separate, independent legal organizations. They are tied together by fully interlocked governing bodies. The governing body of the ALA-APA is the ALA-APA Council, whose members are those individuals concurrently serving on the ALA Council. Within the policies established by the ALA-APA Council, the ALA-APA is managed by the board of directors, whose members are those individuals concurrently serving on the ALA Executive Board. The ALA-APA Bylaws are available at www.ala-apa.org/bylaws.
15. Drawn from the ALA List (http://joblist.ala.org/home/index.cfm?site_id=21926); the California Library Association-Career Center (www.cla-net.org/networking/opening_search.asp); the Florida Library Jobs website (www.floridalibraryjobs.org); *Library Journal*'s Jobzone (http://jobs .libraryjournal.com/); Colorado's Library Jobline (https://twitter.com/libraryjobline); and New York Job Openings (www.nysl.nysed.gov/libdev/libjobs.htm); RAILS (Illinois) (https://www .railslibraries.info/jobs).
16. The Toolkit and Training program were originally developed by 2002–2003 ALA President Maurice J. (Mitch) Freedman's Better Salaries and Pay Equity for Library Workers Task Force as part of the Campaign for America's Librarians.
17. In a *Public Libraries* forum, Cameron Johnson (2002) observed, "unions can help make libraries better by offering a collaborative model for employee relations that management might want to emulate. . . . Union leadership consists of grassroots workplace politics: talking to employees at all levels, building consensus, discussing, persuading, and acting democratically."
18. See ALA-APA, "Start a Union" (http://ala-apa.org/improving-salariesstatus/unions/start-a-union/).
19. The Corporation for National and Community Service is a federal agency that engages more than 5 million Americans in service through its core programs—Senior Corps, AmeriCorps, and the Social Innovation Fund.
20. See Charlotte-Mecklenberg Library, Volunteers (https://www.cmlibrary.org/volunteer). A statewide study for Florida reported volunteers contributed time equivalent to 722 full-time staff (nearly 29,000 hours per week) serving in all areas of the state's public libraries—shelving books, checking material in and out, staffing reference and information desks, and providing behind-the-scenes support (Driggers and Dumas, 2011).
21. Fargo Public Library. www.cityoffargo.com/CityInfo/Departments/Library/Volunteers/; Provo City Library (UT) www.provolibrary.com/volunteers; Ridgefield Library (CT) www.ridgefield library.org/about/volunteer_opp.shtml.
22. For a complete list of LB21c grants see https://www.imls.gov/grants.
23. Information on the SPECTRUM Scholarship Program is available at www.ala.org/offices/ diversity/spectrum.
24. See the following websites for more information:

    - American Indian Library Association (AILA, www.ailanet.org)
    - Asian/Pacific American Librarians Association (APALA, www.apalaweb .org)
    - Black Caucus of the ALA (BCALA, www.bcala.org)
    - Chinese American Librarians Association (CALA, www.cala-web.org)
    - REFORMA—National Association to Promote Library and Information Services to Latinos and the Spanish-Speaking (www.reforma.org).

25. See New York State Library, Continuing Education for Public Librarian Certification (www .nysl.nysed.gov/libdev/cert/conted.htm). A wide range of options for professional development is available. Approved programs from accepted providers include formal classes or courses, workshops, seminars, lectures, institutes, webinars, e-courses, library conference programs, or other relevant programs.

26. See the Mexico State Library Continuing Education website (www.nmstatelibrary.org/services-for-nm-libraries/continuing-education) and the Montana State Library Continuing Education and Certification website (http://msl.mt.gov/library_development/training/).
27. See the web pages of the ALA Emerging Leaders Program (www.ala.org/educationcareers/leadership/emergingleaders) and Learning Round Table. (www.ala.org/learnrt/). The Mission of the Learning Round Table is to promote quality continuing education and staff development for all library personnel.
28. The Texas Library Association's 2017 theme was "Own Your Profession" (www.txla.org/annual-conference).
29. See the following sources for award details: ALA Ernest A. DiMattia, Jr. Award for Innovation and Service to Community and Profession (www.ala.org/awardsgrants/ernest-dimattia-jr-award-innovation-and-service-community-and-profession); PLA Allie Beth Martin Award (www.ala.org/pla/awards/alliebethmartinaward); "Bourne: LJ's 2017 Librarian of the Year" (http://lj.libraryjournal.com/2017/01/managing-libraries/jill-bourne-ljs-2017-librarian-of-the-year/#_.). "Illinois Library Association, 2016 Award Winners," (https://www.ila.org/about/awards/2016-ila-award-winners); New Jersey Library Association, Librarian of the Year (https://njla.org/awards); Pennsylvania Library Association, Trustee of the Year Award (https://www.palibraries.org/page/2016AwardWinners).

REFERENCES

ALA-APA. (2014a) *Advocating for better salaries toolkit* (5th ed.). http://ala-apa.org/files/2014/05/2014-ala-apa-better-salaries-toolkit-2.pdf.

ALA-APA. (2014b). State/regional certifications. http://ala-apa.org/certification-news/stateregional-certifications/.

American Library Association. Affiliates and their websites. www.ala.org/groups/affiliates/affiliates.

American Library Association. List of support staff in libraries. www.ala.org/educationcareers/careers/paths/listsupportstaff.

American Library Association. State and regional chapters. www.ala.org/groups/affiliates/chapters/state/stateregional.

American Library Association. What library directors need to know. www.ala.org/educationcareers/careers/librarycareerssite/whatyouneeddirector.

American Library Association. (2013a). Continuing education (and where to find it). www.ala.org/tools/atoz/continuing-education.

American Library Association. (2013b). *Policy manual.* www.ala.org/aboutala/governance/policymanual.

American Library Association, Learning Round Table. www.ala.org/learnrt/.

American Library Association, Office for Accreditation. (2015a). Off*Accreditation process, policies and procedures.* www.ala.org/accreditedprograms/standards/AP3.

American Library Association, Office for Accreditation. (2015b) *Standards for accreditation of master's programs in library and information studies.* www.ala.org/accreditedprograms/standards.

American Library Association, Office for Diversity, Literacy and Outreach Services. (n.d.). www.ala.org/offices/diversity.

American Library Association, Office for Diversity, Literacy and Outreach Services. (2017). Diversity Counts. (2012). www.ala.org/offices/diversity/diversitycounts.

American Library Association, Committee on Education (2016). *Financial assistance for library and information studies.* www.ala.org/educationcareers/sites/ala.org.educationcareers/files/content/scholarships/2015-2016%20FALIS%20Directory.pdf.

Ames, K. S., & Heid, G. (2009, Winter). The role of the library board of trustees in the construction of a public library. *Georgia Library Quarterly, 46,* 9-14.

Amundsen, J. L. (2015, May 26). Carla Hayden to deliver 2015 Jean E. Coleman Library Outreach Lecture. *ALA News.* www.ala.org/news/press-releases/2015/05/carla-hayden-deliver-2015-jean-e-coleman-library-outreach-lecture.

Anthony, C. (2013). Success is entwined with community. *Public Libraries, 52*(5), 5-6.

Applegate, R., Gibbs, P., Cowser, C. S., & Scarborough, J. (2007, October). Public library trustees: Characteristics and educational preferences. *Public Library Quarterly, 26,* 21-43.

Association of Specialized and Cooperative Library Programs. (n.d.). Century Scholarship. www.ala.org/ascla/asclaawards/asclacentury.

Barriage, S. (2016), The role of the union in promoting social justice, in U. Gorham, N. G. Taylor & P. T. Jaeger (Eds.), *Perspectives on libraries as institutions of human rights and social justice* Bingley, United Kingdom: Emerald Group Publishing Limited, pp. 231–243.

Bass, M. (2013). *The politics and civics of national service: Lessons from the Civilian Conservation Corps, Vista, and AmeriCorps.* Washington, DC: Brookings Institution Press.

Bernier, A. (2009). Young adult volunteering in public libraries: Managerial implications. *The Bowker Annual Library and Book Trade Almanac, 23,* 133-139.

Berry, J. N. (2017, January 4). Jill Bourne: LJ's 2017 Librarian of the Year. *Library Journal, 142,* 28-30. http://lj.libraryjournal.com/2017/01/managing-libraries/jill-bourne-ljs-2017-librarian-of-the-year/#_.

Boise, Idaho. (n.d.). City Code, Chapter 2 Section 4. www.boisepubliclibrary.org/info/board-of-trustees/.

Brown, M. E. (2015). Invisible debility: Attitudes toward the underrepresented in library workplaces. *Public Library Quarterly, 34*(2), 124-133.

Bureau of Labor Statistics, U.S. Department of Labor, *Occupational Outlook Handbook,* 2016-17 Edition, Librarians. https://www.bls.gov/ooh/education-training-and-library/librarians.htm.

California Library Association (n.d.). Hall of Fame. www.cla-net.org/?page=612.

Carlton, A. (2015). 2015 ALA Award Winners: Honoring excellence and leadership in the library profession. *American Libraries, 46,* 32-38.

Charlotte Mecklenburg Library. (n.d.). https://www.cmlibrary.org/about/boardtrustees?utm_source=footer&utm_medium=link&utm_campaign=board-trustees.

Chief Officers of State Library Agencies (COSLA). (n.d.) Member profiles. www.cosla.org/profiles/.

Chief Officers of State Library Agencies. (2015). *Trustee toolkit: Hiring a new director.* www.cosla.org/content.cfm/id/trustee_toolkit_hiring_a_new_library_director.

Code of Virginia. Chapter 2. Local and Regional Libraries. http://law.lis.virginia.gov/vacode/title42.1/chapter2/.

Corporation for National and Community Service. (n.d.). https://www.nationalservice.gov/.

Culver, E., & Gittinger, N. M. (1954, Winter). "A History of the Citizens' Library Movement," *Bulletin of the Louisiana Library Association 17,* 18-20.

Charlotte Mecklenburg Library. (n.d.) https://www.cmlibrary.org/about/board.

Danhoff, P. New voice for America's libraries/A rich history—United for Libraries. (www.ala.org/united/sites/ala.org.united/files/content/about/history.pdf).

Dawson, A., & McCook, K. (2006, Summer). Rebuilding community in Louisiana after the hurricanes of 2005. *Reference and User Services Quarterly, 45,* 292-296.

Denver Public Library. (n.d.). Organizational structure. https://www.denverlibrary.org/content/organizational-structure.

Disability employment policy resources by topic. (n.d.). https://www.dol.gov/odep/about/.

Disaster Information Model Curriculum. https://disasterinfo.nlm.nih.gov/dimrc/disasterinfocurriculum.html.

Driggers, P. F., & Dumas, E. (2011). *Managing library volunteers: A practical toolkit.* Chicago, IL: ALA Editions.

Drummond, C., Coalition to Advance Learning for Archives, Libraries and Museums., & OCLC. (2016). *National agenda for continuing education and professional development across libraries, archives, and museums.* www.oclc.org/content/dam/research/publications/2016/oclcresearch-national-agenda-lams-education-development-2016.pdf.

Fargo Public Library. (n.d.). Volunteer Opportunities. www.cityoffargo.com/CityInfo/Departments/Library/Volunteers.

Garceau, O. (1949). *The public library in the political process: A report of the Public Library Inquiry.* New York, NY: Columbia University Press.

Gay, Lesbian, Bisexual and Transgender Round Table (GLBTRT). (n.d.). Buddy Program. www.ala.org/glbtrt/involved/buddy.

Girmscheid, L., & Schwartz, M. (2014). Pay day. *Library Journal, 139*(12), 22.

Glennon, M. (1997, January/February). Developing and passing a bond issue: A trustee's view. *Public Libraries, 36,* 24-48.

Goodrich, J. (2005, September/October). Staffing public libraries: Are there models or best practices? *Public Libraries, 44,* 277-281.

Guerrero, A. (2015). National Plutocrat Radio: Corporate one-percenters dominate NPR affiliates' board. www. fair.org/home/national-plutocrat-radio/).

Hague, R. (1999). A short history of the Stevens County Rural Library District. *Alki, 15,* 22-23.

Hastings, S. (2015). If diversity is a natural state, why don't our libraries mirror the populations they serve? *roy, 85*(2), 133-138.

Henricks, S., & Henricks-Lepp, G. M. (2014). Multiple constituencies model in the identification of library effectiveness. *Library Management, 35*(8/9), 645-665.

Holt, G. E., & Holt, L. E. (2014). *Success with library volunteers.* Santa Barbara, CA: Libraries Unlimited.

Hunter, C. C. (2016). Diversity & disability. *Public Libraries, 55*(1), 15-16.

ICF, Inc. (2013). Laura Bush 21st Century Grant Program Evaluation (Grant Years 2003-2009). https://www.imls.gov/sites/default/files/legacy/assets/1/AssetManager/LB21%20Evaluation%20Report.pdf.

Institute of Museum and Library Services. (2014). *Public libraries survey: Fiscal Year 2012.* www.imls.gov/research/public_libraries_in_the_us_fy_2012_report.aspx.

Institute of Museum and Library Services. (2016a, July). *Supplementary Tables: Public Libraries Survey Fiscal Year 2014.* https://www.imls.gov/sites/default/files/fy2014_pls_tables.pdf.

Institute of Museum and Library Services. (2016b). *Public libraries in the United States survey. Fiscal Year 2013.* Washington, DC. https://www.imls.gov/sites/default/files/publications/documents/plsfy2013.pdf.

Joeckel, C. B. (1935). *The government of the American public library.* Chicago, IL: University of Chicago Press.

Johnson, C. (2002, May/June). Professionalism, not paternalism. *Public Libraries, 41,* 139-140.

Kelley, H. N. (1999, Fall). Portrait of the Illinois trustee community. *Illinois Libraries, 81,* 222-225.

Kenney, B. (2015). So, you want to be a library director? *Publishers Weekly, 262*(20), 24-25. https://www.publishersweekly.com/pw/by-topic/industry-news/libraries/article/66654-so-you-want-to-be-a-library-director.html.

Kentucky State Board for the Certification of Librarians. (n.d.). http://kdla.ky.gov/librarians/staff development/Pages/certification.aspx.

Kentucky State Board for the Certification of Librarians. (2010). *Certification manual.* http://kdla.ky.gov/librarians/staffdevelopment/Documents/manual.pdf.

Keokuk Municipal Code. Chapter 2.85: Board of Library Trustees www.keokuk.lib.ia.us/about/policies/admin-gov/ordinance.

King County Library System. (n.d.). Volunteering. https://kcls.org/faq/volunteer/.

Kohn, K. (2016). Voter fever: Taxpayers speak on library referenda. *ILA Reporter, 34*(3), 4-7.

Kreamer, J. T. (1990, July/August). The library trustee as a library activist. *Public Libraries, 29,* 220-223.

Lang, S. (2008, September/October). From the other side. *Public Libraries, 47,* 28-29.

Laura Bush 21st Century Grant Program. (n.d.). https://www.imls.gov/grants/available/laura-bush-21st-century-librarian-program.

Laura Bush 21st Century Grant Program Evaluation. (2013). Grant years 2003–2009. https://www.imls.gov/sites/default/files/legacy/assets/1/AssetManager/LB21%20Evaluation%20Report.pdf.

Macikas, B. (2016). The diversity spectrum. *Public Libraries, 55*(1), 7–8.

Madison (ID) Public Library District. (n.d.). Library Board of Trustees. http://madisonlib.org/board-of-trustees/.

Maine State Library. (2015). *Maine Library Trustee Handbook 2015.* Library Development Documents. Paper 10. http://digitalmaine.com/ld_docs/10.

Mainzer, E., & Dipeolu, A. (2015). Doing right by those we serve: Law, ethics and career services for individuals with disabilities. *Career Planning and Adult Development Journal, 31,* 131–141.

Marcum, D. (2016, March 28). Library leadership for the digital age. *Ithaka S+R Issue Brief.* www.sr.ithaka.org/publications/library-leadership-for-the-digital-age/.

McCook, K. (2010). Unions in public and academic libraries. In *Encyclopedia of library and information.* London, United Kingdom: Taylor and Rutledge.

Medical Library Association. (n.d.). Disaster Information Model Curriculum. https://disasterinfo.nlm.nih.gov/dimrc/disasterinfocurriculum.html.

Mehra, B., & Davis R. (2015). Strategic diversity manifesto for public libraries in the 21st century. *New Library World, 116* (1/2), 15–36.

Miller, E. G., & Fisher, P. H. (2007). *Library board strategic guide.* Lanham, MD: Scarecrow Press.

Montana State Library. (n.d.). Continuing education and certification. http://msl.mt.gov/library_development/training/.

Moore, M. Y. (2010). *The successful library trustee handbook* (2nd ed.). Chicago, IL: American Library Association.

Most, L. (2011). Librarians build communities. Scholarship kick-off workshop held at Valdosta State. Second cohort. https://librariansbuildcommunities.wordpress.com/2011/01/22/199/#comments.

National Association of Counties. (2015). Legislative priorities. www.naco.org/sites/default/files/documents/2015_FINAL_Leg%20Priorities-fixed%20-NEW%20LOGO.08.27.15.pdf.

National League of Cities. (2015). Annual report. www.nlc.org/Documents/About%20NLC/NLC%20FY%202015%20Annual%20Report.pdf.

Neale, S. (2013). *Fundraising by Friends of the Library groups: Profitability trends and effectiveness of recent initiatives.* www.ala.org/united/sites/ala.org.united/files/content/friends/orgtools/sally-neale_friends-fundraising_11-16.pdf.

New Mexico State Library. (n.d.). Continuing education. www.nmstatelibrary.org/services-for-nm-libraries/continuing-education.

New York State Education Department. (2015). *Handbook for Library Trustees of New York.* www.nysl.nysed.gov/libdev/trustees/handbook/handbook.pdf. See also Library Trustees Association of New York State. http://librarytrustees.org.

Occupational outlook handbook, 2016–17 edition, Librarians. Bureau of Labor Statistics Department of Labor. www.bls.gov/ooh/education-training-and-library/librarians.htm.

Pennsylvania. Public Library Code. (n.d.). www.statelibrary.pa.gov/Libraries/LawsRegulations/Pages/Pennsylvania-Code-and-Regulations.aspx.

Provo City (UT) Library (n.d.). Volunteer. www.provolibrary.com/volunteers.

Public Library Association. (2016). 2016 Conference. Denver. www.placonference.org/wp-content/uploads/2016/03/PLA2016_Program_Book_Reduced_Spreads.pdf.

Public Library Association. (n.d.). Careers in public librarianship. www.ala.org/pla/tools/careers and LibraryCareers.org www.ala.org/ala/educationcareers/careers.

Public Library Association. (n.d.). Online learning. www.ala.org/pla/onlinelearning.

Public Library Association. (n.d.). PLA Leadership Academy. www.ala.org/pla/education/leadership academy.

Reed, S. G. (2012). *Libraries need friends: A toolkit to create Friends Groups or to revitalize the one you have.* United for Libraries: The Association of Library Trustees, Advocates, Friends and Foundations.

Ridgefield (CT) Library. (n.d.). Volunteer. www.ridgefieldlibrary.org/about/volunteer_opp.shtml.

Rosa, K. (2016, May 2). Notable dissertations. *American Libraries.* https://americanlibrariesmagazine.org/2016/05/02/notable-dissertations-library-student-research/.

Roy, L. (2006). *Bridging boundaries to create a new workforce: A survey of SPECTRUM scholarship recipients, 1998–2003.* Chicago, IL: American Library Association.

Rutledge, M. (2013). Overcoming hidden barriers to board diversity and inclusion. *BoardSource.* www.revisions.org/pubs/Rutledge_Overcoming-Barriers-Board-Diversity-Inclusion_BoardSource2013.pdf.

Rzepczynski, M. (2013, September/October). Survey says. *Public Libraries, 52,* 10–12.

San Luis Obispo Friends of the Library. www.slofol.org.

Schwartz, M. (2016, March 9) Top skills for tomorrow's librarians. *Library Journal.* http://lj.libraryjournal.com/2016/03/featured/top-skills-for-tomorrows-librarians-careers-2016/#_.

SPECTRUM Scholarship Program. (n.d.). www.ala.org/offices/diversity/spectrum.

Stewart, A., Washington-Hoagland, C., Zsulya, C. T., & Library Leadership and Management Association. (2013). *Staff development: A practical guide.* Chicago, IL: American Library Association.

Stone, C., & Stone, D. L. (2015). Factors affecting hiring decisions about veterans. *Human Resource Management Review, 25,* 68–79.

Swan, D. W., et al. (2015). Data file documentation: Public Libraries Survey: Fiscal Year 2013 (IMLS-2015-PLS-02). Institute of Museum and Library Services. Washington, DC. https://www.imls.gov/sites/default/files/fy2013_pls_data_file_documentation.pdf.

Throgmorton, K. (2016). Recruiting and retaining volunteers. *American Libraries, 47*(6), 42–45.

Traska, M. R. (2015). Building a better Board of Trustees. *American Libraries, 46*(11/12), 32–37.

United States. Department of Labor. Bureau of Labor Statistics. (2016). Union members summary. www.bls.gov/news.release/union2.nr0.htm.

Vinopal, Jennifer. (2016, January 13) The quest for diversity in library staffing: From awareness to action. *In the Library with the Lead Pipe.* www.inthelibrarywiththeleadpipe.org/2016/questfordiversity/.

VolunteerMatch. (n.d.) https://www.volunteermatch.org/about/.

Walker, V. L., & Davidson, D. J. (2010). Vital voices: Lessons learned from board members of color. *BoardSource.* https://www.boardsource.org/eweb/.

WebJunction. (n.d.). https://www.webjunction.org/about-us/help.html.

Wisconsin Department of Public Instruction. (2016). *Trustee Essentials: A Handbook for Wisconsin Public Library Trustees.* https://dpi.wi.gov/pld/boards-directors/trustee-essentials-handbook.

Wisconsin Public Library. (2010). Wisconsin Department of Public Instruction. *Wisconsin Public Library standards.* https://dpi.wi.gov/pld/boards-directors/library-standards.

Young, N. J. (2016, May 18). How the bathroom wars shaped America. *Politico Magazine.* www.politico.com/magazine/story/2016/05/2016-bathroom-bills-politics-north-carolina-lgbt-transgender-history-restrooms-era-civil-rights-213902.

CHAPTER 7

The Public Library Building

Emblem of Community Heritage and Embodiment of Community Courage

What is the first picture that comes to mind when you think of a public library? Whether it is a neoclassical Carnegie library, the New York Public Library lions, or the modern Seattle Public Library, most people will agree that library buildings are iconic. This chapter considers the public library building not only as civic memory and source of identity, but also as a collective space. It summarizes the history of public library buildings in the United States and reviews the role of the Library Services and Construction Act. Examples of recent public library architecture and outline design standards, including accessibility requirements are presented and the need for security and disaster planning is also addressed.

CIVIC MEMORY AND IDENTITY

The importance of the library as civic memory and identity to towns large and small has been described with great poetry and artistry in Robert Dawson's photographic essay, *The Public Library*, which includes 681 photographs from the collection of the Library of Congress.[1] The American public library is architecture, community space, and a reflection of the contemporary social landscape.[2] The images in Dawson's book and exhibit document the wide range of architecture of public libraries in America, including those on small-town streets, in shopping malls, on Indian reservations, in national parks, and in large cities. The photographs show that the public library is not only a source for information and knowledge, but that it is also a public commons.

Descriptions of the public library emphasize its centrality to the American landscape. It has been described as the heart of the community: a public good; a third place; the embodiment of the public sphere; an arsenal of democracy; the people's university; part of the educational ecosystem; and an agency for digital inclusion. During the three centuries since the public library was established as an American institution, it has been reinvented, repurposed, and renewed again and again. Shannon Mattern, New School Media Studies scholar, has investigated libraries as multiuse public spaces, anchors in urban redevelopment, civic icons, and showcases of renowned architects. She writes that public libraries are sites where spatial, technological, intellectual, and social infrastructures shape and inform one another (Mattern, 2007, 2014).

The physical buildings that house American public libraries are also manifestations of community spirit created by socially minded women's groups, political interests, and everyday people who vote for millages and raise funds to support local libraries. The idea of the library itself is a catalyst for community spirt in service of the public good.

At the outset of the new millennium, the public library began to be characterized as a community anchor when public officials began to see it as an equity investment with a vital role to play in a community's social and fiscal well-being (St. Lifer, 2001). This concept was developed most clearly by Chicago Mayor Richard M. Daley in partnership with Chicago Public Library Commissioner Mary Dempsey. In 2005, Daley described their collaboration on dozens of new or renovated libraries:

> *Libraries today are community anchors.* When we go out and dedicate a new library, it is amazing how many new volunteers we get from the community itself and how many people look at that amount of investment in a library and see what it means . . . that we're investing that much money in the community. They in turn say, "We're going to start *investing our own time and effort in our own community.*" (Daley, in Holt & Holt, 2010, p. 22).[3]

Yet questions arise. Researchers in the 2015 report *Libraries at the Crossroads* asked, "Should bricks-and-mortar libraries have a smaller physical footprint in their communities?" (Horrigan, 2015). The respondents overwhelmingly replied "*no*." Despite the availability of online information, libraries still occupy a prominent spot in people's minds and hearts as a *place.* Cynthia Nitikin and Josh Jackson, of the Project for Public Spaces (2009) said, "the dawn of the 'information superhighway' threatened to make [libraries] less relevant, even obsolete. Yet now, these institutions are as prominent as ever, with a wave of innovation as the next generation of libraries extend their mission well beyond the storage of knowledge." According to Robert Pasicznyuk (2014), director at Colorado's Douglas County Libraries, "There are a number of communities that long for something beyond virtual communities. That desire becomes a reality in library makerspaces big and small. In each of these examples, the library is only realizing what it was originally conceived to be—a place where the community convenes around its commitment to literacy and lifelong learning."

When there are so few places for the public, the idea of the public library is more important than ever. The project "Reimagining the Civic Commons" explains:

> Our civic assets were once the pride of our communities. Our libraries, parks, community centers, and schoolyards served rich and poor alike as neutral ground where common purpose was nurtured. But as communities became segmented by income, technology advanced and needs changed, support for civic assets declined. Americans spend less time together in social settings, trust each other less and interact less with people whose life experiences are different. (http://civiccommons.us/)

Cities must preserve and nurture space for public gatherings where all can enter with no pressure to purchase. Elmborg (2011) explicitly warns librarians against using the marketing terminology regarding creating spaces that has so infused library management, because the spirit of the public sphere—that which enlivens public discourse—is not aligned with consumer culture. Library space is not for sale to the highest bidder.

In a world where war and terrorism exist, the public library represents so much that is good in the human spirit. This was especially apparent in New York after the terror attacks in 2001, where libraries offered places of hopeful continuation of culture and human hope. In her notes on *Reading Room: A Catalog of New York City's Branch Libraries* (2016) architectural photographer Elizabeth Felicella (2016) documents 210 branches of New York City's public library system as "part and parcel of the evolution of modern public life . . . places that reflect and shape our best and changing aspirations as a society and as individuals within it (Felicella, 2016)."

Public libraries often collect local history and have thus become spaces that symbolize community heritage. For instance, Pittsburgh was once called the "Workshop of the World"; the city's Carnegie Library maintains a historical Iron and Steel collection that documents mill owners, workers, labor practices, and conflicts. South Carolina's Charleston County Public Library employs a public historian to stimulate community involvement to explicate the history of the region dating back to 1790. The Newark (NJ) Public Library houses, maintains, and develops the Puerto Rican Community Archive, which preserves the history of New Jersey's Puerto Rican residents (Schull, 2015). These initiatives are more than centers of learning; they are essential for maintaining a sense of place in their cities. "Placemaking" is a concept that requires community participation. Libraries may be designed by architects, but good planning processes involve the community. A library is not simply a lovely building plopped into an empty space. As the Project for Public Spaces (2009) explains,

> Placemaking inspires people to collectively reimagine and reinvent public spaces as the heart of every community . . . With community-based participation at its center, an effective Placemaking process capitalizes on a local community's assets, inspiration, and potential, and it results in the creation of quality public spaces that contribute to people's health, happiness, and well being.

Libraries are often beautiful spaces that symbolize civic and cultural pride. We need only search "beautiful libraries" to be besieged by click bait; for instance, *TechInsider* (Weller, 2016) chronicled "the most beautiful libraries in each state," offering a breathless cyber tour of the libraries of the United States.[4] Unsurprisingly, library literature exalts library spaces; *Library Journal* and *Public Libraries* offer glimpses into spaces that capture our imagination. For instance, a *Public Libraries Online* story on the Alice Virginia and David W. Fletcher Branch of the Washington Free Library (Maryland) in Hagerstown (figure 7.1) features its expansive, glass-enclosed, multistory circular atrium, designed to resemble the old Hagerstown roundhouse of the Western Maryland Railroad. Library Director Mary Baykan explained that the library is a symbol of the area; therefore, it was important "to include functionality and aesthetics, along with symbolism reflecting the history of Washington County" (Smith, 2014).

The public library building demonstrates that people will come together and contribute funds to support an agency that supports lifelong learning and equal access to information. The library building is an emblem of the belief that all people are entitled to the right to knowledge, creativity, and an expansion of human capabilities.

THE BEGINNING OF THE PUBLIC LIBRARY BUILDING

"Built by the People and Dedicated to the Advancement of Learning"

The first public libraries in America were not stand-alone facilities. They were in churches, clubs, storefronts, and civic buildings. Even the Boston Public Library was initially located

FIGURE 7.1 Image of Alice Virginia and David W. Fletcher Branch, Washington County, MD

SOURCE: Featured in *Public Libraries Online,* June 2014 (http://publiclibrariesonline.org/2014/06/a-library-as-a-symbol-for-the-community/). Photo by Jeffrey Smith.

in a public-school building (Boston Public Library, n.d.). This soon changed. A library was built in Boston on Boylston Street in 1858. The collection was moved in 1895. The library is described in *A Handbook to the Art and Architecture of the Boston Public Library: Visitors Guide to the McKim Building, Copley Square, Its Mural Decorations and Its Collection.* The Boston Public Library facing Copley Square is one of Boston's proudest monuments, and perhaps the most admired, discussed, and influential public building of the American architectural of the nineteenth century. It marks the supreme achievement of its architect, Charles F. McKim, whose challenge was to erect a civic building of commanding presence that did not overpower the Richardsonian Romanesque of Trinity Church. The solution resulted in the first outstanding example of Renaissance Beaux Arts academicism in the United States (Wick, 1977, pp. 13–14).

There are numerous histories of other early public library buildings that provide insight into the place these buildings held in the life of the communities. Public libraries were often built with donor funds (though that is not a universal truism), and were visible symbols of the magnanimity of wealthy donors. The study *Henry Hobson Richardson and the Small Public Library in America: A Study in Typology* (Breisch, 2003) focuses on the architect, whose Crane Memorial Library in Quincy, Massachusetts (1879–1881) has been ranked among America's favorite buildings.[5] Other histories, such as that of Montana's Anaconda Public Library (Geil, 1998), Cleveland Public Library (1925); the New York Public Library (Reed, 2011); and the San Francisco Public Library (Wiley, 1996) are guaranteed to delight the library historian.

The most widespread influence on early public library architecture was the philanthropy of Andrew Carnegie, who funded the building of hundreds of public libraries in America between 1886 and 1919.[6] The 1,688 Carnegie libraries are the single largest collection of historic buildings in America. Initially, each community that received a Carnegie building grant was able to develop its own library architecture, and buildings were varied in style and space use. Midway through the program (in 1911), the Carnegie Corporation issued a publication called "Notes on Library Buildings" that provided suggested guidelines for libraries built with Carnegie funds. The variety of architectural styles for the Carnegie-funded libraries included Italian Renaissance, Beaux-Arts, Classical Revival, Spanish Revival, Prairie, Tudor Revival, and "Carnegie Classical" (Bobinski, 1969). Communities in the United States initially tended to think of public libraries as civic landmarks and expressions of community pride, and perhaps less attention was paid to functionality. Carnegie's gifts helped communities to adopt the idea of the public library as a logical community service with some basic standardization of structure.

> **▸ FACT**
>
> Andrew Carnegie spent over $56 million to build 2,509 libraries throughout the English-speaking world—which would be $1,600,000,000.00 in 2015 dollars.*
>
> ———
>
> *Philanthropy of Andrew Carnegie. Columbia University Libraries. See http://library.columbia.edu/locations/rbml/units/carnegie/andrew.html. For inflation see Dave Manuel www.davemanuel.com/.

There have been several studies of these libraries. *Carnegie Libraries across America: A Public Legacy* (Jones, 1997) illustrates the variety of architectural styles of Carnegie libraries nationwide.[7] *Free to All: Carnegie Libraries and American Culture, 1890–1920,* examines the funding, design, staffing, and use of monumental urban central libraries and of more functional urban branch libraries and small-town libraries (Van Slyck, 1995). George Bobinski's classic study, *Carnegie Libraries: Their History and Impact on American Library Development,* details the process of the library program and how it was administered (1969). Figure 7.2 shows the Paris-Bourbon County, Kentucky, restoration of a 1904 Carnegie library.

Many Carnegie libraries are listed in The National Register of Historic Places.[8] Fred Schlipf (2014) has evaluated the challenges in remodeling and expanding Carnegie-era library buildings and suggests possible solutions.

FUNDS FOR PUBLIC LIBRARY CONSTRUCTION: PRIMING THE PUMP WITH LSCA

Thirty years after the Carnegie program ended, ALA's National Plan for Public Library Service (1948) assessed the status of the nation's public library buildings and found the situation dire:

> The present [physical plant of the public library] is barely 50 percent adequate for existing public library services. And for the extension of library service to the 35 million people now entirely without public libraries, a great new building program must be undertaken. (Joeckel & Winslow, 1948, p. 29)

Although specifics were not given regarding design, general statements of accessibility, functionality, and the functionality of a "modern educational center," meeting rooms, film viewing space, and listening areas were set forth in the National Plan.

FIGURE 7.2 2017 AIA Kentucky Honor Award, Paris-Bourbon County (KY) Public Library

SOURCE: Paris-Bourbon County (KY) Public Library. Design by EOP Architects (www.eopa.com), Lexington, KY. Photo by Phebus Photography.

The 1956 Public Libraries Division's ***Public Library Service: A Guide to Evaluation, with Minimum Standards*** stated, "The public library building should serve as a symbol of library service. It should offer to the community a compelling invitation to enter, read, look, listen and learn" (ALA, PLD 1956, p. 56). These guidelines were used to argue for the federal legislation to support libraries, which was successfully passed in 1956 as the Library Services Act, which evolved into the Library Services and Construction Act (LSCA) in 1966 (Drennan, 1967).

A full picture of the scope of LSCA funding in libraries would require a study of the reports of individual states. Unfortunately, these do not exist in a single convenient location. Some are in the ERIC database, and some are archived by individual states. For example, Rhode Island has a historical note at its Office of Library and Information Services that explains in detail how federal funding, in collaboration with state and local funding and donations, brought $123 million for library construction since 1966.[9]

> **▸ FACT**
>
> Between 1965 and 1996 over $300 million in LSCA federal funds were granted through the state library agencies for the construction of new library buildings, as well as expansion and remodeling (McCook, 2011, p. 190, note 1).*
>
> ---
>
> *U.S. Department of Education, Office of Educational Research and Improvement. 2011. Biennial Evaluation Report, 1995–1996: Public Library Construction and Technology Enhancement Grants to State Library Agencies (CFDA No. 84-154).

The scope of federal support over the 30 years of LSCA funding is shown in figure 7.3. A review of the library literature during the

LSCA era demonstrates how important library activism has been for maintaining services. Stories of state-level lobbying for local matches, congressional hearings to reinstate funds cut by President Ronald Reagan, and the street-fighting energy of librarians all over the United States show how librarian activists managed to sustain appropriations during times of duress.[10]

The Library Services and Construction Act, as the name implies, expanded the capacity of libraries through federal funding for buildings and services. The story of the competition behind the design and building of the central Chicago Public Library in 1987 is one of the best-documented events in public library building history, and one that is illustrative of the meaning of public library buildings. The problem of building a civic monument for Chicago was viewed as a clear choice between two distinct alternatives. One option was to build a static, tranquil space conducive to the search for knowledge that would project an image of solidity and permanence, a structure that would express civic dignity and monumentality. A second option was to create an image that would reflect the dynamism of the city, symbolizing the active collection of information rather than the contemplation of knowledge. The video *Design Wars* follows the architects and builders in competition to design the Chicago Public Library as they tried to accommodate issues of functionality,

Public Library Construction and Technology Enhancement Grants to State Library Agencies (CFDA No. 84.154) Funding History

Funding History*

Fiscal Year	Appropriation	Fiscal Year	Appropriation
1965	$30,000,000	1987	$22,050,000
1970	7,807,250	1988	22,143,100
1975	0	1989	21,877,520
1980	0	1990	18,572,036
1981	0	1991	18,833,395
1982	0	1992	16,383,640
1983	50,000,000	1993	16,252,571
1984	0	1994	17,436,160
1985	24,500,000	1995	17,436,160
1986	21,102,000	1996	16,041,620

* There is no time limit for the expenditure of these funds.

FIGURE 7.3 Public Library Construction and Technology Enhancement Grants to State Library Agencies (CFDA No. 84.154) Funding History

SOURCE: Public Library Construction and Technology Enhancement Grants to State Library Agencies (CFDA No. 84.154). https://www2.ed.gov/pubs/Biennial/95-96/eval/603-97.pdf.

safety, public appeal, and express a vision of Chicago (MARZ Associates, in association with WGBH, Boston, 1989).

The design selected in 1988, a Beaux-Arts building by Hammond, Beeby, and Babka, Inc., has been characterized as aesthetically and architecturally fitting the city like a glove, with its monumental and decorative, yet profoundly public, innovative, and urban-appropriate form. As hoped, the central library (figure 7.4), named the Harold Washington Library Center after the city's first African-American mayor (1922–1987), sparked a revitalization of Chicago's South Loop District after it opened in 1991 ("Six Chicago Architects," 1989; Lane, 1989).

The story of community-wide engagement in the selection of the design for the Chicago Public Library is emblematic of the importance of the library as a great public space (Dawson, Moyers and Patchett, 2014; Kent and Myrick, 2003). Public libraries that reach into the heart of a community may be monumental central libraries or small intimate branches. During the LSCA construction grant period, many communities found opportunities to build public libraries that not only provided educational and recreational needs but also provided a great public space during a time of expansive suburbanization and growth in edge cities.

The LSCA was replaced in 1996 when President Bill Clinton authorized the Library Services and Technology Act (LSTA). At that point, federal funding focused on technology enhancement, rather than physical spaces. Although there is less federal support for buildings, funding programs continue as local and state collaborations. For example, New York

FIGURE 7.4 Chicago Public Library—Harold Washington Library Center

SOURCE: Reprinted by permission of the Chicago Public Library.

Public Libraries: Five-Year Cost Summary

	2012	2013	2014	2015	2016
New Buildings	34	27	29	38	32
Additions, Renovations, Remodels	73	47	55	54	59
Total Funds	$603,961,651	$361,793,970	$583,252,852	$688,935,437	$634,499,203

FIGURE 7.5 Public Libraries: Five-Year Cost Summary

SOURCES: Data from Fox, 2015, "Working in Harmony," *Library Journal* 140(19), 34; Fox, 2016, "Open for Business," *Library Journal* 141(19), 34.

appropriated $14 million in capital funds for public library construction in its 2015 state budget—up to 75% of approved costs of acquisition, construction, renovation, or rehabilitation of public libraries or public library system headquarters. Minnesota offers the Library Construction Grant program, a competitive dollar-for-dollar matching grant program that provides public libraries with funding for renovation, construction, and improvement projects that result in more accessible library facilities.[11] Each state is different, but most states provide some funds for construction of new library buildings.

The annual number of buildings and expenditures on public library buildings are reported annually by *Library Journal* (see figure 7.5).

Library construction can be a major force for community revitalization. In San Francisco, voters approved issuance of a $106 million bond program to build and refurbish 24 neighborhood branch libraries. This measure initiated a nearly $200-million campaign to update, revitalize, and preserve the San Francisco Branch Library system, known as the Branch Library Improvement Program (BLIP). Speaking to the success of the program in 2015, Mayor Ed Lee stated:

> While the focus of the BLIP program was to ensure seismic safety and full accessibility, the 24 completed library projects have gone so much further to bridge the technology divide; create safe and welcoming spaces for children, teens, and community; and offer educational opportunities that enable all our residents to succeed in the 21st century economy. Our civic efforts have provided needed resources so our residents, our youth, our families and our seniors can all share in our City's prosperity. (San Francisco Public Library, 2015)

Over $634 million were spent on public library buildings (new and additions, renovations, and remodels) in 2016. The annual *Library Journal* series on public library buildings reported 32 new facilities completed in Fiscal Year 2016 in communities throughout the United States at a total cost of $397,152,182. Local funds were the main source of support, coming in at $371,719,254. Local gifts and donations to support the construction of new libraries totaled $14,388,312. States contributed $15,025,234. Federal support for new construction was $350,000 (Fox, 2016).

Another 59 buildings had additions, renovations, or remodeling costing $397,152,182. Funding for this construction came predominantly from local sources ($199,559,402) followed by gifts and donations ($32,636,393), state funds ($2,787,038) and federal funds $2,423,000 (Fox, 2016).

When natural disasters strike, rebuilding the library is often a rallying point for community renewal. For example, when the Cedar Rapids (IA) Public Library was damaged by the Cedar River flood in 2008, the city chose to rebuild it, spending $45 million on a certified U.S. Green Building Council Leadership in Energy and Environmental Design (LEED) Platinum building (see figure 7.6). The new 94,000-square-foot building includes expanded space for youth, flexible meeting spaces, a café, a green roof, and views of the nearby park and cityscape (Murvosh, 2014). When Louisiana's New Orleans Regional Library was damaged by Hurricane Katrina in 2005, the city built five new branches, using funds from Energy Efficiency and Conservation Block Grants, damage reimbursements from the Federal Emergency Management Agency, state Community Development Block Grants, and municipal bonds (Schwartz, Cornog & Warburton, 2012).

BUILDING SHOWCASES

New Construction

Each year, in addition to articles that appear on new building in local newspapers or state association publications, *American Libraries* and *Library Journal* present summaries of the year's library architecture, additions, renovations, and adaptive reuse. Full of sumptuous photographs, these annual features demonstrate community commitment to public library

FIGURE 7.6 Cedar Rapids (IA) Public Library

SOURCE: Design by OPN Architects. Photo by Wayne Johnson, Main Street Studio; courtesy of OPN Architects.

buildings. *Library Journal* has published the biennial Library Building Awards of the American Institute of Architects (AIA) and ALA since 1963.

The 1966 *ALA Bulletin* explained why it awarded the first-place winner:

> The only First Honor Award was in the Public Library category. It was presented to the Magnolia branch of the Seattle Public Library . . . the jury commented: "This relatively small and sensitively designed library presents a friendly and inviting face to its users. The plan is simple and well organized; the choice of native materials makes it a handsome example of Northwest regional architecture . . . Its respect for the site contributes greatly to the successful solution to the requirements of the program." (p. 577)

The 1972 report began:

> A good building must serve well the functions carried on within . . . It should permit these functions to be well organized, well defined, and well related . . . Every building makes some kind of statement, but if the building is to be a good piece of architecture, the statement must be honest and expressive of the true character of the building . . . A building must be kind to its users . . . to be successful in the ultimate sense, a building must also be kind to its environment. (p. 521)

Design and ideas about placemaking have changed since the 1970s, but similar themes still pervade today's awards; the winning libraries fit well in and are connected to their environment, whether a busy downtown respite or a suburban gathering place. They are "kind to their users." They are designed to help people use the space well. A few highlights indicate the range and scope of recently completed, renovated, or repurposed public library buildings.

New construction in 2015 included new main libraries in Palo Alto, California; Hudson, Colorado; Baton Rouge, Louisiana; South Hadley, Massachusetts; Ely, Minnesota; Billings, Montana; and Tiverton, Rhode Island. The new main library in Baton Rouge, Louisiana, (figure 7.7) takes full advantage of its location within a community park to offer an immersive experience with nature. A three-story glass wall offers views of a botanical garden, and a central plaza connects the library to gardens, soccer fields, a new café and a rooftop terrace (Morehart, 2015).

Many new branches were opened in 2015, including Denver, Colorado; Sarasota and Miami-Dade, Florida; Atlanta, Georgia; Louisville, Kentucky; and Milwaukee, Wisconsin. The Northeast Dade-Aventura Branch of Florida's Miami-Dade Public Library System (shown in figure 7.8) maximizes exterior spaces with courtyards and covered terraces.

Joint-Use Libraries

The joint-use library has been defined as libraries of two or more different types of libraries amalgamating to offer collections and services that neither could have afforded to offer individually (Miller, 2001). This might be a public library and a school library, or a public library and a college/university library. The public library system in Broward County, Florida, and Nova Southeastern University (Cisse, 2013) share space and collections. The physical and administrative merging of the San Jose State University and San Jose Public Library to form the Martin Luther King Jr. Library in San Jose, California, demonstrated that two

FIGURE 7.7 Main Library, East Baton Rouge (LA) Parish Library at Goodwood

SOURCE: Design by Library Design Collaborative: A Joint Venture. Photo by Josh Peak.

FIGURE 7.8 Northeast Dade-Aventura Branch, Miami-Dade (FL) Public Library

SOURCE: Design by Miami-Dade County Internal Services Department. Photo by Miami-Dade Public Library System.

existing libraries with different missions, clients, and bureaucracies could not only share a building but also successfully integrate operations (Agee, 2014). In Virginia Beach, a joint-use library of 125,000 square feet was opened in cooperation with Tidewater Community College (Free, 2013). Case studies of various joint-use libraries have been discussed in *Joint Libraries: Models That Work* (Gunnels, Green, & Butler, 2012)

There are also joint-use *facilities* such as Hewitt, Texas, where a joint library and city hall comprise a 26,500-square-foot building that allows for direct flow among multipurpose rooms, the library, municipal court, and council chambers (Smith, 2014). In 2016 the Public Library ALA/IIDA Library Interior Design Award went to the Mill Woods Library, Seniors' Centre and Multicultural Facility in Alberta, Canada. The senior center is in the upper portion, and the library is on the ground floor. The Carmel Mountain Ranch Library in San Diego combines an activity center and library (Bernard, 2016).

Mitchell Park Library and Community Center in Palo Alto, California, shown in figure 7.9, replaces two outdated facilities. The LEED Platinum-certified building celebrates the community's heritage by incorporating a large existing oak tree in the courtyard into the building's design (Morehart, 2015).

Repurposed Spaces and Adaptive Reuse of Buildings

Public library buildings also provide the opportunity for repurposing or adaptive reuse of older buildings. If the building was a landmark, the architects often strive to retain historic features. Recent repurposed buildings include the Centennial Library in Midland, Texas, a former retail store, and the Athens-Limestone (AL) Public Library, which was transformed from an abandoned grocery store. In Wisconsin, the Madison Public Library and the Meadowood Neighborhood Center revitalized an empty storefront, and allowed both entities to use a commercial-grade kitchen in the joint community room. The Garland Smith Pub-

FIGURE 7.9 Mitchell Park Library and Community Center, Palo Alto, CA

SOURCE: Photography by Cortez Media Group. Design by Group 4 Architecture, Research + Planning, Inc.

lic Library of Marlow, Oklahoma, is a renovated National Guard Armory (Fox, 2015). The Kansas City (MO) Main Library was relocated to a former bank in 1999 (KCLibrary.org). Features of the former bank provide some unique and delightful spaces, such as a movie theater in the old vault.

The Corvallis-Benton County (OR) Public Library, Monroe Community Library shown in figure 7.10 is a part of the last remaining freight depot in Benton County, constructed and restored as an addition to the depot. Original historical features, including graffiti, were preserved, and solar and geothermal energy sources were added. The Southeast Branch, Nashville Public Library, in Antioch, Tennessee (shown in figure 7.11), is both repurposed *and* joint use. It is a former J. C. Penney department store and shares space with a community center.

BRANCHES

Many public libraries have extended services beyond the central library by developing branch systems or providing bookmobile services, collaborating through joint-use libraries,

FIGURE 7.10 Corvallis-Benton County (OR) Public Library, Monroe Community Library

SOURCE: Design by Broadleaf Architecture.

and facilitating online access via mobile devices. The Public Library Survey Data Element Definitions states:

A branch library is an auxiliary unit of an administrative entity which at minimum includes:

1. Separate quarters
2. An organized collection of library materials
3. Paid staff
4. Regularly scheduled hours when it is open to the public.[12]

> ▶ **FACT**
>
> In 2015 there are 7,769 public library branches.*
>
> ---
>
> *See IMLS, Public Library Survey (2016). Number of public libraries with branches and bookmobiles, and number of service outlets, by type of outlet and state: Fiscal year 2014, p. 10, Table 3. https://www.imls.gov/sites/default/files/fy2014_pls_tables.pdf.

Although main libraries might embody a sweeping grand architectural statement, branch libraries tend to be more personal and in touch with the local neighborhood, or function as the heartbeat of the community (Putnam and Feldstein, 2003). In a report for the Center for an Urban Future, the scope of services of the branches of the New York City Public library was described as an increasingly critical part of the city's human capital system, yet undervalued by policymakers and increasingly threatened in today's digital age (Giles, 2013).

FIGURE 7.11 The Southeast Branch, Nashville Public Library, Antioch, TN

SOURCE: HBM Architects, Design Architect, and Lose & Associates, Architect of Record.

Branch libraries serve their communities by providing convenient locations and access to materials and information that link to the wider world of what libraries offer. In her discussion of the branches at nine locations of the Wichita Public Library, in which she focuses on the Alford Regional Branch Library, Jean Hatfield (2008) characterizes the branch library as a community center.

The Branch Librarian's Handbook (Rivers, 2004) describes the variety of branch services. Branch libraries can afford to be innovative and responsive to their local community. Programs like the Library Partnership, a neighborhood resource center of the Alachua County Library District in Gainesville, Florida, merges branch and social services (Florida Library, 2009). Green public art is showcased at the Pearl Avenue branch of the San Jose (CA) Public Library (Blumenstein, 2009). The Clear Lake City-County Freeman Branch Library of Houston received a generous bequest that financed community free access to classes and makerspace tools. The Jocelyn H. Lee Innovation Lab became the first dedicated makerspace in Harris County (TX) Public Library system (Ferrell, 2016).

Branch libraries can also be responsive to the culture of their patrons, or even address tragedies in their neighborhoods. In the wake of the shooting at the Pulse nightclub in Orlando, Florida, on June 12, 2016, the Orange County Library System's Hiawassee Branch collected photographs of flowers, gifts, and displays from the vigil held on June 13 to post on the Orlando Memory heritage site (Peet, 2016).

Figure 7.12 shows that there are 16,559 stationary public library outlets in the country. Of these, 8.890 are central or main libraries and 7,669 are branches. There are 659 bookmobiles.

RESOURCES ON BUILDING DESIGN

There have been a number of new or updated books on library buildings. Sannwald's *Checklist of Library Building Design Considerations,* (2016), now in its 6th edition, provides a complete inventory for building with a special focus on Americans with Disabilities Act (ADA) factors, provides a complete inventory for building with a special focus on ADA federal building code. *Public Library Buildings: The Librarian's Go-To Guide for Construction, Expansion, and Renovation Projects* showcases the reinvention of the library building, and discusses features such as art galleries, digital archives, makerspaces, and Friends' book sales areas (Charbonnet, 2015).

Libraries: A Design Manual (Lushington, Rudorf, & Wong, 2016) is a handbook on planning libraries. It features contributions by experts in architecture and library science who analyze specific aspects of the building type and presents a typology of some 40 exemplary international projects that provides inspiration and a range of options.

For those interested in networking, the Building and Equipment Section of ALA's Library Leadership and Management Association (LLAMA BES) provides opportunities to exchange ideas about building issues with other professionals.[13] LLAMA BES brings together librarians and design professionals to analyze, discuss, and share information about buildings, equipment, and furnishings. Topics at its conferences include library site selection; building planning and architecture; library furniture and equipment; interior design; maintenance and security of buildings and property; and disaster recovery. Additional resources for space planning are available at the WebJunction (2015) site for space planning.

State libraries provide additional information about public library building requirements. The extraordinarily important document *Public Library Space Needs: A Planning*

State	Number of public libraries	Number of libraries with		Number of outlets						
				Stationary outlets					Bookmobiles[1]	
					Central libraries		Branches			
		Branches	Bookmobiles	Total[2]	Total	Response rate[3]	Total	Response rate[3]	Total	Response rate[3]
Total[4]	9,070	1,556	546	16,559	8,890	100.0	7,669	100.0	659	100.0
Alabama	218	20	12	292	216	100.0	76	100.0	14	100.0
Alaska	79	6	1	95	79	100.0	16	100.0	1	100.0
Arizona	90	23	8	220	85	100.0	135	100.0	11	100.0
Arkansas	58	37	2	233	54	100.0	179	100.0	2	100.0
California	184	116	36	1,117	167	100.0	950	100.0	53	100.0
Colorado	113	36	10	258	96	100.0	162	100.0	13	100.0
Connecticut	182	27	4	229	182	100.0	47	100.0	4	100.0
Delaware	21	3	2	32	19	100.0	13	100.0	2	100.0
District of Columbia	1	1	0	26	1	100.0	25	100.0	0	100.0
Florida	82	50	18	531	63	100.0	468	100.0	24	100.0
Georgia	63	56	12	395	63	100.0	332	100.0	13	100.0
Hawaii	1	1	1	50	1	100.0	49	100.0	2	100.0
Idaho	102	17	10	143	99	100.0	44	100.0	11	100.0
Illinois	623	45	19	780	623	100.0	157	100.0	19	100.0
Indiana	237	71	23	427	236	100.0	191	100.0	25	100.0
Iowa	534	9	3	558	534	100.0	24	100.0	3	100.0
Kansas	318	13	3	366	317	100.0	49	100.0	5	100.0
Kentucky	119	38	74	206	119	100.0	87	100.0	75	100.0
Louisiana	68	52	24	340	68	100.0	272	100.0	28	100.0
Maine	228	2	1	234	228	100.0	6	100.0	1	100.0
Maryland	24	24	9	187	15	100.0	172	100.0	16	100.0

FIGURE 7.12 Number of Public Libraries with Branches and Bookmobiles, and Number of Service Outlets, by Type of Outlet and State: Fiscal Year 2014

[CONTINUED ON FOLLOWING PAGE]

SOURCE: https://www.imls.gov/sites/default/files/fy2014_pls_tables.pdf.

FIGURE 7.12 [CONTINUED ON FOLLOWING PAGE]

State	Number of public libraries	Number of libraries with		Number of outlets						
				Stationary outlets					Bookmobiles[1]	
					Central libraries		Branches			
		Branches	Bookmobiles	Total[2]	Total	Response rate[3]	Total	Response rate[3]	Total	Response rate[3]
Massachusetts	368	36	4	462	368	100.0	94	100.0	4	100.0
Michigan	388	59	8	643	384	100.0	259	100.0	9	100.0
Minnesota	137	24	7	356	129	100.0	227	100.0	8	100.0
Mississippi	52	38	2	235	52	100.0	183	100.0	2	100.0
Missouri	149	46	17	361	138	100.0	223	100.0	27	100.0
Montana	82	16	4	115	82	100.0	33	100.0	4	100.0
Nebraska	263	3	7	282	263	100.0	19	100.0	7	100.0
Nevada	21	13	3	85	18	100.0	67	100.0	3	100.0
New Hampshire	219	5	0	224	219	100.0	5	100.0	0	100.0
New Jersey	281	37	12	424	281	100.0	143	100.0	12	100.0
New Mexico	87	11	1	114	87	100.0	27	100.0	1	100.0
New York	756	52	4	1,065	755	100.0	310	100.0	7	100.0
North Carolina	80	65	21	385	69	100.0	316	100.0	23	100.0
North Dakota	73	3	11	76	72	100.0	4	100.0	11	100.0
Ohio	251	99	36	709	239	100.0	470	100.0	53	100.0
Oklahoma	117	9	2	212	116	100.0	96	100.0	4	100.0
Oregon	129	24	7	221	126	100.0	95	100.0	7	100.0
Pennsylvania	455	47	17	621	451	100.0	170	100.0	23	100.0
Rhode Island	48	8	1	70	47	100.0	23	100.0	1	100.0
South Carolina	42	34	31	192	40	100.0	152	100.0	31	100.0
South Dakota	112	7	5	144	112	100.0	32	100.0	5	100.0
Tennessee	186	28	3	286	186	100.0	100	100.0	3	100.0

FIGURE 7.12 [CONTINUED]

State	Number of public libraries	Number of libraries with		Number of outlets							
				Stationary outlets						Bookmobiles[1]	
					Central libraries		Branches				
		Branches	Bookmobiles	Total[2]	Total	Response rate[3]	Total	Response rate[3]		Total	Response rate[3]
Texas	548	70	6	865	546	100.0	319	100.0		7	100.0
Utah	72	20	15	126	56	100.0	70	100.0		16	100.0
Vermont	155	3	4	157	154	100.0	3	100.0		4	100.0
Virginia	91	63	19	357	83	100.0	274	100.0		22	100.0
Washington	62	23	12	344	54	100.0	290	100.0		27	100.0
West Virginia	97	26	7	173	97	100.0	76	100.0		8	100.0
Wisconsin	381	20	6	460	378	100.0	82	100.0		6	100.0
Wyoming	23	20	2	76	23	100.0	53	100.0		2	100.0
Outlying areas											
American Samoa	1	1	0	2	1	100.0	1	100.0		0	100.0
Guam	1	1	0	6	1	100.0	5	100.0		0	100.0

1. A bookmobile is a traveling branch library. It consists of at least one of the following: (1) A truck or van that carries an organized collection of library materials; (2) paid staff; and (3) regularly scheduled hours (bookmobile stops) for being open to the public.
2. Total stationary outlets is the sum of central and branch libraries.
3. Response rate is calculated as the number of libraries that reported the item, divided by the total number of libraries in the survey frame.
4. Total includes the 50 states and the District of Columbia but excludes outlying areas and libraries that do not meet the FSCS Public Library Definition. Of the 9,070 public libraries in the 50 States and DC, 7,347 were single-outlet libraries and 1,723 were multiple-outlet libraries. Single-outlet libraries are a central library, bookmobile, or books-by-mail-only outlet. Multiple-outlet libraries have two or more direct service outlets, including some combination of one central library, branch(es), bookmobile(s), and/or books-by-mail-only outlets.

NOTE: Data were not reported by the following outlying areas (Northern Marianas and Virgin Islands). Missing data were not imputed for nonresponding outlying areas.

Outline, by Anders C. Dahlgren was issued in 2009 by the Wisconsin Department of Public Instruction, Public Library Development Office. It introduces the concept of the "design population," which focuses on the actual scope of use rather than defined geographical service areas. Librarians and trustees can use the outline to estimate space needs based on a library's service goals. The outline organizes space requirements into six categories along with formulas for estimating needs. Examples include:

- Collection space for books, periodicals, nonprint resources, and digital resources. A general average for books housed in different environments is 10 volumes per square foot. This is predicated on housing a normal variety of adult trade books on full-height shelving 84 or 90 inches tall installed with a three-foot aisle, with the top and bottom shelves left vacant for future expansion.
- Reader seating space, which will vary depending on type of use (e.g., general reading, intensive use by youth doing schoolwork) and size of population. This requires at least 30 square feet per seat.
- Staff work space, that is, the work stations needed to support a library's service program. Each work station will need 125 to 150 square feet.
- Nonassignable space--about 25% of total space—for heating and cooling equipment, storage, corridors, and custodial space.

The categories assessed by Dahlgren provide a convenient overview of the library spaces that need to be considered in building design.[14]

ACCESSIBILITY AND UNIVERSAL DESIGN

> Libraries play a catalytic role in the lives of people with disabilities by facilitating their full participation in society. Libraries should use strategies based upon the principles of universal design to ensure that library policy, resources and services meet the needs of all people.
>
> **—Library Service for People with Disabilities, ALA Policy B.9.3.2**

Universal Design addresses designing products, places, and experiences to make them accessible to as broad a spectrum of people as possible, without special modifications or adaptations. It can also be applied to architectural remodels or renovations.[15] Take the case study of the Haston library in North Brookfield, Massachusetts, an elegant, Richardsonian structure built in 1894 of granite with a red slate roof. In a short article that includes figures and floor plans, architect Philip O'Brien details the steps needed to remodel a historic building to provide access to people with disabilities. He recommends "access strategies that are durable, maintainable, and integrated into the existing fabric and circulation of your building," and notes that "changes that accommodate both the handicapped and able-bodied reduce cost and consolidate supervision requirements and go a long way toward providing universal access" (O'Brien, 2011).

The standards issued under the Americans with Disabilities Act (ADA) address access to buildings and sites nationwide in new construction and alterations (U.S. Access Board). The ADA affects more Americans than any other civil rights legislation (Davis, 2015). It was created to eliminate discrimination in many areas, including access to private and public services, employment, transportation, and communication. The U.S. Access Board is responsible for developing and updating the ADA Accessibility Guidelines (ADAAG). These guidelines are used by the Department of Justice (DOJ) and the Department of Transportation (DOT) to set enforceable standards that the public must follow.

The American Library Association has adopted the Library Services for People with Disabilities Policy, part of which is reprinted in figure 7.13.[16]

Library Services for People with Disabilities (Excerpt)

The American Library Association recognizes that people with disabilities are a large and neglected minority in the community and are severely under-represented in the library profession. Disabilities cause many personal challenges. In addition, many people with disabilities face economic inequity, illiteracy, cultural isolation, and discrimination in education, employment and the broad range of societal activities. . . . ALA, through its divisions, offices and units and through collaborations with outside associations and agencies, is dedicated to eradicating inequities and improving attitudes toward and services and opportunities for people with disabilities.

Library Services for People with Disabilities Policy

3. Facilities

The ADA requires that both architectural barriers in existing facilities and communication barriers that are structural in nature be removed as long as such removal is "readily achievable." (i.e., easily accomplished and able to be carried out without much difficulty or expense.)

The ADA regulations specify the following examples of reasonable structural modifications: accessible parking, clear paths of travel to and throughout the facility, entrances with adequate, clear openings or automatic doors, handrails, ramps and elevators, accessible tables and public service desks, and accessible public conveniences such as restrooms, drinking fountains, public telephones and TTYs. Other reasonable modifications may include visible alarms in rest rooms and general usage areas and signs that have Braille and easily visible character size, font, contrast and finish.

One way to accommodate barriers to communication, as listed in the ADA regulations, is to make print materials available in alternative formats such as large type, audio recording, Braille, and electronic formats. Other reasonable modifications to communications may include providing an interpreter or real time captioning services for public programs and reference services through TTY or other alternative methods. The ADA requires that modifications to communications must be provided as long as they are "reasonable," do not "fundamentally alter" the nature of the goods or services offered by the library, or result in an "undue burden" on the library.

FIGURE 7.13 Library Services for People with Disabilities (Excerpt)

SOURCE: ASCLA, History of the Policy (www.ala.org/ascla/asclaissues/historylibrary).

The ASCLA "Library Accessibility-What You Need to Know" toolkit series of 15 tip sheets was developed to help librarians manage access issues. These include, but are not limited to, patrons with physical disabilities; cognitive, mental, or emotional illnesses; learning and/or developmental disabilities; service animals; and those needing assistive technologies. All of these patrons' needs have an impact on designs for public library facilities. In 2012 updates to the ADA Standards for Accessible Design went into effect to create wayfinding signage for those with visual impairments (Humrickhouse, 2012).

> **▶ TASK**
>
> Take a walk around your local public library—inside and out. Imagine being in a wheelchair (unless you already are). Are there areas for improvement? What could make the environment more comfortable or easy to use for people with any disabilities?

GREEN AND SUSTAINABLE BUILDING

Green building principles began to be incorporated into library building plans during the first decade of the twenty-first century (Antonelli, 2008). The ALA Social Responsibilities Round Table (ALA-SRRT) Task Force on the Environment addressed sustainability issues in 2001 with the Libraries Build Sustainable Communities project. This program served as a model for libraries at the 2002 United Nations World Summit on the Environment (Stoss, 2009). Greening Libraries is a landmark book in librarianship that provides an overview of green development (Antonelli & McCullough, 2012).

Using the criteria of the U.S. Green Building Council's Leadership in Energy and Environmental Design (LEED) performance system, a green building is one that is built incorporating the following design elements:

- sustainable site selection and development
- water conservation
- energy efficiency
- local resources, material conservation, and waste reduction
- indoor environmental quality
- innovation in design (Green Libraries, n.d.).

LEED certification helps to create healthier, more productive places; encourages energy and resource-efficient buildings that reduce stress on the environment, and saves taxpayer money. The USCBC predicts that LEED-certified buildings will directly contribute $29.8 billion to U.S. Gross Domestic Product by 2018.

Sustainability, Living Buildings, LEED, and Green Libraries are hallmarks of public library building concerns in the twenty-first century. Colorado's Rangeview Library District is the first carbon-positive library in the United States—thanks to solar panels, a geothermal heating and cooling system, and a gift of carbon-offset credits. The Anythink branch in Brighton that opened in September 2009 offsets 167,620 pounds of carbon dioxide, which is 16% more than it is anticipated to use annually. Environment-friendly features include geothermal heating and cooling, solar tubes that capture natural light that is used to illuminate interior spaces, and motion-sensor lighting controls ("New Colorado Facility," 2009).

In 2015 the American Library Association Council passed a Resolution on the Importance of Sustainable Libraries. Libraries are uniquely positioned and essential to help the communities they serve to become sustainable, resilient, and regenerative.[17]

Recent publications about library buildings and renovation increasingly reflect green practices.[18] In *Ecology, Economy, Equity: The Path to A Carbon-Neutral Library,* Henk (2014) uses the "three E's" of sustainability—ecology, economy, equity—as a foundation to trace the history of sustainability and reviews the process of building a carbon-neutral library. *The Green Library Planner: What Every Librarian Needs to Know Before Starting to Build or Renovate* (Carr, 2013) and Eco-Library Design (Flannery & Smith, 2013) provide additional philosophical and pragmatic approaches to ecologically friendly building practices.

The Living Building Challenge is "the world's most rigorous proven performance standard for buildings. People from around the world use [its) regenerative design framework to create spaces that, like a flower, give more than they take."[19] Rebecca Miller (2015) believes that living buildings could be the ultimate expression of resilience: "The Living Building Challenge . . . takes the idea that a library is a living, breathing thing out of the concept phase and into action by defining standards and moving toward them. The library world has the opportunity, perhaps even the responsibility, to help make the challenge a reality."

One award-winning library that sought LEED Gold certification, the recently redesigned Chinatown Branch of the Chicago Public Library, incorporated ancient Feng Shui principles to create the building's three-sided, pebble-like shape. Design partner Brian Lee stated, "We hope the building creates a memorable architectural statement that embodies twenty-first-century Chinatown. We are incredibly proud of its design and its position as a library of the future in Chicago's urban fabric" (Wang, 2016).

BOOKMOBILES

National bookmobile day is celebrated each year on the Wednesday of National Library Week (figure 7.14).[20] According to IMLS data, there are 679 bookmobiles in use in the United States.

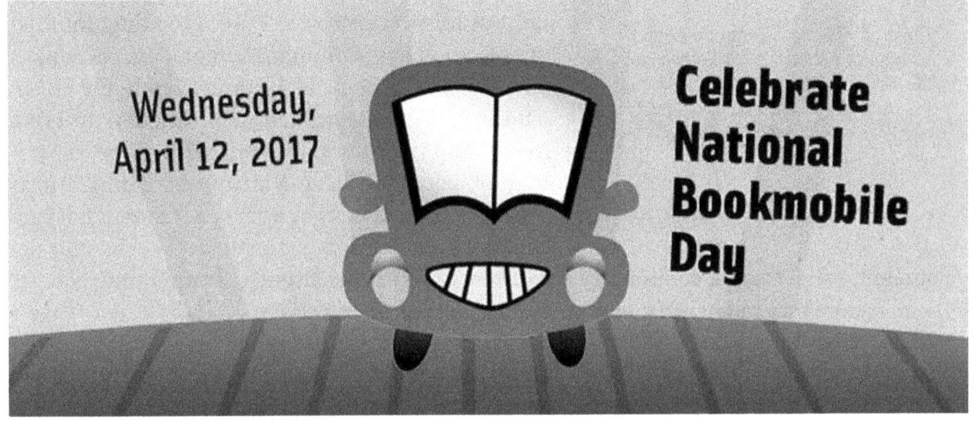

FIGURE 7.14 National Bookmobile Day, 2017

SOURCE: ALA Office for Diversity, Literacy, and Outreach Services, National Bookmobile Day (www.ala.org/offices/olos/nbdhome).

Historian Derek Attig (2014) has studied the roles that bookmobiles play in an effort to build what some reformers called "common consciousness," a sense of cultural and spiritual connection. A recent history details the rise and fall of bookmobiles in America. The number of bookmobiles peaked in 1965 at 2,000 but had dropped to 696 in 2011 (Ortwein, 2015).

ALA sponsors a parade of bookmobiles at its annual conferences in collaboration with the Association of Bookmobile and Outreach Services and the Association for Rural and Small Libraries (ALA, ODLOS, 2017). Resources that provide public libraries with a range of cultural and technical support to extend service to meet diverse programming and outreach needs (especially for rural communities) are provided at the ALA ODLOS website (www.ala.org/offices/diversity). Today's bookmobiles do not only cart books around; they are also outfitted with Wi-Fi and other technologies.

The Association of Bookmobile and Outreach Services (ABOS) publication *National Bookmobile Guidelines* (2008) provides criteria for management, staffing, collection development, funding, and vehicle construction and maintenance from chassis to tires. The annual bookmobile conference sponsored by ABOS showcases many case studies and exemplary programs for mutual support and service development of bookmobile librarians.

DISASTERS AND PUBLIC LIBRARIES

The Federal Emergency Management Agency (FEMA) has declared hundreds of events as disasters in the twenty-first century. Based on a governor's request, the president may declare that a major disaster or emergency exists, thereby activating an array of federal programs to assist in the response and recovery effort (FEMA Declaration Process, n.d.). Jaeger, Langa, McClure, & Bertot (2006) found that after disasters patrons came to libraries for access to communication tools, to use recharging stations, and to find out about disaster and recovery resources. The library itself might become a command center for the city or food distribution, or even a temporary shelter. Bishop and Veil (2013) characterized public libraries as post-crisis information hubs, providing Internet access to enable community members to request aid, help find missing family and friends, file FEMA and insurance claims, and help residents to begin rebuilding their lives. Patin's (2016) autoethnography of post-Hurricane Katrina rebuilding efforts focuses on the library as a source of community resilience because of its contribution to economic development, social capital, community competence, and information and communication (p. 64)—all factors that can help a community bounce back after a crisis.

> ▶ **FACT**
>
> Libraries have been identified as an essential service during disasters.*
>
> —
>
> *Robert T. Stafford Disaster Relief and Emergency Assistance Act, Public Law 93–288, as amended, 42 U.S.C. 5121 et seq. Located in United States Code, Title 42. The Public Health and Welfare, Chapter 68. Disaster Relief.

The Cedar Rapids flood (2008), Joplin tornado (2011), Superstorm Sandy (2012), Oklahoma and Colorado wildfires (2012), Colorado floods (2013), California earthquake (2014), South Carolina floods (2015), Oregon severe winter storms, straight-line winds, flooding, landslides, and mudslides (2016), and Hurricane Hermine (2016) are just a few recent natural disasters that have affected communities and libraries.[21]

The Stafford Act, which authorizes FEMA to provide federal assistance, has designated libraries as an essential service to meet immediate threats to life and property resulting from major disasters such as floods, hurricanes, or tornado.[22]

The Hurricane Preparedness and Response Project (located at the Information Institute at Florida State University) prepared libraries to assist in reducing a state's disaster risk during weather-related catastrophes. This initiative sought to clarify and raise awareness of the roles of public libraries in hurricane/disaster preparedness and response situating public libraries as essential service points in times of crisis (Brobst, Mandel, & McClure, 2012).

The Library as Safe Haven: Disaster Planning, Response, and Recovery (Halsted et al., 2014) provides an eight-step approach to developing a risk assessment plan, instructions on how to draft a one-page service continuity plan; and sample disaster plans. *Disaster Response and Planning for Libraries* (Kahn, 2012) includes information on preparing for technology recovery, damage-prevention equipment, and reproducible checklists and forms. "Librarians and Libraries Respond to Disasters," a bibliography maintained by the Disaster Information Management Research Center of the National Library of Medicine, chronicles library support of communities during times of crisis. The Flint Public Library collects the stories of residents living through the water crisis in Flint, Michigan (Greenberg, 2016).

Safety, Security, and Patron Interaction

Although we certainly want to maintain facilities that are open to everyone, occasionally people with mental health problems can pose a safety problem for other patrons and librarians. Such problems can be addressed by staff who monitor patron behavior and use customer service skills to defuse challenging situations. In *Library Security: Better Communication, Safer Facilities* (2015), Albrecht discusses how to prevent and respond to violent situations, including techniques for verbal de-escalation. Security and safety audits are discussed in *The Facility Manager's Guide to Safety and Security* (Henderson, 2016).

Public space safety and security have been studied from legal, design, and policy perspectives by community planners. Németh and Schmidt (2007) have observed that "although security is necessary for creating spaces the public will use, making it a top priority is often criticized for restricting social interaction, constraining individual liberties, and unjustly excluding certain populations." One way to demonstrate rationale is via transparency about policies.[23] For example, the Norfolk (MA) Public Library publishes its Safety and Security Policy (2014), which declares

> This policy provides guidance and direction for Library staff and patrons in the pursuit of creating and maintaining a safe and secure environment, and in responding to events that may affect patrons and Library operations. Safety and Security is a shared responsibility. Library staff and patrons are responsible to make all reasonable efforts to ensure their safety and security while on Library premises.

Trapskin (2008) has discussed security in the context of changing patterns of library use: libraries are no longer passive repositories of information but lively commons where people can share ideas in person or online. This shift brings with it not only record numbers of library visits but also increasing security incidents. Today's library administrators need to address security threats proactively. Two basic proactive solutions are to pay greater attention to the design of collaborative and other spaces and to actively promote positive interactions between staff and patrons.

"Problem situations, not problem patrons," is how Slavick (2009) characterizes difficult interactions with users who might be homeless, afflicted with mental, emotional, or physical illness, or suffering from substance abuse. He suggests active listening, empathizing, staying on topic, and maintaining an impersonal but flexible approach to diffuse problem situations.

Another positive approach has been described by staff members of the Fairfax County, (VA) Public Library, who state they do not have a problem behavior philosophy, but rather a customer service philosophy:

1. Every customer who uses our libraries should feel welcomed, valued, and respected.
2. All our rules are applied humanely, courteously, and fairly to all.
3. Every day is a new beginning. Except in extreme cases, we should not presume that a problem will occur because of past experience.
4. Every customer is entitled to their individual style of use of the library as long as it does not interfere with the rights of others.
5. Not all behaviors are problem behaviors.
6. Actions should be taken in a calm, reasonable fashion only after obtaining sufficient evidence that a problem really exists. (Waller and Bangs, 2007)

A recent article notes that a wide variety of patron actions, from drug use and public intoxication to abusive language, can be disruptive and dangerous. Library staff must be on the lookout for dangerous conduct, and libraries must articulate policies on how the offending patrons should be treated by enacting policies appropriate for local communities (Dixon, 2016). Gun laws require close monitoring, as well; the right to bear arms in public spaces, including libraries, has gone before the courts recently and several states have ruled that libraries cannot declare the property to be a gun-free zone (Goldberg, 2014).

Civil Disturbances

Public libraries have proven to be a source of stability during times of civil disturbance. In 2014 the Ferguson (MO) Municipal Public Library, became a model in the way it reacted to the crisis and the aftermath of riots brought on by the shooting of Michael Brown, a young African-American man, by local police (Berry, 2015). Schools in Ferguson were closed for a week but the library remained open for over 200 children and businesses. In April 2015 riots broke out in Baltimore following the funeral service for Freddie Gray, an African-American man who died in police custody. People clashed violently with Baltimore law enforcement, burned cars, and looted businesses, and more than 200 arrests were recorded. The Enoch Pratt Free Library stayed open.[24] With the schools closed the children needed a place to go (Peet, 2015). The decision to stay open despite the threat of continued violence attracted praise and support both nationally and internationally, but librarian Melanie Townsend Diggs insisted it wasn't an act of heroism. She told *American Libraries:*

> This is our life every day. We are public servants every day. At the end of the day, what happened on Monday [during the height of the unrest] was service oriented . . . We were giving the best service to our customers and our community that we can give. We do that every day. (Cottrell, 2015)

Librarian of Congress Dr. Carla D. Hayden, who was CEO of Enoch Pratt Free Library at this time of civil disturbance, was selected to present the 2015 Jean E. Coleman Library

Outreach Lecture.[25] Dr. Hayden's commitment to the centrality of the library to all communities has led her to the helm of the greatest library in the United States.

CONCLUSION

In 1999, repurposing plans were developed to relocate the main Kansas City (MO) Public Library to the former First National Bank. Although the century-old building, a true masterpiece of craftsmanship replete with marble columns, bronze doors, and ornate moldings, required remodeling and a fifth-floor addition, it provided the framework for a modern and impressive urban library. Through a public-private partnership headed by the Downtown Council, and utilizing funds from federal, state and municipal sources, corporations, foundations, individuals, and the library district itself, the library raised the nearly $50 million needed for the project (Kansas City Public Library, n.d.). A speech given by Vartan Gregorian, then president of the Carnegie Corporation, to supporters of the project is a profound testimony to the importance of the public library to the community. (See figure 7.15.)

There are many different ways to think about public library buildings. They are civic spaces, safe havens, and spaces for learning. They are also places of memory, civic renewal, and social action. They are places for civic engagement. They are busy because of the pa-

"Libraries as Acts of Civic Renewal"

Excerpts from a Speech by Carnegie Corporation President Vartan Gregorian to the Kansas City Club

Libraries contain the heritage of humanity, the record of its triumphs and failures, its intellectual, scientific and artistic achievements and its collective memory. They are a source of knowledge, scholarship and wisdom. They are an institution, withal, where the left and the right, God and the Devil, are together classified and retained, in order to teach us what to emulate and what not to repeat. But libraries are more than repositories of past human endeavor, they are instruments of civilization. They are a laboratory of human aspiration, a window to the future and a wellspring of action. They are a source of intellectual growth, and hope. In this land and everywhere on earth, they are a medium of progress, autonomy, empowerment, independence and self-determination. They have always provided—and I would suggest, always will provide—a place and space for imaginative recreation, for imaginative rebirth. That is because the library is a transcendent institution, being able to surpass the limitations of time and space. The library is an oasis, a place for reflection, for contemplation, for privacy, for the renewal of one's imagination and the development of one's mind.

FIGURE 7.15 "Libraries as Acts of Civic Renewal": Excerpts from a Speech by Carnegie Corporation President Vartan Gregorian to the Kansas City Club

SOURCE: Gregorian, Vartan, 2002, "Libraries as Acts of Civic Renewal" (Speech), Kansas City Public Library. Used with permission of Carnegie Corporation of New York.

trons and the librarians who make it their *third space* (i.e., neither a home nor commercial space). Communities continue to fund them because of their significance, and their usefulness in good and hard times.

NOTES

1. "Robert Dawson's extensive survey provided the perfect opportunity for the Library of Congress to represent the public library's role in the twenty-first century. His photographs also offer a fascinating comparison to our interior and exterior views of libraries newly built at the start of the twentieth century," Helena Zinkham, Director for Collections and Services at the Library of Congress. The Dawson collection is the largest acquisition of library photography by the Library of Congress since the early 1900s. See "News from the Library of Congress" (2015). https://www.loc.gov/today/pr/2015/15-190.html.
2. From 1994 to 2015, Dawson photographed 526 of the 16,536 public libraries in 48 states and the District of Columbia. The images provide documentation of the wide range of architecture of public libraries in America—those on small-town streets, in shopping malls, on Indian reservations, in national parks, and in large cities. The photographs illustrate the role of public libraries, not only as sources for information and knowledge but also as a public commons. This online gallery is posted at www.robertdawson.com/index.html.
3. The Chicago Public Library during the Dempsey years was the focus of study of exemplary community-building. See Putnam & Feldstein (2003), "Branch Libraries: The Heartbeat of the Community," in *Better Together: Restoring the American Community.*
4. In 2016 *TechInsider* showcased the most beautiful library in each state. The list included past and current winners of the American Institute of Architects and the American Library Association awards and included states that had never won. See Weller (2016), "The Most Beautiful Library in Each U.S. State" (www.techinsider.io/most-beautiful-library-in-all-50-states-2016-7).
5. The Thomas Crane Memorial Library of Quincy, Massachusetts, also known as the Richardson building, is the original library building designed by Henry Hobson Richardson and funded by Albert Crane in honor of his father, Thomas Crane. Considered Richardson's masterpiece of library architecture, the building was ranked 43rd out of 150 works of architecture recently selected as America's Favorite Architecture. Its foundation is of Quincy granite, the upper structure of North Easton granite, and the trimming of Longmeadow brownstone. See http://thomascranelibrary.org/about/richardson-building.
6. There were hundreds more built in other countries, including the United Kingdom, Ireland, Canada, Australia, South Africa, New Zealand, the Caribbean, Mauritius, Malaysia, and Fiji. See Anderson (1963) and Prizeman (2011).
7. Indexed by state, place, and building, including street address, date of construction, and current use of each library.
8. The National Register of Historic Places was established by the U.S. National Park Service (NPS). See the Focus Digital Library, an enterprise system for managing NPS digital assets including photos, documents, drawings, maps, and GIS images (http://focus.nps.gov/nrhp). See also Schlipf (2014) for an interesting analysis of the challenges of remodeling and expanding Carnegie-era library buildings.
9. The Rhode Island Statewide Library Program was activated July 1, 1964, in response to a heightened interest in statewide library cooperation and the federal legislation that became the Library Services and Construction Act (LSCA). The construction aspect of the LSCA was considered an intrinsic part of improving library service, and motivated local efforts to supplement federal seed money. The 1965 Annual Report from Rhode Island to the U.S.

Department of Health, Education, and Welfare's Office of Education states that "the outdated, inappropriate, inconvenient, and inadequate housing of public libraries became acutely real upon examination." By October of 1964 the State Plan for Construction had been submitted to and approved by the U.S. Office of Education (www.olis.ri.gov/grants/construction/planning/history.php).

10. These were the pre-Internet days when librarians spent time writing letters and making visits to state and national legislators. State and national journals were used to rally the library community. See, for example: "Stories of All Libraries Built, Remodeled, or That Received Equipment Grants (South Dakota) under the LSCA, 1965-1970" (1971); "Library Community Rallies against LSCA Threat" (1976); "Carter Signs LSCA Extension" (1977); "N.E. State Library Coalition Opposes LSCA Cutbacks" (1981); and "New LSCA library building boom: First reports from Ohio & California." (1983).
11. States have different approaches to budgeting and programs for library construction. For examples, see Arizona State Library, Archives and Public Records, State Grants-in-Aid Construction Guidelines (www.azlibrary.gov/sites/azlibrary.gov/files/libdev_sgiac_funded_12-21-2015.pdf); Minnesota State Library Service. Library Construction Grants (http://education.state.mn.us/MDE/StuSuc/Lib/StateLibServ/LibAccessImpGrant/index.html); New York State Library; and Division of Library Development, Public Library Construction Grant Program. (www.nysl.nysed.gov/libdev/construc/14m/faq.htm#c1). Funds may be used to remove architectural barriers from a library building or site; remediate conditions hazardous to health or safety; renovate or expand an existing building for use as a library; or to reconstruct a new library. The Minnesota program is authorized biennially by the Legislature and funded from the sale of General Revenue Obligation Bonds. The 2014 Minnesota Legislature allocated a total of $2,000,000 to the program.
12. The IMLS FY 2014 PLS includes the following elements: Data Files (CSV and SAS formats); APIs (State Summary); Administrative Entity; Outlet Datasets; Documentation Supplementary Tables; and Data Element Definitions. See https://www.imls.gov/research-evaluation/data-collection/public-libraries-survey/explore-pls-data/pls-data.
13. The LLAMA Buildings and Equipment Section sponsors committees on architecture for public libraries; functional space requirements; interior design awards; library buildings awards; library interiors, furnishings and equipment; and safety and security of buildings. See www.ala.org/llama/sections/bes.
14. Anders C. Dahlgren, author of *Public Library Space Needs: A Planning Outline,* has written an author's note to the 2009 edition that summarizes the history of this important work: "With Extensive Support from Wisconsin, Department of Public Instruction's Editors, Publication No. 8210, Public Library Space Needs: A Planning Outline" appeared in 1988. A revision was published online in 1998. Since that original publication, a number of state library agencies and state library associations have modeled similar recommended processes. In 2007, the Library Buildings and Equipment Section of the International Federation of Library Associations published "IFLA Library Building Guidelines: Developments and Reflections," which includes a variation on the Outline as its recommended method for establishing a library's space need.
15. From the description of Universal Design for Libraries and Librarians, a course sponsored by the Library Information Technology Association of ALA in summer 2016:

    > This course will present an overview of universal design as a historical movement, as a philosophy, and as an applicable set of tools. Students will learn about the diversity of experiences and capabilities that people have, including disabilities (e.g., physical, learning, cognitive, resulting from age and/or accident), cultural backgrounds, and other abilities. The class will also give students the

opportunity to redesign specific products or environments to make them more universally accessible and usable (www.ala.org/lita/universal-design).

16. See also ALA Policy B.2.1.20, Services to Persons with Disabilities (Old Number 53.1.20), which provides rationale based on the First Amendment:

    The First Amendment to the U.S. Constitution mandates the right of all persons to free expression and the corollary right to receive the constitutionally protected expression of others. A person's right to use the library should not be denied or abridged because of disabilities. The library has the responsibility to provide materials "for the interest, information, and enlightenment of all people of the community the library serves." (See also the Library Bill of Rights.) "When information in libraries is not presented in formats that are accessible to all users, discriminatory barriers are created." (www.ala.org/aboutala/governance/policymanual/updatedpolicymanual/section2/53intellfreedom)

17. See Resolution on the Importance of Sustainable Libraries:

    The American Library Association (ALA), on behalf of its members: 1. recognizes the important and unique role libraries play in wider community conversations about resiliency, climate change, and a sustainable future and begins a new era of thinking sustainably in order to consider the economic, environmental, and socially equitable viability of choices made on behalf of the association; 2. enthusiastically encourages activities by itself, its membership, library schools and state associations to be proactive in their application of sustainable thinking in the areas of their facilities, operations, policy, technology, programming, partnerships, and library school curricula; and 3. directs the ALA Executive Director to pursue sustainable choices when planning conferences and meetings and to actively promote best practices of sustainability through ALA publications, research, and educational opportunities to reach our shared goal of vital, visible, and viable libraries for the future. Adopted by the Council of the American Library Association Sunday, June 28, 2015, in San Francisco, California. (www.ala.org/aboutala/sites/ala.org.aboutala/files/content/governance/council/council_documents/2015_annual_council_documents/cd_36_substainable_libraries_resol_final.pdf)

18. The ALA Social Responsibilities Round Table Task Force addressed sustainability issues in 2001 with the Libraries Build Sustainable Communities project.
19. The Living Building Challenge (see https://living-future.org/lbc/) is a building certification program, advocacy tool, and philosophy that defines the most advanced measure of sustainability in the built environment and acts to rapidly diminish the gap between current limits and the end-game positive solutions we seek. The Challenge is comprised of seven performance categories called Petals: Place, Water, Energy, Health & Happiness, Materials, Equity and Beauty. Petals are subdivided into a total of 20 Imperatives, each of which focuses on a specific sphere of influence. This compilation of Imperatives can be applied to almost every conceivable building project, of any scale and any location—be it a new building or an existing structure. See http://living-future.org/lbc.
20. National Bookmobile Day celebrates bookmobiles and the dedicated library professionals who provide this valuable and essential service to their communities. National Bookmobile Day is coordinated by the ALA Office for Diversity, Literacy and Outreach Services, the Association of

Bookmobile and Outreach Services (ABOS), and the Association for Rural and Small Libraries (ARSL; www.ala.org/offices/olos/nbdhome).

21. See the FEMA Disaster Declarations annual list (https://www.fema.gov/disasters/grid/year).
22. Section 403 of the Stafford Act authorizes FEMA to provide federal assistance to meet immediate threats to life and property resulting from a major disaster. Specifically, Section 403(a)(3)(D) allows for the provision of temporary facilities for schools and other essential community services when related to saving lives and protecting and preserving property or public health and safety. Libraries have been designated an essential service. This policy dates in 2011—the change had its roots in the exception that was made in 2009 to assist the flood-damaged Cedar Rapids Library in Iowa (Kelley, 2011). See also https://www.fema.gov/media-library-data/1383153669955-21f970b19e8eaa67087b7da9f4af706e/stafford_act_booklet_042213_508e.pdf.
23. Security camera policies are often available to the public. See, for example, the policy of the Elizabeth (NJ) Public Library at www.elizpl.org/trustees%20docs/SecurityCameras.pdf.
24. In recognition of her efforts to keep the Enoch Pratt Free Library and its branches open and continually engaged with the Baltimore community during the civil unrest in the wake of the death of Freddie Gray, Dr. Carla D. Hayden, CEO of the Enoch Pratt Free Library in Baltimore, was selected by the Advisory Committee of the ALA Office for Diversity, Literacy, and Outreach Services to deliver the 2015 Jean E. Coleman Library Outreach Lecture.
25. The 14th Librarian of Congress. (2016). *Library of Congress Magazine, 5*(5), 2–3. Dr. Carla D. Hayden, CEO of the Enoch Pratt Free Library in Baltimore, delivered the 2015 Jean E. Coleman Library Outreach Lecture June 29, 2015. www.ala.org/offices/olos/olosprograms/jeanecoleman/jeanecoleman.

REFERENCES

2016 Library Design Showcase. (2016). *American Libraries, 47*(9/10), 43. https://americanlibrariesmagazine.org/2016/09/01/2016-library-design-showcase.

Agee, A. (2014). Ten years later: A joint library evolves. *Journal of Academic Librarianship, 40*(5), 521–528.

Albrecht, S. (2015). *Library security: Better communication, safer facilities*. Chicago, IL: ALA Editions.

American Library Association. Library service for people with disabilities, ALA Policy B.9.3.2. www.ala.org/aboutala/governance/policymanual/updatedpolicymanual/tableofcontents#section2.

American Library Association. (1966). Third Library Building Awards. *ALA Bulletin 60*(6), 576–583.

American Library Association. (1972). 1972 Library Buildings Awards program. *American Libraries 3*(5), 521–527.

American Library Association, Office for Diversity, Literacy and Outreach Services. (2017). National Bookmobile Day, www.ala.org/offices/olos/nbdhome.

American Library Association, Public Libraries Division. Coordinating Committee on Revision of Public Library Standards. (1956). *Public library service: A guide to evaluation, with minimum standards*. Chicago, IL: American Library Association.

Anderson, F. (1963). *Carnegie Corporation library program, 1911–1961.* New York, NY: Carnegie Corporation.

Antonelli, M. (2008, Fall). The green library movement: An overview of green library literature from 1979 to the future of green libraries. *Electronic Green Journal, 27.* http://escholarship.org/uc/item/39d3v236.

Antonelli, M., & McCullough, M. (2012) *Greening libraries*. Los Angeles: Library Juice Press.

Association of Bookmobile and Outreach Services. (2008). *National bookmobile guidelines*. www.abos-outreach.org/2008BookmobileGuidelines.pdf.

Attig, D. (2014). *Here comes the bookmobile: Public culture and the shape of belonging.* Unpublished doctoral dissertation, University of Illinois-Urbana. http://hdl.handle.net/2142/49657.

Bernard, M. (2016). 2016 ALA/IIA Library Interior Design Awards. Contract, *57*(8), 64.

Berry, J. N. (2015). 2015 Gale/LJ library of the year: Ferguson Municipal Public Library, MO, Courage in crisis. *Library Journal, 140*(10), 28-32.

Bishop, B., & Veil, S. R. (2013). Public libraries as post-crisis information hubs. *Public Library Quarterly, 32*(1), 33-45.

Blumenstein, L. (2009, Spring). San Jose's green art. *Library Journal: Library by Design,* 24-25.

Bobinski, G. S. (1969). *Carnegie libraries: Their history and impact on American library development.* Chicago, IL: American Library Association.

Boston Public Library (n.d.). Restoration of the McKim building. www.bpl.org/central/mckim.htm#history.

Breisch, K. A. (2003). *Henry Hobson Richardson and the small public library in America: A study in typology.* Cambridge, MA: MIT Press.

Brobst, J. L., Mandel, L. H., & McClure, C. R. (2012). Public libraries and crisis: Roles of public libraries in hurricane/disaster preparedness and response. In C. Hagar (Ed.), *Crisis information management: Communication and technologies* (pp. 155-173). Cambridge, United Kingdom: Woodhead.

Carr, M. M. (2013). *The green library planner: What every librarian needs to know before starting to build or renovate.* Lanham, MD: Scarecrow Press.

Carter signs LSCA extension. (1977). *American Libraries, 8*(11).

Charbonnet, L. (2015). *Public library buildings: The librarian's go-to guide for construction, expansion, and renovation projects.* Santa Barbara, CA: Libraries Unlimited.

Cisse, S. (2013). Partnering with public library services: A town and gown affair. *Collaborative Librarianship, 5*(3), 208-210.

Cleveland Public Library. (1925). *Main library of the Cleveland public library.* Cleveland, OH.

Cottrell, M. (2015, May 15). Libraries respond to community needs in times of crisis: Baltimore, Ferguson just two recent examples of libraries offering refuge. *American Libraries.* https://americanlibraries magazine.org/2015/05/15/libraries-respond-to-community-needs-in-times-of-crisis/.

Dahlgren, A. C. (2009). *Public library space needs: A planning outline/2009.* Wisconsin Department of Public Instruction, Public Library Development. http://dpi.wi.gov/pld/pdf/plspace.pdf#page=5.

Davis, L. J. (2015). *Enabling acts: The hidden story of how the Americans with Disabilities Act gave the largest US minority its rights.* Boston, MA: Beacon Press.

Dawson, R., Moyers, B. D., & Patchett, A. (2014). *The public library: A photographic essay.* New York, NY: Princeton Architectural Press.

Dixon J. A. (2016). Safety first. *Library Journal, 141*(9), 29-31.

Drennan, H. T. (1967). Federal funds for facilities. *ALA Bulletin, 61*(9), 1054-1057.

Elmborg, J. K. (2011). Libraries as the spaces between us: Recognizing and valuing the third space. *Reference and User Services Quarterly, 50*(4), 338-350.

Federal Emergency Management Agency Declaration Process. (n.d.). https://www.fema.gov/disaster -declaration-process.

Felicella, E. (2016, September). *Reading room: A catalog of New York City's branch libraries.* Center for Architecture. http://cfa.aiany.org/index.php?section=upcoming&expid=320.

Ferrell, P. (2016). Stories from the innovation lab: Markers of success. *Texas Library Journal, 92*(1), 6-9.

Flannery, J. A., & Smith, K. M. (2013). *Eco-library design.* Dordrecht, Germany: Springer.

Florida library merges branch, social services. (2009, August). *Library Journal, 134,* 10.

Fox, B. (2015, November 16). The year in architecture 2015: Working in harmony. *Library Journal.* http://lj.libraryjournal.com/2015/11/buildings/year-in-architecture-2015-working-in-harmony/.

Fox, L. (2016). Branching out. *Library Journal, 141*(10), 16.

Free, D. (2013). Tidewater Community College, City of Virginia Beach open joint-use library. *College and Research Libraries News, 74*(8), 398-400.

Geil, M. (1998). *Anaconda's treasure: The Hearst Free Library*. Anaconda, MT: The Library.

Giles, D. (2013). *Branches of opportunity*. Center for an Urban Future. https://nycfuture.org/pdf/Branches_of_Opportunity.pdf.

Goldberg, B. (2014). Taking aim at the reality of guns in libraries. *American Libraries, 45*(1/2), 16-17.

Green libraries. (n.d.). www.greenlibraries.org.

Greenberg, W. (2016, March 31). Flint Public Library to archive stories of residents living through the water crisis. Michigan Radio [Internet. http://michiganradio.org/post/flint-public-library-archive-stories-residents-living-through-water-crisis#stream/0.

Gregorian, V. (2002). Libraries as acts of civic renewal. https://www.carnegie.org/media/filer_public/d7/9c/d79c6501-1966-4b48-809b-108d4bf7c4cd/ccny_speech_20021017_libraries.pdf.

Gunnels, C. B., Green, S. E., & Butler, P. M. (2012). *Joint libraries: Models that work*. Chicago, IL: American Library Association.

Halsted, D. D., et al. (2014). *Library as safe haven: Disaster planning, response, and recovery*: Chicago, IL: Neal-Schuman.

Hatfield, J. (2008, July/August). Doing what we do best. *Public Libraries, 47*, 19-20.

Henderson, J. W. (2016). *The facility manager's guide to safety and security*. Boca Raton, FL: Taylor & Francis.

Henk, M. (2014). *Ecology, economy, equity: The path to a carbon-neutral library*. Chicago, IL: ALA Editions.

Holt, L. E., & Holt, G. E. (2010). *Public library services for the poor: Doing all we can*. Chicago, IL: ALA Editions.

Horrigan, J. (2015). *Libraries at the crossroads*. Pew Research Center. www.pewinternet.org/2015/09/15/2015/Libraries-at-crossroads/.

Humrickhouse, L. (2012). New ADA rules take effect. *American Libraries 43*, (5/6): 24-25.

Jaeger, P. T., Langa, L., McClure, C. R., and Bertot, J. C. (2006). The 2004 and 2005 Gulf Coast hurricanes: Evolving roles and lessons learned for public libraries in disaster preparedness and community services. *Public Library Quarterly 25*(3-4), 199-214.

Joeckel, C. B., & Winslow, A. (1948). *A national plan for public library service*. Chicago, IL: American Library Association.

Jones, T. (1997). *Carnegie libraries across America: A public legacy*. Washington, DC: Preservation Press.

Kahn, M. B. (2012). *Disaster response and planning for libraries* (3rd ed.). Chicago, IL: American Library Association.

Kansas City Public Library. (n.d.). *Library history: Overview*. https://www.kclibrary.org/library-history.

Kelley, M. (2011, January 19). Cedar Rapids new public library helped spur FEMA change. *Library Journal*.

Kent, F., & Myrick, P. (2003, April). How to become a great public space. *American Libraries, 34*, 72-76.

Kranich, N. (2010, Fall). Promoting adult learning through civil discourse in the public library. *New Directions for Adult and Continuing Education, 127*, 15-24.

Kranich, N. (2013). Libraries and strong democracy: Moving from an informed to a participatory 21st century citizenry. *Indiana Libraries, 32*(1), 13-20.

Lane, C. K. (1989). Chicago Public Library competition. *Chicago Architectural Journal, 7*, 6-27.

Library community rallies against LSCA threat. (1976). *Library Journal, 101*, 568.

Lushington, N., Rudorf, W., & Wong, L. (2016). *Libraries: A design manual*. Basel : Birkhäuser.

MARZ Associates, in association with WGBH, Boston. (1989). *Design wars* [VHS]. Boston, MA: WGBH Educational Foundation.

Mattern, S. (2007). *The new downtown library*. Minneapolis, MN: University of Minnesota Press.

Mattern, S. (2014). Libraries as infrastructure. Places. https://placesjournal.org/article/library-as-infrastructure/.

McCook, K. (2011). *Introduction to public librarianship* (2nd ed.). New York, NY: Neal-Schuman Publishers.

Miller, R. (2015, October 2). Real-world barriers. *Library Journal*. http://lj.libraryjournal.com/2015/10/opinion/editorial/real-world-barriers-expanding-on-a-tradition-of-access-editorial/.

Miller, W. (2001). Joint-use libraries: Introduction. *Resource Sharing and Information Networks, 15*, 131-150.

Morehart, P. (2015). From the past, the future. *American Libraries, 46*(9-10), 40-47.

Murvosh, M. (2014). The comeback kids. *Library Journal,* 1–6.

N.E. state library coalition opposes LSCA cutbacks. (1981). *Library Journal, 106,* 929–930.

Németh, J., & Schmidt, S. (2007). Toward a methodology for measuring the security of publicly accessible spaces. *Journal of the American Planning Association, 73* (Summer), 283–297.

New Colorado facility becomes first carbon-positive library. (2009, December 12). *American Libraries Online.* www.americanlibrariesmagazine.org.

New LSCA library building boom: First reports from Ohio & California. (1983). *Library Journal,* 1.

Nitikin, C., & Jackson, J. (2009). *Libraries that matter. Project for public spaces.* www.pps.org/reference/librariesthatmatter-2/.

Norfolk (MA) Public Library. (2014). Safety and security policy. http://library.virtualnorfolk.org/Public_Documents/NPL_docs/SAFETY%20SECURITY%20POLICY%2005212014.pdf.

O'Brien, P. (2011, Fall). Is your library accessible? *Library Journal,* 9–11.

Ortwein, O. (2015). *Bookmobiles in America: An illustrated history.* CreateSpace Independent Publishing Platform.

Pasicznyuk, R. (2014, July/August). Libraries as a reflection of a community's needs and values. *Public Libraries, 53,* 12–17.

Patin, B. (2016). Through hell and high water: A librarian's autoethnography of community resilience after Hurricane Katrina. *Mediatropes 5*(2), 58–83.

Peet, L. (2015, May). Baltimore's Enoch Pratt Free Library provides haven in troubled times. *Library Journal, 140*(8).

Peet, L. (2016). Libraries respond to Orlando tragedy. *Library Journal, 141*(12), 14–16.

Prizeman, O. (2011). *Philanthropy and light: Carnegie libraries and the advent of transatlantic standards for public space.* Farnham, Surrey, United Kingdom: Ashgate.

Project for Public Spaces (2009, December 31). *What is Placemaking?* www.pps.org/reference/what_is_placemaking/.

Putnam, R. D., & Feldstein, L. M. (2003). Branch libraries: The heartbeat of the community. In *Better together: Restoring the American community* (pp. 34–54). New York, NY: Simon and Schuster.

Reed, H. H. (2011). *The New York Public Library: Its architecture and decoration.* New York, NY: Norton.

Reimagining the civic commons. (n.d.). http://civiccommons.us/.

Rivers, V. (2004). *The branch librarians' handbook.* Jefferson, NC: McFarland.

San Francisco Public Library (2015). *Reinvesting and renewing for the 21st century: A community and economic benefits study of San Francisco's branch library improvement program.* https://sfpl.org/pdf/about/commission/ReinvestingRenewing.pdf.

Sannwald, W. W. (2016). *Checklist of library building design considerations.* 6th edition. Chicago, IL: ALA Editions.

Schlipf, F. (2014). Remodeling and expanding Carnegie-era library buildings. *Library Trends, 62*(3), 556–580.

Schull, D. D. (2015). *Archives alive: Expanding engagement with public library archives and special collections.* Chicago, IL: ALA Editions.

Schwartz, M., Cornog, M., & Warburton B. (2012). Hurricane Katrina-damaged libraries reopen. *Library Journal, 137*(9), 13.

Six Chicago architects: Impressions of the Chicago Public Library competition. (1989). *Chicago Architectural Journal, 7,* 28–37.

Slavick, S. (2009, November/December). Problem situations, not problem patrons. *Public Libraries, 48,* 38–42.

Smith, J. (2014, June) A library as a symbol for the community. *Public Libraries Online.* http://publiclibrariesonline.org/2014/06/a-library-as-a-symbol-for-the-community/.

St. Lifer, E. (2001, January). The library as anchor. *Library Journal, 126,* 59–61.

Stories of all libraries built, remodeled, or that received equipment grants under the LSCA, 1965–1970. (1971). *South Dakota Library Bulletin, 57*(3), 231–249.

Stoss, F. (2009). How and why we got here today: A history of the ALA Task Force on the Environment. *SRRT Newsletter 168*. http://libr.org/srrt/news/srrt168.php#6.1.

The 14th Librarian of Congress. (2016). *Library of Congress Magazine, 5*(5), 2–3.

Tomkins County, New York. (2015). 2015 Community Foundation Library Grants from the Rosen Fund and additional Community Foundation Funds. www.cftompkins.org/news-and-events/news/2015/03/2015-community-foundation-library-grants-from-the-rosen-fund-and-additional-community-foundation-funds/.

Trapskin, B. (2008, September). A changing of the guard: Emerging trends in public library security. *Library and Archival Security, 21*, 69–76.

U.S. Department of Education, Office of Educational Research and Improvement. (1996). *Biennial evaluation report, 1995–1996: Public library construction and technology enhancement grants to state library agencies* (CFDA No. 84-154). www.ed.gov/pubs/Biennial/95-96/eval/603-97.pdf.

Van Slyck A. A. (1995). *Free to all: Carnegie libraries and American culture, 1890–1920*. Chicago, IL: University of Chicago Press.

Waller, E., & Bangs, P. (2007, September/October). Embracing the problem customer. *Public Libraries, 46*, 27–28.

Wang, L. (2016). LEED Gold-seeking Chicago Chinatown library embodies ancient Feng Shui. *Inhabitant.* http://inhabitat.com/leed-gold-seeking-chicago-chinatown-library-embodies-ancient-feng-shui/.

WebJunction. (2015). Resources for Space Planning in Libraries. www.webjunction.org/documents/webjunction/WebJunction_039_s_Focus_on_Space_Planning_for_Libraries.html.

Weller, C. (2016). The most beautiful library in each US state. www.techinsider.io/most-beautiful-library-in-all-50-states-2016-7.

Wick, P. A. (1977). *A handbook to the art and architecture of the Boston Public Library: Visitors guide to the McKim Building, Copley Square, its mural decorations and its collections*. Boston, MA: Associates of the Boston Public Library.

Wiley, P. B. (1996). *A free library in this city: The illustrated history of the San Francisco Public Library*. San Francisco, CA: Weldon Owen.

CHAPTER 8

Youth Services in Public Libraries

History, Core Services, Challenges, and Opportunities

Alicia K. Long

> It should be noted that this specialization [youth services] has attracted and continues to attract some of the most idealistic (while also realistic) members of the profession, who have produced some of the most imaginative and responsive programs in the modern public library.
>
> **—Statement at the Centennial of the American Library Association, 1976 (Fenwick, 1976, p. 350)**

The Institute of Museum and Library Services (IMLS) compiles statistics for all library services in the annual Public Libraries Survey (PLS). In the latest IMLS report, which includes data from public library services for the year 2014, the representation of children and young adults' programs demonstrates the scope of these services. The report's table 10 shows that out of 4,476,171 programs that took place in public libraries, 57.4% were children's programs and 9.5% were young adult's programs. For every 1,000 children, 228.8 attended library programs, as did 21.8 per 1,000 young adults (IMLS, 2016, Table 11).[1]

As these figures show, library collections, programs, and services dedicated to young people constitute an integral part of most (if not all) public library systems in the United States. Public library leaders are well aware of the importance of developing specific services for children and youth in their communities. However, this was not always the case; it was not until the second half of the nineteenth century and the beginning of the twentieth that the efforts of the early pioneers of youth librarianship started to take shape. In the late nineteenth and early twentieth centuries, librarians who specialized in youth services began to form professional organizations and create dedicated programs that addressed the particular needs of children, and later, teenagers. It soon became apparent that 1) youth services seemed to attract the most innovative professionals; 2) children were responsible for bringing adults to the library; and 3) those who went to the library as children grew up to be loyal patrons (and library supporters) as adults.

In the majority of the historical overviews of public librarianship, children and services to children are credited with driving the growth of libraries (Jenkins, 2000). However, in spite of this long history, the centrality of services to youth is still not always at the forefront of the decisions, policies, and agendas of the library profession. This chapter briefly summarizes the history of services to youth in public libraries in the United States and explores the state of youth services by addressing the knowledge and competencies needed for professionals who serve youth, the main characteristics of the children and adolescents served, and a selection of some of the most successful programs being implemented in libraries throughout United States.

HISTORY

The origins of library services for children in the United States can be traced back to the development of educational opportunities for youth in nineteenth-century American society. Children were considered an economic and civic asset, and there were structures to shape their morals. There was a growing realization that they had educational needs, as well as an "increasing awareness of children as children." A number of social agencies both public and private started providing services to guide and educate youth. Some of the first libraries dedicated to children were Sunday school libraries, which provided not only religious books but also volumes on other topics (Walter, 1941).

> ▶ **FACT**
>
> In 1803 Caleb Bingham (a bookseller) donated 150 children's books to the Salisbury, Connecticut, library to start a collection for children. In 1810, the town allocated funds to expand the collection, making it the first public library to allocate funds to children services/collections.

The idea of providing library access to children came to national attention with the establishment of public libraries in the mid-1850s, along with the consequent growth of literature for children, and changing attitudes toward the improvement of child welfare. The first public libraries that offered services to children established age restrictions on library use and specific selection of books being published for children, as found in Fletcher's 1876 report, *Public Libraries in the United States of America; Their History, Condition, and Management.*

The creation and organization of services to children and young adults was, in fact, a result of the work of individual pioneers who championed the need for children's rooms, special collections, and trained librarians to work with children (Larson, 2015; McDowell, 2009; Miller, 2003; Walter, 2010). See figure 8.1.

With the advent of the twentieth century, specific professional education for children's librarianship began to develop at institutions like Baltimore's Enoch Pratt Library and the Carnegie Library of Pittsburgh (Fenwick, 1976). The American Library Association's Section for Children's Librarians was organized in 1900; Louise Seaman Bechtel was appointed as the head of a juvenile department of Macmillan Publishing in 1919; and that same year Frederick Melcher organized the American Booksellers Association's first Children's Book of the Week.

The years 1920 to 1950 were a time of consolidation, standardization, and broadening horizons for library service to children (McDowell, 2009). During the Depression, public library circulation soared, and circulation to children represented about 40 to 45% of the total. Children's librarians continued to provide services that had been established earlier: individual reader guidance, book selection, and provision of reading promotion materials. Storytelling programs provided a literacy experience for older children and li-

Key Figures in the History of Youth Services

Selected Key Figures of Library Services to Youth, Nineteenth and Twentieth Centuries

CAROLINE HEWINS was a librarian at the Hartford (CT) Public Library. Starting in 1882, she published eight yearly reports titled *Readings of the Young,* considered the beginnings of youth librarianship research.

EMILY HANAWAY was serving as the principal of a grammar school when she opened a reading room for children in 1895. Later this became a branch of the New York Free Circulating Library.

MARY WRIGHT PLUMMER was a librarian at Pratt Institute. She designed the first children's room in a public library in 1895.

ANNE CARROLL MOORE was a children's librarian at Pratt Institute. She started story hours for children in 1896 and later campaigned for children's rooms in all branches of the New York Public Library, where she worked from 1906 to 1941.

AUGUSTA BAKER was a storyteller and author who worked at the New York Public Library from 1937 to 1974 and conducted research about the portrayal of African Americans in children's books.

CHARLEMAE HILL ROLLINS was a children's librarian at the Chicago Public Library from 1927 to 1963, and a scholar of African American literature for children.

PURA BELPRÉ became the first Puerto Rican librarian at the New York Public Library in 1921, where she held regular bilingual story-times for Latino children from New York's neighborhoods.

MARGARET A. EDWARDS was considered a pioneer of YA services. She joined the Enoch Pratt Free Library in 1932, and started her work to promote services for children and young adults, which included taking horse-drawn wagons to youth in poor neighborhoods of Baltimore.

Note: In 1996, the National Association to Promote Library and Information Services to Latinos and the Spanish-speaking, also known as REFORMA, created a book award to celebrate excellence in children's literature for and by Latinos/as. Now implemented as a collaboration between REFORMA and ALSC, the award carries the name of "Pura Belpré Medal" to honor this Latina pioneer. *The Stories I Read to the Children* is a 2013 book edited by Lisa Sánchez González, about the life and writings of Belpré.

FIGURE 8.1 Key Figures in the History of Youth Services

braries instituted youth and preschool story hours. Special rooms for teens were created, with the first designated area for children established in 1925 at the Cleveland Public Library. In 1930 the American Library Association established the Young People's Reading Round Table.

In 1941 three constituencies within the American Library Association (children's librarians, young peoples' librarians, and school librarians) formed the Division of Libraries for Children and Young People, and appointed Mildred Batchelder as the Executive Secretary. With the mid-century publication of the Public Library Inquiry series of reports,[2] library leaders and administrators recognized that children were in part responsible for drawing adults to the library, therefore acknowledging the need to provide specific services (Jenkins, 2000; Larson, 2015; Walter, 2010). The 1950 Public Library Inquiry volume by Robert Leigh stated that public libraries' children's rooms and children's librarians contributed greatly to the "classic success of the public library" at the time (Jenkins, 2000, p. 104). Nevertheless, despite this growing realization, no specific section of the Public Library Inquiry reports is dedicated to in-depth study of this success, nor were the development of youth services addressed in formal studies. Statistical reports, analyses, and research all reflected a focus on adult services. This historical lack of formal research and the tendency to dismiss the importance of youth librarianship has been lamented by researchers trying to conduct serious inquiry on the field (Jenkins, 2000; Miller, 2003).

THESE PICTURE BOOKS introduce children to two of the foremothers of library services for children:

- *Miss Moore Thought Otherwise: How Anne Carroll Moore Created Libraries for Children,* written by Jan Pinborough and illustrated by Debby Atwell.
- The *Storyteller's Candle/La velita de los cuentos* (about Pura Belpré), written by Lucía González and illustrated by Lulu Delacre.

There were a number of state and federal court cases that affected the provision of education after World War I. For instance, the 1947 case *Mendez v. Westminster School District* held that the segregation of Mexican and Mexican American students was unconstitutional, and the 1954 *Brown v. Board of Education* decision declared that separate but equal educational facilities were inherently unequal.

While those landmark cases affected the public educational system, desegregation in public libraries took place at varying rates and as part of the broader civil rights movement that advocated an end of segregation in all public spaces. The 1960s protests, sit-ins, and other efforts to desegregate public facilities, especially in the South, included libraries as targets for desegregation. Services for children were inherently part of the struggle because until the end of Jim Crow laws children of color were not allowed in the White-only libraries of the South (Crestwell, 1996).

From the 1950s until 1975, an increase of media in formats other than the book impacted library services. The 1956 Library Services and Construction Act (LSCA) provided federal funding for public libraries to experiment with new outreach programs for the unserved (Walter, 2001). Changing demographics made supporting the teaching of basic reading literacy skills and providing collections that appealed to minorities a higher priority for city libraries.

Young adults became a more visible focus of librarians with the establishment of the ALA Young Adult Services Division in 1957. Federal education funding during the 1960s and early 1970s provided money to purchase school library books and to hire school librarians (Miller, 2003). This inspired discussion and research on school library-public library cooperation, shared collection building, and other joint ventures, which extend to the present day (Woolls, 2001). The work of Margaret A. Edwards of the Enoch Pratt Library in Baltimore discussed best practices in services for teens (Walter & Meyers, 2003).

During the 1970s and 1980s funding became a major issue in library services, and public libraries were required to document and assess the impact of their services in order to justify financial support (Walter & Meyers, 2003; Walter, 2010). ALA and PLA task forces specified and defined goals, policies, and recommendations to implement and quantify services (ALA, 1984; Rollock, 1988; Walter, 2010). Circulation statistics, quantitative evaluation methods, and accountability were required to validate effectiveness and justify the use of taxes to administer services and programs. Public libraries wrote mission statements, and strategic planning became a means for connecting information to libraries. Measurement of children's services was, however, minimal. The publication of *Output Measures for Public Libraries* in 1987 did not include specific services for children, except for "Preschoolers Door to Learning" (Walter, 2010). At the time, about half of all public library users were under the age of 18, with one-quarter between the ages of 12 and 18 (U.S. NCES, 1988). In addition, during the 1970s and 1980s, more schools had established school libraries because of the requirements of the Elementary Secondary Education Act (ESEA) that had been passed in 1965. As a result, public library professionals redefined their services and there was a switch in focus to preschool children and day-care centers (Miller, 2003).

In 1992, the American Library Association's Young Adult Services Division (YASD) was reorganized as the Young Adult Library Services Association (YALSA). Publications such as *Competencies for Libraries Serving Youth: Young Adults Deserve the Best* (YALSA, 2010; developed 1981) and *You Are Not Alone* (1986) were some of the first publications about services to teens for librarians. Lists of "Quick Picks" for reluctant readers and "Best Books for Young Adults" became popular with young library patrons. Children's services statistics were not included in the 1987 Output Measures for Public Libraries; therefore, in 1992, Virginia Walter released a youth services-specific publication, *Output Measures for Public Library Service to Children.* YALSA followed ALSC's lead and Walter produced *Output Measures and More: Planning and Evaluating Public Library Services for Young Adults* (1995). These publications marked a shift in youth librarians' perception of the services they provided. The tools were used to formulate budget requests, to evaluate outcomes of programs and grant-sponsored events, and to plan and justify services according to the children and youth's needs (Walter, 2010).

Another milestone for youth services came as a result of the 1996–1997 ALA presidency of Mary Somerville, under the theme: "Kids Can't Wait . . . Library Advocacy Now!" which emphasized a focus on youth services and youth services librarians.

At the outset of the twenty-first century, the Urban Libraries Council initiative "Public Libraries as Partners in Youth Development," supported by the DeWitt Wallace Reader's Digest Fund, called for teen-friendly library spaces, more relevant materials and services, increased computer access and instruction, improved customer service, and a review of policies on hours and fines (Meyers, 2001).

PLA's Early Literacy Project began in 2000 in partnership with the National Institute of Child Health and Human Development (NICHD), which released the National Reading Panel's landmark report, Teaching Children to Read: An Evidence-Based Assessment of the Scientific Research Literature on Reading and Its Implications for Reading Instruction, which provided research-based findings concerning reading development in America's children

(National Reading Panel, 2000). The initiative based on this work, Every Child Ready to Read @ your library (ECRR), provided research-based findings on how children learn to read, including the importance of early childhood experiences that promote literacy development.

The new century brought an emphasis on multiple literacies, an expansion of the concept of knowledge sharing and creation, and a more holistic view of children and teens, which expanded the library's role beyond providing good books, fun programs, and a nice space to read. An example of this new vision is Walter's *Twenty-First Century Kids, Twenty-First Century Librarians* (2010), which reviews the history, assesses the present, and forecasts the future of children's services in public libraries. Walter analyzes the legacy of children's services that libraries inherited in the twenty-first century by focusing on six traditional core values and describing five concepts of the child served at the library: the child as reader, as a child of the information age, as a community member, as a global citizen, and as an empowered person. These perspectives are not mutually exclusive; Walter provides them to address the different needs of youth in order to plan services accordingly.

Many of the milestone developments in the history of library services to youth left a legacy of specialized programs and resources, increased information and best practices, and inspired the development of professional organizations to help the youth services librarians who will serve the twenty-first-century children and teens. Indeed, public library leaders and administrators should be well aware that the success of their libraries' children and youth programs not only shines a positive light on the image of their library systems, but also directly impacts their communities by contributing to civic involvement and cultural and educational enrichment.

FROM CORE SERVICES TO CIVIC ENGAGEMENT AND INNOVATION

The types and characteristics of library services provided to youth today have evolved dramatically in the past century and a half. Twenty-first-century youth programming still includes storytime sessions, storytelling events, and summer reading programs, but youth services librarians are also at the forefront of developing new ways to engage children and teens in services and programs that spark innovation and discovery. In a way, professionals interested in youth services are at a crossroads in the evolution of youth librarianship. The definitions, models, and traditional services of the past are not sufficient to serve the young adults and children of the twenty-first century.

In an age of new paradigms, the young user is seen more as a citizen to be engaged than as a passive patron to be served. As proposed by Lankes (2011), many libraries are now facilitating the creation and sharing of knowledge in their communities. Youth services librarians realize that the youngest citizens can add cultural meaning to their communities, just as adults do, and that "getting it right makes it imperative that we give teens [and children] a place of their own in our libraries" (Walter & Myers, 2003, p. viii). Advances in technology complement traditional ways of engagement by providing innovative opportunities for youth to create. In this spirit, learning labs, digital studios, programs with focus on STEM (science, technology, engineering, and math) content, 3D printers and robotics, augmented reality (AR), popular-culture trivia contests, fandoms, and comics conventions are some of the newer additions to the array of services for children, teens, and young adults found in today's public libraries (Gorman & Suellentrop, 2009; Larson, 2015; Naidoo, 2014).

To better understand the scope and characteristics of library services for children and youth in the twenty-first century's public libraries, the content of this chapter addresses the following main aspects of library services to youth: the professional; the user; and their interaction through services, resources, and programs.

The Youth Services Library Professional

In the United States, two main divisions of the American Library Association (ALA) specialize in services for children and youth in public libraries: the Association for Library Services to Children (ALSC), and the Young Adults Library Services Association (YALSA). These two national-level associations provide public librarians with resources and professional enrichment to develop their skills and enrich their practices.[3]

In 1989 ALSC developed a list of core competencies for librarians working with children, the ALSC Competencies for Librarians Serving Children in Public Libraries (2015). These have undergone several revisions, with the most recent in 2015. These competencies cover all aspects of the job of a librarian serving children, and range from attitudes such as "demonstrating respect for diversity and inclusion of cultural values" (ALSC, 2015, p. 3) to skills including identifying "the digital media needs of children and their caregivers" (p. 3), along with an array of other competencies. Fulfilling these competencies or recommending that professionals who aspire to serve children achieve, maintain, and develop them will ensure that "children receive the highest quality of library service as defined in the ALA Bill of Rights and its interpretations" (p. 2). All competencies are grouped by areas of service as shown in figure 8.2.

YALSA, which provides professional development for librarians who serve young adults or teenagers, also developed their version of core competencies for librarians serving young adults (YALSA, 2010). These competencies were first published in 1981 with subsequent reviews, and the latest version was completed in 2010. As of 2016, YALSA is working on an update, expected to be completed in 2017. Public library administrators should pay special attention to these skills and abilities when employing librarians to serve their libraries'

ALSC Competencies

Competencies for Librarians Serving Children in Public Libraries: Areas of Service

Area I. Commitment to Client Group
Area II. Reference and User Services
Area III. Programming Skills
Area IV. Knowledge, Curation, and Management of Materials
Area V. Outreach and Advocacy
Area VI. Administrative and Management Skills
Area VII. Professionalism and Professional Development

FIGURE 8.2 ALSC Competencies

SOURCE: ALA, Competencies for Librarians Serving Children in Public Libraries (www.ala.org/alsc/edcareeers/alsccorecomps).

teenagers and young adults. Young Adults Librarians' competencies are also grouped by areas, as shown in figure 8.3.

The organization also created training kits to prepare youth librarians to develop these competencies.[4] In August of 2015, YALSA announced that it was creating digital badges for professionals who wished to demonstrate on their portfolios, websites, and other career materials that they had achieved the competencies needed for serving young adults. The press release announcing the initiative stated:

> Librarians, library workers and library students with an interest in young adult library services can complete learning-based tasks and develop skills tied directly to the seven competency areas covered in YALSA's Competencies for Librarians Serving Youth (YALSA, 2010). Participants will develop projects in one of seven areas to show proficiency in that area. Once proficiency is proven, participants will earn digital badges that can be displayed in virtual spaces, such as social media websites or online resumes. (Munguia, 2015).[5]

ALSC's and YALSA's lists of competencies address the particular needs of children and youth, respectively, demonstrating expectations of librarians focusing on different age groups. The short-sighted assumption that the only requirement to serve youth is a deep knowledge of children's (or young adult) literature has never been more inaccurate than now. Youth services professionals must prioritize discovery and exploration, promote innovation, value an inclusive mindset, and have a strong command of digital technologies—in addition to mastery of traditional skills such as knowledge of children's literature, reading, and storytelling abilities, implementation of children's programs and events, and organizational skills.

Librarians or library professionals working with youth need to stay current on the latest developments in children's and young adult literature, education, and technology, and

YALSA Competencies

Competencies for Librarians Serving Youth: Young Adults Deserve the Best—Areas of Service

Area I. Leadership and Professionalism
Area II. Knowledge of Client Group
Area III. Communication, Marketing & Outreach
Area IV. Administration
Area V. Knowledge of Materials
Area VI. Access to Information
Area VII. Services

FIGURE 8.3 YALSA Competencies

SOURCE: YALSA's Competencies for Librarians Serving Youth: Young Adults Deserve the Best (www.ala.org/yalsa/guidelines/yacompetencies2010).

participate in enrichment and collaboration with other professionals in their fields and related spheres. Both ALSC and YALSA offer many professional-development opportunities for their members, including national conferences, symposia, and virtual meetings and training, all of which contribute to the success of services to youth, and consequently to library services in general.

One of the most valued competencies for professionals working with children and youth is being comfortable with and skilled in the practice of collaboration. Public librarians working with youth will benefit from collaborating, with the staff in the school libraries that serve the same constituents. A good piece of advice for public youth librarians is to be aware of the services and materials provided by the American Association of School Librarians (AASL). There is a common ground of knowledge that both public libraries and educational institutions share about the youth they both serve, and therefore a strong connection between them will enrich both sides and benefit their users. Public librarians need to be aware of trends in the school systems, and remain knowledgeable about current educational standards, curricula, and assessment methods being applied in the public schools' system in order to support and understand the needs of students and teachers. Some ways to work together include partnerships between public and school librarians, developing joint programs, maintaining communication about assignments and curriculum needs, and partnering for summer reading.

> **▶ FACT**
>
> In 2010, state leaders developed a set of common standards for mathematics and language arts for all public schools nationwide, known as the Common Core. The AASL had previously developed the Standards for the 21st Century Learner, a set of learning standards for assessing the development of students' information literacy skills. School librarians now use both sets of standards when planning services for students.*
>
> *The AASL developed a "crosswalk" that helps librarians correlate the information literacy standards to the Common Core. More information can be found at www.ala.org/aasl/standards/crosswalk.

Public librarians who wish to develop their understanding of educational reforms such as the Common Core can take advantage of webinars and other training opportunities from the AASL and PLA, such as the Common Core and the Public Librarian: Reaching Patrons and Students.[6] Because public librarians serve students doing homework and research outside of school, it is vital that youth librarians and school librarians maintain good communication at the least, and develop collaborative programs if possible.

Rebecca Power, a Georgia librarian, led one such collaborative project between the Cobb County, Georgia, Public Schools and the Cobb County Public Libraries. Power explains: "In the past, school media specialists thought to themselves, 'How can I get my students to read more over the summer?' while youth services librarians thought, 'How can I get my patrons to read more during the summer?' Two different minds with the same objective." After the public/school libraries partnership, Power concluded "The result was the most successful summer reading program on record for each partner" (Hill, 2015). The AASL and PLA are collaborating in a website based on the training mentioned above.

Public education impacts public librarianship; librarians and administrators should be aware of changes in the schooling system so that they can meet the needs of students and advocate for student information needs. A recent example of a policy decision at the national level that will have an impact in the lives of students and the services that the public libraries provide to them is the December 2015 signing of the bill Every Student Succeeds Act (ESSA), a law that ensures funding for resources and services in public schools, including school libraries. The American Library Association was involved in the drafting of the bill. "With a good school library and a good public library, your public library experience is much better," said ALA's Washington Office's director Emily Sheketoff (Peet & Vercelletto, 2016).

In addition to the schools, community partnerships also play a significant role in providing services to youth in today's libraries. Partnering with other local institutions or organizations benefits public library programming and the children and teens who participate by expanding the scope of programs and services, including outreach to nonlibrary users. Sports clubs, after-school care providers, religious organizations, preschool and day-care centers, and community health providers are some examples of possible partners. These community organizations should be actively sought to engage in the programs that the library offers, and vice versa.

Motivated by new models of services to young adults proposed by YALSA in The Future of Library Services for and with Teens: A Call to Action, Adrienne Strock (2014) discussed some benefits of establishing partnerships with community organizations. "Partnering can relieve us of the burden of being an expert in all things as we push the realm of library services to provide more dynamic opportunities for teens in order to provide them with necessary 21st century skills," Strock (p. 15) stated, giving examples from Idaho's Meridian Library District partnerships with Boys and Girls Clubs, Parks and Recreation, bike shops, and other community groups.

The User: Children, Young Adults, And Their Caregivers

Whom does a youth services librarian serve? Infants, children, and teens. But caregivers, families, teachers, and other adults invested in children's lives are also an important part of the youth services librarian's population.

In both sets of competencies mentioned for librarians serving children and those for young adults (ALSC, 2015; YALSA, 2010), there is a section dedicated to make sure professionals have knowledge of and commitment to their client group. For example, one of the competencies requires that librarians have an understanding of the theories of infant, child, and adolescent development (ALSC, 2015, p. 3). As much as teachers and those in the educational field need to have a deep knowledge of learning theories and developmental psychology, for library professionals working with youth it is imperative that they not only know, but understand their users, especially because children's developmental characteristics change dramatically from one year to the next, as they grow.

It is, in fact, very important that youth librarians develop their knowledge of the child from infant to young adulthood. From decisions about the building, materials, and décor to selections of collection materials or appropriate content, the child's psychosocial characteristics inform every librarian's decision related to how to better serve them (Gorman & Suellentrop, 2009; Larson, 2015).

Knowledge of the child has also changed over the years. It is important for librarians to stay current on the latest research and information. Research in brain development, behavioral expectations at different stages, and classifications and treatment of special conditions, for example, has yielded many new developments that should be considered for library's purposes. When discussing the need for developing a "sensory-enhanced story time" at the Douglas County Libraries, librarians explained: "Everyone is welcome at each of our library story times, but we began this story time because some find greater enjoyment in its modified environment of a closed room where lighting and music are lower, movement and conversation are encouraged, and there are multiple ways to engage through the senses." What began as a service for children on the autism spectrum started attracting other users who just felt more comfortable in the new environment (Baldassari-Hackstaff, Kerber, Krovontka, & Olson, 2014).

Children's services usually include collections and programs for babies, toddlers, preschoolers, and school-age children. Libraries did not historically consider the needs of teenagers when planning buildings and collections; when they did, young adults were considered to be either "big children" or, just as their name states, younger versions of adults. Now "YA" stickers on book spines and teen spaces are found in most library systems. Even tweens (those children too old to be children, but not officially teenagers) have such specific needs that they drive a set of programs (Thompson, 2013). In all these ranges and stages, the group's specific needs, behaviors, and expectations guide the selection of programs and their implementation, and professionals must make sure that they understand what those are.

Knowledge of age-specific characteristics is not guaranteed merely by earning an ALA-accredited Master in Library Science degree. As Virginia Walter pointed out when reflecting on who serves children in libraries:

> because the [ALA Accreditation] Standards do not require any program to offer courses related to library services for young people, a student has no guarantee that he or she will be able to specialize in—or even be taught the basics of—children's librarianship. And no public library can assume that a graduate of an ALA-accredited program has received any relevant training (2014, p. 27).

Some library systems are implementing their own skills-training for their librarians, such as New York's program on Early Childhood Literacy (Ready to Read)[7] or Pennsylvania's Preschool Connections program. But smaller or rural systems might need to be creative, seek external funding, or rely on librarians who take their own initiative to attend webinars and workshops, or encourage training in more creative ways (Walter, 2014).

In addition to the specific characteristics of each developmental stage, the multicultural and diverse character of today's communities does not permit libraries to ignore the diversity of its target population, which is especially important in regard to children. Children are growing up in an increasingly diverse world, and the library workers who design, prepare, and implement services need to embrace and celebrate this diversity. Children's literature has made great strides in addressing diversity, especially in recent years. This will be discussed further in terms of collections and programs, but it is very important to point out the need to ensure multicultural or diverse representation and awareness of the librarians and workers who will work with these children and their families. Library administrators and leaders need to be conscious about the diversity of their employees, the "Whiteness" that has pervaded librarianship historically, and the cultural competencies that are needed in libraries today. "Culturally competent LIS professionals must be able to embrace the diversity of all communities regardless of race, ethnicity, gender, sexual orientation, and socioeconomic status" (Montiel-Overall, Nuñez, & Reyes-Escudero, 2016, p. 21). Topics such as diversifying librarianship as a profession are especially relevant in regard to youth services. "In [a] culturally supportive environment, you, your young patrons, and other members of your library community will all come to understand and to appreciate our many human differences," wrote Denise Agosto in 2001. The statement is still relevant 15 years later.

It is also important to note that diversity of children, youth, their families, and the librarians who serve them includes all types of diverse populations, not only cultural or ethnic groups. GLBTQ+ children, teens, and parents, families with members who have special needs or abilities, families of gifted and talented youth, children, and teens on the autism spectrum, adoptive families, multiracial families, and homeschooled children are just examples of the diversity of individuals who cross the public libraries' doors and who enrich the sphere of youth services in public libraries (Naidoo & Park, 2013).

An added benefit of librarians serving youth is that they get to interact with patrons of all ages, as children usually come accompanied by their families, caregivers, educators, and other adults related to them. Public relations and customer service are as important for youth librarians as they are for the rest of the library's staff.

The Interaction: Services, Resources, and Programs

Spaces for Children and Teens

Children's or teens' areas tend to be favorite spots in many library buildings, especially those that are newly built or renovated. Let us be frank: colorful and youth-friendly spaces are visually attractive. They are picture-perfect spots to attract media and market the library to the community. There is a reason why many of the most recent renovations in libraries all over the United States focus on their children and/or teen areas. It is, however, interesting to discover that not much about the organization of spaces has changed over the years, even if the needs and the ways in which youth interact with knowledge have (Bon, Cranfield, & Latimer, 2011). As with any other area, the process of constructing or remodeling youth spaces should begin with an assessment of the users' specific needs. Youth are often opinionated, and their voices can be a great resource for decision making. Aligning the spaces with the educational, recreational, and social needs of children, teens, and their families should guide the planning. Most basic library building manuals agree: "defining how services, activities, and collections will satisfy those needs drives the various elements of design such as color, furniture, flooring, shelving and lighting" (Feinberg & Keller, 2010).

Examples abound of both creative and attractive features being used in children's areas of library buildings all over the country. From existing spaces being transformed with natural light and bright colors like the second floor of the Central Library of the Boston Public Library, to the East Hampton (New York) Library's addition of a reference desk shaped like a boat and 10-foot tall lighthouses, architectural firms find attractive designs for almost every budget (Morehart, 2015). Redesigning the children's and/or youth areas is one of the best investments a public library can make, and one that will probably have an impact on library usage as a whole.[8]

Spaces for young adults (YA) also have seen a surge of remodeling projects or construction of attractive teen areas in many public libraries. However, in many cases, the improvements have been made again without consideration for the changing paradigm of services to youth, and the result has been only a change in appearance. "Lacking YA spatial knowledge, libraries commonly design and enact space largely in ignorance of what constitutes normal and appropriate YA public behavior" (Bernier, Males, & Rickman, 2014, p. 167). Even considerations such as postural needs of teenagers and young bodies have been left out of furniture selections or configurations (Bernier & Males, 2014). LIS professionals working with youth need to make sure to bring the research and their knowledge of the youth they serve to the table when building or design decisions are made.

Virtual Spaces

Today, the spaces where youth (and adults) meet transcend the physical world. The public library's virtual presence directly impacts its outreach and usage by the population at-large, but this aspect is even more important in regard to youth services. The children and youth who use today's libraries are digital natives.[9] They do not know a world without Internet services or online communications, so it is true that the library's virtual presence will impact outreach to these populations.

> ▶ **FACT**
>
> Thanks to the convenience provided by mobile devices, especially smartphones, 92% of teens (ages 13 to 17) reported going online daily—including 24% who said they go online "almost constantly," according to a 2015 study from Pew Research Center (Lenhart, 2015).

For a long time, the library's web presence consisted merely of a searchable catalog and a calendar of events. Lately, however, with more and more people digitally connected throughout their waking hours, what is usually called the "virtual library" provides an opportunity to be present in the lives of children and youth. With the abundance of social media channels and applications, the children, youth, and young families will relate better to a library presence that meets them where they are, physically or online.

Libraries' presence in social media outlets is indeed where outreach is more important than ever. A library that is ubiquitous and constantly interacting in the most popular online platforms is a library that is present in its users' lives. Whether Facebook, Instagram, Tumblr, Twitter, SnapChat, or whatever platform is trending at the time this is being read, in youth services librarians should be active participants in the spaces where many of the youth congregate. Moreover, these tools are becoming increasingly interactive and offer new opportunities for youth librarians to communicate with their users and families.

The use of social media or technological tools to reach out youth services' audience needs to be strategically planned, specifically designed with children, youth, and families in mind, and aligned with the library's general plans. In a 2015 Library Technology Report, David Lee King gave an example of using social media in a way that is consistent with a library's strategic implementation of services. "For example, my library has a strategic goal of helping children ages 0-5 get ready to read by kindergarten. Obviously, we're not going to go after a 3 year-old on Twitter! But it makes a lot of sense for us to start attempting to reach young parents, ages 20-35" wrote King (2015, p. 23).

Another example is using texting/SMS services to communicate with teens and families. Some libraries are experimenting with using free texting reminder services to send out announcements of programs or events, asking users to sign up for them, and sending reminders when the event approaches. Megan Robinson, a youth services librarian in Manatee County, Florida, related her experiments with this new technology as part of a pilot project for her library's teens: "It [the text reminder application Remind] has wonderful possibilities such as linking to our event web pages, sharing capabilities with friends and family, instant gratification, information about library services, and links to surveys to collect feedback data on how the service is being run" (Robinson, 2015, personal communication). The development of applications that send notifications to users is also being employed by libraries such as the Orange County (Florida) Library System and the Allen County (IN) Public Library to send parents and caregivers early literacy tips or suggestions to improve school readiness (Landgraf, 2015).

Reference

Just as with adult services, reference interactions are still an important aspect of a youth services librarian's job. Children and youth reference services are very specific. Being acquainted with educational methodologies and curricula is paramount for successful reference services. Young patrons have homework and research needs, and reading constraints mandated by their schools' guidelines. Librarians need to be aware of reading level classifications of books such as Advanced Reader (AR), Lexile Levels, Leveled Readers, and similar systems, as well as their communities' science fair's schedules, important speech or spelling contests, and so on. "When children and their families come in looking for a 'level M' book, it's a huge cause of frustration for my circulation staff. A trained children's librarian should be aware of developments such as this and be able to offer recommendations" (Kaser 2015).

> **▶ FACT**
>
> Homeschooled students are children ages 5 to 17 in a grade equivalent to at least kindergarten and not higher than 12th grade who receive instruction at home instead of at a public or private school either all or most of the time. Approximately 3% of the school-age population was homeschooled in the 2011–2012 school year, a total of 1,773,000 students (U.S. Dept. of Education, 2014).

In addition to formal schooling practices, public library's youth services normally serve homeschooled students. For families who homeschool their children, libraries provide excellent opportunities to complement their curricula and help to foster enjoyment of books and learning. In many cases, for these families the public library is the main source of materials and information, as well as of enrichment programs related to special topics such as art, music, or science, with the added benefit of opportunities for socializing. Even if some librarians are reluctant to engage with homeschoolers because of a lack of understanding or prejudice, most realize that they can become the most frequent users (Furness, 2008). Cheryl Blankenship, a librarian from Briggs Lawrence County, Ohio, reflected on the fact that her library's staff had some concerns at the beginning of a biweekly program designed for homeschoolers. However, she stated that overall it was a positive experience because "the library is gaining a group of patrons who are actively using our facilities and materials, while the families are gaining an opportunity to come together, having their needs for socialization and educational materials met" (Blankenship, 2008).

The ubiquity of online interactions might prove an asset for reference services. Just as with adult services, the old tradition of walking to the reference desk to ask a librarian for help can be complemented by newer methods of librarian-user interaction. Most public libraries offer text, e-mail, and other virtual reference services such as "Ask a Librarian" for all patrons. It is possible, then, that youth services librarians will discover that virtual reference by chat or SMS conveniently suits younger users. Research on the effectiveness of these practices is at its outset, but it will be interesting to assess the use of virtual reference by children or teens. For example, a study by Luo and Weak (2013) showed that teens most commonly used SMS reference services for help with simple questions related to homework and research projects.

Collections

Many librarians who work in youth services are avid readers of children's or YA literature. Some (hopefully many) also took graduate-level courses on selecting and evaluating materials for youth. It is, however, extremely difficult to keep up with the books and other materials available. In addition to the selection of materials, all aspects of collection development, acquisitions, and technical services for the children's or young adults' collections need to be supervised by youth services librarians. Many library systems have centralized collection development policies and staff, for example, these may be combined with adult collections or managed from a central location. In other cases, the youth services area has its own policies and practices (Larson, 2015). In both cases, youth services librarians should be involved in selection, deselection, policy setting, and technical processing of the materials for the children or young adult collections.

The latest statistical report from the Institute of Museum and Library Services (IMLS) indicates that in 2014, children's collections accounted for 35.4% of total circulation in all public libraries in the nation (IMLS, 2016, table 8). With children's materials accounting for more than a third of total circulation, it is necessary to make sure that library directors, supervisors, and children's librarians create policies and practices to develop great collections.[10]

Evaluation and selection of materials are among the most important aspects of the youth librarian's job. This part of the process cannot be done correctly without youth services personnel's input. As Larson pointed out, "It doesn't take a lot of skill to figure out that the collection probably needs the latest best sellers, but the librarian who is working directly with the children will know whether it is likely that the newest title in a specific series is still being voraciously read by young readers in the community" (Larson, 2015, p. 30).

Youth librarians use a combination of selection tools: professional publications, lists of "best of" or "notable" titles, professional literature, and other sources. Selection aids for youth services librarians include:

- *Book Links*
- *School Library Journal*
- *Kirkus Reviews*
- *The Horn Book*
- *AudioFile Magazines*
- Center for Children's Books (CBC) *Bulletin*
- Cooperative Children's Books Center (CCBC) lists
- Professional associations blogs and newsletters
- Book awards lists

YOUTH MEDIA BOOK AWARDS

In professional circles, children's book awards are known as the Oscars of children's literature. Although some of the more important awards for children's and young adult literature are announced annually by the American Library Association's divisions and affiliates during their Midwinter Meeting (at an event known as the Youth Media Awards), there are other important awards at the national level being presented by different organizations. Book award selection committees put a serious amount of work into reading, evaluating, and voting on hundreds of books published each year. Librarians can feel grateful of this work being done so that they are able to identify the best books of each year for their collections.

As mentioned before, ALA divisions such as ALSC and YALSA, and affiliates such as REFORMA (the National Association to Promote Library and Information Services to Latinos and the Spanish Speaking) and BCALA (Black Caucus of the American Library Association) announce their awards together. Other ethnic associations (such as the American Indian Association or the Asian/Pacific American Library Association, for example) have different schedules or hold separate events, but they also present awards to the best books about their cultures. There are also other important awards to consider from different organizations that are for specific genres or formats (figure 8.4).

KEY BOOKS AND MEDIA AWARDS FOR CHILDREN AND YOUNG ADULTS IN THE UNITED STATES

ALA Youth Media Awards

A deep knowledge of children's literature is very valuable for librarians, but when time is of the essence, it is helpful to rely on these professionally approved recommendations to supplement their personal knowledge of their audience and its needs. Youth librarians can, at certain points in time, implement "Needs Assessment" projects to re-evaluate collections or sections of the collection and adjust accordingly (Larson, 2015).

Books are obviously not the only material available for children and teenagers, but they do continue to be the main part of libraries' youth collections. Books are usually categorized by format or by genre, and each library system identifies the best system of organization for its community (Cerny, Markey, & Williams, 2006; Larson, 2015). Some libraries are experimenting with new sections and even new classification systems that they believe respond better to their populations' needs. When the children's staff at Connecticut's Darien Library questioned whether there was a better way to organize books: "The answer was a resounding 'yes,' and the result was a total rethinking of how children's books can be arranged for public use" (Parrott & Gattullo, 2013). Not all libraries will respond well to doing away with the Dewey Decimal Classification System, but it is important to have youth services personnel who understand collection usage to evaluate decisions like these.

Genres and sections of the collection are also fluid and can be adapted to changes in literature. The growing number of graphic novels and the increased popularity of genres like manga or anime also introduce changes to young adults' sections in many libraries. "Japanese animation and Japanese comics are enjoying a huge surge of popularity," wrote Nina Exner, a librarian from North Carolina. And even if its popularity seemed to have increased in recent years, "it has been popular among devoted fans—sometimes but not always self-labeled as 'otaku'—for years, and those fans span genders, ages, and interests" (Exner, 2012, p. 28).

Diversity in the Collection

Recent discussion about the need for a more diverse representation in the books being published and in libraries' collections is an encouraging trend. Tables of award-winning books (see, e.g., figure 8.4) now include specific awards for ethnic minorities or underrepresented populations, indicating that material collections for youth in public libraries need to reflect

Selected Book Awards

AWARD	AGE GROUP	TYPE/CATEGORIES	SPONSOR
Caldecott Medal	Children	Picture books	ALSC
Newbery Medal	Children	Author	ALSC
Theodor Seuss Geisel Award	Children	Beginning readers	ALSC
Robert F. Sibert Medal	Children	Informational	ALSC
Schneider Family	Children and YA	Disability experience	ALA
Batchelder Award	Children	Translation to English	ALSC
Odyssey Award	Children and YA	Audiobooks	ALSC-YALSA
Andrew Carnegie Medal	Children	Videos	ALSC
Michael L. Printz Award	YA	Young Adult literature	YALSA
Stonewall Medal	Children and YA	GLBT experience	GLBTRT
Coretta Scott King Medal	Children and YA	African American	EMIERT
Pura Belpré Medal	Children	Latino American	REFORMA-ALSC
National Book Award for Young People	Children	Young people's literature	National Book Foundation
Boston Globe-Horn Book Award	Children and YA	Picture books, fiction and poetry, and nonfiction	The Horn Book
Orbis Pictus Award	Children	Nonfiction	NCTE
Asian/Pacific American Awards for Literature	Children and YA	Children's, YA, and picture book (Asian American)	APALA
American Indian Youth Literature Award	Children and YA	Picture book, middle school, and YA (Native American)	AILA
Américas Award	Children and YA	Primary and secondary readers (Latino American)	CLASP

FIGURE 8.4 Selected Book Awards

all sections of our communities and the world, as is the birth of a campaign that turned into the organization called We Need Diverse Books (wndb.org). It is important to note that all children, young adults, and families who walk through the public library's doors need to find a collection that is global and inclusive. Notice the emphasis on the word *all,* because not only do members of those "special" groups need to see themselves reflected in books—everyone needs to read and learn about people who are not like themselves. To implement these inclusive practices, youth librarians must be "culturally competent." As Naidoo wrote: "Passionate, culturally competent librarians are the foundation for change within the library profession." In today's conflicted world, it is important that personnel "understand the power of both print and digital children's media to shape a child's view of the world and to build bridges of understanding" (2014, p. 3).

> **▶ FACT**
>
> The Cooperative Children's Book Center (CCBC) compiles yearly statistics of books for children published in the United States that are by or about people of color or first/native nations.*
>
> *The yearly statistics compiled by the CCBC are available at http://ccbc.education.wisc.edu/books/pcstats.asp.

Materials for children and teens include more than books, whether these are print, electronic, or audiobooks. Librarians are also curators of new technologies, games, software, and applications that help users interact, learn, and explore. In addition to these, public libraries usually include other types of materials in their collections, such as toys, manipulatives, early literacy kits, etcetera (Burke, 2016). In 2015, a patron of the Hillary Rodham Clinton Children's Library in Little Rock, Arkansas, donated a number of musical instruments for children to add to the library's collection. Now children can take home drums, a guitar, a violin, a trumpet, or other instruments for 28 days (Children's Library, 2015). Exploration, creativity, and interaction are highly encouraged because the public library is a space where children can create knowledge.

Censorship

One last consideration about collections is the importance of intellectual freedom in youth services. Due to the ages of the patrons served by children's and teens' librarians, the issue of challenges to specific materials is relevant. Public libraries require very clear and public collection development policies that include the criteria for selection and deselection, the procedure for requesting reconsiderations, and the advisory group, committee, or person(s) who will be responsible for evaluating the challenges submitted (Gorman & Suellentrop, 2009; Larson, 2015). Clear policies usually satisfy all sides when there is a controversy, but this is not always the case. Challenges to children's materials may be due to age appropriateness, violence, sexually explicit content, or graphic or obscene language, among others.[11]

Youth librarians and their supervisors or administrators should be prepared to defend their patrons' freedom to read. Public libraries do not serve *in loco parentis*; only a child's guardian should be able to control the books the children under his or her care should read. Likewise, if parents or guardians have objections about materials that are in the library, librarians need to be clear that just as they have control over their own children's readings, they do not have control over what other children read. As Pat Scales, former Chair of the ALA Office for Intellectual Freedom, explained when talking about how to discuss censorship with young children, "the most important point to get across, regardless of age, is that everyone has the right to make his or her reading choices, and only parents have control over what their kids read. If you are successful in conveying that, then you will have just introduced them to the principles of intellectual freedom" (Scales, 2015, p. 12). Banned Books Week, an annual celebration of the freedom to read sponsored by ALA, is a good opportunity for youth services librarians to reinforce these concepts with families and parents (American Library Association, Office for Intellectual Freedom, 2016).

PROGRAMS AND INITIATIVES

"Public library story-times are a cherished memory for many adults. In many libraries, story-times are the highest profile part of the children's librarian's job" (Larson, 2015, p. 91). Discussing ideas and themes related to story times will certainly transcend the scope of this chapter. But it should suffice to say that, even if this practice is a core feature of children's services, there are many other ways both classic and new to implement programming for the children and teenagers of today.

In this section we will describe some of the most important initiatives or programs that could be used or adapted for public libraries, trying to showcase a representative sampling of programs for all age groups.

Summer Reading Programs (SRP)

"According to the American Library Association, over 95% of public libraries offer a summer reading program" (Larson, 2015, p. 136). Developed mainly to keep children occupied and interested in reading over the summer, these programs quickly became the best way to reduce what in education is called the "summer slide"—the tendency for students to fall behind in their academic success after the summer break, for lack of reading. Initially these types of programs were just basic reading promotion. Today, many libraries spend the whole year preparing, developing, and investing time in creating elaborate summer programs that include series of (usually weekly) events for different age-groups, competitions, tracking of readings with logs and other systems, prizes, and big ticket events with performers and contracted providers.

Many states or consortia create a common theme for the public library systems in their geographical region and develop resources, ideas, and marketing and promotional materials based on the theme. The Collaborative Summer Library Program (CSLP) is a consortium of states working together to provide summer reading program materials for children, teens, and adults. In 2015, for example, many library systems in the United States followed their theme "Every Hero Has a Story," and libraries implemented creative superhero-related activities that enticed patrons of all ages. Renowned author Kate DiCamillo talked about this in an interview during her year as National Ambassador for Young People's Literature:

> By the time the summer reading opportunity came along, it was just like, yes. Let me. I'm a kid who grew up going to the summer reading program every year at the public library. I love talking to kids about that. It's just been the most natural thing in the world for me to do while I'm out doing the ambassador stuff. (Gershowitz, 2015, p. 15)

The Urban Libraries Council report *Public Libraries and Effective Summer Learning: Opportunities for Assessment* (2016) provides suggestions for action and future research on the educational opportunities for summer learning in public libraries.[12]

Every Child Ready to Read (ECRR) www.everychildreadytoread.org

This initiative of ALA's ALSC and PLA divisions originated in 2000 as a response to new developments in research on brain development and learning, such as the National Institute of Child Health and Human Development (NICHD)'s report from the National Reading Panel (Ash & Meyers, 2009). ECRR is a parent-education initiative that teaches parents how to be their children's first teachers. In 2016, the ECRR initiative won the American Society of Association Executives (ASAE) "Power of A Summit and Gold Awards."[13] The press release states:

> traditionally, early literacy programs focus on children, rather than parent education. ECRR increases public library impact on early literacy through changing caregiving behaviors and developing library staff skills. Through a focus on active learning, ECRR creates a library environment that supports early literacy and offers hands-on opportunities for families.[14]

DIA: Diversity in Action http://dia.ala.org

DIA began as "El Día de los Niños, El Día de los Libros" (The Day of the Children, The Day of the Books.) This was an initiative created by author Pat Mora and REFORMA to celebrate the joy of reading, or what Mora called "bookjoy." Adopted by the ALSC, the initiative was transformed into "Diversity in Action," which is described as "a nationally recognized initiative that emphasizes the importance of literacy for all children from all backgrounds [and] a daily commitment to linking children and their families to diverse books, languages and cultures" (dia.ala.org/content/about-día). April 30 is the traditional date recognized in many countries as the day of the children, which is why it was chosen to promote special events and celebrations especially for that date, although programs can be adapted for any time of the year or even annual events.

Teen Read Week (TRW) http://teenreadweek.ning.com[15]

The website explains that "'Teen Read Week' [TRW] is a national adolescent literacy initiative created by the Young Adult Library Services Association (YALSA). It began in 1998 and is held annually in October. Its purpose is to encourage teens to be regular readers and library users." A YALSA committee of young adult librarians works on this initiative. It usually has a theme or slogan (for example, in 2016 their promotional materials proclaim "Read for the fun of it" in several languages), and ALA prepares marketing materials and toolkits to use for marketing. Sometimes organizations or associations establish grants and book giveaways related to the program.

Teen Tech Week (TTW) http://teentechweek.ning.com

Similar to TRW, this YALSA initiative focuses on digital resources and technology. During Teen Tech Week youth services or teen librarians showcase digital resources and services that are available for teens. Technological resources, tools, and programs at many libraries offer teens more opportunities to succeed in school, prepare for college, and to be ready for careers.

Prime Time Family Literacy http://primetimefamily.org

Prime Time Family Literacy is a humanities-based literacy program. It was originally created by the Louisiana Endowment for the Humanities (LEH) in 1991 but it has since been adopted by many other states. In 2015 "Prime Time" became an incorporated organization. The family literacy program is described as "a set of unique, humanities-focused, and outcomes-based programs designed to engage new and underserved children and families" (Prime Time, Inc., 2016).

Additional Programs

In addition to the trademarked programs mentioned, many libraries continue to implement successful programs, and create new ones as the needs of children and teens change. Some examples of programs that are being implemented based on needs are:

Fandom conventions (or "cons") such as local versions of Comic Con, Nerd Con, and variants, where children or teenagers dress up as favorite characters from popular fandoms and participate in "cosplay" (costume play) activities, contests, workshops, fairs, etc.

Popular culture programs based on popular books, series, or films. Harry Potter, Doctor Who, and Star Wars, are some recent examples for which librarians organized events, displays, and activities, many times allowing teens to participate in the planning.

Brick/builders clubs. Many libraries formed clubs for children using toy building blocks such as Legos. Children, teens, or families can build projects based on themes suggested by librarians, or use the bricks during unstructured playtime.

Maker movement, innovation hubs, and digital labs. As technological tools such as 3D printers, robotics kits, computers, and digital video, recording, or photography equipment proliferate, many libraries are creating innovation hubs, creativity studios, and similar spaces where they host events and programs that foster tinkering and discovering.

Gaming. Many public libraries became hubs for gamers to gather and exchange items, ideas, or strategies. At the writing of this chapter, the success of the public release of Augmented Reality (AR) games such as "Pokémon Go" provided a new type of engagement as libraries became landmarks (gyms or stops) in the virtual landscape of this game (Spina, 2016).

Gardening/cooking. Health-related library programs for the whole family are often created to promote both healthy eating and community building. Some libraries also design programs specifically with children and youth in mind, which might include classes and/or plots of land to do cooperative gardening.

Health and Job Fairs. Many public libraries provide space and resources for community partners and organizations for job fairs or health fairs. Although these types of programs are targeted at adults, in some cases they can be planned for children and youth (e.g., career fairs for students who will soon be entering college).

Social Services. Rather than fairs or one-time events, some public libraries partner with community organizations to provide regular free social services that help fulfill basic needs in their communities. Examples of these include health screening days, food services for children during summer breaks, and so on.[16]

THE FUTURE OF YOUTH SERVICES: CHALLENGES AND OPPORTUNITIES

The main role of public libraries' youth services is as a community's partner in facilitating the enrichment, education, and creation and discovery of knowledge by its younger generations. The methods and tools that they use to reach these younger patrons and the trends and types of programs and services that they provide have evolved and will continue to do so. But the main purpose will always be the facilitation of knowledge via human interaction.

There are many challenges to fulfilling that purpose. The structure created by PLA to assess library services will be used to address some of these challenges. In this way, youth service librarians, their supervisors, and the libraries' leadership will be able to evaluate their progress and assess their success (or lack thereof) in confronting and overcoming the challenges.

PLA's Project Outcome[17] identified seven essential library service areas to assess, which "could be easily and directly linked to improving or changing patrons' knowledge, behavior, skills/application, and awareness." (PLA, 2016). The seven areas are: Civic/Community Engagement, Digital Inclusion, Early Childhood Literacy, Economic Development, Education/Lifelong Learning, Job Skills, and Summer Learning (PLA, 2016). All seven can be applied to youth services, and two of them are in fact the direct responsibility of the youth services department.

When reflecting on the future of children's and youth services, we believe that three of the seven outcomes will be particularly challenging. These are Civic/Community Engagement, Digital Inclusion, and Early Childhood Literacy.

Civic/Community Engagement Challenge: Diversity

We discussed diversity and multicultural issues in this chapter, with regard to diversifying collections, programs, and staff, as well as facilitating the development of cultural competence by library staff at all levels. In fact, even if the issue is timely and it seems to be a recent concern, it is important to note that the issue of diversity in children's and youth services was introduced by children's services pioneers such as Augusta Baker, Charlemae Rollins, Pura Belpré, and others (Horning, 2015). Not only do we still have a long way to go to reach an ideal situation, but we are now seeing how frequently discrimination, intolerance, racism, and hate surface in our communities. In a society where movements such as Black Lives Matter or We Need Diverse Books are still needed, there are numerous opportunities to take action. Libraries can respond by becoming places of rest among the chaos, but also spaces for dialogue and open discussion and critical analysis (Koester & Lonial, 2015). The role of libraries in social justice and community-building will continue to be crucial.

Socioeconomic disparities in our societies serve as catalysts for other problems. Public libraries are main actors in the community conversation, and as such can play an important role by providing services that promote inclusion and problem-solving. It will require many different members of the society working together to address current socioeconomic inequalities such as unemployment, lack of access to basic resources such as health and education, the digital divide, and so on. In order for librarians to make a difference in their communities, partnerships are now and will continue to be key. Public libraries have unique opportunities to create programs that address those needs. Many organizations provide funding for libraries to implement initiatives, including federal grants and institutions such as the Institute of Museum and Library Services (IMLS). A recent example is the P3 (Performance Partnership Pilots for Disconnected Youth) initiative, which helps state, local, and tribal governments test new strategies to improve outcomes for low-income disconnected youth aged 14 to 24. Libraries should take advantage of opportunities like these to make a difference in their communities (DeVoe, 2015).

Digital Inclusion Challenge: Access for All

Public libraries, including youth services, have traditionally provided access to information in the most democratic and equitable manner. The digital divide, gaps in access, attacks on privacy, and cyber security threats are increasingly common. Youth librarians will need to prepare to face those types of challenges by staying true to the core values of the profession such as universal access, intellectual freedom, and defense of privacy and confidentiality. The challenge will be to promote awareness of the services that the public library provides in defense of citizens' rights, including their rights in the digital world.

Youth librarians also serve as mentors for children, youth, and families navigating the world of new media technologies, social media, and other interactions. Librarians want to guide children, youth, and families across the new frontiers of the digital landscape, just as they have for literacy, reading, and print books. However, it is important to remember "that no matter the technology, no matter the constraints and pressures put on librarians to ready young children for school, it is most important to focus on the community, on the family, and on the child and how librarians can become the best media mentors for them" (Mills, Romeijn-Stout, Campbell, & Koester, 2015, p. 32). A 2014 American Library Association report on the Children's Internet Protection Act provides useful information for public libraries (Batch, 2014).

Early Childhood Literacy Challenge: Educational Attainment

Early childhood education and literacy is among the most important youth services. Studies indicate that the level of literacy that children develop in their early years is a predictor of academic success for the rest of their education. Twenty-first-century research has shown that "the connection between early literacy experiences and a child's later success as an independent reader had never been so firmly established" (Ash & Meyers, 2009).

The future of public libraries can hold the key to educational attainment and success in their communities. Even before children start school, libraries play a role in their development by facilitating programs for them and educating families and caregivers on the importance of reading, talking, and interacting with children from infancy.

The future of youth services is full of possibilities, but likely to be plagued with obstacles. Library leadership must provide youth librarians with a secure, innovative, and well-funded environment. As Virginia Walter wrote, "I would argue today that the children's librarians who are privileged to spend their workdays with young people also must be given the supports and opportunities to do their jobs well" (2014, p. 28).

With the support of their leaders and characteristic creativity, youth librarians will be able to face future challenges by taking advantage of opportunities to grow as professionals, and collaborating and exchanging ideas with those outside of the profession who contribute to the development of children, youth, and their families.

NOTES

1. These facts were retrieved from tables 10, 10a, 11, and 11a from the IMLS report found here: https://www.imls.gov/sites/default/files/fy2014_pls_tables.pdf.
2. The Public Library Inquiry reports consisted of seven volumes published after 1949. Jenkins (2000) mentions that Oliver Garceau's 1949 volume (*The Public Library and the Political Process*) describes the "children's room as 'one of the busiest, as well as one of the pleasantest places in the library' and credits children's librarians with primary responsibility for the development of modern children's literature" (p.104).
3. For those readers outside the United States and those with a global perspective, it is suggested that you explore the resources and information of the "Libraries for Children and Young Adults Section" of the International Federation of Library Associations (IFLA): www.ifla.org/about-the-libraries-for-children-and-ya-section.
4. For more information on the *Young Adults Deserve the Best* training kits, see www.ala.org/yalsa/sites/ala.org.yalsa/files/content/YADeserveBrochure_FINAL_rev2013.pdf.
5. See http://yalsabadges.ala.org for information on the "Badges for Learning" system being developed to award badges for YALSA competencies. http://yalsabadges.ala.org.
6. See the AASL webinar "The Common Core and the Public Librarian" (www.ala.org/aasl/ecollab/ccss101).
7. In 2013, the State Library of New York identified early literacy for the development of a statewide training for public library staff to implement the "Ready to Read" program. In 2014, the State Library received $50,000 in federal funds for an IMLS 2014/2015 Laura Bush 21st Century Program Planning Grant. Read more: www.nysl.nysed.gov/libdev/earlylit/training.htm.
8. In 2011/2012, YALSA developed a set of guidelines for libraries that are planning to renovate or build new young adult spaces: The *Teen Space Guidelines* can be downloaded from: www.ala.org/yalsa/guidelines/teenspaces.
9. John Palfrey is an author who, in spite of not being a librarian, has addressed the role of librarians in the digital competencies of youth. One of his first works on this topic is 2010's *Born Digital: Understanding the first generation of digital natives.* Philadelphia: Basic Books.
10. Facts retrieved from IMLS tables 8 and 8a (https://www.imls.gov/sites/default/files/fy2014_pls_tables.pdf).
11. For more information on the definitions of challenged and banned books, the reasons, and lists of books, please visit the Office for Intellectual Freedom of the ALA and the Banned Books website (www.ala.org/bbooks/about).
12. The report *Public Libraries and Effective Summer Learning* can be accessed via the IMLS website's announcement of 2016 grants for summer learning (https://www.imls.gov/news-events/project-profiles/accelerate-summer-public-libraries-evolving-summer-reading-programs).
13. Find more information about the Power of A Awards at www.thepowerofa.org/awards/.

14. Press Release: www.ala.org/news/press-releases/2016/07/pla-receives-asae-power-summit-and-gold-awards-every-child-ready-read.
15. YALSA's Teen Read Week website contains resources and opportunities to share activities related to Teen Read Week events; see http://teenreadweek.ning.com/.
16. The state of Florida, for example, partnered in 2016 with the USDA Summer Food Service Program to provide "Summer BreakSpot" in many library locations across the state. More information is available at www.summerfoodflorida.org.
17. Project Outcome delineates seven areas to assess public library services. Before this project, in 2008 the *Public Library Association* (PLA) released the "service responses" in Sandra Nelson's *Strategic Planning for Results.* Those 18 responses could be used as an organizational structure to encompass all youth services roles (Long & McCook, 2011). The service responses belonged to four concepts of library service: the public sphere, cultural heritage, education, and information. The challenges for the future of youth services mentioned in this chapter could still be encompassed in those four underlying areas that are central to the role of public libraries in the community.

REFERENCES

Agosto, D. (2001). Bridging the culture gap: Ten steps toward a more multicultural youth library. *Journal of Youth Services in Libraries, 14*(3), 38–41.

American Library Association. (1984). *Realities: Educational reform in a learning society.* Chicago, IL: American Library Association.

American Library Association, Office for Intellectual Freedom. (2016). Banned Books Week: Celebrating the freedom to read. www.ala.org/bbooks/bannedbooksweek.

Ash, V., & Meyers, E. (2009, Spring). Every child ready to read @your library. *Children and Libraries, 7,* 3–7.

Association for Library Service to Children. (2015). *Competencies for librarians serving children in public libraries.* www.ala.org/alsc/edcareeers/alsccorecomps.

Baldassari-Hackstaff, L., Kerber, S., Krovontka, R. A., & Olson, L. R. (2014). "Sensory-enhanced storytime at Douglas County libraries." *Public Libraries, 53*(1), 36–42.

Batch, K. R., (2014). *Fencing out knowledge: Impacts of the Children's Internet Protection Act 10 years later.* American Library Association. Office for Information Technology Policy. http://connect.ala.org/files/cipa_report.pdf.

Belpré, P. (2013). *The stories I read to the children: The life and writing of Pura Belpré, the legendary storyteller, children's author, and New York public librarian.* L. Sánchez-González (Ed.). New York, NY: Center for Puerto Rican Studies.

Bernier, A., & Males, M. (2014). YA spaces and the end of postural tyranny. *Public Libraries, 53*(4), 27–36.

Bernier, A., Males, M., & Rickman, C. (2014). "It is silly to hide your most active patrons": Exploring user participation of library space designs for young adults in the United States. *Library Quarterly, 84*(2), 165–182.

Blankenship, C. (2008). Is today a homeschool day at the library? *Public Libraries, 47*(5).

Bon, I., Cranfield, A., & Latimer, K. (2011). *Designing library space for children.* Berlin/Munich, Germany: DeGruyter.

Burke, J. (2016). *Neal-Schuman library technology companion: A basic guide for library staff.* Chicago, IL: Neal-Schuman, 2016.

Cerny, R., Markey, P., & Williams, A. (2006). *Outstanding library service to children: Putting the core competencies to work.* Chicago, IL: American Library Association.

Children's Library in Little Rock now lending musical instruments. (2015, February 11). *Arkansas Matters.* www.arkansasmatters.com/news/news/childrens-library-in-little-rock-now-lending-musical-instruments.

Crestwell, S. (1996, Summer/Fall). The last days of Jim Crow in southern libraries. *Libraries and Culture, 31,* 557–573.

DeVoe, T. (2015). Nine pilots announced in new federal effort to serve disconnected youth. Institute of Museum and Library Services. www.imls.gov/news-events/upnextblog/2015/10/nine-pilots-announced-new-federal-effort-serve-disconnected-youth.

Exner, N. (2012). Anime-zing in North Carolina: Library views of anime fans. *North Carolina Libraries, 70*(1). www.ncl.ecu.edu/index.php/NCL/article/view/324.

Feinberg, S., & Keller, J. (2010). *Designing space for children and teens in libraries and public places.* Chicago, IL: ALA Editions.

Fenwick, S. I. (1976). Library services to children and young people. *Library Trends, 25,* 329–360.

Furness, A. (2008). *Helping homeschoolers in the library.* Chicago, IL: ALA Editions.

Garceau, O. (1949). *The public library in the political process: A report of the Public Library Inquiry.* New York, NY: Columbia University Press.

Gershowitz, E. (2015). An interview with Kate DiCamillo. *Horn Book Magazine, 91*(6), 14-24.

Gorman, M., & Suellentrop, T. (2009). *Connecting young adults and libraries.* New York, NY: Neal Schuman.

Hill, N. M. (2015) Public and school libraries: Missions in compliment or conflict? *Public Libraries, 54*(3), 14–19.

Horning, K. T. (2015). Milestones for diversity in children's literature and library services. *Children and Libraries, 13*(3), 7–11.

Institute of Museum and Library Services. (2016, July). *Supplementary Tables: Public Libraries Survey Fiscal Year 2014.* https://www.imls.gov/sites/default/files/fy2014_pls_tables.pdf.

Jenkins, C. (2000, Winter). The history of youth services librarianship: A review of the research literature. *Libraries and Culture, 35,* 103–140.

Kaser, G. (2015, January 26). Ten things a children's librarian needs to know. *Public Libraries Online.* http://publiclibrariesonline.org/2015/01/ten-things-a-childrens-librarian-needs-to-know/.

King, D. L. (2015). Social media teams. *Library Technology Reports 51*(1): 22–25.

Koester, A., & Lonial, A. (2015). About race: A community event shifts from celebrating diversity to discussing race. *School Library Journal. 61*(6), 34-36.

Landgraf, G. (2015). Libraries explore a variety of mobile options. *American Libraries, 46*(1/2), 14–15.

Lankes, R. D. (2011). *The Atlas of New Librarianship.* Cambridge, MA: MIT Press.

Larson, J. (2015). *Children's services today: A practical guide for librarians.* Lanham, MD: Rowman & Littlefield.

Lenhart, A. (2015). *Teens, social media, and technology overview 2015.* Pew Research Center. www.pewinternet.org/2015/04/09/teens-social-media-technology-2015/.

Long, A. K., & McCook, K. P. (2011). Youth services. In McCook, K. P. (Ed.), *Introduction to public librarianship,* 2nd. ed., (pp. 241-281). New York, NY: Neal Schuman.

Luo, L., & Weak, E. (2013). Text reference services: Teens' perception and use. *Library and Information Science Research, 35*(1), 14-23. doi:10.1016/j.lisr.2012.03.002.

McDowell, K. (2009). Surveying the field: The research model of women in librarianship, 1882–1898. *The Library Quarterly, 79*(3): 279-300.

Meyers, E. (2001, February). The road to coolness: Youth rock the public library. *American Libraries, 32,* 46–48.

Miller, M. L. (2003). Public library service to children. In *Encyclopedia of Library and Information Science* (pp. 2397-2407). New York, NY: Marcel Dekker.

Mills, J. E., Romeijn-Stout, E., Campbell, C., & Koester, A. (2015). Results from the young children, new media, and libraries survey. *Children and Libraries, 13*(2), 26–35.

Montiel-Overall, P., Nuñez, A. V., & Reyes-Escudero, V. (2016). *Latinos in libraries, museums, and archives: Cultural competence in action! An asset-based approach.* Lanham, MD: Rowman & Littlefield.

Morehart, P. (2015). From the past, the future. *American Libraries, 46*(9–10), 40–47.

Munguia, N. G. (2015, August 11). YALSA announces Badges for Learning continuing education offering. www.ala.org/news/press-releases/2015/08/yalsa-announces-badges-learning-continuing-education-offering.

Naidoo, J. C. (2014). *Diversity programming for digital youth.* Santa Barbara, CA: Libraries Unlimited.

Naidoo, J. C., & Dahlen, S. Park. (2013). *Diversity in youth literature: Opening doors through reading.* Chicago, IL: American Library Association.

National Center for Education Statistics. (1988). *Services and resources for young adults in public libraries.* Washington, DC: U.S. Government Printing Office.

National Reading Panel. (2000). *Report of the national reading panel: Teaching children to read: An evidence-based assessment of the scientific research literature on reading and its implications for reading instruction.* Washington, DC: National Institute of Child Health and Human Development, National Institutes of Health.

Output measures for Public Libraries. (1987). https://books.google.com/books/about/Output_Measures_for_Public_Libraries.html?id=lLjgAAAAMAAJ.

Palfrey, J. (2010). *Born digital: Understanding the first generation of digital natives.* Philadelphia, PA: Basic Books.

Parrott, K., & Gattullo, E. (2013). Throwing Dewey overboard. *Children and Libraries, 11*(3), 3–33.

Peet, L., & Vercelletto, C. (2016). ESSA signed into law. *Library Journal, 141*(1), 12–14.

Prime Time, Inc. (2016). About us. www.primetimefamily.org/about-us/.

Public Library Association. (2016). *Webinar: Project Outcome: An Integral Part of the Planning Process.* www.ala.org/pla/onlinelearning/webinars/archive/projectoutcomeplanning.

Robinson, 2015, personal communication. Megan Robinson, a youth services librarian in Manatee County, Florida.

Rollock, B. T. (1988). *Public library services for children.* Hamden, CT: Shoe String Press.

Scales, P. (2015). It's about choice. *School Library Journal, 61*(8), 12.

Spina, C. (2016, July 12). Pokémon GO: What do librarians need to know? *School Library Journal.* www.slj.com/2016/07/technology/applications/pokemon-go-what-do-librarians-need-toknow/.

Strock, A. L. (2014, Fall). Reaching beyond library walls: Strengthening services and opportunities through partnerships and collaboration. *Young Adult Library Services,* 15–17.

Thompson, S. B. (2013). Don't forget the tweens. *Public Libraries, 52*(6), 29–30.

U.S. Department of Education, National Center for Education Statistics. (2014). *Parent and family involvement in education: National Household Education Surveys Program.* https://nces.ed.gov/programs/digest/d13/tables/dt13_206.10.asp?current=yes.

U.S. National Center for Education Statistics. (1988). *Services and resources for young adults in public libraries.* Washington, DC: U.S. Government Printing Office.

Urban Libraries Council. *Public libraries and effective summer learning: Opportunities for assessment.* www.urbanlibraries.org/filebin/documents/Public_Libraries_and_Effective_Summer_Learning_web.pdf.

Walter, F. K. (1941, July/August). A poor but respectable relation—The Sunday school library. *Library Quarterly, 12,* 734.

Walter, V. A. (1995). *Output measures and more: Planning and evaluating public library services for young adults.* Chicago, IL: American Library Association.

Walter, V. A. (2001). *Children and libraries: Getting it right.* Chicago, IL: American Library Association.

Walter, V. A. (2010). *Twenty-first century kids, twenty-first century librarians.* Chicago, IL: American Library Association.

Walter, V. A. (2014). Who will serve the children?: Recruiting and educating future children's librarians. *IFLA Journal, 40*(1), 24–29. doi: 10.1177/0340035214522110.

Walter, V. A., & Meyers, E. (2003). *Teens and libraries: Getting it right.* Chicago, IL: American Library Association.

Woolls, B. (2001, Spring). Public library-school library cooperation: A view from the past with a predictor for the future. *Journal of Youth Services in Libraries, 14,* 8–10.

Young Adult Library Services Association. (2010). *YALSA's competencies for librarians serving youth: Young adults deserve the best.* Chicago, IL: American Library Association. www.ala.org/ala/mgrps/divs/yalsa/profdev/yadeservethebest_201.pdf.

CHAPTER 9

Reader and Adult Services

To Survive, to Flourish, to Create*

Kathleen de la Peña McCook and Katharine Phenix

American public libraries were established in the mid-nineteenth century to provide opportunity for continuing education and access to resources that individuals could not afford. As we have seen from the founding documents of the Boston Public Library, the collection was intended for adults who had left school to have access to works of general culture or research into any branch of useful knowledge (Boston Public Library, 1852, p. 8). A century later this concept had become internalized by Americans as a "library faith" that the public library made a difference in peoples' lives and supported the democratic process (Garceau, 1949).

On the eve of the new millennium, the American Library Association adopted the statement "Libraries: An American Value," which declared: "Free access to the books, ideas, resources, and information in America's libraries is imperative for education, employment, enjoyment, and self-government" (1999). The value of public libraries today is measured by many services beyond distribution of print materials. The authors of *Libraries, Human Rights, and Social Justice,* consider that library *services* make libraries "utterly unique and irreplaceable in their communities" (Jaeger, Taylor, & Gorham, 2015, p. 52).

Why do public libraries provide such a variety of services to adults today? What is the philosophy that informs the collections, programs, and one-to-one assistance that comprises the work of public librarians for adults in the twenty-first century? There is a growing recognition of the importance of developing human capabilities. Human development—or the human development approach—is about expanding the richness of human life, rather than simply the richness of the economy in which human beings live (UN Human Devel-

* This is a difficult set of services to characterize as the national association that addresses them has changed direction and focus over the years. The Reference and User Services Association (RUSA) of the American Library Association is the current Division focused on services to adults and evolved from the merger of the Reference and Adult Services Divisions. RUSA is a member community engaged in advancing the practices of connecting people to resources, information services, and collections as stated in the 2015 *New Strategic Plan for RUSA. Reference and User Services Quarterly, 55*(1), 9–10. See also the RUSA website: www.ala.org/rusa/sites/ala.org.rusa/files/content/about/rusa-strategic-plan.pdf.

opment Reports Office). All people deserve autonomy, agency, and dignity. Recent research in the economics of human development contributes to capability theory by showing how internal capabilities—skills—are formed and how they can be measured (Heckman, 2015, 2016). Public libraries are positioned by history and conviction to provide resources and services that promote human capabilities.

Public libraries are a key societal instrument in helping adults survive, flourish, and create. This chapter reviews the evolution of adult services from provision of collections to lifelong learning to realization of human capabilities. The lens of human capabilities, notably defined and explored by Frances Stewart (2013) and Martha Nussbaum (2011, 2016), allows us to grant public libraries centrality in the goal of a human-development approach to social institutions. As the human-capabilities paradigm has become accepted by educators and librarians, the rationale for expanding types of service provision has a greater basis in human development. This is an approach focused on people and their opportunities and choices (UN Human Development Report). It is an approach that helps us understand that adult services in public libraries are as expansive as astronomy night in the library parking lot, as personal as a sewing class, as compassionate as helping the homeless, or as true as recommending *The Everglades: River of Grass* to a conservationist club in south Florida.[1]

Adult use of the public library still primarily comprises the circulation of books in a variety of formats—what librarians have named, and in some cases still call "readers services."[2] Libraries offer many varied programs and services, but the most important activity of a public library for adults remains, as of the time of this writing, inclusive provision of books and other media for reading, listening, and viewing (IMLS, 2016, p. 13; Swan et al., 2014, pp. 19–20).

Lifelong learning, digital inclusion, and the variety of programs that comprise broad adult services are also important to the public library mission. These include access to computers, Wi-Fi, and makerspaces; financial and health literacy programs; job and career programs; guidance in applying for government assistance programs such as Medicare and insurance subsidies; and cultural programs. In this chapter, we primarily address reader services and lifelong learning as adult services. We then identify other services for adults, which will vary from library to library. Throughout we have tried to provide a geographical variety of sources with documentation.

INCLUSION AND ACCESSIBILITY

We begin this chapter by stating that inclusion, accessibility, diversity, civil rights, justice, and equity must underlie all program development. Libraries operate within a tripartite model of access: physical, intellectual, and social (Jaeger, Taylor, & Gorham, 2015). Library users have a range of abilities and characteristics that may preclude access, including language barriers, vision impairment, neurodiversity, and mobility. In *Creating Inclusive Library Environments: A Planning Guide for Serving Patrons with Disabilities,* Kowalsky and Woodruff (2017) highlight ways that libraries can provide barrier-free access. Digital inclusion also offers critical new challenges to equitable public service (Thompson, Jaeger, Taylor, Subramaniam, & Bertot, 2014).

The reason why this is so important is because people do not always have equal access to good schools, computer training, or books. People come from different backgrounds, and they do not always experience a welcoming environment in the world. The library should be a place that welcomes everyone, and that begins with the staff who design spaces, build collections, and create services. The work of the American Library Association Office for Diversity, Literacy and Outreach Services supports equity and inclusion as fundamental values of the association, and its work should inform service.[3]

Jennifer Hoyer (2013, p. 60) states, "libraries that reach out to socially excluded members of their community are stronger for it as they embrace a greater part of their mandate to provide information access." In *Public Libraries and Social Justice* (2010), John Pateman and John Vincent make a strong argument that libraries should address the gap between rich and poor. In 2015, an Anythinker named Hannah Martinez won the Lucy Schweers Award for Excellence in Paralibrarianship for her Any Ability program, which serves adults with disabilities ("Anythink Staff Member Wins," 2015). Inclusion means affirming the "Prisoners' Right to Read" (ALA, 2014) for incarcerated people who are residents of public library service areas (Drabinski & Rabina, 2015), and remembering the needs of families of people in correctional facilities. It also means addressing the needs of the poor and homeless (Miller, 2015; Gehner, 2010; Holt & Holt, 2010).

> **▶ FACT**
>
> Adults mainly use the public library to borrow books—over *two billion* books each year.* Bob Holley of Wayne State University believes people come to libraries for fun "stuff" to read or view and that the importance of pleasure reading for public library users is one of the main reasons libraries will survive (Holley, 2015/2016).*
>
> ---
>
> *See ALA Fact Sheet (2015). Public library use. www.ala.org/tools/libfactsheets/alalibraryfactsheet06#usagelibs. We refer to books regardless of format or means of access, which includes printed books, audiobooks, e-books either circulated as physical items or downloads. For detailed discussion on Work, Expression, Manifestation, and Item (WEMI) see Tillett (2003), Koster (2009), FictionFinder (2009), and FictionFinder (n.d.), Note that the 2016 and 2017 *Library Journal* Star libraries will measure both virtual circulation and Wi-Fi use.

READER SERVICES

> We read in slow, long motions, as if drifting in space, weightless. We read full of prejudice, malignantly. We read generously, making excuses for the text, filling gaps, mending faults. And sometimes, when the stars are kind, we read with an intake of breath, with a shudder, as if someone or something had "walked over our grave," as if a memory had suddenly been rescued from a place deep within us—the recognition of something we never knew was there, or of something we vaguely felt as a flicker or a shadow, whose ghostly form rises and passes back into us before we can see what it is, leaving us older and wiser.
>
> **—Manguel, 1996, p. 303**

Providing materials for reading, viewing, and listening for pleasure is a central focus for public libraries. Acquiring, organizing, and making current collections available in multiple formats (e.g., print, large-print, ebooks, and audiobooks) is a primary function of the twenty-first-century public library,[4] so librarians should be aware of and understand the role of reading in the lives of library users (Rolstad & McCook, 1993). Duncan Smith, founder of NoveList, observed that patrons "know that reading—including leisure reading—is an important and essential part of their personal and their community's inspiration infrastructure. For a majority of our regular and long-term users, it is the primary reason they use and value their library" (Smith, 2015).[5]

That All May Read: National Library Service for the Blind and Physically Handicapped

It is essential that public librarians act as advocates for readers with different vision and physical abilities. The 2017 publication of *Revised Standards and Guidelines of Service for Library of Congress Network of Libraries for the Blind and Physically Handicapped* included the work of many librarians. These guidelines provide appropriate service standards for the development and deployment of LC/NLS network library services and activities, including direct patron services, collection development and management, outreach efforts, and the production of local materials (Association of Specialized and Cooperative Library Agencies, 2017). These should be kept in mind by every public librarian every day to ensure that patrons in need are connected to the library. The free library service was established by the Pratt-Smoot Act in 1931 to provide blind adults with books in an embossed format; amended in 1934 to include sound recordings (talking books); and expanded in 1952 to include children, in 1962 to provide music materials, and again in 1966 to include individuals with physical limitations that prevent the reading of regular print.

The American Library Association Forum for Library Services to Individuals with Physical, Learning, Social, Cognitive and Health Disabilities seeks to inform library staff about the information, communication, technology, and format needs of people with these types of disabilities and how to meet them through programs, guidelines, and the Internet (ASCLA, PLuSCH Forum, n.d.).

Barbara Mates, former head of the Ohio Library for the Blind and Physically Disabled, has produced a guide, *Assistive Technologies in the Library,* to help librarians serve all patrons using assistive technologies (Mates & Reed, 2011). The intersection of disability, accessibility, inclusion, and libraries for equitable library service is the topic of the 2015 publication, *Accessibility for Persons with Disabilities and the Inclusive Future of Libraries* (Wentz et al., 2015). As librarians plan and develop reader services the needs of all patrons should always be considered.

Key Works in Reading History

The history of recreational reading has been addressed by Esther Carrier in *Fiction in Public Libraries, 1876–1900* (1965) and *Fiction in Public Libraries, 1900–1950* (1985). She provides a comprehensive analysis of the historical debate between adherents of "quality" fiction and those who felt that fiction of all types should be included in collections. Librarians responsible for collection development and readers' advisory services are most effective when they understand the history and sociology of reading and its role in the lives of library users. Karetzky's (1982) summary of the history of reading research provides an intellectual guide to the work of early reading theorists. Knowledge of the investigations of reading provides an intellectual basis for public library collection development.

Milestone works on the sociology of reading include *Reading Interests and Habits of Adults* (Gray & Munroe, 1929); *What People Want to Read About* (Waples & Tyler, 1931);

Living with Books (Haines, 1935); *The Geography of Reading* (Wilson, 1938); *Lost in a Book: The Psychology of Reading for Pleasure* (Nell, 1988); *Readers, Reading, and Librarians* (Katz, 2001); and *Reading Matters: What the Research Reveals about Reading, Libraries and Community* (Ross, 2006). Several recent works illustrate the persistence of reading as an essential aspect of the creative lives of adults. These works examine reading and the meaning of reading.

- *Book Reading* (Perrin, 2016)
- *Browsings: A Year of Reading, Collecting, and Living with Books* (Dirda, 2015)
- *Libraries and the Reading Public in Twentieth-Century America* (Pawley & Robbins, 2013)
- *Main Street Public Library* (Wiegand, 2011)
- *A Few Good Books* (Maatta, 2010)
- *A Reader on Reading* (Manguel, 2010)

These works can help reader services librarians understand their patrons and build collections that respond to the entire community of readers. Librarians who know the history of reading and reading cultures, and who try to strike a balance between collections comprised of popular books, classic books, and meaningful books that lead to introspection and understanding serve their readers well.

The shaping of collections that will cause the intake of breath and rescued memory, is a trust that the public grants librarians. Librarians have struggled with the role that they should play in selection for years. In 1953, Lester Asheim's classic "Not Censorship but Selection" expressed this tension. In the early 1990s, many professionals essentially abdicated the responsibility of book selection in favor of a "Give 'Em What They Want" philosophy (Rawlinson, 1990). Sarah Ann Long, an ALA President, (2001, p. viii) noted, "We were fitting in with a tide of stylish opinion that was sweeping the country that was both anti-intellectual and antiauthority." The public, though, has shown an appreciation for some clarity in book selection, as expressed by Vivian Gornick: "I cannot help thinking, 50 years ago in the Bronx, if the library had responded to my needs instead of shaping my needs, what sort of reader would I have become?" (1998, p. 40). Today, many librarians have adopted demand-driven acquisition (DDA) or patron-driven acquisition (PDA), which focuses on providing library materials at a user's point of need. Approval plans attempt to help the library collect everything that might be desired in the future. DDA is the standard method of just-in-time library collecting, whereas approval plans are a prime example of just-in-case collecting (Arndt, 2015; Roll, 2016).

Librarians will likely always struggle with selection because they have limited funds. The main thing to remember is that all of our patrons have a right to be not only educated, but also entertained by reading materials, on their own terms. Catherine Ross has created two models of leisure reading in public libraries: "Reading with a Purpose" and "Only the Best" (2009). The impact of reading on readers is also discussed by Ross in *The Pleasures of Reading* (2014).

Circulation

Circulation of books is the oldest public library service. The management of the collection has changed over the years, in line with philosophy of librarians regarding reading, and technologies to enhance library services. The earliest concerns were registering borrowers, lost cards, handling late books, establishing reserves, conduct at the circulation desk, book drop problems and the personality of circulation librarians (Flexner, 1927).[6] New media formats, as they began to be purchased such as vinyl recordings, films, video tapes, audio tapes, CD-ROMS, and DVDs dictated a need for new procedures for their storage and circulation.

New services such as reciprocal borrowing between and among public, academic, and special libraries gave librarians more flexibility in collection development. For instance, the cutting-edge Illinois Regional Library Council allowed borrowing among multiple jurisdictions (Hamilton & Brown, 1973). Interlibrary loan was facilitated through union catalogs. Public libraries were early adopters of fax and photocopiers to share periodical articles. Through the history of librarianship, articles about format challenges that demonstrate the adaptability of librarians to changing patron needs have been published. Today, floating collections (Johal, 2012) and self-check-out have changed the way libraries provide materials. Ayre (2015) explained:

> In our remodeled library, we've added several self-check-out units and 90% of all checkouts are happening at those units. Instead of dropping material into outside, stand-alone book drops (with decidedly un-ergonomic bins inside), we've provided a drive-up return that is part of an automated materials handling (AMH) system that immediately checks-in and rough sorts all returns.

When librarians adopt new technologies and services, though, they should look at any possible drawbacks. Patron-driven self-hold systems allow patrons to request materials, pick them up, and check them out of the library without assistance by staff members. Though convenient, this may violate patron privacy (Stevens, Bravender, & Witteveen-Lane, 2012; Perez, 2011).

> ▶ **FACT**
>
> In 2016, 30 stand-alone public library systems and 19 library consortia in the United States set a new record for lending more than one million digital books. (OverDrive, 2017).

Digital delivery of e-books and streaming services are growing segments of public library circulation (Expanding Access, 2012; Scardilli, 2014). The vendor OverDrive, working with libraries, lends e-books, audiobooks, streaming video and periodicals to users, hosts and manages the digital library, helps libraries build collections, and provides tools to measure circulation.[7] Although these collections appear to be an important part of library services, Sendze (2012) points out that libraries pay hundreds of thousands of dollars to license books from a vendor—but do not own any of it.

Other sources of digital services are Midwest Tap's Hoopla, which offers digital music, movies, audiobooks, e-books, and comics for loan; Total BooX, an iPad, iPhone and Android app for books; the 3M Cloud Library; and Kanopy, a collection of films, documentaries and more. Music from Freegal can be downloaded from many public libraries as well.

Because libraries are purchasing materials (especially online materials) from so many different sources, it is crucial that they do not bury them under multiple locations within the library's website. The website can either help or hinder locating materials. Librarians should focus on a clean and easily navigable website design to ensure that their own public interface is not a barrier to use.[8] Discovery products will also help patrons find materials. Library catalogs (or OPACs) search the physical collection of the library. Discovery systems (or next-generation catalogs) overlay and are able to search the entirety of the library collection, including the physical collection, databases, and other digital materials, thus increasing exposure of items in the collection that one would have to log in to through a separate interface (Discovery Product Functionality, 2014).

From the days of rubber date stamps to today's digital delivery, librarians have demonstrated creativity and flexibility when developing the circulation function. Safeguarding privacy, maintaining equity of access for people with different abilities, and supporting discovery of a rich reading, viewing, and listening collection remain essential library functions.

> **▶ FACT**
>
> Nearly four in ten Americans read print books exclusively; just 6% are digital-only book readers (Perrin, 2016).

Readers' Advisory Services

Readers' Advisory (RA) services, comprehensively described by Flexner (1941) at the New York Public Library, waned after World War II as librarians focused resources on information services (Dilevko & Magowan, 2007). But when the Internet changed the face of reference services in the late twentieth century, RA services rebounded. This growth was in large part due to the publication of Saricks and Brown's *Readers' Advisory Service in the Public Library* (1989). According to Wyatt (2014), this book:

> shifted the ways librarians were suggesting books from a haphazard approach based on a book's general popularity and on the readers' advisor's own personal preferences to a systematic and tested framework focused on patron preferences. Moreover, in an era when reference services and processes were given significant attention and care, Saricks and Brown provided librarians with a well-developed process for RA that could make an equal claim to professionalism. Their work was also an early and crucial step in convincing librarians that they not only could offer RA service but that they should do so. (p. 29)

The book signaled that the provision of such service was important—just as important as providing reference assistance.

There is a wide range of widely known popular sources as well as more specialized resources for RA. Some of the resources that support readers' advisory service include:

- guides such as *The Readers' Advisory Guide to Historical Fiction* (Baker & Klaassen, 2015) and *The Readers' Advisory Guide to Genre Blends* (McArdle, 2015)[9]
- the Read On . . . series from Libraries Unlimited (2006–)[10]
- the Genreflecting series (Libraries Unlimited)[11]
- NoveList, a package of products that helps libraries connect with readers (https://www.ebscohost.com/novelist), including NextReads, a book suggestion tool (https://www.ebscohost.com/novelist/our-products/nextreads)
- Fiction_L, an electronic mailing list devoted to readers' advisory topics such as book discussions, booktalks, collection development issues, booklists, and bibliographies, and a wide variety of other topics of interest to librarians, book discussion leaders, and others with an interest in readers' advisory[12]
- Whichbook (www.openingthebook.com/whichbook), a product that enables millions of combinations of factors and then suggests books which most closely match reader needs
- Bookbrowse.com[13]

- the What's Next: Books in Series Database from Michigan's Kent District Library (www2.kdl.org/libcat/whatsnext.asp)
- EarlyWord, News for Collection Development and Readers Advisory Librarians (www.earlyword.com).
- LibraryReads, a monthly list of the top 10 books selected by public library workers (http://libraryreads.org)
- websites such as Stop You're Killing Me (www.stopyourekillingme.com/)
- social networking platforms like LibraryThing (www.librarything.com) and GoodReads (https://www.goodreads.com/), both of which are owned wholly or partially by Amazon
- state and local groups such as the Maryland Readers' Advisory Interest Group, Adult Reading RoundTable (Chicago Area); Seattle Public Library blog, Shelf Talk; and Jefferson-Madison Regional Library (Charlottesville, Virginia) Reader's Corner.[14]

Burke and Strothmann's 2015 study aimed to discover how the library website might facilitate RA. They found that including RA forms on the website is an effective outreach tool, and can help connect readers to books and promote the library's collections. They also found that the OPAC (online public access catalog) is not only a door to the collection, but also used to look for reviews, read-alikes, and links to Novelist or Goodreads.

Readers' Advisory is an important service, but the RUSA CODES CONVO (October 2016) revealed that some librarians did not feel prepared to provide thoughtful, whole-library based readers' advisory. The advice they gave each other was to listen, listen, listen. Some even said, in the spirit of community connection and human kindness, that the actual book recommendation is less important than the conversation, because that person will come back for more conversation.[15]

Another movement in the library sphere is to make the materials in the library more visible on the Internet. To this end, Zepheira (2014) brings to light "dark library content" via the 2014 LibHub Initiative, which pledges "I believe the visibility of libraries and their collections enriches the Web's resources and enhances the experience of those served by access to quality content." Anythink Libraries was one of 12 libraries experimenting with using new, linking format of coding which would make library content available directly on the Web. Colorado, Anythink (a revolution of Rangeview Libraries) partners with Zepheira as founding partner of the LibHub Initiative.[16]

Book Groups

Book groups and book clubs account for millions of sales of books per year. Libraries not only sponsor book groups, but provide book-group resources (Wu, 2011). Book groups are a long-standing phenomenon of American cultural life that now take place in both real space and cyberspace (Fuller & Rehberg, 2013). Some sources that will help librarians organize or facilitate book groups include:

- *Reading Group Guides,* an online community for reading groups at the Book Report Network website, provides over 4,000 reading guides for discussion. Reading Group Choices selects discussible books and suggests discussion topics for reading groups. It produces a printed guide distributed nationally to libraries, reading groups, book stores, community book festivals, and individuals.

- *The Facilitator's Handy List of Ground Rules, Guidelines and Everything Else* (https://www.kclibrary.org/book-clubs/guidelines), by Kaite Mediatore Stover, Director of Reader's Services at the Kansas City Public Library. She has suggestions for before, during, and after book group discussions, complete with a list of 22 general discussion questions and 7 more for discussing books no one in the group likes.
- The Women's National Book Association sponsors National Reading Group Month for "Celebrating the Joy of Shared Reading." ALA's *Booklist* partners with them yearly to publish the annual selection of great group reads.[17]
- The web-based *Goodreads* lists over 7,000 online book clubs for book lovers of almost any imaginable genre. For example, there are 339 members of the dystopian book club; 7,326 members in the paranormal club, and 347 in the urban fantasy group. Many librarians are active on Goodreads—for their own reading pleasure, to keep up with the latest book trends, and also to connect with readers.

Nancy Pearl,[18] author of *Book Lust: Recommended Reading for Every Mood, Moment, and Reason; Book Lust to Go: Recommended Reading for Travelers, Vagabonds, and Dreamers; More Book Lust; Book Crush: For Kids and Teens*, provides a list of "Book Group Do's" on her website. She emphasizes that it is important to enjoy the experience of reading new books and discussing them and for group leaders to guide the discussion and handle difficult members (www.nancypearl.com). One excellent example of library support of book groups is Novel Conversations: Think, Read Talk, a collaboration of the Indiana Humanities Council and libraries in the state.[19]

Many libraries organize summer reading clubs for adults as well as those for children and young adults. Parents can sign up for summer reading along with their children, which is an excellent opportunity to market the library's reading clubs. Saricks (2015) also discusses how to choose which books will be read by a club. The Collaborative Summer Library Program (CSLP) established in Minnesota in 1987, offers a model for sharing artwork, themes, and incentives that other libraries have borrowed (www.cslpreads.org/about/).

The 2017 theme from the CLSP is *Build a Better World/Construye un mundo major;* 2018's is *Music,* and 2019's is *Space.* The website (www. cslpreads.org/about/) includes sample programs for all age groups, as well as a list of diversity resources for inclusive programming for people with autism, hearing, vision, or mobility disabilities, learning or emotional disabilities, as well as people living in poverty, in alterative families, or people who speak a language other than English.

And, of course, Oprah's Book Club revolutionized reading by organizing national conversation about serious books (Rooney, 2005.) In *Reading Oprah,* Farr describes how Oprah trusted readers to take on formidable titles and read them with a growing confidence and skill. "Then, they would talk about them, giving them a life beyond the reader and text" (Farr 2004).

▶ TASK

Visit your local library's catalog. Search for a current popular title (go to the best-seller lists if you do not read popular books). How many formats is the book available in? Does the interface include ratings and book discussion from other users? How does the library's website help you find books that you like?

Mass Readings Events

The *One Book, One Community Planning Guide* is a key resource developed for librarians building community-wide reading programs. Mass Reading Events are evidence of a robust book culture. In *Reading Beyond the Book: The Social Practices of Contemporary Literary Culture,* we are presented with an exploration of social practices inspired by the sharing of books in public spaces (Fuller & Rehberg, 2013). The One Book, One Community (OBOC) model that grew out of the 1998 Seattle-based program initiated by Nancy Pearl represents an intersection of traditional forms of reading and reading practices with the communication technologies of the twenty-first century that promote shared reading on a wide scale, (Harder, Howard, & Sedo, 2015). Some libraries focus on local authors and history. Many have author presentations, film screenings, and other events to bring the community together and create a shared experience of literature.

Promoting Books and Reading

Librarians promote books and reading in their community in a variety of ways. There are author programs, such as the Eagle Valley Library District (CO) Local Author Expo and Notable Books Programs at the Sacramento Public Library.[20] Some librarians use social networking sites like Pinterest to inspire others with their creative book displays (see the Watertown [WI] Public Library's pins for inspiration).[21] Creative displays can have significant impact on circulation. Anythink Libraries' *Visual Merchandising Guidelines* provide ideas and innovative methods to put the collection forward. Though these take extra effort, rewards can be enormous. When Anythink implemented a display-driven rebranding in 2009, it nearly doubled its circulation from just under 700,000 in 2008 to more than 1.3 million in 2012 (Vinjamuri, 2015).

Excitement around an author reading deepens experiences of books for readers (Peet, 2015b). Hooper's (2016) *Librarian's Guide to Book Programs and Author Events* provides suggestions for programming that target book lovers and includes interviews from librarians in the field. He uses book group discussion questions compiled by Katharine Phenix during her time as chair of the Notable Books Council in 2014 (Hooper, p. 63). Booktalks are another way to enhance interest in specific books (Booktalking; http://nancykeane.com/booktalks/). The 2016 Delaware Humanities Forum, in collaboration with the Dover Public Library, commemorated the centennial of the Pulitzer Prizes with a series of reading and discussion sessions and writing workshops.[22] Anythink Libraries (Rangeview, CO), along with five other Colorado libraries, hosted another Pulitzer centennial supported by the Colorado Humanities Council entitled "The American West as Living Space."

The Center for the Book at the Library of Congress fosters a national appreciation and love of reading. It was established in 1977 under the aegis of then Librarian of Congress Daniel J. Boorstin, who saw great value in the Library of Congress actively promoting books and reading. The Center invites people of all ages to discover the fascinating people, places, and events that await you whenever you read.[23] Its website Read.Gov provides resources about state centers for the book, state book festivals, and literary awards. For further reading, look to the 2010 special issue of *Libraries and the Cultural Record:* "John Y. Cole: Librarian, Bookman, and Scholar," which is dedicated to the director of the Center for the Book (Maack, 2010).

State Center Affiliates for the Book, usually located at state libraries, develop activities that promote each state's book culture and literary heritage. For instance, the Michigan Center for the book, located at the State Library of Michigan, aims to generate interest in the state's books and authors with lists of books. The Nebraska Book Festival, sponsored by the Nebraska Center for the Book, is supported by the Nebraska Library Commission.

Book festivals at the national, state, and local level attract thousands of people celebrating reading. First Lady Laura Bush (2001–2009)[24] worked with the Library of Congress to begin the Washington, DC, National Book Festival in 2001 (Kniffel, 2001; 2008). President and First Lady Michelle Obama were honorary cochairs from 2008 to 2016.[25]

Listening to Books and Viewing Videos

Former first lady Laura Bush speaks at the 2010 National Book Festival.

Photo by Barry Wheeler, Library of Congress.

Technology not only promotes books, but offers an alternate form of reading. Audiobooks make up a growing portion of library circulation, and librarians have created listening lists similar to recommended reading lists (Saricks, 2011). Audiobooks (and listening groups) can offer an excellent means of connecting to literature for people who are unable to read for any reason (Morgan, 2014; Lundh & Johnson, 2015).

The Listen List: Outstanding Audiobook Narration seeks to highlight outstanding audiobook titles that merit special attention by general adult listeners and the librarians who work with them. The list of winning titles is produced by the Listen List Council of RUSA CODES. The Listen List is annotated to stress the appealing elements of the title, and includes listen-alikes to guide listeners to additional audio experiences.

The ALA Video Round Table (VRT) was founded in 1988 (as the ALA Video Interest Group) to provide "a unified voice for video advocacy in the areas of legislation, professional guidelines for collections today, such as those related to streaming and digital media, and other issues." The VRT honors Notable Videos for Adults each year—not feature films, but videos of a performance, an educational title, or a how-to, geared toward an adult audience.

Streaming videos are available through Hoopla, OverDrive, and other vendors (Ennis, 2013). Duncan and Peterson's *Creating a Streaming Video Collection for Your Library* (2014) offers advice to librarians who want to establish a streaming video collection using vendor licensing and fair use guidelines.

Books Honored by Librarians

Librarians are extraordinarily active on local, state, national, and international book award committees, devoting countless hours to reading and discussing new books. This engagement infuses and enriches their daily work. For over 60 years, the Notable Books Council of the Reference and User Services Association (RUSA) of ALA has produced an annual list of recommended books. The Andrew Carnegie Medals for Excellence in Fiction and Nonfiction, selected in cooperation with ALA *Booklis*t staff, a bookstore owner, and a member of the RUSA committee, are chosen from a long and short list to recognize the single best fiction and nonfiction books each year for adult readers. The Reading List Council of RUSA produces the Reading List, an annual best-of list composed of eight different fiction genres for adult readers: Adrenaline, Fantasy, Historical Fiction, Horror, Mystery, Romance, Science Fiction, and Women's Fiction. The Sophie and Arthur Brody Foundation sponsors The Sophie Brody Medal, which honors the U.S. author of the most distinguished contribution to Jewish literature (fiction and/or nonfiction) for adults published in the United States in the preceding year, as well as the Sophie Brody Award for Jewish literature.

Other national librarian recognition of books includes the Asian Pacific American Librarians Association Literature Awards; the Black Caucus of the American Library Association Literary Award; the Chinese American Library Association Best Book Award; and the Stonewall Book Awards given by the Gay, Lesbian, Bisexual, and Transgender Round Table of ALA.[26]

Many state library associations also give literary awards. These are usually awarded to authors residing in the state; for instance, the Alabama Author Awards are awarded by the Alabama Library Association.[27] The Idaho Library Association gives the Idaho Book Award to encourage the writing and publishing of books about Idaho by Idahoans.[28] The Wisconsin Library Association Literary Award must be written by a person who was born in Wisconsin, or is currently living in Wisconsin, or lived in Wisconsin for a significant length of time.

One of our favorite awards is the International Dublin Literary Award. At €100,000, it is one of the richest literary prizes in the world. Books are nominated by invited public libraries in cities throughout the world—making the award unique in its coverage of international fiction. Titles are nominated on the basis of "high literary merit" as determined by the nominating library. In 2017 the winner was José Eduardo Agualusa for *A General Theory of Oblivion* (Dublin Award, 2017).

Lifelong Learning as an Enduring Reason for Library Growth

> If there's anything we're trying to do in this library and the library world, it is to build a learning culture . . . the most important thing is . . . the creation of an imaginative world for children and . . . adults that opens their minds to the world.
>
> **—Crosby Kemper, Kansas City Public Library (IMLS Focus, 2015)**

Creating a Nation of Learners is the title of the current strategic plan of the IMLS.[29] "Learning in Libraries," a 2015 forum convened by IMLS, explored participatory learning and opportunities for libraries to be agents of workforce development with passage of the Workforce Innovation and Opportunity Act of 2014 (IMLS Focus). This is a twenty-first-century continuation of the struggle between progressive and neoliberal theories of lifelong learning. The American Library Association has identified lifelong learning as one of the core values on which librarianship rests (ALA, Core Values, 2004). In assessing this core value, Elmborg noted that "Lifelong Learning as an ALA Core Value means something different depending on whether we see it through the lens of administrative progressivism or progressive pedagogy" (2016, p. 554).

Since public libraries were first established, many provided support to adults seeking self-education. However, tensions were felt throughout the twentieth century between librarians who thought that libraries should focus on collection development and those who felt that educational services were also important. The conflict is evident in the ALA presidential addresses of Hiller C. Wellman (1915), and Walter L. Brown (1917), who took different approaches to the public library responsibility for adult education.

Much of the justification throughout the 1920s and 1930s for the establishment of library service came from a desire for adult education, which might include basic literacy, education for specific individual goals, or general education. In his history of the adult-education movement in the United States, Knowles (1977, p. 115) observed that by the 1920s, "the library moved from a custodial function to educational."

Publication of Learned's *The American Public Library and the Diffusion of Knowledge* (1924) underscored the public library's growing acceptance of adult education as an important aspect of its mission.[30] Adult services scholar Margaret E. Monroe (1963) characterized Learned's book as "a perceptive synthesis and orderly summation of significant services already envisioned and initiated in public libraries" (p. 29).

The American Public Library and the Diffusion of Knowledge also provided the intellectual justification for ALA to take action by forming the Commission on the Library and Adult Education. The Commission's report, *Libraries and Adult Education* (1926), studied the role of adult education and became the foundation of the subsequent expansion of adult services in public libraries. ALA then established a Board on Library and Adult Education, which reported activities in the journal *Adult Education and the Library* (1924-1930) and later the *ALA Bulletin.* These included research, the Reading with a Purpose Project, and ongoing work with the American Association for Adult Education (Coleman, 2008, p. 124). Elmborg (2016) has observed that at this time other entities were concerned with lifelong learning including the Settlement House movement, the Granges, and Melvil Dewey's idea of "home education" as supported by libraries (p. 539).

John Chancellor was appointed to ALA headquarters staff in 1934 to assess adult education development in public libraries. The Board on Library and Adult Education was reorganized as the Adult Education Board (Stevenson, 1954, p.226). Libraries were viewed as being deeply conscious that they were an adult education agency. Readers' Advisory services gained acceptance, and librarians began to interact with other adult education agencies. The American Association for Adult Education published *The Public Library—A People's University* and characterized it as a sound bulwark of a democratic state (Johnson, 1938, p. 79).[31] Johnson's motivations, though, have been questioned by Latham (2010), who points to Johnson's engagement with social power brokers who viewed the public library as an avenue of social control. Even so, librarians appropriated Johnson's catchphrase, "the people's university," and used it to cement the role of the public library in American society.

Swain (1995) explored the expansion of readers' services during the New Deal, including supervised reading rooms, bookmobiles, and rural library services. The Library Adult Education Board suggested that libraries provide services for nonreaders and individuals with limited reading ability. The board recommended that librarians establish good working relationships with other community organizations because nonreaders could best be reached through contacts with literacy and adult basic education classes and social agencies (Birge, 1981, p. 60; Coleman, 2008, p.128).

By the late 1930s, librarians began to use the broader term "adult services," but projects within ALA under the rubric of adult education continued. These included the establishment of the Adult Education Section within the Public Library Division in 1946, the American Heritage Project, 1951-1954 (Preer, 1993),[32] and the creation of the Office of Adult Education within ALA, which awarded sub-grants of $1.5 million to libraries to stimulate adult education activities (1951 to 1961). Funds were provided to promote Great Books and political education, emphasizing discussion groups. A national survey of 1,692 public libraries conducted by Helen Lyman, *Adult Education Activities in Public Libraries,* was published in 1954—the first effort to describe the scope of adult services across the United States.

Margaret E. Monroe identified a variety of library services provided by libraries to adults during the first half of the twentieth century that incorporated aspects of adult education.[33] The history of public librarians with literacy and lifelong learning shows coalitions of librarians, educators, and funders working together to enhance the lives of adult learners and new readers. During the 1960s many library services were bolstered by funding during the federal War on Poverty and other outreach services to the underserved (Weibel, 1982).

The concept that libraries supported the democratic process provided librarians with an ongoing rationale that has been useful for promoting support of libraries and is tied closely to the idea of adult lifelong learning. Gilton (2012) demonstrates that public librarians can promote learning by combining the elements of Information Literacy Instruction (ILI) with traditional practices of public libraries.

As this book goes to press, the Workforce Innovation and Opportunity Act has given new emphasis to the workforce aspects of lifelong learning as summarized in a 2016 ALA Fact Sheet (figure 9.1).

The National Endowment for the Humanities (NEH) and State Humanities Councils have been long-standing partners with public libraries to promote lifelong learning. They support research, education, preservation, and public programs. By working closely with these organizations, public librarians can extend community dialogue about reading to topics of current importance. Library historians seeking to capture the library experience from the users' viewpoint and those of others involved with libraries can clarify the role of libraries in the life of the individual and in the intellectual, cultural, and social lives of those who live in the United States.

In recognition of the Endowment's ongoing support of libraries, in 2016 the American Library Association celebrated the Endowment's fiftieth anniversary with a special session that highlighted the NEH-funded Great Stories Club project. The event featured *March,* the first installment of the graphic novel trilogy created by Congressman John Lewis, Andrew Aydin, and Nate Powell (NEH, 2016).

NEH Chairman William Adams emphasized the vital role libraries play in our democracy: "There is no democracy without the act of memory." He encouraged libraries to continue to preserve and share the history of the civil rights movement. Congressman Lewis shared stories about growing up on a sharecropping farm and his important civil rights leadership. He described how, as a child, he was not given a library card because it was a privilege only afforded to white patrons at his library. He asked the 1,000 librarians in attendance at the event to "keep the faith" and to dedicate themselves to equality and inclusion for all (NEH, 2016). In 2016 many public libraries were included in the NEH *Latino Americans: 500 Years of History* grants,[34] which gave them another tool for inclusive programming.

Examining the library experience will further increase understanding of the extent to which librarians have attempted to mediate between the reader and the book to lead the reader to "high" culture (Carpenter, 1996). The meaning of carefully developed library collections, expert readers' advisory service, and the importance of books in our society is reinforced by the power of the humanities. In *The Art of Freedom,* Earl Shorris (2013) shows that the difference between a comfortable life and a life of poverty is often the failure of poor people to enter political life—a life that requires reflection. What better way to enter the reflective world than to engage in lifelong learning for knowledge?

Each U.S. state has a Humanities Council that is affiliated with NEH. Examples of lifelong learning supported by state councils in 2016 include Idaho's "Let's Talk About It" Program and Louisiana's "Reading in Literature and Culture."[35] Research corroborating the importance of public libraries to lifelong learning is reported in the 2016 Pew study, *Libraries and Learning* (Rainie, 2016), which found that the majority of respondents were highly

The Workforce Innovation and Opportunity Act: Summary of Library Provisions

After over 15 years, Congress reauthorized the Workforce Investment Act in 2014, calling it the Workforce Innovation and Opportunity Act (WIOA). WIOA will help job seekers and workers access employment, education, training, and support services to succeed in the labor market. This legislation now recognizes the part libraries can play in assisting these job seekers and be integrated into the state and local plans to deliver these crucial services.

The Workforce Innovation and Opportunity Act would strengthen the capacity of public libraries to support workforce investment in local communities by including the following provisions:

- Ensure State Workforce Development Boards develop strategies for technological improvements to facilitate access to, and improve the quality of, services and activities provided through the one-stop delivery system, including improvements to enhance digital literacy skills (as defined in section 202 of the Museum and Library Services Act) under section 101(d)(7)—Functions of the State Workforce Development Board.
- Ensure Local Workforce Development Boards develop strategies for using technology to maximize the accessibility and effectiveness of the local workforce development system by increasing access to services and programs of the one-stop delivery system, such as improving digital literacy skills under section 107(d)(7)(C)—Functions of the Local Workforce Development Board.
- Authorize employment, education, and training programs provided by public libraries as additional one-stop partners under section 121(b)(2)(B)(vii)—Additional One-Stop Partners.
- Prohibit any department, agency, officer, or employee of the United States to exercise any direction, supervision, or control over the selection of library resources under section 129(c) (6)—Prohibitions.
- Authorize adult education and literacy activities provided by public libraries as an Allowable Statewide Employment and Training Activity under section 134(a)(3)(A)(viii)(II)(dd)—Allowable Statewide Employment and Training Activities.
- Authorize a public library as an eligible provider of adult education and literacy services under section 203(5) (F)—Definition of Eligible Provider.
- Include a definition of "workforce preparation activities" that specifically includes digital literacy skills under section 203(17)—Definition of Workforce Preparation Activities.

FIGURE 9.1 The Workforce Innovation and Opportunity Act: Summary of Library Provisions [CONTINUED ON FOLLOWING PAGE]

SOURCE: ALA Office of Government Relations, The Workforce Innovation and Opportunity Act: Summary of Library Provisions (www.ala.org/advocacy/advleg/federallegislation/workforce).

FIGURE 9.1 [CONTINUED]

- Authorize technical assistance activities related to the development and dissemination of proven models for addressing the digital literacy needs of adults, including older adults under section 242(c)(1)(C)—National Leadership Activities.
- Encourage support for national, regional, or local networks of private nonprofit organizations, public libraries, or institutions of higher education to strengthen the ability of those organizations to meet various performance requirements under section 242(c)(2)(B)—National Leadership Activities.

satisfied with library services designed to meet educational needs. The study further determined that women and members of minority groups found the library essential.

Literacy

The American Library Association's Committee on Literacy adopted the definition of literacy from the Organisation for Economic Co-operation and Development Programme for the International Assessment of Adult Competencies:

> Literacy is the ability to identify, understand, interpret, create, communicate and compute, using printed and written materials associated with varying contexts. Literacy involves a continuum of learning in enabling individuals to achieve their goals, to develop their knowledge and potential, and to participate fully in their community and wider society (www.ala.org/advocacy/literacy-clearinghouse).

Historical examples of public library literacy services are included in studies by Jean E. Coleman, founding director for the Office for Diversity, Literacy and Outreach Services (1996) and the volume *Literacy and Libraries: Learning from Case Studies* (DeCandido, 2001). Fundamental questions about the focus of public libraries and the provision of adult literacy services were addressed in 2001 when the ALA Committee on Literacy was established. Discussion at this time contended that librarians should pair adult lifelong learning theory with literacy to make a broad commitment to "learning for life" (McCook & Barber, 2002). George Demetrion (2005) has examined the role of adult literacy in the life of the United States in his monograph *Conflicting Paradigms in Adult Literacy Education: In Quest of a U.S. Democratic Politics of Literacy*. His historical review provides a convincing argument for a stronger commitment to adult literacy by librarians.

Literacy continues to be a focus of public libraries, although over the years there have been ebbs and flows.[36] The lifelong learning continuum includes the 29% of people in the United States who cannot read above the eighth-grade level (Cooper, 2014); people for whom English is a second language; and people who want to grow and expand intellectual capabilities and cultural competence throughout their time on earth. When IMLS places the learner at the center of its mission, and lifelong learning is a key feature of its long-range plan, we see that this continues a century-old history of connecting libraries to literacy. Through collections, programs, and partnerships, libraries are an essential and trusted component of the nation's learning ecosystem, providing opportunities for lifelong, and "life-wide" learning (IMLS, *Creating a Nation of Learners*).

In 2013 the American Library Association reaffirmed its commitment to basic literacy with a resolution (see figure 9.2).

This commitment is made real by IMLS and the U.S. Department of Education's Office of Career, Technical, and Adult Education (OCTAE) work to help libraries and federally funded adult education programs designed to enhance skills, literacy, employability, and quality of life for low-skilled Americans. IMLS and OCTAE share resources, disseminate information about adult education-library partnerships, and provide training opportunities for library staff (IMLS, 2014). Recent examples of grants to promote literacy include the Providence (RI) Public Library's program, which pairs libraries and community partners to develop service plans and programs for adult English literacy, and the District of Columbia Public Library's General Equivalency Diploma (GED) Institutes, which help prepare instructors to teach struggling teens and adults GED preparation (IMLS 2014).

Librarians can work collaboratively with the Commission on Adult Basic Education (COABE), which promotes adult education and literacy programs (e.g., Adult Basic Education, Adult Secondary Education, English for Speakers of Other Languages, Family Literacy, Skills Development, Workforce Development), and other state, federal, and private programs that assist undereducated and/or disadvantaged adults to function effectively. COABE publishes the *Journal of Research and Practice for Adult Literacy, Secondary, and Basic Education.*

The ALA Office for Diversity, Literacy and Outreach Services, in partnership with ProLiteracy, received a grant from the Institute of Museum and Library Services to develop online training and supporting resources to better equip librarians and library staff to serve adult learners in 2015. The grant puts into practice the priorities outlined in *Adult Literacy through Libraries: An Action Agenda,* a collaborative project of ProLiteracy, ALA, and the On-

Resolution Reaffirming ALA's Commitment to Basic Literacy

Resolved, that the American Library Association (ALA), on behalf of its members:

1. Reaffirms and supports the principle that lifelong literacy is a basic right for all individuals in our society and is essential to the welfare of the nation;
2. Reaffirms the core value of basic literacy as foundational for people of all ages and is the building block for developing other literacies;
3. Encourages appropriate ALA units and Divisions to actively participate in the Association's Literacy Assembly; and
4. Urges appropriate ALA units and libraries of all types to make basic literacy a high priority by incorporating literacy initiatives into programs and services for all users.

FIGURE 9.2 Resolution Reaffirming ALA's Commitment to Basic Literacy

SOURCE: Adopted by the Council of the American Library Association June 30, 2013.

ondaga County (NY) Public Library. The new project's goal is to increase and expand adult literacy services in public libraries across the nation (ALA-ODLOS, 2015).

Additionally, the Workforce Investment Act of 2014 included basic literacy (see figure 9.1, above).

Adult Services as Expanding Human Capabilities

How did services for adults in public libraries expand from reader services and educational lifelong learning to the many services we see today? Public librarians have increasingly taken a human capabilities approach—helping communities to survive, flourish, and create. This includes support to labor, financial literacy, elder programs, reference, cultural programming, local history, genealogy, and vocational guidance all of which became part of many public libraries' range of services in the twentieth century (Okobi, 2014; Stephens, 2006). We have seen that even as early as the 1954 Lyman study, services to adults had far extended beyond service to readers and lifelong learning.

By 1957 the organization of services to adults within ALA had outgrown its place within the Public Library Division and was granted division status as the Adult Services Division (ASD). At its founding, ASD identified five aspects of adult services:

- indirect guidance (displays, reading lists)
- advisory services (informed and planned reading)
- services to organizations and groups (exhibits, reading lists, book talks, program planning support)
- library-sponsored programs (films, discussion groups, radio, television)
- community advisory services

The division published the *ASD Newsletter*, which incorporated *the Library Services to Labor Newsletter* in 1964. Librarians created programs such as the Library-Community Project, the Reading for an Age of Change series, and work with adult new readers (Heim, 1986; Phinney, 1967). In 1970, the ASD jointly adopted the policy "Library Rights of Adults: A Call for Action," with the Reference Services Division. Given the common goals of the two divisions, a merger took place in 1972 to form the Reference and Adult Services Division (RASD). Adult services within RASD were the focus of several committees, including the Service to Adults Committee (Hansen, 1995).

> **▸ FACT**
>
> Each adult should have the right to a library that seeks to understand both his needs and his wants and that uses every means to satisfy them.*
>
> ———
>
> *"Library Rights of Adults: A Call for Action—1970" (Hansen, 1995)

Two major studies of adult services were carried out in the 1980s. *The Service Imperative for Libraries* posited four basic adult service functions based on the theories of Margaret E. Monroe: information, guidance, instruction, and stimulation (Schlachter, 1982). *Adult Services: An Enduring Focus for Public Libraries* (an ASE Project) was an assessment and status report on key services for adults as the model had evolved in the late twentieth century (Heim & Wallace, 1990; Heim & Nuttall, 1990). Services to minorities, job seekers, labor, parents, older adults, people with disabilities, and genealogists were examined in the context of the ASE Project, which was overseen by the Service to Adults committee of RASD.[37]

In 1996, the "Adult Services" designation was removed by the ALA Reference and Adult Services Division, and it was renamed the Reference and User Services Association (RUSA). At this point, the use of "adult services" as a type of service designation disappeared from the divisional organizational structure of ALA.[38]

Many aspects of public library services to adults have a connection through the ALA Office of Diversity, Literacy, and Outreach Services, which supports equity and inclusion in library services.[39] From 2001 to 2016, the ALA Office published the *Diversity & Outreach Columns* Blog, highlighting library outreach services, including support for adult new- and non-readers; gay, lesbian, bisexual, and transgender people; incarcerated people and ex-offenders; older adults; people of color; people with disabilities; people experiencing poverty and homelessness; rural, native, and tribal libraries of all kinds; and bookmobile communities. Today the blog is called *Intersections* (http://www.ala.org/advocacy/diversity/odlos-blog/welcome). The Office is the point of contact for the Ethnic and Multicultural Information Exchange Round Table; the Gay, Lesbian, Bisexual, and Transgender Round Table (GLBTRT); the Social Responsibilities Round Table (SRRT); and the Association of Bookmobile and Outreach Services (ABOS).

Affiliate organizations also provide a cultural home for adult services; these include:

- The American Indian Library Association (AILA)
- The Asian Pacific American Librarians Association (APALA)
- The Black Caucus of the American Library Association (BCALA)
- The Chinese American Librarians Association (CALA)
- The National Association to Promote Library & Information Services to Latinos and the Spanish Speaking (REFORMA)

Each of these organizations focuses on different aspects of services to adults—library services to immigrants or literacy for new Americans—that should be considered as public libraries seek to respond to community needs and cultural factors. How did these services evolve?

ADULT SERVICES DURING THE PLANNING ERA (1966-2015): PUBLIC LIBRARY ROLES TO SERVICES RESPONSES

As we have seen in the history of public library standards and measurement, the period after issuance of the 1966 standards was one of great change and reassessment for all aspects of public library planning. This shift in philosophy from issuing standards to a planning model affected adult services as well. As public libraries moved into the planning era, adult services evolved based on each community's needs. Librarians worked to take a place at the table within communities based on local contexts (McCook, 2000). What we see from 1966 to 2015 is an ongoing expansion of library activities that parallel the evolution of adult services. After the widespread adoption of the PLA planning process for public libraries, the PLA delineated 8 main public library roles in 1987, which was increased to 13 service responses in 2001, and then again to 18 service responses in 2008.

These inventories were used to plan and provide a thoughtful look at the range of opportunities that characterized library service development from the 1980s to 2015. Susan Hildreth, writing as president of the Public Library Association, characterized the process in 2007:

> The PLA planning process has long provided assistance for public librarians to envision, evaluate, and respond to community needs with distinctive programs and services. *The New Planning for Results* continues that effort and represents an all-in-one guide that outlines a tested, results-driven planning process, revamped and streamlined to enable librarians to respond quickly to rapidly changing environments. One of the key elements in this planning process is the involvement of the library's community. Library service plans are based on what the community wants and needs, not what the library staff determines is right for the community.[40]

The three sets of service inventories that were used by public librarians during the planning era demonstrate the evolution of all services, and also define the variety of services to adults. Each role and service response over time can be assessed for changing service development. For example, "Reference Library," one of eight defined roles in 1987, became "General Information" in 2001 and was changed to "Get Facts Fast: Ready Reference" in 2008. In an assessment of the state of reference in 2016, Murray noted that "patrons still need, indeed desire and in many cases demand, meaningful interactions with knowledgeable, well-trained reference librarians (or whatever name we might end up calling ourselves)." Each role and response listed in figure 9.3 has a corresponding history reflective of its evolution. These 8 roles were replaced by 13 "service responses" in the 1990s (figure 9.4). These 13 service responses were expanded to 18 in the 2008 volume (figure 9.5).

These roles and responses were defined, described, and analyzed from the 1980s to 2015. They provide a menu of options that adult services in public libraries provided through 2015.[41] In 2015 a new direction in articulating service began.

THE PUBLIC LIBRARY AS THE HELP DESK AND FACILITATOR OF COMMUNITY ENGAGEMENT

Project Outcome is the initiative launched in 2015 by PLA to help public libraries understand and share the true impact of essential library services and programs. It also marks a major shift from the planning process. Areas of focus for measurement of outcomes for adult services include Civic/Community Engagement, Digital Inclusion, Economic Development, Education and Lifelong Learning, and Job Skills.[42]

Public Library Service Roles in the 1980s

- Community activities center
- Community information center
- Formal education support center
- Independent learning center
- Popular materials library
- Preschoolers' Door to Learning
- Reference library
- Research center

Figure 9.3 Public Library Service Roles in the 1980s

SOURCE: *Planning and Role Setting for Public Libraries* (McClure, 1987).

Public Library Service Responses in the 1990s

- Basic literacy
- Business and career information
- Commons
- Community referral
- Consumer information
- Cultural awareness
- Current topics and titles
- Formal learning centers
- General information
- Government information
- Information literacy
- Lifelong learning
- Local history and genealogy

Figure 9.4 Public Library Service Responses in the 1990s

SOURCE: *The New Planning for Results* (Nelson, 2001).

Public Library Service Responses in 2008

- Be an Informed Citizen: Local, National and World Affairs
- Build Successful Enterprises: Business and Nonprofit Support
- Celebrate Diversity: Cultural Awareness
- Connect to the Online World: Public Internet Access
- Create Young Readers: Early Literacy
- Discover Your Roots: Genealogy and Local History
- Express Creativity: Create and Share Content
- Get Facts Fast: Ready Reference
- Know Your Community: Community Resources and Services
- Learn to Read and Write: Adults, Teens and Family Literature
- Make Career Choices: Job and Career Development
- Make Informed Decisions: Health, Wealth and Other Life Choices
- Satisfy Curiosity: Lifelong Learning
- Stimulate Imagination: Reading, Viewing and Listening for Pleasure
- Succeed in School: Homework Help
- Understand How to Find, Evaluate, and Use Information: Information Fluency
- Visit a Comfortable Place: Physical and Virtual Spaces
- Welcome to the United States: Services for New Immigrants

Figure 9.5 Public Library Service Responses in 2008

SOURCE: *Strategic Planning for Results* (Nelson, 2008).

Enhancing existing service data with outcome data offers tremendous potential for many areas of public library planning. The range of public library adult services, in addition to reader services and lifelong learning, are best described by the organizational structure of the ALA Reference and User Services Association (RUSA) as well as guidelines and standards in effect.

RUSA has six specialty sections, each of which provides a community of interest for adult services.

- BRASS—business reference and services section of RUSA.
- CODES—collection development and evaluation section.
- HS (History section)—historical reference or research section.
- ETS—emerging technologies section.
- RSS—reference services section: frontline reference and provision of library and services to special user populations.
- STARS—sharing and transforming access to resources section: interlibrary loan, access services, cooperative reference, cooperative collection development, and other shared library services (ALA, RUSA, About RUSA, n.d.).

In addition to sections that develop programs and continuing education for adult services, RUSA issues guidelines and standards on:

- business information responses
- disaster resources
- financial literacy education in libraries
- genealogy collections
- health and medical reference
- local history
- reference/information services, including behavioral performance
- cooperative reference services
- virtual reference services

RUSA also provides guidelines for special user populations: multilingual collections and services, older patrons, and the Spanish-speaking.[43] Because so many services have been defined and developed, it is crucial that each library assesses community needs to select services to offer. This means, for example, that adult programming that aligns with the library's mission and values will be developed—there is no "one size fits all" model. In his book *Adult Programs in the Library* (2013), Brett W. Lear discusses the components of programming policies and how they align with the library's mission statement.

The alignment of mission and programming is reinforced by the interpretation of the Library Bill of Rights, "Library-Initiated Programs as a Resource." Library-initiated programs support the mission of the library by providing users with additional opportunities for information, education, and recreation. They take advantage of library staff expertise, collections, services, and facilities to introduce users and potential users to the resources of the library. These programs may be cooperative or joint programs with other agencies, organizations, institutions, or individuals.[44]

Some outstanding examples of adult programs today include:

- Cultural Tourism in Kentucky, McCracken (KY) County Public Library
- Lifescapes: Senior Writing Program, Northwest Reno (NV) Library
- What's Underneath Candlewood Lake? New Milford (CT) Public Library
- Estate Planning, Arapahoe (CO) Library District
- Know Dirt, Deschutes (OR) Public Library
- Job Seeker Series, Arlington Heights (IL) Memorial Library
- Pros and Cons of the Iraq War, Carroll County (MD) Public Library (Lear, 2013).

Figure 9.6 depicts the size of programming nationwide. Over 25 million adults attended programs in 2014.

In 2017 the National Impact of Library Public Programs Assessment (NILPPA) was launched to answer two research questions:

1. How can we characterize and categorize public programs offered by libraries today?
2. What competencies and training are required for professionals working with library programming?

A series of surveys will be disseminated to library practitioners to map the existing landscape of library public programming, including program types, topics, formats, audiences, partner relationships and current competencies, and also to identify those skills required in the field (ALA Public Programs Office, 2017).

The library as a facilitator of public access to local resources is addressed in *The Collection All Around* (Davis, 2017) which takes the point of view that libraries can help people discover historical, cultural, and natural riches that they might otherwise overlook. A multifaceted example of adult services made manifest is the intersection of librarianship and the Affordable Care Act in terms of libraries and e-government, computer access and the digital divide, and library neutrality and trust (Bossaller, 2016). "Access to Affordable Care through Public Libraries" provides evidence of how libraries' services might be influenced by both local and internal factors.

The Community Salute is a 2017 initiative of IMLS with the goal of studying how libraries and museums are responding to the needs of veterans and their families and developing new strategies through community partnerships to provide better services.

A model in democratic exchange is provided by the Monroeville (PA) Public Library, which includes "Hot Topics" to guide patrons to reliable online news and information current events. From the Islamic State to the U.S. presidential primaries to local tax issues, visitors get quick access to useful resources vetted by a team of librarians. Putnam (2016) notes, "It's a thoughtful service with a conscious goal: to support the informed citizenry a strong democracy depends on." Mark Hudson, head of adult services at Monroeville Public Library underscores the libraries' role in supporting democracy: "Librarians can help people gain the basic knowledge and understanding they need to participate in debates, engage in effective political action, and make the societies they live in more democratic" (Hudson, 2016).

CONCLUSION

The future of adult services was incisively characterized as having made an unprecedented shift by Kenney (2015), who asked, "So what do people want from us? They want help doing

Adult Attendance at Public Library Programs by State: Fiscal Year 2014

STATE	TOTAL NUMBER OF PUBLIC LIBRARIES	TOTAL ADULT ATTENDANCE
ALL STATES	9070	25,060,000
Alabama	218	279,000
Alaska	79	50,000
Arizona	90	328,000
Arkansas	58	196,000
California	184	2,051,000
Colorado	113	696,000
Connecticut	182	646,000
Delaware	21	64,000
District of Columbia	1	43,000
Florida	82	1,370,000
Georgia	63	297,000
Hawaii	1	29,000
Idaho	102	83,000
Illinois	623	1,083,000
Indiana	237	846,000
Iowa	534	244,000
Kansas	318	289,000
Kentucky	119	467,000
Louisiana	68	496,000
Maine	228	197,000
Maryland	24	379,000
Massachusetts	368	675,000
Michigan	388	864,000
Minnesota	137	287,000
Mississippi	52	183,000

STATE	TOTAL NUMBER OF PUBLIC LIBRARIES	TOTAL ADULT ATTENDANCE
Missouri	149	450,000
Montana	82	81,000
Nebraska	263	119,000
Nevada	21	303,000
New Hampshire	219	225,000
New Jersey	281	1,109,000
New Mexico	87	96,000
New York	756	3,596,000
North Carolina	80	363,000
North Dakota	73	24,000
Ohio	251	1,136,000
Oklahoma	117	324,000
Oregon	129	215,000
Pennsylvania	455	876,000
Rhode Island	48	178,000
South Carolina	42	214,000
South Dakota	112	24,000
Tennessee	186	276,000
Texas	548	1,540,000
Utah	72	239,000
Vermont	155	100,000
Virginia	91	538,000
Washington	62	330,000
West Virginia	97	74,000
Wisconsin	381	439,000
Wyoming	23	49,000

FIGURE 9.6 Adult Attendance at Public Library Programs by State: Fiscal Year 2014

SOURCE: Institute of Museum and Library Services, 2016. Supplementary Tables: Table 11. Public Libraries Survey Fiscal Year 2014, July 2016 (https://www.imls.gov/sites/default/files/fy2014_pls_tables.pdf).

things, rather than finding things. . . . Sometimes it is assistance with the technology we offer at the library—downloading e-books for example. But often it's more involved: creating and improving resumes, conducting job searches, uploading files, seeking insurance information. E-government has landed squarely in the library's lap, and we're finding that citizens regularly need help utilizing government sites."[45]

NOTES

1. See, for example, astronomy night at the Cary (IL) Public Library (www.nsaclub.org/events/2014/10/2/astronomy-night-cary-public-library) and sewing classes at the Kokomo-Howard County Public Library (www.kokomotribune.com/news/area_briefs/library-to-have-sewing-classes/article_cd9334bf-70f2-5d66-8696-0f3866dd239b.html). See also Bardoff (2015), Douglas & Fink (1974), Dowd (2015), and Davis (2009).
2. There is no standardization whether "reader" is singular or plural or where to put the apostrophe (or used at all). For various uses, see the Danville (IL) Public Library, Reader's Services (www.denvillelibrary.org/reader-services/); the East Meadow (NY) Public Library Reader Services (www.eastmeadow.info/books-reading/reader-services/); the Evanston (IL) Public Library Readers' Services (https://www.epl.org/index.php?option=com_content&view=category&layout=blog&id=76&Itemid=291); and the Boston Public Library Reader Services Department (www.bpl.org/research/generalref/).
3. The American Library Association's Office for Diversity, Literacy, and Outreach Services mission is to support

   > library and information science workers in creating safe, responsible, and all-inclusive spaces that serve and represent the entire community. To accomplish this, we decenter power and privilege by facilitating conversations around access and identity as they impact the profession and those we serve. We use a social justice framework to inform library and information science workers' development of resources. We strive to create an association culture where these concerns are incorporated into everybody's everyday work (www.ala.org/offices/diversity).

4. Books and services for readers—what the public at large thinks of as the central purpose of the public library—were addressed in PLA publication, *Strategic Planning for Results* under the service response "Stimulating Imagination" (Nelson, 2008).
5. NoveList is a division of EBSCO with more than 50 employees. For more than 20 years, the NoveList team has continued to innovate and develop solutions for readers' advisory, catalog enrichment, e-mail newsletters, library marketing, and more. But, throughout it all, the core mission continues to be helping libraries help readers. See https://www.ebscohost.com/novelist/about-novelist/the-novelist-story.
6. "The personality of the circulation librarian"—Infinitely patient, perfect control of temper, like people including children, love books, accurate, neat, dependable, adaptable, imaginative and industrious. (W. W. Charters, quoted in Flexner [1927], pp. 274-293).
7. OverDrive provides apps for major devices, One-Step Checkout and OverDrive Read. See http://company.overdrive.com/libraries/public-libraries/.
8. See, for example, the San Francisco Public Library's eLibrary page which is simple, elegant, and linked to social media (http://sfpl.org/index.php?pg=0000000301).
9. Other sources include Baker & Klaassen (2015); Goldsmith (2010); McArdle (2015); Morris, (2012); Moyer & Blau (2008); Moyer & Stover (2010); Saricks (2009); and Spratford (2012).

10. For more details on the Read On series, see www.abc-clio.com/LibrariesUnlimited.aspx.
11. Orr, C., & Herald, D. T. (2013). *Genreflecting: A guide to popular reading interests.* Another book in the Genreflecting Advisory series includes *Graphic Novels: A Genre Guide to Comic Books, Manga, and More* (Pawuk & Serchay, 2017).
12. Fiction_L was created at the Morton Grove (IL) Public Library as a mailing list on readers' advisory issues. Archives contain the complete record of all topics discussed on Fiction_L, from the list's first message in December 1995 up through messages posted in May 2016. Many discussion threads, end with of a compiled list of titles or authors; most of these lists are collected in the Fiction_L Booklist pages (www.mgpl.org/read-listen-view/fl/flmenu/) to make them more easily accessible. As of June 2016, Fiction-L moved to the Cuyahoga County Public Library (https://listserver.cuyahogalibrary.net). The discussion list, which has over 3,000 followers, is described as follows:

    > Fiction_L is an electronic mailing list devoted to reader's advisory topics such as book discussions, booktalks, collection development issues, booklists and bibliographies, and a wide variety of other topics of interest to librarians, book discussion leaders, and others with an interest in reader's advisory. Fiction_L was developed for and by librarians dealing with fiction collections and requests; however, fiction lovers worldwide are welcome to join the discussion. Among the topics discussed have been: genre study, bibliographies, workshops, audiobooks, reading clubs, and print and electronic resources. The discussion is not limited to fiction, but rather covers all aspects of reader's advisory for children, young adults and adults, including non-fiction materials. The collective wisdom of Fiction_L participants has proved very helpful for librarians trying to locate an obscure title for a patron or in creating a booklist for an upcoming event. This list has come up with answers to numerous fiction and non-fiction "stumpers" much to the delight of many patrons, as well as librarians, happy to find the title of a book they read 20 years ago (or just a couple months ago). The only clue to the title may be the picture on the cover or a character's name. Fiction_L, along with its archives and booklists, is an invaluable resource for librarians who want to provide better and more efficient service to their customers. It's the perfect way to ensure that your patrons find a *good* book to read so they don't leave the library empty-handed! The new url is https://listserver.cuyahogalibrary.net.

13. BookBrowse is an online magazine for booklovers—including reviews, previews, "behind the book" backstories, author interviews, reading guides (https://www.bookbrowse.com/).
14. See Readers' Advisory Interest Group (www.mdlib.org/content.asp?contentid=267); the Chicago area's Adult Reading RoundTable (http://03c8e5a.netsolhost.com/wordpress1/about/); the Seattle Public Library's Blog Shelf Talk (https://shelftalkblog.wordpress.com/); the Jefferson-Madison Regional Library Reader's Corner (http://jmrl.org/pr-readers.htm).
15. Archives of the RUSA CODES convos are available at http://lists.ala.org/sympa/arc/codes-convos/2016-10/.
16. Zepheira (http://zepheira.com/solutions/library/libhub/); also, "Anythink partners with Zepheira as founding partner of Libhub Initiative" (https://www.anythinklibraries.org/news-item/anythink-partners-zepheira-founding-partner-libhub-initiative),
17. See Women's National Book Association, National Reading Group Month. www.booklistreader.com/2016/09/21/book-groups/national-reading-group-month-the-2016-great-group-reads/ and www.wnba-books.org.
18. Nancy Pearl, winner of the Women's National Book Association Award, has had an extraordinary

career based on her love and sharing of books. See her website at www.nancypearl.com/?page_id=2.

19. Novel Conversations is a free statewide lending library. The Indiana Humanities lends more than 550 titles, primarily fiction and biography, to reading and discussion groups all over Indiana, including public and school libraries, senior centers, churches, and formal and informal book clubs. Any Indiana resident can request a set of books. The service is free as long as books are either shipped to a public library via the Indiana State Library's INfo Express service or picked up and returned at Indiana Humanities headquarters at 1500 N. Delaware St. in Indianapolis.
20. Notable Books is a monthly Sacramento Public Library series focused on bringing classic works of literature to the Sacramento community in a friendly, casual manner (https://www.saclibrary.org/About-Us/News/2015/November/Upcoming-Notable-Books-events/).
21. The Watertown (WI) Public Library's Pinterest page on book displays includes book cart displays, bulletin boards and holiday extravaganzas. https://www.pinterest.com/wttnpubliclib/library-displays/.
22. The 2016 Delaware Humanities Forum commemorated the centennial of the Pulitzer Prizes with a series of reading and discussion sessions and writing workshops highlighting and exploring recent Pulitzer Prize-winning works in collaboration with the Dover Public Library; see www.dehumanities.org.
23. The Center for the Book at the Library of Congress was established in 1977. The National Book Committee (1954–1974) and the U.S. Governmental Advisory Committee on International Books and Library Programs (1962–1977), merged to became the first Advisory Committee for the Center for the Book. In 2010 a special issue of the journal, *Libraries and the Cultural Record,* was dedicated to the director of the Center for the Book, titled "John Y. Cole: Librarian, Bookman, and Scholar" (Maack, 2010).
24. First Lady Laura W. Bush initiated the Texas Book Festival in 1995 while she was first lady of Texas. See the history of the Texas Book Festival at www.texasbookfestival.org/mission-history/.
25. The Festival news is updated at its blog at the Library of Congress website. www.loc.gov/bookfest/.
26. See the Asian Pacific American Librarians Association Literature Awards (www.apalaweb.org/awards/literature-awards/); Black Caucus of the American Library Association Literary Award (www.bcala.org/index.php/awards/literary-awards/literary-awards-2#); Chinese American Library Association best book award (www.cala-web.org/node/881); and the Stonewall Book Awards given by the Gay, Lesbian, Bisexual, and Transgender Round Table of the ALA (www.ala.org/glbtrt/award).
27. Awards are based on literary merit. An honored author must be an Alabamian by birth or have lived in Alabama for at least five years (www.jclc.org/resources/MaterialsLists/aaa/default.aspx).
28. The purpose of the Idaho Book Award is to recognize and honor one book, selected from among all the books published in any one calendar year, which has made an outstanding contribution to the body of printed materials about Idaho, either through the work's setting or the locality of the author. The award is intended to encourage the writing and publishing of books about Idaho and by Idahoans. See http://idaholibraries.org/idahobookaward/.
29. The current strategic plan continues emphases of IMLS on lifelong learning. The 21st Century Learner Conference, held at the beginning of the twenty-first century in November 2001, reaffirmed the role of the public library as an educational institution. At that conference, Robert S. Martin first librarian to direct IMLS, stated: "There is a difference between information and knowledge, and the most important role of the library is not providing access to information, it is supporting, enhancing, and facilitating the transfer of knowledge—in other words, education" (Martin, 2001). The history of the educational role of the public library has been described by Monroe, 1981; 1991.

30. Julia Wright Merrill, who worked on adult education and extension at ALA during this time has been inducted into the Wisconsin Library Hall of Fame. See http://heritage.wisconsinlibraries.org/entry/julia_wright_merrill_18811961.
31. Johnson as a man of his time who may have seen the public library as an agency of control is discussed by Latham (2010).
32. Funded by the Ford Foundation Fund for Adult Education. See Edelson (1991).
33. The ALA, RUSA Adult Services NoveList Margaret E. Monroe Award is presented to a librarian who has made significant contributions to library adult services (https://www.rusaupdate.org/awards/novelists-margaret-e-monroe-library-adult-services-award/).
34. National Endowment for the Humanities. Museums, Libraries and Cultural Organizations Implementation Grants. This grant program supports projects for general audiences that encourage active engagement with humanities ideas in creative and appealing ways (www.neh.gov/grants/public/museums-libraries-and-cultural-organizations-implementation-grants).
35. Idaho's "Let's Talk About It" (LTAI) Library Program. For thirty years the Idaho Humanities Council has partnered with the Idaho Commission for Libraries and US Bank Foundation to bring book discussion programs to libraries statewide. The program brings together humanities scholars and adult readers in public libraries to read and discuss literature that explores American values, history, and culture (www.idahohumanities.org/?p=lets_talk_about_it). Louisiana Endowment for the Humanities. Readings in Literature and Culture, the LEH's adult reading and discussion series, RELIC, has enrolled nearly 105,000 readers in 63 parishes across Louisiana (www.leh.org/relic/).
36. The connection between public libraries and adult literacy and education organizations has followed changing adult education policies within the federal government. The shift to an emphasis on workforce training grew after the passage of the 1998 Workforce Investment Act. Conflicts over participants' roles, the interpretation of the legislation, and ambiguity about the process of implementation emerged (Hopkins, Monaghan, & Hansman, 2009). The challenges are defined in the *Reach Higher, America* report (National Commission on Adult Literacy, 2008). In the lead-up to reauthorization of the Workforce Investment Act, changes that should be made to provide greater support from the federal government for adult education were addressed at a Council for the Advancement of Literacy Round Table ("Council for Advancement," n.d.). Librarians should be aware of the "learn to earn" movement and recognize that our traditions of "learn to live" are also a rich motivation for adult literacy.
37. In 1983 the Services to Adults Committee of RASD won an ALA Goal Award to conduct a national survey of adult services among 1,758 libraries serving populations of 25,000 or more. This survey, the Adult Services in the Eighties Project, extended the research done by Lyman (1954). The final report is *Adult Services: An Enduring Focus for Public Libraries* (Heim & Wallace, 1990). Complete records of the project, including original surveys, are at the ALA Archives "Adult Services in the Eighties (ASE) Project File" (http://archives.library.illinois.edu/alaarchon/?p=collections/controlcard&id=7005).
38. For the organizational history of adult services within the ALA, see articles by Hansen (1995), McCook (1992), and Heim (1986).
39. For founding and first 25 years of the Office for Diversity, Literacy and Outreach Services see Lippincott & Taffae (1996). See also postings in the Diversity & Outreach blog from 2001–2016 at http://olos.ala.org/columns/.
40. Susan Hildreth was PLA president at the time the PLA Planning Process was developed. She later served as city librarian for the Seattle Public Library and director of the Institute of Museum and Library Services from 2011-2014. She previously served as California state librarian, and city librarian at San Francisco Public Library (Peet, 2015a).

41. For a historical bibliography for each 2008 services response see McCook, 2011, pp. 231–240 and pp. 407–429.
42. Project Outcome: Measuring the True Impact of Public Libraries. Public Library Association. Public libraries offer a broad range of vital community services: digital readiness training, preschool literacy education, employment counseling, workforce development, and outlets for creative expression and communication. Typically, libraries rely on simple attendance counts and anecdotal success stories to measure the effectiveness of their services; however, these statistics are not enough to guide internal strategy or build persuasive arguments to secure library funding. Enhancing existing service data with outcome data offers tremendous potential in many areas of the public library. See www.ala.org/pla/initiatives/performancemeasurement.
43. For links to information on each services response, see www.ala.org/rusa/guidelines/guidelines-by-topic.
44. "Library staff select topics, speakers and resource materials for library-initiated programs based on the interests and information needs of the community." See ALA, Office of Intellectual Freedom, Library-Initiated Programs as a Resource. www.ala.org/advocacy/intfreedom/librarybill/interpretations/libraryinitiated.
45. See Kenney (2015), who continues: "It is assumed that libraries mostly help bridge the digital divide, assisting the poor and disenfranchised in getting online. But it's more complicated than that. Keeping up with the full range technology today is a challenge for everyone, and when users have to fill in a knowledge gap, no matter their educational level or economic status, they're showing up at the reference desk." See also the follow up article "We Need to Talk about Reference" (Albanese & Kenney, 2016).

REFERENCES

Albanese, A. R., & Kenney, B. (2016). We need to talk about reference. *K, 263*(35), 36–38.

American Library Association. (2004). Core values of librarianship. www.ala.org/advocacy/intfreedom/statementspols/corevalues.

American Library Association. (1999). *Libraries: An American value.* www.ala.org/advocacy/intfreedom/americanvalue.

American Library Association. (2013). Resolution reaffirming ALA's commitment to basic literacy. Adopted by the Council of the American Library Association, Sunday, June 30, 2013, in Chicago, Illinois. www.ala.org/aboutala/sites/ala.org.aboutala/files/content/governance/council/council_documents/2013_annual_council_docs/cd_37_literacy%20resol-finalfinal.doc.pdf.

American Library Association. (2015, June 24). ALA's Office for Diversity, Literacy and Outreach Services and ProLiteracy receive IMLS grant to expand adult literacy services. through libraries. www.ala.org/news/press-releases/2015/06/ala-s-office-diversity-literacy-and-outreach-services-and-proliteracy-receive.

American Library Association. Committee on Literacy. (n.d.). www.ala.org/groups/committees/ala/ala-literacy.

American Library Association. Literacy Clearinghouse. (n.d.). www.ala.org/advocacy/literacy-clearinghouse.

American Library Association. Office for Intellectual Freedom. (2014). Interpretation of the Library Bill of Rights. Prisoners' Right to Read. Dates vary. www.ala.org/advocacy/intfreedom/librarybill/interpretations.

American Library Association. Public Programs Office (2017). IMLS Funds $500,000 ALA Research Project to Study Library Programming. *Programming Librarian.* www.programminglibrarian.org/articles/imls-funds-500000-ala-research-project-study-library-programming.

American Library Association. Reference and User Services Association. (n.d.). About RUSA. www.ala.org/rusa/about.

American Library Association. References and User Services Association. (n.d.). Notable Books Council. Notable Books. www.ala.org/rusa/awards/notablebooks.

American Library Association. References and User Services Association. (n.d.). The Reading List. www.ala.org/rusa/awards/readinglist.

American Library Association. References and User Services Association. (n.d.). Sophie Brody Award. www.ala.org/rusa/awards/brody.

American Library Association, Video Round Table. (n.d.). Notable Videos for Adults. www.ala.org/vrt/notablevideos.

Anythink staff member wins Lucy Schweers Award. (2015). https://www.anythinklibraries.org/news-item/anythink-staff-member-wins-lucy-schweers-award.

Arndt, T. (2015). *Getting started with demand-driven acquisitions for E-books: A LITA guide*. Chicago, IL: ALA Editions.

ASCLA PLuSCH Forum. (n.d.) www.ala.org/ascla/asclaourassoc/asclasections/lssps/plusch.

Asheim, L. (1953). Not censorship but selection. *Wilson Library Bulletin, 28*, 63–67.

Association of Specialized and Cooperative Library Agencies. (2017). *Revised standards and guidelines of service for the Library of Congress network of libraries for the blind and physically handicapped*. Chicago, IL: Association of Specialized and Cooperative Library Agencies, American Library Association.

Ayre, L. B. (2015). Liberated from the circulation desk—Now what? *Collaborative Librarianship, 7*(3), 145-147.

Baker, J. S., & Klaassen, A. (2015). *The readers' advisory guide to historical fiction*. Chicago, IL: ALA Editions.

Bardoff, C. (2015) Homelessness and the ethics of information access. *The Serials Librarian, 69* (3-4).

Birge, L. E. (1981). *Serving adult learners: A public library tradition*. Chicago: American Library Association.

Booktalking: Quick and simple. http://nancykeane.com/booktalks/.

Bossaller, J. (2016). Access to Affordable Care through public libraries. *Library Quarterly, 86*(2), 193-212.

Boston Public Library. (1852). *Report of the trustees of the public library to the City of Boston*.

Brown, W. L. (1917, July). The changing public. *ALA Bulletin, 11*, 91-95.

Burke, S., & Strothmann, M. (2015). Adult readers' advisory services through public library websites. *Reference and User Services Quarterly, 55*(2), 132-143.

Carpenter, K. E. (1996). *Toward a history of libraries and culture in America*. Washington, DC: Library of Congress.

Carrier, E. J. (1965). *Fiction in public libraries, 1876-1900*. New York, NY: Scarecrow Press.

Carrier, E. J. (1985). *Fiction in public libraries, 1900-1950*. Littleton, CO: Libraries Unlimited.

Coleman, Brenda Weeks. (2008). *Keeping the faith: The public library's commitment to adult education, 1950-2006* (Doctoral dissertation). University of Southern Mississippi. http://aquila.usm.edu/dissertations/1181.

Coleman, J. E. (1996). *Literacy education programs in public libraries as a response to a socio-educational need: Four case studies*. Doctoral dissertation, Rutgers, the State University of New Jersey.

Collaborative Summer Library Program. (n.d.). www.cslpreads.org/about.

Colorado Humanities. (2010). The American West as living space. www.coloradohumanities.org/content/american-west-living-space-schedule.

Cooper, K. K. (2014). Supporting adult literacy. *Public Libraries, 53*(3), 8-10.

Council for Advancement of Adult Literacy. (n.d.) www.caalusa.org/publications.html.

Davis, J. E. (2009). *An Everglades providence: Marjory Stoneman Douglas and the American environmental century*. Athens, GA: University of Georgia Press.

Davis, J. T. (2017). *Collection all around: Sharing our cities, towns, and natural places*. Chicago, IL: American Library Association.

DeCandido, G. (Ed.). (2001). *Literacy and libraries: Learning from case studies*. Chicago, IL: American Library Association.

Demetrion, G. (2005). *Conflicting paradigms in adult literacy education: In quest of a U.S. democratic politics of literacy.* Mahwah, NJ: Erlbaum.

Dilevko, J., & Magowan, C. F. C. (2007). *Readers' advisory service in North American public libraries, 1870-2005: A history and critical analysis.* Jefferson, NC: McFarland & Co.

Dirda, M. (2015). *Browsings: A year of reading, collecting, and living with books.* New York, NY. Pegasus.

Discovery Product Functionality. (2014). *Library Technology Reports, 50*(1), 5-32.

Douglas, M. S., & Fink, R. (1974). *The Everglades: River of grass.* New York, NY: Ballantine Books.

Dowd, R. (2015). *A librarian's guide to homelessness.* www.imls.gov/research/public_libraries_in_the_us_fy_2012_report.aspx.

Drabinski, E., & Rabina, D. (2015). Reference services to incarcerated people, part I. *Reference and User Services Quarterly, 55*(1), 42-48.

Duncan, C. J., & Peterson, E.D. (2014). *Creating a streaming video collection for your library.* Lanham, MD: Rowman & Littlefield.

Eagle Valley Library District presents local author expo and book fair (2015, November 28). *Vail Daily.* www.vaildaily.com/entertainment/19321533-113/eagle-valley-library-district-presents-local-author-expo.

EarlyWord. News for Collection Development and Readers Advisory Librarians. (n.d.). www.earlyword.com.

Edelson, P. J. (1991) *Socrates on the assembly line: The Ford Foundation's mass marketing of liberal adult education.* Educational Resources Information Archive. ED340885. https://archive.org/details/ERIC_ED340885.

Elmborg, J. (2016). Tending the garden of learning: Lifelong learning as core library value. *Library Trends, 64*(3), 533-555.

Ennis, M. (2013, July). More vendors help libraries stream video. *The Digital Shift.* www.thedigitalshift.com/2013/07/acquisition/more-vendors-help-libraries-stream-video/.

Expanding access to devices, collections, and services. (2012). *Library Technology Reports, 48*(1), 19-24.

Farr, C. K. (2004). *Reading Oprah: How Oprah's book club changed the way America reads.* Albany, NY: State University of New York Press.

FictionFinder: A FRBR-based prototype for fiction in WorldCat. (n.d.). OCLC Research. www.oclc.org/research/themes/data-science/fictionfinder.html.

Flexner, J. M. (1927). *Circulation work in public libraries.* Chicago, IL: American Library Association.

Flexner, J. M., Hopkins, B. C., & American Association for Adult Education. (1941). *Readers advisors at work: A survey of development in the New York Public Library.* New York, NY: American Association for Adult Education.

Fuller, D., & Rehberg, S. D. N. (2013). *Reading beyond the book: The social practices of contemporary literary culture.* New York, NY: Routledge.

Garceau, O. (1949). *The public library in the political process: A report of the Public Library Inquiry.* New York, NY: Columbia University Press.

Gehner, J. (2010). Libraries, low-income people, and social exclusion. *Public Library Quarterly, 29*(1).

Gilton, D. L. (2012). *Lifelong learning in public libraries: Principles, programs, and people.* Lanham, MD: Scarecrow Press.

Goldsmith, F. (2010). *The readers' advisory guide to graphic novels.* Chicago, IL: American Library Association.

Goodreads. (n.d.) https://www.goodreads.com.

Gornick, V. (1998, February 20). Apostles of the faith that books matter. *The New York Times*, p. B40.

Gray, W. S., & Munroe, R. (1929). *The reading interests and habits of adults.* New York, NY: Macmillan.

Haines, H. E. (1935). *Living with books: The art of book selection.* New York, NY: Columbia University Press.

Hamilton, B. A., Brown, E. R., & Illinois Regional Library Council. (1973). *Libraries and information centers in the Chicago metropolitan area.* Hinsdale, IL: Illinois Regional Library Council.

Hansen, A. M. (1995, Spring). RASD: Serving those who serve the public. *RQ, 34*, 314-338.

Harder, A., Howard V. & Sedo, D.R. (2015). Creating cohesive community through shared reading: A Case study of One Book Nova Scotia. Partnership: *The Canadian Journal of Library and Information Practice and Research, 10*(1), 1–21.

Heckman, J. (2015). Creating flourishing lives: The dynamics of capability formation. Amartya Sen Lecture at the Human Development and Capability Association conference held at Georgetown University, September 11, 2015. https://www.youtube.com/watch?v=oO-TqzE4AcE.

Heckman J., & Corbin, C.O. (2016). Capabilities and skills. *Journal of Human Development and Capabilities, 17*(3), 342–359.

Heim, K. M. (1986, Winter). Adult services as reflective of the changing role of the public library. *RQ*, 26, 180–187.

Heim, K. & Nuttall, H. (1990). *Adult services: A bibliography and index: a component of the adult services in the eighties project.* Baton Rouge, LA: Louisiana State University, School of Library and Information Science, Research Center Annex Consulting Group. Also ERIC document ED320609.

Heim, K. M., & Wallace, D. P. (Eds.). (1990). *Adult services: An enduring focus for public libraries.* Chicago, IL: American Library Association.

Hildreth, S. (2007). Engaging your community: A strategy for relevance in the twenty-first century. *Public Libraries, 46*(3), 7-9.

Hildreth, S., & Sullivan, M. (2015). Rising to the challenge: Re-envisioning public libraries. *Journal of Library Administration, 55*(8), 647-657.

Holley, Bob (2015/2016). Why don't public librarians brag more about one of their greatest successes: providing pleasure reading for their patrons? *Against the Grain* 27, p. 58.

Holt, L. E. & Holt, G. E. (2010). *Public library services for the poor: Doing all we can.* Chicago, IL: ALA Editions.

Hooper, B. (2016). *Librarians guide to book programs and author events.* Chicago, IL: ALA Editions.

Hopkins, J. L., Monaghan, C. H., & Hansman, C. A. (2009). Conflict and collaboration: Providers and planners implementing the Workforce Investment Act (WIA). *Adult Education Quarterly*, 59 (May), 208-226.

Hoyer, J. (2013). "Finding room for everyone: libraries confront social exclusion," in Dudley, M., *Public libraries and resilient cities.* Chicago: ALA Editions.

Hudson, M. Quoted in Putnam, L. (2016). How libraries are curating current events, becoming community debate hubs. http://mediashift.org/2016/05/how-libraries-are-curating-current-events-becoming-community-debate-hubs/.

IMLS Focus: Learning in Libraries (2015). https://www.imls.gov/sites/default/files/publications/documents/imlsfocuslearninginlibrariesfinalreport.pdf.

Institute of Museum and Library Services. (2011, 2013). *Creating a nation of learners: Strategic plan, 2012-2016.* https://www.imls.gov/about-us/strategic-plan.

Institute of Museum and Library Services. (2014). *Adults gain skills at the library.* https://www.imls.gov/assets/1/AssetManager/AdultLiteracy.pdfFBossaller.

Institute of Museum and Library Services. (2016, July). Supplementary Tables: Table 11. Public Libraries Survey Fiscal Year 2014. https://www.imls.gov/sites/default/files/fy2014_pls_tables.pdf.

Institute of Museum and Library Services (2017). *Community salute: Libraries and museums serving Veterans and military families.* https://www.imls.gov/sites/default/files/publications/documents/supporting-veterans-military-families-how-begin.pdf.

International Dublin Literary Award. (n.d.). www.dublinliteraryaward.ie/.

Jaeger, P. T., Taylor, N. G., & Gorham, U. (2015) *Libraries, human rights, and social justice: Enabling access and promoting inclusion.* Lanham, MD: Rowman & Littlefield.

Johal, J., et al. (2012). Take the plunge! Implementing floating collections in your library system. *Public Libraries, 51*(3), 13-20.

Johnson, A. (1938). *The public library—A people's university.* Chicago, IL: American Library Association.

Karetzky, S. (1982). *Reading research and librarianship: A history and analysis.* Westport, CT: Greenwood Press.

Katz, W. A. (2001). *Readers, reading, and librarians.* New York, NY: Haworth Information Press.

Kemper, C. (2015) Kansas City Public Library. Welcome and opening remarks, IMLS Focus: Learning in libraries. You Tube video. https://www.youtube.com/watch?v=tBjiKk3180E.

Kenney, B. (2015). For future reference. *Publishers Weekly, 262*(37), 20–21.

Kniffel, L. (2001, October). Authors take center stage at first National Book Festival. *American Libraries, 32,* 16–17.

Kniffel, L. (2008, December). Eight years later: Laura Bush, librarian in the White House. *American Libraries, 39,* 42–47.

Knowles, M. S. (1977). *A history of the adult education movement in the United States.* Huntington, NY: Robert E. Krieger.

Kowalsky, M., & Woodruff, J. (2017). *Creating inclusive library environments: A planning guide for serving patrons with disabilities.* Chicago, IL: ALA Editions.

Koster, L. (2009, November) When is an e-book a book? About cataloging physical items or units of content. https://commonplace.net/2009/11/is-an-e-book-a-book/.

Latham, J. M. (2010, July). Clergy of the mind: Alvin S. Johnson, William S. Learned, the Carnegie Corporations, and the American Library Association. *Library Quarterly, 80,* 249–265.

Lear, B. W. (2013). *Adult programs in the library.* (2nd ed.). Chicago, IL: ALA Editions.

Learned, W. S. (1924). *The American public library and the diffusion of knowledge.* New York, NY: Harcourt.

LibraryReads. (n.d.) http://libraryreads.org.

LibraryThing. (n.d.). https://www.librarything.com/home.

Lippincott, K., & Taffae, S.M. (1996). *Twenty-five years of outreach: A bibliographic timeline of the American Library Association, Office for Literacy and Outreach Services.* ED 396 755 IR 055 926.

Listen List. (n.d.). RUSA, CODES. www.ala.org/rusa/awards/listenlist.

Long, S. A. (2001). Foreword. In R. McCabe, *Civic librarianship: Renewing the social mission of the public library* (pp. vii–ix). Lanham, MD: Scarecrow Press.

Lundh, A. A., & Johnson, G. M. (2015). The use of digital talking books by people with print disabilities: A literature review. *Library Hi Tech, 33*(1), 54–64.

Lyman, H. (1954). *Adult education activities in public libraries.* Chicago, IL: American Library Association.

Maack, M. N. (2010). John Y. Cole: Librarian, bookman, and scholar. *Libraries and the Cultural Record, 45*(1), 1–4.

Maatta, S. L. (2010). *A few good books: Using contemporary readers' advisory strategies to connect readers with books.* New York, NY: Neal-Schuman.

Manguel, A. (1996). *A history of reading.* New York, NY: Penguin.

Manguel, A. (2010). *A reader on reading.* New Haven, CT: Yale University Press.

Martin, R. S. (2001, November 7, 2011). 21st Century Learners Conference, Institute of Museum and Library Services: Reprinted in McCook, *Introduction to public librarianship* (2nd ed.). Neal-Schuman/ALA Editions, pp. 469–473.

Mates, B. T., & Reed, W. R. (2011). *Assistive technologies in the library.* Chicago, IL: ALA Editions.

McArdle, M. M. (2015). *The readers' advisory guide to genre blends.* Chicago, IL: American Library Association.

McClure, C. R. (1987). *Planning and role setting for public libraries: A manual of options and procedures.* Chicago, IL: American Library Association.

McCook, K. (1992, Winter). Where would we be without them? Libraries and adult education activities: 1966–1991. *RQ, 32,* 245–253.

McCook, K. (2000). *A place at the table: Participating in community building.* Chicago, IL: American Library Association.

McCook, K., (2011). *Introduction to public librarianship* (2nd ed.). New York, NY: Neal-Schuman Publishers.

McCook, K., & Barber, P. (2002). Public policy as a factor influencing adult lifelong learning, adult literacy and public libraries. *Reference and User Services Quarterly, 42*(1), 66–75.

Miller, R. (2015, October 2). Real-world barriers. *Library Journal,* http://lj.libraryjournal.com/2015/10/opinion/editorial/real-world-barriers-expanding-on-a-tradition-of-access-editorial/#_.

Monroe, M. E. (1963). *Library adult education: The biography of an idea.* New York, NY: Scarecrow Press.

Monroe, M. E. (1981). The cultural role of the public library. *Advances in Librarianship, 11,* 1–49.

Monroe, M. E., & Heim, K. M. (1991) *Partners for lifelong learning: Public libraries and adult education.* Washington, DC: Office of Library Programs, U.S. Department of Education, Office of Educational Research and Improvement.

Morgan, G. (2014). Reading groups, libraries and social inclusion: Experiences of blind and partially sighted people. *Library Review, 63*(6/7), 1.

Morris, V. I. (2012). *The readers' advisory guide to street literature.* Chicago, IL: ALA Editions.

Moyer, J. E., & Blau, A. (2008). *Research-based readers' advisory.* Chicago, IL: American Library Association.

Moyer, J. E., & Stover, K. M. (2010). *The readers' advisory handbook.* Chicago, IL: American Library Association.

Murray, D. C. (2016). A thirty-year reflection on the value of reference. *Reference & User Services Quarterly, 56*(1), 2–5.

National Commission on Adult Literacy and Council for Advancement of Adult Literacy. (2008). *Reach higher, America: Overcoming crisis in the U.S. workforce: Report of the National Commission on Adult Literacy.* New York, NY: Council for the Advancement of Adult Literacy.

National Endowment for the Humanities. (2016). Celebrating 50 Years of NEH support for library programming. https://www.neh.gov/divisions/public/featured-project/celebrating-50-years-neh-support-library-programming.

Nebraska Library Commission. Nebraska Center for the Book. (n.d.) http://nlc.nebraska.gov/.

Nell, V. (1988). *Lost in a book: The psychology of reading for pleasure.* New Haven, CT: Yale University Press.

Nelson, S. (2001). *The new planning for results: A streamlined approach.* Chicago, IL: American Library Association.

Nelson, S. (2008). *Strategic planning for results.* Chicago, IL: American Library Association.

Next Reads. (n.d.). https://www.ebscohost.com/novelist/our-products/nextread).

NoveList. (n.d.). https://www.ebscohost.com/novelist.

Nussbaum, M. C. (2011). *Creating capabilities: The human development approach.* Cambridge, MA: Belknap Press of Harvard University Press, 2013.

Nussbaum, M. C. (2016): Aspiration and the capabilities list. *Journal of Human Development and Capabilities 17*(3): 301-308.

Okobi, E. A. R. H. (2014). *Library services for adults in the 21st century.* Santa Barbara, CA: Libraries Unlimited.

Orr, C., & Herald, D. T. (2013). *Genreflecting: A guide to popular reading interests.* Santa Barbara, CA: Libraries Unlimited.

OverDrive (2017). Record number of libraries surpass one million ebook and audiobook checkouts with OverDrive in 2016. http://company.overdrive.com/record-number-libraries-surpass-one-million-ebook-audiobook-checkouts-overdrive-2016/.

Pateman, J., & Vincent, J. (2010). *Public libraries and social justice.* Farnham, Surrey, England: Ashgate.

Pawley, C., & Robbins, L. S. (2013). *Libraries and the reading public in twentieth-century America.* Madison, WI: University of Wisconsin Press.

Pawuk, M., & Serchay, D. (2016). *Graphic novels: A genre guide to comic books, manga, and more.* Santa Barbara, CA: Libraries Unlimited.

Pearl, N. (n.d.) *Nancy Pearl.* www.nancypearl.com/.

Peet, L. (2015a). LJ talks to Susan Hildreth. *Library Journal, 140*(3), 20.

Peet, L. (2015b). AUTHOR! AUTHOR!. *Library Journal, 140*(8), 26–29.

Perez, N. (2011). Resolution to protect library confidentiality in self-service hold practices. American Library Association, Intellectual Freedom Blog. www.oif.ala.org/oif/?p=2371.

Perrin, A. (2016, September 1). *Book reading 2016.* Fact Tank: Pew Research Center, 2016-9. www.pewinternet.org/2016/09/01/book-reading-2016/.

Phinney, E. (1967, Summer). Ten years from the vantage point of the executive secretary. *AD Newsletter, 4,* 11-14.

Preer, J. L. (1993, Spring). The American Heritage Project: Librarians and the democratic tradition in the early Cold War. *Libraries and Culture, 28,* 165-188.

ProLiteracy Worldwide. https://www.proliteracy.org.

Putnam, L. (2016). How libraries are curating current events, becoming community debate hubs. http://mediashift.org/2016/05/how-libraries-are-curating-current-events-becoming-community-debate-hubs/.

Rainie, L. (2016). *Libraries and learning.* Pew Research Center. www.pewinternet.org/2016/04/07/libraries-and-learning/.

Rawlinson, N. K. (1990, June). Give 'em what they want! *Library Journal, 115,* 77-79.

Resolution reaffirming ALA's commitment to basic literacy. Adopted by the Council of the American Library Association, Sunday, June 30, 2013, in Chicago, Illinois. www.ala.org/aboutala/sites/ala.org.aboutala/files/content/governance/council/council_documents/2013_annual_council_docs/cd_37_literacy%20resol-finalfinal.doc.pdf.

Roll, A. (2016). Both just-in-time and just-in-case. *Library Resources and Technical Services, 60*(1), 4-11.

Rolstad, G. O., & McCook, K. (1993). *Developing readers' advisory services: Concepts and commitments.* New York, NY: Neal-Schuman Publishers.

Rooney, K. (2005). *Reading with Oprah: The book club that changed America.* Fayetteville: University of Arkansas Press.

Ross, C. S. (2006). *Reading matters: What the research reveals about reading, libraries and community.* Westport, CT: Libraries Unlimited.

Ross, C. S. (2009, Spring). Public libraries, pleasure reading and models of reading. *Library Trends, 57,* 632-656.

Ross, C. S. (2014). *The pleasures of reading: A booklover's alphabet.* Santa Barbara, CA: Libraries Unlimited.

Saricks, J. (2015). At leisure with Joyce Saricks. *Booklist, 111*(15), 25.

Saricks, J. G. (2009). *The readers' advisory guide to genre fiction.* Chicago, IL: ALA Editions.

Saricks, J. G. (2011). *Read on—Audiobooks: Reading lists for every taste.* Santa Barbara, CA: Libraries Unlimited.

Saricks, J. G., & Brown, N. (1989). *Readers' advisory service in the public library.* Chicago, IL: American Library Association.

Scardilli, B. (2014). Streaming video in public libraries. *Information Today, 31*(6), 1-37.

Schlachter, G. A. (1982). *The service imperative for libraries: Essays in honor of Margaret E. Monroe.* Littleton, CO: Libraries Unlimited.

Sendze, M. (2012). The e-book experiment. *Public Libraries, 51*(1), 34-37.

Shorris, E. (2013). *The art of freedom: Teaching the humanities to the poor.* New York, NY: W. W. Norton & Company.

Smith, D. (2015). Readers' advisory. *Reference and User Services Quarterly, 54*(4), 11-16.

Spratford, B. S. (2012). *The readers' advisory guide to horror.* Chicago, IL: ALA Editions.

State Library of Michigan. (n.d.). Michigan Book Lists. www.michigan.gov/libraryofmichigan/0,2351,7-160-54574_36788_36791—-,00.html.

Stephens, A. K. (2006, Spring). Twenty-First Century public library adult services. *Reference and User Services Quarterly, 45,* 223-235.

Stevens, R. S., Bravender, P., & Witteveen-Lane, C. (2012). Self-service holds in libraries. *Reference and User Services Quarterly, 52*(1), 33-43.

Stevenson, G. T. (1954). The ALA Adult Education Board. *ALA Bulletin, 48,* 226-231.

Stewart, F. (2013) *Capabilities and human development: Beyond the individual—the critical role of social institutions and social competencies.* United Nations Development Programme. Human Development

Report Office. *Occasional Paper* 2013/03. http://hdr.undp.org/sites/default/files/hdro_1303_stewart.pdf.

Stop You're Killing Me. (n.d.). www.stopyourekillingme.com/.

Stover, K. M. *The facilitator's handy list of ground rules, guidelines and everything else.* Kansas City Public Library. www.kclibrary.org/?q=book-clubs/guidelines.

Swan, D. W, et al. (2014). *Public libraries in the United States survey: Fiscal Year 2012* (IMLS-2015-PLS-01). Institute of Museum and Library Services. Washington, DC.

Swain, M. H. (1995). A new deal in libraries: Federal relief work and library service, 1933-1943. *American Libraries, 30,* 265-283.

Thompson, K. M., Jaeger, P. T., Taylor, N. G., Subramaniam, M. M., & Bertot, J. C. (2014). *Digital literacy and digital inclusion: Information policy and the public library.* Lanham, MD: Rowman & Littlefield.

Tillett, B. B. (2003). *What is FRBR?: A conceptual model for the bibliographic universe.* Washington, DC: Library of Congress, Cataloging Distribution Service. www.loc.gov/cds/downloads/frbr.pdf.

United Nations Human Development Programme, Human Development Report Office. (n.d.). http://hdr.undp.org/en/humandev.

Vinjamuri, D. (2015). Building a display-driven strategy. *Library Journal, 140*(6), 46.

Waples, D., & Tyler, R. W. (1931). *What people want to read about: A study of group interests and a survey of problems in adult reading.* Chicago, IL: American Library Association.

Weibel, K. (1982). The evolution of library outreach 1960-75 and its effect on reader services: Some considerations. *Occasional Paper* 16. Urbana, IL: Graduate School of Library and Information Science. ERIC ED231376.

Wellman, H. C. (1915, July). The library's primary duty. *ALA Bulletin, 9,* 89-93.

Wentz, B., in Jaeger, P. T., & In Bertot, J. C. (2015). Accessibility for persons with disabilities and the inclusive future of libraries. *Advances in Librarianship 40.* Emerald Publishing.

What's Next? Books in series. (n.d.). http://ww2.kdl.org/libcat/whatsnext.asp.

Widdersheim, M. M. (2015). Governance, legitimation, commons: a public sphere framework and research agenda for the public library sector. *Libri: International Journal of Libraries and Information Services,* 65(4), 237-245.

Wiegand, W. A. (2011). *Main Street public library: Community places and reading spaces in the rural heartland, 1876-1956.* Iowa City, IA: University of Iowa Press.

Wilson, L. R. (1938). *The geography of reading: A study of the distribution and status of libraries in the United States.* Chicago, IL: University of Chicago Press.

Wu, K. (2011). The book club phenomena. *McSweeney's.* www.mcsweeneys.net/articles/the-book-club-phenomena.

Wyatt, N. (2014). We owe our work to theirs. *Reference and User Services Quarterly, 54*(2), 24-30.

Zepheira. (2014). http://zepheira.com/solutions/library/libhub/.

CHAPTER 10

Collaboration and Consortia

Jenny S. Bossaller

There is a long history of cooperation in American libraries. In 1876, the American Library Association's inaugural meeting saw the formation of the Committee on Cooperation in Indexing and Cataloguing College Libraries, believed to be the first effort at widespread cooperation in the United States. The report of the Office of Regents of the University of the State of New York (1878) explained the significance of a movement towards cooperation: "It is safe to say that if the movement, now happily started in this country and proposed in England, is carried on discreetly, there will be a constant tendency toward common methods; and as methods become common, coöperation will be facilitated" (p. 472). In 1901, the Library of Congress began creating the National Union Catalog in order to locate and record the location of every important book in the United States, which was to facilitate borrowing and lending on a national scale. In 1936, Ralph Parker introduced punched cards in libraries, providing the means to automate routine tasks in the library and paving the way towards automated ILL between library consortia (Burns, 2014). Interestingly, outside of libraries in 1937, H. G. Wells wrote a short piece called the World Brain, envisioning a permanent world encyclopedia that would provide access to all the knowledge of humankind; this has read as an early vision of cooperative structures in libraries or of the Internet (note that the piece is a product of its time, espousing controversial subjects such as eugenics).

Although we tend to focus on recent memory, it is important to remember that today's vast cooperative networks had their beginnings long before WWII. Since WWII, technologies have been more ingrained into the daily work of librarians, which has enabled more cooperation.

Cooperation, however, is not only about technology, and libraries do not only cooperate with other libraries. John Curl (2009) wrote that there are cooperatives that fulfill every human need—from childcare to transportation to medicine to schools. His concern is largely with worker exchanges, which might provide an alternative framework to describe the work of library cooperatives and consortia. Curl said that "worker cooperatives are increasingly recognized throughout the world as a necessary element in any sustainable economic system of the future" (p. 7). Cooperatives are encouraged even by the United Nations because they "demonstrate a wide acceptance that global peace and stability require solving the problems of poverty and unemployment, and that cooperatives can help accomplish this" (p. 7). Cooperation across institutions, agencies, and nonprofits across cities and regions increases community resiliency (Patin, 2016; Grace and Sen, 2013). Libraries cooperate with museums and other learning organizations to enhance opportunities for informal learning

(Santo, Peppler, Ching, & Hoadley, 2015) and for cultural preservation (Yarrow, Clubb, & Draper, 2008). Cooperatives of all types enable workers to maximize their efforts—for each other, and for the public good. Thus, there are (at least) two ways to conceive of cooperation: technological and social.

Librarians are, in essence, knowledge workers. Since the ALA was founded, public librarians have made great strides to increase libraries' ability to serve their patrons, and most agree that one of the best ways to do this is through cooperation that maximizes their work for the public good. Today public libraries are connected through a variety of mechanisms including local cooperative agreements, state library agencies, library consortia, multistage regional networks, and national and international cooperatives such as the Online Computer Library Center (OCLC). These entities comprise a creative series of overlapping networks in which public libraries have functioned to expand and extend their services using cutting-edge technologies. Librarians have long worked at the state and national levels to develop policies on all aspects of service from interlibrary loan to cataloging standards. Through state library agencies, librarians have worked on statewide plans, professional development, collaborative grants, cooperative licensing, and massive digitization projects. Cooperation enables librarians to do more things quicker and better. On the flip side, it also maximizes any social agency's impact in the community.

In previous chapters, we have discussed librarians' need to understand political processes at the local and national level. It is also important that librarians recognize the relationships the public library has with larger systems that provide support and connections to additional resources. This is professional networking! Networks provide opportunities to carry on professional connections that enrich careers and strengthen ties to others. The spirit and energy of individual librarians built the foundation of this network. We turn attention in this chapter to the growth of public library cooperation initiatives in the United States, focusing on:

1. Libraries cooperating with each other, through consortia
2. Collaborative Digital Initiatives and Platforms
3. Professional associations
4. Partnerships with the community
5. Training and funding mechanisms to support cooperation

Unfortunately, there are countervailing forces that undermine librarians' efforts to create strong cooperative networks. Especially since the recent economic downturn, public funding for education and libraries (among other social goods) has been reduced generally, but cooperative efforts have also suffered. This is both unfortunate and ironic, given that the premise of cooperatives is to increase sustainability and stretch dollars. Now, as much as ever, librarians need to understand how cooperative efforts might help them maximize their efforts.

COOPERATING WITH EACH OTHER: CONSORTIA, STATE LIBRARIES, AND COOPERATIVES

Groups of collaborating libraries might be called cooperatives, networks, collectives, alliances, and partnerships, or consortia. What exactly is a library consortium? According to the U.S. Code of Federal Regulations, Sect. 54.500, a library consortium "is any local, regional, or national cooperative association of libraries that provides for the systematic and effective coordination of the resources of school, public, academic, and special libraries and information centers, for improving services to the clientele of such libraries." Consortia are generally formal associations, governed and regulated by their members. A useful definition of libraries working together was formulated by Joseph Becker (1979): "when two or more libraries engage formally in a common pattern of information exchange, through communications, for some functionally interdependent purpose, we have a library network" (p. 89).

Horton and Pronevitz's (2015) book *Library Consortia* describe three main areas for cooperation; consortia might engage in some or all of these activities:

1. Components of discovery to delivery (resource sharing, ILL, delivery, shared offsite storage and collection development, shared ILS and technologies, and cooperative digitization, hosting institutional repositories).
2. Shared purchasing activities, such as databases and equipment.
3. Library Empowerment Activities (training, education, professional development, and consulting). Shared virtual reference and summer reading programs are also discussed.

As previously described, libraries have been working together in various kinds of consortial activities since the 1880s. It wasn't until the 1960s and 1970s (what Horton and Pronevitz refer to as the "heyday of consortial development") that widespread library automation enabled the development and growth of several large-scale consortia, including the Online Computer Library System (OCLC), the Western Library Network (WLN), and the Research Libraries Information Network (RLIN) (p. 5). The OCLC (formerly known as the Online Computer Library System) is still the world's biggest library network.

In 1965, 16 libraries began to participate in Henriette Avram's Project MARC (Burns, 2014). Avram was hired to develop an automated cataloging format at the Library of Congress in 1965, after working for the National Security Agency (Schudel, 2006). MARC (Machine Readable Cataloging) was the basis for OCLC. OCLC was the brainchild of Ralph Parker, University of Missouri librarian, and Frederick G. Kilgour of the Ohio College Association. It was built to be a "cooperative, computerized, regional network in which most, if not all, Ohio college libraries will participate" (Burns, p. 94). As Parker said in 1966, such cooperation was only possible by taking a "systems approach to mechanization"; librarians usually direct their efforts towards "the solution of specific problems" (p. 94).

This system was established to solve the problem of scarcity—a need to borrow books from each other efficiently. Such cooperation is only possible by conceptualizing the libraries as part of a system; that system rests on a technological backbone of MARC records that are loaded into a shared system, which we now see manifested in WorldCat. Over the years, OCLC established a network of state and regional providers that essentially granted OCLC control over resource borrowing and sharing. This existed until recently, when regional consortia with buying power and training opportunities changed how consortia work. There are probably many reasons why consortia have changed and why we see a decentralized marketplace for library services; for instance, libraries share many resources and use different methods for sharing resources, such as e-books and institutional repositories, rather than borrowing and lending books. State legislatures and funding agencies want to see competition and bidding; OCLC did have a monopoly. The future is perhaps more dispersed than it was in the past, centralized by a platform that has not yet been completely developed. Perhaps centralization waxes and wanes according to available technologies. We can revisit that idea later.

We most often think of consortia as geographically situated, library-based organizations, and geography is still the basis for many consortia. However, they are not always limited to small areas, and certain functions are online services rather than goods, freeing them from the confines of geography altogether. Consortia are also not static; they grow, merge, and morph. Horton and Pronevitz refer to merged consortia as "megaconsortia" (p. 23), with more mass for greater buying power or leverage than smaller consortia, and certainly more than solo libraries. These mergers, along with a shift to provision of online services and training, have also resulted in a new type of relationship between libraries and providers—they are not peer institutions, but instead nonprofit corporations or vendors. This has also introduced competition in the marketplace among the vendors, with libraries possibly joining multiple consortia for different purposes. These nonprofits provide a variety of services to libraries that focus on helping them cooperatively develop resources. They also provide other services, and those vary from consortium to consortium. Some of them require formal membership, and others have looser membership qualifications.

> **▶ TASK**
>
> Spend some time looking up books and other items in WorldCat. Who owns them? How is WorldCat useful for the average library users? For librarians?

The growth of networks in the late twentieth century was a response to OCLC policy that shared cataloging would take place through networks, rather than individual libraries. Seventeen regional service providers contracted with OCLC to provide support and training for OCLC services. Realizing their shared mission and also that the future of libraries was not necessarily in cataloging, the regional service providers began to morph. Two examples of these are LYRASIS and AMIGOS (see figure 10.1).

In 2008, the boards of PALINET and SOLINET recognized their shared mission and the unprecedented opportunities to expand education, leadership development, technology, and savings for members, while adding critical new initiatives needed for the future. In February 2009, members of these two well-established regional library networks voted to merge, creating LYRASIS. Other organizations, the Bibliographic Center for Research (BCR) and NELINET (a regional network rooted in New England), joined shortly after. LYRASIS "partners with member libraries, archives, and museums and other cultural heritage organizations to create, access, and manage information with an emphasis on digital content, while building and sustaining collaboration, enhancing operations and technology, and increasing buying power" (LYRASIS, n.d., About Us).

State library agencies have been mentioned in previous chapters, but they are worth bringing up again here because of their role as catalysts in public library cooperation. The first state libraries were founded in the 1890s to encourage public library development. Public library leaders in the early twentieth century recognized that the creation of independent public libraries affiliated with municipal governments could not meet the library needs of the nation. Some communities were too small to provide adequate library services based on local taxing districts. The Library Services Act (LSA, 1956) and the Library Services and Construction Act (LSCA, 1964) were principal pieces of legislation for ensuring library service across the nation.

In the early 1960s, the Association of State Libraries initiated a survey to review the status of state library agencies to make recommendations for their future. The 1966 report

The Library Functions of the States identified "coordination and cooperation" as one of the key goals of the State Library Agencies (Monypenny, 1966), a point that was made the following year with strong emphasis in the National Advisory Commission on Libraries (1969) report, *Libraries at Large: Traditions, Innovations and the National Interest.* This report included the recommendation that the LSCA be amended to strengthen state library agencies so that the agencies could "coordinate planning for total library service," setting policy for future library coordination for public libraries.

The ALA Washington Office worked diligently to see that the National Advisory Commission on Libraries' recommendation was implemented through amendments to the LSCA in 1970. State plans were required, but states were given latitude to develop their own services. A sample of state library plans and annual reports are available through the U.S.

Profile: AMIGOS

In 1973, Amigos Library Services began as a regional consortium serving libraries throughout the Southwest United States as an OCLC regional service provider. Amigos focuses on training, consulting, and providing discounts on e-books and databases. It also has a courier service offering low-cost pickup and delivery of ILL items among participating libraries. Membership is available to academic, public, school, and special libraries. They primarily serve Arkansas, Arizona, Illinois, Kansas, Missouri, New Mexico, Oklahoma, and Texas but have member libraries in several other states.

In the late 1970s and early 1980s OCLC worked with consortia such as Amigos to provide support, training, and implementation on their products and services. During that time, many State Libraries used Library Services and Technology Act (LSTA) funds to support their use of OCLC services. There was limited competition between the existing 17 network consortia. Around 2010, OCLC decided to change its business model. It dissolved exclusive contracts with regional providers and began working with individual libraries. This changed their relationships with the regional service providers resulting in changes in the consortial landscape. Several consortia that previously served as regional service providers for OCLC have transformed and are thriving. They include Minitex, OhioNet, the Midwest Collaborative for Library Services, Lyrasis, and Amigos. Some consortia did not survive this change in business practices.

Since 2010, a wave of consortial mergers spread through the United States. The cumulative impact of the economic downturn, the loss of OCLC affiliation and reductions in state funding changed the operating environment for consortia, and mergers provided a way for organizations to continue to fulfill their public purpose in a new way. State-based models have changed as well. Libraries have options for finding services such as training, resources sharing, and group purchasing.

In 2012, the Missouri Library Network Corporation (MLNC) merged with Amigos Library Services, a direct result of OCLC no longer requiring members to work with a corporate partner (one of the 17 regional network providers). This merger was mutually beneficial: it offered the combined membership more leverage in negotiating, additional continuing

FIGURE 10.1 Profile: AMIGOS [CONTINUED ON FOLLOWING PAGE]

FIGURE 10.1 [CONTINUED]

education options, and a continuous role in governance of the merged organization. Tracy Byerly, Amigos' Chief Specialty Officer, explains that the merger worked because the two organizations had similar cultures, membership structures, and shared geographic boundaries. They also had similar services—both offered negotiated discounts on electronic resources and continuing education. Amigos offered courier service, where MLNC was involved in association management. Additionally, they both operated under similar governance model, each having an elected board that is composed of its members and are funded entirely by their membership fees.

Not all consortia do the same thing or have the same focus. For instance, while both Lyrasis and Amigos offer training and discounts on electronic resources, Lyrasis is also home to a strong suite of field digitization and preservation services, including the Digitization Collaborative, disaster preparedness tools, digitization and preservation supplies, preservation toolbox, training, and consulting. Amigos has a robust continuing education offering which includes fundamentals for paraprofessionals, such as training in RDA cataloging, copy cataloging, and management. This mix means that libraries may join more than one consortium.

Department of Education's, Education Resources and Information Center (ERIC). These state plans provide a history of innovation and cooperative efforts. A few abstracts of model plans illustrate the extent of services:

1. Illinois State library—Annual Program LSCA, 1974. This document gives an overview of 16 distinct projects that were being conducted at the time, such as professional development activities, local public library and public library system development, and library services for institutionalized, blind, and physically handicapped people.
2. Wyoming State Library—Five-Year Plan, 1974-1978. This document shows how demographic characteristics of the population drive the planning process. The final component of the plan lists the goal of library service as bringing informational, cultural, and recreational services and materials to all citizens of the state. Specifically, it focuses on: 1) consultant, financial, and reference services; 2) services to the handicapped, the institutionalized, and the disadvantaged; 3) library service to rural areas; 4) research and library development services; and 5) aid with library construction.

Documents such as these demonstrate how, during this period, state libraries helped local libraries coordinate activities to meet targeted community needs. Libraries worked to forge innovative services to extend library resources to the underserved, enhance personnel development, and build the capacity of libraries to respond to the needs of each state's residents.

LSTA and the Future of Libraries

The Library Services Act (LSA, 1956-1964), the LSCA (Library Services and Construction Act, 1964-1996), and the current legislation, the Library Services and Technology Act (LSTA, 1996—present) demonstrate federal commitment to local purposes and priorities. These include a range of services designed to build human capital, expand existing library services, and update the information infrastructure of today's libraries. Today "over 1500 Grants to States Projects are granted each year to libraries that serve the priorities of the LSTA" (IMLS, 2016, https://www.imls.gov/grants/grants-states). The money is funneled to libraries through State Library Administration Agencies (SLAAs).

The passage of the LSTA in 1996 shifted the manner in which the federal government funded state activities. The LSTA is part of the Museum and Library Services Act, which created the Institute of Museum and Library Services (IMLS) and established federal programs to help libraries and museums serve the public. The LSTA's stated 1996 purposes were to:

1. Consolidate Federal library service programs.
2. Stimulate excellence and promote access to learning and information resources in all types of libraries for individuals of all ages.
3. Promote library services that provide all users access to information through State, regional, national, and international electronic networks.
4. Provide linkages between libraries.
5. Promote targeted library services to people of diverse geographic, cultural, and socioeconomic backgrounds, to individuals with disabilities, and to people with limited functional literacy or information skills.

The Grant to State Program allocates "a base amount to each of the SLAAs plus a supplemental amount based on population" (IMLS, n.d.). In 2016, the base amount was $680,000 for each of the 50 states, Puerto Rico, and the District of Columbia, and $60,000 each for the U.S. Territories. Programs serve "children, parents, teenagers, adult leaders, senior citizens, the unemployed, and the business community" with priorities given to programs that address "underserved communities and persons having difficulty using a library." Detailed evaluation plans are required from each SLAA. The planning and evaluation initiative "Measuring Success" was developed to improve the methods of evaluating programs in order to better distribute funds and develop best practices.

The Museum and Library Services Act of 2010 specifically addressed consortial activities as "resource and policy approaches to eliminate barriers to fully leveraging the role of libraries and museums in supporting the early learning, literacy, lifelong learning digital literacy, workforce development, and education needs of the people in the United States" (Museum and Library Services Act of 2010).

Multi-Type Library Cooperatives

One term used for library networks is the multi-type library cooperative (MLC). These are nonprofit cooperatives composed of academic, school, public, and specialized libraries in a specific region that aim to improve access to materials, as well as to provide a space for librarians to share their expertise. The MLC emerged as a solution to resource sharing in the 1970s. It is difficult to generalize about MLCs, because even more than state library agencies, MLCs developed directly in response to local needs, evolving from the efforts of librarians working through professional associations in collaboration with state library agencies. The MLC was an evolution in the long push for larger units of library service, first described in the 1920s and legitimized by the LSA, which called for state plans to promote service to rural areas. The 1967 addition of Title III to the LSTA specifically promoted multi-type library development, and the PLA issued standards for this type of library cooperative, entitled *Minimum Standards for Public Library Systems, 1966.* The library system, as discussed in the standards, was intended to provide accessibility through branches, cooperating libraries, and bookmobile stops, plus a pool of resources and services used in common by all the outlets.

The increased scope of the MLCs in the 1970s and 1980s strongly contributed to public library development and acted as a mechanism to help equalize services for all people. Consulting services and continuing education provided by the MLCs rendered support to small libraries without professional staff. Some MLCs purchased core collections to share among member libraries or coordinated cooperative collection development. By 1990 standards were established for MLCs and state laws consolidated to support further development (ASCLA, 1990; Fiels, Neumann, and Brown, 1991). Librarians working in MLCs or system environments find support locally, but also through two units of ALA: the Association of Specialized and Cooperative Library Agencies (ASCLA) and the Public Library Systems Community of Practice of the PLA.

Two examples of current multitype library collectives (one state and one citywide) are RAILS, in Illinois, and Baynet, a member organization centered in the San Francisco Bay area.

1. RAILS: Reaching Across Illinois Library System (RAILS) "serves approximately 1300 academic, public, school, and special library agencies in northern and west-central Illinois. Services include interlibrary delivery, shared catalog support, continuing education, consulting, talking books advisory service, shared e-book collection, cooperative purchasing, and more" (www.railslibraries.info/). Any library can apply to become a member. There are no membership fees, but all members must agree to comply with the ILLINET Interlibrary Loan Code and provide reciprocal borrowing to other members. Public library members must complete annual public library reports, as required by the State Library Act, and must also assess "possibilities for library services to unserved areas" (Membership Requirements, RAILS).
2. BayNet: Bay Area Library and Information Network. "As a multi-type library association, BayNet represents librarians and information professionals from all varieties of organizations. Our mission is to strengthen connections among all types of San Francisco Bay Area Libraries and Information Centers, and to promote communication, professional development, cooperation, and innovative resource sharing." A current job list, news about member libraries, news about current events in local libraries, and free or low-cost training opportunities provide ways for librarians in the Bay Area to connect. They host a free annual meeting with speakers and social activities. BayNet is not a consortium, but a member organization that librarians and information professionals from all types of libraries can join on an individual basis.

The organizations are quite different because RAILS is comprised of libraries, and BayNet is for individuals. However, they are both collectives, offering training and benefits for members.

The National Library Service for the Blind and Physically Handicapped

Perhaps the most long-standing example of cooperating is the National Library Service for the Blind and Physically Handicapped. This service was established with Pratt-Smoot Act, which was signed into law by President Herbert Hoover in 1931:

> That there is hereby authorized to be appropriated annually to the Library of Congress, in addition to appropriations otherwise made to said Library, the sum of $100,000, which sum shall be expended under the direction of the Librarian of Congress to provide books for the use of the adult blind residents of the United States, including the several States, Territories, insular possessions, and the District of Columbia.
>
> Sec. 2. The Librarian of Congress may arrange with such libraries as he may judge appropriate to serve as local or regional centers for the circulation of such books, under such conditions and regulations as he may prescribe. In the lending of such books preference shall at all times be given to the needs of blind persons who have been honorably discharged from the United States military or naval service. (https://www.loc.gov/nls/act1931.html)

In 1952, the National Library Service for the Blind was expanded to include services for children. In 1962, it began to distribute music, and in 1966 it was again expanded to serve people with physical disabilities that prevent reading regular print materials (https://www.loc.gov/nls/reference/guides/annual.html).

According to Amy Nickless, Special Service librarian at Missouri's Wolfner Talking Book and Braille Library, from the late 1930s through the 1970s the St. Louis location "filled both an educational and social need in the area as the Wolfner Library also served as a community center for the blind . . . Many societies and organizations for the blind used the library as its home base and social events, such as dances, were held on a regular basis" (personal communication, October 6, 2010). Today, Nickless says that the biggest cooperation between libraries involves the interlibrary loan of locally produced items, such as local histories and local interest topics (Missouri authors, history, setting, etc.). This includes many children's books. According to Nickless, one way that librarians who work within the network cooperate is by sharing their internal and external newsletters, which helps them learn about programming in other libraries.

Joint-Use Libraries

Sometimes librarians might find that it is in their community's best interest to establish joint-use libraries. These are also called combined libraries, dual-use libraries, co-managed libraries, or cooperative libraries. The ALA's fact sheet and bibliography about joint-use libraries explains that joint-use libraries "are those where two separate library service providers use the same building to serve distinct clienteles. Such libraries are most often public libraries combined with school library media centers or public libraries combined with academic libraries, but other types exist" (American Library Association, 2012).

There are also libraries that combine city and a college or university; for instance, San Jose has a joint-use library shared by San Jose State University and the City of San Jose; they share the Dr. Martin Luther King, Jr. Library, with the City Library Director and the University Library Dean "co-managing" the Library. The agreement is an important part of any consortium or joint-use library because it outlines the rights and responsibilities (fiscal, spatial, programmatic, etc.) of each entity. This 65-page document demonstrates the complexity of such agreements.

LOCAL HISTORY: COOPERATING WITH THE COMMUNITY AND WITH OTHER LIBRARIES

Many public libraries have, for years, collected local history materials in their local history reference collections (LHRCs). Archives and historical societies might collect rare or vulnerable materials, designating public libraries as collectors of local newspapers, yearbooks, cemetery records, and other items that their patrons donate. LHRCs provide a means of teaching, researching, and understanding the past. Establishing LHRCs is one step, but digitization of some of the materials might also be required. This means that libraries should think about not only how they will establish and maintain their local collection, but also how they might help people who live outside of the community to use the digitized collection. Both require planning, thought, and coordination.

Working with the Community: Establishing a Local History Collection

Kathy Marquis and Leslie Waggener (2015) and the RUSA Local History committee provide guidelines for establishing a local history collection (2012). Marquis and Waggener explain that when starting out, the library should begin by examining the patron base, space, and budget to determine what is feasible and desirable to collect. Some commonly collected, locally published materials found in public libraries are atlases, county histories, video/audio recordings, cookbooks, guidebooks, biographies, and publications about local institutions—material that is unique to the area. The guidelines suggest that prior to establishing an LHRC, a collection development policy that includes how to deal with local materials should be established, and to determine (and write down!) what is within the scope of the collection and what falls outside.

Small public libraries are likely not equipped to deal with preservation or security of rare items. This means that they must be selective about what they collect; if the library were to have an open call for donations, the public might expect to have their documents properly preserved rather than used. They do not recommend collecting institutional or organizational records (e.g., meeting minutes), personal papers, photographs, scrapbooks, or artifacts. The library should find out if other organizations are collecting local materials, and remember that the best place for archival materials is where they will be most easily found. The RUSA (2012) Local History Committee has issued "Guidelines for Establishing Local History Collections," which emphasize that the library should establish and maintain a dialog between local institutions (museums, academic libraries, local archives), societies

MOBIUS is only one example of many consortia. Marshall Breeding (2016) explained that "current technology architectures can be used to create multi-tenant platforms in which a single instance of the software can support thousands of libraries" (p. 10). The systems can be expanded almost infinitely, and Breeding recommends that any library considering replacing its ILS needs to investigate options for joining a consortium—it will save the library money, time, and will vastly improve library services to patrons.

Consortium Profile: MOBIUS

MOBIUS was founded in 1998 as a resource-sharing initiative for academic libraries across Missouri. It was originally funded by the legislature and was underneath the University of Missouri system. It became a not-for-profit corporation in 2010, which gave it the latitude to expand its services, especially out of the state. It began with 50 academic libraries, but now has 75 members, including "65 academic libraries, 5 public libraries, 4 special libraries, and the Missouri State Library, serving a total of 184 physical branches" (MOBIUS, 2016).

The consortium has expanded to provide services beyond state boundaries to libraries in Iowa, Oklahoma, and Texas. Its expansion is largely due to the addition of these out-of-state public libraries and academic libraries. The growth and expansion offers lessons in resource sharing, technical expertise, and management with a strong vision for the future of collaboration and cooperative services.

Why Public Libraries?

MOBIUS was founded for academic libraries' resource sharing, similar to so many other consortia. All of the libraries operated on Innovative Interface's ILS (III) system, and were organized by "clusters," which were the names given to the servers, primarily focused on geographic regions (with the University of Missouri system having its own server). The clusters' data fed (and still feeds) into the shared central server, called the Inn-Reach system. MOBIUS offered member libraries help with all technical issues, help with vendor negotiations, and training.

The current director of MOBIUS, Donna Bacon, was formerly the Distance Reference Manager of the Springfield-Greene County Library, which was the first public library in MOBIUS. She said that when they first joined MOBIUS there was some question about why a public library would want to be a part of the consortium. They soon learned why: circulation went up across the board. "If you want your circulation to go up, join a consortium . . . Once you start mixing academic and public libraries together, things really change" (D. Bacon, personal communication, October 3, 2016). Why? Public users want the academic materials; they serve distance learning students who don't have an academic library nearby. Students participating in National History Day need research materials. Academic library users have access to current popular materials. The unique holdings in the Art Museum, theological schools, Osteopathic Institute, and other members contribute to an incredible diversity of material that benefits all of the member libraries. Their materials complement each other, and because of the variety they can better meet their mission of providing equal access to resources for patrons, and services to libraries.

[CONTINUED ON FOLLOWING PAGE]

[CONTINUED FROM PREVIOUS PAGE]

The MOBIUS office took on a second project in 2012: the Evergreen Library Project. Evergreen is an open-source ILS for consortia that was developed by the Georgia Public Library Service in 2006. The Missouri Evergreen project began when the director of MOBIUS and the State Librarian initiated conversations regarding a project that would expand resources to public libraries. MOBIUS is under contract from the Missouri State Library, funded by LSTA, to implement and manage Missouri Evergreen. That includes staff, servers, and migration/training costs. Missouri Evergreen gives smaller libraries the ability to put their holdings into an ILS (some were still using card catalogs prior to joining the consortium), and provide databases to the public.

While many people see open-source systems as a way to save money, they are actually "expensive to run. You're shifting your money from paying a vendor to paying staff, and programmers are not cheap" (D. Bacon, 2016). For the first year, MOBIUS contracted with Equinox, a company founded by the people that developed Evergreen to help them learn to manage the systems. After the first year they were able to manage it on their own, and have steadily continued to grow. They are currently moving their services from a local data center to Google Cloud Services. They are also waiting for III to develop an API that will connect the III system to the Evergreen system.

Remember, the consortium is not only about computers; it is about materials that must be transported efficiently. This requires extensive coordination. The consortium has developed a labeling, bagging, boxing, borrowing, and transport system for the materials, with the goal of keeping the cost as low as possible for the members. Their cost-analysis found that borrowing from within the consortium was much cheaper than using traditional ILL. However, most of the smaller libraries simply did not do much ILL before entering the consortium so an accurate before-and-after analysis may not be possible.

To sum it up, the original goal of MOBIUS was to increase access to academic materials across the state. The addition of public libraries to MOBIUS added to the diversity of both the public and academic libraries. Missouri Evergreen is a separate system that MOBIUS manages, but there are hopes to eventually merge the two. This is an example of systemic thinking. Creating and nurturing such a complicated system requires an understanding of the mechanics, but also intelligent decision-making, political connections, and strong leadership.

(both genealogical and historical), and agencies (county, city, and state). Public libraries should not be in competition with local historical or genealogical societies.

Archives emphasize preservation rather than access. This is a leap for a public librarian to make, but necessary if the public is entrusting the library with precious materials. The entire lifecycle (acquisition, collection, use, and disposal) of archival materials differs from that of library materials. For instance, Marquis and Waggener (2011) discuss the reference process for archival collections: the patron identifies the materials she wishes to consult in advance and makes an appointment; gloves are frequently worn, and the patron might only be given one archival box at a time to examine. Can the library support such requirements? Think of the LHRC in terms of public trust: the public is entrusting you to preserve their materials. It is a collaboration between the library and the public to preserve and share treasures, but the rules of the game should be clear.

Digitization of Local Materials

Digitization is recommended for items that will be used beyond the library's walls. Embarking on a digitization project lies outside of the scope of this chapter. Please consult a current book on digitization projects if you are interested in the technical aspects of digitization.

From city- to statewide platforms for digital heritage to national and international cooperative projects, librarians and archivists are creating ways to connect anyone with access to the Internet to digitized and born-digital content. Exactly how are digitization projects cooperative? They involve collaborations with the community itself for development. They also require establishing and following technological workflows, using existing standards created through cooperation and collaboration. Without standards and the idea that they will eventually need to "talk to" each other, they will be stand-alone projects, which are much less useful than those that can contribute to large, collaborative projects.

Larger public libraries might have both archives and local history collections, with the staff, expertise, and funding to properly support both. Here, let's turn to some large digital collections that demonstrate collaboration on the local and national level. They are rooted in their community, but they all also contribute to the Digital Public Library of America (DPLA), which is explained in figure 10.2.

Boston Public Library

The venerable BPL's archival collections digitized books and manuscripts, newspapers, photographs, and sound archives. Some of the online collections focus on Boston's history, mixing narratives about local history with photographs and other digitized representative pieces from the collection.

> **▶ TASK**
>
> Explore a DPLA collection. Find out who contributed the items. Explore the map. How and why does it work?

Chicago Collections

"Together we keep Chicago's history and culture alive: the member institutions of Chicago Collections collaborate, uniting their resources, to offer access and exciting learning experiences to both the general public and academic researchers." There are a variety of members, including universities, research libraries, societies, historical associations, and public libraries. The Chicago Collections includes archives, manuscripts, and objects from members' collections. Explore Chicago Collections is "a free, centralized, web-based search engine and record-finding tool where researchers, teachers, and students are able to locate or access over 100,000 maps, photos, and letters": primary source materials that are searchable by topic, and are included in "library guides, digital exhibits, and educational materials" (Chicago Public Library, 2016). It has a cooperative reference network to help people use the collections, and hosts educational and community events.

Internet Archive

The American Libraries collection contains, as of 2016, over two million items of material contributed from libraries across the United States from the Library of Congress, archives, colleges, and universities, and local public libraries. It includes a wealth of genealogical material, yearbooks, local history, newspapers, and audio files.

Cooperating with Each Other: Professional Associations

Librarians were one of the first occupational groups in the United States to organize as a professional association. The American Library Association was established in 1876, and it has since provided a means for librarians to discuss, plan, solve problems, and develop cooperative initiatives. This chapter is about collaboration, and one of the first ALA committees was, in fact, specifically focused on collaboration: the committee on shared cataloging. The publication *Public Libraries in the United States of America: Their History, Condition, and Management: Special Report* (U.S. Bureau of Education, 1876) included histories of and statistics about libraries. This aided librarians' efforts at cooperation by providing context

Profile: The Digital Public Library of America

The Digital Public Library of America (DPLA) is a platform for digital content. It was created in 2010 with the goal of bringing the dispersed collections "of America's libraries, archives, museums, and cultural heritage sites, and making them freely available to students, teachers, researchers, and the general public." This ambitious goal aims to bring these various collections into a single searchable space; it is a massive aggregation of digital collections. It includes (as of October 2016) over 14 million items. There are many ways of looking at the collection; the website itself includes a timeline, map, and curated exhibitions. It also has an open API, which "enables new and transformative users of our digitized cultural heritage." As of 2016, developers have created 34 apps that connect to the DPLA via the API to allow users to use the collections in a variety of ways. Some of the apps also connect to Europeana, the shared digital platform for Europe.

The keyword for DPLA (and other massive digital projects) is interoperability, which is only possible when everyone understands and adheres to standards. The interoperability of the DPLA discovery framework is made possible by metadata that describes content and resources. The metadata also connects US holdings to holdings in other countries—in, for instance, the Europeana platform. Individuals and small libraries cannot contribute to the DPLA. Libraries, historical societies, and other entities that wish to contribute content must join a hub.

"Service hubs" are responsible for compiling records from contributors. The aggregated data is then uploaded and available for reuse through the DPLA API (Gregory and Williams, 2014). Gregory and Williams describe the process that DigitalNC followed to contribute as a hub to DPLA. They worked with the DPLA to determine the metadata schema and required fields; assess and set up a feed aggregator; review metadata fields provided by the data providers, and harvest feeds from data providers on a monthly basis. The DPLA only has a few required fields, and the hubs must decide which fields they will require of contributors. Cooperation and compliance assures that the data contributed by libraries and historical societies will work with the DPLA and Europeana. DPLA and Europeana can be searched simultaneously, providing access to both libraries' resources through the "Search DPLA and Europeana" app.

FIGURE 10.2 Profile: The Digital Public Library of America

of growth and development. The *Library Journal*, the official publication of ALA until 1908 when the *ALA Bulletin* began publication, also contributed to the capacity of librarians to work together and share ideas. Thus, from its beginning in 1876, librarians found two key elements—baseline data and a mechanism for ongoing communication—that paved the way for collaborative progress.

Today, ALA is an umbrella organization that includes many smaller units and divisions. Units include the Association for Library Collections and Technical Services; Association for Library Services to Children; Association of Library Trustees, Advocates, Friends and Foundations; Library Leadership and Management Association; Library Information Technology Association; Reference and User Services Association; and the Young Adult Library Services Association. These smaller groups develop and share best practices, establish standards, communicate and examine successes and failures, and nurture new members. The Division of Public Libraries was formed within ALA in 1944 and merged with the Library Extension Division in 1950 to become the Public Library Division. In 1958 this division was reorganized as the Public Library Association (PLA), which today is the overarching national professional association for public librarians, with a membership of nearly 9,000 members in 2016 (see figure 10.3).

Each of these units and divisions have, over the years, developed cooperative projects, formulated standards and guidelines, recommended best practices, and provided opportunities for librarians to collaborate to improve and expand the quality of public library services. Twice yearly (at ALA Annual Conferences and Midwinter Meetings) 15,000 to 20,000 librarians from all over the United States meet to plan, exchange ideas, and learn about

Profile: The Public Library Association (PLA)

Mission Statement

The Public Library Association enhances the development and effectiveness of public library staff and public library services. This mission positions PLA to:

- Focus its efforts on serving the needs of its members
- Address issues which affect public libraries
- Commit to quality public library services that benefit the general public

Core Purpose (2014)

To strengthen public libraries and their contribution to the communities they serve.

Core Organizational Values (2014)

PLA is dedicated to:

- Visionary Leadership.
- Member Focus.
- Integrity and Transparency.

FIGURE 10.3 Profile: The Public Library Association (PLA) [CONTINUED ON FOLLOWING PAGE]

FIGURE 10.3 [CONTINUED]

- Openness, Inclusiveness, and Collaboration.
- Excellence and Innovation.

PLA Goals (2014)

- **Advocacy and Awareness:** PLA plays a major role in public library advocacy and in influencing public perception about the library.
- **Leadership and Transformation:** PLA is a leading source for learning opportunities to advance transformation of public libraries and helps to position the library's institutional and professional orientation from internal to outward toward the community.
- **Literate Nation:** PLA is a leader and valued partner of public libraries' initiatives to create a literate nation.
- **Organizational Excellence:** PLA is positioned to sustain and grow its resources to advance the work of the association.

PLA offers a variety of learning opportunities for its members, including:

- biannual conferences and training institutes for leaders
- live and on-demand webinars and online classes on topics such as measuring effectiveness, collection development, and technology
- a wide range of publications and workbooks, including a set dedicated to the Service Responses
- advocacy training and resources

PLA's recent initiatives are Digital Literacy, Family Literacy, and Performance Measurement.

PLA also publishes a magazine (available online and in print): Public Libraries (http://publiclibrariesonline.org/), offering librarians a way to stay on top of the latest news, articles, and book reviews for and about public libraries. The website also has a podcast and videos—all ways to stay connected to the larger world of public libraries between conferences.

new developments in the field. In addition to these two major conferences, the PLA holds its own biennial national conference to provide continuing education for the nation's public librarians. Library workers at all levels benefit from joining some association because it allows them to form a community of practice outside of their own libraries, deepening their connection to the profession at large and enabling them to participate in continuing education.

State or regional associations that are ALA chapters provide a parallel but local opportunity to meet and collaborate. Chapters promote general library service and librarianship within their geographic area, provide geographic representation to the Council of the American Library Association, and cooperate in the promotion of general and joint enterprises within ALA and other library groups. Fifty-seven state and regional library association chapters are affiliated with ALA, each including at least one committee or section that addresses public library issues. Generally, these associations hold an annual conference, as well as workshops and programs during the year.

National and state library associations serve the broad community. However, some librarians find their professional home in specialized organizations. Two representative organizations outside of ALA are the Urban Libraries Council and the Association for Rural and Small Libraries.

- The Urban Libraries Council (ULC; www.urbanlibraries.org) was founded in 1971. The ULC focuses on "education/lifelong learning, workforce and economic development, public safety, health and wellness, safety and environmental sustainability" (www.urbanlibraries.org/about-us-pages-13.php). Member libraries are located throughout the United States and Canada, and service communities from approximately 30,000 to more than 8 million residents. The ULC "provides a forum for library leaders to share best practices and innovative ideas that inspire programs that support 21st century learning, a strong economy, and an active democracy."
- The Association for Rural and Small Libraries (ARSL; http://arsl.info/) is a network of librarians that "provides resources and support that empower those in small and rural libraries to deliver excellent service for their communities." The ARSL meets annually and via a members-only listserv, and provides a space for people who work in small libraries to exchange ideas and conversation. It also advocates for small and rural libraries, acting as a liaison with legislatures.

People do come to conferences to learn about what other librarians are doing in their libraries to develop and grow programs and enhance services, but a frequent topic at these meeting is, indeed, collaboration amongst themselves. The conferences provide a venue to explore how to best pool resources and work together for the public good. The 1996 PLA conference offered 19 sessions that were tagged with "collaboration"—with each other and with the community. It is clearly not only a buzzword, but a way of thinking about libraries' roles and places in the community. This is not only a phenomenon in the United States; collaboration is a frequent topic of conversation at IFLA and library associations around the world.

COMMUNITY OUTREACH: COOPERATING WITH OTHER GROUPS

At this point, it is worth returning to the most fundamental purpose of public libraries: serving the community. Although libraries have realized their role as resource providers in successful communities for decades, there has been a shift in emphasis from only providing information services to realizing the full extent of community involvement. The ULC Civic Engagement Report (2011) said, "Libraries are at the heart of the communities they serve, and civic engagement is at the heart of where libraries are going in the 21st century. Moving from a community resource to a civic engagement leader is a logical step in the evolution of public libraries" (p. 14). One report begins by asking, "As communities develop strategies to address important issues and needs, communicating those strategies to the public is essential. And what community program reaches more of the general adult public in a learning environment than the public library?" (International City/County Management Association, 2011, p. 1). Many libraries have new job positions specifically created to work with community agencies, reflecting an emphasis on this value. The library sees a cross-section of its citizenry and is uniquely positioned to understand a wide variety of needs. A fundamental premise is engaging with others, rather than working alone.

Within any city there are numerous cultural and social service agencies, many of which offer possibilities for partnerships with libraries. What exactly is community, and how does the public library fit into it? A community is a physical place, but being a member of a community includes a sense of belonging. Public libraries are a place for people to belong—culturally and intellectually, regardless of their backgrounds. In 2001, Ronald McCabe wrote *Civic Librarianship* (McCabe, 2001); he said that "cultural confusion and division continue to damage our national life" (p. xiii). Libraries can be one of the catalysts that solve civic problems. The public library's primary mission is to enlighten the citizenry by providing access to educational and entertainment materials. Whether or not they patronize them, most people think that libraries do a good job of meeting this goal, as the Pew Research Center found: "Citizens believe that libraries are important community institutions and profess interest in libraries offering a range of new program possibilities" (Horrigan, 2015). In the next breath, however, the report says that people are visiting libraries less! If libraries are so valuable to people and have such a prominent space in our shared imagination, how can that be? Robert Putnam (2001) said that we are a nation "bowling alone," turning away from shared experiences and civic duties. If the library is an important communal, civic, and shared learning space, we need to both find a way to counter Pew's findings that people are visiting libraries less, and then to prove that we are doing so. Beginning with a grim examination of current funding woes for public libraries across the United States and Canada in an age of austerity, Huber and Potter (2015) offer a counterattack to survive, succeed, and grow.

Huber and Potter describe a process of finding inefficiencies in current practices to reallocate funding for community connections (see figure 10.4). An important component of their model of stewardship is tracking impact throughout the process and using reports to demonstrate the library's worth to funding agencies, including the city and granting agencies. One of the principles of the book is purposeful partnering based on identified "cracks" in the community pyramid. The central idea is that the library should create meaningful partnerships across the city to fill in those cracks, thus entrenching the library in the areas that are most needed.

This concept is taken even further in *Public Libraries and Resilient Cities,* which explores the roles that that public libraries can play in promoting ecologically, economically, and social resilient communities (Dudley, 2013). Dudley describes programs that involve the library in initiatives as diverse as community gardens, successful immigration, summer food distribution, and ecological sustainability.

In their 2013 book on the community-centered library, *Transforming Libraries, Building Communities,* Edwards, Robinson, & Unger identify seven strategic roles for the library to reposition itself as a more community-centered institution: 1) as a civic action center; 2) a center for sustainability; 3) as a cultural reflection of the community; 4) as a community center for diverse populations; 5) as a center for the arts; 6) as a university; and as 7) champion of youth. In its role as a civic action center, they see the library as not only supporting an informed citizenry but providing a forum through opportunities for civic engagement and civil discourse (Edwards, Robinson, & Unger, p. 6).

Developing Community-Led Public Libraries proposes creating meaningful and sustained relationships with local communities. Community-led libraries will acknowledge that the community—not service providers—is expert on its needs. A needs-based community-led approach will enable public library services to target the socially excluded and underserved so that the library will become an agent of social justice and social change (Pateman & Williment (2013, p. 2).

One of the common focuses of these books is that they all focus on community partnerships. They have found that libraries can do this best by working with other community groups. This can help them make the best use of their resources and to maximize governmental or nonprofit investments.

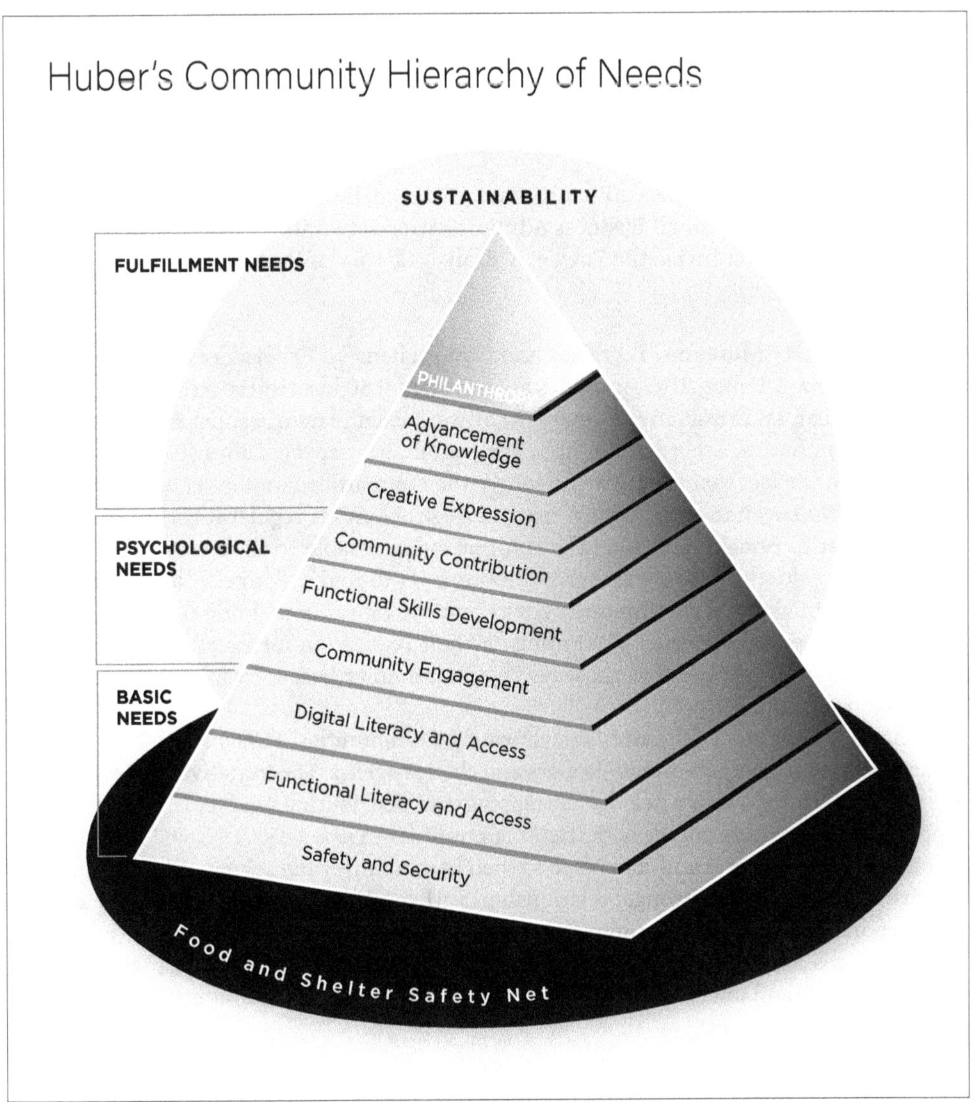

FIGURE 10.4 Huber's Community Hierarchy of Needs

SOURCE: Huber & Potter, 2015.

Some other public library initiatives tackling critical health and social issues in the community are:

- Realizing a lack of access to healthy foods, libraries are among the sites (including public housing and low-income senior citizen housing) that host the Baltimarket program, which enables people access to healthy foods that are chosen online and delivered on-site once a week (www.baltimarket.org/virtual-supermarket/).
- When the Flint, Michigan, water supply was destroyed by political malfeasance, the Flint Public Library provided guidance and information.
- REFORMA and ALA have passed the "Resolution in Support of Immigrants' Rights to Free Public Library Access." The Greensboro (NC) Public Library's Glenwood Branch established a Multicultural Resource Center for speakers of other languages who are learning English, including tutoring, conversation clubs, software in a specialized ESL computer lab, and citizenship classes.
- When a tornado damaged Birmingham, Alabama, homes and businesses in 2015, the U.S. Small Business Administration set up its disaster loan outreach center inside the Powderly Branch Library of the Birmingham Public Library.

The IMLS report "Museums, Libraries and Comprehensive Experiences" (Walker, Lundgren, Manjarrez, & Fuller, 2015) provides an overview of 50 local initiatives in economically distressed urban and rural environments that were exemplars of cooperation between libraries and museums. According to the report, about 20 years ago, libraries began to come to terms with the fact that they were no longer the main information provider. At the same time, museums began to experience a "patronage problem" as regular museum-goers aged. Realizing that to remain not only relevant, but indispensable to their communities, they began to more closely engage with their communities to find a distinct role in community building, placemaking, and community revitalization. Libraries and museums are especially trusted as "neutral conveners," "trading on their reputation for excellence, community trust, and institutional presence in ways that community-based organizations and many public agencies cannot" (p. 9).

The ALA's initiative "Libraries Transforming Communities" (LTC) seeks to strengthen librarians' roles as core community leaders and change-agents. The initiative addresses a critical need within the library field by developing and distributing new tools, resources, and support for librarians to engage with their communities in new ways. LTC will help libraries become more reflective of and connected to their communities and achieve a domino effect of positive results, including stronger relationships with local civic agencies, nonprofits, funders and corporations, and greater community investment in civility, collaboration, education, health and well-being. ALA also hopes to shift public discourse away from past themes about libraries in crisis and toward talk of libraries as agents of positive community change.

Community Information Referral

Outside of partnerships with local groups, public libraries have a long history of providing information about the community to citizens. This service technically falls under reference work, but it is worth mentioning here because it is founded in cooperation with the social service agencies. A community information referral hub is like a central node in the network of providers; the librarians need to be in contact with all of the other providers in order to make referrals, and the outside organizations should be aware that the library is serving as a hub so that they can refer people to the library if a request falls outside of their scope.

Poe (2006) explains that the mass movement of people into cities during the post-WWII period precipitated a need for Information and Referral (I&R) services. In 1968, "the Enoch Pratt Free Library and the University of Maryland's library school . . . began researching the possibility of providing I&R services. In 1970, the research became reality when the Public Information Center opened" (pp. 36–37). The 1970s were the defining period for I&R. The Detroit Public Library's Information Place was a model library organized to provide community information, as conceptualized by its director, Clara S. Jones. Many other libraries followed suit when the U.S. Office of Education began funding this activity, and in 1977, 196 libraries reported that they were involved in I&R (Childers, 1984).

In a visionary article written for *American Libraries* in 1979, Arthur Curley discussed information and referral as a revolution that would bring information from the people to the people. The classic work covering practical case studies and the actual delivery of library-based I&R, *Information and Referral: Public Libraries,* provided an intellectual and philosophical analysis of the profession's work to develop I&R in the 1970s (Childers, 1984). The appropriate role of libraries in I&R and community information was defined at the national level in the 1983 National Commission on Libraries and Information Science report, which recommended that community information and I&R are best accomplished with an interdisciplinary coordination of social service agencies and libraries.

I&R and community information services were formally put into action by the Community Information Section of the PLA beginning in 1979. The section developed standards for information and referral for over 25 years, producing four editions of *Guidelines for Establishing Community Information and Referral Services in Public Libraries* (Maas & Manikowski,1997).

With the advent of the Internet, community networking emerged as a complement to I&R systems (whether library-based or not). Librarians were well represented among early rounds of grantees from the Telecommunications and Information Infrastructure Assistance Program (McCook, 2000). Committed community information librarians utilized new technologies to serve community information needs. In 1999 the possibilities of yoking I&R and electronic web-based information as the Internet exploded were addressed in *The Community Networking Handbook* (Bajjaly, 1999).

In 2000, the Federal Communications Commission assigned 2-1-1 to serve as the three-digit number for access to information and referral services. Involvement by librarians in the implementation of the 2-1-1 initiative is a natural evolution of the profession's long activity in community information services (McCook, 2000; Chepesiuk, 2001).

An outstanding example of a networked 2-1-1 center is LINC, the Library Information Center at the Memphis Public Library (www.memphislibrary.org/linc/211.htm). LINC, in conjunction with United Way of the Mid-South, is the local source for community resources. The center maintains a large, comprehensive database of human services organizations, government agencies, and volunteer groups, which can be accessed by dialing 2-1-1.

Durrance, Pettigrew, and Unruh (2002) identified the contributions libraries make as providers of community information. They view the library and its staff as uniquely qualified to coordinate the provision of community information in local communities, especially as it becomes widely available in digital formats and distributed by multiple agencies. This service model has grown in importance as e-government has expanded. As pointed out by Jaeger and Bertot (2009), patrons now seek assistance from public librarians for a range of government services. The roles of e-government service provider and digital ombudsman find librarians providing advice and specific techniques for applying and integrating various digital and Internet-enabled services.

This service response is also supported by the work of ALA's Government Documents Round Table. See, for example, Morrison (2008) on ways to support library users with e-government resources at the local, state, and national levels and especially the GODORT quarterly publication *Documents to the People.*

Health Literacy

Barbara Jones (2016) called librarians "first responders" in the nation's health literacy crisis. Health literacy is "the degree to which an individual has the capacity to obtain, communicate, process, and understand basic health information and services to make appropriate decisions." Low health literacy has a high cost, and research has found that over 1/3 people in the United States have poor health literacy. Patients are asked to make decisions about their own health treatments and disease processes, and according to the Pew Research Center (Fox, 2013), 50% of adults look for health information online to either self-diagnose or bring to their care provider. Public librarians are well-equipped to help people make better decisions; they can offer skills as searchers and evaluators of information, provide free access to the Internet, provide instructional session in personal health research, and connect people to local health services. Many libraries partner with public health departments, doctors, public gardens, bike repair initiatives, food and nutrition groups, and hospitals, and behavioral/ mental health providers to bring programming and services to the library.

Some examples of health in public libraries include:

- Ignacio Albarracin (ALA Mover and Shaker 2015 and digital services coordinator at the San Antonio Public Library) tackled "the growing prevalence of obesity, diabetes, and teen pregnancy among working-class, Spanish speaking San Antonians" by writing health articles for the local newspaper, consulting with local community health organizations, and embedding the library "into these community health initiatives to amplify their effectiveness" (*Library Journal*, 2015).
- The Kansas City Public Library partnered with the Truman Medical Center and Health Sciences Institute of Institute of the Metropolitan Community College, offering free access to health, nutrition, and wellness information, hosting weight loss groups and exercise classes and distributing surplus food.
- The Lawrence (KS) Public Library found that it was located in a food desert (an area without access to fresh food). To help provide access to healthy foods for people in its community, it partnered with a local grocer, taking orders for food at the library and serving as a distribution station.

There are some excellent resources to which librarians who want to do health programming can turn. For instance, Webjunction's program *Health Happens in Libraries* (www.webjunction.org/explore-topics/ehealth.html) is a program that aims to magnify "the role of public libraries as key contributors to community health." This program provides resources (such as webinars and access to materials that libraries can distribute) to libraries who want to be involved with their community's health.

The National Library of Medicine also has a wide variety of resources for libraries. Aside from the excellent evidence-based information that it compiles about health, medicines, and supplements in MedLinePlus it also has program tools and kits that librarians can use. For instance, its website provides instructions about how to teach a class on finding health information, how to evaluate health information, and how to talk to doctors. It also supplies information for all ages that can be used for programming at the library, or in conjunction with nursing homes, community centers, and local health departments. It has a traveling exhibit program (https://www.nlm.nih.gov/hmd/about/exhibition/booktraveling.html) that libraries can reserve for display in their library. The effectiveness of any of these programs will be enhanced when the library partners with other community groups because the library will be able to reach more people.

▶ TASK

Write down four health problems in your community. How could your public library amplify the effectiveness of health prevention strategies through partnerships?

Measuring Impact

Volumes have been written about measuring the impact of library services. Although it is certainly enticing to become involved in a wide variety of community projects, we also have to be prepared to assess the programs themselves. Fortunately, Project Outcome, the Public Library Association project dedicated to helping public libraries understand and share the true impact of essential library services has selected Civic/Community Engagement as one of seven service areas for which to define and measure outcomes (Teasdale, 2015). Project Outcome is a "free toolkit offering libraries access to training, data analytics, and standardized surveys that measure outcomes in seven key library service areas: civic/community engagement, digital learning, childhood early literacy, economic development, education and lifelong learning, job skills, and summer reading." The Impact Survey (https://impactsurvey.org) is an online survey tool designed specifically for public libraries that want to better understand their communities and how people use their public technology resources and services.

Similarly, the *National Impact of Library Public Programs Assessment (NILPPA)* carried out in 2014 by ALA, with funding from IMLS and in partnership with New Knowledge Organization Ltd., was the first step to answer questions about programs in libraries:

- What are the current best practices in this service? Who initiates public programming in libraries?
- What criteria guide program selection?
- What competencies and training lead to excellence as a library programmer?
- What kinds of community partners are most suitable?
- How is funding obtained?
- How are public issues identified? And, ultimately, what is the impact of library programs, individually and collectively, on the people who attend?

This is a long-term, multifaceted research framework that seeks to understand the characteristics, audiences, impacts, and value of programming in libraries at the national level. The stated purpose of this project is to "ensure public and private sector leaders have the information they need to make strategic investment decisions that will further leverage the infrastructure and expertise of libraries." Funders, policy makers, educators, librarians, and libraries' institutional and civic partners may benefit from the findings of this study.

PUBLIC LIBRARY LEADERSHIP

Carla Hayden was sworn into office as the 14th Librarian of Congress in August 2016. She was the CEO of the Enoch Pratt Free Library in Baltimore from 1993 until her appointment, leading the library and the city through a period of public demonstrations against police injustice. The libraries of the Enoch Pratt Free Library stayed open in service of their mission "to provide equal access to information and services that empower, enrich, and enhance the quality of life for all." Dr. Hayden was President of ALA in 2003–2004. She was named the Librarian of the Year by *Library Journal* in 1995. The recognition and honor she received for her passion and activism for equality of access demonstrates that public librarians who are deeply embedded in their communities do, indeed, make a difference.

Dr. Hayden is now our most recognized (former) public librarian, but at the turn of the millennium the American Library Association elected two back-to-back presidents, Sarah Ann Long (1999-2000) and Nancy Kranich (2000-2001), who were ardent in their commitment to the importance of civic engagement, community building, and community engagement to public libraries.

The leadership of public libraries at the national level as represented by the presidents of the PLA from 1945 to 2012 is shown in figure 10.5. These individuals have represented large and small public libraries from every region of the United States. The contributions of these presidents and association activists to the development of public libraries through their focus on advocacy, the political process, strategic planning, and program provision are part of the rich heritage of connections that has laid the groundwork for the enduring institution that is the twenty-first-century public library.

CONCLUSION

Have librarians built a World Brain? Fortunately, no; we are working on something much more humane and better. Librarians have, indeed, built technological innovations that enable widescale sharing of resources. The systems are continuing to improve all the time, as ILSs and consortia respond to new possibilities offered by less expensive and more powerful servers. However, they also recognize the importance of taking care of humans. Perhaps the most important idea from this chapter is that librarians are members of widespread groups within both the local community and across the country. In order to provide the best services, they must nurture connections, listen and learn, assess, and act. This happens with deep connections, continuous assessment, listening, and action.

REFERENCES

American Library Association (2012). "Joint Use Libraries: A bibliography." *ALA Fact Sheet 20*. www.ala.org/tools/libfactsheets/alalibraryfactsheet20.

Presidents of the Public Library Association from 1945 to 2012

2017-2018	Pam Sandlian Smith, Director, Anythink Libraries, Adams County, CO
2016-2017	Felton Thomas Jr., Director, Cleveland Public Library, Cleveland, OH
2015-2016	Vailey Oehlke, Director of Libraries, Multnomah County Library, Portland, OR
2014-2015	Larry Neal, Director, Clinton-Macomb Public Library, Detroit, MI
2013-2014	Carolyn Anthony, Director, Skokie Public Library, Skokie, IL
2012-2013	Eva Poole, Director of Libraries for the Denton Public Library, Denton, TX
2011-2012	Marcia A. Warner, Director, Grand Rapids, Public Library, MI
2010-2011	Audra L. Caplan, Director, Harford County Public Library, Belcamp, MD
2009-2010	Sari Feldman, Executive Director, Cuyahoga County Public Library, OH
2008-2009	Carol Sheffer, Director, Round Lake Library, NY
2007-2008	Jan Sanders, Director, Pasadena Public Library, CA
2006-2007	Susan Hildreth, State Librarian of California
2005-2006	Daniel L. Walters, Executive Director, Las Vegas-Clark County Library District, NV
2004-2005	Clara Nalli Bohrer, Director, West Bloomfield Township Public Library, MI
2003-2004	Luis Herrera, Director, Pasadena Public Library, CA
2002-2003	Jo Ann Pinder, Director, Gwinnett County Public Library, GA
2001-2002	Toni Garvey, Director, Phoenix Public Library, AZ
2000-2001	Kay Runge, Director, Scott County Library System, IA
1999-2000	Harriet Henderson, Director, Louisville Public Library, KY
1998-1999	Christine L. Hage, Director, Rochester Hills Public Library, MI
1997-1998	Ginnie Cooper, Director, Multnomah County Library, OR
1996-1997	Linda Mielke, Director, Carroll County Public Library, MD
1995-1996	LaDonna Kienitz, City Librarian, Newport Beach, CA
1994-1995	Judy Drescher, Director, Memphis/Shelby County Public Library, TN
1993-1994	Pat A. Woodrum, Executive Director, Tulsa City-County Library System, OK
1992-1993	Elliot Shelkrot, Director, Free Library of Philadelphia, PA
1991-1992	June Garcia, Extension Services Administrator, Phoenix Public Library, AZ
1990-1991	Charles M. Brown
1989-1990	Sarah Ann Long
1988-1989	Melissa Buckingham
1987-1988	Susan S. Kent
1986-1987	Kathleen M. Balcom
1985-1986	Patrick O'Brien
1984-1985	Charles W. Robinson
1983-1984	Nancy M. Bolt
1982-1983	Donald J. Sager
1981-1982	Agnes M. Griffen
1980-1981	Robert Rohlf
1978-1980	Ronald A. Dubberly

FIGURE 10.5 Presidents of the Public Library Association from 1945 to 2012

[CONTINUED ON FOLLOWING PAGE]

FIGURE 10.5 [CONTINUED]

1976–1978	Genevieve M. Casey
1974–1976	Dorothy M. Sinclair
1973–1974	Lewis C. Naylor
1972–1973	David Henington
1971–1972	Effie Lee Morris
1970–1971	Andrew Geddes
1969–1970	June E. Bayless
1968–1969	Willard O. Youngs
1967–1968	Helen E. Fry
1966–1967	David Marshall Stewart
1965–1966	Alta Park
1964–1965	William Chait
1963–1964	Ransom L. Richards
1962–1963	Clara E. Breed
1961–1962	Harold L. Hamill
1960–1961	Elinor Walker
1959–1960	James E. Bryan
1958–1959	Lura G. Currier
1957–1958	Arthur H. Parsons, Jr.
1956–1957	John T. Eastlick
1955–1956	Mildred W. Sandoe
1954–1955	Ruth W. Gregory
1953–1954	Jack B. Spear
1952–1953	Ruth Rutzen
1951–1952	Harold F. Brigham
1950–1951	Helen M. Harris
1949–1950	John S. Richards
1948–1949	Louis M. Nourse
1947–1948	Forrest B. Spaulding
1946–1947	Carl Vitz
1945–1946	Amy Winslow—Provisional officers until permanent officers elected.
1944–1945	Amy Winslow—Provisional officers until permanent officers elected.

Association of Specialized and Cooperative Library Agencies (ASCLA). (1990). *Standards for cooperative multitype library organizations.* Chicago, IL: American Library Association.

Bajjaly, S. T. (1999). *The community networking handbook.* Chicago, IL: ALA Editions.

BayNet (2017). "About" https://baynetlibs.org/about/.

Becker, J. (1979). Network functions. In A. Kent & T. J. Galvin (Eds.), *The structure and governance of library networks.* New York, NY: Marcel Dekker.

Breeding, M. (2016). Better together: shared technology infrastructure for collaboration and resource sharing. *Computers in Libraries, 36* (7).

Burns, C. S. (2014). Academic libraries and automation: A historical reflection on Ralph Halsted Parker. *Portal: Libraries and the Academy, 14*(1), 87-102.

Chepesiuk, R. (2001, December). Dial 211: Libraries get involved with a new social service initiative. *American Libraries, 32*, 44–46.

Chicago Public Library. (2016). Programs and Initiatives. http://chicagocollections.org/about/historical-cultural-educational-programs-and-initiatives/.

Childers, T. (1984). *Information and referral: Public libraries.* Norwood, NJ: Ablex.

Curl, J. (2009). *For all the people: Uncovering the hidden history of cooperation, cooperative movements, and communalism in America.* Oakland, CA: PM Press.

Curley, A. (1979, July). Information from the people to the people. *American Libraries, 10*, 316–320.

Dudley, M. (2013). *Public libraries and resilient cities.* Chicago, IL: American Library Association.

Durrance, J. C., Pettigrew, K. E., & Unruh, K. T. (2002). *Online community information: Creating a nexus at your library.* Chicago, IL: American Library Association.

Edwards, J. B., Robinson, M. S., & Unger, K. R. (2013). *Transforming libraries, building communities: The community-centered library.* Lanham, MD: Scarecrow Press, 2013.

Fiels, K. M., Nuemann, J., & Brown, E. R. (1991). *Multitype library cooperation state laws, regulations and pending legislation.* Chicago, IL: Association of Specialized and Cooperative Library Agencies.

Fox, S. (2013). Health and Technology in the U.S. Washington, DC: Pew Research Center. www.pewinternet.org/2013/12/04/health-and-technology-in-the-u-s/.

Grace, D., & Sen, B. (2013). Community resilience and the role of the public library. *Library Trends 61*(3), 513–541.

Gregory, L., & Williams, S. (2014). On being a hub: Some details behind providing metadata for the Digital Public Library of America. *D-Lib Magazine, 20*(7/8). https://doi.org/10.1045/july2014-gregory.

Horrigan, J. (2015). *Libraries at the crossroads.* Washington, DC: Pew Research Center. www.pewinternet.org/2015/09/15/2015/Libraries-at-crossroads/.

Horton, V., & Pronevitz, G. (2015). *Library consortia: Models for collaboration and sustainability.* Chicago, IL: ALA Editions.

Huber, J., & Potter, S. (2015). *The Purpose-Based Library: Finding your path to survival, success, and growth.* Chicago, IL: American Library Association.

Ignacio Albarracin | Movers & Shakers 2015—Digital developers. (2015, March 19). *Library Journal.* http://lj.libraryjournal.com/2015/03/people/movers-shakers-2015/ignacio-albarracin-movers-shakers-2015-digital-developers/#_.

International City/County Management Association (2011). Maximize the potential of your public library: A report on the innovative ways public libraries are addressing community priorities. file:///Users/bossallerj/Desktop/MaximizeYourPublicLibrary.pdf.

Jaeger, P. T., & Bertot, J. C. (2009, Winter). E-government education in public libraries. *Journal of Education for Library and Information Science, 50*, 39–49.

Jones, B. (2016, October). Public health and public libraries: Librarians as health literacy first responders. Paper presented at the annual meeting of the Missouri Library Association, Springfield, MO.

Library Services Act (LSA, 1956).

Library Services and Construction Act (LSCA, 1964).

LYRASIS. (n.d.). https://www.lyrasis.org/about/Pages/default.aspx.

Maas, N. L., & Manikowski, D. (1997). *Guidelines for establishing community information and referral services in public libraries* (4th ed.). Chicago, IL: American Library Association.

Marquis, K., & Waggener, L. (2011). Historical collections: Is adding one right for your public library? *Public Libraries 50*(2), 42–48.

Marquis, K., & Waggener, L. (2015). What to collect? Building a local history reference collection at your library. *American Libraries 46*(7/8), 26–29.

McCabe, R. B. (2001). *Civic librarianship: Renewing the social mission of the public library.* Lanham, MD: Scarecrow Press.

McCook, K. P. (2000). *A place at the table: Participating in community building.* Chicago, IL: American Library Association.

Membership Requirements. Reacting Across Illinois Library System (RAILS). https://www.railslibraries.info/content/27.

MOBIUS. (2016). https://mobiusconsortium.org/about-mobius.

Monypenny, P. (1966). *The library functions of the states.* Chicago, IL: American Library Association.

Morrison, A. M. (2008). *Managing electronic government information in libraries.* Chicago, IL: American Library Association.

Museum and Library Services Act of 2010. S. 3984—111th Congress.

National Advisory Commission on Libraries. (1969). *Libraries at large: Traditions, innovations, and the national interest* (D. M. Knight & E. S. Nourse, Eds.). New York, NY: R. R. Bowker.

Nickless, A. (2010, October 6). Personal communication.

Pateman, J., & Williment, K. (2013). *Developing community-led public libraries: Evidence from the UK and Canada.* Farnham, Surrey, United Kingdom: Ashgate Publishing Limited.

Patin, B. (2016). Through hell and high water: A librarian's autoethnography of community resilience after Hurricane Katrina. *Mediatropes 5*(2), 58-83.

Poe, J. (2006). Information and referral services: A brief history. *The Southeastern Librarian, 54*(1), 8.

Public Library Association. (1967). *Minimum standards for public library systems, 1966.* Chicago, IL: American Library Association.

Putnam, R. D. (2001). *Bowling alone: The collapse and revival of American community.* New York, NY: Touchstone.

RAILS: Reaching Across Illinois Library System (2016). https://www.railslibraries.info/.

Reference and User Services Association. (2012). Guidelines for establishing local history. collections. www.ala.org/rusa/resources/guidelines/guidelinesestablishing.

Santo, R., Peppler, K., Ching, D., & Hoadley, C. (2015). "Maybe a maker space? Organizational learning about maker education within a regional out-of-school network." *FabLearn: Conference on Creativity and Fabrication in Education,* Stanford, CT.

Schudel, M. (2006, May). Henriette Avram, "Mother of MARC," Dies. *Library of Congress Information Bulletin,* 130-132.

Teasdale, R. (2015, May 28). Project Outcome launch: Seven surveys to measure impact. *Public Libraries Online.* http://publiclibrariesonline.org/2015/05/project-outcome-launch-seven-surveys-to-measure-impact/.

University of the State of New York. (1878). Annual report of the Regents of the University, to the Legislature of the State of New-York. The Board. https://books.google.com/books?id=FTQdAQAAIAAJ.

Urban Libraries Council (2011). Civic Engagement: Stepping up to the Civic Engagement Challenge. www.urbanlibraries.org/filebin/pdfs/ULC_Civic_Engagement_Report.pdf.

U.S. Department of the Interior. Bureau of Education. (1876). *Public libraries in the United States of America: Their history, condition, and management. Special report.* Champaign, IL: Government Printing Office. Reprint, as Monograph Series, no. 4.

Walker, C., Lundgren, L., Manjarrez, C., & Fuller, S. (2015). *Museums, libraries and comprehensive initiatives: A first look at emerging experience.* Washington, DC: Institute of Museum and Library Services. https://www.imls.gov/sites/default/files/publications/documents/museumslibrariesandcomprehensiveinitiatives.pdf.

Webjunction (2017). Health Happens in Libraries. www.webjunction.org/explore-topics/ehealth.html.

Yarrow, A., Clubb, B., & Draper, J.-L. (2008). *Public libraries, archives and museums: Trends in collaboration and cooperation.* (IFLA Professional Reports: 108). The Hague, IFLA www.ifla.org/publications/ifla-professional-reports-108?og=49.

CHAPTER 11

Technology in Public Libraries

An Overview of the Past, Present, and Future

Richard J. Austin and Diane Austin

Imagine that you are a public librarian arriving at work. You enter the library through an electronic door counter, using a keycard for security. You turn on the computers at the public service desks, turn on the networked public computers, finish and distribute an agenda for a staff meeting focusing on e-books and programs in the makerspace. You note that a book order needs to be processed, that there are two book carts waiting for check-in, and several e-mails from vendors to answer. Before the library has even opened, you have used nine different technology systems. When patrons start coming in, they head straight to the computers to apply for jobs, check their social media, look for books to check out, and read foreign-language newspapers. Today, you have classes in online genealogy, computer basics, and robotics for children. It is clear that technology is a big part of the public library! However, you also have an art class, a yoga class over the lunch hour, and a book talk with a local author. Your first-Monday knitting group will be in at six tonight. Again, there are those books to check in . . . the library is clearly not *only* about technology.

> ▶ **TASK**
>
> Go to your local library's web page or look at their newsletter and look at programming and website design. How much is digital? How much is "analog"?

Let's consider this proposition: public libraries respond to their community's information needs. If we want to think about technology in public libraries, we can start by thinking about the purposes of technology in relation to information. Many theorists have said that we live in "an information society" (Webster, 2014). However, "the information society" is very difficult to define or pinpoint. When did we become an information society? If society has shifted, what does that mean for public libraries?

According to Parsons (2016), "we live in an information age: a period in history when information is easy to access and affects many aspects of everyday life, from economy to politics and social relationships" (p. 2). Davis and Shaw (2011) describe the information society:

> We are said to be living in an information society—even though historians disagree as to when it began and definitions of information vary. We can easily see some impacts of information on society (such as information overload . . .), but others are hard to

> identify. . . . Even if it is difficult to define, the notion of an information society is so common that we need at least a brief list of its major characteristics:
>
> - Major changes occur in information technologies.
> - Large portions of the economy deal with information.
> - Information networks are a major feature in our lives.
> - Information available for our use is extensive—continually growing (pp. 5–6).

It is true that information technologies (or more simply technology) play an important role in many (but not all) people's lives; information technologies affect our personal, professional, and educational lives, and even our relationships. This is particularly true for people working in information or information-related organizations. Marshall Breeding writes a yearly *Library Technology Report.*[1] In 2015 he declared that:

> Technology permeates almost every aspect of libraries, archives, museums, corporations, and other organizations where information professionals carry out their work. All information professionals make use of technology tools in their portfolio of responsibilities, and an understanding of how technology can be leveraged to better serve their communities will help professionals use these tools more effectively. Beyond using technology as part of their daily tasks, some information professionals are responsible for managing some aspect of their organization's technology tools and infrastructure, making it even more important for these leaders to understand the various ways technology can be used today, and how knowledge of technology trends can guide their decision making (p. 250).

In 2017 America supports 9,091 public library administrative units with 16,543 stationary service outlets and 699 bookmobiles (IMLS, 2016). These provided about 97% of the U.S. population with access to information and services (IMLS, 2016, p. 1). There were 285,395 public-access Internet computers available at public libraries in FY 2014 (IMLS, 2016, p. 37). A recent Pew survey of public library users over the age of 16 found that "77% say free access to computers and the Internet is a 'very important' service of libraries" (Zickuhr, Rainie, & Purcell, 2013). Most people, then, who want access to technologies can obtain access in a public library. However, we still hear about a "digital divide." What exactly is the digital divide? Hertz (2011) said that most people "would answer that it has to do with those who have access to technology and those who don't. Ten years ago, they would have been right . . . We are [now] looking at a different kind of divide . . . from an access issue to a *kind of access* divide." The digital divide refers to who has access to computers and advanced technologies, and the ability to use them as they need to participate in all aspects of society. Although cell phone adoption has risen sharply, enabling most people access to the Internet, smartphones are inadequate for filling out job applications and other tasks that people must be able to perform. Differences in access are still marked by socioeconomic status, geography, and age. Creating training and spaces for hands-on experience in makerspaces and labs, using emerging technologies such as 3D printing, is another way that librarians can help to close the digital divide.

The University of Maryland's Digital Inclusion Survey tracks many of the metrics that characterize the efforts of public libraries to close the digital divide. In the 2014 survey, Bertot, Real, Lee, McDermott, and Jaeger (2015) summarized these efforts:

> When librarians provide individuals with the hardware, software, and broadband and Wi-Fi connectivity needed to interact with online information and services, they have

> bridged the digital divide through *access* to technologies. When librarians help patrons use these systems to find the information they need and understand how to use a range of technologies and information sources, they improve *adoption* in their communities. *Digital inclusion* combines these two concepts that transcends just meeting the needs of individuals, instead giving individuals the resources needed to succeed in the digital age. (p. xi)

Technology is, however, constantly changing and evolving. This presents numerous issues for organizations that rely on technology to run their operations and, as is the case in public libraries, for making sure that the technologies and related services provided to their patrons are as up-to-date as possible. This is a problem that Breeding has studied extensively. In 2015 he explained that information organizations must constantly adapt to ways that content is delivered and how their patrons will access that content (Breeding, 2015b, p. 250).

The primary purpose of this chapter is to provide MLIS students and new public librarians with an introduction or macro-level overview of the technological environment they will likely see as they move into positions in public library systems in the United States. It looks at both the daily workflow of staff and the technologies the library uses to connect to library patrons. There will be a brief examination of the history of technology use in public libraries and the evolution of those technologies. It will further examine the technology requirements and related skills that should be part of the knowledge base for all public librarians.

This chapter is not a how-to guide and does not cover the detailed workings of computers or how to use the different technologies found in today's public libraries. It takes Parsons (2016) over 900 pages to detail how computers and related technologies work. Burke (2016) requires over 200 pages to review the technologies used in libraries today. When you are ready to dig deeper into computers and related technologies in use in libraries today, Burke is a good place to start. However, because this field changes so rapidly, we suggest subscribing to relevant blogs and professional journals to stay up-to-date as well.

INFORMATION TECHNOLOGY IN PUBLIC LIBRARIES: A BRIEF HISTORY

Libraries are rooted in technology. From the first records archives in Sumeria to the typical public library in a large city, they exist because of a need to store and find information. Historically speaking, they were built to serve the political and economic needs of the state (Rubin, 2016).

After the printing press, punched cards may have been the next important technology applied in libraries and information-related organizations. Punched cards had been developed as early as the 1830s by English mathematician Charles Babbage for use in a mechanical calculating device. An early applied use of punched cards was by Herman Hollerith for the 1890 U.S. Census (Parsons, 2016). Black (2007) discusses the introduction of pre-computer technologies in libraries in the early to mid-twentieth century:

> In the late-nineteenth and early-twentieth centuries a range of important new technologies of information emerged in response to the growth and increasing complexity of organizations and their operations. One such technology was the punched-card machine, a direct forerunner of the computer in terms of the information management function in organizations. Punched-card technology first appeared in libraries in the 1930s, in the United States. (p. 291)

The second technology Black (2007) discusses is the development and introduction of microphotography. Although microphotography had been developed in the late nineteenth century, it was not until the 1930s that the technology was refined and put into widespread use and ideas to combine this technology with punch card technology first emerged. Black (2007) describes one of the major ideas to do this; "in the 1930s and 1940s punched-card technology was matched with microphotography to give birth to the idea of a machine called the Rapid Selector, as an 'information retrieval' panacea to the problem of information chaos" (p. 295). In 1945 American Massachusetts Institute of Technology engineer Vannevar Bush proposed a refinement of the Rapid Selector technology into a device that he called the Memex (Bush, 1945). Rayward (2014) describes the Memex as

> an iconic version of what we would now call a scholar's workstation. Nevertheless, it belonged firmly to the predigital era in that its recording, retrieval, and display mechanisms were based on automatically microfilming documents and searching the microfilm in new ways. (p. 693)

Some abortive attempts to create practical devices combining these technologies continued into the late 1940s, but no successful devices of this type were ever released. By that time, however, it was becoming clear that the future of devices to perform these types of functions would be based on computer technology. Black (2007) summarizes his analysis thus:

> by the 1950s the writing was effectively on the wall for both punched-card and microfilm systems. In 1951 the computer became available commercially and, even though for a while microfilm took on a new lease of life as microfiche (produced from computer records) and punched cards were for a short time used in conjunction with computers, in little over a generation it had come to dominate library functions, from circulation to information retrieval. (p. 297)

Thompson (2009) states that "The first experiments with computers for library applications occurred in the 1950s" (p. 9). During this time IBM was involved in the early development work on library circulation systems (Thompson, 2009). As illustrated in figure 11.1, by the 1960s the integration of computerized (automation) systems into libraries was well under way and would proliferate during the 1970s.

The six major technological developments identified by Burke (2016) that impact today's libraries and broadly chronicle the evolution of computers and related technologies since the introduction of commercially available computers in the early 1950s are:

- library systems and the MARC record
- personal computers (PCs)
- online searching
- audiovisual or media items (e.g., film, phonograph records, film strips, slides, VHS tapes, CDs, DVDs, MP3s, etc.)
- the Internet
- a society that wants and requires technology

An important addition to this list is the development and widespread introduction of Wi-Fi and related wireless technologies and the devices that use these technologies such as smartphones and tablets. This combination of wireless technologies and devices drive today's adoption to mobile services.

Figure 11.1 lists each technological development, the general timeframe for its development and/or introduction, and additional sources for basic information about each topic.

Thompson (2009) also provides a decade-by-decade account of the history of library technology (pp. 9-17). To a large extent, it is the evolution of the eight technologies or technology-related items that have shaped the work-related activities and services provided in public libraries in the twenty-first century. More broadly, most of these items have played a significant role in shaping the information society in which we live today.

PUBLIC LIBRARIANSHIP AND TECHNOLOGY SKILLS

This section focuses on the technologies that librarians use in their daily activities and looks at the technological skills that all public librarians should have or develop. As discussed earlier, the pace of technological change today is very fast and will probably accelerate as we move into the future. Librarians must be agile with technology, adaptable, and willing to learn. Changes in community demographics and culture, economic and political conditions, and technologies all affect how librarians perform their job and how they conceptualize services. Abram (2015) identifies three categories of trends or changes affecting information professionals and organizations: lifestyle and societal trends, facility and service trends, and technology trends (p. 44), and eleven important technology or technology-related trends: online learning, wireless availability, digital download kiosks, mobile device arenas,

Major Technological Developments since the Introduction of Commercial Computers

Technology or related development	Development or introduction date	For historical background information, see
MARC record	Mid-1960s	Rubin, 2016, pp. 176–178
Library systems and MARC record	Late 1960s	Burke, 2016, p. 8
Early time sharing online search systems (e.g., Dialog, LexisNexis, etc.)	Mid-1960s, in some libraries by early 1970	Bourne & Hahn, 2003, pp. 141–144
Audiovisual or media items	Various	Burke, 2016, pp. 10–11; Parsons, 2016
The Internet (and World Wide Web)	Early 1960s; ARPANET 1969; World Wide Web, early 1990s	Parsons, 2016, pp. 164–177; 234-277; Davis & Shaw, 2011, p. 84
Personal computers (PCs)	Kits (Altair, Apple I) 1976; Assembled (Apple II) 1978; (IBM PC) 1981	Parsons, 2016, pp. 539–541
A society that wants and requires technology	1990 to present	Burke, 2016, pp. 12–13
Wi-Fi and related devices	Wi-Fi (IEEE 802.11 standard) 1997; iPhone 2007; iPad 2010	Parsons & Oja, 2014, pp. 192–205); Burke, 2016, p. 11

FIGURE 11.1 Major Technological Developments since the Introduction of Commercial Computers

live-streaming, e-book readership, user-created content, cloud computing, computer training space, 3-D printers, and virtual libraries.

How Did We Arrive at This Moment in History?

All of these current technologies are centered on digital information. When did digital communication begin driving change in libraries? Parsons (2016) states that the move to digital communication was no less than a revolution: "the digital revolution is an ongoing process of social, political, and economic change brought about by digital technology, such as computers and the internet" (p. 3). Some historians date the beginning of the digital revolution to the early 1980s, whereas others look to World War II for its origins. Information-related organizations such as libraries experienced the revolution early, with computers and mechanization widely affecting librarianship by the late 1960s or early 1970s.

Before the late 1980s, though, few frontline workers had direct contact with the computers (mainframes) used in their operations. Customers and consumers had even less. Parsons (2016) describe this period as the "Data Processing" era of computing, which was characterized by mainframe computers that were

> huge, complex, and expensive devices. They existed in limited numbers, primarily housed in big corporations and government agencies. Computers were operated by trained technicians. Each computer installation required specialized software.... Back then, processing components for computers were housed in closet sized cabinets that did not usually include a keyboard or display device. Computers were accessed using the keyboard and display screen of a terminal. Terminals had little processing capability of their own, so they were used to enter data and view results produced by software that ran on the main computer. (p. 4)

The earliest commercial Online Public Access Catalogs (OPACs) date back to late 1960s and early 1970s. These early OPACs were often stand-alone systems (or dumb terminals) and the data they contained were basically a computerized version of the library's card catalog. Library patrons could search for items by using a terminal and searching for the title, author, or subject of a work.

Parsons (2016) describes the period beginning in the early to mid-1980s as the "Personal Computing" era. This period was marked by the rapid development and widespread adoption of personal computers such as the Apple II and IBM PC. The early 1990s saw the dawn of the "Network Computing" era, distinguished by connections of multiple computers or servers to networks that enabled sharing files and data. This era also saw the introduction of the first laptops, providing users with mobility. It was also marked by the development of the World Wide Web and the first browsers that allowed users to more easily access it. Bertot (2009) states that "Public libraries were early adopters of Internet-based technologies and have provided public access to the Internet and computers since the early 1990s" (p. 81).

How did public libraries become the anchor institutions that provide public-access computing in so many communities? Public access to the Internet was a natural extension of library service. In 1993, ALA held the forum, Telecommunications and Information Infrastructure Policy Issues, to provide a mechanism for the library community to identify national policy issues, questions, and principles in the areas of telecommunications and information infrastructure. Public librarians proved to be highly capable environmental scanners and moved quickly to implement new technologies into their daily work. Libraries were already public information providers, and many librarians were actively building websites and helping people connect to online information.[2]

Recognizing the complexity of issues relating to information policy, ALA established the Office for Information Technology Policy in 1995, which focuses on enhancing the ability of ALA's Washington Office of Government Relation to follow and influence national issues relating to electronic access to information as a means to ensure the public's right to a free and open information society. The Library Services and Technology Act (LSTA) of 1996 (introduced as part of the Museum and Library Services Act), which replaced the LSCA, emphasizes technology in the criteria for its grants to libraries. The LSTA has helped libraries to create the technological infrastructure required to obtain and use electronic resources through funding based on required state plans.

The Telecommunications Act of 1996 and provisions for universal service funded through the E-Rate (Schools and Libraries Universal Service Support Mechanism, n.d.) solidified the library's' role in public computing. The Act made possible an annual subsidy of $65 million for discounted telecommunication rates to libraries and schools. Through the E-Rate, libraries have been able to add telecommunications infrastructure (Federal Communications Commission, 2016). The Schools and Libraries Program of the Universal Service Fund makes discounts available to eligible schools and libraries for telecommunication services, Internet access, and internal connections. In 2014 the FCC rebooted the E-Rate to meet the needs of twenty-first-century digital learning.[3]

Between 1997 and 2003, the Bill and Melinda Gates Foundation made grants to more than 5,800 libraries in the United States, installed more than 25,000 PCs and trained 7,000 librarians so that libraries would be equipped to provide Internet service and computer applications to the public. The Gates donations—the largest gift to U.S. public libraries since Carnegie—amounted to $200 million for 25,000 computers in over 5,800 libraries. The focus was low-income communities where 10% of the population were below the federal poverty line (Bill and Melinda Gates Foundation, 2001).

In a 2003 interview with *American Libraries* Bill Gates observed:

> I didn't really realize that librarians are often working without much acknowledgment of the important role they play. The program was valuable. Together, these discounts and grants made it possible for libraries of all sizes, even in the least well-funded areas, to afford Internet connections. In fact, the first U.S. library grants targeted the areas with the least access to the Internet with the goal of using libraries as a means to close the digital divide. (Kniffel, 2003)

Other Gates' initiatives included the Native American Access to Technology Program, Internet services, and training for U.S. public libraries serving low-income communities, and "Staying Connected," which provided assistance with public computer hardware upgrades, training for library staffs, expansion of broadband coverage and technical support.

The convergence of support from LSTA, Universal Service through E-Rate, and the Gates Foundation philanthropy provided U.S. public libraries with the means to incorporate new technologies and integrate electronic services as enhanced performance standards for public libraries throughout the nation. These new standards became generally accepted through the LSTA planning process.

Technology does not stand still, though. Parsons (2016) defines the "Cloud Computing" era as the next major shift in digital technologies. Cloud computing is not associated with a specific device or technology; it is marked by "the idea that consumers use their computers or handheld devices to access applications, storage, and other computing resources supplied by Internet-based servers, rather than from their local devices" (Parsons & Oja, 2014, p. 329). Parsons and Oja continue: "cloud computing encompasses most Internet-enabled activities including Webmail, Google searching, social networking, blogging, and photo share. The concept of cloud computing is that apps and data are available any time, from anywhere, and on any device" (p. 329). Breeding (2015b) said that "Cloud computing includes a variety of models, each with its own distinct characteristic and functionality" (p. 252). This enables much greater mobility, and has thus driven the development of mobile devices such as tablets and smartphones.

INFORMATION TECHNOLOGY IN PUBLIC LIBRARIES TODAY

Today's librarian works in an environment that is infused with complex and constantly changing technologies. Is there a base level of knowledge that librarians need today? Lawson, Kroll, and Kowatch (2010) refer to 10 "hard skills" that librarians must have. At least seven of these require the use of or knowledge of technology: reference, instruction/training, collection development, database searching, network/systems administration, web design, research, and cataloging (Lawson et al., 2010, pp. 58–59). Similarly, Burke (2016) lists 15 "job tasks" that librarians and library staff perform on a regular basis; of the 15 job tasks identified, at least 12 require the use of or knowledge of computer technology: reference, instruction, collection development, circulation, cataloging, library/IT systems, library administration, acquisitions, periodicals and serials, media/audiovisual, distance library services, and interlibrary loan (Burke, 2016, p. 19). In a more general discussion of the technology skills needed for information professionals today, Shontz and Murray (2012) state:

> Technology skills are essential in an information job, but acquiring the right ones can be tricky. Technology changes so quickly that what's hot today won't be applicable two years from now. Focus on learning concepts rather than specific software. It's important to be comfortable with technology, including computer programs, databases, presentation software, office applications, and other commonly used technologies. (p. 41)

They conclude with another important recommendation for librarians: "When it comes to technology, the more tools and applications you're exposed to, the easier it becomes to pick up new skills" (Shontz & Murray, 2012, p. 42).

In an effort to provide librarians and potential librarians with the technology guidelines needed for their jobs, some state library associations, individual public library systems, and other professional organizations have generated lists of core technology competencies and library technology skills as an aid for their employees or potential employees; Webjunction (2014) compiled these sets into a document entitled "Competency Index for the Library Field."

These lists can be helpful but must be updated regularly to remain so. Thompson (2009) warns that:

> The idea of core competencies for technology is not something that can be perfectly defined and then fixed in place. There is not one list of competencies that is appropriate for every institution. Different sizes and types of libraries have different technology skill needs. What's more, as libraries change, so do their technology needs. (p. 3)

Even though competencies and skills are a moving target, libraries and information-related organizations do continue to develop and use core competencies for various reasons (Thompson, 2009). Identifying core competencies, as in the following list, can help:

1. Define job descriptions, classifications, and hiring criteria
2. Establish employee orientation and performance evaluation standards
3. Develop training and professional development programs
4. Improve or change library services
5. Improve of change the technology support structure (p. 5)

In the context of public libraries, core competencies can be seen as a measure of the knowledge base or technology skill set of librarians and potential librarians. Del Bosque and Lampert (2009) investigated the gap between the technology skill set of novice librarians (under nine years of professional employment) and the technology expectations of their employers. They report that

> Even if a position description does not require any specific technical skill, new librarians are prime candidates within the organization to be asked to work on technology-related projects, sometimes outside the normal scope of their duties, such as website redesign, digitization projects, or investigating Web 2.0 services for users. (p. 262)

So what strategies should librarians use to learn about or keep up-to-date with rapidly changing technologies? This is an important issue for libraries as employers and to the librarians that provide services directly to the communities they serve. Del Bosque and Lampert's (2009) survey of novice librarians identified seven strategies to keep up-to-date with technologies:

- Stay curious and explore new things.
- Keep up on reading (journals, news media, books, listservs).
- Use technology as a tool (blogs, wikis, RSS aggregators).
- Take online classes, workshops, and webinars.
- Attend conferences.
- Join committees and get involved in new initiatives.
- Participate in research and scholarship.

There are many organizations that provide webinars and conferences. For instance, the American Library Association (ALA), Library and Information Technology Association (LITA), and the Public Library Association (PLA) all hold large conferences and publish journals, but state association conferences and local training opportunities can be just as valuable. All librarians working with the public should also spend time trying new technologies. Hold technology fairs in the library. Take new devices home and learn how to enjoy them. Try to break them (your patrons will!). Remember that much of your experimentation and testing will take place outside of the workplace. Also remember that you can often download and test shareware before buying a fully functional version. Remember, if you are a student, that many software companies and universities offer lower pricing for students. To keep your equipment up-to-date, lower cost student rates are also often available for the purchase of hardware, such as laptops and software.

KINDS OF TECHNOLOGY

"Technology" is a nebulous term; here, we will look at the components of technology using six broad categories: hardware and operating systems, software, the Internet, the World Wide Web, wireless networks, cloud computing, library specific systems and technologies, electronic resources and digital libraries, and evolving technologies and technology-related activities. Each of the six categories contain a number of related technologies. Recent surveys of the technologies used by librarians on a regular basis in their jobs and the technologies made available to patrons will be used to establish the relative importance of a specific technology and to gauge the likelihood that public librarians will use and need to know about it. Important terminology and concepts will also be discussed. The facts and figures here are likely ephemeral, but the point is not: librarians need to be aware of their options in order to make intelligent decisions for their library. They need to be adept with a variety of tools and platforms so that they can troubleshoot problems and identify solutions for technology problems.

Burke's (2016) survey found that librarians are involved with technologies as follows:

Technology activity	Percentage of librarians reporting involvement
Public or staff printers	82.4%
Teaching technology	71.8%
Scanners and similar devices	67.7%
Design and management of library website	48.6%
Fax machines	40.4%
Purchasing technology	32.5%
Computer security	27.2%
Technology installation	16.2%
Network management	8.1%

Hardware and Operating Systems

Hardware is the generic term used to refer to the variety of devices that can be used to run programs or applications, store data, connect to online services of various types, etc. Devices such as servers, desktop computers, all-in-ones, laptops, 2-in-1s, tablets, smartphones, and peripheral devices (monitors, printers, scanners, etc.) are all different kinds of hardware. Peripheral devices, such as mice and keyboards, monitors, and printers, are either hardwired to computers via a cable or wirelessly via a Wi-Fi network or Bluetooth connection. Operating systems (OSs) are included in this category because every action performed by a computer is controlled or governed to some extent by its operating system software.

Today, most computers and laptops have both an Ethernet connector and a wireless ethernet card to receive Wi-Fi transmissions. Most Wi-Fi networks tend to be fairly short-range and localized (a room, building, restaurant, house, etc.). The key device needed to create a Wi-Fi network is the transmitter (router).

Servers (network servers or file servers) are computers that are used to house the software applications, data, library websites, and other types of resources that are accessed over a network by library employees and patrons (depending on the configuration of the library's technology). Servers can be multipurpose or specialized; a dedicated web server might house the library website, provide access to the Internet, or handle e-mail. A library might also have a file or application server. Servers generally have more powerful processors, run faster (because of more random access memory [RAM]), and have larger storage capacities (hard drives) than the average library computer or public access computer (PAC). The operating systems (OSs) used by servers can include Windows, Mac, or open source Linux-based programs. Servers, much like the mainframes from earlier times, are usually maintained by specially trained library employees.

There are different kinds of computers used by library staff and the public. A library might have desktops, laptops, or all-in-one computers (a type of computer in which the processor, monitor, and speaker are contained in a single unit, with either wired or wireless peripherals). Both PC and MAC versions are available. Depending on how they are used, computer specifications can vary widely. Powerful processors and large amounts of RAM are needed for applications such as video editors and other memory or processing power intensive applications or programs. A basic PC used for web browsing, e-mail, social media, and word processing can be a less powerful, simpler (and cheaper) computer. Most libraries use Windows-based PCs, although Macs are becoming more common. A few libraries use the Linux operating system (Burke, 2016).

The widespread use of Wi-Fi and related technologies has driven the development and adoption of mobile devices, such as iPads and other tablets, 2-in-1s, e-book readers, and, of course, smartphones. Libraries are making these technologies available to their patrons; Bertot et. al. reported in 2015 that 20.7% of public libraries made tablet computers and 25.5% made e-readers available to their patrons.

One problem with these devices, for librarians, is that they buy e-books, e-magazines, and other materials, and they should ensure that what they buy is compatible (or optimized) across all devices, so they should know something about operating systems. The operating systems on iPads are some version (depending on model) of the Apple iOS mobile operating system. Other tablets use a variety of OSs including versions of Android (technically Linux based), Windows, and other Linux-derived OSs (such as Google Chrome). Most 2-in-1 computers run a Windows OS. E-book readers or e-readers are similar to tablets but are optimized to read e-books and periodicals. They do not have operating systems per se but have special displays that use electronic paper technology to improve the contrast and readability of e-books. A smartphone is basically a sophisticated type of cell phone that can be used to access the Internet. Similar to tablets, smartphones can be used to download and run a variety of applications (apps or programs).

Printers and Peripherals

Printers are often the bane of the librarian's existence. Printing is an important service that most libraries make available to their patrons, but printers do require a lot of maintenance.

They come in a variety of types, sizes, and capabilities. At the time of this writing, laser printers were the most common, generally used for black and white text oriented printing. Ink jet printers are another option that can produce both black-and-white and color copies. Multifunction or all-in-one printers are usually ink jets that can also be used for scanning, copying, and faxing. There are also specialty printers such as color lasers and large-format printers to make posters or other oversized items. Like other peripherals, most printers can be networked so that they are available to all employees in a facility. They can also be accessed wirelessly via Wi-Fi or Bluetooth. Bluetooth is fairly short ranged wireless signal and is used to connect individual devices to one another. Bluetooth is now installed on a variety of devices such as smartphones, game controllers, tablets, and computers of all types. Bluetooth is used to connect these devices to printers, speakers, headsets, keyboards, mice, and other peripherals.

In 2015, Bertot et al. reported that 79.9% of public libraries had color printers for patrons, 39.4% offered wireless printing, and 8.3% had large-format printers available. Choosing a printer is an important decision. Consider maintenance, cost of the ink, configuration of your public access computers stations, compatibility, and overall cost of the printer when making a purchasing decision.

Scanners are another important type of peripheral found in libraries. In 2015, Bertot et al. found that 62.5% of libraries provided scanners for patrons to digitize images and documents. At one time scanners were stand-alone devices that were attached to computers, requiring specialty software; fortunately, they are easier to use now. Scanners come in a variety of sizes and types such as photo/slide scanners and large-format scanners. Although much of day-to-day scanning might be performed now using all-in-one printers, libraries with a local history section or digital media area should look at the high-resolution book scanners and other specialty scanners.

There are other pieces of hardware or system requirements that a library will need to purchase, such as barcode readers and self-checkout kiosks, both of which play important roles in the circulation activities of the library. However, those are generally purchased through specialized library vendors.

Makerspaces

Many libraries are investing in advanced technology creation spaces, which might be called informal learning spaces, makerspaces, recording or production studios, robotics studios, fablabs, or hackerspaces. Such spaces require substantial knowledge about technology to maintain, and they can be quite expensive to set up, depending on the technologies in which the library invests. Some makerspaces focus on crafting and sewing, but many others have STEAM equipment, such as

> video production equipment, recording devices, drawing tools and equipment, circuit boards, electrical wiring, electronic equipment, saws, drills, screwdrivers, routers, wood and metal working tools, 3-dimensional copying and printing machines, computer equipment, charging stations, and wood, metal, plastic and composite supplies and materials, glue, solvents, nails, screws, and other working parts. (Moorefield-Lang, 2015)

These may require significant investment. There are many grades of 3-D printers, laser printers, and engravers (for instance), with prices for the home hobbyist to the professional lab. The good news is, there are many resources for librarians who want to learn more about this emerging and quickly growing service in libraries, such as *The Makerspace Librarian's Sourcebook* (Kroski, 2017), which "delves into 11 of the most essential technologies and tools most commonly found in makerspaces, ranging from 3D printers, Raspberry Pi, Arduino, and wearable electronics to CTC, Legos, drones, and circuitry kits."

Important to Remember

When considering the overall range of hardware purchases in the library, note two factors:

1. Libraries are ethically and legally obligated to ensure that they have accessible computers for all of their patrons. This means that they might need to invest in keyboards for low-vision patrons as well as other specialty peripheral devices to make their computers easier to use for people with various physical abilities. The ALA Library Services for People with Disabilities Policy is quite specific:

   > Library materials must be accessible to all patrons including people with disabilities. Materials must be available to individuals with disabilities in a variety of formats and with accommodations, as long as the modified formats and accommodations are "reasonable," do not "fundamentally alter" the library's services, and do not place an "undue burden" on the library. Examples of accommodations include assistive technology, auxiliary devices and physical assistance . . .
   >
   > Well-planned technological solutions and access points, based on the concepts of universal design, are essential for effective use of information and other library services by all people. Libraries should work with people with disabilities, agencies, organizations and vendors to integrate assistive technology into their facilities and services to meet the needs of people with a broad range of disabilities, including learning, mobility, sensory and developmental disabilities. Library staff should be aware of how available technologies address disabilities and know how to assist all users with library technology. (ALA "Library Service for People with Disabilities. Policy Statement," 2001)

2. Children have special needs; larger libraries generally have a computer area set aside for children, with special keyboards and smaller chairs.

> ▶ **TASK**
>
> Go to your local library and list every piece of hardware that you can see. What is new? What needs updating? How many people are using it, and what are they using?

Software

Application software (also known as applications, apps, or programs) is the coded instructions that tell a computer how to perform some action or task. For the purposes of this section, we will focus on software that librarians report using on a regular basis. Librarians need to know about available software options. They must also invest the time to learn new software skills that can enable them to create better presentations to their boards, help their patrons get better jobs, and spend less time working on their budgets.

Before looking at specific software, however, a brief examination of software licensing and open source software is needed. Like most intellectual property, copyright protection is afforded to software authors and grants them the same exclusive rights to copy, distribute, sell, and modify their software program. When software is installed, users are often presented with an end-user license agreement (EULA), which the user must agree to before the program can be installed. The license agreement generally spells out the terms that must be adhered to when the software is installed. The terms usually discuss any restrictions, for example, how many installations are allowed, that no modifications can be made to the program, and so on. Open source software is sometimes assumed to be the same as freeware, but this is not the case. Corbly (2014) states that "With open source products, the copyright holder gives others the right to study, modify, and distribute the software free of charge to anyone for any purpose" (p. 66). The code, itself, is actually (as of the time of this writing) "open."

Office suites and related productivity software appear to be the most widely used type of software by librarians and library staff. Burke (2016) reports that 96.8% of librarians surveyed use e-mail on a regular basis, 91.0% use word processing software (Microsoft Word and Google Docs), 83.0% use spreadsheets (Excel), 69.8% use presentation software (PowerPoint and Prezi), and 22.8% use database software (Access) (pp. 20–23). Basic versions of Microsoft's Office suite include Word, Excel, PowerPoint, Access, and the Outlook program for e-mail. Microsoft Office may be the most widely used office suite in the United States and is available in Windows, Mac, and Linux versions. Many libraries and educational institutions, though, are turning to Google Docs, GoogleSheets, and other programs available on the cloud via the Google office suite. Google Docs can be run directly from the Web or downloaded to run offline. Because these programs are not installed on a local computer, they have the advantage of working across mobile devices such as tablets and smartphones, and documents and projects can easily be shared for collaboration. GoogleDocs are compatible with Microsoft Word. Such qualities as mutual compatibility and ease of sharing and accessing shared documents are key. Workspaces, for librarians and patrons, can be fluid, mobile, and collaborative.

> **▶ TASK**
>
> Go to the ALA Privacy Toolkit (www.ala.org/advocacy/privacy confidentiality/toolkitsprivacy/privacy). Identify and discuss ways that library can protect patron privacy on the Internet.

The Internet

The purpose of the Internet is to enable communication and sharing. Knowledge of how it works should be fundamental for librarians. We know that we need browsers on our computers, but what browsers should a library install? Again, we need to be attuned to what our users are most familiar with while ensuring that our computers do not compromise patron data or put our own networks at risk. In order of popularity, Google Chrome, Apple Safari, Microsoft Internet Explorer, and Mozilla Firefox dominated the market in 2015 (StatCounter, 2015). Libraries have an obligation to ensure patron safety. Some browsers collect more personal data and expose patrons to greater risk of hacking. ALA's Privacy Toolkit is a must-read for any librarian working with PACs.[4] The Library Freedom Project encourages librarians to install the Tor browser (an encrypted routing system for online communication) on their computers. As the Library Freedom Project (2015) explains, "libraries are our most democratic public spaces, protecting our intellectual freedom, privacy, and unfettered access to information, and Tor Project creates software that allows all people to have these rights on the Internet. What's more, Tor Project is Free and Open Source Software (FOSS), which is the best defense against government and corporate surveillance."

CONNECTIONS: LIBRARY 2.0 AND 3.0

Librarians have many widely available tools on the Internet to connect with their patrons—for instance, to advertise programs and new services. One way to do that is through blogs, social networks, and other Web 2.0 technologies. The progression of these tools into libraries is worth noting. The concept of Web 2.0 is more than just a stepped-up version of the Internet and Internet technologies. It reflects the efforts of designers and users to change the way the World Wide Web is experienced. Web 2.0 includes the emerging phenomena of social networks and media, interactive communications, various "glue" technologies, and the development of diverse content and multimedia. This socially, more connected version of the Web is facilitated by software and applications such as blogs, wikis, podcasts and vodcasts, Really Simple Syndication (RSS) feeds, microblogging and messaging, tagging, and a myriad of other resources. The essence of Web 2.0 is to allow users to create and interact with content directly on the Web (Cormode & Krishnamurthy, 2008; Anderson, 2012).

Web 2.0 was the launching pad for the idea of Library 2.0. Kwanya, Stilwell, and Underwood (2013) outline four accepted principles of Library 2.0 on discourse and practice:

1. *The library is everywhere:* on devices, portals, virtual learning environments, etc. The library is reproduced wherever and whenever the user needs it.
2. *The library has no barriers:* information resources available from the library are readily available to users with minimal barriers.
3. *The library invites participation:* it draws on the collective intelligence of all librarians and the user community in platforms such as wikis, blogs, and social bookmarking systems.
4. *Library 2.0 uses flexible best of breed systems:* interoperability and mixing of systems allow all users to install systems to effectively deliver library services.

The popularity and use of social media and other Web 2.0 applications continue to grow and change, but it can be difficult to keep up with new platforms and trends. A summary of various Web 2.0 software, applications, and functions is presented in figure 11.2.

But what does the third generation of the Web, often referred to as the Web 3.0 or the Semantic Web, bring to libraries? Is there a difference between it and Web 2.0, and if so, what is the difference (Berners-Lee, Hendler, & Lassila, 2001)? According to Kwanya, Stilwell, and Underwood (2013) "it is generally accepted that Web 3.0 combines the Semantic Web, Web 2.0 applications and artificial intelligence" p. 191); they propose the following five principles to distinguish Library 2.0 from Library 3.0 (pp. 192–193):

1. *The library is intelligent:* artificial intelligence systems offer library users the services that they want and need.
2. *The library is organized:* the Semantic Web enables users to find information even on the Invisible Web (i.e., pages that aren't indexed by most search engines).
3. *The library is a federated network of information pathways:* the search environment of the library is comprehensive. Barriers to disparate information sources disappear in an open network.
4. *The library is apomediated:* that is, "can use social mediation of information" (p. 193); the library is a trusted aid in finding the best information, and conversation is facilitated by social media.
5. *The library is "my library":* library users are able to customize content, layout, and navigation to create a personalized library experience.

For the library as a service organization, though, Web 3.0 allows for the utilization of openly accessible data sets that can help it make decisions or analyze user preferences. Libraries can use their own data or readily available big data sets (such as the many sets found on data .gov) to determine user needs and services.

We do not see the various generations of Web 1.0, 2.0, and 3.0 as freestanding and mutually exclusive, but as an evolution toward meeting the future needs of life on the Web.

Libraries certainly purchase quantities of online materials, and they work with vendors to ensure that the materials are available through the library's interface. However, librarians still must ensure that their own institutions' websites are usable and that people who come into the library can access the materials both on the library's hardwired network and on their own devices.

People expect to be able to interact with web content, which has increased demands on the library. Searching, viewing, streaming, interacting with the library and all of its content—in the catalog, databases, multimedia, e-books, magazines, music—all originate in the library's website. Library website administrators should consider using content management systems (CMSs), such as Drupal so that their websites have a consistent interface and organization.

Library-Specific Systems and Technologies

"Library automation" and "data processing" were early terms used to describe efforts to computerize daily work activities such as acquisition, cataloging, circulation, public access (catalog), and so on.[5] Marshall Breeding (2015b) has observed: "From the earliest years of computing, software has been developed to help information organization automate their work" (p. 255). Early automation efforts both increased efficiency of routine tasks of librarians and of sharing books between libraries. This automation "opened up a software market aimed at libraries, permitting the purchase of individual modules (e.g., a stand-alone circulation system) or all of the modules combined into a suite, referred to as integrated library system (ILS) software" (Burke, 2016, p. 53). The software packages have standardized language and protocols that allow the modules to communicate with each other.

Today most libraries are likely to have some type of ILS system. Very small libraries might not require an ILS, but if any library wants to participate in cooperative borrowing and lending they should invest in some kind of ILS.

Examples of Current Web 2.0 Technologies and Applications

BLOGS/WEBLOGS: Sites that contain short, user-generated articles or commentaries (text or other media posts) facilitated by content management software. Includes blog sites such as WordPress, LiveJournal, and Blogger.

WIKIS: Users can access and edit content from the front end through content management systems (CMS), such as Wikipedia or MediaWiki.

TAGGING: Social bookmarking allows users to find, retrieve, store, organize, and share sites and files through applications such as Delicious or Jumper.

LIVE STREAMING MEDIA: An alternative to downloading; users receive a real-time, constant feed of media to their devices.

SOCIAL NETWORKS: Sites for maintaining personal and professional connections and sharing information and content between users, such as MySpace, Facebook, Qzone, Google+, and LinkedIn.

MICROBLOGGING: Present tense communication and real-time text and media information tools such as Twitter, Tumblr, and EdModo. Conversations are real time and not threaded as with blogs.

RSS FEEDS: Summarize details of content and publish updates to subscribed users. Includes apps such as NewzCrawler, gReader (Android), and NetNewsWire (iOS).

MASHUPS: A site or application that creates content from more than one source. Sometimes content is overlaid (like Google Maps) and sometimes it is merged into a web page that contains user's information or services along with other linked web services or information, like Amazon.

SOCIAL CATALOGING: Helps users organize and store lists and descriptions of various media, including sites like Library Thing and Good Reads.

MEDIA SHARING: Allow users to upload and share various media, including audio, video, electronic documents, and images and podcasting, vodcasting, and streaming media software/applications such as Spotify, iTunes, SlideShare, PhotoBucket, Flickr, Instagram, and YouTube.

URI SHORTENING SERVICES: Make links more useable by reducing the number of characters in the URL, such as Tiny URL or Bit.Ly.

FIGURE 11.2 Examples of Current Web 2.0 Technologies and Applications

There are three basic types of library systems: integrated, nonintegrated, and stand-alone (Burke, 2013). In an integrated library system, the required modules are purchased from a single vendor or manufacturer who designs, installs, maintains, trains users, and makes modifications as needed to the system. This is often referred to as a "turnkey operation," which enables a library to quickly put the system into use. Nonintegrated systems are basically made up of modules from multiple vendors. An integrated ILS is more likely to offer a seamless experience for both librarians and patrons, but the need for more modules will add to the cost.

An ILS will always require funding, but there are some ways to reduce costs. An ILS is software that is installed on a server (or multiple servers). Some libraries might find that it is better for them to invest in a turnkey system with proprietary software, and have the vendor manage it for them in a cloud-based system; others will look to open source options, such as Evergreen or Koha, installed on a local server. Another option is to share system management with other libraries in a cooperative agreement or to join a consortium.

With proprietary software, the library is usually licensed to use the software and does not have access to the source code to be able to make changes to the program. In contrast, open source software makes the source code available to the library that owns it. Bilal (2014) states that "Open source ILS software [provides] access to the program source code (the actual computer program the developer has created) for modification and free distribution" (p. 4).

The most-used library systems by number of installations and library type have been identified by Breeding (2016). For midsized and large libraries, the top four systems were Symphony (by SirsiDynix), Aleph (by Ex Libris), Voyager (by Ex Libris), and EOS.Web (by SirsiDynix) (p. 32). For smaller and school libraries, the top three systems were Destiny Library Manager (by Follett), Concourse (by Book Systems), and Atrium (by Book Systems) (p. 32). OCLC's WorldShare Management Services and Innovative Interfaces (III)'s Sierra Systems are other important competitors, though III is more competitive among academic libraries. The vendor landscape is constantly changing because of innovations, mergers, and acquisitions.

There are 11 frequently used types of ILS modules: OPAC or discovery services, cataloging, circulation, acquisitions, serials, interlibrary loan, authority control, media management, electronic resources management, digital asset management, and (for schools) a textbook management module (Bilal, 2014, pp. 1–2). The functions of most of the modules listed here are fairly obvious, but a few may not be.

The first module type we examine will be the OPAC or discovery services module. As mentioned earlier in the chapter, Online Public Access Catalogs (OPACs) were among the earliest of library activities to be automated and as such have been a component of ILS systems or stand-alone modules in libraries for decades. But today new products are being introduced to improve the search experiences of library patrons. These programs or modules are called "discovery services" or "discovery interfaces." Jacobsen (2011) describes discovery interfaces:

> Discovery interfaces are one of the hottest new trends in the library Online Public Access Catalogue (OPAC) sphere, although currently usage is primarily limited to academic and public libraries. A discovery interface provides a more intuitive and productive experience for users, whether searching a library catalogue, an article index, or any other data source. It is a layer of software that sits on top of any existing database or integrated library system (ILS), such as Inmagic Genie, ingesting records in many

> formats, including MARC and XML, and providing a best-of-breed, web-based search interface for users (para.1).

Breeding (2015a) discusses discovery interfaces as a component of discovery services platforms (programs or modules): "Discovery services facilitate access to resources for library patrons. These products include a discovery interface that presents a variety of features related to the search and retrieval of materials from library collections, patron self-service requests, and a variety of other capabilities" (p. 22).

Capabilities of discovery interfaces are discussed by Bilal (2014): "a *discovery interface* supports many features, including, but not limited to, searching by author, title, phrase, and keywords combined with Boolean operators (AND, OR, NOT)" (p. 6). A variety of discovery interfaces are available today including Blacklight, VuFind, Destiny Quest, Primo, WorldCat Local, and Encore.

A newer version of discovery interfaces is also coming into use, described by Bilal (2014) as:

> a cloud based *next-generation discovery interface* that goes beyond federated searching to enrich the user's information discovery experience. This service is based on the *open platform* framework and harvests data from aggregated scholarly e-resources including eBooks, journal articles, newspaper articles, and digital repositories. A discovery service integrates with a library's collections to provide access to a library's print and digital contents in a single interface. (p. 7)

Bilal also observes, "Discovery services are implemented in academic and large-sized libraries. Currently, most ILS companies that target small libraries are utilizing discovery interfaces rather than discovery services" (p. 7). Some of the discovery service products on the market include Primo Central Index, Summon, and EBSO Discovery Service.

Other two-module types are the authority control and digital asset management modules. The authority control module is where the subject headings for MARC 21 bibliographic records created in the cataloging module are created and managed. The purpose of the digital asset management module "is to organize, and maintain digital collections, repositories, images, digitized texts, and other materials in a digital format" (Bilal 2014, p. 11).

A final important library centric technology is "radio frequency identification" or RFID. Burke (2016) defines RFID as:

> A method used by libraries to protect their physical collections by placing a small tag on each item: the tag consists of a computer chip with an antenna attached, and security gates or self-checkout systems can then read them to complete their functions. (p. 208)

Rubin (2016) states that "RFID tags are easier to use than bar codes because they don't need to be aligned and can be read from considerable distances" (p. 211). Beyond securing the physical collection, RFID can be also used to improve a variety of library activities including circulation (check-out/check-in) and shelf organization and accuracy. RFID has been in use in libraries for over a decade and has replaced or supplemented both barcodes and security strips. Despite their widespread use, some still have privacy concerns, which ALA has addressed in best practices recommendations.

ELECTRONIC RESOURCES AND DIGITAL LIBRARIES

> The first eBook was born out of Michael Hart's vision of what the Internet would become. In 1971, Hart typed the Declaration of Independence into a mainframe and shared it with a few other people, giving birth to what would eventually be known as Project Gutenberg. Since that time, the humble electronic text has become tremendously more complicated. File format, digital rights management (DRM), hardware, and licensing all play crucial roles in how we consume eBooks. (Sheehan, 2013, p. 2)

Recent studies have found that over 90% of public libraries have e-book collections, and over 25% circulate e-readers and tablets (Burke, 2016; Bertot et. al., 2015). E-books are only the tip of the iceberg, though. Librarians work with all types of recorded information and texts. The generation of librarians who are retiring soon have seen vinyl records, filmstrips, audiocassettes, laser discs, and VHS tapes appear then weeded from the shelves as they were replaced by CDs, DVDs, Playaways, and download-only media. Remember, "as today's information professionals survey their workplaces, what they see is in some ways a world apart from those who staffed their same offices just a few decades ago" (Gregory & Rudersdorf, p. 94).

Librarians might work in two spaces—digital and physical—today. What exactly is a digital library? Davis and Shaw (2011) define it as:

> a library in which collections are stored in digital formats and are accessible by computers via networks such as the internet. Born digital collections are composed entirely of resources designed and produced electronically. Digital libraries may also be created by digitizing paper-based information resources. (p. 116)

More generically, "the digital library goes by many names but generally involves information products and services that are organized, described, and delivered through technology" (Gregory and Rudersdorf, 2015, p. 94). The digital library is a 24/7 space that exists in tandem with the physical library. Just like the physical space, its collection and environment (the interface and organization) require just as much TLC. The shift from analog formats (paper, microforms, etc.) to digital or electronic formats has profoundly changed the way librarians do their jobs, and it reminds us that new librarians need to be adept with technology and willing to explore new options.

Today, public libraries collect a wide range of electronic resources, such as a mix of any or all of following:

- electronic books (e-books)
- local historical content
- periodicals, including electronic journals (e-journals) and databases, and popular magazines
- electronic reference collections
- downloadable movies, TV shows, music, audiobooks
- online learning tools for technology, languages, etc.

New and established vendors of electronic resources showcase their products at ALA and state conferences. With all of the new and improved products, how does a library decide which resources to collect? In "Key Issues for E-Resource Collection Development," Johnson et al. (2012) state that there are some commonalities between physical book collection development and electronic resource collection development, such as currency, cost or value, accuracy, and duplication of current resources. As with physical collection development, each library must begin by gauging community needs.

There are some special considerations for electronic resources. For instance, how is the resource made available to patrons? Is authentication problematic? Do users require any special hardware or software? Is the resource stored on-site or remotely? How many people can access the resource at the same time? Is it easy to use? "Licensing, access, networking, pricing, ownership, and rapidly changing technology and standards" (Johnson et al., 2012 p. 7)—all bear on the ultimate value of the resource to the library and patrons.

Once the library has purchased products, they must market them to current and potential users. The Reference and User Services Association (RUSA) document "Guidelines for the Introduction of Electronic Information Resources to Users" is a helpful checklist that covers planning, testing, staff education, user education, publicity, and assessment or evaluation of the products once they have been introduced to the public.

Beyond the library's purchased items, there are many freely available items online that the library should point its users toward; for instance, the Library of Congress and the Digital Public Library of America (DPLA) each have large holdings that are valuable to history buffs, genealogists, and students. Integrating these collections into the catalog or the website can ensure that even patrons in small towns have access to world-class holdings.

Evolving Technologies and Technology Related Activities

The Maker Movement in libraries certainly exemplifies the expression "what is old is new again." Bertot et al. reported that in 2015, only 3.0% of public libraries provide development technologies (e.g., sandbox machines, makerspaces/creatorspaces) for patrons, 2.6% provide 3-D printers, and 23.8% provide gaming consoles (e.g., Xbox, PlayStations) (p. 9). However, including these is a growing trend. Libraries have the potential to break down traditional barriers to technologies; as Holman (2015) pointed out, the maker culture leans heavily toward white, affluent males.

Makerspaces are a new way for libraries to engage users and expand services to the community. Makerspaces afford library patrons opportunities to learn, engage, create, discover, and socially interact with numerous kinds of high- and low-tech media. From 3D printing to coding to gaming to googly eyes, feathers, and felt, makerspaces allow patrons to spend time in their community library engaging, creating, building, problem-solving, critically thinking, playing, and learning (Moorefield-Lang, 2015).

Because this chapter is about technology, we will focus on high-tech makerspaces (not to discount the value of crafting spaces). The modern makerspace movement found its roots in the 1990s with global technology groups, now known as hackerspaces, where technology enthusiasts collaborated in exploration and innovation. MIT professor Neil Gershenfeld launched his hands-on tech course "How to Make (Almost) Anything" in 1998 and spearheaded his "Fab Labs" with a National Science Foundation (NSF) grant in 2001 (Enis, 2015). Events such as Maker Faire, which debuted in 2006, instilled the concept of learning and community and inspired spaces for gathering, creating, and innovating (Dougherty, 2012). Fontichiaro (2015) reports:

> Beginning around 2011, many information organizations leveraged past authority as resource providers and extended into providing experiences in-house, shifting from "check out our DIY materials and leave" to "check out and linger." Forming spaces that may be named makerspaces, digital labs, or production studios, along with activities for creators known as "makers," many information organizations are experimenting with how to invite in new patrons while expanding services for existing patrons. (p. 193)

Although only 3% of libraries had makerspaces in 2015, that number is growing. In 2016 IMLS awarded a National Leadership Grant to the Brooklyn Public Library to pilot BKLYN Link, a community-driven mesh network that will provide free broadband access and a technology-based fellowship program for young adults ages 18 to 24.[6] Library makerspaces might include an updated Fab Lab, recording studios, creative STEM (science, technology, engineering, math) and STEAM (science, technology, engineering, arts, math) education spaces, DIY crafting workspaces, and coding boot camps. Makerspaces are another way libraries serve the educational and economic needs of a community. They provide space for small business and individual innovation and product design, for students to learn STEM-related concepts, or for individuals to express their creativity (Burke, 2016).

Funding for makerspaces has come from community reinvestment from individual benefactors, library budget line items, and grants. Depending on the desires of the community served, makerspaces may be state-of-the-art, high-tech ventures or be run with very little capital beyond human resources and ingenuity.

Maker programs are growing. They offer a community a place to share, create, innovate, and play, all for learning's sake. It is an informal movement, with no specific list of requirements, equipment, or activities (Britton, 2012). It is also a social movement, that transforms education and educational spaces such as libraries and school media centers, moves beyond formalized learning, and encourages exploration and innovative thinking, which are within the role of the evolving library. One needs only to look at conference schedules and ALA publications to find a wealth of materials about how to set up a new makerspace.

Disaster Planning

With so much investment in technology, and utter dependence on having technology that functions, libraries should have a plan for backing up and recovering their data should a natural or manmade disaster strike. The Library and Information Technology Association (LITA) guide *Technology Disaster Response and Recovery Planning* (Mallery, 2015) provides guidance in developing a strategic response and recovery plan. Two case studies reinforce the need for preparedness and offer practical advice for being a good steward of a library's digital resources.

CONCLUSION

As part of the preparation to become a library and information professional, knowledge of technology is critical. This includes an awareness of the historical evolution of technologies, technologies currently in use, and emerging and future technologies. Library professionals must continuously enhance their knowledge and skills throughout their careers by engaging in professional development activities such as attending conferences, using a variety of technologies on a regular basis, and keeping up-to-date with both applied and scholarly research.

NOTES

1. Overview of all reports are available at *Library Technology Reports Document Depository* (www.librarytechnology.org/repository/item.pl?id=21672).
2. In 1994 public librarians were among the first community-service workers to apply for a series of grants for model programs that demonstrated innovative use of network technology. At the Newark Public Library, funds were used to support the Newark Electronic Information Infrastructure Demonstration Project. The New York Public Library, working with the Literacy Assistance Center of New York City, tested networked information resources for people with limited literacy skills at 30 neighborhood branches. The Danbury Public Library developed a model community Freenet planning process for the state of Connecticut. Three counties in southeast Florida (Broward, Dade, and Palm Beach) developed a Free-Net training infrastructure coordinated by SEFLIN, the South East Florida Information Network. The Salem (OR) Public Library developed OPEN (Oregon Public Electronic Network) to enhance the exchange of information between governments and citizens.
3. On December 11, 2014, the FCC took the next step in modernizing the E-Rate program by adopting the Second E-Rate Modernization Order, which sets out to maximize options for schools and libraries seeking to purchase high-speed broadband and adjusted the E-Rate spending cap to $3.9 billion. Among other provisions, the Order took further steps to improve the overall administration of the program and maximize the options schools and libraries have for purchasing affordable high-speed broadband connectivity. See Universal Service Program for Schools and Libraries (E-Rate) (https://www.fcc.gov/general/universal-service-program-schools-and-libraries-e-rate).
4. During 2015-2016, the ALA Intellectual Freedom Committee approved several new privacy guidelines intended to assist librarians, libraries, schools, and vendors with developing best practices for online privacy and data management and security. (See www.ala.org/advocacy/library-privacy-guidelines-e-book-lending-and-digital-content-vendors.) These include:
    - Library Privacy Guidelines for E-book Lending and Digital Content Vendors
    - Library Privacy Guidelines for Data Exchange Between Networked Devices and Services
    - Library Privacy Guidelines for Public Access Computers and Networks
    - Library Privacy Guidelines for Library Websites, OPACs, and Discovery Services
    - Library Privacy Guidelines for Library Management Systems
    - Library Privacy Guidelines for Students in K-12 Schools
5. See, for instance, "Proceedings of the Clinic on Library Applications of Data Processing" 1963-1998, which have been digitized through the Open Content Alliance at the University of Illinois at Urbana-Champaign (https://www.ideals.illinois.edu/handle/2142/348).
6. A mesh network is a wireless network that uses radio nodes, laptops, cell phones, and other wireless devices to provide reliable access to the Internet. BPL will conduct community-asset mapping in three low-income Brooklyn neighborhoods to identify which community is best positioned to host a mesh network, plan the technical structure of the network, develop user policies and procedures, and create a "playbook" of strategies and tools for deepening community engagement and launching a mesh network. The project team will also design a technology-based youth fellowship program to teach young adults how to install and maintain the mesh network and pilot a five-month abbreviated version of the fellowship. See Owens (2016).

REFERENCES

Abram, S. (2015). Librarianship: A continuously evolving profession. In S. Hirsh (Ed.), *Information services today: An introduction* (pp. 41-52). Lanham, MD: Rowman and Littlefield.

American Library Association. (2001, January 16). Library service for people with disabilities. Policy statement. www.ala.org/ascla/resources/libraryservices.

Anderson, P. (2012). *Web 2.0 and beyond: Principles and technologies*. Hoboken, NJ: CRC Press.

Aqil, M., Ahmad, P., & Siddique, M. (2011). Web 2.0 and libraries: Facts or myths. *DESIDOC Journal of Library and Information Technology, 31,* 395-400. http://publications.drdo.gov.in/ojs/index.php/djlit/article/view/1198/534.

Bauerlein, M. (2008). *The dumbest generation: How digital age stupefies young Americans and jeopardizes our future (or, don't trust anyone under 30)*. New York, NY: Penguin.

Berners-Lee, T., Hendler, J., & Lassila, O. (2001). The Semantic Web--A new form of Web content that is meaningful to computers will unleash a revolution of new possibilities. *Scientific American, 284*(5).

Bertot, J. C. (2009). Public access technologies in public libraries: Effects and implications. *Information Technologies and Libraries, 28*(2), 81-92.

Bertot, J. C., Real, B., Lee, J., McDermott, A. J., & Jaeger, P. T. (2015). *2014 digital inclusion survey: Survey findings and results.* Information Policy and Access Center, University of Maryland. http://digitalinclusion.umd.edu/sites/default/files/uploads/2014DigitalInclusionSurveyFinalRelease.pdf.

Bilal, D. (2014). *Library automation: Core concepts and practical systems analysis.* Santa Barbara, CA: Libraries Unlimited.

Bill and Melinda Gates Foundation. (2001). The Bill & Melinda Gates Foundation's U.S. Library Program distributes final round of grant applications. www.gatesfoundation.org/Media-Center/Press-Releases/2001/02/US-Library-Program-Grants.

Black, A. (2007). Mechanization in libraries and information retrieval: Punch cards and microfilm before the widespread adoption of computer technology in libraries. *Library History, 23,* 291-299. doi: 10.1179/174581607x254785.

Blank, G., & Reisdorf, B. C. (2012). The participatory web. *Information, Communication and Society, 15,* 537-554. doi: 10.1080/1369118X.2012.665935.

Bourne, C. P., & Hahn, T. B. (2003). *A history of online information services, 1963-1976.* Cambridge, MA: MIT Press.

Breeding, M. (2015a). Library services platforms: A maturing genre of products. *Library Technology Reports, 51*(4), 37.

Breeding, M. (2015b). Managing technology. In S. Hirsh (Ed.), *Information services today: An introduction* (pp. 250-261). Lanham, MD: Rowman and Littlefield.

Breeding, M. (2016). Library systems report 2016: Power plays. *American Libraries, 47*(5), 30-43.

Britton, L. (2012). The makings of a makerspace, part 1: Space for creation, not just consumption. *Library Journal.* www.thedigitalshift.com/2012/10/public-services/the-makings-of-maker-spaces-part-1-space-for-creation-not-just-consumption/.

Burke, J. J. (2013). *Neal-Schuman library technology companion: A basic guide for library staff* (4th ed.). Chicago, IL: Neal-Schuman.

Burke, J. J. (2016). *Neal-Schuman library technology companion: A basic guide for library staff* (5th ed.). Chicago, IL: Neal-Schuman.

Bush, V. (1945, July). As we may think. *The Atlantic Monthly, 176*(1). www.theatlantic.com/magazine/archive/1945/07/as-we-may-think/303881/.

Carlsson, H. (2015). Researching public libraries and the social web, 2006-2012. *Journal of Documentation, 71,* 632-649. doi: http://dx.doi.org/10.1108/JD-03-2014-0046.

Casey, M., & Savastinuk, L. (2007, October 31). We know what Library 2.0 is and is not [LibraryCrunch Web Log Post]. www.librarycrunch.com/2007/10/we_know_what_library_20_is_and.html.

comScore. (2015). *comScore reports September 2015 U.S. smartphone subscriber market share.* https://www.comscore.com/Insights/Rankings/comScore-Reports-September-2015-US-Smartphone-Subscriber-Market-Share.

Corbly, J. E. (2014). The free software alternative: Freeware, open-source software, and libraries. *Information Technology and Libraries, 33*(3), 65–75.

Cormode, G., & Krishnamurthy, B. (2008). Key differences between Web 1.0 and Web 2.0. *First Monday, 13*(6). Retrieved from http://firstmonday.org/ojs/index.php/fm/article/view/2125/1972.

Davis, C. H., & Shaw, D. (Eds.). (2011). *Introduction to information science and technology.* Medford, NJ: Information Today Inc.

Del Bosque, D., & Lampert, C. (2009). A chance of storms: New librarians navigating technology tempests. *Technical Services Quarterly, 26,* 261-286. doi: 10.1080/07317130802678878.

Dougherty, D. (2012). The Maker Movement. *Innovations 7*(3), 11-14.

Emanuel, J. (2013). Digital native librarians, technology skills, and their relationship with technology. *Information Technology and Libraries, 32,* 20-33. http://ejournals.bc.edu/ojs/index.php/ital/article/view/3811/pdf.

Enis, M. (2015, July 6). Meet your maker. *Library Journal 140*(12), 24-26.

Federal Communications Commission. (2016). Universal Service Program for Schools and Libraries. Retrieved from https://www.fcc.gov/general/universal-service-program-schools-and-libraries-e-rate.

Fontichiaro, K. (2015). Creating culture and makerspaces. In S. Hirsh (Ed.), *Information services today: An introduction* (pp. 192-198). Lanham, MD: Rowman and Littlefield.

Gilroy, A. A. (2001, January). Telecommunications discounts for schools and libraries: The "E-Rate" program and controversies. Congressional Research Service, Library of Congress.

Gregory, L., & Rudersdorf, A. (2015). Digital resources: Digital libraries technology. In S. Hirsh (Ed.), *Information services today: An introduction* (pp. 94-105). Lanham, MD: Rowman and Littlefield.

Hazra, S. (2015). Application of Web 2.0 in library services: Are we ready? *International Journal of Emerging Research in Management and Technology, 4*(7), 50-54. http://ermt.net/docs/papers/Volume_4/7_July2015/V4N7-133.pdf.http://ermt.net/docs/papers/Volume_4/7_July2015/V4N7-133.pdf.

Hertz M.B. (2011, October 24). A new understanding of the digital divide. [Blog post]. Retrieved from https://www.edutopia.org/blog/digital-divide-technology-internet-access-mary-beth-hertz.

Hirsh, S. (Ed.). (2015). *Information services today: An introduction.* Lanham, MD: Rowman and Littlefield.

Holman, W. (2015). Makerspace: Towards a new civic infrastructure. *Places Journal.* https://placesjournal.org/article/makerspace-towards-a-new-civic-infrastructure/.

Institute of Museum and Library Services. (2016). *Public libraries in the United States survey: Fiscal year 2013.* https://www.imls.gov/sites/default/files/publications/documents/plsfy2013.pdf.

Jacobsen, J. (2011, September 27). Discovery interfaces: A new OPAC for Libraries [Blog post]. Retrieved from www.andornot.com/blog/post/Discovery-Interfaces-A-New-OPAC-For-Libraries.aspx.

Johnson, S., Evensen, O., Gelfand, J., Lammers, G., Sipe, L., & Zilper, N. (2012). *Key issues for E-Resource Collection Development: A Guide for Libraries.* Ed. by IFLA's Acquisition and Collection Development Committee, including Jérôme Fronty, Joseph Hafner, Judy Mansfield and Regine Schmolling. www.ifla.org/files/assets/acquisition-collection-development/publications/electronic-resource-guide-en.pdf.

Kniffel, L. (2003). Bill Gates: Why He Did It. *American Libraries,* (11). 48.

Kroski, E. (Ed.). (2017). *The makerspace librarian's sourcebook.* Chicago, IL: ALA Editions.

Kwanya, T., Stilwell, C., & Underwood, P. (2013). Intelligent libraries and apomediators: Distinguishing between Library 3.0 and Library 2.0. *Journal of Librarianship and Information Science*, 45(3), 187-197.

Lawson, J., Kroll, J, & Kowatch, K. (2010). *The new information professional: Your guide to careers in the digital age.* New York, NY: Neal-Schuman.

Library Freedom Project (2015). TOR Exit Relays In Libraries: A New LFP Project. Retrieved from https://libraryfreedomproject.org/torexitpilotphase1/#more-778.

Mahmood, K., & Richardson, J. V., Jr. (2011). Adoption of Web 2.0 in US academic libraries: A survey of ARL library websites. *Program, 45*(4), 365–375.

Mallery, M. (2015). *Technology disaster response and recovery planning: A LITA guide*. Chicago, IL: American Library Association.

McCook, K. (2011). *Introduction to Public Librarianship*. 2nd ed. New York, NY: Neal Schuman.

Moorefield-Lang, H. (2015). Change in the making: Makerspaces and the ever-changing landscape of libraries. *Techtrends: Linking Research and Practice to Improve Learning, 59*, 107–112. doi: 10.1007/s11528-015-0860-z.

Moorefield-Lang, H. (2015). User agreements and makerspaces: a content analysis. *New Library World 116*(7/8), 358–368.

Owens, T. (2016). Libraries leading in equitable digital access and connectivity. IMLS Office of Library Services. https://www.imls.gov/news-events/upnext-blog/2016/10/libraries-leading-equitable-digital-access-and-connectivity.

Parsons, J. J. (2016). *New perspectives on computer concepts 2016: Comprehensive* (Enhanced ed.). Boston, MA: Cengage Learning.

Parsons, J. J., & Oja, D. (2014). *New perspectives on computer concepts 2014: Comprehensive* (17th ed.). Boston, MA: Cengage Learning.

Rayward, W. B. (2014). Information revolutions, the information society, and the future of the history of information science. *Library Trends, 62*, 681–713. doi: 10.1353/lib.2014.0001.

Reference and User Services Association (2012). Guidelines for the introduction of electronic information resources to users. www.ala.org/rusa/resources/guidelines/guidelinesintroduction.

Riley-Huff, D. A., & Rholes, J. M. (2011). Librarians and technology skill acquisition: Issues and perspectives. *Information Technology and Libraries, 30*(3), 129–140.

Rubin, R. E. (2016). *Foundations of library and information science* (4th ed.). New York, NY: Neal-Schuman.

Schuessler, J. (2014, April 22). The digital public library of America marks a year of rapid growth. *The New York Times*. http://artsbeat.blogs.nytimes.com/2014/04/22/digital-public-library-of-america-marks-a-year-of-rapid-growth/?_php=true&_type=blogs&ref=arts&_r=1.

Sheehan, K. (2013). *The eBook Revolution: A primer for librarians on the front lines*. Santa Barbara, CA: Libraries Unlimited.

Shontz, P. K., & Murray, R. A. (2012). *What do employers want? A guide for library science students*. Santa Barbara, CA: Libraries Unlimited.

StatCounter. (2015). *StatCounter global stats: Top 9 desktop, mobile and tablet browsers in the United States from July 2008 to Oct. 2015*. http://libraries.pewinternet.org/2013/01/22/library-services/.

Thompson, S. M. (Ed.). (2009). *Core technology competencies for librarians and library staff: A LITA guide*. New York, NY: Neal-Schuman.

Webjunction (2014). Competency Index for the Library Field. Retrieved from: https://www.webjunction.org/content/dam/WebJunction/Documents/webJunction/2014-03/Competency-Index-2014.pdf.

Webster, F. (2014). *Theories of the information society*. New York: Routledge.

Zickuhr, K., Rainie, L., & Purcell, K. (2013, Jan. 22). Library services in the digital age. Part 4: What people want from their libraries. Pew Internet. http://libraries.pewinternet.org/2013/01/22/part-4-what-people-want-from-their-libraries/.

CHAPTER 12

Global Perspectives on Public Libraries

Clara M. Chu and Barbara J. Ford

> The public library, the local gateway to knowledge, provides a basic condition for lifelong learning, independent decision-making and cultural development of the individual and social groups.
>
> **—IFLA/UNESCO Pubic Library Manifesto, 1994**

Up to this point, this book has focused on the American public library. The American and British library systems developed in the same era and share much common ground. However, there are many other models of public library development across the world. They developed according to each government's agenda and along with their educational systems, under colonial and postcolonial conditions. Many countries do not have tax supported library systems, and others consider their national library to be the public library. Equal access to all reading materials, as is voiced in this book, is not a universally held right.

There are some excellent books that detail the development of libraries around the world. *Global Library and Information Science* (Abdullahi, 2009) provides brief overviews of public libraries by region. *International Dictionary of Library Histories* (Stam, 2016) provides a worldwide survey of public libraries and some important landmarks, giving a global snapshot of public library development. *The Encyclopedia of Library and Information Science* (2009) and Wikipedia both provide overviews of the development of libraries in various countries.

This chapter discusses global development of public libraries briefly, but it focuses on the future. It is framed by a new international agenda, the 17 Sustainable Development Goals (SDGs) and 169 targets that constitute the United Nations 2030 Agenda, adopted on 25 September 2015. This document provides details on this ambitious agenda to eradicate poverty, tackle inequality and injustice, and manage climate change globally by the year 2030, calling on public libraries to play key local and national roles in sustainable development. The SDGs (https://sustainabledevelopment.un.org/sdgs) cover:

1. No Poverty—End poverty in all its forms everywhere.
2. Zero Hunger—End hunger, achieve food security and improved nutrition and promote sustainable agriculture.

3. Good Health and Well-being—Ensure healthy lives and promote well-being for all at all ages.
4. Quality Education—Ensure inclusive and equitable quality education and promote lifelong learning opportunities for all.
5. Gender Equality—Achieve gender equality and empower all women and girls.
6. Clean Water and Sanitation—Ensure availability and sustainable management of water and sanitation for all.
7. Affordable and Clean Energy—Ensure access to affordable, reliable, sustainable, and clean energy for all.
8. Decent Work and Economic Growth—Promote sustained, inclusive, and sustainable economic growth, full and productive employment, and decent work for all.
9. Industry, Innovation and Infrastructure—Build resilient infrastructure, promote inclusive and sustainable industrialization, and foster innovation.
10. Reduced Inequalities—Reduce income inequality within and among countries.
11. Sustainable Cities and Communities—Make cities and human settlements inclusive, safe, resilient, and sustainable.
12. Responsible Consumption and Production—Ensure sustainable consumption and production patterns.
13. Climate Action—Take urgent action to combat climate change and its impacts by regulating emissions and promoting developments in renewable energy.
14. Life Below Water—Conserve and sustainably use the oceans, seas, and marine resources for sustainable development.
15. Life on Land—Protect, restore, and promote sustainable use of terrestrial ecosystems, sustainably manage forests, combat desertification, and halt and reverse land degradation and halt biodiversity loss.
16. Peace, Justice and Strong Institutions—Promote peaceful and inclusive societies for sustainable development, provide access to justice for all and build effective, accountable, and inclusive institutions at all levels.
17. Partnerships for the Goals—Strengthen the means of implementation and revitalize the global partnership for sustainable development.

The International Federation of Library Associations and Institutions (IFLA) was actively engaged in the process of creating the SDGs, ensuring that access to information, culture, Information and Communication Technologies (ICTs) and universal literacy, all critical roles of libraries would be incorporated in the 2030 Agenda. Whether they address climate change or labor rights, public libraries are civic institutions that serve as lifelines to their communities, and must work actively with their communities and organizations to strengthen local social, economic, or environmental conditions. More specifically, public libraries anywhere in the world, regardless of their varying levels of resources, can engage in advancing the SDGs to build thriving communities and contribute to the collective impact of a global sustainable development agenda.

HISTORY AND PURPOSE OF PUBLIC LIBRARIES: A WORLD VIEW

The United Nations Educational, Scientific and Cultural Organization (UNESCO) first issued the Public Library Manifesto in 1949, then revised it in 1972 and again in 1994. The manifesto was prepared in cooperation with the International Federation of Library Associations and Institutions (IFLA) and can be read in over 20 languages on the IFLA website (www.ifla.org). The latest available Public Library Manifesto (IFLA/UNESCO, 1994) has several sections, including mission, funding, legislation, networks, operation, management, and implementation. The manifesto proclaims that UNESCO believes "in the public library as a living force for education, culture, and information, and as an essential agent for the fostering of peace and spiritual welfare through the minds of men and women." To supplement the UNESCO manifesto, many countries in all parts of the world have their own declarations and policies, adopted by their library professional associations or government agencies, about the mission and purpose of public libraries.

The history of public libraries is virtually unique to each country. Each country's public libraries have developed along different lines, with varying degrees of government interest, citizen involvement, mechanisms for financial support, and structure. Changes in public libraries can occur very rapidly as the national situation changes or evolves slowly when resources are limited or there is no impetus for change. The exact number of public libraries in the world today is difficult to know because at present there is no single list of the world's public libraries. It is estimated that worldwide there are over 320,000 public libraries and over 230,000 are in developing countries.

The 2009 *UNESCO Framework for Cultural Statistics* is an attempt to define reliable international comparable information and statistics in order to develop evidence-based policies that includes some information about libraries (UNESCO, 2009). OCLC Global Library Statistics (www.oclc.org/en/global-library-statistics.html) include data, if available, for the total number of libraries, including public libraries by OCLC regions for the Americas, Asia Pacific, Europe, the Middle East, and Africa. The Bill and Melinda Gates Foundation is building a Global Libraries Data Atlas (www.glatlas.org), an online source for data collected by grantees. A French map is available from the Association des Bibliothécaires de France (www.abf.asso.fr). At LibWeb (www.lib-web.org) over 8,000 webpages from libraries in 146 countries are listed so that libraries worldwide can be found online. With great differences in distribution, financial support, and population characteristics, few general statements can possibly apply universally to public libraries. However, since the middle of the nineteenth century the tax-supported, open-to-all public library has become a part of the cultural life of many nations.

Public libraries have often been created in communities around the world as part of a societal change process, to become a source of knowledge and a basis for lifelong learning. Periods of turbulence and rapid change often result in renewed focus on what the public library has to offer. The public library can become an informal classroom to ensure that groups are included in governmental processes and have equal access to knowledge and information. Today in some countries, public libraries are seen as a potential line of defense against threats to democracy and social disintegration and a way to provide broad access to all to the tools of the digital age.

Adaptation to changes in technology and digital information has led to discussions of the role of the public library. Public libraries range from those that make use of the latest technology, such as those found in Singapore, to camel delivery services in Africa, and from print, multimedia-, and Internet-based institutions to libraries building on oral traditions in countries with low literacy rates. In recent years many countries have been renewing public libraries in light of the Internet and digitization. An international comparison of public access to information and telecommunications technology through libraries and other structures shows varied approaches (Gomez, 2012). Equal access to information, the need to promote information literacy, and lifelong learning are key concepts for the future of public libraries. Substantial investment in infrastructure has been necessary and is essential to foster the growth of technical skills among the populations served. Libraries also serve as community anchors and places where everyone is welcome. Increasingly, libraries in developing countries are helping governments achieve their development goals.

There are a variety of forms of "public libraries." Although most public libraries are government-supported there are also other types of libraries available to the public. Community libraries might be supported by nongovernmental organizations, foundations, and nonprofit organizations, among others. Read Global (www.readglobal.org), which has developed community libraries in India, Nepal, and Bhutan to inspire rural prosperity, is an example of such an organization. In some countries, such as Colombia, banks support strong public libraries. The Goethe Institute often provides public access to information and reading rooms in their locations around the world. U.S. and European embassies also offer libraries and sources to the public.

WORLDWIDE SNAPSHOT

This section discusses the general development of public libraries and then focuses on three individual countries with close affiliation to the United States—Great Britain, Canada, and Mexico.

In Africa the planned development of libraries was rare until after the 1920s. Subscription libraries existed in South Africa as early as 1838 and were later developed into the public library system. Libraries in Lagos, Nigeria, were founded and supported by the British Colonial Office and funded by the Carnegie Corporation. The first national public library service established by statute in sub-Saharan Africa was the Ghana Library Service in 1948. Public library development in Africa escalated in the 1960s and 1970s with local librarians trained abroad. Today new partners are assisting and supporting public libraries. In Tanzania in 2016 a public library and resources center was financed by China to support the country's economic progress. Governments and foundations from North America and Europe have supported the development of public libraries in Africa.

Public libraries in the areas encompassed by the former British Empire generally followed a similar pattern of development. Originating as institutions such as subscription libraries for the wealthy elite, libraries slowly broadened their scope to include service to all. After independence, the trend toward service to all continued. In the English-speaking Caribbean region, organized public library services were created in the nineteenth century after financial assistance from the Carnegie Corporation and British Council helped set up library services. Provision for public library development in India has been included in its five-year plans since independence from colonial rule, but public library services are available by and large only to urban residents. The Delhi Public Library in India was established as a pilot project in 1951 in cooperation with UNESCO and became a model public library for South Asian countries. Progress is being made in the development of rural libraries in India, but it is challenging to convince communities that information can be a vital resource for development.

Although private libraries developed quite early in Islamic history, public libraries are a recent development in Islamic countries. New public library buildings and expanded services in countries like the United Arab Emirates are notable in recent years. The Qatar National Library is a recent important public library that may well serve as a model for others in the region. In Bhutan and the Maldives, public libraries are virtually nonexistent. Public library services in southeast Asia range from initial development in Thailand to a broad-based joint effort in Malaysia, where public library development is the responsibility of state, federal, and local government authorities, to the remarkable development in Singapore, where the National Library operates the public library system. In 1966, public libraries were opened in Nepal with the assistance of the Danish International Development Agency, UNESCO, and the Nepal National Library. Development of public libraries in the Pacific islands dates primarily from after World War II. Following political changes, there has been considerable recent interest in and development of all libraries including public libraries in Myanmar.

In China, public libraries did not exist before their introduction through missionaries in the early 1900s. After the communist government takeover, however, it decreed in 1957 that public libraries were to be part of a system to inculcate citizens with patriotism and socialism and make them good Party members. China's Cultural Revolution in 1966 led to the closure or destruction of many public libraries. Since that time, certain cities and provinces have slowly reestablished public libraries (Yitai & Gorman, 2000). New public library buildings have been constructed in many cities and policies are being developed for library services as part of the drive to modernize. Opened in 2013, the Guangzhou Library (www.gzlib.gov.cn/english/index.jhtml) in the south of China is a large-scale library with over 100,000 square meters of constructed space, 7.33 million books (print and electronic combined), 4,000 seats, 500 computers, and an average of 20,000 daily users. Moreover, the national library network has grown stronger and more widespread.

The pattern was similar in the Balkan countries, where public libraries emerged in the mid-nineteenth century as part of a national emancipation movement. During the post-World War II period, the communist states supported large-scale programs to change their library systems and libraries to political propaganda tools for mass indoctrination of Marxist-Leninist ideology. Poor infrastructures and the absence of national standards and trained personnel have slowed recent attempts to automate library services in the Balkans. In Central and Eastern Europe, following the communist era various organizations (e.g., the Mellon Foundation, Soros Foundation, Gates Foundation, and the Council of Europe) poured significant funding into automation and infrastructure upgrades.

In Finland, nationalism and the quest for education established public libraries in the 1860s, followed in the 1920s by written standards enforced by library inspectors. Sweden's combination of education and religious movements facilitated the creation of public libraries, originally aimed at the lower classes. In the mid-nineteenth century, reading societies in Iceland evolved into public libraries in rural parts of the country. Spain's public library movement, as defined by a 1901 ruling, has led to a service orientation toward the public. The proliferation and growth of Iberian libraries after the 1970s has been remarkable. Both Spain and Portugal have modernized their libraries with the advent of the Internet and web-based digital technology. Spain held its first national conference on public libraries in 2002, with papers and discussions illustrating the innovative programs existing in Spain's public libraries.

Great Britain

The growth of public libraries in Great Britain is one example of how development has taken place in a pattern most like that of the United States. The Public Libraries Act of Great Britain, passed in 1850, provided for funding the establishment and maintenance of a public library open to all and supported by taxes. The act was motivated by the instabilities of the time, including the Industrial Revolution, and public libraries were conceived as help for the working class, contributors to economic growth, and cultivators of democracy. New libraries did not reach significant numbers until donations from the Carnegie Corporation of New York began in the 1880s. By the 1960s and 1970s library service became more a matter of national government concern and funds were provided to put up new buildings, expand holdings, and hire more staff. By the 1970s public libraries in the United Kingdom had moved toward larger units of service and the national government was providing some funding. In 1997 the British arts minister announced a fund to bring local public libraries to the forefront of the information technology revolution. The complexity of the role of the public library has been explored by Black (2000, p. 71), who exhorts librarians "to resurrect the true, radical essence of its philosophy: the enhancement and emancipation of the self within the context of progress and social justice." A 2008 literature review covered the attitudes of public library staff toward social inclusion policy and disadvantaged groups, and found that the concept of social inclusion remains at the core of current public library policy and strategy (Birdi & Wilson, 2008). In 2016, the UK Department of Culture, Media and Sport issued a report about the ambition for public libraries from 2016-2021 (UK Department for Culture, Media and Sport, 2017). At the same time, British public libraries are facing the greatest financial crisis in their history, having lost a quarter of their staff as hundreds of libraries have closed.

Canada

Canada's first libraries were mostly held by rich families and religious institutions and not open to the general public. There were subscription libraries that required membership dues. By the late 1700s public libraries were beginning to be established. Due to Canada's size and diversity, the modern public library developed slowly based on each of the provinces' specific conditions and took on a variety of forms including school district libraries and association libraries. In the late 1800s tax support for library services began to be legislated. After 1900 Carnegie grants began to aid in building construction and expansion of collections and services. Today's public libraries in Canada are governed by provincial statutes and primarily financed by municipal tax revenues and other local revenues, with some provincial grants supplementing local funding. They are hubs of community activities with varied programs and activities and support for multicultural issues. Of note is Canada's leadership in multicultural library services, especially its Multilingual Biblioservice (MBS), a central distribution system established in 1973 by the National Library of Canada to address the growing need for books in languages other than English and French, and to strengthen Canada's policy on multiculturalism. The MBS was intended to supplement local library collections but some smaller libraries became dependent on these materials due to their decreasing financial and human resources. The MBS ended its successful service in 1994 as a result of a review by the National Library of Canada.

As in many parts of the world, Canadian public libraries have been subject to political and economic trends. In the 1960s public libraries received support to expand services and improve buildings. In 1999, public libraries were serving 93% of the Canadian population (Schrader & Brundin, 2002, p. 15). Since then public libraries have again faced financial challenges and consolidations. Issues of concern to public libraries include staffing, technological change, library book rate, funding, and services to aboriginal people (Wilson, 2008). In early 2016 the Canadian Library Association voted to dissolve due to the size and diversity of the country and its libraries, and the provincial emphasis of libraries and library associations.

Mexico

The first Spanish libraries in Mexico were in monasteries and served a religious mission. Public libraries began to be formed in the late 1700s and served primarily the Spanish oligarchy. The Mexican War of Independence from 1810 to 1821 led to an understanding of the need for public libraries by several local governments. With much of the population illiterate, the institutions continued to serve a select group. A National Library became a goal and was established in 1867 although illiteracy and limited education continued. In 1921 a Ministry of Public Education was founded with plans to start a nationwide public library program. The Ministry created around 2,500 libraries across Mexico but there was inadequate continuing support. The project was abandoned in 1940 and some of the libraries disappeared. Libraries in Mexico languished until the late 1970s, when a national plan was developed for a library system (Lau, 2010). The existing system was assessed and library workshops for staff were organized. Mexico's National Program of Public Libraries was announced in 1984 with deadlines for establishment of public libraries in capital cities and municipalities. Over the next five years a system of public libraries was put in place. Each town with a population of at least 5,000 people has its own public library. Library policies and collection development are determined by the federal government; building construction and facilities maintenance are the responsibility of state governments, and staff hiring and payroll are handled by municipal governments. Internet access is a crucial issue and libraries have benefited from outside donations, in particular, from the Bill and Melinda Gates Foundation. Issues today include the ongoing struggle to serve the general population, access to tools of learning, bridging the gap in Internet connectivity, and diverse indigenous populations. The Biblioteca Vasconcelos in Mexico City is a beautiful new library holding close to half a million books, dedicated to José Vasconcelos, philosopher, politician, and former director of the National Library of Mexico.

IFLA: A GLOBAL VOICE FOR PUBLIC LIBRARIES

IFLA and UNESCO

The International Federation of Library Associations and Institutions (IFLA) is the leading international body representing the interests of library and information services and their users. It is the global voice of the library and information profession, with over 1,400 members from nearly 150 countries. The roots of IFLA are in the International Congress of Librarians and Booklovers held at Prague in 1926. It was there that Gabriel Henriot, then president of the Association des Bibliothécaires Francais (now the Association des Bibliothécaires de France) and professor at the American Library School in Paris, recommended the creation of a standing international library committee, to be elected by individual national organizations. The impetus was part of the international movement to promote cooperation across national frontiers that followed World War I.

One year later, in 1927, IFLA was founded in Edinburgh during the celebration of the fiftieth anniversary of the Library Association of the United Kingdom. IFLA's first constitution was approved in 1929 at the First World Congress of Librarianship and Bibliography in Rome. Wieder and Campbell (2002) tell the story of IFLA's first 50 years, primarily summarizing early development and pointing out the importance of IFLA's formal agreement with UNESCO. Founded in 1946, UNESCO assumed the goal of assisting libraries and promoting the development of documentation, library, and archival services as part of national information infrastructures. IFLA was officially recognized as the principal nongovernmental organ for UNESCO's cooperation with professional library associations in Oslo in 1947. At the same time, UNESCO promised financial support for the execution of IFLA's program. Although financial support has not been forthcoming, IFLA and UNESCO continue to collaborate on information, literacy, and cultural projects.

In recent years, the advent of computer and telecommunications technology that permits the international exchange of information in digital format and the governmental reform movement has renewed interest in public libraries. Eradicating the digital divide has become a major topic of concern for national governments, private foundations, nongovernmental organizations, and the computer industry. A core value of IFLA is the belief that people, communities, and organizations need universal and equitable access to information, ideas, and works of imagination for their social, educational, cultural, democratic, and economic well-being.

Documents developed by IFLA, including the IFLA Internet Manifesto and The Glasgow Declaration on Libraries, Information Services and Intellectual Freedom, illustrate the importance of these issues. IFLA actively supported the World Summit on the Information Society in Geneva in December 2003 and in the second phase in Tunis in December 2005. Advocacy has become a focus of activities for IFLA, and projects like training and creating guidelines for increasing the effectiveness of library associations and developing library leaders are important. The Lyon Declaration on Access to Information was adopted in 2014 and was helpful in getting libraries and access to information included in the United Nations-negotiated Sustainable Development Goals for its 2030 Agenda.

IFLA's strategic directions include libraries in society, information, and knowledge, cultural heritage, and capacity building. IFLA has developed a toolkit on libraries and the United Nations' post-2015 development agenda. Increasing and improving library advocacy and developing strong international and national libraries policies and standards, including addressing multicultural issues, are priorities for IFLA.

Since the mid-1960s, the objectives of public libraries in many parts of the world have been the subject of regular review to examine whether they respond adequately to the needs of communities. Because of social change, there have been increased demands for citizens for improved access to information and education while advances in the production and distribution of information have increased expectations. The public library has traditionally responded to such demands and has become vital to many governments and a focal point for the aspirations of citizens. The role of public libraries in communities cannot be overlooked, as they are often the most successful focal point of local democratic life and support continuous lifelong learning.

Public Libraries Section of IFLA and Standards and Guidelines

The IFLA Public Libraries Section provides an international forum and network for the development and promotion of public libraries. The goals, objectives, and strategies of the section are developed within the context of the principles enshrined in the Public Library Manifesto, the Lyon Declaration, and the IFLA strategic directions. The Public Libraries Section is looked to for professional direction and guidance.

Public libraries have important responsibilities in providing the public with access to information. The IFLA Section on Statistics and Evaluation, the UNESCO Institute for Statistics, and the International Organization for Standardization recognize that comparison of statistical results among institutions and countries will never be possible if data and data collection methods have not been clearly defined and standardized. In 1998, UNESCO's World Culture Report showed that the unequal distribution of public libraries in the world can lead to inequity and imbalance. It appears from the statistics and literature about public libraries that there is a strong relationship between the level of development and the use of public libraries, and that development often increases public library use. As the projects for better global library statistics move forward, there has been progress in identifying the ways in which library support contributes to an improved quality of life for all people.

In 1973 IFLA published "Standards for Public Libraries," which was reissued with slight revisions in 1977. In 1986 this document was replaced by "Guidelines for Public Libraries." As their titles suggest, they represent two different approaches to providing practical guidance to librarians. The introduction to the 1973 standards stated that separate standards were not considered desirable because the general objectives in all countries were the same, the modifying factor being the pace at which development could take place. The 1973 version therefore provided a range of quantitative standards, including the size of collections and administrative units, opening hours, staffing levels, and building standards. The 1986 guidelines took a different view, recognizing that when needs and resources vary so widely there can be no common standards for services. The guidelines offered not rules but advice, based on experience drawn from many different countries and useful for general application. The guidelines recognized that recommendations on desirable levels of library service, based on past experience in quite different circumstances, are bound to be unreliable and misleading.

The next approach to standards took the form of consultative meetings in Amsterdam (1998), Bangkok (1999), and Jerusalem (2000) to develop a set of guidelines for the twenty-first century that were framed to provide assistance to librarians in any situation to develop an effective public library service related to the requirements of their local community.

The IFLA Public Library Service Guidelines, Second Edition, was published in 2010 updating the 2001 version (Koontz & Gubbin, 2010). The guidelines address the following areas:

- the mission and purposes of the public library
- legal and financial framework
- meeting the needs of customers
- collection development
- human resources
- management of public libraries
- the marketing of public libraries

These guidelines and standards can be relevant to any public library at some point in its development. Where public libraries cannot meet all the standards and recommendations immediately, it is hoped that they provide a target for the future. The Guidelines are available in a number of languages.

Under IFLA's leadership, people around the world are becoming aware of the key role of public libraries in providing access to information to help everyone participate in civil society and develop their country. Countries are slowly learning the role that information can play in solving problems and advancing national development goals. Some parts of the world still face challenges to gain access to technology that allows public libraries to be linked with networks internationally. Some countries do not have national information policies or a national information infrastructure. Public librarians are collaborating and working beyond traditional boundaries with public information networks for citizens and providing opportunities for lifelong learning. Digitization is enabling sets of images to be stored, indexed, and made accessible to the public. A good balance between print collections and electronic materials is needed. Networking can transform and revitalize public libraries. In many countries, public libraries are working to provide access to new technologies and to make use of the IFLA/UNESCO Guidelines for Development (IFLA, 2001).

Other parts of IFLA have also developed standards and guidelines that are useful for public libraries. Units that focus on special populations have developed guidelines for babies and toddlers, children, young adults, Braille users, prisoners, persons with dyslexia, mobile libraries, multicultural communities, and hospital patients and the elderly and disabled in long-term care facilities, among others. The sections on information literacy, indigenous matters, and people with special needs and special interest groups on lesbian, gay, bisexual, transgender and queer; religions; and women also offer important opportunities for dialogue on issues of importance to libraries.

The IFLA document *The Role of Libraries in Lifelong Learning* (Häggström, 2004), describes the role of libraries as important prerequisites for an informed democratic knowledge society. "Meeting User Needs: A Checklist for Best Practices" (IFLA, 2008) provides practical guidance for public libraries in understanding their users' and potential users' needs through consultation, survey, and feedback. This objective follows from the general guidance provided in Chapter 3 of Guidelines for Development 2008 and is a helpful tool that provides examples from around the world.

The value of public libraries to their community, also referred to as return on investment (ROI), is an important topic. The blog and website of the Public Libraries Section includes some studies that address these issues. Evaluation and impact data are very helpful and needed in advocating for support of libraries.

The Lyon Declaration on Access to Information and Development was launched in 2014 and states clearly that access to information supports development by empowering people to:

- exercise their civil, political, economic, social, and cultural rights
- learn and apply new skills
- make decisions and participate in an active and engaged civil society
- create community-based solutions to development challenges
- ensure accountability, transparency, good governance, and empowerment
- measure progress on public and private commitments to sustainable development.

Public libraries help ensure that everyone has access to, and is able to understand, use, and share information that is necessary to promote sustainable development and democratic societies.

As the United Nations works on the future of global development and the post-2015 agenda, access to information is recognized as important to enabling citizens to make informed decisions and to supporting governments in achieving development goals. IFLA has developed *Toolkit: Libraries and the UN post-2015 Development Agenda* (2015), outlining how libraries can help guarantee access to information. This toolkit should help library institutions and organizations who signed the Lyon Declaration to work with their countries to uphold the public's right to access information and data while respecting privacy, to recognize the importance of an open Internet, to ensure the provision of information by governments, and to measure the impact of access to information and data.

Public Librarians Sharing Expertise

IFLA is not the only place public librarians gather to share ideas and discuss worldwide issues related to the future of public libraries. The Next Library Conference (www.nextlibrary.net) is an international gathering of library professionals and innovators mostly from public libraries who are making changes to support learning in the twenty-first century. Created by Denmark's Aarhus Public Libraries and first held in 2009, the conferences explore the evolving role of the public library. At Next Library events, public librarians from around the world gather to learn, create, and develop new ideas and programs. The International Librarians Network (www.interlibnet.org) is run by volunteers and has a peer mentoring program to help librarians develop international networks. Participants are matched with others outside their countries and supported by regular contact and discussion. Regional meetings among countries with similar backgrounds are also helpful in sharing ideas and expertise. Foundations and funders also sometimes provide opportunities to meet and share ideas. There is much to learn from public libraries around the world and how they serve the public.

User Services, Collection Development, and Intellectual Freedom

The range of possible services offered by public libraries varies considerably because the public library has a very broad charge and serves all. Most public libraries offer separate services for children and adults. In much of the world students are often the greatest users of public libraries, which provide a quiet place to study or an important source of information for homework or family and personal needs.

Collections are the concrete expressions of the public library's mission, and issues relating to the preservation of intellectual freedom and guaranteeing the right to read are central to collection development. In developing countries, there may be less opportunity to develop balanced collections, because space is valuable and the cost of acquiring materials limits the number and selection of materials. Libraries often import expensive materials from abroad and therefore shipping expenses and issues related to customs and import duties can present difficulties in the acquisition process. In some cases, collections may be largely or wholly dependent on international donations, in which cases libraries have little or no control over the selection of the materials, including the number, subject matter, genre, and format, that they receive.

Electronic books (e-books) and other electronic resources are now part of the range of online services public libraries offer. Issues such as cost, distributors' lending restrictions, publishers' licensing restrictions, the need for electronic reading devices (e.g., computer, tablet, smartphone, etc.), and reliable power supplies limit the ability of many public libraries worldwide to offer electronic materials and for their users to access them. Nonprofit organizations, such as EIFL (Electronic Information for Libraries) and IFLA, as well as regional library federations, are educating the professional community on access issues and advocating for better information access. The IFLA 2014 eLending Background Paper defines terms and presents major issues regarding eBooks and libraries worldwide. A complementary document is the IFLA Principles for Library eLending (2013). IFLA's web page on eLending for Libraries (www.ifla.org/elending) is a go-to resource for librarians across the globe, and its eLending and eBooks updates keep librarians current.

Africa has its own unique challenges, because its libraries were often founded to serve educated urban populations and not those with primarily oral traditions. However, Kigongo-Bukenya (Abdullahi, 2009) sees new initiatives such as reading tents, village reading room programs, and the New Partnership for African Development as catalysts for the utilization of information within African communities. Historically, the public library may not have been a notable success in Africa because it is an imported institution that African governments have never financed at levels that allow it to be effective (Sturges & Neill, 1998). These days a reading society, which needs library services, is developing in Africa. Therefore, libraries must be stocked to meet the needs of the children and students who are the primary clientele.

Elsewhere in Africa, some rural information and cultural centers have been developed to find new ways to reach the general public with library service. Rural audio libraries have been founded to address the preservation and transmission of oral cultures in Mali, Swaziland, Zimbabwe, and Tanzania. A lending service provided out of a van or truck or by bicycle or camel may serve towns that cannot support a library building or librarian. The distribution of book boxes to remote rural areas is a typical way of responding to needs for materials to read where a room is available and people cannot be served in any other way.

In 2010, the EIFL Public Library Innovation Programme (EIFL-PLIP) commissioned research to strengthen understanding of the role of public libraries in Africa. The 2011 report "Perceptions of Public Libraries in Ethiopia, Ghana, Kenya, Tanzania, Uganda and Zimbabwe" shows that respondents from six African countries consider public libraries to be potential contributors to community development in areas such as health, employment, and agriculture. However, public libraries were found to be small and under-resourced, and respondents associate them with traditional book lending and reference services rather than with innovation and technology. Over a decade later, in 2016, at the African Library and Information Association and Institutions' (AfLIA) two-day 2nd African Public Libraries Summit, a picture of progress is evident. The online proceedings (AfLIA, 2016) include papers on innovation, transformation of spaces, digital libraries, etc. The next regional conference will take place in 2017 as the 2nd African Library and Information Association and Institutions (AfLIA) and 4th African Library Summit (AfLIA, 2016); one of its sub-themes will address public libraries: "National/Public/Community Library Services Leading the Realisation of the Development Agenda."

In some parts of the world, community action spontaneously created new public libraries. Senegal's tiny libraries, which are found in community centers in the suburbs of Dakar and funded by local societies and donor organizations, are a case in point. Working with the Soros Foundation, Haitian communities developed community libraries around the country. In Mexico, new presidential leadership has led to the creation of a substantial number of new public libraries in the early part of the twenty-first century.

Article 19 of the Universal Declaration of Human Rights provides the basis for discussion of intellectual freedom and access to information. In 1997 IFLA created a committee focusing on the Freedom of Access to Information and Freedom of Expression (FAIFE) to speak for all libraries on their role regarding intellectual freedom. IFLA's executive board strongly endorsed FAIFE as an essential activity for the federation to support as a priority for libraries and a crucial activity for IFLA. The main task for FAIFE is to promote freedom of speech and emphasize the vital role of the library as the doorway to information and knowledge. In 2001 the first IFLA/FAIFE World Report on Libraries and Intellectual Freedom was published. The report and others that follow include a short, factual summary of the situation in a number of countries, including the general situation concerning libraries, librarianship, and intellectual freedom; specific cases of challenges of censorship or other violations of intellectual freedom; the legislation of libraries and intellectual freedom; and library association positions related to intellectual freedom including professional codes of conduct or ethics. The IFLA/FAIFE World Report Series now comprises two publications, the *World Report*, published biannually, and the *Theme Report*, published in alternate years. Starting in 2010, the Report has been published as a web tool (http://db.ifla-world-report.org/home/index) with two interfaces for browsability, one by country and the other by topic.

FAIFE has developed training programs and materials to enhance access to information including access to information on HIV/AIDS through libraries, access to health information through libraries, the IFLA *Manifesto on Transparency, Good Governance, and Freedom from Corruption* (2014), and IFLA *Internet Manifesto* (2014). These are useful as libraries around the world address these important issues. FAIFE issues statements as issues of a critical nature arise to express IFLA's stance on freedom of access to information and freedom of expression. Three statements issued in 2016 reveal concerns of a global nature and include the IFLA FAIFE Statement on the Continued House Arrest of Natalya Sharina, as Moscow Prosecutor General's Office Refuses to Sign Her Indictment; the IFLA Statement on Net Neutrality and Zero-Rating; and the IFLA Statement on the Right to be Forgotten.

Because of the important role of information in contemporary society, a new class of people who are information-poor has emerged, resulting in what is often referred to as the digital divide. Many cannot buy computers and many who own them cannot use them effectively. Public libraries that have the technology and skills have a responsibility to aid and guide those who do not. By providing access, training, and the chance to experiment, public libraries can help users meet their educational needs. The importance of strong, well-funded public libraries for economic and social development in contemporary society cannot be underestimated.

The EIFL Public Library Innovation Award is presented to public libraries that improve people's lives. Its winners are a source of ideas and inspiration for the development of public library services that support community development and, in many cases, with the use of digital technologies. Since 2011 nine different calls have been issued and 33 winners from public and community libraries in developing and transition countries in Africa, Asia, Europe, and Latin America have received the award.

Migration for political, educational, economic, social, and environmental reasons has given rise to more diverse communities around the world. Such diversity transforms communities and results in the development of transnational connections, which means individuals have connections to their home country as well as to other countries where extended families now reside. For example, García Lopez, Caridad Sebastián., and Morales García (2012) note that "Spain has evolved into a pluralistic societal space, shared by citizens of different nationalities who talk different languages and display a large variety of cultural characteristics." They cited a fourfold increase in the number of foreign-born citizens in the 2000s. The Libraries for All: European Strategy for Multicultural Education (ESME) Project is an example of an European integration strategy to provide resources for public libraries to serve multicultural communities (see http://librariesforall.eu), including guidelines, a manual, needs assessments, and a compilation of best practices around the world. As an example of best practice, Birgit Lotz's *Libraries Serving Diverse Communities: Multicultural Library Services of the Public Library of Frankfurt* (2011) is a library service profile that libraries can model to describe who they are serving and what multicultural services they are providing.

In 2012 IFLA's Section on Library Services to Multicultural Populations published the IFLA/UNESCO Multicultural Library Manifesto Toolkit (2012) to support the implementation of the manifesto, which was endorsed by UNESCO in 2009 and is available in 24 languages. It is well documented in the professional literature that best practices in multicultural services are found in countries in North America, Europe, and Australasia. Libraries in other parts of the world are beginning to show a similar commitment in providing multicultural services such as China, where since 2012 the Nanjing Library has been providing training on the use of computers and electronic resources to rural migrant workers, seniors, children, laid-off workers, and other vulnerable groups (Bing, 2015).

"The Alexandria Proclamation on Information Literacy and Lifelong Learning" (2005) states that:

> Information Literacy lies at the core of lifelong learning. It empowers people in all walks of life to seek, evaluate, use and create information effectively to achieve their personal, social, occupational and educational goals. It is a basic human right in a digital world and promotes social inclusion of all nations.

Although public librarians have taught library instruction since the introduction of computers in libraries, they have also been delivering basic computer skills training. However, the teaching of information literacy (IL) is not widely practiced in public libraries in many parts of the world, and lags behind IL instruction in academic libraries. Andrew Lewis (n.d.), writing on the CILIP Information Literacy Group blog, thinks that the challenge lies in the public library's diverse users, which makes it difficult to develop targeted IL instruction that can be more relevant and instructive to users. Crawford and Irving's 2013 book on information literacy and lifelong learning noted the link that exists between public libraries and schools in the UK and Europe in developing information literacy skills.

In addition to literacy and information literacy, public libraries in the twenty-first century need to support the development of complementary or multiple literacies. "21st Century Literacies in Public Libraries" was the theme of the IFLA Public Libraries Section's 2016 satellite meeting, which covered digital, civic, health, and multiple literacies among other forms of literacy.

Public libraries are making room to create makerspaces, which enable users to imagine, design, create, and learn. Although a makerspace doesn't need to have the latest digital technologies, many include 3-D printers, software, materials, and tools to work on electronic and robotic projects, as well as traditional crafts. Makerspaces not only support innovation but intergenerational learning to preserve traditional practices to promote cultural and economic development and learning.

Initiated and funded by the Danish Agency for Culture and Realdania, the Model Programme for Public Libraries is "a web-based inspiration catalogue and tools . . . to communicate new knowledge, best practice and inspiration for brand new space/function interplay for library developers." These resources support public libraries to design physical spaces that meet local needs, and are informed by local knowledge and the recognition that digitization and individualization are critical societal developments. Since 2014 the Programme has made an annual award to the world's best new public library of the year. The 2016 award was presented at the conclusion of the Public Libraries Sections Program at the 2016 IFLA WLIC in Columbus, Ohio. These libraries serve to inspire the design and redesign of public libraries and are a showcase of the public library as a civic treasure.

Governance and Funding

The public library is generally the responsibility of local and national authorities, supported by specific legislation and financed by national and local governments. Private funds provide important supplements in many locations. International financial support can be of benefit, but strong local government support is necessary for development of new programs and maintenance of existing services. The constraints on libraries often relate to the lack of funds and therefore the lack of facilities, materials, and staff salaries. Disruptions, including political and economic conflicts, poverty, war, and disease, can erode the hard work and achievements of libraries. International case studies of public libraries and their national policies provide ideas of how countries vary (Helling, 2012).

In many countries, public libraries are faced with diminishing financial resources. At the same time, ways of delivering information are expanding and librarians think that public libraries should provide information in print and nonprint formats. The use of electronic information often increases financial pressures. Funding is one of the major challenges for public libraries around the world, and public libraries are reacting in a number of ways to these changes. Recruiting volunteers to reduce personnel costs, raising costs for patrons by initiating annual charges, charging for lending some items, and assessing different rates for different services have been among the strategies used. Promoting the public library in an effective way has become essential, and one strategy to achieve this is through cooperation with social and cultural organizations. Sponsorship of projects for public libraries by the private sector is also becoming more common. For example, libraries around the world often look to companies to sponsor reading programs and other activities. As a case in point, Spanish public libraries count on 99% public funding, and between the 2008 financial crisis and 2014 there was a 60% decrease in funding coming from the national General State Budgets, which funds both public and academic libraries (Merlo-Vega & Chu, 2015). The line item for libraries in the General State Budgets is dedicated to infrastructure and the cooperative purchase of information resources, leading to reduced or no investment in library buildings and in the purchase of materials in public libraries. In 2012 and 2013, many public libraries had no acquisition budget, at a time when unemployment, in 2013, was 26.1%, the highest rate Spain has experienced. Despite these challenges, public libraries have survived due to imaginative solutions, and engagement with and support from their communities.

The UNESCO Public Library Manifesto (see figure 12.1), prepared in cooperation with IFLA, states that the public library shall in principle be free of charge. However, there is an ongoing discussion among libraries about payment for services. Some argue for equal and easy access to free services, and others insist that fiscal concerns and market mechanisms point to the need to charge for selected services. Some libraries are introducing registration

UNESCO Public Library Manifesto

November 1994

Freedom, prosperity and the development of society and of individuals are fundamental human values. They will only be attained through the ability of well-informed citizens to exercise their democratic rights and to play an active role in society. Constructive participation and the development of democracy depend on satisfactory education as well as on free and unlimited access to knowledge, thought, culture and information.

The public library, the local gateway to knowledge, provides a basic condition for lifelong learning, independent decision-making and cultural development of the individual and social groups.

This Manifesto proclaims UNESCO's belief in the public library as a living force for education, culture and information, and as an essential agent for the fostering of peace and spiritual welfare through the minds of men and women.

UNESCO therefore encourages national and local governments to support and actively engage in the development of public libraries.

The Public Library

The public library is the local centre of information, making all kinds of knowledge and information readily available to its users.

The services of the public library are provided on the basis of equality of access for all, regardless of age, race, sex, religion, nationality, language or social status. Specific services and materials must be provided for those users who cannot, for whatever reason, use the regular services and materials, for example linguistic minorities, people with disabilities or people in hospital or prison.

All age groups must find material relevant to their needs. Collections and services have to include all types of appropriate media and modern technologies as well as traditional materials. High quality and relevance to local needs and conditions are fundamental. Material must reflect current trends and the evolution of society, as well as the memory of human endeavour and imagination.

Collections and services should not be subject to any form of ideological, political or religious censorship, nor commercial pressures.

Missions of the Public Library

The following key missions which relate to information, literacy, education and culture should be at the core of public library services:

FIGURE 12.1 UNESCO Public Library Manifesto [CONTINUED ON FOLLOWING PAGE]

SOURCE: The Manifesto is prepared with the International Federation of Library Associations and Institutions (IFLA). www.unesco.org/webworld/libraries/manifestos/libraman.html.

FIGURE 12.1 [CONTINUED]

1. creating and strengthening reading habits in children from an early age;
2. supporting both individual and self conducted education as well as formal education at all levels;
3. providing opportunities for personal creative development;
4. stimulating the imagination and creativity of children and young people;
5. promoting awareness of cultural heritage, appreciation of the arts, scientific achievements and innovations;
6. providing access to cultural expressions of all performing arts;
7. fostering inter-cultural dialogue and favouring cultural diversity;
8. supporting the oral tradition;
9. ensuring access for citizens to all sorts of community information;
10. providing adequate information services to local enterprises, associations and interest groups;
11. facilitating the development of information and computer literacy skills;
12. supporting and participating in literacy activities and programmes for all age groups, and initiating such activities if necessary.

Funding, Legislation and Networks

- The public library shall in principle be free of charge. The public library is the responsibility of local and national authorities. It must be supported by specific legislation and financed by national and local governments. It has to be an essential component of any long-term strategy for culture, information provision, literacy and education.
- To ensure nationwide library coordination and cooperation, legislation and strategic plans must also define and promote a national library network based on agreed standards of service.
- The public library network must be designed in relation to national, regional, research and special libraries as well as libraries in schools, colleges and universities.

Operation and Management

- A clear policy must be formulated, defining objectives, priorities and services in relation to the local community needs. The public library has to be organized effectively and professional standards of operation must be maintained.
- Cooperation with relevant partners—for example, user groups and other professionals at local, regional, national as well as international level—has to be ensured.
- Services have to be physically accessible to all members of the community. This requires well situated library buildings, good reading and study facilities, as well as relevant technologies and sufficient opening hours convenient to the users. It equally implies outreach services for those unable to visit the library.

FIGURE 12.1 [CONTINUED]

- The library services must be adapted to the different needs of communities in rural and urban areas.
- The librarian is an active intermediary between users and resources. Professional and continuing education of the librarian is indispensable to ensure adequate services.
- Outreach and user education programmes have to be provided to help users benefit from all the resources.

or subscription charges for public library membership. These strategies become more common with political and economic changes and reductions in funds.

IMPLEMENTING THE MANIFESTO

Decision makers at national and local levels and the library community at large, around the world, are hereby urged to implement the principles expressed in the Manifesto.

A trend in local government in some parts of the world is to merge libraries into larger bodies of leisure, culture, or education. For example, since 2004 Library and Archives Canada combines the holdings, services, and staff of both the former National Library of Canada and National Archives of Canada. The head of a library service may be a librarian who also manages programs outside the library sector, or a nonlibrarian who is responsible for a range of services including libraries. Certain countries in some parts of the world, faced with diminishing governmental resources, have considered radical changes. One option is to contract out the public library service, so that it is provided by an outside company on behalf of a local or central government body. Many jurisdictions have not chosen to adopt this course, since most librarians think it is important that the public library is an independent and impartial institution that provides education, culture, recreation, and information to all.

IMPACT AND ADVOCACY

Networking and resource sharing are especially essential today. No single library can buy everything its users need. Public libraries are increasingly used for education and personal development and as information resource centers. Economic necessity and the need to increase the effectiveness of individual libraries have spurred cooperative efforts among groups of libraries to achieve equity of access. Many new library networks are multi-type and broker remote access to information. With electronic sources of information becoming key to the provision of reference and information services, networks are becoming more common and more essential.

Information about the current state of public libraries in Europe has been facilitated by the creation of the European Union and the European Commission. A green paper on the role of libraries in the information society was issued in 1997 (Thorhauge, Larsen, Thun, & Albrechtsen, 1997). Nations in northern Europe were shown to have relatively higher percentages of their population registered as borrowers from public libraries. In 2008, the European Union launched a vast online library, which offers access to millions of books, maps, recordings, photographs, archival documents, paintings, and films from its member states' national libraries and cultural institutions. Europeana.eu is a site that aims to provide new ways for people to explore Europe's heritage.

A 2016 report for the European Parliament discusses the impact that public libraries can have on the intellectual and cultural development of citizens with a focus on their role in providing open public space for learning, culture, and social communication (European Parliament Committee on Culture and Education, 2016). PL2020 brings together library organizations and advocates from across the European Union to raise awareness of the value of public libraries as partners for social and economic development under the Europe 2020 strategy. PL2020 promotes how libraries are contributing to European policy objectives in social inclusion, digital inclusion, and lifelong learning (www.publiclibraries2020.eu). They provide grants to support advocacy projects at all levels. The PL2020 website provides numbers and stories that illustrate what public libraries are doing and how libraries empower citizens. These kinds of collaborative efforts help illustrate how libraries change lives.

In countries such as Malaysia and Singapore, public libraries are being built on a planned basis with strong direction by the national library. The role of the public library as a cultural center is key in some countries. In Bulgaria, public libraries are housed in cultural centers, and in the United Kingdom most metropolitan public libraries are administered as part of a leisure or cultural directorate. With social, technological, and telecommunications advances, one of the responses of public libraries has been to create large units of administration and to fund coordinating mechanisms. In 2001 Mexico held its first international conference on public libraries, with speakers from Germany, Canada, Spain, the United States, France, Italy, and Mexico.

Librarians have in recent years begun to address the issue of the value of the public library in terms of the ways in which libraries contribute to the economic development of the local community. An Australian management consultant asserts that politicians and librarians underestimate the current and potential economic value of public libraries and suggests that the benefit created is twice as much as the funds spent (Haratsis, 1995). Consultants in New Zealand developed a cost-benefit methodology for assessing the value of library output (New Zealand Library and Information Association, 1996). The role of the library in economic development can involve a wide range of activities, from encouragement of literacy to the provision of specialized business services. With financial constraints and the perceived need to provide new services while maintaining book and multimedia collections and delivering specialized services to minority groups, there are discussions about which services are basic—and therefore should be free of charge—and which might be fee-based. Many libraries face stable or diminishing budgets as well as the need to provide new services and meet increased demands. One example of how libraries have responded to these challenges is illustrated by actions of Spanish librarians during economic crisis and reveal the impact of libraries as social justice institutions, the role of librarians as agents of change, and the value of community grassroots efforts when governments are not providing needed resources and services (Merlo-Vega & Chu, 2015).

UNESCO's 2010 global monitoring report on the Education for All initiative, Reaching the Marginalized, discusses the scale of deprivation. The report identifies disadvantages in education worldwide and assesses the effectiveness of national policies in combating marginalization. Literacy is an important aspect of the fight against marginalization and public libraries can be a factor. The Global Impact Study of Public Access to Information and Communication Technologies implemented by the University of Washington's Technology and Social Change Group was a five-year project (2007–2012) to generate evidence about the impacts of public access to information and communication technologies. Using data from Botswana, Chile, and the Philippines, the study shows that "a central impact of public libraries is promoting digital inclusion, information access, and development of ICT skills through technology provision, particularly for marginalized populations and those who face challenges using and benefiting from computers and the internet." The study states that "both users and non-users reporting positive impacts and a willingness to pay to maintain the existence of public libraries" (Sey et al., 2013). The Global Impact Study website (www.globalimpactstudy.org) has useful information on the impact of libraries including surveys, in-depth studies, publications, and information about research design. This information should be helpful to public libraries as they continue to seek funding and support from governments and other sources.

International Library Development Initiatives

Public libraries around the world have received targeted support from philanthropic organizations, such as the Carnegie Corporation, Bertelsmann Foundation, British Council, Book Aid International, IREX, Elsevier Foundation, and the Bill and Melinda Gates Foundation, among others. When countries have fewer resources, public libraries may be viewed as a new concept imported from the West. At the beginning of the last century, Andrew Carnegie was instrumental in spreading the influence of libraries through countries that were part of the former British Commonwealth. Carnegie provided funds for over 2,800 public library buildings, most of them in the English-speaking world. Carnegie required a community to donate space for the building and provide for the operating expenses. In recent years the Carnegie Corporation has focused on libraries in Africa. The focus of foundations and organizations has moved from buildings and books to information and technology and transforming libraries to community hubs. Other library development initiatives not provided by philanthropic organizations are also discussed in this section.

Bill and Melinda Gates Foundation

The Bill and Melinda Gates Foundation Global Libraries Initiative (www.gatesfoundation.org) supports libraries throughout the world to help individuals improve their lives through information and technology. The foundation gave its first grants in 1997 and announced in 2014 that it is planning to conclude its work and funding for Global Libraries in 2018. The focus was on research and innovation; training and leadership; delivery of information; and impact, advocacy, and policy. The International Network of Emerging Library Innovators (INELI) (www.libraryinnovators2.com) was established in 2011 to create a pool of future library leaders to redefine public libraries for the future and build and sustain public libraries around the world. In order to leave the field strong, the foundation is identifying and funding legacy partners including the American Library Association's Pubic Library Association, the International Federation of Library Associations and Institutions, and the Technology and Social Change Group at the University of Washington Information School.

The foundation has worked in 16 countries and through intermediaries in 5 additional countries. The foundation has supported projects such as the Abre Tu Mundo (Open Your

World) project in Chile, which has given Chilean residents no-cost access to computers and the Internet in Chile's 368 public libraries, as well as training on the use of new information technologies and the generation of local content for the Internet (www.biblioredes.cl).

The Access to Learning Awards funded by the foundation were given annually to a public library or similar organization outside the United States that showed a commitment to offering the public free access to information technology through an existing innovative program. Awards have included projects like the following: a network of 19 public libraries in Bogotá that offers no-cost access to digital information in some of the city's poorest neighborhoods; the Helsinki Information Gas Station, a portable unit providing immediate information by phone, fax, or text messages; a project in Bangladesh that converts indigenous boats into mobile libraries that provide free computer and Internet stations and training to agricultural communities; Rural Education and Development (READ) in Nepal, which works with villages to build self-supporting libraries funded through community projects that provide free access to the Internet, books, and multimedia tools; a technological solution in remote underprivileged communities that is helping preserve culture and bring indigenous Australians into local libraries; an innovative mobile technology program that provides computer access and training to remote, indigenous communities in Mexico's Veracruz state; a government-run program in Sri Lanka to increase digital literacy among the nation's poorest residents living in remote rural areas; and the Arid Lands Information Network in Kenya, Uganda, and Tanzania.

IREX

The Beyond Access project of the International Research and Exchanges Board (IREX) works with local partners in eight countries to transform libraries into modern community information hubs to power social and economic development (www.beyondaccess.net). Activities focus on access to information, community literacy, and employability. Projects include modernizing libraries for a changing society in Myanmar, integrating libraries into Uruguay's information and telecommunications strategy to increase digital inclusion, increasing access to information and economic opportunities in Peru, and helping public libraries partner to power Georgia's economic and social development. Projects in Bangladesh, Ethiopia, and Mali focus on integrating local libraries and technologies for early reading programs and community literacy.

Electronic Information for Libraries (EIFL)

The Electronic Information for Libraries (www.eifl.org) consortium, launched in late 1999, provides a structural solution to the digital divide in content access. The consortium serves an estimated 9 million users through several thousand libraries in more than 60 developing and transitional countries. EIFL works with libraries to enable access to knowledge for education, learning, research, and sustainable community development. It supports open access including online, free, and unrestricted availability of peer-reviewed literature and access to commercial e-resources through its licensing program. EIFL is an independent foundation governed by a board elected by national consortia belonging to the network, which receives some core operating support from the Open Society Institute but is increasingly supported by its membership.

EIFL's Public Library Innovation Programme, which began in 2011, enables public libraries to develop new services using digital technology. They give small grants focusing on a variety of topics and build librarians' capacity to innovate. Awards for contributing to community economic well-being include one to the Belgrade City Library to help people manage their money. Awards for social inclusion include one to Croatia to build trust between Roma and Croatian children. Public libraries empowering women and girls includes a grant to a Guatemalan library to empower talented women weavers. For creative use of ICT in public libraries, a public library in Poland established an ICT laboratory that enables people to compose music, produce movies, make moving robots, and other projects. Awards for public libraries contributing to literacy include a municipal library in Moldova that created a summer learning center in a city amusement park. In Ukraine, a public library contributes to literacy by using a computer game to teach children and adults to read and write using the Ukrainian alphabet. Awards were also given for public libraries contributing to community health and to open government.

Open Society Institute, Soros Foundation

The Open Society Institute (OSI) is a private operating and grant-making foundation based in New York City that serves as the hub of the Soros Foundation's network, a group of autonomous foundations and organizations in more than 50 countries (www.opensociety foundation.org). OSI and the network implement a range of initiatives that aim to promote open societies by shaping government policy and supporting education, media, public health, and human and women's rights, as well as social, legal, and economic reform. Following the dissolution of the Soviet Union, OSI's Library Program helped libraries transform themselves into public and service-oriented centers for their communities, with model libraries that functioned as civic information centers in Russia and eight Central and Eastern European countries with support from local governments. OSI's work to support access to information in Haiti is also notable. The OSI Information Program works to increase access to knowledge, empower civil society groups, and protect civil liberties in the digital environment. Grants are available for organizations, which are generally invited to submit proposals.

Bertelsmann Foundation

Since its inception in 1977, the Bertelsmann Foundation (www.bfna.org) has conducted projects in the sphere of public libraries where they emphasize the construction and promotion of model libraries as well as the development of future-oriented methods of library management. The Bertelsmann Foundation International Network of Public Libraries worked to pool international know-how to strengthen the exchange of experience among public library experts, to develop concepts for modern library management, and, above all, to promote the transfer of such model solutions into practice. With 16 experts from 10 countries, the network created a forum in which people could share information and expertise to increase the effectiveness and efficiency of libraries. The two modules are 1) international research and 2) preparation of model solutions on issues of modern library management and implementation of these solutions at the practical level to test their suitability for everyday use. Volume 1 of a series of case studies sponsored by the Bertelsmann Foundation *International Network of Public Libraries* (Windau, 1999) outlines successful solutions. The report of the Canterbury Public Library (which serves the city of Christchurch, New Zealand) and the methodology used to evaluate its ability to meet the challenges of the twenty-first century provides guidelines and recommendations on how to implement change in a meaningful way. The Bertelsmann Foundation has changed its focus to improving education, shaping democracy, strengthening economics, advancing societies, promoting health, and vitalizing culture.

British Council

Since 1934 librarians in the British Council (www.britishcouncil.org) have created an international library network and helped lay the foundations of public library systems in the developing world (Coombs, 1988). The council maintained its own libraries, administered book aid schemes, encouraged professional interchange and education, and ran courses in librarianship. In 1959, the public library development scheme that emerged to sponsor public library systems was created more or less from scratch. The areas of most intense activity were West and East Africa. By the 1970s the council felt the need to provide integrated and more sophisticated information service. More recently, people have questioned the relevance of the British model, based partly on the fact that appropriate materials were difficult to acquire from indigenous publishers. Although the focus of the British Council has changed and now offers less support for this work, in 2016 a new network of libraries across Pakistan was launched at the inaugural ceremony of a new purpose-built library in Lahore. A maker library project to create a dialogue between makers in the UK and South Africa was launched in 2014.

Mortenson Center for International Library Programs

The Mortenson Center for International Library Programs at the University of Illinois at Urbana-Champaign designs programs for library and information workers to exchange ideas and upgrade their knowledge and skills through experiences and study visits (www.library.illinois.edu/mortenson). This is achieved through a structured program of skills development, formal coursework, consultation with library and library school faculty, and literature reviews, as well as library tours and conferences. The Center also develops international partnerships to develop librarians internationally, strengthen international ties among librarians and libraries worldwide for the promotion of international education, understanding, and peace. Since 1991 librarians from over 90 countries have participated in these programs. In 2016, it launched its Libraries for Peace initiative (http://librariesforpeace.org) to advance the Center's mission to strengthen international ties among libraries and librarians worldwide for the promotion of international education, understanding, and peace. It consists of a website and social media that provide resources for libraries and others to learn about what libraries are doing to promote peace, how they can initiate their own efforts, and where these actions are taking place; to discuss and share ideas of libraries and peacebuilding; and to serve as an information hub for an international library celebration and action day for peace. This Libraries for Peace (L4P) Day calls on libraries and librarians around the world to annually observe the International Day of Peace on September 21, and to pledge to act to advance peace.

Book Donation Programs

Several hundred book donation programs operate throughout the world, which function with varying degrees of success. The key is to be certain that funds are not spent to send books that are not needed or outdated materials. Book Aid International is a major donor of new and used books. It supports libraries in Africa by sending new books.

The Canadian Organization for Development through Education, the Norwegian Agency for Development Cooperation, and other agencies have provided funding for libraries. A number of useful workshop meetings devoted to the organization of library services have been heavily facilitated by IFLA's Action for Development through Libraries Programme (ALP) (www.ifla.org). In French-speaking Africa, a network of centers was set up to provide access to information media. The cultural center as focus for information activity is a well-established concept in francophone West Africa. An example is Senegal, where the Ministry of Culture provides each administrative region of the country with a major cultural center that generally includes library activities.

Other Initiatives

There are many other initiatives that support library and information work in different countries or regions of the world. Read Global (www.readglobal.org) partners with rural communities to develop libraries and community centers in Nepal, Bhutan, and India. The centers are owned and operated by the local community and include a library, computer room, women's section, children's room, and training area. A sustaining enterprise or small business (tractor rentals, sewing cooperatives, community radio stations, etc.) creates local jobs and generates profit to support the ongoing cost of the center. Room to Read (www.roomtoread.org) focuses on literacy and gender equality in education. It collaborates with communities and local governments across Asia and Africa to develop literacy and the habit of reading among primary school children and supports girls to complete secondary education. The Elsevier Foundation (www.elsevierfoundation.org) and its Innovative Libraries grant program supports capacity-building in developing countries through training, infrastructure, and preservation of information. It has given out 50 grants over 10 years. In 2016 it ended this program and launched two new initiatives focusing on innovations in health information and research in developing countries. The Asia Foundation (www.asiafoundation.org) has supported programs to enhance the potential of libraries in Myanmar, Vietnam, Mongolia, Nepal, and Thailand among others. The Riecken Foundation (www.riecken.org) supports over 60 libraries in rural Honduras and Guatemala. It offers books, programs, and access to technology, and helps to develop local leadership. The governments of Sweden, Denmark, Norway and other European countries have long provided support for libraries and library associations.

In the end, each country and community must decide what kind of public library is needed and develop the local support to ensure its success. International programs can help, but local support and leadership are essential.

COMMUNITY OUTREACH AND SERVICES

An international comparison of public library services and statistics at the end of the twentieth century revealed that of the wide range of services provided, books, interlibrary lending, and children's services are nearly universal (Hanratty & Sumsion, 1996). The library is for many people the reason for coming to the central city and is considered by people of many cultures to be a safe and non-threatening environment.

Public Libraries and the Information Society, prepared for the European Commission, proposes a vision for public libraries for the twenty-first century. This report outlines the necessity of developing national policies and strategies for public libraries and the importance of continuing education for librarians (Thorhauge et al., 1997). The report discusses how the public library fulfills a variety of functions, serving as local cultural center, local learning center, general information center, and social center. Libraries can help all people prosper in an information society and be a key part of the educational system. Public libraries are a critical component for a civil society and lifelong learning, education, and democratic process in an open society.

Similar evaluations took place in other parts of the world, including discussions of the barefoot librarian in Africa (Onwubiko, 1996). Access to knowledge and lifelong learning is vital in democracies. Unequal access to information and technology, as well as information illiteracy, may create additional social divisions, but public libraries can help, and changes in government can lead to opportunities to renew public libraries. Administrative reform can lead to changes, but most countries remain committed to financing them by public budgets.

Outreach services such as bookmobiles, electronic information delivery, and cooperation with other libraries to improve services are important. Bookmobiles can expand service by reaching out to people who cannot get to a library. Those managing public libraries must find a balance between varied goals, such as using marketing techniques and providing a collection that is not based on commercial interests. The introduction of the Camel Library Service by the Kenya National Library Service is an innovative approach to delivering services to those with a nomadic lifestyle (Atuti, 1999). Rahman (2000) reports on the status of rural and small libraries in Bangladesh, describing the reality of isolation, poor telecommunications infrastructure, and neglect faced by many rural libraries around the world that sometimes serve illiterate populations.

Libraries respond to community needs in ways that are most appropriate to their settings and resources. Camel book boxes, bicycle book carts, donkey-drawn book carts, and other programs illustrate ingenious ways librarians respond to community needs and deliver services. Mali has a library in a railway car that serves 10 communities along the railway line. In Zimbabwe, a donkey cart is used as a means of conveyance. Pack mules have been used in South America to transport collections of books to remote communities. Bicycles can move information workers and small quantities of materials at low cost over difficult terrain. The Ideas Box, created by Libraries Without Borders, is a portable multimedia kit for refugee and vulnerable populations that can be delivered to a refugee camp. When set up, it offers multimedia information resources that would be encountered in a public library, including print materials, e-books, tablets, software, a large digital screen, and seating (www.ideas-box.org).

The number of displaced people around the world has increased, whether they stay within their own national borders as internally displaced persons (IDP) or leave their homeland to seek asylum in the hope of being accepted as refugees by another country. The last few years have been notable because of the great number of Syrians fleeing to Europe as refugees. EBLIDA (The European Bureau of Library, Information and Documentation Associations) has created the resource web page, on "Public Libraries in Europe Welcome Refugees," while IFLA's Public Libraries Section has compiled examples and stories of public libraries responding to the refugee crisis, particularly in Europe, in the document "Responding! Public Libraries and Refugees."

IFLA's Action for Development through Libraries Programme (ALP) has been the primary vehicle for delivering the professional development strand of its Advocacy Framework through training based on policy and guidelines developed by IFLA's core activities or sections. ALP is an important mechanism for developing plans to extend library service.

The IFLA (2009) Public Libraries Section has issued "10 Ways to Make a Public Library Work," which suggests ideas for public library development:

1. Develop public library buildings emphasizing community and cultural spaces, not just physical stores of knowledge.
2. Liberate our services using the World Wide Web 2.0 and look toward Web 3.0 and 4.0.
3. Connect with our communities and educate and train people. Librarians and information scientists can act as educators and personal knowledge advisors and not just keepers of keys or Internet gateways.
4. Develop a "worldwide wisdom"—a global knowledge and understanding—by creating international cultural pathways on the web.
5. Work internationally to erode barriers and censorship while respecting all cultures.
6. Support our staff with continued training and encouragement to be proactive.
7. Develop our digitized collections services and knowledge—the hybrid library—knowledge, education, and information in diverse forms.
8. Improve accessibility to our catalogs and databases, especially for users with visual impairments.
9. Establish national and international standards on the Internet environment.
10. Public libraries as cultural storehouses—the live environment alongside the recorded one—archives, museums, libraries, and culture combined: a "comby library" (https://www.ifla.org/files/assets/public-libraries/publications/10-ways-to-make-a-public-library-work.pdf).

Telecommunication infrastructures vary widely among nations. Donations of computer information systems are increasingly common, but internal funds may not be available for ongoing maintenance and upgrades. Digital and Internet-based projects provide new opportunities for public libraries. In countries without a strong public library tradition, it is difficult to show relevance and need for the Internet and technology. The Internet democratizes information and empowers users, and public libraries can be gateways to information and assist people in learning how to use these resources.

Today library cooperation is a major means for providing services, and libraries throughout the world have become more connected to each other through systems and networks, making it easier to share resources. Systems, networks, and databases make it possible to search for information in other libraries. As the local gateway to information, the public library must meet the information needs of a community by using not only their collection, but also those of others. The changing financial situation for public libraries and rapidly changing technology mean that skilled leadership and staff are essential. Moreover, the increasing diversity of communities also means libraries need to find solutions to deliver multicultural and multilingual services and resources.

Library cooperation is not limited to working with other libraries, but also involves cooperating with other cultural and memory associations. These cross-sector activities among libraries, archives, and museums (LAM) are critical to the future development of these institutions. Professionally, they have developed distinct practices and cultures, but collaboration among LAM is important for cross-fertilization of cultural heritage practices, including the collection, organization, and access of cultural heritage materials and cultural programming. Yarrow, Clubb, & Draper (2008) have issued the report "Public Libraries, Archives and Museums: Trends in Collaboration and Cooperation," which describes new opportunities for cross-sector activities for public libraries.

THE ROAD AHEAD FOR PUBLIC LIBRARIES WORLDWIDE

Public librarianship follows a variety of models in different parts of the world, including technology centers, cultural centers, and study centers, among others. As society continues to undergo ideological, political, cultural, social, economic, and technological changes, public libraries must develop policies and strategies that demonstrate their relevance. Libraries are perceived to be at a crossroads in their history. People wonder whether they will have a central place in the electronic society or remain on the margins, and whether they will be able to attract the funds to provide the varied resources and programs needed by the public.

Issues of censorship and the wide range of materials available on the Internet, copyright and intellectual property rights, and providing services free at the point of delivery are key components of future public library services. Public libraries play an essential role in providing and organizing electronic materials for use and in helping and training users to use digital resources. Users demand that libraries provide not only the software and hardware needed, but also the professional support to help independent learners use resources. By participating in the international interest section or group of national library associations or in international associations such as IFLA, and attending the IFLA congress and other international conferences, librarians can work to be part of world librarianship.

The global library community has many challenges and opportunities ahead, including the right to education as outlined in the International Covenant on Economic, Social and Cultural Rights. The aims and objectives of education have moved toward a growing consensus in international human rights law that education should enable the individual to freely develop his or her own personality and dignity, to participate in a free society, and to respect human rights (Kalantry, Getgen, & Koh, 2010: 262). These goals can be supported by public libraries and the librarians who staff them to provide equal and open access to information for all. Likewise, public libraries have taken up the challenge and opportunity to support the United Nations's *Transforming Our World: The 2030 Agenda for Sustainable Development* (2015). IFLA has compiled examples of libraries, most of which are public libraries, that are advancing the SDGs in their recently released report *Access and Opportunity for All: How Libraries contribute to the United Nations 2030 Agenda* (2016). These are but a few examples of what public libraries are already doing and serve as best practices for public libraries as vital contributors to sustainable community development.

Afterword: Working in Public Libraries Internationally

This chapter may inspire librarians to seek work in a library abroad and experience firsthand how public library development and services around the world varies. The opportunity will be professionally enriching, but finding employment in public libraries in other countries can be a challenge due to issues such as credentialing, knowledge of the country and community, and familiarity with cultures and languages. If libraries seek employees from other countries, it is often because they are seeking special skills and experiences. Changing economic and social environments can have an immediate and direct impact on international opportunities.

Working internationally requires special personal and professional traits. Traits include openness to uncertain and unknown issues and environments. It may require bridging low- and high-tech environments and using cross-cultural communication and strong problem-solving skills. Realistic expectations are essential. Salary and benefits, as well as employers' requirements, may differ and are likely to vary by country. Immigration and work visa issues must be understood and addressed.

There are some things that library and information professionals interested in working in other countries can do. They can begin conversations with librarians in other countries through organizations such as the International Librarians Network (http://interlibnet.org). They can contact librarians who hold positions they would like to secure. Students can get to know international students and take courses with an international focus and/or write papers and work on projects that focus on international issues. They can work with the alumni association of their library and information science school to connect with alumni in other countries.

Volunteer opportunities such as with the Peace Corps or non-government organizations, including book distribution and literacy programs, can provide valuable experience for international employment and be a stepping stone to working or volunteering in public libraries. International job exchanges are also a way to gain international experience. Work for library-related vendors and multinational corporations sometimes has an international component. International schools and educational institutions also hire international librarians. Intergovernmental organizations such as the United Nations and its related bodies and UNESCO can also provide opportunities. International library organizations such as IFLA hire librarians from around the world. Churches and other religious organizations may also offer international library-related work. The U.S. Department of State hires information resources officers to work in various world regions. The U.S. military also hires librarians to work in public, school, and military libraries on bases around the world.

There is no one centralized source to locate international job opportunities. Some helpful resources include:

- Doffek, P. Library and Technology Jobs: International Library Jobs. http://guides.lib.fsu.edu/c.php?g=352933&p=2383381.
- The Global Librarian. International LIS Jobs. http://thegloballibrarian.tumblr.com/internationalLISjobs.
- Hawkins, K. S. (March 16, 2016). "Jobs and internships abroad." In *International Librarianship*. www.ultraslavonic.info/intllib.html.

Professional associations can also be resources:

- International Federation of Library Associations and Institutions (IFLA). LIBJOBS (A mailing list for librarians and information professionals seeking employment.) www.ifla.org/mailing-lists%20.
- IRRT International Exchanges Committee, American Library Association. International Employment Opportunities and Funding Sources for Librarians. www.ala.org/irrt/irrtcommittees/irrtintlexc/internationalemployment.

- The Chartered Institute of Library and Information Professionals (CILIP). LIBEX: International Job Exchange. www.cilip.org.uk/membership/benefits/advice-support/international-job-exchange-libex.

These sources may quickly become out-of-date and be replaced by new resources. Thus, an Internet search for new sources is recommended.

International job opportunities in public libraries are few compared to opportunities to work in school or academic libraries. Finding international employment opportunities often requires library experience and always requires resourcefulness and persistence.

REFERENCES

Abdullahi, I. (2009). *Global library and information science.* Munich, Germany: K. G. Saur.

African Library and Information Association and Institutions (AfLIA). (2016). Proceedings of the 2nd African Public Libraries Summit. http://ocs.aflia.net/index.php/ap12/ap12/schedConf/presentations.

African Library and Information Association and Institutions. (2016). 2nd African Library and Information Association and Institutions (AfLIA) and 4th African Library Summit. http://aflia.net/web/pages/news-events/call-for-papers-2nd-aflia-conference-4th-african-library-summit-2.

Association des Bibliothécaires de France (2017). www.abf.asso.fr/.

Atuti, R.M. (1999). Camel library service to nomadic pastoralists: The Kenyan scenario. *IFLA Journal, 25,* 152-158.

Bates, M. J., & Maack, M. N. (Eds.). (2009). *Encyclopedia of Library and Information Science* (3rd ed.). Boca Raton, FL: CRC Press.

Beyond Access (2017). http://beyondaccess.net/.

BiblioRedas (2017). www.biblioredes.cl/.

Bill & Melinda Gates Foundation (n.d.). Global Libraries Atlas. https://www.glatlas.org/Account/Login?ReturnUrl=%2F.

Bing, W. (2015). Nanjing Library's efforts on intellectual freedom. *Chinese Librarianship: An International Electronic Journal* (CLIEJ), *39,* 7-18. www.iclc.us/cliej/cl39wang.pdf.

Birdi, B., & Wilson, K. (2008). The public library, exclusion and empathy: A literature review. *Library Review, 57*(8), 576-592.

Black, A. (2000). *The public library in Britain, 1914-2000.* London, United Kingdom: British Library.

British Council (n.d.). www.britishcouncil.org.

Coombs, D. (1988). *Spreading the word: The library work of the British Council.* London, United Kingdom: Mansell.

Crawford, J., & Irving, C. (2013). *Information literacy and lifelong learning: Policy issues, the workplace, health and public libraries.* Oxford, United Kingdom: Chandos Publishing. www.sciencedirect.com/science/book/9781843346821.

EBLIDA (The European Bureau of Library, Information and Documentation Associations). (n.d.) Public libraries in Europe welcome refugees. www.eblida.org/activities/public-libraries-in-europe-refugees.html.

EIFL Public Library Innovation Programme (EIFL-PLIP). (2011). Perceptions of public libraries in Ethiopia, Ghana, Kenya, Tanzania, Uganda and Zimbabwe. www.eifl.net/resources/perceptions-public-libraries-africa-0.

Encyclopedia of library and information science. (2009). London: Taylor & Francis.

European Parliament Committee on Culture and Education (2016). Public libraries—Their new role. www.europarl.europa.eu/RegData/etudes/STUD/2016/585882/IPOL_STU(2016)585882_EN.pdf.

García López, F., Caridad Sebastián, M., & Morales García, A. M. (2012). Comparative analysis of the development of multicultural library services in the Spanish public library network (2007-2010). *Information Research, 17*(4). http://InformationR.net/ir/17-4/paper554.html.

GatesFoundation.org (2017). Global libraries: Strategy overview. The Bill and Melinda Gates Foundation Global Libraries Initiative.

Global Impact Study (2013). www.globalimpactstudy.org.

Gomez, R. (Ed.) (2012). *Libraries, telecentres, cybercafes and public access to ICT: International comparisons.* Hershey, PA: Information Science Reference.

Guangzhou Library (2017). www.gzlib.gov.cn/IntroductionToGZL.

Häggström, B.M. (2004). *The role of libraries in lifelong learning: Final report of the IFLA project under the Section of Public Libraries.* http://archive.ifla.org/VII/s8/proj/Lifelong-LearningReport.pdf.

Hanratty, C., & Sumsion, J. (1996). *International comparison of public library statistics.* Loughborough, United Kingdom: Loughborough University, Library and Information Statistics Unit.

Haratsis, B. (1995). Justifying the economic value of public libraries in a turbulent local government environment. *Australasian Public Libraries and Information Services, 8,* 164–172.

Helling, J. (2012). *Public libraries and their national policies: International case studies.* Oxford, UK: Chandos Publishing.

International Federation of Library Associations and Institutions (IFLA). (2001). The public library service: IFLA/UNESCO guidelines for development (IFLA Publications 97). Prepared by a working group of the section of Public Libraries chaired by Philip Gill. Munich, Germany: K. G. Saur. www.ifla.org/files/assets/hq/publications/archive/the-public-library-service/pub197.pdf.

International Federation of Library Associations and Institutions. (2002). The Glasgow declaration on libraries, information services and intellectual freedom. www.ifla.org/publications/the-glasgow-declaration-on-libraries-information-services-and-intellectual-freedom.

International Federation of Library Associations and Institutions. (2005). *Beacons of the information society: The Alexandria proclamation on information literacy and lifelong learning.* www.ifla.org/publications/beacons-of-the-information-society-the-alexandria-proclamation-on-information-literacy.

International Federation of Library Associations and Institutions. (2008). *Meeting user needs: A checklist for best practices.* http://archive.ifla.org/VII/s8/proj/Mtg_UN-Checklist.pdf.

International Federation of Library Associations and Institutions. (2009). *10 ways to make a public library work.* www.ifla.org/en/publications/10-ways-to-make-a-public-library-work-update-your-libraries.

International Federation of Library Associations and Institutions. (2009). IFLA/UNESCO multicultural library manifesto. www.ifla.org/node/8976.

International Federation of Library Associations and Institutions. (2012). IFLA/UNESCO multicultural library manifesto toolkit. www.ifla.org/node/8977.

International Federation of Library Associations and Institutions. (2013). IFLA principles for library eLending. www.ifla.org/elending/principles.

International Federation of Library Associations and Institutions. (2014). IFLA 2014 eLending *background paper.* www.ifla.org/files/assets/hq/topics/e-lending/documents/2014_ifla_elending_background_paper.pdf.

International Federation of Library Associations and Institutions. (2014). *Internet manifesto.* www.ifla.org/publications/node/224.

International Federation of Library Associations and Institutions. (2014). *Lyon declaration on access to information and development.* www.lyondeclaration.org.

International Federation of Library Associations and Institutions. (2014). *Manifesto on Transparency, Good Governance, and Freedom from Corruption.* https://www.ifla.org/publications/ifla-manifesto-on-transparency-good-governance-and-freedom-from-corruption.

International Federation of Library Associations and Institutions. (2015). *Toolkit: Libraries and the UN post-2015 development agenda.* www.ifla.org/publications/toolkit—libraries-and-the-un-post-2015-development-agenda.

International Federation of Library Associations and Institutions. (2016). *Access and opportunity for all: How libraries contribute to the United Nations 2030 Agenda.* www.ifla.org/publications/node/10546.

International Federation of Library Associations and Institutions. (2016). *IFLA FAIFE statement on the continued house arrest of Natalya Sharina, as Moscow Prosecutor General's Office refuses to sign her indictment.* www.ifla.org/publications/node/10844?og=30.

International Federation of Library Associations and Institutions. (2016). *IFLA statement on net neutrality and zero-rating.* www.ifla.org/publications/node/10700?og=30.

International Federation of Library Associations and Institutions. (2016). *IFLA statement on the right to be forgotten.* www.ifla.org/publications/node/10320?og=30.

IFLA & Committee on Freedom of Access to Information and Freedom of Expression (FAIFE). (2001). *IFLA/FAIFE World Report: Libraries and Intellectual Freedom.*

IFLA & UNESCO. (1994) *The IFLA/UNESCO Public Library Manifesto.* www.ifla.org/en/publications/iflaunesco-public-library-manifesto-1994.

IFLA Public Libraries Section. (n.d.). *Responding! Public libraries and refugees.* www.ifla.org/files/assets/public-libraries/publications/library_service_to_refugees_0.pdf.

IFLA Public Libraries Section. (2009). 10 ways to make a public library work/Update your libraries. https://www.ifla.org/files/assets/public-libraries/publications/10-ways-to-make-a-public-library-work.pdf.

International Librarians Network (2017). www.interlibnet.org.

Kalantry, S., Getgen, J. E., & Koh, S. A. (2010). Enhancing enforcement of economic, social, and cultural rights using indicators: A focus on the right to education in the ICESCR. *Human Rights Quarterly, 32,* 253-310.

Kigongo Bukenya, I. (2009). Public Libraries. In Abdullahi, I. (Ed.), *Global library and information science* (pp. 21-44). Munich, Germany: K. G. Saur.

Koontz, C., & Gubbin, B. (2010). *IFLA public library service guidelines.* Berlin, Germany: De Gruyter/Saur.

Lau, J. (2010). Mexico: Libraries, archives and museums. *Encyclopedia of Library and Information Science.* (3rd ed., pp. 3624-3646). Boca Raton, FL: CRC Press.

Lewis, A. (n.d.). Where does information literacy fit in within public libraries? CILIP Information Literacy Group Blog. www.informationliteracy.org.uk/sectors/il-public-libraries/.

Libweb (n.d.). Library servers via WWW. www.lib-web.org.

Lotz, Birgit. (2011). *Libraries serving diverse communities: Multicultural library services of the Public Library of Frankfurt.* Johannesburg, South Africa: Goethe-Institut. www.goethe.de/ins/za/joh/pro/lib/Lotz_Libraries%20serving%20diverse%20communities.pdf.

Lyon Declaration on access to information and development (2014). www.lyondeclaration.org.

Merlo-Vega, J. A., & Chu, C. M. (2015). Out of necessity comes unbridled imagination for survival: Contributive justice in Spanish libraries during economic crisis. *Library Trends 64*(2), 299-328.

Model programme for public libraries. (n.d.) http://modelprogrammer.slks.dk/en/about-the-programme/intro/.

Mortenson Center for International Library Programs (n.d.). www.library.illinois.edu/mortenson.

New Zealand Library and Information Association. (1996). *Valuing the economic costs and benefits of libraries: A study prepared for the N Strategy.* Wellington: New Zealand Library and Information Association.

Nextlibrary.net (n.d.). www.nextlibrary.net.

OCLC (2017). Global Library Statistics. https://www.oclc.org/en/global-library-statistics.html.

Onwubiko, C. P. C. (1996). The practice of Amadi's barefoot librarianship in African public libraries. *Library Review, 45,* 39-47.

Open Society Institute (n.d.). www.opensocietyfoundation.org.

PL2020 (2014). Public libraries 2020: Building stronger EU Communities. www.publiclibraries2020.eu/.

Rahman, F. (2000). Status of rural and small libraries in Bangladesh: Directions for the future. *Rural Libraries, 20,* 52–64.

READ Global: Inspiring Rural Prosperity (2016). www.readglobal.org.

Room to Read (n.d.). www.roomtoread.org.

Riecken Foundation (n.d.). www.riecken.org.

Schrader, A. M., & Brundin, M. R. (2002). National Core Library Statistics Program statistical report, 1999: Cultural and economic impact of libraries on Canada. https://www.gov.uk/government/consultations/libraries-deliver-ambition-for-public-libraries-in-england-2016-2021/libraries-deliver-ambition-for-public-libraries-in-england-2016-2021.

Sey, A., Coward, C., Rothschild, C., Clark, M., & Koepke, L. (2013). Public libraries connecting people for development: Findings from the Global Impact Study. https://digital.lib.washington.edu/researchworks/handle/1773/23885.

Stam, D. H. (Ed.). (2016). *International dictionary of library histories.* New York: Routledge.

Sturges, P., and Neill, R. (1998). The quiet struggle: Information and libraries for the people of Africa. 2nd. ed. London: Mansell.

Thorhauge, J., G. Larsen, H.-P. Thun, & H. Albrechtsen. (1997). *Public libraries and the information society.* Luxembourg: European Commission.

UK Department for Culture, Media & Sport (2017). Libraries Taskforce: Research programme. https://www.gov.uk/government/publications/libraries-taskforce-research-programme.

UNESCO. (1998) *World culture report 1998: Culture, creativity and markets.* France: UNESCO.

UNESCO. (2009). *The 2009 UNESCO framework for cultural statistics (FCS).* www.uis.unesco.org/culture/pages/framework-cultural-statistics.aspx.

UNESCO. (2010). *Education for all global monitoring report—2010. Reaching the marginalized.* New York, NY: Oxford University Press.

United Nations. (n.d.). *Sustainable development goals.* https://sustainabledevelopment.un.org/sdgs.

United Nations. (2015). *Transforming our world: The 2030 Agenda for Sustainable Development.* https://sustainabledevelopment.un.org/post2015/transformingourworld.

Wieder, J., & Campbell, H. (2002). IFLA's first fifty years. *IFLA Journal, 28,* 107–117.

Wikipedia. https://www.wikipedia.org.

Wilson, V. (2008). Public libraries in Canada: An overview. *Library Management, 29*(6/7), 556–570.

Windau, B. (Ed.). (1999). *International network of public libraries* (Vols. 1–6). Lanham, MD: Scarecrow Press.

Yarrow, A., Clubb, B., & Draper, J.-L. (2008). *Public libraries, archives and museums: Trends in collaboration and cooperation.* The Hague, The Netherlands: IFLA Headquarters, 2008 (IFLA Professional Reports: 108). www.ifla.org/publications/ifla-professional-reports-108?og=49.

Yitai, G., & Gorman, G. E. (2000). *Libraries and information services in China.* Lanham, MD: Scarecrow Press.

AFTERWORD

What We Do

Katharine Phenix

My library serves the same mix of people as do most suburban library systems. We have families coming to Music and Movement programs on Thursdays, there are several older gentlemen who check out DVDs and look for the most recent *Linn's Stamp News* and a Harry Bosch title by Michael Connolly. As the adult services librarian, I work with plenty of ladies who have time to participate in one of the book clubs I lead. We regularly give away shower kits in the summer and sleeping bags in the winter that are put together by the Teen Advisory Board. We have compiled phone numbers and addresses for food banks, mental health resources, and local shelters appropriate for our people who are experiencing homelessness. I've been a public librarian for 37 years, and worked as support staff in an academic library for 7 years. I probably came to the profession because of the engraving above the doors of my hometown library: "You shall know the truth, and the truth shall make you free"; by way of another quote, "knowledge is power"; and finally, "power to the people." I absolutely believe that democracy requires an educated population and that access to information is a human right.

At work today I got a hug that did not come from a coworker. I didn't do much to deserve it. This is how it happened: I'm hanging out beside the Tech "perch." A woman approaches. She seemed harried. I took her to a public computer. I revealed where the USB port was on the monitor. I helped navigate the photo folder on a flash drive. We cropped the birthday cake out of the picture and saved it to the desktop, and then we attached it to an e-mail. I also managed to keep an accompanying four-year old from wandering away. The computer skills were, for the moment, beyond this woman's abilities. Her aunt had just passed away. The newspaper obit required a photo before noon. We needed an appropriate picture of Aunt Barbara and her lovely smile. Maybe this bereaved patron will come back for one of our computer classes when she has recovered from her grief, but for now, the technology she needed was available and the library staff were there to help. She was grateful, and so I got a hug.

We see a lot of people in times of crisis. We are also there for people experiencing major life transitions. For example, I scanned and e-mailed divorce papers yesterday, and faxed a hastily compiled resume before a 5:00 pm deadline. Our teen librarian prevented a likely suicide attempt last week. Our security guard has been using jumper cables daily on a woman's car. She lives in it, and has to leave the library parking lot every evening. We have 30 public computers and 12 laptops for checkout. And really, what public library ever has enough copies of *What to Expect When You're Expecting, A Child Called It,* and GED study guides?

Several hugs ago I helped a group of three women identify and print a few important documents. They had literally just come from the doctor. The mother been diagnosed with an advanced, incurable cancer. Her sister and daughter were with her to help find all the right medical documents and legal forms she would need to put her affairs in order. That hug was a group hug. They were so pleased to be able to get it all done in one trip. I was grateful to be in the presence of such humility and bravery. Public library workers are often asked to be part social worker, part medical professional, and part psychiatrist. It is a rare privilege to be viewed as an authoritative resource for all of life's little inconveniences: Fix my cell phone? Identify this insect? Format my resume? In 2016 I attended a daylong conference entitled *The Library as a Refuge,* which featured presentations by a member of Northern Colorado Pride, representatives of the Poudre River Library District Outreach Services to Spanish speakers, the social workers employed by Denver Public Library, and a nurse from Dementia Friendly Communities (Colorado Library Association, 2016). These are the people who represent the people we are trying to serve better.

Speaking of hugs, I asked a few of my colleagues from other libraries about their thoughts on the future of the public library. What is it about this institution that will endure? What are the small acts of library workers that fulfill the grand promises of policy makers and board members who declare the library to be a "third place," a "refuge," and the "heart of the community?" Without any prompting, my fellow library workers answered my question with, literally, hug stories. We should be storytellers. We are just now starting to share these stories to remind people that the public library will endure. In the 1970s, authors of a report written in response to what was known as the Lacy Report asserted that a librarian should "serve as both the *motivator* and *supplier* of aspirations for the dispossessed and disorganized," and "focus[ing] on needs and services for *people*—not institutions" (Mathews & Lacy, 1970).

LIBRARY FUTURE FATIGUE

That was in the 1970s. Will the public library of the future still be a library that we recognize? Will it meet the needs of the same populations we work with today? Apparently, there is something presently called "Library Future Fatigue" (Schwartz, 2016), it does seem as though it is an oft heard question. Since 2014 there has been an ALA Summit for the Future of Libraries called "Libraries from Now On: Imagining the Future" (Bolt, 2014); there is also PLA Strategic Plan and Goal Areas (2014-2017), a Global Libraries Initiative, the Research Institute for Public Libraries at the Aspen Institute (2015-2016), The Future of Libraries: Ours to Create Now (2015), and "The Future of Libraries Summit Report."[1] "The Future of Libraries: Do We Have Five Years to Live?" was the name of a two-day institute held in Vancouver in 2013 (Haycock, 2013). The 2016 Knight News Challenge asked "How Might Libraries Serve 21st Century Information Needs?" In fact, ALA has established a Center for the Library of the Future which is keeping track of 23 trends from Aging Advances to Urbanization. Please visit its website (www.ala.org/transforminglibraries/future) to find a compendium of material addressing the future. Historically, the future library was a memex machine (Bush, 1945). Now Memex is the name of a search technology developed by DARPA (Defense Advanced Research Projects Agency) used for web crawling (http://open catalog.darpa.mil/MEMEX.html).

We library workers hear it all the time. "Now that everything is online, do we really need libraries?" "Do librarians just read all day?" "Do you volunteer here or are you paid?" And we counter with the famous quote "Google can bring you back 100,000 answers, a librarian can bring you back the right one" (which is often attributed to Neil Gaiman)[2] or we use the analogy "your librarian, human search engine." Finally, most of us know by heart

Mark Y. Herring's 2001 article "10 Reasons Why the Internet is No Substitute for a Library" (which is now available as a handsome poster).

Considering what the future might look like for all of us, futurist Thomas Frey writes

> Yes, many of you are still reading newspapers, watching TV, reading books and magazines, and listening to radio. But a growing number are finding digital substitutes for traditional news. For young people, Facebook, Instagram, Reddit, Twitter, YouTube, Vine, and Instagram are their only news sources. When it comes to talking to your family and friends are you more likely to use Skype, send a text message, chat with them while playing Destiny, send photos, use Facetime, or Google hangouts? (Frey, 2016)

It's not just a North American moment. Here's what IFLA summarized in a report of a three-year study.

> Trend report-related discussions in 30 countries triggered vibrant and passionate debate around the future role of libraries. There was general consensus on the need for libraries to adapt and evolve to deliver new services to wider audiences. Concerns were expressed that libraries could be at risk of forfeiting their natural role as pace setters in key areas including information literacy, intellectual property and data management. At the same time, it was also recognised that there is an on-going tension between embracing new technological opportunities whilst maintaining current functions to serve existing audiences. (IFLA Trend Report, 2016).

KEEPING UP TECHNOLOGICALLY

Libraries must keep up with the technological times. When a young man (no phone, just released from jail) needs to get on a computer to communicate with his girlfriend on Facebook, we had better have the tools—the most up-to-date browsers, software, operating system, and bandwidth needed to assist him. Even in a public library, *especially* in a public library, it is much more important to have an updated edition of Chrome than the latest edition of the telephone directory. I don't remember when I was last asked for a criss-cross directory or referred to the physical *World Almanac.*

How do we serve our newest populations when they reach our shores and borders? We offer computers loaded with Skype and teach Google Hangouts so they can keep in touch with family. We don't just lend books; we lend personal HotSpots, laptops, e-readers, and Kill-a-Watt electrical use monitoring devices. For us, reference work is not so much a look-up as a question of cultural context. The answers aren't in reference books any more.

Our challenges are to stay true to our professional service imperatives while navigating future waters. For example, the preservation of patrons' privacy was once a matter of consciously obliterating circulation data. Now we are sure to use codes on our hold slips inserted in requested books and shelved on the self-service hold shelves. We negotiate privacy in our partnerships with third-party content providers such as Overdrive and Amazon, and with the ILS vendors we use. Or at least we inform our patrons of intrusive metadata collection of reading preferences. For the privacy of Internet users, the Library Freedom Project urges librarians to sign the "Library Digital Privacy Pledge" to use the *HTTPS* protocol to make library digital services more secure. The American Library Association promotes privacy with its Privacy Tool Kit (2016) because

> Privacy is essential to the exercise of free speech, free thought, and free association. Lack of privacy and confidentiality chills users' choices, thereby suppressing access to ideas. The possibility of surveillance, whether direct or through access to records of speech, research and exploration, undermines a democratic society (www.ala.org/advocacy/privacyconfidentiality/toolkitsprivacy/privacy).

ALA also offers ways to celebrate Choose Privacy Week in the first week in May.

Science fiction author Ray Bradbury typed *Fahrenheit 451* in the basement of the Powell Library at UCLA for $0.10/half hour. Access to a typewriter must have been just as limited then as much of the technology we provide to our library users is today. Is the usage of a library 3-D printer any different from a typewriter or word processor? Which new medical device will be prototyped, or new song recorded, or code written on computers and studio equipment at the library? We are fostering not just budding writers and artists, but also coders (Sphero, Ozobot, Dot and Dash), architects (Keva Planks), and engineers (Lego Mindstorm). Ernest and Julio Gallo used pamphlets they found in the basement of the Modesto Public Library to learn how to commercially make wine. Instead of purchasing markers and wool for our adult/teen programs, our budgets expand to provide Arduinos, Raspberry Pi, screenwriting software, Wacom tablets, and a SparkFun Redstick. We aren't cutting edge or trailing edge but we do support innovation. We don't just do sewing programs anymore; we sew with conductive thread to make LEDs light up. When comparing the public library involvement with Hour of Code or Teen Tech Week to National Library Week or Day of Dialog, it seems that we are still providing the place and possibilities for our communities as we always have. Just remember that the first use of punch cards was at the Boston Public Library in 1934 (Black, 2007). What would Andrew Carnegie have thought about free Wi-Fi?

MISSION STATEMENTS

The primary services of the public library have morphed the institution from "the people's university" to "the people's office," "the people's IT center," and now "the people's incubator" (Wapner, 2016).

Our mission statements allow us the leeway to remain true to our earliest promises of access to information, education, and entertainment. Here are some examples of a public library mission statement. Add "with a computer" to any one of those statements and you've described what we do daily. You can find more mission statements at the Urban Libraries Council website (www.urbanlibraries.org/mission-statements-pages-236.php).

- The Seattle Public Library brings people, information, and ideas together to enrich lives and build community.
- Read, Learn, Discover!
- Information, Imagination, Inspiration.
- Preserving Yesterday, Informing Today, Inspiring Tomorrow.
- We open doors for curious minds.

A new twist on library work is that we are a center of activity and not a reference point. Joan Frye Williams has used the analogy that we are no longer the grocery store—we are now the kitchen. In the old days, we referred our patrons (never by pointing!) to materials they could take home to help them learn to paint, or whittle, or sew, or repair. We called the library a "portal" and our guidance was called either "reference" or "advisory." Now when people come to the library, they come to "do" as often as they come to "get." As Brian Kenney (2015) noted, "So what do people want from us? They want help doing things, rather than finding things. You could argue that users have always wanted this, and you'd be right. But the extent of this shift in recent years is unprecedented in the history of library services." He goes on to say that much of the work we do is with technology. Working librarians everywhere have struggled with the great discussion about whether to "touch the device" or "take over the keyboard" when assisting with new technologies. Ranganathan (1931) says save the time of the reader (p. 336.) We help with resumes and Excel spreadsheets, use Zamzar to reformat files, and assist customers with products because Amazon and Kobo aren't around to provide customer support. (Interestingly, no one has come into the library for help with changing points and plugs in their engines, and some of us could do that, too.)

Libraries with studios offer recording equipment and time slots for making music, so a librarian with recording skills is a valuable resource. The most-wanted new hires can code, or weave, or facilitate a podcast. If you are interviewing for a public library job, the interview is more than likely to include an exercise in teaching your new bosses a new skill, or showing your juggling prowess (yes, this really happened). Not only can a patron pick up (or download and print) a tax form, but we also have county volunteers available to help review and file the form. Consider the vision statement of the R-Squared Conference on Risk and Reward:

> Faced with diminishing budgets, new technologies and changing customer needs, the traditional library faces extinction. We must adapt and innovate to transform from a quiet storehouse of books to a dynamic center of free engagement with knowledge (www.rsquaredconference.org/about/vision).

LIBRARY AS PLACE (AND NOT PLACE)

The reason people come to us to help solve their problems, help them with transitions, and share hugs is that we have a very long history of service to all, and a reputation for doing it very well.

> But now that I see the wreck that could have been, without Miss Richey, I'm of a fearsome mind to throw my arms around every living librarian who crosses my path, on behalf of the souls they never knew they saved. (Kingsolver, 2015)

As a place we want to be your third place—not home, not school or work, but a shared space. I have heard Dennis Lehane, Connie Willis, Jeanette Winterson, Val McDermid, and Nancy Pearl address large groups of library workers and say something similar. I can't wait until one of the teens of Adams County, Colorado, keynotes a library conference and says, "I don't know what I would have done if it were not for my public library and the help I got from the librarians to find my next great read, my voice, and myself." And in my daily work, when not involved in a program (read-aloud Shakespeare, weaving, mindfulness, making nutritious smoothies or organic cleaning products), I am almost always working one-on-one with someone. Libraries are simultaneously a single place (third place, gathering place, safe space, brick-and-mortar building) and at the same time everywhere, all the time, 24/7 through its virtual branches, chat space, readers' advisory links, databases, and downloadables. There are many opportunities in the social networking space for librarians to connect with their communities. You can find libraries on Facebook, Twitter, Tumblr, Pinterest (The World's Catalog of Ideas), Instagram, Skype, Snapchat, and no doubt on whatever comes next.

Providing apps for smartphones and tablets is another enterprise designed to create the virtual branch. The Calgary Public Library has an app called "Grow a Reader" available for iPhone or Android that teaches parents and caregivers how to develop early literacy skills in young children. This is a long way from black flannel board, but does essentially the same thing. More old services become new with online book clubs for the homebound, virtual reference, and personalized, template-based readers' advisory to add to the virtual package. My library provides a Skype connection to free legal aid services once a month from the district court. The lawyer lives in rural Elbert County and provides service to three branches of our library in one 2-hour time slot. There are also e-books, digital audio, streaming film, TV shows, and graphic novels available for borrowing from patrons in very remote places. Although once we were thrilled to place our catalogs online to share cataloging data and holdings in library-specific websites, now we strive to remain relevant by positioning our digitized matter into the larger web arena. Consider Zepheira, which sponsors the LibHub initiative (LibHub.org). This program was initiated by the Library of Congress and takes library catalogs that are in MARC format and uses BIBFRAME to reformat them to make them browser-searchable. The Libhub Initiative Pledge states "I believe everyone benefits from the visibility of libraries and their content on the Web."

As Denver City Librarian Michelle Jeske notes:

> Being able to showcase our rich collections and fabulous Western History and Genealogy resources more readily on the web is very exciting—and timely. This initiative will make these resources more discoverable and the library more relevant and accessible in the eyes of our community (www.libhub.org/sponsors-partners).

VIDEO [DID NOT KILL] THE RADIO STAR[3]

This era of librarianship is one rife with the concept of "disrupting convention," which might be shorthand for "this is not your father's library." "Shhh is a Four-Letter Word" reads one library t-shirt provided by the Anythink libraries. For the last several years library workers around the world have participated in Outside the Lines: Libraries Reintroduced (https://www.getoutsidethelines.org), an effort to get out and demonstrate the new creativity and innovation occurring in public libraries near them. At our summer reading kickoff, we invited a mariachi band to stroll and sing around the library. Several people commented that they never thought they would see *that* in a library.

As I look back on my years of library service I know that several pebbles I dropped made ripples into the wider world. Television did not signal the end of radio; the paperback did not destroy great literature; the music collection is going all digital and soon DVDs and Blu-ray (which replaced videotapes) on the shelf will give way to streaming through cyberspace.

Despite dire warnings libraries endured as Ask.com; AskJeeves; Google Helpouts, ChaCha, Yahoo Answers came and went, flashes in the pan. The library developed by Occupy and the phenomenon of "little free libraries" illustrates our common need to share content.

I've ridden the technology train as far as I am likely to go and settled back into whole-library readers' advisory. Nothing beats a conversation about books, music, and film. Books may not be our brand, but reading is. Do you see that arrow up there on the left-hand corner? It means go back one screen. If you can read the screen you can navigate the Internet. I have brought technology to the greatest generation because my book club people have discovered Alice Munro, Bryce Courtenay, and Shakespeare on our Sony e-readers and iPads. As a public librarian I can sign application forms to bring in audio, digital, and radio services to the print-disabled supplied by the Colorado Talking Book Library (www2.cde.state.co.us/ctbl/). In my career I've been given flowers, candy, free coffee, popcorn, and a Japanese fan because of doing, you know, this and that. We are raising readers and inventors, reintroducing play to adults, and staffing experience zones where people can watch webcams, or learn rug hooking, or do Zentangles in places where books used to be. We don't want to be buildings full of books that people come to, we want to be a place that people come to be surrounded by books.

Our future is as much about the people in our communities as it is about the library as place and platform. Note this research from library school faculty:

> A significant shift has occurred in information organizations. The shift de-emphasizes the physical collections (to include digital content) to focus more on individuals and the communities that they serve, in particular how institutions can facilitate community and individual change and transformation through learning, making, content creation, and other forms of active and interactive engagement. (Bertot, Sarin, & Percell, 2015.)

Jessamyn West, rural Vermont librarian, moss lover, and my hero as a one-time Burning Man librarian spoke at the Harvard Innovation Lab in November 2016. Her slides are online (www.librarian.net/talks/knight/LIL.pdf). Her talk, a cautionary tale of developing user-friendly technology, was called "Innovation vs. Liberation." Her concluding slide reads "The library comforts the afflicted and comforts the comfortable. It's for EVERYONE." Then she concludes "Because everyone deserves some damned comfort" (West, 2016).

Embrace change. I started my career by stamping books with *Date Due* and filing pocket cards in order by using multicolored paper clips. I have endured the use of microfiche and CD-ROM catalogs. I used Dialog and DOS. I have updated my library vocabulary from *card catalog* to *OPAC*. The top technologies in the libraries in which I've worked have been WordPerfect and Print Shop on the Apple IIe. I spent 2 years at netLibrary feeling like I might be hastening my own demise while expanding access to the world's knowledge through e-books and audio. Now I know that e-books are just another format somewhere beyond the clay tablet and rag paper, but by no means the last vehicle of content. Librarians will be there, collecting, organizing, and making it available to anyone who comes in the door, or portal, or hologram.

As you go forth, be kind.

NOTES

1. "On July 31st 2015 the Library and Information Association of New Zealand Aotearoa and Te Rōpū Whakahau cohosted Taking Libraries to 2025: The Future of Libraries Summit at the

Michael Fowler Centre in Wellington" (www.lianza.org.nz/our-work/projects/future-libraries-summit). A full report is available at www.lianza.org.nz/sites/default/files/Future%20of%20Libraries%20Summit%20Report.pdf.

2. These words are woven into the carpet at the Duke University Medical Center Library. After staff posted a photograph to the library's Facebook page, it was picked up and reposted by best-selling author Neil Gaiman, author, library supporter, and source of the quote.
3. With a tip of the hat to The Buggles.

REFERENCES

American Library Association. (n.d.). Libraries of the Future. Center for the Future of Libraries www.ala.org/transforminglibraries/future.

American Library Association. (2016). Privacy Tool Kit. www.ala.org/advocacy/privacyconfidentiality/toolkitsprivacy/privacy.

Bertot, J. C., Sarin, L. C., & Percell, J. (2015, August 1). Re-envisioning the MLS: Findings, issues, and considerations. College Park, MD: University of Maryland, College of Information Studies. http://mls.umd.edu/wp-content/uploads/2015/08/ReEnvisioningFinalReport.pdf.

Black, A. (2007). Mechanization in libraries and information retrieval: Punch cards and microfilm before the widespread adoption of computer technology in libraries. *Library History, 23,* 291–299. doi: 10.1179/174581607x254785.

Bolt, N. (2014). Libraries from now on: Imagining the future of libraries ala summit on the future of libraries-Report to ALA membership. *ALA Connect.*

Bush, V. (1945). As we may think. *The Atlantic Monthly, 176*(1). www.theatlantic.com/magazine/archive/1945/07/as-we-may-think/303881/.

Colorado Association of Libraries. (2016). Libraries as Refuge: A CoPLA Workshop. www.cal-webs.org/events/EventDetails.aspx?id=830885.

Frey, T. (2016). Twelve Critical Skills for the Future. www.futuristspeaker.com/business-trends/twelve-critical-skills-for-the-future/.

Haycock, K. (2013). The Future of Libraries: Do We Have Five Years to Live? http://kenhaycock.com/future-libraries-five-years-live-2/.

Herring, M. Y. (2001). Ten reasons why the Internet is no substitute for a library. *American Libraries, 32*(4), 76–78.

How might libraries serve 21st century information needs? (2016). https://www.newschallenge.org/challenge/how-might-libraries-serve-21st-century-information-needs/brief.

IFLA Trend Report 2016 Update. http://trends.ifla.org/update-2016.

Kenney, B. (2015, September 11). Where reference fits in the modern library. *Publisher's Weekly,* September 11, 2015. www.publishersweekly.com/pw/by-topic/industry-news/libraries/article/68019-for-future-reference.html.

Kingsolver, Barbara. (2014). How Mr. Dewey Decimal Saved My Life, in Dawson, Robert. *The Public Library: A Photographic Essay.* New York, Princeton Architectural Press, 78.

LibHub: Leading, learning, and linking. LibHub.org.

Library and Information Association of New Zealand Aotearoa. (2015). Future of libraries 2015.

Mathews, V. H. & Lacy, D. (1970). *Response to change: American libraries in the seventies* (p. 42). Bloomington, IN: Indiana State University. 1970 ERIC document ED 044 131, p 42. https://eric.ed.gov/?id=ED044131.

Public Library Association. (2014, June). Strategic plan and goal areas (2014–2017). www.ala.org/pla/about/strategicplan.

Ranganathan, S. R. (1931). *The five laws of library science.* Madras: The Madras Library Association.

Research Institute for Public Libraries at the Aspen Institute. (2015–2016). https://ripl.lrs.org.

rSquared: The Risk and Reward Conference 2012. Telluride, Colorado. www.rsquaredconference.org/about/vision.

Schwartz, M. (2016, September 20). Future fatigue. *Library Journal.* http://lj.libraryjournal.com/2016/09/lj-in-print/future-fatigue-designing-the-future/#_.

Wapner, C. (2016, June). The people's incubator: Libraries propel entrepreneurship. *OITP Perspectives, 4.* www.ala.org/advocacy/sites/ala.org.advocacy/files/content/ALA_Entrepreneurship_White_Paper_Final.pdf.

West, J. (2016, November 28). Innovation vs. liberation. Keynote at Harvard Library Innovation Lab. www.librarian.net/talks/knight/LIL.pdf.

ABOUT THE AUTHORS AND CONTRIBUTORS

AUTHORS

Kathleen de la Peña McCook is Distinguished University Professor, School of Information, University of South Florida in Tampa. The Chicago Public Library named McCook as a Charlotte Kim Scholar in Residence in 2003, where she did a systemwide series of events on the role of the public library in building communities. She was visiting scholar for the Laura Bush 21st Century Librarian Program, "Librarians Build Communities" at Valdosta State University, Department of Library and Information Studies, 2009–2011. She has contributed to many books on librarianship, including *Information Services Today*; *Service Learning*; and *Libraries and Democracy: The Cornerstones of Liberty*. She is a member of the editorial boards of the journals *Progressive Librarian* and *The Library Quarterly*. McCook was Dr. Jean E. Coleman Library Outreach Lecturer for the ALA Office for Diversity, Literacy and Outreach Services in 2010, speaking on Librarians and Human Rights. She was honored with the REFORMA Elizabeth Martinez Lifetime Achievement (LAA) Award in 2016.

Jenny S. Bossaller is Associate Professor at the University of Missouri's School of Information Science & Learning Technologies. She earned her MA in Library Science in 2005, worked at the MOBIUS consortium from 2005 to 2008 and a PhD in Information Science and Learning Technologies in 2010. She has been active in state, national, and international conferences and committees, including the Missouri Library Association, ALA, ALISE, ASIS&T, and IFLA. She has served on the editorial board of RUSQ for the past four years. Her scholarship covers a wide range of topics, such as free speech, public librarians' role in the Affordable Care Act, library management, equity, education, indigenous knowledge, and reference work. Her teaching focuses on information access, public libraries, and intellectual freedom. She is the co-PI on the Public Library Leadership (PuLL) project, which aims to develop new public librarian leaders with an awareness of community needs, and which involves work with many public librarians across Missouri.

CONTRIBUTORS

Diane Austin is completing a PhD in Curriculum and Instruction/Instructional Technology at the University of South Florida's College of Education. She earned an MA in Instructional Systems from the Pennsylvania State University. An instructor, instructional designer, and technologist, Ms. Austin teaches undergraduate and graduate students web design, curriculum, instructional technology, and instructional media. She actively represents the

USF School of Information and collaborates with various organizations including Florida schools and libraries, the American Library Association, Florida Library Association, Tampa Bay Library Consortium, and the Florida Association for Media in Education.

Richard J. Austin is a senior instructor at the University of South Florida's School of Information. He holds a PhD in Information Studies from Florida State University, an MLIS. in Library and Information Science from the University of South Florida, and a Master's of Business Administration from Lehigh University. Dr. Austin has been the director of the University South Florida's Undergraduate Information Studies program, where he teaches technology- and information-related courses in both the undergraduate and graduate programs.

Clara M. Chu is director of the Mortenson Center for International Library Programs and Mortenson Distinguished Professor at the University of Illinois at Urbana-Champaign. She specializes in the information needs, uses, and barriers faced by multicultural communities. Dr. Chu publishes, presents, and consults internationally in English and Spanish, and serves on the editorial boards of *Libri* and *Library Trends*. Active in professional associations, she served as the 2014/15 President of the Association for Library and Information Science Education and is the ALA representative on the National Commission for UNESCO. She is the recipient of numerous honors from professional organizations. She obtained her MLS and PhD from the University of Western Ontario.

Loida Garcia-Febo is an international library consultant, researcher, and expert on topics such as human rights, advocacy, and services to multicultural populations. She has taught in 20 countries in 5 continents; served communities as an academic, public, school, and special librarian; and advocated on behalf of libraries at the United Nations. Ms. Loida-Garcia has been a member of the Governing Board of IFLA and member of the Executive Board of the American Library Association. She was elected ALA president for 2017-2018.

Barbara J. Ford is Mortenson Distinguished Professor Emerita, Mortenson Center for International Library Programs, University of Illinois at Urbana-Champaign Library. She is a past president of ALA and former Assistant Commissioner of the Chicago Public Library. She served as an elected member of the International Federation of Library Associations and Institutions governing board. Ms. Ford began her international work as a Peace Corps volunteer in Panama and Nicaragua in the 1970s and has since worked with library projects around the world. She has been recognized with awards for her significant contributions and dedication to international librarianship by ALA and the Chinese American Librarians Association.

Alicia K. Long teaches multicultural materials for children and young adults at the University of South Florida's School of Information, and works as librarian and access services supervisor at the State College of Florida Libraries. She has been an ALA Spectrum Scholar (2009) and Emerging Leader (2012). Ms. Long is active in REFORMA, is a book reviewer and chair and past member of the Pura Belpré Award Selection Committee. She also presents programs in public libraries as discussion leader, storyteller, and facilitator of early childhood literacy programs.

Katharine Phenix is an adult services librarian (aka Adult Guide) at Anythink Libraries, Huron Street Branch in Rangeview, Colorado. Ms. Phenix began her library career in sixth grade, her library work in college, and her public library career as a circulation librarian at the Westminster (CO) Public Library. She has reviewed software for the *Wilson Library Bulletin* and worked at netLibrary, an early provider of e-book content. She was as an interlibrary loan librarian with the Adams County (CO) Library System, and as an adult services librarian before, during, and after its transition to Anythink, a revolution of Rangeview Libraries. Katharine engineered the first online bookmobile in 1985, has chaired the ALA Council Committee on the Status of Librarianship and the RUSA Notable Books Council, was a member of the selection committee for the 2015 ALA Carnegie Medal Award for Excellence in Fiction and Nonfiction, and served on the Progressive Librarian Coordinating Council and its editorial board.

Lynn C. Westney retired in 2009 as associate professor emerita from the University of Illinois at Chicago. As an academic reference librarian and collection development specialist for over a quarter of a century, Ms. Westney has compiled and edited 15 annual reference books, written peer-reviewed articles and book chapters, edited a quarterly column on history and computing, and presented papers at scholarly conferences worldwide. An active member of ALA, she served as chair of several committees and held elected positions in two RUSA sections, ANSS and BRASS.

INDEX

References to notes are indicated by "n" following the page number (e.g. 198n11); references to figures are indicated by *f*.

#

"10 Ways to Make a Public Library Work" (IFLA), 372
"12 Ways Libraries Are Good for the Country," 5
21st Century Librarian (LB21) program, 63, 176, 178, 186n22
2030 Agenda, 347-348, 354, 373

A

Abram, Stephen, 325
access
  1963 Access Study, 54-55
  equity of, 53-56, 66, 71, 362, 364-366
Access to Learning Awards, 367
Access to Public Libraries (ALA), 54-55, 88
accessibility and universal design, 208, 212-214, 221n15, 258, 260
accountability, 61, 81-93, 96-97, 121, 315-316. *See also* Project Outcome
"An Act Providing for the Establishment of Public Libraries" (1849), 28
ADA (Americans with Disabilities Act), 208, 212-214
Adams, William, 270
administration, 31-32, 93-95, 143-144, 152-157
Adult Education Board, 37, 44n26, 67, 269
Adult Programs in the Library (Lear), 278
Adult Services: An Enduring Focus for Public Libraries (Heim & Wallace), 274, 284n37
adult services
  human development and, 257-258, 274-275
  inclusion in, 258-260
  programs, 278-279, 280*f*
  reader services, 259-275
advocacy, 66, 122-123, 128, 136, 151-152, 308*f*, 364-370
affiliate organizations, 56, 179, 183, 244-245f, 275
Africa, 350, 358, 370-371
African Americans
  Black Caucus of the ALA (BCALA), 56, 179, 183, 186n24, 268, 275, 283n26
  Carnegie libraries for, 34, 44n21
  in the Jim Crow era, 1-2, 17n2, 31, 34, 41, 53, 232
  segregation and, 17n2, 34, 41, 46n34, 54-55, 232
Akron-Summit County (OH) Public Library, 144, 148*f*
ALA. *See* American Library Association (ALA)
Alabama, 41, 120, 138n22, 177, 268, 283n27, 312
Albarracin, Ignacio, 314
Albrecht, Steve, 217
Alemanne, Nicole D., 11
"Alexandria Proclamation" (IFLA), 360
Alice Virginia and David Fletcher Branch, Washington Free Library, Hagerstown, MD, 195, 196*f*
Alire, Camila, 136
Allie Beth Martin Award, 72n4, 183-184, 187n29
ALSC (Association for Library Services to Children), 235-238, 244-245, 248
American Association of School Librarians (AASL), 237, 252n6
American Civil Liberties Union (ACLU), 68
American FactFinder, 60
American Indian Library Association (AILA), 3-4, 56, 71, 179, 183, 186n24, 275. *See also* Native Americans
American Libraries (journal), 5, 12, 13, 60, 132, 202, 313, 327
American Library Association (ALA)
  accredited degree programs, 159, 162*f*, 164, 170-173*f*, 185n11, 239
  Adult Education Board, 37, 44n26, 67, 269
  affiliate organizations, 56, 179, 183, 244-245f, 275
  Association for Library Services to Children (ALSC), 235-238, 244-245, 248

Black Caucus (BCALA), 56, 179, 183, 186n24, 268, 275, 283n26
Board on Library and Adult Education, 37, 44n26, 269
Bulletin of the American Library Association, 38, 203, 269, 307
Center for the Future of Libraries, 14, 18n11, 182, 380
Commitment to Basic Literacy, 273*f*
Committee on Library Extension, 37
Committee on Literacy, 272
Committee on Rural, Native, and Tribal Libraries of All Kinds, 3
Committee on Work with the Foreign-Born, 2, 36
continuing education by, 181
Enlarged Program, 37
ethnic affiliate organizations of, 56, 179, 183, 244-245f, 275
founding of, 30, 35-36
Gay, Lesbian, Bisexual, and Transgender Round Table, 13, 56, 180-181, 268, 275, 283n26
Libraries Transform Campaign, 14, 18n11, 136, 139n35-36, 312
Library Extension Board, 45n30, 107
Library History Round Table (LHRT), 31, 44n15
Library Leadership and Management Association (LLAMA), 208, 221n13
Library War Service, 36-37
Office for Diversity, Literacy, and Outreach Services, 179, 185n8, 222n20, 223n24, 272-273, 281n3, 284n39
Office for Information Technology Policy (OITP), 7-8, 11, 61-62, 327
Office for Library Advocacy, 66, 122, 136
overview, 307-309
PLA. *See* Public Library Association
policy statements, 13, 69, 71, 333
presidents, 5-7, 8, 15, 123, 136, 233, 261, 268, 316
Privacy Toolkit, 334-335, 382
Public Awareness Office, 136, 139n35
Public Libraries Division, 88, 198
Reference and User Services Association (RUSA), 257, 264, 267, 275, 278, 302, 341
Social Responsibilities Round Table (SRRT), 18n9, 56, 60, 71, 73n14, 89, 214, 275
United for Libraries, 128, 139n28, 149-151, 174-175
Young Adult Library Services Association (YALSA), 233, 235-238, 244-245, 248-249, 252n8, 253n15
American Library Association Council, 5, 39, 45n29, 60, 107, 165, 215
American Library Association-Allied Professional Association (ALA-APA), 156, 164-165, 174, 186n14
American National Standards Institute (ANSI), 97n5
The American Public Library and the Diffusion of Knowledge (Learned), 37, 269
Americans with Disabilities Act (ADA), 208, 212-214
America's Star Libraries ratings, 81, 93-94, 99n24
AMIGOS, 296, 297*f*-298*f*
Amundsen, J. L., 158
anchor institutions, libraries as, 11, 65, 194, 326-327
Andrew Carnegie Medal, 245*f*, 267
Anthony, Carolyn, 82, 317
Anythink Libraries, 264, 266, 317, 384
Apostles of Culture (Garrison), 30
architecture. *See* buildings and construction
Arsenals of a Democratic Culture (Ditzion), 2, 30
Asheim, Lester, 261
Asian/Pacific American Librarians Association (APALA), 56, 179, 186n24, 245*f*, 275, 283n26
Asplund, Julia Brown, 31
association awards, 95-96
Association for Rural and Small Libraries (ARSL), 183, 216, 223n20, 309
Association for Library Services to Children (ALSC), 235-238, 244-245, 248
Association of Specialized and Cooperative Library Agencies, 180, 300
associations, professional, 306-309, 374-375
athenaeums, 24, 30, 43n4
Atlanta Public Library, 54
audiobooks, 245*f*, 267
Aurora (IL) Public Library, 144, 146*f*
Austin, Diane, 321, 389-390
Austin, Richard J., 321, 390
author programs, 266
Avram, Henriette, 295
awards
  for books, 243-245, 267-268
  for librarians, 68-69, 183-184
  for libraries, 93-96, 100n26-29
  for support staff and trustees, 183-184
  See also America's Star Libraries ratings
Ayre, Lori B., 262

B

Bailey, Barbara, 68
Baker, Augusta, 231, 250

Baltimore, civil unrest in, 12, 17n6, 158, 185n8, 218, 223n24-25, 316
Banned Books Week, 67, 247, 252n11
Bass, Melissa, 175
bathrooms, legislation on, 180
Battles, David. M., 31, 41
Baykan, Mary, 195
BayNet, 300-301
Becker, Joseph, 295
Becker, Patti C., 40
Becker, Samantha, 96
Bedford (MA) organizational chart, 144, 145*f*
Belpré, Pura, 231, 232, 245, 250
Berelson, Bernard, 40, 46n33, 67
Berman, Sanford, 60
Bernier, Anthony, 175
Berry, John N., 1, 58, 74n20
Bertelsmann Foundation, 368-369
Bertot, John C., 128, 216, 314, 322-323, 326, 331-332, 341
Bilal, Dania, 338-339
Bill and Melinda Gates Foundation, 63-64, 135, 327, 349, 366-367
Bill of Rights, Library, 67-69, 180, 235, 278
Bingham, Caleb, 230
bisexual persons, 13, 56, 180-181, 268, 275, 283n26, 356
Bishop, Bradley W., 12, 216
Black, Alistair, 323-324, 352
Black Caucus of the ALA (BCALA), 56, 179, 183, 186n24, 268, 275, 283n26
Blankenship, Cheryl, 242
blind persons, 260, 301
blogs, 335, 337
Bluetooth, 332
Board on Library and Adult Education, 37, 44n26, 269
boards of trustees. *See* trustees, boards of
Bobinski, George, 197
Boise, Idaho, 113-114
book festivals, 267, 283n24
book groups, 264-265
The Book Industry (Miller), 40
BookBrowse, 263, 282n13
bookmobiles, 106, 208-211*f*, 215-216, 222n20, 275, 322, 371
books
- awards for, 243-245, 267-268
- banned and challenged, 67-68, 247, 252n11
- borrowed annually, 259
- donations, 369-370
- electronic, 262, 331, 340, 358
- on librarians, 232
- per capita recommendations, 86
- promotion of, 266-267
- on reading, 261

Books, Bluster, and Bounty (Swetnam), 33
booktalks, 266
Boorstin, Daniel J., 266
Bossaller, Jenny S., xvi, 70, 293, 389
Boston Public Library
- Board of Trustee structure of, 29, 107
- building and collections, 43n12, 195-196, 240, 257, 305
- founding of, 2, 26-30, 43n12, 107, 257

Bourne, Jill, 184
Bowerman, George F., 67
branch libraries, number of, 206-211
Bray, Thomas, 23-24
Brazil (Indiana), 33-34
Breeding, Marshall, 303, 322-323, 328, 336, 338, 339
Bridging Cultures (NEH), 134, 139n30
British Council, 369
broadband adoption, 64-65, 343n3
Brooklyn (NY) Public Library, 70, 94, 121, 176, 342, 343n6
Brown, Michael, 12, 218
Brown, Nancy, 263
Brown v. Board of Education, 46n34, 232
Brown v. Louisiana, 55
Bryan, Alice I., 40
budgets
- examples, 124, 130*f*-132*f*
- library construction and, 201, 221n11
- trustees and, 130*f*, 144, 150

buildings and construction
- accessibility and universal design, 208, 212-214, 221n15
- civic memory and, 193-195
- funding for, 32-35, 198-201
- green and sustainable, 214-215, 222n17-19
- history of, 32-35, 195-197
- joint-use libraries, 203-206
- LSCA and, 197-202, 220n9
- safety and security, 217-218

Bulletin of the American Library Association, 38, 203, 269, 307
Bureau of Education, 26, 43n4, 44n25, 72n6
Bureau of Labor Statistics, 158
Burke, John J., 323-325*f*, 328, 330, 334, 339
Burke, Susan K., 264
Buschman, John, 69-70
Bush, Laura, 176, 178, 267

C

California, 33, 40, 111, 114, 160*f*-163*f*, 176-177, 205*f*, 280*f*
California Library Association, 14, 18n10, 124-128, 184
Canada, 352-353, 364
career development, 181-183
career opportunities, 157, 165-170, 186n15, 374
Carmichael, James V., 31
Carnegie, Andrew, 9, 32-34, 44n19, 197, 366
Carnegie Corporation, 44n21, 139n30, 197, 219, 350, 366
Carnegie Denied (Martin), 34
Carrier, Esther, 260
Carter, Jimmy, 57, 106
cartoons, newspaper, 152, 153*f*
A Catalyst for Change (IMLS), 15, 133
Cedar Rapids (IA) Public Library, 17n7, 167-168, 202, 223n22
censorship, 66-69, 246-247, 252n11, 359
Center for the Book, 266-267, 283n23
Center for the Future of Libraries, 14, 18n11, 182, 380
certification
  LEED, 205, 214-215
  professional, 156, 164-165, 181, 185n13, 186n25
Chancellor, John, 38, 269
Chartered Institute of Library and Information Professionals (CILIP), 375
Chase, Peter, 68
Chicago Collections, 305
Chicago Public Library
  architecture, 199-200*f*, 215
  community building by, 11, 17n4, 194, 200, 220n3
  design/build competition, 199-200
  Harold Washington Library Center, 200
  intellectual freedom policy, 67-68
  key figures, 11, 194, 231
Chicago Public Library Foundation, 135
Chief Officers of State Library Agencies (COSLA), 64, 85, 91-92, 99n23, 111, 114, 153-154
Children's Internet Protection Act (CIPA), 63, 122-123, 251
children's services. *See* youth services
China, 351, 360
Chinese American Librarians Association (CALA), 56, 179, 183, 186n24, 268, 275, 283n26
Christian, George, 68
Chu, Clara M., 347, 380
circulating libraries, 25, 43n5
circulation, 261-263, 266-267
citizenry, informed, 5, 7, 63, 74n17, 91, 115, 277*f*, 310
Civic Librarianship (McCabe), 310
civic memory, 193-195
civil disturbances, 12, 218-219
civil rights, 41, 53-55, 89, 212-213, 232, 270
Clinton, Bill, 200
Clinton, De Witt, 26
Coates, Ta-Nehisi, 14
Coleman, Jean E., 272
collaboration
  for community outreach, 309-316
  consortia and, 293-299, 303-304
  by cooperatives, 86-87, 106, 113-114, 293-302
  in local history collections, 302-305
  by state library agencies, 54, 91, 107-111, 123, 294, 296-297
Collaborative Summer Library Program (CSLP), 247, 265
The Collection All Around (Davis), 279
collection development, 243, 260-262, 341, 357-361
The Colonial Book in the Atlantic World (Amory and Hall), 23
colonial times, 23-25
Colorado, 12, 98n9, 98n12, 144, 147*f*, 160*f*-163*f*, 214, 266
Colorado Talking Book Library, 385
Colored Carnegie Library, 34, 44n21
Committee on Library Extension, 37
Committee on Literacy, 272
Committee on Work with the Foreign-Born, 2, 36
Common Core, 237, 252n6
Common School movement, 25-27, 43n7
community anchor institutions, 11, 65, 194, 326-327
community commons, libraries as, 1, 8-14, 69-70, 90, 193-195, 220n2, 277*f*
community engagement, 82, 92, 250-251, 276-279
Community Foundations and the Public Library report, 135
Community Hierarchy of Needs, 311*f*
community information referral, 312-314
community outreach, 309-316, 370-373
community-based planning, shift to, 53, 56-59, 62-63, 89-91
computers, types of, 331. *See also* technology
conferences
  ALA and PLA, 36, 82, 97n1, 181-182, 307-309, 329
  continuing education and, 181-182, 307-308
  international, 357

R-Squared Conference on Risk and Reward, 383
state and regional, 58, 90-91, 182-183
White House Conferences, 54, 57-58, 61, 73n8
Connected Learning program, 65
Connecticut Four, 68-69
Connuscio, Carolyn, 10
consortia, 293-299, 303-304
construction. *See* buildings and construction
continuing education, 181-183
Cooperative Children's Book Center (CCBC), 243, 246
cooperatives, 86-87, 106, 113-114, 293-302
Corbly, James E., 334
core values, xvi, 7-8, 54-56, 66-72, 268-274
Corsaro, James, 34
Corvallis-Benton County (OR) Public Library, 206
COSLA (Chief Officers of State Library Agencies), 64, 85, 91-92, 99n23, 111, 114, 153-155
county library systems, 86-87, 105-111, 113-114
Crawford, John, 360
Creating a Nation of Learners (IMLS), 7, 268
Creating Capabilities (Nussbaum), 96
Creating Inclusive Library Environments (Kowalsky and Woodruff), 258
Crowe, Linda, 184
Cultural Crusaders (Passet), 33
cultural heritage, 16, 70, 306, 373
Culture in Transit, 70
Curl, John, 293
Curley, Arthur, 5, 17n3, 313
Cuyahoga (OH) County Public Library, 93, 282n12, 317*f*

D

Dahlgren, Anders C., 212, 221n14
Daley, Richard M., 11, 194
Dana, John Cotton, 36
data collection, 17n1, 59, 81-93, 98n9. *See also* statistics
Davies, Nicolle I., 152
Davis, Charles H., 321, 325*f*, 340
Davis, Jeffrey T., 279
Davis, Rebecca, 179
Dawson, Alma, 41
Dawson, Robert, 193, 220n1-2
"Declaration for the Right to Libraries" (ALA), 15-17
Del Bosque, Darcy, 329
Demetrion, George, 272
democracy, 1-2, 4-8, 15*f*-16*f*, 66-72, 269-270, 279, 362*f*
Dempsey, Mary, 11, 17n4, 194, 220n3
Denver (CO) Public Library, 143-144, 147*f*, 184n1
Developing Community-Led Public Libraries (Pateman and Williment), 310-311
Dewey, Melvil, 34-36, 269
DIA: Diversity in Action, 248
DiCamillo, Kate, 247
Diggs, Melanie Townsend, 12, 218
digital divide, 64, 135, 251, 279, 322-323, 354, 367-368
digital inclusion, 64-65, 82, 250-251, 322-323
Digital Inclusion Survey, 64, 322-323
digital libraries, defined, 340
digital literacy, 64-65, 116, 271*f*-272*f*
Digital Public Library of America (DPLA), 70, 135-136, 305, 306*f*, 341
DigitalLearn.org, 64
digitization projects, 25, 305
Dillinger, Susan, 93
Dillingham, Walter J., 134
directors, library, 31-32, 93-95, 143-144, 152-157
disabilities
building accommodations for, 208, 212-214
library workers with, 180
services for people with, 71, 213, 222n16, 258-260, 265, 301, 333
Disaster Information Management Research Center, 13, 217
disasters, 12-13, 202, 216-217, 223n21-22, 342
discrimination, 34, 54-56, 213, 250. *See also* segregation
Dismantling the Public Sphere (Buschman), 70
Ditzion, Sydney, 2, 25-26, 30, 31, 34
diversity
in collections, 245-246, 248, 250
of staff, 177-179
donation programs, for books, 369-370
Dudley, Michael, 310
Duncan, Cheryl J., 267
Durrance, Joan, 313
Dziedzic, Donna, 93-94

E

early literacy, 65, 91, 121, 233-234, 248, 251, 384
East Baton Rouge (LA) Parish Library, 203-204*f*
e-books, 262, 331, 340, 358
e-circ, 81
Ecology, Economy, Equity (Henk), 215

Edge Initiative, 64-65, 82, 100n31
Education
adult, 37, 38, 44n26, 45n31, 268, 269, 273, 284n30, 284n36
continuing education, 181-183
as core value, 66
lifelong learning, 16, 66, 268-272, 277, 349-350, 360
Edwards, Julie B., 15, 310
Edwards, Margaret A., 231, 233
e-government, 281, 314
Electronic Information for Libraries (EIFL), 358-359, 367-368
electronic resources, 340-342
Elmborg, James, 194, 268-269
Elsevier Foundation, 370
Enlarged Program, 37
Enoch Pratt Free Library
civil disturbances and, 12, 17n6, 185n8, 218, 223n24-25, 316
Margaret A. Edwards and, 231, 233
equity of access, 53-56, 66, 71, 362, 364-366
E-Rate program, 63, 122-123, 137n1, 327, 343n3
Estes, Rice, 54
ethnic affiliate organizations, 56, 179, 183, 244-245f, 275
Europe, 360, 364-365, 370-371
evaluations
of outcomes (*see* outcomes)
of services, 121-122
Every Child Ready to Read (ECRR), 234, 248
Every Student Succeeds Act (ESSA), 63, 74n21, 238
EveryLibrary, 128, 139n29
Exner, Nina, 244

F

Facebook, 92-93, 241, 337, 381
facilities. *See* buildings and construction
families, service to, 16, 238-242, 247-252
Farr, Cecilia K., 265
Farwell, Bob, 95
Federal Communications Commission (FCC), 11, 63, 137n1, 313, 327, 343n3
Federal Emergency Management Agency (FEMA), 12, 17n7, 216, 223n21-22
federal government, 38-39, 105-106, 123-127*f*. *See also* funding; legislation
Federal-State Cooperative System (FSCS), 84, 97n6-98n7
Felicella, Elizabeth, 194-195
Feminist Task Force, 44n17, 56
Fencing out Knowledge study, 122-123
Ferguson (MO) Municipal Public Library, 12, 17n5, 95, 176, 218
Fiction_L, 263, 282n12
Figueroa, Miguel, 182
First Amendment, 7, 16, 55, 69, 222n16
Fisher, Patricia H., 144
Fletcher, Cynthia N., 38
Flexner, Jennie M., 263
Flint Public Library, 13, 217, 312
Florida
library buildings, 203, 204*f*
services and initiatives, 13, 208, 253n16
statistics on, 106, 108*f*, 137n3, 160-163*f*, 171*f*, 186n20, 280*f*
Florida Library Association, 92-93, 100n28
Fogarty, John F., 41-42
Fontichiaro, Kristin, 341-342
Forbidden Books in American Public Libraries (Geller), 67
Ford, Barbara J., 347, 390
foundation funding, 129, 134-136, 139n31, 366-370
Foundations of the Public Library (Shera), 26-27, 30
free public libraries, 27-28, 37, 129
freedom, intellectual, 8, 17n3, 66-69, 246-247, 252n11, 357-359
Freedom of Access to Information and Freedom of Expression (FAIFE), 359
Freedom of Information Act (FOIA), 123
freedom of inquiry, 4-5, 67-68, 144
freedom to read, 66-69, 246-247, 357-369
Frey, Thomas, 381
Friends of Libraries, 107, 122,123, 128,151, 174-175, 208
funding
from Bill and Melinda Gates Foundation, 63-64, 135, 327, 366-367
for buildings and construction, 32-35, 198-201
global, 361-364
from Grants to States Program, 63, 75n24, 116-121, 133, 138n24, 198-199*f*, 299
through library foundations, 129, 134-136, 139n31
overview, 123-136
per capita data, 124-128f, 132
state library agencies and, 75n24, 115, 120-121, 132-133, 199*f*, 299
fundraising, 128, 134, 139n31, 174-175

G

Gale Cengage Learning Library of the Year, 95
gaming, 249, 341
Garceau, Oliver, 40, 83, 105, 252n2

Garcia, Tonya, 184
Garcia-Febo, Loida, 8-10, 390
Garmer, Amy, 149
Garrison, Dee, 30, 44n17
Gates, Bill and Melinda, 63-64, 135, 327, 349, 366-367
Gay, Lesbian, Bisexual, and Transgender Round Table, 13, 56, 180-181, 268, 275, 283n26
Geller, Evelyn, 67
gender equality, 348, 370
gender identity/expression, 13, 56, 179, 180-181, 239, 275, 356
Georgia, 31, 44n21, 54, 107-108*f*, 128*f*, 160*f*-163*f*, 237, 280*f*
Georgia Public Library Service, 114, 138n17
Gershenfeld, Neil, 341
Gerstenfeld, Victoria, 184
global libraries
  advocacy and, 364-370
  community outreach by, 370-373
  IFLA and, 252n3, 348-349, 353-361, 370-374
  overview, 347-353
  rural, 350, 358, 364, 367, 370-371
  standards, 355-357, 363, 372
  statistics on, 349, 355, 370
GoodReads, 264, 265
Gorham, Ursula, 128
Gornick, Vivian, 261
governance, 107-111, 143-157, 184n1-185n8, 361-364
government
  access to information on, 90, 123, 277*f*, 281, 314
  advocacy and, 122-123
  federal, 38-39, 105-106, 123-127*f* (*see also* funding; legislation)
  global, 349-354, 361-364, 370
  local, 86, 106-111, 113-114, 124, 361-364
  relation to libraries, 38-39, 106-107
  types of, 106-114
  See also democracy
The Government of the American Public Library (Joeckel), 30, 107
Government Publications for the Citizen (McCamy), 40
Grants to States Program, 63, 75n24, 116-121, 133, 138n24, 198-199*f*, 299
Gray, Freddie, 12, 17n6, 185n8, 218, 223n24
Great Britain, 352
Green, Edith, 41-42
Greene County (OH) Public Library, 168-170
Gregorian, Vartan, 219
Groton (CT) Public Library, 30
Gubbin, Barbara A.B., 183

H

Habermas, Jürgen, 69
Hamer, John H., 32
Hamilton-Pennell, Christine, 92
Hanaway, Emily, 231
Handbook for Library Trustees of New York State, 151
handbooks, trustee, 151-152
handicapped persons. *See* disabilities
hardware, 330-333
Harold Washington Library Center, 200
Harris, Michael, 29-30
Hartford (CT) Public Library, 157, 231
Hatfield, Jean, 208
Hayden, Carla D., 17n6, 53, 185n8, 218-219, 223n24-25, 316
health literacy, 250, 314-315
heart, libraries as, 8-10, 309
Heart of the Community (Christensen and Levinson), 9
Held, Ray, 111
Henderson, Carol C., 58
Henk, Mandy, 215
Henke, Kelsey, 128
Hennen, Thomas J., 99n24
Hennen's American Public Library Ratings (HALPR), 99n24
Hewins, Caroline, 231
Hiatt, Peter, 89
Hildenbrand, Suzanne, 31
Hildreth, Susan, 275-276, 284n40, 317
Hill, Lister, 42
Himmel, Ethel, 14-15, 61, 73n16, 90
Hiring a New Library Director (COSLA), 153-155
"History and Status of Native Americans in Librarianship" (Patterson), 2, 4, 31, 53
The History of Public Library Access for African Americans (Battles), 31, 41
Holley, Bob, 259
Holman, Will, 341
Holt, Glen E. and Leslie E., 144, 175, 194
home rule, 113, 138n12-13
homeless people, 13-14, 18n9, 60, 73n14, 177*f*, 275
homeschooled students, 242
Hooper, Brad, 266
Hoopla, 262, 267
Horrigan, John B., 42n21
Horton, Valerie, 295-296
Houghtaling, June, 91
household income, 124, 128*f*
How Americans Value Public Libraries (Pew), 8
Hoyer, Jennifer, 259
Hoyt, Dolores. J., 25

Huber, John J., 310-311*f*
Huerta, Isabel, 184
human capabilities, xviii, 96,100n30, 100n31, 195, 257-258, 274
human development, 96-97, 100n30-32, 257-258, 274-275
human resources. *See* staff
human rights, 71-72, 359-360, 373
Human Rights and Social Justice (Wronka), 71
Hunger, Homelessness, and Poverty Task Force, 18n9, 60, 73n14
Hunter, Chrystna, 180
Hurricane Katrina, 12, 135, 176, 202, 216
Hurricane Preparedness and Response Project, 13, 217
Hurricane Rita, 12, 135
hurricanes, 12-13, 135, 176, 202, 216-217

I

Idaho, 113-114, 143, 170, 268, 270, 283n28, 284n35
IFLA (International Federation of Library Associations and Institutions), 252n3, 348-349, 353-361, 370-374, 381
ILA Reporter, 152, 153*f*
Illinois
  collaboration in, 114, 262, 300
  development of libraries in, 38, 43n4, 44n22, 56, 107
  RAILS (Reaching Across Illinois Library System), 165, 300-301
  statistics on, 108*f*, 128*f*, 152, 160-163*f*, 171*f*, 280*f*
  See also Chicago Public Library
Illinois Regional Library Council, 262
Illinois State Library, 298
IMLS. *See* Institute of Museum and Library Services (IMLS)
impact, measuring, 61, 81-93, 96-97, 121, 315-316. *See also* Project Outcome
Impact Survey, 65, 82, 97n2, 315
Implementing for Results (Nelson), 61, 74n16, 90
income, household, 124, 128*f*
Index of Public Library Service, 82, 93
Indiana, 33-34, 92, 107-108*f*, 160*f*-163*f*, 265, 280*f*, 283n19
indigenous peoples of the Americas. *See* Native Americans
Information 2000 (NCLIS), 58
Information and Culture (journal), 44n23, 115
The Information Film (Waldron), 40
Information Services and Use (NISO), 84, 97n5
information society, 321-322, 364, 371
information technology, 62-63, 322, 323-325, 328-330
informed citizenry, 5, 7, 63, 74n17, 91, 115, 277*f*, 310
Innovation and the Library (Pungitore), 89
Inouye, Alan, 11
Institute of Museum and Library Services (IMLS)
  data and reports by, 15, 17n1, 124, 133, 229, 243, 252n1, 312
  establishment of, 53, 74n19, 115, 299
  funding of tribal libraries, 3
  LSTA and, 8, 53, 62-63, 115-121, 132-133, 299
  Public Libraries Survey (PLS), 84-85, 98n11, 138n26, 159, 229
  state library agencies and, 81, 85, 98n9, 114-115, 121, 299
  strategic plans, 7, 11, 65, 268
integrated library systems (ILSs), 336, 338-339
intellectual freedom, 8, 17n3, 66-69, 123, 246-247, 252n11, 357-359
Intellectual Freedom Manual (ALA), 69
International Dublin Literary Award, 268
International Federation of Library Associations and Institutions (IFLA), 252n3, 348-349, 353-361, 370-374, 381
International Librarians Network, 357, 374
international libraries. *See* global libraries
international library conferences, 357
Internet
  broadband adoption, 64-65, 343n3
  digital divide, 64, 135, 251, 279, 322-323, 354, 367-368
  digital inclusion, 64-65, 82, 250-251, 322-323
  filtering, 63, 122-123
  history of library access to, 326-327
  as major technological development, 324-325*f*
  net neutrality, 123
  privacy and, 334-335, 343n4, 381-382
  universal service, 63, 122-123, 137n1, 327, 343n3
Internet Archive, 305
Iowa, 31, 107-108*f*, 113, 160*f*-163*f*, 223n22, 280*f*
IREX, 367
Irving, Christine, 360

J

Jackson, Irene Dobbs, 54
Jackson, Josh, 194
Jacobsen, Jonathan, 338-339
Jaeger, Paul T., 14, 30, 71, 128, 216, 314, 322
Jeske, Michelle, 384
Jim Crow era, 1-2, 17n2, 31, 34, 41, 53, 232

job listings, 157, 165-170, 186n15, 374
job titles, 165*f*
Joeckel, Carlton B., 30, 39, 45n31, 86-87, 107, 149
Johnson, Alvin S., 2, 269, 284n31
Johnson, Linda E., 94
Johnson, Lyndon B., 42, 55, 57
Johnson, Sharon, 341
joint-use libraries, 203-206, 301-302
Jones, Barbara M., 69, 314
Jones, Plummer A., 36
Jones, Virginia Lacy, 55
Josey, E. J., 41, 136
Journal of Human Development and Capabilities, 100n30
journals, state, 54, 72n1, 221n10
Jumonville, Florence, 111
Junto, 24, 42n3

K

Kansas, 69-70, 95, 160*f*-163*f*, 206, 219, 280*f*, 314
Kansas City Public Library, 69, 219, 314
Karetzky, Stephen, 260
Katrina (hurricane), 12, 135, 176, 202, 216
Kemper, Crosby, 268
Kennedy, John F., 42
Kenney, Brian, 152-153, 279-281, 285n45, 383
Kentucky, 25, 34, 114, 160*f*-163*f*, 165, 198*f*, 279, 280*f*
Keokuk, Iowa, 113
Kevane, Michael, 37, 44n25
Kilgour, Frederick G., 295
King, David Lee, 241
King County (WA) Library System, 95, 96, 176
Knight News Challenge, 70, 135-136, 139n33, 380
Knott, Cheryl, 2, 17n2, 31, 41, 44n16, 53
Koehler, Wallace C., 2
Kowalsky, Michelle, 258
Kowatch, Kelly, 328
Kranich, Nancy, 5-7, 12, 316
Kroll, Joanna, 328
Kunitz, Stanley, 67
Kwanya, Tom, 335

L

Lacy, Dan, 57, 380
Ladenson, Alex, 35
Lamont, Bridget L., 56
Lampert, Cory, 329
Lang, Shirley, 152
Langa, Lesley, 216
Lankes, R. David, 234
Las Vegas-Clark County Library, xv, 317*f*
Latham, Joyce M., 38, 67, 269, 284n31
Latinos, 56, 71, 179, 183-184, 231, 245*f*, 278
Laura Bush 21st Century Librarian (LB21) program, 176, 178, 186n22
laws. *See* legislation
Lawson, Judy, 328
League of Library Commissions, 37-38
Lear, Bernadette A., 35, 44n23, 115
Lear, Brett W., 278
Learned, William S., 37, 269
Lee, Jean, 322
LEED certification, 205, 214-215
legal basis of libraries, 105-111, 123, 137n3
legislation
- advocacy and, 122-123
- basic areas of, 111, 137n9
- in the development of public libraries, 27-30, 35, 40-42, 55-56
- examples of, 111-114, 129*f*
- Library Services Act (LSA), 5, 40-42, 84, 87-88, 115, 296, 299
- Library Services and Construction Act (LSCA), 5, 40-42, 53-56, 59-60, 197-200, 220n9, 232
- Library Services and Technology Act (LSTA), 8, 53, 62-63, 115-121, 132-133, 299, 327
- Museum and Library Services Act (MLSA), 62-63, 74n19, 115, 120, 271, 299
- state, local, and regional, 111-114, 129*f*
- UNESCO on, 363
- Workforce Innovation and Opportunity Act, 106, 137n2, 270, 271*f*-272*f*

Leigh, Carma Zimmerman, 40
Leigh, Robert D., 39-40, 232
Leininger, Michele, 153
Lemony Snicket Prize for Noble Librarians Faced with Adversity, 17n5, 69
lesbians, 13, 56, 180-181, 268, 275, 283n26, 356
Lewis, Linda K., 31
librarians. *See* public librarians
"Librarians and Libraries Respond to Disasters," 13, 217
Librarians Build Communities (LBC), 176
libraries
- joint-use, 203-206, 301-302
- legal basis of, 106-107
- public (*see* public libraries)
- right to, 15-17, 274
- rural (*see* rural libraries)
- school district, 25-26, 43n6, 107
- social, 24-25, 27-29, 42n4-43n4

libraries, *continued*
traveling, 31, 35, 38, 44n22
tribal, 3-4, 60, 73n13, 107, 275
Libraries, Human Rights, and Social Justice (Jaeger et al.), 71, 257
"Libraries: An American Value" (ALA), 5, 257
Libraries and Adult Education (ALA), 37, 269
Libraries and Democracy (Kranich), 5-7
"Libraries as Acts of Civic Renewal" (Gregorian), 219
Libraries at Large (NACL), 57, 297
Libraries at the Crossroads (Horrigan), 42n1, 194
"Libraries Can Save Divided America" (Smith), 11-12
"Libraries Change Lives" (ALA), 15-17
Libraries for the Future, 135
Libraries Transform Campaign, 14, 18n11, 136, 139n35-36, 312
Library 2.0 and 3.0, 335-336
Library Administration Division (LAD), 55
library agencies, state. *See* state library agencies
"Library and Information Studies and Human Resource Utilization," 159, 164*f*
The Library as Place (Buschman and Leckie), 69
library automation, 336
Library Bill of Rights, 67-69, 180, 235, 278
library buildings. *See* buildings and construction
Library Company of Philadelphia, 24, 42n3
Library Connection, 68-69
Library Consortia (Horton and Pronevitz), 295-296
library directors, 31-32, 93-95, 143-144, 152-157
Library Extension Board, 45n30, 107
library faith, 9, 83, 257
The Library Functions of the States (Monypenny), 54, 297
"Library Future Fatigue" (Schwartz), 380
Library History Round Table (LHRT), 31, 44n15
Library Journal, 30, 58, 93, 95, 96, 99n24-25, 100n27, 201-203
Library Journal/Gale Cengage Learning Library of the Year, 95
Library Law and Legislation in the United States (ALA), 111, 137n9
Library Leadership and Management Association (LLAMA), 208, 221n13
Library of Congress, 25, 193, 220n1, 266-267, 283n25, 293, 384
Library Security (Albrecht), 217
library service responses, 61, 73n15, 74n17, 90-91, 253n17, 275-277
Library Services Act (LSA), 5, 40-42, 84, 87-88, 115, 296, 299
Library Services and Construction Act (LSCA), 5, 40-42, 53-56, 59-62, 197-200, 220n9, 232
Library Services and Technology Act (LSTA), 8, 53, 62-63, 115-121, 132-133, 299, 327
Library Statistics Working Group, 84, 98n8
Library Support Staff Certification (LSSC), 164-165, 185n13
Library Technology Report, 241, 322, 343n1
Library War Service, 36-37
The Library's Public (Berelson), 40, 46n33
lifelong learning, 16, 66, 268-272, 277, 349-350, 360
Lincove, David A., 68
literacy
adult literacy, 272-274, 284n36
digital literacy, 64-65, 116, 271*f*-272*f*
early literacy, 65, 91, 121, 233-234, 248, 251, 384
health literacy, 250, 314-315
importance of libraries to, 16
Living Building Challenge, 215, 222n19
local government, 86, 106-111, 113-114, 124, 361-364
local history collections, 195, 302-305
Long, Alicia K., 229, 390
Louisiana, 55, 64, 74n22, 105n1, 160*f*-163*f*, 202-204*f*, 280*f*
LSA (Library Services Act), 5, 40-42, 84, 87-88, 115, 296, 299
LSCA (Library Services and Construction Act), 5, 40-42, 53-56, 59-62, 197-200, 220n9, 232
LSTA (Library Services and Technology Act), 8, 53, 62-63, 115-121, 132-133, 299, 327
Lukensmeyer, Carolyn, 7
Lunch at the Library programs, 14, 18n10
Luo, Lili, 242-243
lyceums, 27
Lyman, Helen, 269, 274
Lynch, Mary Jo, 98n7
Lyon Declaration on Access to Information and Development, 354, 356-357

M

Macikas, Barbara, 179
Madison (WI) Public Library, 94, 135, 205
Madison (ID) Public Library District, 143, 184n1
Maine, 151, 160*f*-163*f*, 171*f*, 280*f*
Maine Library Trustee Handbook, 151
makerspaces, 208, 249, 332-333, 341-342, 360
Malone, Cheryl K., 31, 41, 44n16
Managing with Data (Hernon et al.), 85
Mandel, Lauren H., 11

Manguel, Alberto, 259, 261
Mann, Horace, 26–27
Marcum, Deanna, 70, 152
Marquis, Kathy, 302, 304
Martin, Lowell, 88
Martin, Robert Sidney, 34, 35, 115
Martinez, Hannah, 259
Maryland, 107, 108*f*, 124, 125*f*, 160–163*f*, 280*f*, 322. *See also* Enoch Pratt Free Library
mashups, 337
mass reading events, 265–266
Massachusetts
  development of libraries in, 23–32, 35
  legislation, 112–113*f*
  library buildings, 196, 203, 212, 220n5
  Regulations for Regional Library Systems, 114
  statistics on, 108*f*, 160–163*f*, 170–171*f*, 280*f*
  Town of Bedford organizational chart, 144, 145*f*
  See also Boston Public Library
master's degrees, ALA-accredited, 159, 162*f*, 164, 170–173*f*, 185n11, 239
Mates, Barbara, 260
Mathews, Virginia H., 57, 380
Mathiesen, Kay, 71
Mattern, Shannon, 193
Mattson, Kevin, 5
McCabe, Ronald, 310
McCamy, J. L. and J. T., 40
McClure, Charles R., 11, 216
McCook, Kathleen de la Peña, xvi, 92, 284n38, 285n41, 389
McDermott, Abigail, 322
McMullen, Haynes, 24, 27
meal programs, 14, 18n10
Measures that Matter project, 85
Measuring Success, 121, 299
Mehra, Bharat, 179
mercantile libraries, 24, 28–29, 43n4
Merrill, Julia Wright, 38, 105, 284n30
metrics, 81–93, 121. *See also* Project Outcome
Mexico, 353, 359, 365
Meyer, Elizabeth G., 41
Miami-Dade Public Library System, 203–204*f*
Michigan, 31, 65, 120, 129*f*, 160*f*–163*f*, 217, 266–267, 312
Michigan Reads! program, 65
Mickells, Gregory, 94
Midland-Reporter Telegram, 11–12
Miksa, Francis, 30, 44n17
Milam, Carl H., 39–40, 45n28, 87
Miller, Ellen G., 144
Miller, Rebecca, 64, 215
Miller, William, 40
Minimum Standards for Public Library Systems (PLA), 55–56, 88, 300
minorities, 2, 31, 53, 56, 60, 245–246. *See also* African Americans; Latinos; Native Americans
mission statements, 59, 89, 120, 307*f*, 382–383
Missouri, 96, 160*f*–163*f*, 170, 176, 297, 303–304
Mitchell Park Library and Community Center, 205
MLS degrees, ALA-accredited, 159, 162*f*, 164, 170–173*f*, 185n11, 239
mobile devices, 241, 331, 384
MOBIUS, 303–304
Molz, Redmond K., 39, 45n31, 73n7
Money and the Moral Order (Hamer), 32
Monroe, Margaret E., 269–270, 274
Moon, Eric, 54
Moore, Anne Carroll, 231, 232
Moore, Mary Y., 144
"More and Better Libraries" slogan, 105
Morris, Sharon P., 153
Morrison, Andrea M., 314
Mortenson Center for International Library Programs, 369
Mouet, Gerardo, 95
multi-type library cooperatives (MLCs), 299–300
municipal libraries, 26, 29, 106–111, 113, 144
Murray, David C., 276
Murray, Richard A., 328
Museum and Library Services Act (MLSA), 62–63, 74n19, 115, 120, 271, 299

N

Naperville (IL) Public Library, 93–94
Nashville Public Library, 9, 135, 207*f*
National Advisory Commission on Libraries (NACL), 57, 297
National Agenda for Continuing Education and Professional Development, 181
National Association to Promote Library and Information Services to Latinos and the Spanish Speaking (REFORMA), 56, 71, 179, 183, 186n24, 231*f*, 244–245*f*, 312
National Bookmobile Day, 215, 222n20
National Center for Educational Statistics (NCES), 83–84, 97n7–98n7
National Commission on Libraries and Information Science (NCLIS), 3–4, 54, 57–60, 60, 73n13, 74n20, 98n7
National Endowment for the Humanities (NEH), 134, 270, 284n34

National Impact of Library Public Programs Assessment (NILPPA), 279, 315
National League of Cities, 105
National Library of Medicine, 13, 217, 315
National Library Service for the Blind and Physically Handicapped, 260, 301
National Medal for Museum and Library Service, 94-95
National Plan for Libraries, 39, 45n29
National Plan for Public Library Service, 39, 86-87, 197
National Policy Agenda for Libraries (OITP), 7-8, 62
National Register of Historic Places, 32, 197, 220n8
National Resources Planning Board (NRPB), 45n31, 87
National Safe Place Program, 13, 18n8
Native Americans, 2-4, 31, 53, 60, 73n13, 107, 245*f*. *See also* American Indian Library Association (AILA)
natural disasters, 12-13, 202, 216-217, 223n21-22
NCLIS (National Commission on Libraries and Information Science), 3-4, 54, 57-60, 60, 73n13, 74n20, 98n7
Nebraska, 114, 120, 160*f*-163*f*, 267, 280*f*
Nelson, Sandra, 61, 74n16-17, 90-91, 253n17, 277*f*, 281n4
Németh, Jeremy, 217
net neutrality, 123
networking, professional, 294. *See also* collaboration
New Deal, 37-38, 66, 269
New England, 23-28, 43n5
New Hampshire, 25, 28, 43n5, 149, 150*f*, 160-163*f*, 280*f*
New Hampshire Statutes: Library Trustees, 149, 150*f*
New Mexico, 31, 65, 109*f*, 121, 160*f*-163*f*, 172*f*, 181, 280*f*
The New Planning for Results (Nelson), 61, 74n16, 276, 277*f*
New York, 26, 34-35, 121, 128*f*, 151, 160*f*-163*f*, 181, 280*f*
New York City, 24, 70, 194-195, 207, 343n2, 368
New York Public Library, 32, 134, 194-196, 207, 231, 263, 343n2
Newark (NJ) Public Library, 195, 343n2
newspaper cartoons, 152, 153*f*
Next Library Conference, 357
Nickless, Amy, 301
Nitikin, Cynthia, 194
Nocek, Jan, 69
Norfolk (MA) Public Library, 217
North Carolina, 45n27, 65, 92, 133, 143, 160*f*-163*f*, 175, 280*f*
Not Free, Not for All (Knott), 2, 31, 41, 44n16, 53
Notable Books programs, 266, 283n20
NoveList, 260, 263, 281n5
Nussbaum, Martha C., 96, 258

O

Oak Park (IL) Public Library, 124, 130*f*
Obama, Barack, 74n21
Obama, Michelle, 94, 100n26, 267
OCLC, 182, 294-297, 338, 349
O'Donnell, Ruth, 93
Office for Diversity, Literacy, and Outreach Services, 179, 185n8, 222n20, 223n24, 272-273, 281n3, 284n39
Office for Information Technology Policy (OITP), 7-8, 11, 61-62, 327
Office for Intellectual Freedom, 66-67, 246-247, 252n11
Office for Library Advocacy, 66, 122, 136
Ohio, 14, 38, 73n12, 128*f*, 148*f*, 160*f*-163*f*, 280*f*, 295
Oja, Dan, 328
One Book, One Community (OBOC), 265-266
Open Society Institute, 368
operating systems, 330-331
Oprah's Book Club, 265
Orange County (FL) Library System, 208, 242
ordinances, local, 113-114
organizational charts, 144-148*f*
Otis (CT) Library, 95
outcomes, 61, 81-93, 96-97, 121, 315-316. *See also* Project Outcome
Outcomes Based Evaluations (OBE), 61
Output Measures for Public Libraries (PLA), 59, 89, 233
outreach services, bookmobile, 106, 209*f*-211*f*, 215-216, 222n20, 275, 322, 371
Outside the Lines, 384
OverDrive, 262, 267, 281n7
Oxnard, California, 114

P

packhorse libraries, 38
Paris-Bourbon County (KY) Public Library, 197-198*f*
Parker, Ralph, 293, 295
Parsons, June J., 321, 325*f*, 326, 328
Part of Our Lives (Wiegand), 30, 83-84
Pasicznyuk, Robert, 194

Passet, Joanne E., 33
Pateman, John, 259
Pathways to Excellence (NCLIS), 3-4, 60
Patin, Beth, 216
PATRIOT Act, 68-69
patrons, interactions with, 217-218
Patterson, Lotsee, 2-4, 31, 53, 73n13
Paul Howard Award for Courage, 68-69
Pawley, Christine, 31, 35, 261
Pearl, Nancy, 265-266, 282n18-283n18, 383
Peich, Alysia, 38
people's university, libraries as, 2, 37-38, 193
Performance Measurement Task Force (PMTF), 82
peripheral devices, 330-333
personnel. *See* staff
Peterborough Town Library, 28, 43n8
Peterson, Erika D., 267
Pettigrew, Karen E., 313
Pew Research Center, 65, 310, 314
Phenix, Katharine, 257, 266, 279-385, 391
Philadelphia libraries, social reach of, 10
philanthropy, 27, 32-35, 197, 366
PLA. *See* Public Library Association (PLA)
place, sense of, 69-70, 383-384
PLA*metrics*, 85
planning
community-based, shift to, 53, 56-59, 62-63, 89-91
National Plan for Public Library Service, 39, 86-87, 197
Planning for Results series, 14-15, 53, 61, 73n16-74n17, 90-91, 99n21, 276-277*f*
strategic, 7, 11, 61, 65, 268
Planning and Role Setting for Public Libraries (McClure), 59, 89, 276*f*
Planning for Results (Himmel and Wilson), 14-15, 61, 73n16, 90
A Planning Process for Public Libraries (PLA), 59, 89
PLDP (Public Library Development Program), 58-59, 61, 89-90, 99n19
Plummer, Mary Wright, 231
Poe, Jodi, 313
police, shootings by, 12, 176, 218
"Policy on Library Services to the Poor" (ALA), 60, 73n14
politics, involvement in, 105-106, 136, 152
The Politics of an Emerging Profession (Wiegand), 36
poor people, 13-14, 18n9, 60, 73n14, 270, 327, 347
position announcements, 157, 165-170, 186n15, 374
position titles, 165*f*
Post-War Standards for Public Libraries (Joeckel), 39, 45n31, 87
Potter, Steven V., 310-311*f*
Power, Rebecca, 237
Pratt-Smoot Act, 260, 301
Prime Time Family Literacy, 249
printers, 331-332
privacy, 262-263, 334-335, 343n4, 381-382
Privacy Toolkit, 334-335, 382
problem patrons, 217-218
professional associations, 306-309, 374-375
professional development, 181-183
programs
adult, 278-279, 280*f*
children's, 65, 121, 247-250
Progressive Librarians Guild, 71
Project for Public Spaces, 194-195
Project Outcome, 61, 81-83, 97n3, 250, 253n17, 276, 315
Pronevitz, Greg, 295-296
Public Awareness Office, 136, 139n35
The Public Librarian (Bryan), 40
public librarians
abilities of, 158-159
awards for, 68-69, 183-184
books honored by, 267-268
certification, 156, 164-165, 181, 186n25
continuing education, 181-183
as defenders of intellectual freedom, 66-69, 123
diversity of, 177-179
education, 36
with MLS degrees, 159, 162*f*, 164, 170-173*f*, 185n11, 239
motivations of, 30
number of, 161*f*-162*f*, 171*f*-173*f*
recruitment, 176-177, 178
salaries, 156, 158, 165, 174
technology skills of, 325-329
women as, 31-32
working internationally, 373-375
public libraries
from the 1690s to 1960s, 23-42
from the 1960s to the present, 53-72
as anchor institutions, 11, 65, 194, 326-327
awards for, 93-96, 100n26-29
buildings (*see* buildings and construction)
as community commons, 1, 8-14, 69-70, 90, 193-195, 220n2, 277*f*
core values, xvi, 7-8, 54-56, 66-72, 268-274
criticism of, 29-30
democracy and, 1-2, 4-8, 15*f*-16*f*, 66-72, 269-270, 279, 362*f*
evolution, 14-17
future of, 14, 18n11, 299, 373, 380-381, 384-385

public libraries, *continued*
  global (*see* global libraries)
  governance, 107-111, 143-157, 184n1-185n8, 361-364
  as heart of the community, 8-10, 309
  legal basis, 105-111, 123, 137n3
  number of, 1, 17n1, 106, 108*f*-110*f*, 171*f*-173*f*, 207, 209*f*-211*f*, 349
  as the people's university, 2, 37-38, 193
  as public sphere institutions, 69-70, 193-194
  public support of, 8-9, 14, 15-17, 42n1, 136
  role of, 53-54, 61, 89-90, 250, 310, 356-359, 364-365
  rural (*see* rural libraries)
  as safe havens, 11-14, 158, 217
  service responses of, 61, 73n15, 74n17, 90-91, 253n17, 275-277
  staffing (*see* staff)
Public Libraries and Resilient Cities (Dudley), 310
Public Libraries and Social Justice (Pateman and Vincent), 259
Public Libraries Division, 88, 198
Public Libraries in the United States of America report, 30, 84, 230, 306
Public Libraries Survey (PLS), 84-85, 98n11, 138n26, 159, 229
The Public Library (Dawson), 193, 220n1-2
The Public Library (Johnson), 2, 269
Public Library Association (PLA)
  awards from, 95-96, 100n28
  continuing education by, 181-182
  history, 5, 54, 56, 307
  mission statement, 59, 89, 307*f*
  Planning for Results series, 14-15, 53, 61, 73n16-74n17, 89-91, 99n21, 276-277*f*
  presidents, xv-xvi, 284n40, 316-318*f*
  profile of, 307*f*-308*f*
  Project Outcome initiative, 61, 81-83, 97n3, 250, 253n17, 276, 315
  Statement of Principles, 6-7, 89, 99n18
Public Library Data Service, 82, 85, 99n13
"The Public Library: Democracy's Resource," 5, 6-7
Public Library Development Program (PLDP), 58-59, 61, 89-90, 99n19
The Public Library in the Political Process (Garceau), 40, 83, 105, 252n2
The Public Library in the United States (Leigh), 40
Public Library Inquiry, 4-5, 39-40, 45n32, 83, 87, 105, 232, 252n2
Public Library Manifesto, 347, 349, 361-364*f*
The Public Library Mission Statement and Its Imperatives for Service (PLA), 59, 89
Public Library Principles Task Force, 5, 6-7
Public Library Space Needs (Dahlgren), 208-212, 221n14
public sphere, library as, 69-70, 193-194
Public Urban Library Service Education project, 176
Puerto Rican Community Archive, 195
Puerto Rico, 8-10, 120, 195, 231, 299
Pungitore, Verna L., 89, 99n17, 99n19

Q

quality of life, 8, 96-97
Quincy, Josiah, 28

R

Raber, Douglas, 4-5, 39-40, 45n32, 90
racial minorities. *See* minorities
racial segregation, 17n2, 34, 41, 46n34, 54-55, 232
RAILS (Reaching Across Illinois Library System), 165, 300-301
ratings and rankings, 81, 93-94, 99n24
Read Global, 350, 370
reader services, 259-275
readers' advisory, 263-264, 282n12
Readers' Advisory Service in the Public Library (Saricks and Brown), 263
reading
  books on, 261
  freedom in, 66-69, 246-247, 357-369
  mass reading events, 265-266
  promotion of, 266-267
Reading Room (Felicella), 194-195
reading rooms, 25, 38, 269
Ready Set Kindergarten! program, 121
Real, Brian, 322
Reclaiming the American Library Past (Hildenbrand), 31
recruitment, 176-177, 178
Reference and User Services Association (RUSA), 257, 264, 267, 275, 278, 302, 341
reference services, 242-243
referenda, 124-128, 152
REFORMA, 56, 71, 179, 183, 186n24, 231*f*, 244-245*f*, 312
refugees, 371
Report of the Trustees of the Public Library to the City of Boston, 2, 23, 26, 29-30, 43n12
Report on the Public Libraries of the United States (Smithsonian), 84
Research Institute for Public Libraries (RIPL), 85, 98n12, 100n31

"Response to Change" (Mathews and Lacy), 57
revenue, operating, 124-127
RFID, 339
Rhode Island, 25, 43n4-5, 160-163*f*, 170, 198, 220n9, 280*f*
rights
  civil, 41, 53-55, 89, 212-213, 232, 270
  human, 71-72, 359-360, 373
  to libraries, 15-17, 274
  to reading, 66-69, 246-247, 357-369
Rita (hurricane), 12, 135
Robinson, Megan, 241-242
Robinson, Melissa S., 15, 310
Rollins, Charlemae Hill, 231, 250
Rosa, Kathy, 128
Rosenwald, Julius, 41
Roughen, Patrick, 41
Roy, Loriene, 3-4
R-Squared Conference on Risk and Reward, 383
RSS feeds, 335, 337
Rubenstein, Ellen, 10
Rubin, Richard, 325f, 339
rural libraries
  ALA Committee on Rural, Native, and Tribal Libraries, 3
  Association for Rural and Small Libraries, 183, 216, 223n20, 309
  development of, 37-38, 41-42, 88
  global, 350, 358, 364, 367, 370-371
  grants for, 121
  Internet access and, 11, 137n1
Rutledge, Merryn, 149

S

Sacramento (CA) Public Library, 166, 266, 283n20
safe havens, libraries as, 11-14, 158, 217
Safe Place program, 13, 18n8
safety and security, 217-218
Saint Paul (MN) Public Library, 124, 131*f*
salaries, 156, 158, 165, 174
Samek, Toni, 55
San Francisco, 196, 201, 281n8, 300
Sannwald, William W., 208
Santa Ana (CA) Public Library, 95
Saricks, Joyce G., 263, 265
"Save Our Library Committee," 152, 153*f*
Scales, Pat, 246-247
Schlipf, Fred, 197
Schmidt, Stephan, 217
school district libraries, 25-26, 43n6, 107
School of Library Economy, 36
Seale, Maura, 12
Seattle Public Library, 13, 134, 193, 203, 264, 282n14, 382
security and safety, 217-218
segregation, 17n2, 34, 41, 46n34, 54-55, 232
selection aids, 243
self-check-out, 262
Sendze, Monique, 262
sense of place, 69-70, 383-384
September 11th terror attacks, 68, 194
servers, 331
service responses, 61, 73n15, 74n17, 90-91, 253n17, 275-277
sexual orientation/expression, 13, 56, 179, 180-181, 239, 275, 356
Shaw, Debora, 321, 325*f*, 340
Shera, Jesse H., 26-27, 30
Shontz, Priscilla K., 328
shootings, by police, 12, 176, 218
Shorris, Earl, 270
SLAAs. *See* state library agencies
Slavick, Steven, 217-218
smartphones, 241, 322, 331, 384
Smith, Duncan, 260
Smith, Mark, 11-12
Smith, Maureen Millea, 183-184
Smithsonian Institution, 84
Smith-Towner bill, 37
social change, 53-59, 72n2, 311
social justice, 71-72, 250-251, 257-259, 311
social libraries, 24-25, 27-29, 42n4-43n4
social media, 241, 336, 337
Social Responsibilities Round Table (SRRT), 18n9, 56, 60, 71, 73n14, 89, 214, 275
social services, 250
software, 333-334
Sohier, Elizabeth Putnam, 35
Somerville, Mary, 233
Soros Foundation, 359, 368
South Dakota, 65, 160*f*-163*f*, 170, 172*f*, 280*f*
Spanish libraries, 9-10, 353, 361, 365
Spanish speakers, 56, 71, 179, 183-184, 231, 244-245*f*, 278
Spaulding, Forrest, 67, 318*f*
SPECTRUM scholarship program, 179, 186n23
staff
  awards for, 183-184
  certification of, 156, 164-165, 181, 185n13, 186n25
  continuing education, 181-183
  with disabilities, 180
  diversity of, 177-179

staff, *continued*
number of, 160*f*-163*f*, 171*f*-173*f*
overview, 158-174
recruitment, 176-177, 178
salaries, 156, 158, 165, 174
unions and, 174, 186n17-18
See also public librarians
Stafford Act, 12, 17n7, 216, 223n22
standards
global, 355-357, 363, 372
national, 5, 38, 53-54, 86-91
post-war, 39, 45n31, 87
state, 91-93, 99n22
state library agencies and, 91-93
state library agencies
Chief Officers of State Library Agencies (COSLA), 64, 85, 91-92, 99n23, 111, 114, 153-154
collaboration by, 54, 91, 107-111, 123, 294, 296-297
funding and, 75n24, 115, 120-121, 132-133, 199*f*, 299
IMLS and, 81, 85, 98n9, 114-115, 121, 299
legislation and, 111-113*f*
standards and, 91-93
state library associations, 54, 59-60, 91, 124-128, 151, 177, 182-183, 268
state library commissions, 35-38
State Library of North Carolina, 92, 133
Statement of Principles (PLA), 6-7, 89, 99n18
states
funding by, 132
grants to, 63, 75n24, 116-121, 133, 138n24, 198-199*f*, 299
journals of, 54, 72n1, 221n10
operating revenue, 124-127
specialized services by, 42, 46n38
standards of, 91-93, 99n22
statistics on, 108*f*-110*f*, 124-128, 160*f*-163*f*, 171*f*-173*f*, 209*f*-211*f*, 280*f*
statistics
global, 349, 355, 370
outcomes and, 81-85, 93, 97n5, 99n22-25, 121-122
on states, 108*f*-110*f*, 124-128, 160*f*-163*f*, 171*f*-173*f*, 209*f*-211*f*, 280*f*
on youth services, 229, 233, 243, 246
STEAM equipment, 332. *See also* makerspaces
Stearns, Lutie, 31, 35, 36
Stewart, Andrea, 181
Stewart, Frances, 96-97, 100n32, 258
Stielow, Frederick J., 34
Stilwell, Christine, 335
Strategic Planning for Results (Nelson), 61, 74n16, 90-91, 253n17, 277*f*, 281n4
A Strategy for Public Library Change (PLA), 56-57, 89
streaming services, 262, 267, 337
Stripling, Barbara, 15-17
Strothmann, Molly, 264
summer meal programs, 14, 18n10
summer reading programs, 237, 247-248, 265
Sundstrom, William A., 37, 44n25
sustainability, 214-215, 222n17-19, 311*f*, 347-348
Sustainable Development Goals (SDGs), 347-348, 354
Swain, Martha H., 38, 269
Swetnam, Susan H., 33

T

Taffae, Sara M., 74n22-75n22
tagging, 337
task forces, 56, 61, 82, 233. *See also specific task forces*
taxation, 26-30, 34, 84, 123-124, 128-130*f*. *See also* funding
TechInsider, 195, 220n4
technology
history of library use, 323-328
information technology, 62-63, 322, 323-325, 328-330
kinds of, 330-335
library-specific, 336-339
major developments in, 324-325*f*
overview, 321-323
privacy and, 334-335, 343n4, 381-382
skills needed for, 325-329
See also Internet
Teen Read Week, 248, 253n15
Teen Tech Week, 249
teens. *See* young adults
Telecommunications Act of 1996, 63, 122, 137n1, 327
terror attacks, 68, 194
Texas, 14, 124, 128*f*, 160*f*-163*f*, 205, 280*f*, 283n24
Texas Library Association, 182, 187n28
texting services, 241, 242-243
Thomas Jr., Felton, xv-xvi, 317*f*
Thompson, Susan M., 324-325, 328-329
Ticknor, George, 27, 29-30
Todaro, Julie, 8, 123
Topeka and Shawnee County (KS) Public Library, 70, 95
Torrey, Jesse, 25

"Toward a Broader Definition of the Public Good" (Curley), 5
Toward a National Program for Library and Information Services (NCLIS), 57-58
Transforming Libraries, Building Communities (Edwards et al.), 15, 310
transgender persons, 13, 56, 180-181, 268, 275, 283n26, 356
Trapskin, Ben, 217
traveling libraries, 31, 35, 38, 44n22
tribal community libraries, 3-4, 60, 73n13, 107, 275
Trustee Essentials handbook, 152
trustees, boards of
  awards for, 183-184
  at Boston Public Library, 5, 29, 107
  budgets and, 130*f*, 144, 150
  New Hampshire Statutes on, 149, 150*f*
  organizations for, 150-152
  responsibilities of, 144, 149, 150*f*
Turning the Page (ALA), 136
Twenty-First Century Kids (Walter), 234
Twitter, 241, 337, 381, 384
Tyler, Alice, 31

U

Underwood, Peter, 335
Unger, Kelley R., 15, 310
unions, 174, 186n17-18
United for Libraries, 128, 139n28, 149-151, 174-175
United Kingdom, 352
United Nations 2030 Agenda, 347-348, 354, 373
United Nations Educational, Scientific, and Cultural Organization (UNESCO), 347, 349-351, 353-356, 360, 361-364*f*, 365
United States, number of public libraries in, 1, 17n1, 106, 108*f*-110*f*, 171*f*-173*f*, 207, 209*f*-211*f*, 349
universal design, 208, 212-214, 221n15
Universal Service program, 63, 122-123, 137n1, 327, 343n3
University of Illinois at Urbana-Champaign, 343n5, 369
University of Washington, 82, 97n2, 366
Unruh, Kenton T., 313
Urban Libraries Council, 64-65, 82, 96, 100n29, 233, 248, 309, 382
U.S. Bureau of Education, 26, 43n4, 44n25, 72n6
U.S. Unified Community Anchor Network, 65
USA PATRIOT Act, 68-69
USDA Summer Meals Toolkit, 14, 18n10
Utah, 120, 138n22, 160*f*-163*f*, 280*f*

V

Valdosta State University, 176
values, core, xvi, 7-8, 54-56, 66-72, 268-274
Vattemare, Alexandre, 28, 43n10
Veil, Shari R., 12, 216
Vermont, 25, 43n5, 110*f*, 160-163*f*, 172*f*, 280*f*
Video Round Table (VRT), 267
Vincent, John, 259
Vinopal, Jennifer, 179
Virginia, 111, 160*f*-163*f*, 280*f*
virtual spaces, 241-242
volunteers, 175-176, 177, 186n20
vulnerable populations, 10-11, 360, 371. *See also* homeless people; poor people

W

Waggener, Leslie, 302, 304
Waldron, Gloria, 40
Walter, Virginia, 233-234, 239, 252
Washington (state), 110*f*, 128*f*, 160*f*-163*f*, 172*f*, 176, 280*f*
Washington Free Library (MD), 195, 196*f*
Washington Office (ALA), 58, 62, 122, 139n34, 297, 327
Washington State Library, 114, 138n17
Watson, Paula D., 31, 35
Weak, Emily, 242-243
Web 2.0 and 3.0, 335-337, 372
webinars, 82, 97n3, 128, 182, 252n6
WebJunction, 182, 314-315, 328
West, Jessamyn, 385
Westney, Lynn C., 33-34, 391
"What Should Be the Federal Government's Relation to Libraries?" (ALA), 39
Whichbook, 263
White House Conferences, 54, 57-58, 61, 73n8
White Trash (Isenberg), 72n3
Wiegand, Wayne A., 14, 30, 36, 68, 83-84, 261
Wi-Fi, 325*f*, 331. *See also* Internet
Wight, Edward A., 40
Wight, John Burt, 28
wikis, 335, 337
Wilkins, Barratt, 132
Wilson, William James, 14-15, 61, 73n16, 90
Wisconsin, 113, 114, 137n11-138n11, 159, 160*f*-163*f*, 205, 268
Wisconsin Free Library Commission, 31, 35
Wisconsin Library Hall of Fame, 105n2, 284n30
women, role of, 31-32, 33-36, 44n17
women's clubs, 2, 31, 33, 35
Women's National Book Association, 265

Woodruff, John, 258
Woolfolk, Steven, 69
Workforce Innovation and Opportunity Act, 106, 137n2, 270, 271*f*-272*f*
Works Progress Administration (WPA) projects, 38-39
World War I, 36-37
World War II, 4, 39-40, 68, 87, 351
Wronka, Joseph, 71
Wyatt, Neal, 263
Wyoming, 114, 159-163*f*, 170, 182, 280*f*, 298
Wyoming State Library, 114, 298

Y

YALSA (Young Adult Library Services Association), 233, 235-238, 244-245, 248-249, 252n8, 253n15
Young, Neil J., 180
Young Adult Library Services Association (YALSA), 233, 235-238, 244-245, 248-249, 252n8, 253n15
young adults
  collections for, 243, 244
  knowledge of and commitment to, 238-240
  mobile device use by, 241
  programs for, 248-249, 253n15
  spaces for, 240-241
youth services
  competencies for, 235-238
  core services, 234-243
  future of, 250-252
  history, 229-234
  programs for, 65, 121, 247-250
  sample job description, 168-170
  spaces for, 240-242
  statistics, 229, 233, 243, 246

Z

Z39.7 standard, 84
Zepheira, 264, 282n16, 384

Printed in the USA
CPSIA information can be obtained
at www.ICGtesting.com
LVHW080550051124
795642LV00001B/3